MOON HANDBOOKS

MICHIGAN

LAURA MARTONE

D1041147

Contents

Discover **Michigan**

Michigan, a state known mainly for motors and Motown, possesses much diversity; its offerings are varied and often unexpected. Boasting more than 11,000 inland lakes, it contains countless art galleries, award-winning wineries, and championship golf courses. The length of its lighthouse-studded coastline is second only to Alaska.

Out-of-towners who consider it a typical Midwestern state, with frigid winters and flat cornfields, will be surprised. Though winters are indeed cold, the topography is amazingly diverse. The multifaceted state is a dramatically changing landscape of windswept beaches, rushing rivers, pine forests, remote islands, rugged mountains, impressive waterfalls, enormous sand dunes, and surrounding lakes so massive they resemble never-ending seas.

Unlike the urban metropolis of Detroit, most of Michigan has a small-town vibe, especially in the north. On a typical summer day, you could spend the morning on the shores of Lake Michigan, watching sailboats drift on the vibrant blue waters; then explore quaint coastal communities like Petoskey; and finish the day by picking wild blueberries amid the shady pines of northeastern Michigan.

Nothing compares to traveling along serpentine country roads in autumn, flanked by apple orchards and crimson maple trees. While most tourists visit in spring and summer, winters have grown more popular, too. Despite bitter cold and heavy snowfalls, adventurers enjoy skating across frozen lakes, riding snowmobiles through glistening forests, or braving the isolated hinterlands of the Upper Peninsula.

Divided into two extremely distinct peninsulas – the mitten-shaped Lower Peninsula and the breathtaking Upper Peninsula – Michigan is the only U.S. state that is surrounded by four of the five Great Lakes. How apt that its name is derived from the Native American word *Michigama*, meaning "large lake."

The Lower Peninsula boasts a wealth of rural areas, nostalgic villages, college campuses, resort towns, and the urban centers of Detroit and Flint. Recently, places like Traverse City have seen more tourists, and yet the Upper Peninsula – a vast tract of forests, beaches, and mountains – has remained elusive to many. The U.P. is often overlooked by Michiganders as well as the rest of the nation.

The key to appreciating Michigan is to embrace its diversity. Given so much to see, do, eat, and experience, your love affair with this remarkable state will forever evolve.

Planning Your Trip

▶ WHERE TO GO

Detroit and Southeast Michigan

When considering Detroit, many think of both its musical and automotive heritage as well as its reputation for crime and corruption. Visitors are often surprised by the cultural attractions that abound in southeastern Michigan, from ethnic enclaves like Hamtramck to impressive museums like The Henry Ford. Detroit is also ideal for those seeking an active nightlife; the city boasts three major casino resorts, in addition to one in nearby Windsor.

The Thumb

This region sees fewer crowds than the towns along Lake Michigan. Travelers who appreciate a slower pace and more old-fashioned vibe will enjoy fishing in Lake Huron, touring ancient petroglyphs, strolling through small coastal villages, exploring Frankenmuth, a Bavarian-style village known for its year-

Frankenmuth's picturesque River Place shops

IF YOU HAVE...

- **ONE WEEK:** Visit the Southwest Coast and Northwest Michigan.
- **TWO WEEKS:** Add Mackinac Island, Northeast Michigan, and the Heartland.
- **THREE WEEKS:** Add Detroit and the Thumb.
- **FOUR WEEKS:** Add the Upper Peninsula.

round Christmas store, observing birds in the Shiawassee National Wildlife Refuge, and visiting historic sites within the region.

Ann Arbor and the Heartland

This is the only region not bordered by at least one of the Great Lakes. Still, this vast region contains scenic lakes, college sports teams, unique cultural attractions like Kalamazoo's Air Zoo, and some of the state's largest cities. The Heartland could keep you busy for weeks, especially once you've discovered the enormous casino in Mount Pleasant.

The Southwest Coast

Michigan's most compact region, this shoreline is certainly the easiest to visit. Traveling from Harbor Country to the White Lake area requires less than a three-hour drive—but, oh, what a drive! Along the way, you'll spy sand dunes, lighthouses, art galleries, resort towns and coastal state parks, and the state's only major amusement park. This region also constitutes one of two key wine-producing areas in the state.

Traverse City and Northwest Michigan

Every summer, tourists flock to Traverse City, the self-proclaimed "cherry capital of the world." This area is popular among visitors, due to the wondrous Sleeping Bear Dunes, the wild rivers of Manistee National Forest, the wineries of the Leelanau Peninsula, and the lovely bays, lakes, and beaches. Northwest Michigan is also known for its superb golf courses and ski resorts.

Mackinac Island and Northeast Michigan

With its pine forests, canoeing rivers, inland lakes, and championship golf courses, Northeast Michigan is an outdoor enthusiast's paradise. The area's biggest attraction, the auto-free Mackinac Island, is definitely a step

Colonial Michilimackinac, Northeast Michigan

back in time, luring visitors with its quaint shops, carriage rides, and historic hotels.

The Eastern Upper Peninsula

Most travelers reach the U.P. by crossing the Mackinac Bridge into St. Ignace. From here, you can explore many cultural attractions, including lighthouses, a shipwreck museum, and the Soo Locks near Sault Ste. Marie. You'll find terrific fishing spots like the Manistique Lakes, excellent canoeing rivers like the Two Hearted, incredible views at Pictured Rocks National Lakeshore, and acres of forest land.

The Western Upper Peninsula

For seekers of solitude, this region promises all that and more. Although the Keweenaw Peninsula boasts a wealth of historic mining sites, and the Ironwood area has a number of popular ski resorts, much of this region consists of vast wilderness areas, including some of the highest mountains in the Midwest. Here, backpackers can lose themselves within expansive forests, kayakers can explore the frigid waters of Lake Superior, and the truly daring can venture to isolated Isle Royale.

▶ WHEN TO GO

fall colors at Lake of the Clouds in the Porcupine Mountains, Western Upper Peninsula

Summer is the most popular time to visit Michigan—people flock here for the beaches, inland lakes, and major events like the National Cherry Festival. July is typically the warmest month. In northern Michigan, it's also the buggiest. Time a camping trip in mid-June or after mid-August, when the mosquitoes and black flies are less bothersome.

Autumn may be the best time to visit. Days are cool, night skies are clear, bugs are gone, and fall colors are outstanding. For peak color, the second week of September in the U.P. and the second week of October for the Lower Peninsula are the best times.

Winter usually descends in December in the U.P., in January in the L.P., and can stick around through March. For snow sports, February is your safest bet to ensure good cover.

Spring emerges in southern Michigan in early May, working its way northward. With moderate temperatures and blossoming trees, spring is ideal for foliage lovers.

▶ BEFORE YOU GO

Reservations may be necessary, especially for popular B&Bs during the summer. Michigan is a seasonal place—some attractions and accommodations are only open late spring–early fall. If you come during the off-season, make sure to call ahead.

Your best bet for navigating this sprawling state is to bring your own vehicle or rent a car. All major airports have rental car services.

What to Take

Foreign travelers will need passports, adapter plugs, and current converters; anyone planning to travel to and from Canada should have proper identification as well. All visitors should be prepared for a variety of weather conditions—even in summer, jackets and umbrellas may be necessary. Attire is casual, though nicer restaurants and churches appreciate business casual. If your plans include golfing and bird-watching, you might want to bring your favorite clubs and binoculars. Fishing gear, canoes, bicycles, and other such equipment are easy enough to rent once you get here.

Explore Michigan

Given a place as large, as diverse, and as unassuming as Michigan, it helps to have a few itineraries in mind before hitting the road. Here's a small selection of the state's finest sights and sensations.

▶ THE BEST OF MICHIGAN

Whether you're a long-time resident or a first-time visitor to the Great Lakes State, you should set aside some time to experience Michigan's most beloved sights and activities. Consider taking the following tour of the state's top cultural and natural attractions.

Detroit to Kalamazoo

If you've started your Michigan adventure in the Motor City, head west to Dearborn, where you'll encounter The Henry Ford, a fascinating complex of interactive historic exhibits. Attractions include the Henry Ford Museum, a repository of automobile, aviation, and other all-American displays, Greenfield Village (which presents seven historic districts), an IMAX movie theater, the Benson Ford Research Center, and tour buses leaving for the Ford Rouge Factory Tour, a five-part excursion culminating with a walk through the Ford F-150 truck assembly plant.

From Dearborn, head west along the I-94 corridor, through cities like Ann Arbor and Battle Creek. Two notable sights are the Marshall Historic District, an area that encompasses hundreds of 19th-century homes and businesses, and Kalamazoo's Air Zoo, an enormous complex devoted to aviation, boasting full-motion flight simulators, historic airplanes, a space center, and more.

Saugatuck to Traverse City

From Kalamazoo, continue west on I-94 and head north on U.S. 31, toward the Art Coast, a cluster of art galleries in the towns of Saugatuck, Douglas, and Fennville. After spending some time amid the area's shops, restaurants, and inns, drive north through Holland, Muskegon, and Manistee, en route to the incredible Sleeping Bear Dunes National Lakeshore, a marvelous 35-mile stretch of beaches, islands, and dunes along Lake Michigan. From here, head east on M-72 to Traverse City, an ideal base from which to explore gorgeous Grand Traverse Bay, popular with boaters and surrounded by several scenic resort towns, golf resorts, and award-winning wineries.

Air Zoo

Sleeping Bear Dunes

Grand Traverse Lighthouse

MUSIC AND MOTOR CARS

Detroit's most well-known nicknames – Motown and the Motor City – underscore its rich musical and automotive heritage, which stretches back to the early decades of the 20th century. Visitors will find an array of museums, historic sites, concert venues, nightclubs, and annual festivals that celebrate the city's contributions to American music and industry. Here are a few of southeastern Michigan's best offerings:

MUSEUMS AND HISTORIC HOMES

In the Detroit area, tour the region's vintage car collections, musical heritage exhibits, and former auto baron homes. Begin in downtown Detroit, where the GM Renaissance Center presents the **GMnext Showroom,** a 44,000-square-foot display of vintage vehicles, concept cars, and new models.

Afterward, head to the Cultural Center and view an authentic auto assembly line at the **Detroit Historical Museum.** At the nearby **Charles H. Wright Museum of African American History,** music lovers learn about performers such as John Lee Hooker and Aretha Franklin. Just a bit north, the **Motown Historical Museum** is a small repository of costumes, records, photographs, and other memorabilia that celebrate the likes of Marvin Gaye, Diana Ross, Stevie Wonder, and The Temptations, artists who helped make "Hitsville U.S.A." a household term.

For a unique treat, head west to Dearborn to **The Henry Ford,** a museum complex that explores American history and industry, including Ford's childhood home, a collection of presidential limousines, **Greenfield Village,** and a walk through a Ford truck assembly line. History buffs may also enjoy touring **Fair Lane,** Henry Ford's former Dearborn estate, and the **Edsel & Eleanor Ford House,** a Cotswold-style mansion in Grosse Pointe Shores.

DETROIT'S MUSICAL NIGHTLIFE

For decades, Detroit has been a favored city among musicians as varied as Smokey Robinson, Bob Seger, and Eminem. Following a day of museum-hopping, venture into the Theater District, where the **Music Hall Center for the Performing Arts** has, for eight decades, hosted legendary musical acts. Later, head over to one of Detroit's legendary nightclubs; two winners are **Baker's Keyboard Lounge** and **Flood's Bar & Grille,** both of which offer live jazz music and delicious soul food.

YEARLY CELEBRATIONS

In January, auto lovers can attend the **North American International Auto Show,** which promises a first look at the latest innovative vehicle designs from manufacturers around the world. Two other car-related celebrations include the **Woodward Dream Cruise,** a mid-August event featuring thousands of vintage cars in nine Detroit suburbs, and the **Detroit Belle Isle Grand Prix,** a challenging Indy car race that occurs every Labor Day weekend. Also that weekend, the **Detroit International Jazz Festival** presents nearly 100 open-air jazz concerts alongside the Detroit River.

Dearborn's nostalgic Greenfield Village

Mackinac Bridge to Munising

Expect a two-hour drive on U.S. 31 from Traverse City, through the towns of Charlevoix and Petoskey, to the amazing five-mile-long Mackinac Bridge, currently the world's third longest suspension bridge. After crossing the bridge and passing through St. Ignace, head north on I-75 to Sault Ste. Marie for a look at another engineering marvel, the Soo Locks, through which massive freighters pass between Lakes Huron and Superior.

Head west through the Hiawatha National Forest to the Tahquamenon Falls, the second largest waterfall east of the Mississippi. Near the Whitefish Point Light Station, you'll find the Great Lakes Shipwreck Museum, the only museum dedicated to the perils of maritime transportation on the Great Lakes. Farther west along the Lake Superior coast lies Pictured Rocks National Lakeshore, a fabulous stretch of sand dunes, desolate beaches, sandstone cliffs, and shady forests.

a clear view of "Big Mac" from the Old Mackinac Point Lighthouse

enjoy the Keweenaw National Historical Park, a collection of old copper-mining sites, structures, and downtown districts spread throughout the peninsula. Adventurous hikers, backpackers, kayakers, and wildlife enthusiasts can take a ferry ride to Isle Royale National Park, a wild, isolated archipelago in the northern reaches of Lake Superior.

Straits of Mackinac to the Thumb

Once you're done exploring the Upper Peninsula, head south to Mackinaw City and board a ferry for Mackinac Island, a charming vacation spot that has long banned automobiles in favor of bicycles and horse-drawn carriages. Rife with Victorian mansions, this nostalgic island offers a true step back in time. Back on the mainland, drive south through the Gaylord golf mecca, a large concentration of top-notch golf courses, and make a stop at Hartwick Pines State Park, home to the largest stand of virgin white pines in the Lower Peninsula. Continue south on I-75, toward the Bavarian-style town of Frankenmuth, site of German shops and festivals, all-you-can-eat chicken dinners, and a year-round Christmas store.

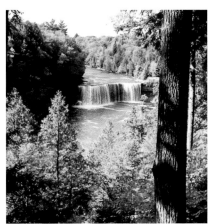

a view of Tahquamenon Falls through the surrounding trees

The Keweenaw Peninsula

If you're willing to venture farther into the wilds of the U.P., head west on M-28/U.S. 41 to the Keweenaw Peninsula, where history buffs will

THE UPPER PENINSULA'S NAUTICAL PAST

Lake Superior, the vast freshwater lake that spreads north of the Upper Peninsula's northern border, has for centuries served as a major transportation route for Native Americans, explorers, tourists, and various industries. Several historic lighthouses dot the coastline, some of which still provide navigational assistance to passing vessels. Despite the presence of such aids, however, shallow reefs and violent storms have led to hundreds of shipwrecks in Lake Superior over the years. Today, numerous maritime museums and underwater preserves reveal this fascinating shipping heritage. Visitors can hit the highlights in a five-day tour of the U.P.'s northern shore.

DAY ONE

From the Mackinac Bridge, head north on I-75 to Sault Ste. Marie, Michigan's oldest city, where you can watch ships passing through the incredible **Soo Locks** or opt for an up-close view aboard a **Soo Locks Boat Tour,** which offers a two-hour trip through the American and Canadian locks and along each nation's shore. After lunch, spend the afternoon at the intriguing **Museum Ship Valley Camp,** which contains over 100 exhibits, including two lifeboats from the stricken *Edmund Fitzgerald* and four aquariums filled with various fish from the Great Lakes region. Head a few blocks east to the **River of History Museum,** which chronicles the history of those who explored and helped to tame the St. Mary's River. Stay overnight in Sault Ste. Marie, perhaps at the quaint **Longships Motel.**

DAY TWO

Following breakfast, drive west along the shore of Whitefish Bay. Stop in Bay Mills, where the 1871 **Point Iroquois Light Station,** now a maritime museum, invites visitors to tour a restored light keeper's home and climb the tower for a pleasant view of the river and bay. Next, visit the 1849 **Whitefish Point Light Station,** the oldest operating lighthouse on Lake Supe-

Soo Locks Boat Tour

rior and now part of a complex that includes the **Great Lakes Shipwreck Museum,** which chronicles several tragic shipwrecks, including the *Edmund Fitzgerald.* Experienced divers might want to take a detour and explore the **Whitefish Point Underwater Preserve,** a fascinating area that encompasses 18 excellently preserved shipwrecks in the cold, clear, deep waters of Lake Superior. Afterward, you can stay in a nearby campground or roadside motel.

DAY THREE

In the morning, consider joining a guided tour of the 1874 **Au Sable Light Station** on the eastern end of Pictured Rocks National Lakeshore. Alternately, you can take a narrated glass bottom boat tour of **Alger Underwater Preserve,** which protects a handful of intact shipwrecks near Grand Island. After your boat trip, head farther west along the Lake Superior shore and spend the afternoon in the historic port of Marquette. The **Marquette Maritime Museum** is a particularly intriguing attraction, housing an interactive pilot house, several exhibits about shipwrecks, Native Americans, and the U.S. Coast Guard, and an impressive collection of lighthouse lenses; the museum also offers informative tours of the 1866 **Marquette Harbor Lighthouse.** After dinner, consider staying at the lovely 1896 **Big Bay Point Lighthouse Bed and Breakfast,** one of the nation's few lighthouse inns; hopefully, you've reserved a room well in advance.

DAY FOUR

After breakfast, take a leisurely four-hour drive via Country Road-550 and U.S. 41 to the tip of the Keweenaw Peninsula. Here, you can join a narrated round-trip cruise through Copper Harbor's formerly bustling port, to the 1866 **Copper Harbor Lighthouse,** where a host will guide visitors through the historic complex, which includes shipwreck artifacts, a small maritime museum, and incredible lake views. Those seeking a challenge can opt instead for exploring the **Keweenaw Underwater Preserve,** a 103-square-mile area containing at least nine

Eagle Harbor Light

shipwrecks, including the oldest known one in Lake Superior.

From Copper Harbor, head south to Eagle Harbor, where the fog signal building beside the 1871 **Eagle Harbor Light** now serves as a maritime history museum. Exhibits feature the area's past shipwrecks, the United States Lighthouse Service, and the perils facing long-ago lighthouse keepers. As the day winds down, stop for dinner in one of the peninsula's several family-friendly restaurants and head south to Ahmeek, where you can stay overnight in the romantic **Sand Hills Lighthouse Inn,** constructed in 1919 and now serving as a Victorian-style bed-and-breakfast. Reservations might be necessary here, too.

DAY FIVE

True history buffs should rise early, head south to Houghton, and take the morning boat ride to **Isle Royale.** Here, you'll encounter a number of historic maritime sites, including the **Edisen Fishery** and the 1855 **Rock Harbor Lighthouse,** now a museum operated by the National Park Service. Stay overnight in the waterfront **Rock Harbor Lodge,** then return to the mainland via the six-hour *Ranger III* boat ride the next morning.

▶ HISTORIC LIGHTHOUSES

During the 19th and early 20th centuries, the Great Lakes served as the principal transportation routes for the industries in this region. Consequently, lights were needed to alert vessels of their proximity to shore. More than 100 lighthouses were erected along Michigan's coastline and its surrounding islands. Although a few structures have since eroded to time, most remain intact and many are still operational. Some of the preserved lighthouses have become inns, museums, or private homes. Others are closed to the public, but nearly all can be viewed—and photographed.

Detroit to the Thumb

Though not the most popular area for lighthouse viewing, it contains several lights, such as the still-active Detroit River Light in Lake Erie, that are situated offshore and can be seen via boat or plane. Two worth a look are the Grosse Ile North Channel Range Front Light, a 50-foot-tall tower lit in 1906, and opened to the public once a year, and the Livingstone Memorial Lighthouse, a unique 65-foot-tall marble structure on Belle Isle.

the *Huron* Lightship, docked on the St. Clair River

From the Detroit area, head north on I-94 to Port Huron, where you can tour the *Huron* Lightship, which retired in 1970 as the last lightship in service on the Great Lakes and is now a National Historic Landmark. Visitors are welcome to explore this vessel, which is docked on the St. Clair River, as well as the nearby Fort Gratiot Light, the oldest light in Michigan. Established in 1829, this 86-foot-tall brick structure is still active today. After touring Port Huron's lighthouses, grab some dinner at one of the city's many fine eateries and stay the night, perhaps even at the lovely Thomas Edison Inn.

The next day, drive north on M-25, skirting the Thumb's coast. The first lighthouse you'll spy is the active Port Sanilac Light, established in 1886 and now a private residence. Farther north, the 1885 Harbor Beach Lighthouse, while still active, is only accessible by boat. Near Port Hope, the operational 89-foot-tall Pointe aux Barques Lighthouse, lit in 1857, is now a museum. If you have time, head up to Port Austin and charter a boat to view the 1878 Port Austin Reef Light, situated offshore and still active today. Stay over in Port Austin, where the historic Garfield Inn provides comfortable accommodations and The Bank 1884 offers fine dining in a casual setting.

the Fort Gratiot Light in Port Huron

Northeast Michigan

On the third day, venture west on M-25 to Bay City, hop onto I-75, and continue along U.S. 23, which traces the Lake Huron shore. There are several historic lighthouses in this area, some of which are inactive and can only be viewed by boat. In Tawas Point State Park, about three hours from Port Austin, you'll spy the operational Tawas Point Lighthouse, one of the state's most well-kept lights. Farther along U.S. 23, you'll find the Sturgeon Point Lighthouse, built in 1869 and still active today—as both a lighthouse and a maritime museum. You can either camp for the night in Harrisville State Park or head to Alpena, which has hotels, eateries, and a lighthouse of its own: the 1914 Alpena Light, a skeletal red structure near the Thunder Bay River.

Spend the next day exploring the rest of the Lake Huron shore, where you'll find the 1832 Thunder Bay Island Light and the 1905 Middle Island Lighthouse, both accessible via boat. Some of the mainland-based lights worth exploring include the 1840 Old Presque Isle Lighthouse, now a museum; the 1871 New Presque Isle Lighthouse, also open to the public; and the 1897 Forty Mile Point Light, a 52-foot-tall lighthouse with attached keeper's quarters. En route to the Mackinac Bridge, you'll encounter the octagonal 1884 Cheboygan Crib Light, which was relocated from the Cheboygan River, and the castle-like Old Mackinac Point Lighthouse, erected in 1892 and now a fascinating museum. From here, you can reach several island and offshore reef lights via boat—though you should take care in these potentially dangerous waters. Two of the most interesting are the 1874 Spectacle Reef Light, an impressive example of a monolithic stone lighthouse, and the 1895 Round Island Light in the Straits of Mackinac. There's no shortage of hotels and restaurants along this coast, from Rogers City to Mackinaw City.

Northwest Michigan and the Southwest Coast

From Mackinaw City, head south on I-75 and U.S. 31. Continue driving until you reach Charlevoix, where you can view the Charlevoix South Pierhead Lighthouse, then take a ferry to Beaver Island, home to the 1858 Beaver Head Lighthouse and the 1870 St. James Harbor Light. Back on the mainland, head toward Traverse City, where you'll find the 1870 Old Mission Point Lighthouse and the 1858 Grand Traverse Lighthouse, a well-preserved structure in Leelanau State Park. Here, visitors can climb the lighthouse tower, stroll through the museum, and enjoy sandwiches and pastries in the gift shop. Spend the night in Traverse City, which offers a wide array of accommodations.

Spend the last two days of your lighthouse tour exploring the Lake Michigan coastline,

Old Mission Point Lighthouse

an area rife with museums, hotels, camp-grounds, restaurants, and, of course, light-houses. In Leland, board a passenger ferry and head to South Manitou Island, where you can tour the 100-foot-tall South Manitou Island Lighthouse, erected in 1872.

Back on the mainland, take M-22 south to Empire, to find the newest light, the cylindri-cal Robert Manning Memorial Lighthouse, erected in 1991 to honor a longtime resident. Farther down M-22, you'll find the opera-tional 1858 Point Betsie Lighthouse, a lovely brick structure with attached keeper's quarters, and the 1932 Frankfort North Breakwater Light, an offshore light that can be viewed from the mainland. Via U.S. 31, visit the active 1927 Manistee North Pierhead Light; the 112-foot-tall 1867 Big Sable Point Lighthouse in Ludington State Park; the 1924 Ludington North Pierhead Light, a white pyramidal structure at the end of the breakwater; and the 1874 Little Sable Point Light in Silver Lake State Park.

Continuing south on U.S. 31, you'll see the 1875 White River Light Station, now a maritime museum; visitors can climb the spiral staircase for an incredible view of Lake

Little Sable Point Light

Michigan. Farther south, you'll encounter four vivid red, operational structures: the 1903 Muskegon South Pierhead Lighthouse, the Grand Haven South Pier Lighthouses, a range-light system linked by a catwalk, the 1872 Holland Harbor Light, and the 1903 South Haven South Pierhead Light. The last stop on your whirlwind lighthouse tour is the St. Joseph North Pierhead Lights, the second range-light system still in existence in the Great Lakes region.

the Manistee North Pierhead Light at sunset

SUN, SAND, AND SERENITY

Due to its enormous coastline, the Great Lakes State has its share of fantastic beaches and beach towns.

Saugatuck's Oval Beach

- **Warren Dunes State Park:** Situated north of Sawyer, this park offers three miles of sandy beaches, with incredibly high dunes. Beachcombers and swimmers crowd the southern end every summer. Farther inland, hikers and bird-watchers will find a bit more solitude.

- **Oval Beach:** Families flock to this popular Saugatuck-area beach, where swimmers can enjoy relatively warm waters in summer and adventurers can explore the nearby dunes.

- **Holland State Park:** One of Michigan's loveliest and most accessible beaches lures hundreds of swimmers and sunbathers on summer weekends. The park offers campgrounds, volleyball courts, amazing sunsets, a nearby boating lake, and terrific lighthouse views.

- **Grand Haven State Park:** Easy to reach from downtown, this sandy swimming beach is usually crowded with sun-seekers and metal-detecting enthusiasts in summer. Others come for the fishing pier, campground, picnic area, and photo-worthy lighthouses.

- **Muskegon State Park:** Part of a diverse 1,165-acre park, this two-mile stretch of sand attracts tons of swimmers, beachcombers, surfers, and picnickers every year. Head inland for hiking, fishing, and other recreational opportunities

- **Silver Lake Sand Dunes:** Perhaps the highlight of Oceana County, this stretch of sand is favored among off-road enthusiasts – the only place in the state where off-road dune driving is allowed.

- **Sleeping Bear Dunes National Lakeshore:** It's a must that you visit this natural wonder during your trip to Michigan. Here, you'll find a curvy stretch of Lake Michigan shoreline, with some of the tallest dunes in the state, and ideal places to canoe, fish, hike, and, in winter, ski.

- **Pictured Rocks National Lakeshore:** Although the U.P.'s Lake Superior coast isn't ideal for swimmers – given the lake's frigid temperatures year-round – the beaches here are perfect for beachcombers, bird-watchers, hikers, and sea kayakers with wetsuits. For relative solitude, venture toward Grand Sable Dunes.

- **Tawas Point State Park:** East of Tawas City, this park is noted for its pure white sandy beach, its warm waters, its well-preserved lighthouse, and its incredible view of the sunrise over Lake Huron.

- **Port Crescent State Park:** Near the tip of the Thumb, this park offers three miles of sandy beaches and dunes. Less popular than spots along Lake Michigan, here you'll have a better chance of finding peace and quiet amid the great outdoors.

▶ A TASTE OF WINE COUNTRY

Tabor Hill Winery

In recent years, Michigan has gained a reputation for crafting award-winning wines, rivaling those of France, Australia, California, and other well-known wine-producing regions. Although wineries are dispersed throughout the state, Michigan has two main winemaking areas in the Lower Peninsula—along the Southwest Coast and around Grand Traverse Bay. Both regions, which contain more than 30 wineries, benefit from a lake effect climate that protects the vines with snow cover in winter and extends the growing season for up to a month.

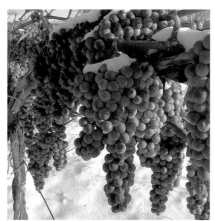

grapevines amid a snowy Michigan winter

For at least a week—preferably during summer or early fall—wine connoisseurs can tour the wineries along the Lake Michigan coast, sampling Michigan's finest. Of course, it helps to have a car.

Lake Michigan Shore Wine Trail

There are 11 wineries and several tasting rooms along this stretch of the Southwest Coast, from Union Pier to Saugatuck. Take a couple of days to experience the best of them.

Begin with the southern half of the wine trail, just east of Harbor Country. To reach these inland vineyards, take Red Arrow Highway to Lemon Creek Road. At the 200-acre Lemon Creek Winery and Fruit Farm, visitors can sample wines in the tasting room, take an informal tour of the vineyard, and pick whatever fruit is in season.

Afterward, drive south on Burgoyne Road, turn right onto Mount Tabor Road, and stop at the Tabor Hill Winery and Restaurant, known for its mid-priced, award-winning wines. Following a tour or tasting, have lunch in the first-rate restaurant, which offers an ever-changing menu of fine dishes, from elk chops to swordfish.

Your last stop of the day should be The

Round Barn Winery, which lies west of Tabor Hill. This family-owned winery, distillery, and brewery invites visitors to tour the vineyard, sample wines in the unique farmhouse, and take a winemaking class. Afterward, drive north to St. Joseph, where you can stay the night in The Boulevard Hotel Inn & Bistro, a terrific spot to enjoy dinner (or breakfast) on an outdoor terrace overlooking Lake Michigan.

The following day, head east on I-94 to M-40, where you'll find two long-standing wineries in Paw Paw. The first, the family-owned St. Julian Winery is actually the oldest and largest winery in the state; it provides year-round tours and tastings. Just up the road lies Warner Vineyards, the state's second oldest winery, offering self-guided tours and a wonderful deck on which to sip champagne. Before heading north to the Leelanau Peninsula, veer toward the coast, where towns like Saugatuck offer diversions of their own. In South Haven, stay at The Last Resort B&B Inn and have a casual meal at fun-loving Clementine's.

The Round Barn Winery

Leelanau Peninsula

Following breakfast, head north on U.S. 31 to Traverse City, just over a three-hour trip. From here, wineries and tasting rooms stretch north along either shore of the West Arm of Grand Traverse Bay. After dining in one of Traverse City's downtown eateries, drive west on M-72, toward the Leelanau Peninsula, which nurtures at least 18 wineries. Take County Road 651 north to Cedar, follow Schomberg Road to French Road, and spend the afternoon sampling merlot and other vintages at Chateau Fontaine Vineyards & Winery, a long-ago potato farm and cow pasture now transformed into 22 acres of grapevines. Head east to Suttons Bay, where you'll find Black Star Farms, a fascinating winery, distillery, creamery, and farmers market, with a tasting

the inn at Black Star Farms, near Suttons Bay

TOP TEN GOLF COURSES

Spring through fall, Michigan is one of the world's finest golfing destinations. Known as "America's summer golf mecca," the Gaylord area alone has over 20 courses, and the U.P. offers a number of seasonal choices, too. While the state has several private clubs – such as Oakland Hills Country Club, which hosted the 2008 PGA Championship – there's also a wide array of public courses.

- **St. Ives Resort:** On the road from Grand Rapids to Cadillac, you'll find this popular resort, celebrated for its pair of spectacular 18-hole courses.

- **Arcadia Bluffs Golf Course:** Located along a gorgeous stretch of Lake Michigan shoreline, this world-class 18-hole golf course has long been considered the best public course in the state, by golfers and golfing magazines alike.

- **Grand Traverse Resort and Spa:** With luxurious accommodations, excellent dining, a top-notch spa, an indoor water park, a 24-hour dog care facility, and three on-site golf courses, this 900-acre resort has easily become one of Michigan's finest golfing destinations.

- **A-Ga-Ming Golf Resort:** Overlooking lovely Torch Lake, not far north of Traverse City, this long-standing resort presents two 18-hole courses: Torch and the relatively new Sundance.

- **Shanty Creek Resorts:** Divided into three villages – Cedar River, Schuss, and Summit – this enormous resort features several dining, lodging, and spa options, numerous downhill skiing runs, and four championship golf courses.

- **Boyne Highlands Resort:** Just north of Petoskey, this year-round resort offers superb lodging, four spectacular golf courses, and access to a wealth of seasonal activities, from fishing to dog sledding.

- **Hidden River Golf & Casting Club:** Between Petoskey and Mackinaw City, you'll find this handsome resort, which appeals to golfers as well as fly fishers.

- **Black Lake Golf Club:** Operated by the UAW, this magnificent golf course is part of the union's 1,000-acre family center, which sits astride picturesque Black Lake.

- **Garland Resort:** Considered one of the state's most beautiful resorts, this family-owned destination presents four magnificent golf courses amid the woods of northeastern Michigan.

- **Treetops Resort:** This year-round resort keeps visitors busy with downhill skiing in winter, activities like tennis and biking in summer, and, of course, five stunning golf courses.

Shanty Creek Resorts

the year-round Chateau Chantal winery

room and a luxurious bed-and-breakfast (an ideal, if pricey, place to spend the next four nights).

Over the following three days, feel free to explore some of the other wineries that line this picturesque peninsula. Take special note of several locales in Suttons Bay, including Raftshol Vineyards, a former dairy enterprise and cherry orchard that now produces over 1,000 cases of bordeaux varietal red wines annually; Chateau de Leelanau Vineyard & Winery, which presents a tasting room not far from Grand Traverse Bay; Ciccone Vineyard and Winery, a Tuscan-inspired winery and tasting room owned by Madonna's father; and L. Mawby Vineyards, offering a year-round tasting room and annual picnic events. You should also stop by Leelanau Cellars, which is situated north of Suttons Bay and provides a fine tasting room for sampling everything from riesling to bacco noir.

Old Mission Peninsula

If your taste buds haven't yet wearied of reds and whites, you should spend the last day of your weeklong wine tour amid the seven wineries of the Old Mission Peninsula, accessible via Traverse City. Make sure to explore two wineries in particular: Chateau Grand Traverse Winery and Chateau Chantal, both of which offer complimentary tastings, winery tours, and luxurious accommodations with incredible views.

Of course, if you have time to spare, feel free to continue your own wine-tasting adventure, either retracing your steps to wineries you might have missed or venturing out into the rest of Michigan, where numerous other vineyards and tasting rooms await.

DETROIT AND SOUTHEAST MICHIGAN

Although Detroit's official motto—*Speramus meliora. Resurget cineribus.*—resulted from a catastrophic fire that nearly destroyed the fledgling town in 1805, its meaning—We hope for better things. It will rise from the ashes.—could just as easily refer to modern times. This is a city, after all, that has witnessed its share of soaring highs and crushing lows, and yet has always managed to come back swinging.

Detroit truly hit the map when Henry Ford's assembly line transformed the town—and the world—forever. With the assistance of the "Big Three" (Ford, General Motors, and Chrysler), the Motor City thrived during the first half of the 20th century. Reliance on a single industry, however, inevitably led to downswings that mimicked those of the auto industry, plunging the racially divided metropolis into years of crime and unemployment—modern problems that have often been exaggerated by the national media.

But the Motor City is defined less by its adversity and more by its innovation and fortitude. Crime is not the crippling issue it once was, and development has helped to revitalize the downtown area. Unofficially nicknamed the Renaissance City in the 1970s, Detroit has finally begun to shed its troubled past. Although it's still a work-in-progress, this tenacious town—also known for its Motown music, rock 'n' roll vibe, and legendary sports figures—has improved its tarnished image since the turn of the new millennium, and nowhere is that more apparent than along the waterfront.

Dominating the Detroit skyline, the once-

SOUTHEAST MICHIGAN

HIGHLIGHTS

Belle Isle: Situated on the Detroit River, between Windsor, Ontario, and the Motor City, Belle Isle has long been a treasured spot for visitors and area residents alike. Highlights include a zoo, a swimming beach, a conservatory, a golf course, the Dossin Great Lakes Museum, four fishing piers, and numerous historic edifices (page 32).

Greektown: One of several ethnic enclaves in the Detroit metropolitan area, this historic neighborhood invites visitors to experience Greek culture at its best. Here, you'll find the long-standing Pegasus Taverna, the rousing Opa! Fest, and, nowadays, a flashy casino (page 36).

The Cultural Center: Art and culture lovers flock to this part of Midtown, which boasts two art museums, three history museums, a new science center, an anthropology museum, several well-preserved Victorian structures, plus nearby theaters and art galleries (page 36).

Hamtramck: Founded at the turn of the 20th century, this village has long lured Polish immigrants and other Europeans. While the neighborhood is more culturally diverse these days, visitors can still come here for Polish sausages, European baked goods, and traditional artwork (page 51).

The Henry Ford: At this one-of-a-kind complex, visitors can view Henry Ford's childhood home, Thomas Edison's Menlo Park laboratory, President Kennedy's limousine, Rosa Parks' bus, and a working 19th-century farm. From here, you can also hitch a ride to the Ford truck assembly plant for an informative walking tour (page 54).

Woodward Dream Cruise: Begun in 1995 as a small fundraiser for the Ferndale community, this annual mid-August parade down Woodward Avenue, from Ferndale to Pontiac, has become the world's largest one-day automotive event, luring 1.5 million people and 40,000 classic cars from around the globe (page 58).

Detroit River International Wildlife Refuge: Established in 2001, North America's first international wildlife refuge includes islands, marshes, coastal wetlands, and waterfront terrain along the lower Detroit River and western shoreline of Lake Erie. Though public access is limited, the Lake Erie Metropark unit is popular among hikers, bird-watchers, anglers, and cross-country skiers (page 61).

LOOK FOR **[** TO FIND RECOMMENDED SIGHTS, ACTIVITIES, DINING, AND LODGING.

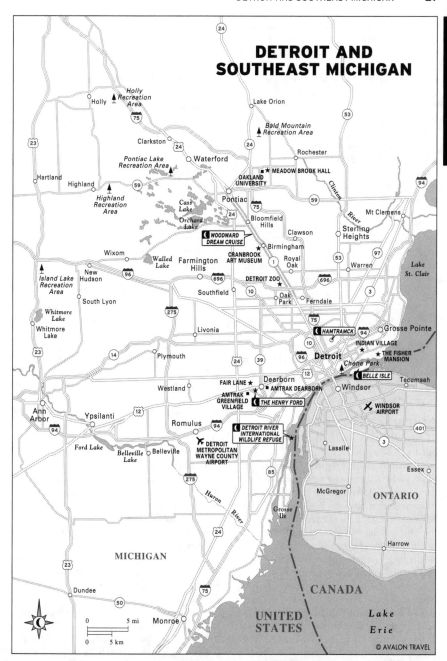

DETROIT AND SOUTHEAST MICHIGAN

© AVALON TRAVEL

controversial Renaissance Center has undergone an extensive renovation, transforming the distinctive office, hotel, and retail complex into the world headquarters of General Motors. In addition, the city has embarked upon an ambitious development project along the Detroit River, which it shares with Windsor, Canada. When completed, the Detroit International Riverfront will comprise a new harbor, an expanded Tri-Centennial Park, and a network of biking and jogging trails. Other recent downtown enhancements include a new ballpark for the Detroit Tigers, an adjacent football stadium for the Detroit Lions, and three casino resorts.

Detroit's many suburbs have also experienced a revival, marked by the opening of such attractions as the Holocaust Memorial Center in Farmington Hills and the Arab American National Museum in Dearborn, both of which celebrate the rich diversity of Detroit's people. Beyond the greater Detroit metropolitan area, visitors will discover a wealth of activities in Southeast Michigan, from skiing on Mount Holly to watching the Woodward Dream Cruise. Despite decades of struggle, it seems that Detroit and its surrounding towns are finally on the upswing, once again affirming the city's 200-year-old motto.

ORIENTATION

Almost prophetically, early Detroit was laid out like the spokes of a wheel. The plan—laid down by Judge Augustus Woodward, the first chief justice of the new Michigan territory—foreshadowed the city's major industry by more than a century. Woodward arrived in 1805 to find no more than a burned-out trading post on the narrow straits of the river—hence the name, *Détroit,* which means "straits." While little else remains of Woodward's grandiose plans to make Detroit the "Paris of the Midwest," the city's main streets—Jefferson Avenue, Gratiot Avenue, Woodward Avenue, Grand River Avenue, Michigan Avenue, and Fort Street—still echo that early hexagonal grid, shooting off at diagonal angles from a central axis. Woodward serves as the city's

main dividing line, splitting the landmass and its residents into east and west.

Compared to most U.S. urban areas, Detroit isn't too difficult to navigate. Though the city, its suburbs, and the rest of Southeast Michigan constitute a sprawling tapestry of distinct neighborhoods and communities, several bisecting highways and interstates make it easy to get around. For instance, I-75 snakes through downtown Detroit, linking southern towns like Monroe to northern destinations like Royal Oak, Pontiac, and Holly. Other major routes include I-96 from Lansing; I-696, which passes through Farmington Hills, Southfield, and Ferndale; and I-94, which cuts across the southern part of the Heartland, passes north of Detroit's Cultural Center and west of the Grosse Pointe suburbs, and heads north toward Port Huron.

PLANNING YOUR TIME

Southeast Michigan is a relatively small area, easy to traverse with a car. Several major routes link Detroit and its suburbs to other parts of the state, including I-75 from Flint, I-96 from Lansing, or I-94 from Battle Creek. Getting here via other forms of transportation is also a snap. The Detroit Metropolitan–Wayne County Airport (DTW) serves as a hub for Northwest Airlines. In addition, Amtrak serves Dearborn, Detroit, Royal Oak, Birmingham, and Pontiac. Greyhound also offers regular bus services to three stations in the area.

Unlike other parts of Michigan, Detroit and its suburbs aren't terribly dependent on the shifting seasons. Most museums, shops, and restaurants are open in winter as well as summer. No matter when you visit, however, you'll need at least three days to explore the region's key attractions, such as downtown Detroit and the Henry Ford complex in Dearborn. Five days is preferable, especially if you plan to make a trip across the border to Windsor, Ontario, in Canada.

Just remember that Detroit is a big, unpredictable city. Crime can be a concern here. Tourist areas, such as the waterfront and the Cultural Center, are well patrolled, but it's important to stay vigilant even in relatively safe areas. For added protection, always travel with someone else, hide your money and identification beneath your clothing, and leave valuable jewelry back at home. It's also helpful to know the location of a few different police stations, just in case.

For more information about Detroit and its suburbs, consult the **Detroit Metro Convention & Visitors Bureau** (211 W. Fort St., Suite 1000, Detroit, MI 48226, 313/202-1800, www.visitdetroit.com) or **Travel Michigan** (800/644-2489, www.michigan.org).

HISTORY

Few think of Detroit as an old city. But it is, in fact, one of the Midwest's oldest, founded in 1701 by Antoine de la Mothe Cadillac for Louis XIV of France.

Early Detroit was alternately ruled by the British and the French. In 1763, Pontiac, the Ottawa war chief, ordered an attack on British posts all over Michigan. Tired of the abuse suffered by the British army, Pontiac united the many Indian nations living around Detroit in a determined effort to capture the fort and restore French rule. Chiefs of the Ottawa, Huron, Potawatomi, and Chippewa tribes attended a secret war council. According to legend, however, a squaw tipped off the British, and Pontiac's men were met by a waiting British army. Rebuffed and defeated, Pontiac was later assassinated in 1769. Today, Pontiac's Rebellion is still regarded as one of the most formidable Native American uprisings in American history.

In 1783, Britain yielded the area to the United States in the Treaty of Paris. Local tribes, however, disputed the U.S. claim, so it wasn't until 1796 that Detroit finally unfurled the stars and stripes. The city fell again during the War of 1812 but was recaptured by the Americans a year later. Despite discouraging reports from initial settlers, people continued to pour in from the East. Between 1830 and 1860, the population doubled with every decade, and the city became best known as a nucleus of beer brewing and stove making.

By the turn of the 20th century, the auto industry had changed everything, making Detroit the fifth-largest U.S. city. The state's first self-propelled vehicle was likely a steam-powered car built by John and Thomas Clegg of Memphis, Michigan, in 1884. Later, Ransom Olds of Lansing developed a gasoline-powered auto and founded the Olds Motor Vehicle Company. In 1896, Charles C. King, an engineer and auto designer, drove the first car through the streets of Detroit; in the same year, Henry Ford tested his Quadricycle, which chugged along fairly well, despite no brakes and no reverse gear.

It was Ford and his later perfection of the assembly line that changed the face of the city—and America—seemingly overnight. Between 1905 and 1924, thousands of immigrants poured in from all over the world, attracted by Henry Ford's then-unheard-of wage of $5 per day. By 1917, 23 companies were busy in Detroit and its suburbs assembling vehicles for an ever-eager public. The Motor City had arrived.

By the 1930s and 1940s, Detroit was the place to be. Lively and full of energy, it was home to after-hours bars known as "blind pigs" (police—"pigs"—turned a "blind eye" to Prohibition-era hideouts that served liquor) and "black and tan" clubs where people of all races mingled. But things began to sour after World War II. As in other U.S. cities, the middle class began to head for the suburbs. Bigger and better freeways took people farther and farther away from the heart of the city, leaving behind vacant storefronts, vacant houses, empty streets, and empty lives too soon filled by poverty and crime.

The 1960s were difficult years. One bright spot was the birth of the Motown Sound, which began in Berry Gordy, Jr.'s tiny basement studio. Like the city, Motown had a hard-driving beat, and it quickly took over airwaves across the country. Detroit became known for producing more than cars, with Hitsville U.S.A. churning out rhythmic Top-10 tunes by artists such as Marvin Gaye, Little Stevie Wonder, the Supremes, and Smokey Robinson and the Miracles.

The late 1960s brought massive unrest to the country and the worst race riot in Detroit's history. In 1967, Detroit was the site of one of 59 racial "disturbances" around the country, a tragedy in which more than 43 people were killed. The nightly news in cities throughout the world showed a Detroit in flames, leaving a lasting impression on the country and a deep scar on the city's psyche.

The riots touched off an even greater exodus, the infamous "white flight" that left Detroit with a black majority in less than five years. By the 1970s, downtown had become a virtual desert after business hours. Controversial mayor Coleman Young, who ruled for more than 20 years, once said you could shoot a cannon down Woodward in those years without hitting a soul.

Today, some four million people call Detroit and its suburbs home. They comprise myriad ethnic groups, with more than 840,000 African Americans in the metropolitan area and the country's largest population of Bulgarians, Chaldeans, Belgians, and Arabs (the most outside the Middle East).

While the city has courted big business almost since the first horseless carriage jounced awkwardly off the assembly line, Detroit has never been a major tourist destination. An active tourism bureau has attempted to change that, with frequent events for national and international media and an aggressive campaign to attract visitors from other parts of the country as well as Europe and Japan.

In 1996, the much-celebrated anniversary of the "birth" of the car turned an international spotlight on the city, with favorable reports in both *The New York Times* and *USA Today*. Detroit responded with a centennial bash and invited the entire world. In 2001, the city celebrated its third century with exhibitions, events, and a month-long riverfront party with visits that included both tall ships and the Temptations. Stevie Wonder led the homecoming concert, which attracted approximately one million people (ironically, more than the city's current population). While city boosters don't expect flashy events such as these to erase the memories of Detroit in flames during the 1967 riots, they hope that they'll help to heal the wounds that have too long plagued the city—and perhaps ameliorate more recent troubles, such as Mayor Kwame Kilpatrick's 2008 resignation and subsequent felony conviction for obstruction of justice.

Sights

ON THE WATERFRONT

Motown's earliest history was made on its waterfront, so a tour is a fitting start to any exploration of the city. If it's a sunny day (regardless of the season), stroll the boardwalk near **Hart Plaza** (www.hartplazadetroit.com) and watch for one of the thousands of hulking freighters that pass annually.

Once, the waterfront, with its active port, was the city's livelihood. During the 20th century, however, Detroit turned its back on its former front door, choosing to erect faceless factories and anonymous office towers along its riverbanks instead of the more gracious green spaces popular during the previous century. Luckily, recent efforts have strived to correct the mistake: when completed, the **Detroit International Riverfront** (www.detroitriverfront.org) will comprise over five miles of public parks and plazas, linked by a continuous riverwalk.

For now, strollers can enjoy small stretches of the riverwalk and places like the 11-acre Hart Plaza, site of the breathtaking Horace E. Dodge Fountain, designed in the 1970s by Isamu Noguchi. It sends more than one million gallons of water per hour into the air via more than 300 streaming nozzles and jets.

GM Renaissance Center

Next to Hart Plaza is the gleaming GM

Renaissance Center (www.gmrencen.com), known to Detroiters as RenCen. Soaring high into the sky, this fortress-like, 73-story hotel/office/retail complex dominates the Detroit skyline, with seven steel towers containing more than 5.5 million square feet of space, including a 1,300-room Marriott hotel, two foreign consulates, and dozens of restaurants, stores, and movie theaters.

Of course, the road to the RenCen's present incarnation was rather rocky at best. The project was originally proposed by Henry Ford II, in part as a response to the 1967 riots. Ford—always a powerful name in Detroit—used his considerable influence to convince friends and foes alike to invest in the riverside complex. With big-name retailers such as Gucci and Cartier, it was intended to draw suburbanites back downtown. But it didn't work. The RenCen was a huge white elephant from the moment it opened in 1977. Designed by John Portman, best known for building hotel atriums, it was a confusing maze of circles and elevators that ultimately led nowhere. By 1983,

many of the original retailers had pulled out and most of the investors had defaulted on their loans.

The center received a much-needed facelift and helpful new directional signs in the mid-1980s, but it never became the city's much-heralded savior. Through the 1980s and much of the 1990s, the RenCen was supported by the various businesses—including Ford, ANR Pipeline, and others—who have kept offices here. In 1996, however, it received a huge shot in the arm with General Motors' announcement that it had purchased the landmark to use as its new world headquarters. In a major boost for the city, GM moved the majority of its workers into the RenCen in 1999. A major internal reorganization followed, leaving the space a bit less confusing.

The RenCen is still the largest privately financed development in U.S. history, with more than $380 million contributed by private investors. Representing a huge investment in the city's future, it is worth seeing on that basis alone. Once inside, you'll need a map to

© DETROIT METRO CVB

the Detroit People Mover passing below the GM Renaissance Center

navigate. Otherwise, you can take a free one-hour tour through this Detroit landmark. Tours depart from the GM Wintergarden, a tropical atrium overlooking the Detroit River, and feature sights like a vintage auto collection, the world's tallest vertical glass sculpture, and a breathtaking view of the Detroit and Windsor skylines.

◖ Belle Isle

At one time, 30 million tons of cargo were transported along the Detroit River, linking the city with more than 200 overseas ports. Nowadays, you can still feel the water's tug on Belle Isle (E. Jefferson Ave. and E. Grand Blvd., www.fobi.org), accessible via the Douglas MacArthur Bridge. This 985-acre urban sanctuary, stranded a half-mile out in the river, has been a public park since 1879, when the city purchased it for a now paltry $200,000 from the heirs of a wealthy local family.

Named after the then-governor's daughter, Isabelle Cass, it was designed in 1883 by Frederick Law Olmsted, of New York's Central Park fame. One of the city's most underrated

(and often neglected) jewels, the park gets a little rowdy on summer weekends, when teenagers from surrounding neighborhoods cruise the narrow streets and pathways looking for action. Although patrolled by both mounted police and squad cars, it's not a safe place to be at night.

On weekdays, however, it's peaceful, especially off-season. Belle Isle is a haven for birdwatchers and for families who flock here to fish from the piers, relax on Detroit's only swimming beach, and tour the vintage glass **Anna Scripps Whitcomb Conservatory,** small zoo, or intriguing **Dossin Great Lakes Museum** (100 Strand Dr., 313/833-5538, www.detroithistorical.org, 11 A.M.–4 P.M. Sat.–Sun., free). The museum traces the development of Great Lakes–area shipping from sailing vessels to modern freighters, many of which can still be seen from the riverfront.

Other visitors to Belle Isle come to jog, circle the island by bike, play golf, or just set up a picnic lunch under one of the gazebos and watch passing freighters. Boating enthusiasts wander around the 65-foot-tall marble **Livingstone**

Memorial Lighthouse, which operated from 1882 to 1930, or check out the pleasure craft docked at the 1923 **Detroit Yacht Club.** Admission to the island is free, though there has been an ongoing debate about charging a nominal admission to help defray maintenance costs.

It isn't the island's first controversy. Native Americans called Belle Isle "Rattlesnake Island" because of the number of snakes. Later, hogs were brought in by 18th-century settlers to destroy the rattlers, giving rise to the name Isle au Cochon ("Hog Island" in French) until 1845, when it was rechristened Belle Isle. Throughout its long history, the island has been used both as a dueling ground and as a place of quarantine for troops, most recently during the cholera epidemic of 1932.

Pewabic Pottery

Farther east along Jefferson Avenue, not far from Belle Isle, is another oasis, Pewabic Pottery (10125 E. Jefferson Ave., 313/822-0954, www.pewabic.com, 10 A.M.–6 P.M.

Mon.–Sat., noon–4 P.M. Sun.). Founded by Mary Chase Perry Stratton in 1903, this arts-and-crafts pottery is housed within a picturesque Tudor Revival building. Best known for their innovative and iridescent glazes, shown to great advantage in the tiles commissioned for many of the city's civic and residential structures, Pewabic tiles can be found in the stunning 1929 art deco Guardian Building, several downtown People Mover stations, and the Shedd Aquarium in Chicago.

Now a nonprofit ceramic arts center and a living museum, Pewabic continues to produce the handcrafted vessels and architectural tiles that brought it initial fame. Visitors peer into huge, fiery kilns on a self-guided tour during business hours. A landmark of Detroit's arts community, the pottery is a pilgrimage for potters and ceramic artists from around the country as well as the site of popular workshops for all ages. But don't look for the secret to the pottery's lustrous glaze—Stratton took it to the grave, leaving her successors to carry on with only an approximation of the original formula.

the Anna Scripps Whitcomb Conservatory on Belle Isle

Riverboat Tours

For a terrific view of Detroit's skyline, consider taking a ride on the Detroit River, the world's busiest international waterway. **Diamond Jack's River Tours** (313/843-9376, www. diamondjack.com, tours 1 P.M. and 3:30 P.M. Thurs.–Sun., $15 adults, $13 seniors 60 and over, $11 children 6–16) offers two-hour narrated riverboat cruises mid-June–August. There are two departure points for these informative tours: Detroit's Hart Plaza and Wyandotte's Bishop Park.

DOWNTOWN DETROIT

Tours of Pewabic will whet your appetite for the city's other vintage architecture. Backtrack along Jefferson to Woodward Avenue, which marks your entrance to the city's official downtown business district. While this area is still quiet after business hours, it hops during the day with office workers who toil in the banks, insurance companies, and other corporations.

The first stop on any architectural tour is the **Wayne County Building** on the east end of Cadillac Square, an early example of the Italian Renaissance style in Michigan. Built from 1895 to 1902, it's one of the oldest buildings in the city. Look up to see its ornamental cornices—they depict "Mad Anthony Wayne" conferring with the Indians.

A few blocks away is the art deco **Guardian Building** (500 Griswold St., www.guardianbuilding.com), a 40-story, Aztec-inspired local landmark. Friendly guards in the 1929 superstructure are usually pleased to share tidbits about the breathtaking building or point you in the right direction for a self-guided tour of its Pewabic-accented interior.

Several blocks north, the buildings of Woodward Avenue cast a long shadow over **Harmonie Park** (www.harmoniepark.com). If Woodward's desolation threatens to overwhelm you, this elegant enclave will restore your hope in the city's future. New energy has transformed a formerly deserted area into the city's hottest nightspot. Much of the credit goes to local architectural firm Schervish Vogel Merz, who believed in the area long before anyone else saw a future in its warehouse-style buildings and vintage storefronts. Today, the area is surrounded by pubs, galleries, and airy artists' lofts.

Theater District

Not far from Harmonie Park lies the official entrance to Detroit's Theater District. Once the city's most exclusive address, the neighborhood known as Brush Park had deteriorated almost to the point of no return before local boy Mike Ilitch—owner of the nationwide Little Caesars Pizza chain as well as the Detroit Tigers baseball and Detroit Red Wings hockey teams—stepped in and bought the aging **Fox Theatre** (2211 Woodward Ave., 313/983-6611, www.olympiaentertainment.com) in 1988.

What followed was a painstaking and often slow $8 million restoration that eventually returned the gaudy yet glamorous structure to its original glory. The 5,000-seat Fox is truly a marvel of 1920s architecture. Built in 1928 by William Fox, it was designed in the style of an Arabian tent. The exotic Thai-Byzantine style borrows motifs from a range of cultures, including Persian, Burmese, Indian, Thai, and Chinese. There are gold-leafed, hand-stenciled walls, marble-finish pillars, gold-tusked elephants, winged lions, a sunburst ceiling, and dreamlike decorative figures throughout. The lobby is six stories high, with 300,000 sparkling glass jewels, loads of brass, and a 13-foot, two-ton stained-glass chandelier.

The restoration was remarkably successful. Today, the Fox is one of the nation's most successful theater operations, with almost nightly presentations, including touring Broadway musicals, big-name concerts, restored film epics, and other special events. You can't miss the 125-foot multicolored neon marquee, which stretches to the 10th floor of the Fox office building. And here's a bit of trivia: During the 1920s, the Fox was the first theater in the United States to sell candy on-site.

Spurred by the resounding success of the Fox, other theaters soon followed. One contrast to the cavernous Fox is the intimate **Gem and Century Theatres** (333 Madison Ave., 313/963-9800, www.gemtheatre.com), a joint

DOWNTOWN
DETROIT

THEATER DISTRICT

HARMONIE PARK

TRAPPERS ALLEY

GREEKTOWN

BRICKTOWN

CORKTOWN

Elmwood
Central Park

Ford Field

Comerica Park

Detroit River

Detroit-Windsor Tunnel

To Belle Isle and Chene Park

To Canada

To Mexicantown

ROMA CAFÉ ▼
★ EASTERN MARKET
● SHORECREST MOTOR INN
★ MUSIC HALL CENTER FOR THE PERFORMING ARTS
PIZZAPAPALIS TAVERNA
▼ OPUS ONE
★ SECOND BAPTIST CHURCH
★ THE ATHENEUM
★ DETROIT MARRIOTT AT THE RENAISSANCE CENTER
RENAISSANCE CENTER
■ WAYNE COUNTY BUILDING
GEM THEATRE ★
★ DETROIT OPERA HOUSE
■ DIAMOND JACK'S RIVER TOURS
FOX THEATRE ★
★ THE FILLMORE DETROIT
COLUMBIA
■ GUARDIAN BUILDING
★ HART PLAZA
● DETROIT RIVERSIDE HOTEL
(OLD) TIGER STADIUM ★
● CORKTOWN INN

0   400 yds
0   400 m

© AVALON TRAVEL

cabaret-style venue with 450 seats. Founded in 1928 by a women's group hoping to have an "uplifting influence on the community," the Gem degenerated into a vaudeville house and a sleazy strip joint before foresighted businessman Chuck Forbes, owner of most of the city's vintage theaters, restored it as a complement to the Fox and a stop for national comedy acts, small plays, and musical revues. It reopened in 1992. Threatened by the new Comerica Park ballpark—home to the Detroit Tigers—it was moved to its present location in 1998. As the world's largest commercial building to be moved, it even made the pages of *Guinness World Records.*

Luciano Pavarotti and Dame Joan Sutherland were just a few of the big names who jetted into Motown in 1996 to attend the opening of the restored **Detroit Opera House** (1526 Broadway St., 313/237-7464, www.motopera.org). Designed in 1922 by C. Howard Crane as a vaudeville stage, the 7,000-square-foot theater served as a parking garage for most of the 1970s. David Di Chiera, the former university professor who founded the Michigan Opera Theatre in 1971 as a way to bring opera to kids, did the seemingly impossible when he raised $36 million for the opera's 2,700-seat new home. Today, it acts as an important cultural resource, luring Broadway musicals as well as opera and ballet productions.

Other area theaters include the **Fillmore Detroit** (2115 Woodward Ave., 313/961-5450, www.livenation.com), a live music venue built in 1925 as the State Theatre, and the **Music Hall Center for the Performing Arts** (350 Madison Ave., 313/887-8500, www.musichall.org), built in 1928 by the widow of auto baron John Dodge for the production of "legitimate" theatrical productions. Its stage has been graced by luminaries such as Lucille Ball, W. C. Fields, Martha Graham, Ella Fitzgerald, Lillian Hellman, and others. The acoustically perfect 1919 Orchestra Hall, now known as the **Max M. Fisher Music Center** (3711 Woodward Ave., 313/576-5111, www.detroitsymphony.com), is home to the acclaimed Detroit Symphony Orchestra.

◖ Greektown

Once a pioneer farm and now the city's best-known ethnic area, Greektown has long been a bright spot downtown and one of the few districts that jumps after midnight. With its many lively Greek restaurants and the Trappers Alley shopping and entertainment complex, this restored stretch of Monroe Street attracts both natives and visitors. (It also attracts parking enforcement officers, so if you park at one of the plentiful metered spots around Monroe, be sure to bring plenty of change.)

At the core of it all is a Greek neighborhood that dates back to 1915. Although most of the original residents have moved to the suburbs and the majority of restaurants and bakeries have gone upscale, you'll still find a few coffeehouses where old-timers gather to drink strong coffee or sip sweet retsina and play cards. One original grocery remains: Open the rusty screen door of the **Athens Grocery/Bakery** (527 Monroe St., 313/961-1149), and you'll walk past windows full of neatly arranged loaves of bread, sinfully sweet Greek pastries, and shiny tins of pungent imported olives.

Other highlights include two of Detroit's most notable churches. **Old St. Mary's Church** (646 Monroe St., 313/961-8711, www.oldstmarysdetroit.com), one of the city's most beautiful Roman Catholic structures, dates to 1841 and serves as Detroit's third oldest Catholic parish. Meanwhile, the **Second Baptist Church of Detroit** (441 Monroe St., 313/961-0920, www.secondbaptistdetroit.org) was established in 1836 by several former slaves who had left the First Baptist Church due to discrimination against African Americans. Once a stop on the Underground Railroad, the original church was replaced by the present one after a devastating fire in the early 1900s.

◖ The Cultural Center

Head north along Woodward Avenue from downtown, and you'll run right into the Cultural Center, part of Midtown Detroit (www.detroitmidtown.com). Bordered by bustling Wayne State University to the west and the Detroit Medical Center to the east, this

© DETROIT METRO CVB

Greektown at night

is where you'll find most of the city's art and civic museums.

Wander the streets of "Old Detroit" (or at least an idealized version of them) in the basement of the 80,000-square-foot **Detroit Historical Museum** (5401 Woodward Ave., 313/833-1805, www.detroithistorical.org, 9:30 A.M.–3 P.M. Wed.–Fri., 10 A.M.–5 P.M. Sat., noon–5 P.M. Sun., $6 adults, $4 seniors 60 and over, $4 children 5–17). You'll trudge along irregular cobblestones that once lined city streets past re-creations of barber shops, grocery stores, and other vintage businesses. The display, which opened in 1951 and has been among the museum's most popular, traces three periods of Detroit history (albeit a decidedly Eurocentric version of it).

The permanent exhibit "Frontiers to Factories" traces the city's history from a trading post to an industrial giant, with a walk-in diorama from the 1750s, a railway station, and a mock, turn-of-the-20th-century exposition. Other highlights of the collection include the Glancy Train display, one of the world's largest; special exhibits about Detroit's leaders, symbols, and entertainment venues; and an exhibition simply named "Motor City," which traces the history of the car, the city, and the people who changed the world when they came to work here. The exhibit's highlight is the "body drop," a segment of a 1953 assembly line in which the outer shell of a later-model Cadillac is lowered from the ceiling onto an engine body set up on an eye-level platform. It was taken from the assembly line at the now-demolished Clark Street Cadillac plant.

Detroit has always been a blue-collar town, yet city founders amassed enough green during the heyday of the auto industry to fund what eventually became one of the country's finest art museums. The **Detroit Institute of Arts** (5200 Woodward Ave., 313/833-7900, www.dia.org, 10 A.M.–5 P.M. Wed.–Thurs., 10 A.M.–10 P.M. Fri., 10 A.M.–6 P.M. Sat.–Sun., $8 adults, $4 children 6–17) attracts more than 500,000 visitors each year. The sometimes-confusing 100-plus galleries contain some of the greatest art treasures of the world, including works by Van Gogh, Rodin, Rembrandt, Brueghel, and other masters.

The museum strives to present an encyclopedic collection, with a multicultural scope that traces creativity in all of its forms, from prehistory through the present. Important collections include the French Impressionist, Italian (the largest outside Italy), German Expressionist, African, Asian, Native American, and 20th-century. It's worth hunting for the museum's generally accepted best works, including Rodin's pensive *Thinker,* Brueghel's *Wedding Dance* (look closely and you may see some remnants of paint on the bulging codpieces; they were once painted over), Van Eyck's tiny treasure, *St. Jerome in His Study,* Romare Bearden's colorful *Quilting Time,* and Rembrandt's enlightened *Visitation.*

While the building may seem to be full of art made by and for the ruling class, the city's workers have the last laugh in the breathtaking *Detroit Industry* frescoes. Mexican muralist Diego Rivera captured the droning monotony of the assembly line in 27 huge panels surrounding the museum's central courtyard. Rivera spent nine months in Detroit in 1933 before unveiling the series to great controversy. A visionary Edsel Ford stood up to virulent criticism of the Mexican socialist's frescoes, which were damning in their innate criticism of capitalism. Many city leaders wanted the walls whitewashed as soon as the scaffolding came down, but Ford stood firm, defending the murals, which, unlike another series in New York's Rockefeller Center, were saved.

Relax and rest your feet with a cup of java or something stronger in the Kresge Court Café, a soaring green and light-filled space modeled after Florence's Bargello Palace. If you're visiting on a weekend, stick around long enough to take in a movie at the museum's acclaimed 1,150-seat **Detroit Film Theatre** (313/833-3237), which offers important premieres by new and established directors and is one of the few venues in the city to show restored, rarely seen classics in their correct aspect ratios. *Variety* called it "the best buy for cineastes in America."

Another highlight of the city's Cultural Center is the **Detroit Science Center** (5020 John R St., 313/577-8400, www.detroit-sciencecenter.org, 9 A.M.–3 P.M. Mon.–Fri., 10 A.M.–6 P.M. Sat.–Sun., $13 adults, $12 children 2–12), which reopened to the public in July of 2001. The recently renovated center includes a digital planetarium, two science stages, the state's only IMAX dome theater, and areas devoted to motion, life sciences, matter, energy, waves, and vibration. Other intriguing attractions in this area include the **Charles H. Wright Museum of African American History** (315 E. Warren Ave., 313/494-5800, www.maah-detroit.org, 9 A.M.–5 P.M. Tues.–Sat., 1–5 P.M. Sun., $8 adults, $5 seniors 62 and over, $5 children 3–12) and the **Museum of Contemporary Art Detroit (MOCAD)** (4454 Woodward Ave., 313/832-6622, www.mocadetroit.org, 11 A.M.–5 P.M. Wed. and Sat.–Sun., 11 A.M.–8 P.M. Thurs.–Fri., free), the Cultural Center's newest addition.

New Center District

The neighborhood known as "New Center" (named in part as an optimistic effort to replace the city's ailing downtown) was once best known for its most famous resident, General Motors. The twin towers of GM's corporate headquarters housed thousands of workers; for decades, its lavish first-floor showrooms were filled year-round with the latest models, hot off the drawing boards located in the upstairs offices.

Much to the chagrin of GM's employees and executives, the corporate headquarters were surrounded by a once-fine neighborhood that had become seedy and derelict. With the clout and bankroll to pull off what few other companies in the world could at the time, GM spent millions upon millions buying, rehabbing, and reselling the old homes in the surrounding neighborhood—redubbed New Center. The idea was to spruce up the company's surroundings, draw its employees and other middle- and upper-income families back downtown, and, hopefully, spur more area redevelopment.

The New Center neighborhood looks pretty good, though GM ended up leaving New Center and moving downtown to the RenCen in 1999. Since then, the GM building (as it's still known by most Detroiters) has struggled to attract tenants. Among those who have moved in are local health care offices and the state of Michigan.

Of the New Center's two main attractions, the **Fisher Building** (3011 W. Grand Blvd., 313/874-4444) is the most interesting. Even if you're not an architecture fan, it's worth seeing for the dazzling ceiling mosaics alone. The Architectural League of New York recognized the Fisher Building as the world's most beautiful commercial structure when it was built in 1928. Albert Kahn, one of the city's best-known architects, made lavish use of expensive materials, including 420 tons of bronze, marble, Minnesota granite, and 24-karat gold. Today, the building's 28-story central tower and two 11-story wings house the Fisher Theater, shops, restaurants, and office space.

Dwarfed by the Fisher Building and the GM Building is the diminutive **Motown Historical Museum** (2648 W. Grand Blvd., 313/875-2264, www.motownmuseum.com, 10 A.M.–6 P.M. Tues.–Sat., $10 adults, $8 children under 13). Known to many across the country as "Hitsville U.S.A.," this is where the Motown Sound exploded from the now-legendary Studio A and soon had teenagers around the country "Dancin' in the Streets."

Berry Gordy, Jr., bought the unremarkable two-story house in 1959 as a fledgling songwriter with a dream of managing singers. Today, the state historic site looks much as it would have in the early 1960s, with an office and tape library filled with reel-to-reel tape machines, company manuals, and newspaper clippings. The second floor re-creates Gordy's 1959–60 apartment, where he and his staff would spend nights packing records to ship to radio stations around the country. The museum's most prized display, however, is the original Studio A, where top tunes such as "Stop in the Name of Love" and "My Girl" were recorded. Diana Ross and the Supremes, Smokey Robinson and the Miracles, Martha and the Vandellas, The Temptations, The Four Tops, Marvin Gaye, Little Stevie Wonder, and the Jackson Five all recorded in this studio during their early careers.

Other artifacts on display in the two museum buildings (at its zenith, the company owned seven buildings along West Grand Boulevard) include rare photos, gold records, flashy costumes, and other memorabilia.

Mexicantown

The smell of fresh tortillas baking at the La Jalisciense factory leads hungry diners and curious visitors to Bagley Street, the main thoroughfare of the city's Mexican district (www.mexicantown.org). Located about five miles from downtown on the city's southwest side, the neighborhood is divided by I-75, so there's an eastern and western side, with shops, restaurants, and homes on both. Here's where you'll find colorful Mexican *mercados* and see elderly Mexican women, heads covered with an old-fashioned lace mantilla, praying the rosary in one of the historic churches, including **Ste. Anne de Detroit** (1000 Ste. Anne St., 313/496-1701, www.ste-anne.org), the city's oldest, founded in 1701. In summer, the area hosts a popular outdoor market on Sunday where you can pick up fresh chili peppers and other spicy souvenirs.

The Mexican restaurants grouped along streets around Bagley provide the area's main income and job base. Forget Taco Bell; this is the real thing. Salt-rimmed margaritas, soft-shell tacos full of spicy meat and onions, and soft, flaky *sopaipillas* rival the best south of the border. Queen of them all is **Xochimilco** (3409 Bagley St., 313/843-0179, 11 A.M.–2 A.M. daily, $4–14) where Mexican art and the eyes of God cover the walls, and where weekend waits can stretch to over an hour. Other fans of Mexican fare prefer Xochi's often-less-crowded competitors, such as **Mexican Village** (2600 Bagley St., 313/237-0333, www.mexicanvillagefood.com, 11 A.M.–11 P.M. Sun.–Thurs., 11 A.M.–1 A.M. Fri.–Sat., $5–18).

SOUTHEAST MICHIGAN

Entertainment and Events

NIGHTLIFE

When the sun goes down, the lights come on around the city. No matter what your style, Detroit has plenty of places where you can party. The city holds a number of options, from alternative bands at **Saint Andrew's Hall** (431 E. Congress, 313/961-8137 or 313/961-6358) to smooth jazz at the long-standing **Baker's Keyboard Lounge** (20510 Livernois Ave., 313/345-6300, www.bakerskeyboard-lounge.com, 5 P.M.–11 P.M. Mon., 11 A.M.–midnight Tues.–Thurs., 11 A.M.–2 A.M. Fri., 4 P.M.–2 A.M. Sat., 4 P.M.–midnight Sun.). Another popular hangout is **Flood's Bar & Grille** (731 St. Antoine St., 313/963-1090, www.floodsdetroit.com, 4 P.M.–midnight Mon., 3 P.M.–2 A.M. Tues.–Fri., 7 P.M.–2 A.M. Sat.–Sun., $5-10 cover), which features jazz, sweet soul, or karaoke nightly.

CASINOS

In 1997, city voters approved a controversial referendum permitting casino gambling within city limits. Over a decade later, three casinos are now open—and remain controversial. Whether gambling is the struggling inner city's angel or devil is still being decided not only at the craps tables, but in the hearts of residents. For those who enjoy rolling the dice, options include **MGM Grand Casino** (1300 John C. Lodge Fwy., 877/888-2121, www.mgmgranddetroit.com), a flashy, art deco palace that draws its inspiration from the Hollywood of yesteryear. Motown in all its glory provides the theme for Detroit's own **MotorCity Casino** (2901 Grand River Ave., 877/777-0711, www.motorcitycasino.com), housed in a former Wonder Bread warehouse and connected by skywalks to downtown restaurants and parking. The **Greektown Casino** (555 E. Lafayette Blvd., 313/223-2999, www.greektowncasino.com) is the city's most spacious, with Las Vegas–style gaming and easy access to the city's liveliest neighborhood. All have on-site restaurants and varying degrees of entertainment.

THE ARTS

Productions at the 5,000-seat **Fox Theatre** (2211 Woodward Ave., 313/983-6611, www.olympiaentertainment.com, show times and ticket prices vary) include touring Broadway musicals, big-name concerts, restored film epics, and other special events. The tiny and jewel-like **Gem and Century Theatres** (333 Madison Ave., 313/963-9800, www.gemtheatre.com, show times and ticket prices vary) is

---

MORE THAN MOTOWN

Detroit has always been a complex town. Its many facets have spawned many monikers – not the least of which honors its status as the birthplace of a groundbreaking musical style. But Motown legends like Aretha Franklin, Martha Reeves, Diana Ross, Smokey Robinson, Mary Wells, Jackie Wilson, and Stevie Wonder aren't the only musically oriented folks to have spent their formative years in and around Detroit. Southeastern Michigan has also nurtured a brood of well-known rock 'n' rollers, including:

- Alice Cooper
- Eminem
- Glenn Frey
- Bill Haley
- Madonna
- Ted Nugent
- Iggy Pop
- Kid Rock
- Bob Seger
- Del Shannon

© DETROIT METRO CVB

the beautifully restored Fox Theatre

a cabaret-style venue for national comedy acts, small plays, and musical revues. The restored **Detroit Opera House** (1526 Broadway St., 313/237-7464, www.motopera.org, show times and ticket prices vary) attracts full-scale productions of opera, ballet, and Broadway musicals.

Other area theaters include the **Fillmore Detroit** (2115 Woodward Ave., 313/961-5450, www.livenation.com, show times and ticket prices vary), a live music venue built in 1925 as the State Theatre, and the **Music Hall Center for the Performing Arts** (350 Madison Ave., 313/887-8500, www.musichall.org, show times and ticket prices vary), which features contemporary ballet, music festivals, and more. For classical music, consider the **Max M. Fisher Music Center** (3711 Woodward Ave., 313/576-5111, www.detroitsymphony.com, show times and ticket prices vary), home to the acclaimed Detroit Symphony Orchestra.

FESTIVALS AND EVENTS

Detroit hosts numerous events and celebrations throughout the year, including January's **North American International Auto Show** (Cobo Hall, 1 Washington Blvd., 313/886-6750, www.naias.com, $12 adults, $6 children 7–12), which still offers the world a first-hand look at what cars will look like in the near and distant future. In late June, the St. Nicholas Greek Orthodox Church holds the annual **Opa! Fest** (760 Wattles Rd., Troy, 248/362-9575, www.opafest.com), a weekend filled with Greek music, traditional Greek folk dancing, and, of course, Greek cuisine, from kabobs and gyros to pastries and wine.

Over Labor Day weekend, there are at least two events worth attending. In Hart Plaza, the **Detroit International Jazz Festival** (313/963-7622, www.detroitjazzfest.com) presents more than 85 free, open-air concerts and a world-class selection of music masters—the largest free jam in the world. The popular "Meet the Artists" series and free clinics in improvisation for students are designed to support the city's vital jazz community and ensure its survival. Concerts are held all over the city in conjunction with the festival, including at Chene Park, home of well-attended annual events and open-air summer concerts.

ELMORE LEONARD'S MOTOR CITY

Born in New Orleans in 1925, Elmore Leonard, the son of a General Motors employee, spent the bulk of his adolescent and teenage years in Detroit. Following high school, he served in the U.S. Navy for three years. After graduating from the University of Detroit with an English degree, he began to write ad copy for clients like Chevrolet. Eventually, however, his love of fiction proved too great an urge to resist.

While maintaining his advertising job, he began to pen Western stories, popular in the 1950s. When the Western market shrank a decade later, Leonard decided to focus on a full-time writing career. Soon, he'd crafted his first crime novel, *The Big Bounce* (1969). Over the ensuing years, he continued to write crime novels (often set in his hometown), gradually gaining a loyal cult following. Adapting several of his stories into screenplays helped to fund his fiction career – until the publication of two best sellers propelled *Time* to christen him the "Dickens from Detroit" in 1984.

Since then, Leonard, who still lives in a Detroit suburb, has continued to write best-selling crime novels, some of which have become popular films, including *Get Shorty* (1995), *Jackie Brown* (1997), and *Out of Sight* (1998). Even his Western tales have made a resurgence: In 2007, Russell Crowe and Christian Bale starred in *3:10 to Yuma*, the second adaptation of his eponymous short story.

If you're curious about Leonard's sharp-tongued take on gritty Detroit, visit the author's official website (www.elmoreleonard.com) or consider perusing the following titles:

UNKNOWN MAN NO. 89 (1977)
When a skillful Detroit process server is hired to search for a missing stockholder, he becomes the unwitting target of a lethal triple-cross.

THE SWITCH (1978)
Hoping to make some easy ransom money, two ex-cons kidnap the wife of a Detroit developer, who, unfortunately for them, has no desire to get her back.

CITY PRIMEVAL (1980)
A dedicated homicide detective strives to stop a psychopathic murderer in the Motor City.

TOUCH (1987)
A former Franciscan monk with faith-healing powers finds it difficult to be a saint in the city.

OUT OF SIGHT (1996)
A career thief forms an unlikely relationship with a sexy U.S. Marshal, which leads them both from sunny Florida to the gritty streets and posh suburbs of Detroit.

MR. PARADISE (2002)
When two roommates – a lingerie model and an escort – get involved with a retired Detroit-based lawyer, murder, greed, and pandemonium ensue.

Meanwhile, Belle Isle is the site of the **Detroit Belle Isle Grand Prix** (www.detroitgp.com), a fact that causes great chagrin to naturalists but brings big bucks to city coffers. Every Labor Day weekend, the birds and bees are drowned out by the drone of roaring Indy cars, which take over the western tip of the island on a 2.1-mile course, considered one of the most challenging in the world. Noise from the event can be heard throughout downtown and as far away as the Grosse Pointes.

SHOPPING
GM Renaissance Center

Downtown shoppers can spend at least a couple hours browsing the boutiques inside the RenCen (www.gmrencen.com). Options run the gamut, from **The Runway** (313/568-7977, 10 A.M.–6 P.M. Mon.–Fri.), which sells high-end women's apparel, to the charming **Renaissance 500 Tobacco Shop** (313/259-6510, 7 A.M.–5:30 P.M.), where the friendly staff provides fine tobacco products and other specialty items.

Eastern Market

There is one place in the city where old and young, Eastsider and Westsider, black and white meet. Bring your wagon or grocery bag to the historic Eastern Market (2934 Russell St., 313/833-9300, www.detroiteasternmarket.com), between Mack and Gratiot Avenues, on a Saturday morning, and you'll find a fragment of old Detroit, a colorful cornucopia of smells, sights, and sounds. In a city that's known great cycles of boom and bust, Eastern Market is as perennial as the fruit and flowers it sells.

Built on the site of an early hay and wood market, this bustling area near Greektown has lured Detroiters since the 1890s. Shoppers come to buy meat, cheese, produce, fruit, and flowers from large, open-air stalls and wholesale/retail specialty shops. Many wholesalers are the descendants of the Belgian, German, and Polish farmers who frequented the market generations ago, or the Italian and Lebanese merchants who began catering to the booming city in the 1920s.

Saturdays are busiest, when the farmers market runs from 6 A.M. to 5 P.M. and thousands of shoppers pour into the area to browse, bargain, and buy among goods that range from fresh chitlins to fresh cilantro. Highlights include the flower stalls (the market is the largest bedding center in the world); the aromas at **Germack's,** the oldest pistachio importer in the United States; and **Rafal Spice Company,** which has more than 400 herbs and spices, 85 kinds of coffee, and a large assortment of hot sauces and perfume oils filling its narrow shelves.

Sports and Recreation

SPECTATOR SPORTS

The Motor City boasts more professional sports teams than most major U.S. cities, and Detroiters are among the country's most loyal fans, with thousands cheering on the home teams at Lions football, Pistons and Shock basketball, Tigers baseball, and Red Wings hockey games. Most are played at sparkling modern suburban stadiums, much like their counterparts across the country.

Historic **Tiger Stadium** (www.tigerstadium.org), situated at Michigan and Trumbull, south of I-75, is still standing—for now. Legendary and longtime home to the Detroit Tigers, it was replaced in April 2000 by the glitzy new **Comerica Park** (2100 Woodward Ave., 313/962-4000, http://detroit.tigers.mlb.com, Apr.–Oct.). Tiger Stadium's future is uncertain, despite ongoing efforts by preservationists who have suggested a number of reuse plans.

While it will never be Tiger Stadium, Comerica Park certainly has its fans. With a family-friendly philosophy that includes a Ferris wheel and a pedestrian museum, it has attracted city and national attention as one of the best of the new breed of ballparks. The location in the heart of the vintage Theater District is also prime.

Just east of Comerica Park is the relatively new Ford Field, home to the **Detroit Lions** (2000 Brush St., 800/616-7627, www.detroitlions.com or www.fordfield.com, Sept.–Dec.). For information about the city's other sports teams, contact the **Detroit Pistons** (The Palace, 5 Championship Dr., Auburn Hills, 248/377-0100, www.nba.com/pistons or www.palacenet.com, Nov.–Apr.), the **Detroit Shock** (The Palace, 5 Championship Dr., Auburn Hills, 248/377-0100, www.wnba.com/shock or www.palacenet.com, Nov.–Apr.), and the

a sold-out crowd at Comerica Park

Detroit Red Wings (Joe Louis Arena, 600 Civic Center Dr., 313/396-7575, http://redwings.nhl.com, Oct.–Apr.).

BIKING

Experienced bikers head for **Highland Recreation Area** (5200 E. Highland Rd., White Lake, 248/889-3750), where 17 miles of trails make up some of the area's most challenging biking, or **Pinckney Recreation Area** (8555 Silver Hill Rd., Dexter Township, 734/426-4913), home to the 17.5-mile Potawatomi Trail, ranked in the nation's top 10 routes.

Accommodations

Detroit offers hotels, motels, and inns to suit all budgets. Although most downtown accommodations are of the business-class, hotel-chain variety, you'll even find a few Victorian-style inns and casino resorts.

$50-150

Close to downtown attractions, the **Detroit Riverside Hotel** (2 Washington Blvd., 313/965-0200, www.detroitriversidehotel.com, $114–150 d) provides luxurious accommodations as well as an indoor pool, a fitness center, and a stylish lounge.

East of downtown, the **Shorecrest Motor Inn** (1316 E. Jefferson Ave., 313/568-3000, www.shorecrestmi.com, $73–161 d) is popular with execs looking to save a buck. The 54-room budget motel, in the shadow of the RenCen, is family-owned and includes business services, clean accommodations, and a decent short-order restaurant (the Clique). West of Detroit's stadiums and theaters, the 150-room **Corktown Inn** (1331 Trumbull St., 313/496-1400, www.corktowninn.com, $60–100 d) is another option for budget-conscious travelers who need little more than clean beds, laundry services, and proximity to Detroit's main attractions.

$150-300

One charming option is 【 **The Atheneum** (1000 Brush Ave., 313/962-2323, www.atheneumsuites.com, $150–299 d), downtown's best all-suite hotel. Located in the heart of Greektown, it borrows classical motifs from the surrounding neighborhood in its 174 luxury suites, all with separate living rooms, marble bathrooms, high-speed Internet access, and other convenient amenities. Another unique choice is the **Detroit Marriott at the Renaissance Center** (GM Renaissance Center, 313/568-8000, www.marriott.com, $229–249 d), which provides terrific views of the Detroit River as well as easy access to the RenCen's shops and restaurants.

For traditional chain lodgings, consider the pet-friendly **Hilton Garden Inn** (351 Gratiot Ave., 313/967-0900, www.hiltongardeninn. com, $170–209 d), located only a block from Comerica Park and Ford Field. You might also try **Courtyard Detroit Downtown** (333 E. Jefferson Ave., 313/222-7700, www.marriott.com, $179–219 d), with 260 oversized rooms, an extensive health club, an enormous indoor pool, and an outdoor aboveground tennis court/running track that offers terrific views of the city's surrounding vintage architecture.

CASINO RESORTS

For even more amenities, consider staying at one of Detroit's three downtown casino resorts. The shimmering 【 **MGM Grand Detroit** (1777 3rd St., 877/888-2121, www.mgmgranddetroit. com, $259–459 d) houses an enormous gaming space, a full-service spa, pampering hotel rooms, live entertainment, and several restaurants, including the Wolfgang Puck Grille. The **MotorCity Casino/Hotel** (2901 Grand River Ave., 866/782-9622, www.motorcitycasino. com, $354–504 d) also promises more than Las Vegas–style games, including a 24-hour fitness center, a luxurious spa, live concerts, varied dining options, and 400 stylish, state-of-the-art rooms and suites. Even Greektown has its own resort, the **Greektown Casino** (555 E. Lafayette Ave., 888/771-4386, www.greektowncasino.com, $119–229 d), which offers a fine steakhouse, a trendy lounge, a wide range of gaming tables and slot machines, and amenities like ergonomic desks, plush bedding, and free parking.

Food

GREEKTOWN

Greektown is a delightful place come mealtime, and most Detroiters have their favorite Greektown restaurant. Top choices include the **Laikon Cafe** (569 Monroe St., 313/963-7058, 11 A.M.–midnight Wed.–Mon., $10–20), **New Parthenon** (547 Monroe St., 313/961-5111 or 313/963-8888, 11 A.M.–3 A.M. daily, $10–25), and the upscale 【 **Pegasus Taverna** (558 Monroe St., 313/964-6800, www.pegasustaverna.com, 11 A.M.–1 A.M. Mon.–Thurs., 11 A.M.–3 A.M. Fri.–Sat., 11 A.M.–midnight Sun., $6–27). All serve specialties that include a tart *avgolemono* (chicken lemon soup), flaky spinach pie, *pastitsio* (Greek macaroni), and flaming *saganaki* cheese, lit with a flourish and a cry of "Opa!" from the waiter. Afterward, many diners wander over to the popular **Astoria Pastry Shop** (541 Monroe St., 313/963-9603, www.astoriapastryshop.com, 8 A.M.–midnight Sun.–Thurs., 8 A.M.–1 A.M. Fri.–Sat., $2–5) for baklava and other Greek and European pastries laid out neatly behind gleaming glass countertops.

Of course, not everything worth seeing in Greektown is Greek. **PizzaPapalis Taverna** (553 Monroe St., 313/961-8020, www.pizzapapalis.com, 11 A.M.–1 A.M. Mon.–Sat., noon–1 A.M. Sun., $6–24) is where Motown meets the Windy City. Only the name is Greek:

SOUTHEAST MICHIGAN

deep-dish pies are the specialty. Meanwhile, **Fishbone's** (400 Monroe St., 313/965-4600, www.fishbonesusa.com, $9–65) is a New Orleans–inspired eatery that opened in the mid-1980s and has been jammed ever since. It serves up surprisingly authentic gumbo ya ya and jambalaya, in addition to ribs, steaks, and seafood.

SOUTH OF GREEKTOWN

South of Greektown, **Opus One** (565 E. Larned St., 313/961-7766, www.opus-one.com, 11:30 A.M.–9 P.M. Mon.–Tues., 11:30 A.M.–10 P.M. Wed.–Thurs., 11:30 A.M.–11 P.M. Fri., 5–11 P.M. Sat., noon–7 P.M. Sun., $10–35) ranks as one of the city's most elegant eateries, with a sophisticated menu that reflects both continental and regional influences. Top off your visit with the warm chocolate cake, accompanied by freshly brewed Jamaican blue java.

CONEY CUISINE

Philly may have the cheese steak and Chicago its deep-dish pie, but Detroit has *the* Coney Island. No, not the amusement part – the hot dog. Detroiters take their coneys very seriously, downing thousands of these hot dogs annually. Curiously, the name Coney Island serves simultaneously as both a destination and a dish.

Family-owned and operated since 1917, **American Coney Island** (114 W. Lafayette, 586/219-0995, www.americanconeyisland.com) is the place where a wiener with skin, beanless chili, onions, and mustard was first called "one with everything." Although this beloved 24-hour eatery now also serves soups, salads, desserts, and spinach pie, it's the dogs that lure a clientele ranging from cops on the beat to fur-clad suburbanites grabbing a bite after a show at the Fox Theatre. American Coney Island has garnered the respect of a long list of celebrities, too, including Michigan governors, famous musicians and athletes, and well-known movie stars like Tim Allen and Jeff Daniels.

THEATER DISTRICT

Detroit's impressive Theater District is home to more than just gorgeously restored entertainment venues; it also boasts a decent array of restaurants, ideal for a pre-show meal. The **Century Grille Restaurant** (333 Madison Ave., 313/963-9800, www.gemtheatre.com, 5–8 P.M. Wed.–Fri., 4–8 P.M. Sat., 11 A.M.–2 P.M. and 3–6 P.M. Sun., $12–29), conveniently situated inside the Gem and Century Theatre Building, has a limited menu of soups, salads, Sunday brunch, and entrées like lamb chops and parmesan-crusted halibut. Theater and dinner packages are often worth considering, too. A more casual option is the **Hockeytown Café** (2301 Woodward Ave., 313/965-9500, www.hockeytowncafe.com, 11 A.M.–close Mon.–Sat., noon–close Sun., $7–24). Though not far from the Fox Theatre, this bustling sports bar is, as the name implies, more popular among sports fans headed to or from nearby Comerica Park or Ford Field. During hockey season, patrons can even hop the restaurant's free shuttles to the Joe Louis Arena. Diners here can anticipate frequent drink specials, vittles like chicken wings and burgers, and a host of high-definition TVs broadcasting a variety of sporting events.

After shopping in the Eastern Market, head over to the **Roma Cafe** (3401 Riopelle St., 313/831-5940, www.romacafe.com, 11 A.M.–10:30 P.M. Mon.–Fri., 11 A.M.–midnight Sat., $13–25), Detroit's oldest Italian restaurant, established in 1890. While classic dishes, such as gnocchi, lasagna, eggplant parmigiana, and tiramisu abound here, you'll also find treats like breaded frog legs, filet mignon, and broiled whitefish.

WOODWARD AVENUE

If you get hungry while exploring the Cultural Center, stop by the **Majestic Café** (4120 Woodward Ave., 313/833-9700, www.majesticdetroit.com, 11 A.M.–2 A.M. daily, $8–25), an eclectic eatery offering hummus, black bean quesadillas, Jamaican jerk chicken, BBQ ribs, and more. It packs in the Wayne State and downtown Medical Center crowds at lunch. For a decidedly fancier experience, make a reservation at **The**

Whitney (4421 Woodward Ave., 313/832-5700, www.thewhitney.com, 11:30 A.M.–2 P.M. and 5–10 P.M. Tues.–Fri., 5–10 P.M. Sat., 11 A.M.–2:30 P.M. Sun., $40–125), Detroit's grandest restaurant, housed in an ornate 115-year-old mansion and offering live entertainment on weekends, plus exquisite dishes such as panéed pork chops with braised spinach, parsnip puree, and apple wood bacon sauce.

NEW CENTER DISTRICT
Even the New Center District has its own gem: the **《 Cuisine Restaurant** (670 Lothrop, 313/872-5110, www.cuisinedetroit.com, 4 P.M.–close Tues.–Sun., $22–90), situated behind the Fisher Building. If you're willing to spend a fair amount, treat yourself to one of Chef Paul Grosz' progression menus, which might include dishes like sea scallop in a citrus coconut glaze, lobster crab bisque, smoked salmon Caesar salad, creamed Alaskan halibut, roasted duck breast with buttered quinoa, and chocolate banana cake. The restaurant also offers a vegetarian progression menu and a superb wine list.

Information and Services

INFORMATION
For free information about Detroit and its suburbs, consult the **Detroit Metro Convention & Visitors Bureau** (211 W. Fort St., Ste. 1000, Detroit, 313/202-1800, www.visitdetroit.com). The two daily newspapers, *The Detroit News* (www.detnews.com) and the *Detroit Free Press* (www.freep.com) are supplemented by a wide variety of suburban dailies and weeklies, as well as the weekly *Detroit Metro Times* (www.metrotimes.com). The *Metro Times* is the city's first—and most successful—alternative rag, with thoughtful reporting on a variety of civic and social issues, extensive entertainment listings (a great place to check out your options on any given night) and consciousness-raising (if not eyebrow-raising) classifieds and want ads. It's distributed freely at bins throughout the city and suburbs. Another good read is *Hour Detroit* (www.hourdetroit.com), a tabloid-size, full-color magazine that's full of thought-provoking and entertaining editorials.

SERVICES
As a major urban center, Detroit has no shortage of necessary services, from banks to mailing centers to grocery stores. The metropolitan area boasts several post offices, including one inside the RenCen. For locations and hours, visit www.usps.com.

Dial **911** for emergency police, fire, or ambulance assistance. In non-emergency situations, call the police at 313/267-4600 or 311 in the city limits. For weather information, call 313/252-2200, ext. 2222. The area code for Detroit and Dearborn telephone numbers is 313. The area code for Oakland County (including Birmingham, Royal Oak, and most of the northern suburbs) is 248. North and east of Detroit, suburbs in Macomb County use an 810 area code.

For medical assistance, you'll find several hospitals in the metropolitan area. One option is the **Detroit Medical Center** (www.dmc.org), which has a number of facilities in the vicinity.

Getting There and Around

Most international travelers arrive by air, while American tourists tend to come via train, bus, or car.

GETTING THERE
By Plane
The **Detroit Metropolitan-Wayne County Airport (DTW)** (734/247-7678 or 800/642-1978, www.metroairport.com) spreads out over some 6,000 acres, 21 miles south of the city in Romulus, just off I-94 and Merriman Road. With 17 airlines, including 6 foreign, Detroit Metro offers service to more than 160 nonstop destinations. Consult the website for current carriers.

Coach service from downtown hotels to the airport is available by reservation. Typically, a one-way ride costs $41–55. For more information, contact **Checker Sedan** (800/351-5466, www.checkersedan.com) or **Metro Airport Taxi** (800/745-5191, www.metroairporttaxi. org).

Detroit Metro has many car rental services, some on-site, others off-site but accessible via a dedicated shuttle service. For details, consult **Avis** (800/331-1212, www.avis.com), **Budget** (800/527-0700, www.budget.com), and **Enterprise** (800/325-8007, www.enterprise.com), or peruse the listings on the DTW website.

By Train
Amtrak (800/872-7245, www.amtrak.com) offers convenient daily service to five metro area stops: Dearborn, Detroit, Royal Oak, Birmingham, and Pontiac. The downtown station is located at 11 West Baltimore Avenue in the New Center, while the suburban Dearborn stop is situated at 16121 Michigan Avenue.

By Bus
Greyhound (1001 Howard St., 313/961-8011 or 800/231-2222, www.greyhound.com) serves downtown Detroit. Be extra careful at the station—it's not located in the best part of town.

Daytime arrivals and departures are always a good idea.

By Car
Many travelers arrive in the Detroit area via car. From Flint or Toledo, take I-75 to downtown Detroit. From Lansing, I-96 heads southeast toward Farmington Hills and Mexicantown. I-94 is another handy route into the city, whether you're coming from Ann Arbor or Port Huron. Several other federal and state highways also make it easy to navigate the Motor City.

GETTING AROUND
By Car
Detroit, not surprisingly, is full of freeways. I-75 is the major north-south thoroughfare, with I-96, I-696, and I-94 heading east-west. Avoid traveling any of these routes during rush hours (generally 6–10 A.M. and 3–7 P.M.) or allow plenty of extra time. It's wise to seek out alternate routes such as I-275, which splits off from I-696, and to pick up a map of the area to ensure you don't get lost (an easy thing to do). Seat belts are required by Michigan law. Rental car companies—including Avis, Budget, and more—can be found at the airport.

Mass Transit
Most would agree that mass transit in Detroit is a joke. (This is the city that invented the car, after all). The **Detroit Department of Transportation (DDOT)** is the state's largest transit system; it serves Detroit and 25 suburban communities. DDOT buses and bus stops are recognizable by their trademark green and yellow colors.

Buses operate on 50 routes during the day and evenings from 6 A.M. until approximately 1 A.M.; 14 of the most popular routes operate 24 hours daily. Consult DDOT (313/933-1300, www.ci.detroit.mi.us/ddot, one-way $1.50) for routes and schedules.

Two other options offer downtown service: the **trolley** and the **Detroit People Mover.**

The red and brass antique trolleys offer limited service along Jefferson Avenue and Washington Boulevard and are used mostly by tourists. The fare is 50 cents. While the People Mover never lived up to high expectations, it's a handy way to travel while downtown, with a bird's-eye view of the city from its elevated track. For 50 cents, you'll get a 15-minute ride along a three-mile track that circles the heart of the business district. Even if you don't ride, it's worth a visit to check out the 13 People Mover stations, which boast works by local artists. The Detroit People Mover (www.thepeoplemover.com, 6:30 A.M.–midnight Mon.–Thurs., 6:30 A.M.–2 A.M. Fri., 9 A.M.–2 A.M. Sat., noon–midnight Sun.) operates through the city's notable areas, including the Civic Center, Greektown, and the Theater District.

Windsor, Ontario

A city of 216,000, Windsor sits along the southern banks of the Detroit River, just across from the Motor City. "Civilized" is the word that comes to mind when Detroiters talk about Windsor. Although separated only by a river, this Canadian city has a virtually nonexistent crime rate, a full plate of excellent restaurants, and a friendly and civic-minded populace who are happy to welcome Yanks. Detroiters have long shuttled back and forth to enjoy Windsor's restaurants, casinos, European-style shops, and terrific riverfront views.

SIGHTS

The **Windsor Wood Carving Museum** (850 Ouellette Ave., 519/977-0823, www.windsorwoodcarvingmuseum.ca, 9 A.M.–4 P.M. Tues.–Sat., free) offers a glimpse into historical carvings, as well as contemporary work by some of Canada's finest craftsmen. The

a view of the Ambassador Bridge from a riverfront sculpture park in Windsor

© CVB OF WINDSOR, ESSEX COUNTY & PELEE ISLAND

expansive one-room museum allows for close-up viewing of most of the pieces. **The Park House Museum** (Kings Navy Yard, 214 Dalhousie St., Amherstburg, 519/736-2511, www.parkhousemuseum.com, 11 A.M.–4 P.M. daily June–Aug., 11 A.M.–4 P.M. Mon.–Fri. Sept.–May, $2 adults, $1.50 seniors, $1 children) has the unique distinction of being the oldest house in the Windsor area and the oldest house from Detroit. The house was built near the mouth of the Rouge River in Detroit in the 1790s, but when the city was turned over to the Americans with the signing of the Jay Treaty, Alexander MacKintosh, a loyalist to the crown, moved the house to Amherstburg in 1796.

SHOPPING

Wander Ouellette, the main drag, and the narrow streets surrounding it. Shops are full of imported clothing and books (both new and used, many with British publishers), and the T-shirt stands are ubiquitous. Standouts are: **Shanfields-Meyers** (188 Ouellette Ave., 519/253-6098, www.shanfields.com, 10 A.M.–5 P.M. daily), with a sparkling array of crystal, including a whole room devoted to Waterford, and a wide selection of discounted china and gifts, and the **World of Habanos** (421 Ouellette Ave., 519/258-5664, www.worldofhabanos.com, 10:30 A.M.–9 P.M. Mon.–Thurs., 10:30 A.M.–midnight Fri.–Sat., 10:30 A.M.–5 P.M. Sun.), which offers Canada's largest selection of aged cigars, including authentic Cuban cigars, as well as accessories such as lighters and humidors.

ACCOMMODATIONS AND FOOD

Windsor is full of nice hotels, including the **Radisson Riverfront Hotel Windsor** (333 W. Riverside Dr., 519/977-9777, www.radisson.com, $139–249 d), which is conveniently located near downtown Windsor and the Detroit River, and offers spectacular views of the Detroit skyline. For a less expensive stay, try the **Travelodge Hotel Downtown Windsor** (33 E. Riverside Dr., 519/258-7774, www.travelodge.com, $70–120 d).

While the shopping is good in Windsor, it doesn't compare to the eating. Top restaurants include **Cook's Shop** (683 Ouellette Ave., 519/254-3377, 5–10 P.M. Tues.–Thurs. and Sun., 5 P.M.–midnight Fri.–Sat., $9–18), a tiny basement eatery where everything is homemade, including the melt-in-your-mouth polenta and pastas prepared tableside on a rolling cart. **The Mini** (475 W. University Ave., 519/254-2221, 11 A.M.–10 P.M. daily, $6–14), which started out with one tiny room (hence the name), expanded as the restaurant's Vietnamese cuisine and fruit slushes caught on with diners from Windsor and across the way. The atmosphere's not much at **Wah Court** (2037 W. Wyandotte St., 519/254-1388, www.wahcourtrestaurant.com, 11 A.M.–10:30 P.M. daily, $8–13), but the more than 30 dim sum selections (available only before 3 P.M.) are first-rate.

INFORMATION

For more information about Windsor, consult the **Convention & Visitors Bureau of Windsor, Essex County & Pelee Island** (333 W. Riverside Dr., Ste. 103, Windsor, Ontario, 519/255-6530, www.visitwindsor.com, 8:30 A.M.–4:30 P.M. Mon.–Fri.).

GETTING THERE AND AROUND

While Windsor has its own airport—the **Windsor International Airport (YQG)** (3200 CR-42, Windsor, 519/969-2430, www.yqg.ca)—most visitors will probably be making a day trip from Detroit via car. Two routes connect Detroit and Windsor: the **Ambassador Bridge** (www.ambassadorbridge.com, $4) and the **Detroit-Windsor Tunnel** (www.dwtunnel.com, $3.75). Claustrophobics tend to opt for the bridge, though the tunnel is faster and more direct.

The Suburbs

Ironically, the same fast cars that made Motown what it was in its heyday are also what crippled it. Bigger and better cars, and more and more efficient freeways only served to take Detroiters farther and farther away from the core city. Most suburbs are bedroom communities that bear little interest for the visitor. Some exceptions include Hamtramck, a Polish neighborhood north of downtown Detroit; Dearborn, where Henry Ford was born and later founded what became one of the state's largest tourist attractions; Royal Oak, home to the Detroit Zoo; Birmingham, home to chic boutiques and fine art galleries; and Grosse Pointe, where Lakeshore Drive still boasts some of the area's finest homes.

◖ HAMTRAMCK

"A Touch of Europe in America," reads the sign approaching Hamtramck (www.hamtramck. com). A Polish stronghold since World War I, its residents have stubbornly withstood annexation. Thus, Hamtramck survives as a "city within a city," 2.5 square miles completely within Detroit city limits. Well known locally, it can be hard to find for the visitor. To get there, take I-75 to the Caniff exit, Exit 55, about 1.5 miles north of I-94.

Named for a German-French Canadian colonel who served during the post-Revolutionary Indian Wars, the strange-sounding hamlet was settled as a village of mostly German farms in 1901, but a new Dodge auto factory and its promise of jobs swelled the population from 3,589 to 45,615 between 1910 and 1920—the largest increase anywhere in the United States. Many were Polish immigrants, earning Hamtramck the nickname "Little Poland." Today, the auto plant is closed and the Polish population has dropped from 90 percent to about 40 percent (the slack is taken up by Albanians and African Americans), but the nickname and culture remain.

Drive along Joseph Campau Street, Hamtramck's main drag, and you'll find Polish bakeries, Polish bookstores, Polish clubs, and shops hawking Polish sausage. There's even a tribute at the corner of Belmont and Joseph Campau Streets to the Polish pope, John Paul II, who visited this ethnic enclave in the mid-1980s. Stop at the **Polish Art Center** for unusual goods such as folk art rugs, leaded glass, Ukrainian-decorated eggs, and *szopkas,* intricate nativity scenes made of tinfoil.

Detroiters have long known about the old-world charms of Hamtramck. Joseph Campau's glass storefronts have a vintage 1930s feel, full of Polish imports, discount clothing, and baked goods and meats. Many Polish suburbanites return with their families on weekends to sip *czarnina* (duck's blood soup), linger over *nalesniki* (crepes), and consume *pierogi* (filled dumplings) before heading home with loaves of fresh pumpernickel or rye and a few Polish pastries such as *paczki* (plump jelly doughnuts) to enjoy later.

Highlights of Polish Hamtramck include the **New Palace Bakery** (9833 Joseph Campau St., 313/875-1334, 6 A.M.–6 P.M. Mon.–Sat.), the most popular of the many bakeries; **Polonia-Jaworowka** (2934 Yemens, 313/873-8432, 11 A.M.–7 P.M. Mon.–Thurs., 11 A.M.–8 P.M. Fri.–Sat., $8–13), housed in a former 1930s food co-op; and **Under the Eagle** (9000 Joseph Campau St., 313/875-5905, 11 A.M.–7 P.M. Mon.–Tues., 11 A.M.–9 P.M. Thurs.–Sun., $4–12), which locals consider one of the best places to indulge in the chewy rye bread, heaping helpings of roast pork loin, tangy sauerkraut, and out-of-the-ordinary dill pickle soup that are the cuisine's strongholds. Afterward, walk it all off with a tour of **St. Florian's** (2626 Poland, 313/871-2778), one of the last of the old Polish churches. Completed in 1926, it holds more than 1,800 faithful and is the site of a popular Strawberry Fest in the spring.

Hamtramck's quirky 1930s flair and cheap rents have attracted artists such as potter/

HOMES OF THE AUTO BARONS

As Detroit grew to become the "motor capital of the world," opportunities to amass great fortunes grew with it. The automobile "royalty" that emerged took on a pampered lifestyle befitting their status and built great estates full of art and intricate workmanship. Now open for tours, these four estates offer visitors the chance to see firsthand how the auto pioneers lived during the heyday of the auto industry.

FISHER MANSION

The only estate within the city limits, the Fisher Mansion (383 Lenox Ave., 313/331-6740, www.detroitiskconlive.com), inspired by William Randolph Hearst's San Simeon, was built by Lawrence P. Fisher of the Fisher Body Company, a talented playboy who once courted actress Jean Harlow and who spent millions of his huge fortune constructing this magnificent riverfront estate. It has been described as "glitz bordering on garish." Completed in 1928, it's most noted for its ornate stone and marble work, exquisite European handcrafted stained glass windows, doors and arches carved from woods imported from India and Africa, and rare black walnut and rosewood parquet floors. More than 200 ounces of gold and silver leaf highlight the decorative ceilings and moldings.

The mansion was neglected after Fisher's death and was purchased for just $80,000 in 1975 by Alfred Brush Ford, great-grandson of Henry Ford, and Elisabeth Reuther Dickmeyer, daughter of legendary United Auto Workers chief Walter Reuther. They restored the mansion and donated it to the International Society for Krishna Consciousness, of which they are members. Today, the mansion serves as the Bhaktivedanta Cultural Center and is also site of the excellent **Govinda's** vegetarian restaurant.

EDSEL & ELEANOR FORD HOUSE

Farther up Jefferson Avenue, where it becomes Lake Shore Road, stands the Edsel & Eleanor Ford House (1100 Lake Shore Rd., Grosse Pointe Shores, 313/884-4222, www.fordhouse.org, 10 A.M.-4 P.M. Tues.-Sat., noon-4 P.M. Sun. Apr.-Dec., noon-4 P.M. Tues.-Sun. Jan.-Mar., closed on major holidays and two weeks in winter, $10 adults, $9 seniors, $6 children 6-12). The Ford House represents a style of living and quality of craftsmanship that is rapidly vanishing, if not completely gone.

The Cotswold-style mansion, designed by noted local architect Albert Kahn, was built in 1929 for Henry Ford's only son, who raised his four children in this house. Much of the interior paneling and furniture was lifted from distinguished old English manors; even the roof is of imported English stones expertly laid by imported Cotswold roofers. What makes the house especially interesting is that it remains much as it did when the Fords lived here. Edsel died in 1943, but his wife, Eleanor Clay Ford, left the estate virtually untouched after that. Throughout is evidence of the Fords' love of art, with copies of masterpieces now replacing the originals that were donated to the downtown Detroit Institute of Arts.

Visitors can take in a 13-minute video about the Fords, an hour-long guided tour that leads them through the distinctive dwelling, and a self-guided tour of the grounds and outer buildings. Highlights include a stylish art deco

jeweler Marcia Hovland and filmmakers Chuck Cirgenski and Janine Menlove. Hollywood-backed *Polish Wedding*, a movie starring Lena Olin, was filmed here in late 1996. With the new wave of artists and filmmakers have come urbane coffeehouses, late-night alternative-music cafés, and colorful studios and shops that add a new hipness to this old-world enclave.

DEARBORN

Home to Ford's international headquarters and the largest collection of Arabic-speaking peoples in the United States, Dearborn is rightly known as "the town that Ford built." There was little here but farmland when Henry Ford was born in a small white farmhouse at the corner of Ford Road and Mercury Drive.

recreation room by famed industrial designer Walter Dorwin Teague; Edsel's personal study, lined with framed family photos and photos of luminaries like Thomas Edison; and the Tudor-style playhouse created in 1930 for daughter Josephine's seventh birthday.

FAIR LANE

Of the four auto baron estates, Henry Ford's Fair Lane (4901 Evergreen Rd., Dearborn, 313/593-5590, www.henryfordestate.org, tours 10 A.M.-3 P.M. Tues.-Sat., 1-4:30 P.M. Sun. Apr.-Dec., 1:30 P.M. Tues.-Fri., 1-3 P.M. Sun. Jan.-Mar., $12 adults, $11 seniors 62 and over, $8 children 6-12) is, surprisingly, the least baronial. By the time it was completed in 1914, Ford had become active in World War I politics and spent a lot of time helping the war effort in Europe. Nonetheless, it is justly listed as a National Historic Landmark.

Fair Lane encompasses more than 1,300 acres. For some, the natural landscape by Jens Jensen is the highlight of a visit; for others, it's the estate's many technical feats, including the extensive six-level hydroelectric power plant created by Ford and his good buddy Thomas Edison. In this house, Ford entertained some of the world's most influential people, including Charles Lindbergh (also a Detroit native), President Herbert Hoover, and the Duke of Windsor. It's an unusual combination of a Scottish baronial structure and the Prairie style developed by Frank Lloyd Wright. Two-hour tours uncover quirky details such as Henry's basement bowling alley and his penchant for birds (he once had 500 birdhouses on the premises) as well as Clara's passion for roses. A small but choice gift shop stocks a wide selection of books on related subjects, and a charming restaurant on the University of Michigan's Dearborn campus is located in the spot that once housed the estate's indoor pool.

MEADOW BROOK HALL

Last but not least is Rochester's Meadow Brook Hall (Adams Rd. and Walton Blvd., 248/364-6200, www4.oakland.edu, tours 11:30 A.M.-2:30 P.M. Mon.-Sun. June-Aug., 1:30 P.M. Mon.-Fri., 11:30 A.M.-2:30 P.M. Sat.-Sun. Jan.-May and Sept.-Nov., holiday walk in Dec., $15 adults, $10 seniors 62 and over, children under 13 free). John Dodge and his brother Horace were among the car makers responsible for Detroit's sudden catapult into big business. John died suddenly in 1920, leaving behind a vast fortune and a widow, Matilda (his former secretary), who remarried a wealthy lumberman, Alfred Wilson, in 1925. Together, Alfred and Matilda toured Europe and dreamed of a grand estate north of the city. They built the 110-room Tudor-style Meadow Brook Hall in the late 1920s for the then-astonishing sum of $4 million. Interiors were copied from drawings of English estates.

Eight decades later, Meadow Brook is still largely intact, in part because Mrs. Wilson left the estate to Oakland University, which still administers the property. Rooms – including a two-story ballroom, game rooms copied from old English pubs, and Matilda's bathroom accented with locally made Pewabic tile – still house original family collections and furnishings. A walk in the surrounding woods reveals a six-room playhouse known as Knole Cottage, built for Frances Wilson, Matilda's daughter.

While in Dearborn, make time for at least a taste of its Arabian culture. Most of Dearborn's Arab citizens live in the neighborhoods that line Warren and Dix. (The Dix neighborhood lies in the shadow of the Ford Rouge Plant, one of the largest factories in the world.) Its working-class residents are more than 90 percent Arab, primarily from Yemen. The south end boasts signs that are in both English and Arabic, headscarves are common on women, and many men wear traditional skullcaps. The restaurants and shops along Dix offer sights and sounds heard in the Arabian peninsula, including a call to prayer broadcast five times daily from a local mosque.

Take some time to visit the fascinating

a lively street scene at Dearborn's nostalgic Greenfield Village

Arab American National Museum (13624 Michigan Ave., 313/582-2266, www.arabamericanmuseum.org, 10 A.M.–6 P.M. Wed. and Fri.–Sat., 10 A.M.–8 P.M. Thurs., noon–5 P.M. Sun., $6 adults, $3 children 6–12), the first museum in the world devoted to Arab American history and culture.

◖ The Henry Ford

Today, Dearborn is best known to tourists as the location of The Henry Ford (20900 Oakwood Blvd., 313/982-6001, www.hfmgv.org, 9:30 A.M.–5 P.M. daily, museum $14 adults, $10 children 5–12), a favorite field trip for local schoolchildren and one of the state's big tourism draws. In the **Greenfield Village** (9:30 A.M.–5 P.M. Apr. 15–Nov. 2, 9:30 A.M.–5 P.M. Fri.–Sun. Nov. 3–Dec. 28, $20 adults, $14 children 5–12), Henry gathered buildings and other structures in an attempt to show how America grew from an agrarian to an industrial society. It's a charming—if disconcerting—time machine, a patchwork quilt of unrelated people and places, where a 16th-century English Cotswold cottage sits a few

hundred yards from an 18th-century New England saltbox. Other features include Ford's childhood home and Thomas Edison's Menlo Park laboratory.

Ford sent his pickers across the Midwest and New England to assemble enough artifacts to fill the 12-acre museum next to the village. Inside is one vast collection after another, including several presidential limousines, the world's greatest holdings of 19th-century farm and kitchen tools (the old washing machines are a stitch), a fine grouping of American furniture, and many artifacts that trace the evolution of the electric light bulb (Edison was a great friend of Ford's; the complex was originally called the Edison Institute).

Worth the price of admission alone is the excellent exhibit known as "The Automobile in American Life," which nostalgically shows the car's effect on the American landscape. There's a 1950s McDonald's sign, complete with oversized golden arches; a 1946 diner from Marlboro, Massachusetts, where an egg salad sandwich cost 15 cents; and a Holiday Inn guest room, circa 1960. The evolution of the auto industry is explained using TV monitors and restored automobiles from each period (to see the cars in chronological order, start at the ramp in front of the Oscar Meyer Wienermobile).

Also worth a peek is the permanent "Made in America" exhibit, which traces the evolution of American manufacturing. Far from dull, it explains technology in an entertaining manner, accented by film clips, including one from the *I Love Lucy* show in which Lucy joins a candy-making assembly line with disastrous results. With thousands of items and the adjacent village, the entire complex is more than a bit overwhelming. A good idea is to split a visit into two days, with one day earmarked to explore each half. You might need even more time if you plan to visit other on-site features like the IMAX movie theater and the Benson Ford Research Center. In addition, tour buses regularly leave for the Ford Rouge Factory Tour, a five-part excursion that culminates with a stroll through the Ford F-150 truck assembly plant.

FARMINGTON HILLS

America's first free-standing **Holocaust Memorial Center** (28123 Orchard Lake Rd., 248/553-2400, www.holocaustcenter.org, 9:30 A.M.–3:30 P.M. Sun.–Thurs., 9:30 A.M.–12:30 P.M. Fri., free) provides a vivid portrayal of the Holocaust. Features include extensive material and state-of-the-art display techniques that enhance this visceral experience.

ROYAL OAK

Heading north on Woodward, Royal Oak is one of the first suburbs you'll encounter after you cross 8 Mile Road. It's the only suburb in the Detroit area where you'll find green hair, unusual pierced body parts, and whips and chains in the window at a boutique called **Noir Leather** (124 W. 4th St., 248/541-3979, www.noirleather.com, 11 A.M.–9 P.M. Mon.–Thurs., 11 A.M.–10 P.M. Fri.–Sat., noon–7 P.M. Sun.). Nowhere else in Michigan will you find a store sign that reads "Absolutely no return on bondage items for sanitary reasons."

Royal Oak was a sleepy (some said dying)

suburb in the 1970s, known only by its nickname—Royal Joke—and as the site of the respected 125-acre **Detroit Zoo** (8450 W. 10 Mile Rd., 248/541-5717, www.detroitzoo.org, 10 A.M.–5 P.M. Apr.–Memorial Day and Labor Day–Oct., 9:30 A.M.–5 P.M. in summer, $11 adults, $7 children 2–12). The zoo, long a popular city attraction, is home to more than 1,300 animals, including the Wildlife Interpretive Gallery, site of a popular hummingbird/butterfly garden, and the Arctic Ring of Fire, which features Arctic species.

In the mid-1980s, the city's gay population was concentrated in Royal Oak, filling the two main commercial streets with vintage clothing and record shops, antique emporiums, and funky coffeehouses. While a few of the original boutiques remain, others have been replaced by high-rent glitzy home furnishings shops and restaurants that now characterize much of the area. Despite this, Royal Oak is still a lively place, where the streets are filled with a pleasing variety of families and punks, gays and straights. Main Street and Washington Avenue, the two main drags, are great spots for window-shopping and people-watching. And it seems as if a new eatery opens almost every day here, giving it one of the best and most extensive restaurant scenes in metro Detroit.

Worthwhile stops include the sinful **Gayle's Chocolates** (417 S. Washington, 248/398-0001, www.gayleschocolates.com, 10 A.M.–6 P.M. Mon.–Tues., 10 A.M.–8 P.M. Wed.–Sat., noon–5 P.M. Sun.), the first in the city to offer cappuccino and espresso (now found on just about every corner). Another feature is the popular juice bar (try the carrot-apple-ginger), but Gayle's heart remains in the chocolate-making facility located upstairs, which churns out some of the best truffles in the country. Also worth a peek are **Lotus Imports** (419 S. Washington, www.lotusimportco.com, 9 A.M.–5 P.M. daily), which stocks ethnic jewelry, clothing, and accessories from all over the world; **Vertu** (514 S. Washington Ave., 248/545-6050, 9 A.M.–5 P.M. Mon.–Sat.), known for its 20th-century designs, including furniture by Eames, Nelson, and Herman

Miller from the 1930–50s; **Dos Manos** (210 W. 6th St., 800/572-4957, www.dosmanos.com, 10 A.M.–6 P.M. daily), for Latin American handicrafts; and **Chosen Books** (120 W. 4th St., www.chosenbooks.net, 9 A.M.–9 P.M. Mon.–Sat., noon–6 P.M. Sun.), metro Detroit's only gay bookstore.

When it's time to eat, you'll be hard-pressed to choose. In the mood for seafood? **Tom's Oyster Bar** (318 S. Main St., 248/541-1186, www.tomsoysterbar.com, noon–midnight Sun.–Thurs., 11 A.M.–1 A.M. Fri., noon–1 A.M. Sat., $7–30) is a branch of the popular East Side eatery that has the area's most extensive selection of—surprise!—oysters, as well as always innovative fresh seafood. **BD's Mongolian Barbecue** 430 S. Main St., 248/398-7755, www.gomongo.com, 11 A.M.–10:30 P.M. Mon.–Thurs., 11 A.M.–11:30 P.M. Fri.–Sat., 11 A.M.–10 P.M. Sun., $7–12) lets you watch as chefs whip up your stir-fry creation on a huge, central grill. It's been so popular, it's opened outposts in other metro Detroit suburbs.

BIRMINGHAM

Naysayers were concerned that downtown Birmingham—a chic enclave of expensive shops and galleries—would shrivel and die when the even more chic Somerset North Shopping Complex (mall is too pedestrian a term) opened on nearby Big Beaver Road late in 1996. Birmingham has proven remarkably resilient, however, and remains a tony 'burb with one of the few thriving downtowns in surrounding Oakland County. Shoppers from all over the metro area come here to see and be seen, to linger in cafés and restaurants, and to exercise their credit cards in the unusual boutiques.

Even if you're not a shopper, Birmingham is worth a trip for its art galleries, one of the most impressive concentrations in the Midwest. Here, you'll even find cutting-edge contemporary art at places like the **Robert Kidd Gallery** (107 Townsend, 248/642-3909, www.robert-kiddgallery.com, 11 A.M.–6 P.M. Tues.–Sat.). More than a dozen influential art outlets are grouped along a section of Woodward north of downtown known as "Gallery Row."

BLOOMFIELD HILLS

For a look at how the other half (actually, the other one percent) lives, turn the wheel north to Bloomfield Hills. Long the suburb of choice for CEOs, Big Three bigwigs, and other members of the city's power brokers, it ranks as the state's richest town as well as the second-wealthiest in the country. Past and present residents have included Detroit Piston captain Isaiah Thomas and the queen of soul, Aretha Franklin. Unlike Grosse Pointe, which still struggles with the remains of its WASPish heritage, it doesn't matter if you're black or white in Bloomfield Hills. Money is the great equalizer.

If Grosse Pointe epitomizes "old money," Bloomfield Hills attracts its newer, shinier counterpart. Huge houses are spread throughout its rolling hills—a geographic anomaly in southeastern Michigan. Most are late 20th century, although older models can be found clustered around Cranbrook, former home of newspaper magnate George Booth, who founded the *Detroit News*. Drive the winding lanes and you'll find Old Tudor, Georgian, and other 1920s-era mansions. One notable exception is the house at 5045 Pon Valley Road, which was designed by Frank Lloyd Wright in 1951.

Cranbrook

Despite its celebrities, Bloomfield Hills remains best known as home to Cranbrook, a renowned, 315-acre arts and educational complex. Here, famed Finnish architect Eliel Saarinen created a lush and lovely refuge for artists and students.

Cranbrook is known throughout the world for the integrated aesthetics of its environment. All buildings, gardens, sculpture, and interiors are treated as an integral and important part of a whole. This creative cohesion is the result of two men, patron newspaper magnate George Booth and artist Eliel Saarinen. Booth, one of the early city expatriates, bought a run-down farm in Bloomfield Hills in 1904 and commissioned noted Detroit architect Albert Kahn to build him a large, Tudor-style mansion there.

© L. DIGGS, PICTURE THIS...

outdoor sculptures at Cranbrook in wintertime

Grandson of an English coppersmith, Booth was a noted proponent of the arts-and-crafts movement, which preached a reunification of life and art. After a 1922 trip to Rome, where he visited the American Academy, he decided to create a school of architecture and design.

While the school is still known throughout the world, equal acclaim is drawn by Cranbrook's **Academy of Art Museum** (39221 N. Woodward Ave., 248/645-3323, www. cranbrookart.edu, 11 A.M.–5 P.M. Wed.–Sun., 11 A.M.–9 P.M. 4th Fri. of each month, $7 adults, $5 students, children under 13 free), with exhibits by prominent faculty and students, and the **Institute of Science** (248/645-3200), a family science and anthropology museum with a fascinating Physics Hall, an extensive mineral collection, a hall of Native American culture, and an observatory that's open to the public Saturday evenings, weather permitting.

GROSSE POINTE

Five cities actually make up the area collectively known as Grosse Pointe on Detroit's far east side. Taken as a whole, Grosse Pointe Shores, Grosse Pointe Farms, Grosse Pointe Woods, the city of Grosse Pointe, and Grosse Pointe Park make up one of the metro area's wealthiest suburbs, a land of landscaped estates, big trees, big homes, and even bigger money.

A summer community in the 1840s, Grosse Pointe began to change about 1910, when wealthy Detroiters sought to separate themselves from the immigrants who crowded the growing city. The wealthiest built mansions that imitated the elegant country houses of England, France, and Italy, importing stone fireplaces and entire rooms that were later incorporated into new construction.

This is where the city's prominent old families settled; many descendants of this founding aristocracy still live here. For years (through roughly the 1950s), prospective home buyers were screened by a Grosse Pointe real estate broker's infamous point system designed to perpetuate WASP homogeneity. Today, you'll find a much more diverse population, although, like most of Detroit's suburbs, it's still predominantly white. Grosse Pointe Park is the most liberal and Democratic, with a number of smaller homes and modest, middle-class 1920s housing. One area, now known as the Cabbage Patch because its early Belgian residents grew the vegetable in their yards, was developed to house servants from the nearby estates.

Many of the largest mansions have been razed, although a few remain along Lakeshore. It's a beautiful drive in any season, with the Detroit River attracting joggers, freighter-watchers, and others who come just to ogle the architecture. To get a peek at the inside of one of the area's original estates, stop at the former **Alger House,** now known as the **Grosse Pointe War Memorial** (32 Lake Shore Rd., 313/881-7511, www.warmemorial.org, 9 A.M.–9 P.M. Mon.–Sat., free). It was originally the home of a founder of the Packard Motor Company and now serves as a community center.

◖ WOODWARD DREAM CRUISE

Begun in 1995 as a small fundraiser for the Ferndale community, this annual mid-August parade down Woodward Avenue has become

© CARL ADAMS/BIRMINGHAM PSD

the Woodward Dream Cruise in Birmingham

the world's largest one-day automotive event, luring 1.5 million people and 40,000 classic cars from around the globe. The Woodward Dream Cruise (www.woodwarddreamcruise. com) stretches 16 miles though Berkley, Birmingham, Bloomfield Hills, Bloomfield Township, Ferndale, Huntington Woods, Pleasant Ridge, Pontiac, and Royal Oak, taking over Woodward Avenue through each of these towns—truly a spectacle to behold. Find your spot early, as it gets very crowded all along the route.

ACCOMMODATIONS

For those who'd prefer not to stay overnight in downtown Detroit, the city's suburbs offer a number of lodging options. **Hampton Inn** (20061 Michigan Ave., Dearborn, 313/436-9600, www.hamptoninn.com, $117–155 d) has a terrific location, overlooking Greenfield Village. The 119 simple but comfortable guest rooms also make this chain a good bet for the budget-minded. Amenities include an indoor pool, free local calls, a continental breakfast, and in-room coffee makers.

Also in Dearborn, the **Hyatt Regency** (600 Town Center Dr., 313/593-1234, www.dearborn.hyatt.com, $109–229 d) is a large steel-and-glass monolith with more than 771 rooms. It's one of the largest in the Hyatt chain. The hotel restaurant, Giulio & Sons, has a lavish Italian-style buffet that's a real bargain. Not far away, the **Ritz-Carlton Hotel** (300 Town Center Dr., 313/441-2000, www.ritzcarlton.com, $249–479 d) was built by Ford money, which still drives this understated 308-room hotel. It attracts power brokers from across the country as well as a few understated rock stars and visiting celebrities. The clubby Grille is known for its excellent, if pricey, continental cuisine.

In Bloomfield Hills, **Radisson** (39475 N. Woodward Ave., 248/644-1400, www.radisson.com, $110–229 d) is a AAA four-diamond property in a prime location. In nearby Birmingham, the ◖ **Townsend Hotel** (100 Townsend St., 248/642-7900, www.townsendhotel.com, $300–500 d) is the posh—if pretentious—European-style hostelry where Paul

McCartney stayed when he performed in Detroit on his last tour. Nothing but the best is good enough here—Belgian linens, pillows of the fluffiest down, yards of marble in the baths, and a restaurant staffed with world-class chefs who cater to the guests' every whim. You'll feel as if you've stepped into a Ralph Lauren ad. Located near Birmingham's fashionable shops and galleries, it's also a favorite stop for afternoon tea, served every afternoon.

FOOD

Detroit's suburbs offer their share of vittles, too. ⟨⟨ **Big Fish** (700 Town Center Dr., Dearborn, 313/336-6350, and 111 W. 14 Mile, Troy, 248/585-9533, www.muer.com, 11 A.M.–10 P.M. Mon.–Thurs., 11 A.M.–11 P.M. Fri., 11:30 A.M.–11 P.M. Sat., 3–9 P.M. Sun., $12–45), part of the Muer seafood restaurant family, is a popular lunch spot that can also get pretty crowded during dinner. Some say the unusual name is a reference to the Big Three execs who power lunch at the original location in Dearborn. Others say it's a reference to the menu, which is mainly seafood. The atmosphere is dark and clubby, accented with fishing and nautical motifs. Specialties include the tangy Martha's Vineyard salad, potato-encrusted whitefish, and any of the excellent daily specials.

The **Speedboat Bar & Grill** (749 Biddle Ave., Wyandotte, 734/282-5750, 11 A.M.–close daily, $6–14) is home of the masterpiece swine burger, maybe the perfect bar burger. It's thick and juicy and served with spicy rings of jalapeño, pepper cheese, chili, and onions fried golden brown. Or you can opt for a brimming bowl of the spicy red chili, a consistent award-winner. This joint is definitely worth a special trip downriver.

Southeast Michigan

In the towns surrounding the Detroit metropolitan area, visitors will find nostalgic downtown districts, historic museums, inland lakes, and recreation areas galore—all a relatively quick drive from Detroit, via interstates and major highways.

GROSSE ILE

Now part of the Detroit River International Wildlife Refuge, Grosse Ile is a lengthy, bottle-shaped island in the Detroit River, just north of the entrance to Lake Erie. While it's not a huge tourist destination, there are two nearby lighthouses worth a look: the **Grosse Ile North Channel Range Front Light,** a white, 50-foot-tall octagonal tower lit in 1906 and deactivated in 1963, and the **Detroit River Light** in Lake Erie, only accessible via boat. While the Grosse Ile Historical Society (734/675-1250) offers an annual one-day tour of the Grosse Ile lighthouse (usually in Sept.), the Detroit River light station, which is still an active navigational aid operated by the U.S. Coast Guard, can only be viewed from the outside.

MONROE

On the banks of the River Raisin, in Michigan's southeast corner, lies the city of Monroe, Michigan's third oldest community. Its location made it the natural crossroads for the Native Americans, the French missionaries, and the fur trappers who settled in the area. Caught between the British Army and the U.S. forces during the War of 1812, Monroe is also the site of the deadliest battle during the war, when after having been pushed back into Canada, the British counterattacked, killing 300 Americans in the Battle of the River Raisin. "Remember the Raisin" became America's rally cry after the Indian allies of the British killed another hundred injured soldiers who were unable to retreat after the battle. In the 19th century, Monroe also became home to General George A. Custer and his wife, Elizabeth.

Of course, with shopping and dining possibilities galore, this quaint town offers more than just history. If you're hoping to stay on the healthy side during your trip, check out the weekly **farmer's market** (20 W. Willow St., 6 A.M.–noon every Sat. year-round, 6 A.M.–noon Tues. in summer and fall) for some locally produced treats. The **Monroe Street Grill** (2 W. Front St., 734/241-1112, 7 A.M.–10 P.M. daily, $4–18) provides a touch of fine dining (but also has more casual fare). Try the artichoke chicken or the beef tips.

To better enjoy the riverfront, you can purchase an inexpensive bike from **Jack's Bicycles** (206 S. Monroe St., 734/242-1400, www.jacksbike.com, 10 A.M.–6 P.M. daily), a fantastic shop with a huge variety of bikes, plus sporty apparel. If you want to splurge on yourself or someone else, check out **Frenchies Fine Jewelry** (15 E. Front St., 734/242-5840, www.frenchiesjewelry.com, 10 A.M.–5 P.M. Mon.–Sat., 10 A.M.–4 P.M. Sun.), where you can browse through their extensive coin, stamp, and fine jewelry collections.

YPSILANTI

Besides being the home of **Eastern Michigan University** (734/487-1849, www.emich.edu), Ypsilanti features two unique museums. The **Michigan Firehouse Museum** (110 W. Cross St., 734/547-0663, www.michiganfirehousemuseum.org, 10 A.M.–4 P.M. Tues.–Sat., noon–4 P.M. Sun., $3 adults, $1.50 children 6–15) offers a look at Michigan's fire-fighting history, while also promoting fire safety and prevention. The **Ypsilanti Historical Museum** (220 N. Huron St., 734/484-0080, www.ypsilantihistoricalsociety.org, 2–5 P.M. Sun.–Tues., free) provides a glance into Ypsilanti's history since its founding in 1860.

Also in Ypsilanti, you'll find the **Riverside Arts Center** (76 N. Huron St., 734/480-2787, www.riversidearts.org), which presents exhibits and performances in the theater space. For a bite to eat, visit **Cady's Grill & Bar** (36 E. Cross St., 734/483-2800, http://cadysgrill.com, 10:30 A.M.–close daily, $9–24), which also houses an impressive wine selection.

PONTIAC

In its heyday, Pontiac was a booming General Motors town. While still the home of several manufacturing plants, it's clear that Pontiac has seen better days. Nevertheless, the town still has a lot to offer for visitors and residents alike.

Perched on 4.5 acres of well-groomed land, the **Oakland County Pioneer and Historical Society** (405 Cesar Chavez Ave., 248/338-6732, www.ocphs.org, 11 A.M.–4 P.M. Tues.–Thurs., $5 adults, $3 children under 13) comprises the Wisner Mansion, the estate to Moses Wisner, one of Michigan's pre–Civil War governors; the Drayton Plains one-room schoolhouse; and the Pioneer Museum. The collection of vintage clothing, from the 19th and early 20th centuries is impressive, as is the collection of military uniforms from the Civil War, the Spanish-American War, World War I, and World War II.

Surprisingly, Pontiac has a thriving club scene, boasting some of southeastern Michigan's hippest joints. **Clutch Cargo's** (65 E. Huron, 248/333-2362, www.clutchcargos.com, hours vary) is a nightclub and music venue that regularly books big-name talent. The **Tonic Club** (29 S. Saginaw St., 248/334-7411, www.tonicdetroit.com, 7 P.M.–2 A.M. Fri.–Sat., 9 P.M.–2 A.M. Sun.) offers multiple dance floors and some of Detroit's hottest DJs. If you're looking for a "spring break" vibe year-round, check out **Tiki Bob's** (25 S. Saginaw St., 248/335-6100, www.tikibobspontiac.com, 9 P.M.–2 A.M. Tues., 10 P.M.–2 A.M. Thurs., 7 P.M.–2 A.M. Fri., 9 P.M.–2 A.M. Sat.).

AUBURN HILLS

In recent years, the Detroit area has seen an influx of outlet malls. One of the biggest and best is located in Auburn Hills. The **Great Lakes Crossing** (4000 Baldwin Rd., 877/746-7452, www.shopgreatlakescrossing.com, 10 A.M.–9 P.M. Mon.–Fri., 11 A.M.–6 P.M. Sun., longer hours during holidays) has almost 200 stores and restaurants. With everything from Brooks Brothers to Nike, the mall is sure to satisfy your shopping fix. The complex also has numerous entertainment opportunities, from the AMC's 25 auditorium theaters to Gameworks, where both kids and adults can play some of the latest games. If you're visiting during the holiday season, plan for huge crowds and long walks from your parking spot.

SPORTS AND RECREATION
Golf

While golfers will find the largest concentration of well-regarded golf courses in the northern half of the Lower Peninsula, southeastern Michigan has a few notable spots as well. One such option is **Shepherd's Hollow Golf Club** (9085 Big Lake Rd., Clarkston, 248/922-0300, www.shepherd-shollow.com, daily Apr.–Oct., $45–85). Situated northwest of Pontiac and Waterford, this scenic championship course offers 27 holes amid 350 acres of rolling, wooded terrain.

(Detroit River International Wildlife Refuge

Perhaps surprising to some, the Detroit area boasts several parks and natural areas, ideal for outdoor enthusiasts weary of the downtown bustle. Perhaps even more surprising, Detroit is the site of North America's first international wildlife refuge. Established in 2001, the Detroit River International Wildlife Refuge (www.fws.gov/midwest/detroitriver) comprises islands, marshes, coastal wetlands, and waterfront terrain along the lower Detroit River and western shoreline of Lake Erie. Though public access is limited, the **Lake Erie Metropark unit,** situated south of Grosse Ile, is popular among hikers, bikers, bird-watchers, anglers, and cross-country skiers.

THE THUMB

Michigan's Lower Peninsula is hard to miss on any U.S. map. Shaped by three of the Great Lakes, it unmistakably resembles a mitten, a hackneyed image for some but nonetheless apt for a state that endures such long, cold winters. As with any normal mitten, there's a thumb-like protrusion—here, the large, rural peninsula along Michigan's southeastern shore, sandwiched between Lake Huron and Saginaw Bay. Called "the Thumb" by locals and tourists alike, this flat, isolated region offers a quiet alternative to bustling Detroit.

Save for peripheral destinations like Port Huron, Frankenmuth, and the cities along I-75, much of this fertile area has been overlooked by contemporary travelers, just as many of Michigan's 19th-century settlers bypassed it in favor of seemingly better farmland elsewhere. The European immigrants who did establish the Thumb's earliest communities embraced the region's bounty by initiating some of Michigan's most critical industries, such as logging, fishing, shipbuilding, and automobile manufacturing.

Today, those who venture off the interstate—rather than zip by, en route to the dunes, hills, and orchards of the north—are treated to a unique place, filled with ample farms, nostalgic towns, and tranquil beaches that boast fewer crowds than those along Lake Michigan. While most tourists aim for the Bavarian-style attractions of Frankenmuth or the cultural diversions of Saginaw and Bay City, the Thumb offers a wealth of other curiosities, many of which relate to the region's diverse history.

Along the Lake Huron shore lie a variety of

© FRANKENMUTH CHAMBER OF COMMERCE/CVB

HIGHLIGHTS

Flint Cultural Center: Some visitors might be surprised to discover such a wealth of art and culture so close to the grittiness of downtown Flint, but this impressive collection of museums and theaters presents enough options, from auto exhibits to ballet performances, to fill several days (page 67).

GM Truck Assembly Plant Tour: GM buildings are prevalent throughout the Flint area, but perhaps the most intriguing is the truck assembly plant, where walking tours allow visitors to see the construction of four-door pickups, from engine placement to frame assembly to road test. Any visit to Flint must include this illuminating tour (page 68).

Crossroads Village and Huckleberry Railroad: In the midst of Flint's modern industrial vibe lies this authentic 19th-century community, which offers a snapshot of long-ago rural life. Families, history buffs, and other curiosity-seekers are welcome to explore the quaint collection of preserved houses, mills, and railroad cars (page 69).

Bronner's CHRISTmas Wonderland: It doesn't matter if it's the height of summer, or if you have enough Bibles and Christmas ornaments to last a lifetime. This enormous, eye-popping repository of holiday goodies, open all year-round, should be a definite stop on any trip to Frankenmuth (page 76).

Bird-Watching near Saginaw: The Saginaw River area abounds with excellent bird-watching sites, from the 9,500-acre Shiawassee National Wildlife Refuge to the less well-known Crow Island State Game Area. Diehards will delight in the plethora of bird species, including swans, egrets, owls, hawks, and bald eagles (page 84).

Sanilac Petroglyphs Historic State Park: During the summer months, those interested in Michigan's earliest inhabitants can hike amid the petroglyphs near the Cass River, several miles south of Bad Axe. Still a mystery after years of study, these ancient drawings are the Lower Peninsula's only known Native American rock carvings (page 92).

Diving in Lake Huron's Underwater Preserves: Scuba divers will find over 35 major shipwrecks, in various stages of deterioration, within the Thumb Area Bottomland Preserve and Sanilac Shores Underwater Preserve, which stretch along Lake Huron's coastline between Port Austin and Lexington (page 98).

Port Huron Museum: With exhibits that relate to Port Huron's arts, history, and marine heritage, the museum encompasses four separate sites, including the *Huron* Lightship, the Thomas Edison Depot, the USCG Cutter *Bramble*, and the town's former library (page 100).

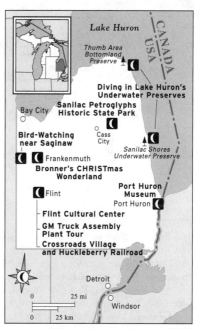

LOOK FOR **(C** TO FIND RECOMMENDED SIGHTS, ACTIVITIES, DINING, AND LODGING.

THE THUMB

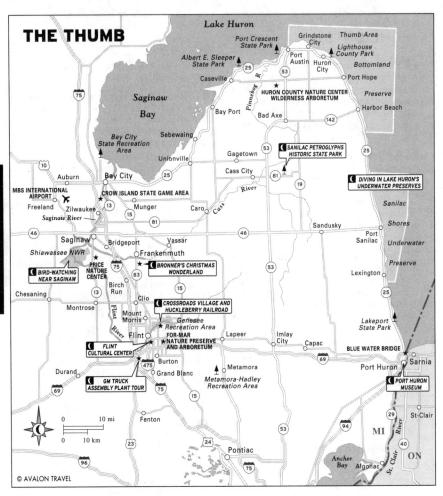

THE THUMB

Lake Huron

Grindstone City
Thumb Area
Port Crescent State Park
Port Austin
Lighthouse County Park
Albert E. Sleeper State Park
Huron City
Bottomland
Caseville
Port Hope
Saginaw Bay
HURON COUNTY NATURE CENTER WILDERNESS ARBORETUM
Preserve
Bay Port
Harbor Beach
Bay City State Recreation Area
Sebewaing
Bad Axe
Unionville
Gagetown
SANILAC PETROGLYPHS HISTORIC STATE PARK
Auburn
Bay City
Cass City
MBS INTERNATIONAL AIRPORT
CROW ISLAND STATE GAME AREA
DIVING IN LAKE HURON'S UNDERWATER PRESERVES
Freeland
Zilwaukee
Munger
Caro
Sanilac
Saginaw River
Saginaw
Bridgeport
Vassar
Sandusky
Port Sanilac
Shores
Shiawassee NWR
Frankenmuth
Underwater
BIRD-WATCHING NEAR SAGINAW
PRICE NATURE CENTER
BRONNER'S CHRISTMAS WONDERLAND
Preserve
Chesaning
Birch Run
Lexington
Montrose
Clio
CROSSROADS VILLAGE AND HUCKLEBERRY RAILROAD
Mount Morris
Genesee Recreation Area
Lakeport State Park
Flint
FOR-MAR NATURE PRESERVE AND ARBORETUM
Lapeer
Imlay City
Capac
FLINT CULTURAL CENTER
Burton
BLUE WATER BRIDGE
Durand
Grand Blanc
Metamora
Port Huron
Sarnia
GM TRUCK ASSEMBLY PLANT TOUR
Metamora-Hadley Recreation Area
PORT HURON MUSEUM
Fenton
MI
St-Clair
0 10 mi
0 10 km
Pontiac
ON
Anchor Bay
Algonac
© AVALON TRAVEL

nautical sights, including the quaint fishing port of Caseville; Port Huron's stunning Fort Gratiot Light, Michigan's oldest lighthouse; and numerous shipwrecks that comprise the Thumb Area Bottomland Preserve. Also intriguing is Flint's Crossroads Village, a community of restored 19th-century buildings that transport visitors to a simpler time, when hoop skirts and hard work prevailed. The Thumb's rarely visited interior offers its own share of historic sites—namely the mysterious Indian petroglyphs south of Bad Axe; Gagetown's

preserved Thumb Octagon Barn, built in the fashion of 1920s-era agricultural structures; and Lapeer's Greek Revival–style homes, part of the National Register of Historic Places.

Outdoor enthusiasts may especially appreciate this laidback region, where bicyclists can explore the Genesee Recreation Area, birdwatchers can view ducks and eagles at the Shiawassee National Wildlife Refuge, and deep-sea anglers can board fishing charters in Port Austin. Various annual events—from car shows to county fairs—make the Thumb an even more enticing stopover before exploring the rest of the Great Lakes State.

PLANNING YOUR TIME

Except for the towns along the I-75 corridor, the Thumb is probably one of the least visited regions in Michigan's Lower Peninsula. For some residents and seasonal visitors, the potential for fewer crowds, even in summer, is perhaps the area's biggest asset. So, whether you're headed south to Detroit, west to Lake Michigan, or north to the Upper Peninsula, you should take some time to visit the villages, beaches, state parks, and cultural attractions that comprise the Thumb.

At minimum, you should reserve three days, though two weeks will allow more time to experience the urban hot spots, interior sites, and Lake Huron coastline. Realistically, you could spend at least two days in each of the destinations along I-75, particularly if you plan to visit museums as well as nearby nature preserves and golf courses. Frankenmuth alone could fill a solid day with its quaint shops, historic structures, Bavarian cuisine, and year-round Christmas store.

Depending on your interests, the coastal towns and interior villages can each be explored in half a day's time. Cultural sites are usually concentrated along the shore or within historic downtown districts, and most towns only offer one main recreation area. In fact, the only two coastal locales that might require multiple days are Port Austin and Port Huron.

Bear in mind that only the major cities, such as Saginaw, have public transit, so reaching the rest of the Thumb will require a vehicle—either your own or a rental car from one of several agencies in the cities along I-75. Since the bulk of the Thumb's attractions lie around its perimeter, it's relatively easy to reach them via car. From Flint, I-75 leads to Bay City, from which M-25 traces the coast to Port Huron, where I-69 returns to Flint, roughly forming a 270-mile loop. Of course, this circuitous route makes it difficult to have one home base while visiting the Thumb.

When preparing your trip, remember that the Thumb is a seasonal place. While a wintertime visit can be fun in a year-round town like Frankenmuth, many of the region's more isolated inns, restaurants, and attractions are only open during the summer. In addition, although most of the Thumb's towns and rural areas are relatively safe to visit, you need to use caution when visiting cities like Flint. As in other urban areas, you should secure your belongings, avoid walking alone at night, and consult residents about other safety concerns.

For more information about the Thumb area, contact the **Thumb Area Tourism Council** (1111 W. Caro Rd., Ste. B, Caro, MI 48723, 989/672-0323, www.thumbtourism. org); the **Tip of The Thumb Heritage Water Trail** (P.O. Box 92, Caseville, MI 48725, www. thumbtrails.com); and the **Huron County Economic Development Corporation** (250 E. Huron Ave., Room 303, Bad Axe, MI 48413, 989/269-6431 or 800/358-4862, www.huron-county.com).

HISTORY

As with the rest of Michigan, the Thumb's original inhabitants were a variety of Native American tribes, some of whom left their remnants behind in the form of ancient rock carvings in Sanilac County. By the early 1800s, many European settlers had bypassed this region in favor of seemingly better farmland in the center of the Lower Peninsula. Some pioneers, however, recognized the Thumb's many benefits, including its timber, fisheries, and fertile land, and began establishing towns like Flint, today the Thumb's largest city. Once an important river crossing on the Pontiac Trail—a link to several Indian routes that crossed the wilderness—Flint owes its existence to Jacob Smith, a Detroit fur trader, who in 1819 persuaded the Ojibwa and Potawatomi Indians to surrender the lands of Saginaw County. Not long after Smith settled on the present site of modern-day Flint, other colonists followed, establishing a post office, a bank, a factory, and other necessary establishments; by 1855, it was an incorporated city.

The Thumb's sleepy personality belies its past as one of the most important lumber centers in the United States. During the mid-1800s, millions of logs were sent down the Saginaw River, to be processed by the waiting mills of Saginaw and Bay City. The explosion of the logging business created the need for log-hauling carts and wagons—all of which were produced in Flint. The thriving timber industry generated great fortunes, many of which were later used to fund the establishment of the auto industry.

Saginaw Bay, meanwhile, witnessed the development of the state's largest commercial fishing industry as well as some of the biggest shipyards ever established on the Great Lakes. But, like many of the industries that helped to fortify the United States, some of these enterprises faded to make room for more modern pursuits.

Travel by ship and by rail eventually gave way to the age of the automobile, igniting southeastern Michigan's most significant industry during the 20th century. By the 1890s, Flint became known for producing road carts, followed by carriage manufacturers and the birth of the Buick Motor Company in 1904. Likewise, when the Thumb's timber was virtually depleted, residents turned to agriculture for a new way of life. Today, the region's commodities include fish, sugar beets, navy beans, corn, various fruits, and, of course, automobiles, the latter of which is still evident in Flint, Saginaw, and Bay City.

Flint and Vicinity

Flint, Michigan. The Vehicle City. Grease-ball Mecca. The birthplace of thud-rockers Grand Funk Railroad, game show geek Bob Eubanks, and a hobby shop called General Motors. A town where every infant twirls a set of channel locks in place of a rattle.... Beer Belly paradise. Gravy on your French fries.... The callus on the palm of the state shaped like a welder's mitt.

–Ben Hamper, *Rivethead: Tales from the Assembly Line*

Gritty Flint is now, and seems like it always has been, a worker's town. The city's economy has long been yoked to General Motors' plants. As long as the plants were booming, the city did well. By the mid-1980s, however, skyrocketing unemployment, corporate downsizing, and increased global competition had challenged the city's financial way of life forever. The city tried to launch an indoor theme park based on car culture, but AutoWorld, expected to boost the local economy and fuel tourism, was an embarrassing failure. Independent filmmaker and native son Michael Moore documented the city

and its relationship with General Motors in the biting satire *Roger and Me,* filling Americans with images that are likely to haunt this weary town forever.

Despite its blue-collar image, Flint hides a rich cultural life. The abrasive Moore is just one of a long line of artists and activists native to the Flint area. Others include assembly line author Ben Hamper, whose book, *Rivethead,* topped *The New York Times* Best-Seller List for several weeks in 1991; novelist Ed Love, author of *Subways Are for Sleeping;* comedienne Sandra Bernhard, best known for her stint on the sitcom *Roseanne;* and 1960s activist and White Panther Party founder John Sinclair. The city's Institute of Music is one of only three locations nationwide chosen as the site of a workshop hosted by New York City's acclaimed Joffrey Ballet School, and in recent years, dedicated locals have revitalized the downtown area, even resurrecting Flint's once celebrated arches along Saginaw Street.

While most of Flint's attractions get little recognition outside the local area, many are well worth visiting, especially for those interested in labor relations or the evolution of the automobile. Surrounding communities, such as Burton and Genesee, also offer a plethora of recreational opportunities, from nature preserves to golf courses.

SIGHTS
◀ Flint Cultural Center

Not far from downtown Flint, the Flint Cultural Center (810/237-7333, www.flintculturalcenter.com) houses several of the city's more notable museums and performance venues, including the Sloan Museum, the Longway Planetarium, The Whiting, the Flint Institute of Arts, the Flint Institute of Music, and the Flint Youth Theatre.

Flint's labor and manufacturing history is told with surprising candor in a 10,000-square-foot permanent exhibit on "Flint and the American Dream" at the city's **Sloan Museum** (1221 E. Kearsley St., 810/237-3450, www.sloanmuseum.com, 10 A.M.–5 P.M. Mon.–Fri., noon–5 P.M. Sat.–Sun., $6 adults, $4 children 3–11). The museum, which focuses on local history and culture, has an impressive collection of neon signs, period clothing, classic motorcycles, and antique automobiles, including the oldest production model Chevrolet in existence. This particular model is worth a look even if you're not a car buff. Exhibits trace the city from Native American hunting and gathering (check out the life-size teepee), through commercial fur trapping and logging, and finally to its identity as an auto manufacturing center. (A 1912 pennant promotes Good Roads Day with the slogan "No More Mud!") Another highlight is the nearby **Buick Gallery & Research Center** (303 Walnut St., 810/237-3440, www.sloanlongway.org, included with Sloan Museum admission), home to the largest collection of vintage, one-of-a-kind, and experimental Buick vehicles, including an M18 Hellcat tank destroyer and a recently restored 1954 Wildcat II.

The **Longway Planetarium** (1310 E. Kearsley St., 810/237-3400, www.longwayplanetarium.com, shows 12:30–3:30 P.M. daily, $5 adults, $4 children 3–11) claims

© JIM CHEEK

THE THUMB

an annual Christmas concert at the Flint Institute of Arts

the state's largest sky screen. The huge, 60-foot domed screen used to reproduce the night sky is as large as those in New York and Chicago. Changing multimedia shows explore the skies, constellations, science fiction, and space travel. Laser shows are offered on Saturday evenings. Call for a current schedule of programs.

Flint Institute of Arts

Like Detroit, Flint benefited from the velvet-lined pockets of a number of wealthy auto industrialists. Generous donations from local citizens built the Flint Institute of Arts (FIA) (1120 E. Kearsley St. in the Cultural Center, 810/234-1695, www.flintarts.org, 10 A.M.–5 P.M. Tues.–Sat., 1–5 P.M. Sun., free, temporary exhibits $7 adults), now the state's second largest museum of the arts. Dedicated to "making art available, accessible and approachable," the permanent collection of more than 7,500 pieces is strong in areas that include contemporary paintings and sculpture, Asian art, African artifacts, glass paperweights, and 19th-century French paintings (predominantly landscapes), including ever-popular works by the French Impressionists. The Bray Gallery houses a fine array of European paintings, furniture, and tapestries that range from the 15th to the 18th centuries.

Buckham Gallery

In downtown Flint, the alternative, artist-run Buckham Gallery (134½ W. 2nd St., 810/239-6334, www.buckhamgallery.org, noon–5 P.M. Wed.–Fri., 10 A.M.–3 P.M. Sat., free, special event prices vary) is dedicated to showing "contemporary cutting-edge art, with no censorship or interference," making for some interesting shows. Established in 1984, the space is also often used for performance art and poetry readings.

GM Truck Assembly Plant Tour

Perhaps Flint's most interesting attraction—and a good way to better understand the city's psyche—is the GM Truck Assembly Plant (G-3100 Van Slyke Rd., 810/232-5758), which offers free tours at 9 A.M. and noon Monday–Friday. The workhorse plant was built in 1947 to make Chevrolets; it was the birthplace of the first Corvairs as well as generations of military vehicles from World War II to the Gulf War. More recently, it has churned out GMC and Chevy vans and full-size pickups. This is the plant where Ben Hamper, aka the Rivethead, worked from 1977 to 1987, but the infamous rivet line has since been replaced by robots. Automation and market forces have slashed the plant's employment from a high of 8,500 to about 2,500 workers today.

DOWNTOWN FLINT

HOLIDAY INN EXPRESS
FLINT FARMERS MARKET
ROBERT T LONGWAY BLVD
FLINT CULTURAL CENTER
BUICK GALLERY & RESEARCH CENTER
THE WHITING
SLOAN MUSEUM
FLINT YOUTH THEATRE
FLINT INSTITUTE OF MUSIC
LONGWAY PLANETARIUM
FLINT INSTITUTE OF ARTS
E 5TH AVE
5TH AVE
N SAGINAW ST
MARTIN LUTHER KING AVE
W 5TH AVE
GARLAND ST
W 4TH AVE
W 3RD AVE
NORTH ST
E BLVD DR
475
CARRIAGE TOWN ANTIQUE CENTER
N 2ND AVE
W 1ST AVE
Flint River
AVON HOUSE BED & BREAKFAST
CHAPO ST
AVON ST
N GRAND TRAVERSE ST
HARRISON ST
UNIVERSITY OF MICHIGAN FLINT
Wilson Park
E 1ST ST
E 2ND ST
E COURT ST
THOMPSON ST
E 3RD ST
W WATER ST
S SAGINAW ST
E KEARSLEY ST
WALLENBERG
E 2ND ST
STEVENS ST
Street Park
River Bank Park
GENESEE TOWERS
W KEARSLEY ST
1ST ST
E 3RD ST
E 4TH ST
AVON PARK DR
E 6TH ST
FLINT AREA CONVENTION AND VISITORS BUREAU
BUCKHAM GALLERY
BEACH ST
CHURCH ST
BILL THOMAS HALO BURGER
E 6TH ST
LAPEER RD
BELLMONT AVE
OAK ST
W 3RD ST
W 4TH ST
W COURT ST
E 5TH ST
E 7TH ST
CITY HALL
W 5TH ST
GENESEE COUNTY ADMINISTRATION
69
0   300 yds
0   300 m
© AVALON TRAVEL

THE THUMB

Veteran auto workers give 90-minute tours, which include a look at "gatekeeping," the dramatic part of assembly when the car's side panel is joined to the vehicle's floor; a visit to the ladder line, where the frame is riveted together; and the finishing line, where the final result is road-tested. Reservations are a must, and remember that only GM vehicles are allowed in the parking lot. Call for more information.

⟨ Crossroads Village and Huckleberry Railroad

After touring the city's modern factories, you'll gain a renewed appreciation for the hardships of the early Industrial Age. The often-hazardous working habits of the pre-industrial 19th century are the focus at the charming but truthful Crossroads Village and Huckleberry Railroad (6140 Bray Rd., 810/736-7100, www.

geneseecountyparks.org, 10 A.M.–5 P.M. Wed.– Sun., for village $10 adults, $8 children 2–12, for village, train, and boat $16 adults, $12.50 children). This restored village has 35 vintage buildings that show a variety of industries, complete with the era's authentic grit, noise, and pervasive smoke. An 1836 gristmill, a sawmill, a cider mill, a print and blacksmith shop, and more give visitors an idea of Genesee County in the mid-1800s. Numerous special weekend events are held throughout the year, especially during holidays.

The 40-minute ride on the Huckleberry Railroad is also a treat; the narrow-gauge train, a collection of vintage wooden coaches and steam locomotives, leads guests through scenic woods and alongside lovely Mott Lake. Also nearby is the **Genesee Belle,** a paddlewheel riverboat that takes visitors on scenic 45-minute cruises on Mott Lake during the summer.

THE SECOND MOTOR CITY: ORIGIN OF THE LABOR MOVEMENT

While Detroit is considered the birthplace of automobile manufacturing, Flint is credited with the start of the American labor movement. As the auto industry grew during the early 20th century, workers from all across the country flocked to factories in Detroit and its surrounding cities, including Flint, Saginaw, and Bay City.

By the 1920s, the industry was booming – until the Great Depression descended upon the nation, causing massive unemployment. In order to save money, car companies began demanding higher productivity for lower wages. Soon, autoworkers were disgusted with the poor working conditions, high-speed assembly lines, and lack of job security. Using solidarity to garner more control, they began to form unions.

In 1935, autoworkers organized the United Automobile Workers of America (U.A.W.), which General Motors (GM) refused to recognize as the bargaining agent for their work-force. When Flint-area workers heard about GM's plan to move work to factories where the U.A.W. had a weaker hold, they initiated Michigan's first large-scale, sit-down strike on December 30, 1936.

Continuing into the new year, the sit-down was an effective way of protest: as long as workers remained in the plant, management could not replace them with others. Unfortunately, Flint's infamous strike resulted in severe riots that ultimately injured 16 workers and 11 police officers.

On March 12, 1937, the sit-down strike finally ended with an agreement under which GM recognized the U.A.W. as their workers' bargaining representative. The success of the U.A.W. inspired the birth of unions across America, jump-starting the modern labor movement and ushering in an age of good wages and extensive benefits for thousands of autoworkers throughout Michigan and the rest of the country.

ENTERTAINMENT AND EVENTS
Nightlife

Though Flint isn't known for its nightlife scene, those seeking respite will find several bars and music clubs in town. If you're looking for a casual hangout, **Kickers Sports Bar & Grill** (5577 S. Saginaw Rd., 810/695-2060, www.kickerssportsbar.com, 11 A.M.–2 A.M. Mon.–Sat., no cover) can keep you busy all night. Besides watching football, basketball, and countless other televised sports, you can play pool, darts, or video games and choose from a wide selection of draft and bottled beers, wines, and cocktails. The grub's not bad either; the extensive menu includes bar favorites like fried pickles, loaded potato skins, and battered mushrooms as well as an assortment of salads, sandwiches, burgers, pastas, pizzas, even ribs and fajitas. The joint also offers plenty of specials, from 25-cent chicken wings on Monday to all-you-can-eat crab legs on Friday, and happy hour specials are available 11 A.M.–9 P.M. every day.

Maxie's Food & Spirits (2500 Hill Rd., 810/232-2500, www.maxiesofflint.com, 11 A.M.–2 A.M. daily, no cover) offers a different atmosphere, with special events every night of the week, including free comedy shows on Sunday, Tuesday karaoke, ladies' night on Wednesday, and rowdy parties through the weekend. In summertime, there's even an outdoor tiki bar, where you'll be treated to tropical drinks, live DJ music, and open pit barbecue until 2 A.M.

For a swankier vibe, stop by **Down the Tracks** (2310 W. Court St., 810/235-2870, 10 A.M.–2 A.M. daily, no cover), a classy lounge where the drinks matter more than the decor. Even more enticing is the **Purple Moon Nightclub** (2525 S. Dort Hwy., 810/424-9579, http://purplemoonnightclub.com, 10 P.M.–2 A.M. Thurs.–Sun., ticket prices vary), a slick, high-energy club, equipped with a gorgeous bar, an enormous dance floor, and

© THE MACHINE SHOP

The Machine Shop

an open stage, where live hip-hop, rock, and tribute bands keep the party hopping.

If your musical tastes run a bit more hardcore, never fear. Since 2002, **The Machine Shop** (3539 S. Dort Hwy., 810/715-2650, www.themachineshop.info, show times and ticket prices vary) has hosted a variety of rock performers, from Blind Melon to Kid Rock.

The Arts

The **Flint Cultural Center,** an unassuming art mecca at the heart of an industrial town, houses several winning performance venues. For concerts, operas, dance shows, and Broadway musicals, reserve your seat at **The Whiting** (1241 E. Kearsley St., 810/237-7337, www.thewhiting. com, show times and ticket prices vary), where recent programs have included *The Wizard of Oz* and an evening with comedian Bill Cosby. Other plays and musicals are featured at the **Flint Youth Theatre** (1220 E. Kearsley St., 810/237-1530, www.flintyouththeatre.com, show times and ticket prices vary), and the nearby **Flint Institute of Music (FIM)** (1025 E. Kearsley St., 810/238-1350, www.thefim.com,

show times and ticket prices vary) presents concerts by the Flint Symphony Orchestra.

Fairs and Festivals

As with the rest of Michigan's Lower Peninsula, Flint-area residents don't need much of an excuse to hold an annual event, especially during the pleasant summer season. In mid-June, the Flint Institute of Arts hosts the **Flint Art Fair** (810/234-1695, www.flintartfair.org, free), which presents the work of over 150 contemporary artists and craftsmen from the U.S., Canada, and places as far away as Bermuda. Art lovers will appreciate the chance to peruse sculpture, glasswork, photography, textiles, and fine jewelry, among other impressive treasures.

In mid-August, the four-day **Back to the Bricks Cruise Weekend** (810/232-8903, www.backtothebricks.org, free) celebrates the region's industrial roots with a parade of classic vehicles, hot rods, sports cars, vintage trucks, and customized motorcycles through downtown Flint. Also in mid-August, the **Genesee County Fair** (Everett A. Cummings Center, G-6130 E. Mount Morris Rd., Mount Morris,

810/687-0953, www.gcf.org, free, special event prices vary) offers a countrified change of pace to Flint's auto-related attractions and events. For a solid week, you'll be treated to livestock shows, agricultural exhibits, pig races, pie-eating contests, and, if you find yourself missing engines, demolition derbies.

SHOPPING

While the Flint area is, by no means, a shoppers' mecca, there are a few stops worth a look. One such place is the **Carriage Town Antique Center** (503 Garland St., 810/234-7146, www.randolphhouse1872.com, 11 A.M.–5 P.M. Tues.–Sun.), a large, recently renovated repository of antique furniture, vintage clothing, and old-fashioned jewelry.

In a region that's well known for its bountiful farms and orchards, it's hard to pass up a produce market. Luckily, the **Flint Farmers' Market** (420 E. Boulevard Dr., 810/232-1399, www.flintfarmersmarket.com, 8 A.M.–5 P.M. Tues., Thurs., and Sat.) is open three days a week; in addition to produce vendors, you'll find a bakery, an art gallery, and a popular eatery known as Steady Eddy's, which offers a surprising number of vegetarian dishes. For more fresh fruit and veggies, you should take a side trip to **Montrose Orchards** (12473 Seymour Rd., Montrose, 810/639-6971, www.montroseorchards.com, 9 A.M.–5 P.M. Mon.–Sat., noon–5 P.M. Sun.), a family-owned farm open mid-May–December. Besides seasonal blueberry fields, pumpkin patches, a bakery, and other market goodies, the farm offers several family-friendly activities, including hayrides.

SPORTS AND RECREATION
Parks and Preserves

The **Genesee Recreation Area** (7004 N. Irish Rd., 810/736-7100, www.geneseecountyparks.org, 8 A.M.–sunset daily, seasons vary throughout park, free) offers a pleasant contrast to Flint's urbanity. It covers more than 4,500 acres along the Flint River off I-475, with beaches, bicycle paths, a boat launch, a campground, fishing sites, and hiking and horse trails.

Southeast of Flint, the 380-acre **For-Mar Nature Preserve and Arboretum** (2142 N. Genesee Rd., Burton, 810/789-8567, www.geneseecountyparks.org, 8 A.M.–sunset Wed.–Sun., buildings close at 5 P.M., free) includes a patchwork of woodlands, restored prairies, open fields, meadows, ponds, and Kearsley Creek, as well as an arboretum planted with specimen trees, shrubs, and vines. Seven miles of up-and-down hiking trails weave through a diverse habitat. Two trails are wheelchair-accessible. An interpretive center has a live bird-viewing area and several animal and reptile displays, including the Foote Bird Museum, which contains more than 600 stuffed and mounted specimens.

Golf

Every summer, golfers flock to Michigan for its numerous, well-groomed courses, and the Flint area, host of the annual Buick Open, is no exception. Just a short drive from the city lie three public 18-hole golf courses: **Brookwood Golf Club** (6045 Davison Rd., Burton, 810/742-4930, www.flintima.org/brookwood, daily Apr.–mid-Nov., $30–40 w/cart); **Captain's Club at Woodfield** (10200 Woodfield Dr., Grand Blanc, 810/695-4653, www.captainsclubatwoodfield.com, daily Apr.–Oct., $25–49 w/cart); and **Fenton Farms Golf Club** (12312 Torrey Rd., Fenton, 810/629-1212, www.fentonfarms.com, daily Apr.–Oct., $25–40 w/cart).

ACCOMMODATIONS

The **Avon House Bed & Breakfast** (518 Avon St., 810/232-6861, www.avonhousebandb.com, $50–60 d) invites visitors to experience life in a Victorian home. The rooms are spacious, furnished with antiques, and a homemade breakfast is included with each night's stay.

The area also has a number of chain hotels, including the **Comfort Inn** (2361 Austin Pkwy., 810/232-4222, www.comfortinn.com, $100–120 d), **Holiday Inn Express** (1150 Robert T. Longway Blvd., 810/238-7744, www.hiexpress.com, $90–160 d), and **Sleep Inn** (2325 Austin Pkwy., 810/232-7777, www.sleepinn.com, $80–100 d).

For something a little different, consider

staying outside of town. Roughly 15 miles north of Flint, the (**Cinnamon Stick Farm Bed & Breakfast** (12364 N. Genesee Rd., Clio, 810/686-8391, www.cinnamonstick-farmbnb.com, $70–140 d) welcomes travelers year-round. Here, the well-appointed, country-style rooms are not the only attraction; guests can fish from a stocked catch-and-release pond, peruse an organic garden, and walk amid the rolling 50-acre countryside.

Camping

Within the Genesee Recreation Area, Genesee County operates the **Wolverine Campground.** Located in the 2,000-acre Holloway Reservoir Regional Park, this summer-only spot has a nice setting in a pine forest, with 195 tent sites, several shower and restroom buildings, a boat launch, and a guarded swimming beach. Reservations are recommended. Contact the **Genesee County Parks and Recreation Commission** (5045 Stanley Rd., 810/736-7100 or 800/648-7275, www.geneseecountyparks.org, $12–22).

FOOD

According to the *The Flint Journal,* **Bill Thomas Halo Burger** (810/238-4607, www. haloburger.com, hours vary, $5–10) serves up the best burgers in town, with 11 locations in the Flint area. The most lively atmosphere, however, is at the (**Big Eazy Grill** (G-5311 Corunna Rd., 810/732-4600, www.flint-food.com/be.htm, 11 A.M.–midnight Mon.–Thurs., 11 A.M.–1 A.M. Fri., noon–1 A.M. Sat., noon–11 P.M. Sun., $12–30), a Cajun-style eatery, complete with an oyster bar and a jazzy lounge; just be aware that the gumbo is unlike any you'll find in New Orleans.

Just off I-75 at the Miller Road exit, **Salvatore Scallopini** (G-3227 Miller Rd., 810/732-1070, www.salvatorescallopini.com, 11 A.M.–10 P.M. Mon.–Thurs., 11 A.M.–11 P.M. Fri.–Sat., noon–10 P.M. Sun., $12–18) is part of a statewide chain known for its authentic Italian cuisine and seafood. An even better choice for Italian dishes is **Pesto's** (G-5275 Miller Rd., 810/732-4390, www.pestos.com, 10:30 A.M.–10 P.M. Mon.–Sat., noon–8 P.M.

Sun., $8–20), where you'll find homemade dressings, scrumptious specials, and desserts big enough for two.

INFORMATION AND SERVICES

Flint offers all the services that a traveler might need or want, from tourism bureaus to pharmacies. For more information about the Flint area, contact the **Flint Area Convention and Visitors Bureau** (502 Church St., 810/232-8900, www.visitflint.travel, 8 A.M.–5 P.M. Mon.–Fri.) or visit www.geneseefun.com. For government issues, contact **City Hall** (1101 S. Saginaw St., www.cityofflint.com) or the **Genesee County Administration** (1101 Beach St., www.co.genesee.mi.us). For local news and events, pick up a daily copy of *The Flint Journal* (www.flintjournal.com or www.mlive.com).

Flint and its surrounding communities have several U.S. post offices, including a **downtown location** (601 S. Saginaw St., 810/257-1526, 10 A.M.–4 P.M. Mon.–Fri.). For late-night drop-offs, try one of the **Burton-area offices** (2333 S. Center Rd., 7 A.M.–11 P.M. Mon.–Sun.). Refer to www.usps.com for more locations in the Flint area.

In case of an emergency, you can contact the **Hurley Medical Center** (1 Hurley Plaza, 810/257-9000, www.hurleymc.com) or the **McLaren Regional Medical Center** (401 S. Ballenger Hwy., 810/342-2000, www.mclaren-regional.org). In addition, there are several area pharmacies, including a 24-hour **Walgreens** (502 S. Ballenger Hwy., 810/424-9270, www. walgreens.com).

Whether you're the victim of an auto accident, a medical emergency, or a crime, it may be necessary to contact the police. If so, you can dial **911** from any mobile or public phone.

While in town, you might need to replenish your travel fund. If so, rest assured that there are plenty of banks in the area, including ones with round-the-clock access. Chase, for instance, has a 24-hour ATM at the **Hurley Medical Center,** the **McLaren Regional Medical Center,** and the **Genesee Towers** (210 W. 1st St., www.chase.com).

GETTING THERE AND AROUND

Visitors can reach Flint via air, train, or car. For information about flights into and out of Flint, contact the **Bishop International Airport (FNT)** (G-3425 W. Bristol Rd., 810/235-6560, www. bishopairport.org). Although this regional airport has limited flights, major carriers like Delta and American Airlines offer daily trips to and from Atlanta, Chicago, Dallas, and other major cities.

It's also possible to travel into Flint via train. **Amtrak** (800/872-7245, www.amtrak.com) offers a route from Chicago, with stops across Michigan, including Kalamazoo, Battle Creek, East Lansing, Flint, and Detroit. For information about schedules, visit the **Flint station** (1407 S. Dort Hwy.).

Given Genesee County's well-designed expressway system, traveling into and around Flint via car is also easy. From Detroit, you can drive northwest on I-75 and connect to I-475, which crosses I-69 and runs directly through downtown Flint. From Saginaw, head southeast on I-75/U.S. 23. Flint is also accessible from Port Huron or Lansing, via I-69, an east-west interstate.

If you arrive in Flint via air or train, you can easily rent a vehicle from various rental agencies:

- **Alamo:** 810/239-4341 or 800/462-5266
- **Avis:** 810/234-7847 or 800/331-1212
- **Budget:** 810/238-8300 or 800/527-0700
- **Enterprise:** 810/235-1101 or 800/261-7331
- **Hertz:** 810/234-2041 or 800/654-3131
- **National:** 810/239-4341 or 800/227-7368

If you'd rather not drive, consider using Flint's public bus system to get around town. For information on routes and schedules, contact the **Mass Transportation Authority (MTA)** (1401 S. Dort Hwy., 810/767-0100, www. mtaflint.org). You might also consider joining a bus tour of the area; for more information, contact **Blue Lakes Charters & Tours** (12154 N. Saginaw Rd., Clio, 800/282-4287, www.bluelakes.com).

Frankenmuth

It would be easy to dismiss Frankenmuth as overcommercialized kitsch. "Michigan's Little Bavaria" once was a quiet and undistinguished German farm town of just more than 4,000, but has since grown to become the state's top tourist attraction, with an estimated three million visitors each year.

Frankenmuth houses the world's largest Christmas store, a two-mile-long street of pseudo-Bavarian shops, and three restaurants that serve all-you-can-eat, family-style chicken dinners. Buoyed by the seemingly endless flow of visitors, the area has expanded over the years to include an 18-hole public golf course and the Midwest's largest outlet mall.

Despite the Bavarian image it relentlessly pushes today, much of Frankenmuth's history echoes that of other Saginaw Valley towns. A group of 15 young Lutherans from an area near Nuremberg founded the city in 1845 (Frankenmuth means "courage of the Franconians"). This optimistic group followed the call to become missionaries in America, with hopes of tending to the growing Saginaw Valley German community and converting the local Ojibwa Indians to Christianity along the way.

The Indians stood steadfast and the Franconians' mission soon failed. Still, more and more Germans immigrated to the area, drawn by abundant opportunities for logging and a growing community. German, in fact, remained the community's principal language until well into the 1920s.

Once the forests were stripped by the logging business, settlers turned to farming. The chicken-dinner craze Frankenmuth enjoys

FRANKENMUTH

CITY HALL/
POLICE DEPT
■ POST OFFICE
W GENESEE ST

To The Timbers
Golf Club
ST. JULIAN
WINERY
E SCHOOL ST

DRURY INN & SUITES ●
SATOW DRUG STORE ★
MAIN STREET TAVERN ★
WILLI'S SAUSAGE COMPANY ■

FAIRFIELD INN BY MARRIOTT ●

W TUSCOLA ST

To St. Lorenz
Lutheran Church

MCCLELLAN'S ■
FRANKENMUTH
WOOLEN MILL
FRANKENMUTH
■ CHEESE HAUS
★ FRANKENMUTH
HISTORICAL MUSEUM
BAVARIAN
INN LODGE
●
■ CHAMBER OF COMMERCE/
CONVENTION & VISITORS BUREAU

ZEHNDER'S OF
FRANKENMUTH
BAVARIAN INN
RESTAURANT
FANTASY CARRIAGE ■
COMPANY
FRANKENMUTH CARRIAGE
COMPANY
THE FORTRESS
GOLF COURSE
■ FRANKENMUTH
RIVER PLACE
FRANKENMUTH
CLOCK
COMPANY

E JEFFERSON ST

WALNUT ST

LIST ST

FRANKENMUTH
JELLYSTONE
PARK
●
MICHIGAN'S OWN
MILITARY AND
SPACE MUSEUM

0   300 yds
0   300 m

To ◖BRONNER'S CHRISTMAS WONDERLAND,
Grandpa Tiny's Farm,
Prime Outlets, and Tony's

© AVALON TRAVEL

Cass River

today started as an attraction for traveling salesmen, but later became a staple of the Detroit Sunday drive set in the 1920s and 1930s. They had more reason to steer toward Frankenmuth in the 1950s, when signmaker Wally Bronner, who sadly passed away in early 2008, opened a Christmas decorating shop as a sideline to his regular business. By the 1970s, the city had been expanded into the Bavarian nerve center it is today.

SIGHTS
Old Frankenmuth

Beneath the commercialism, however, is a genuine German community, where people are old-world friendly and everyone knows everyone else. Old Frankenmuth can still be found in a number of places in town, which are, not surprisingly, the places most tourists skip. **Satow's Drug Store** (308 S. Main St., 989/652-8001, www.satowdrugs.com, 7:30 A.M.–9 P.M. Mon.–Sat., 8 A.M.–4 P.M. Sun., $3–6) has a coffee shop where locals hang out, soups are made from scratch, and prices are reminiscent of the 1950s. The **Main Street Tavern** (310 S. Main St., 989/652-2222, 10 A.M.–2:30 A.M. Mon.–Sat., noon–2:30 A.M. Sun., $4–11) is owned by a former baker from Zehnder's who makes all the fragrant bread and buns on the premises. His cheeseburger is made from local beef and cheese; a house specialty is the pizza made with Italian sausage from Willi's Sausage Company next door. Wash it down with a once-locally made Carling's or a Frankenmuth Pilsner for a delicious meal filled with old-world flair at a reasonable price.

The 1880 **St. Lorenz Lutheran Church** (W. Tuscola and Mayer Rd., 989/652-6141, www.stlorenz.org, 9 A.M.–noon Mon.–Sat. June–Sept., free) houses the largest congregation, east of the Mississippi, of the conservative Missouri Synod of the Lutheran Church. Self-guided tours reveal scenes of Lutheran and Frankenmuth history, an early cemetery, a small museum, and a reconstruction of the first settlers' original log church and parsonage.

THE THUMB

Frankenmuth Historical Museum

The Frankenmuth Historical Museum (613 S. Main St., 989/652-9701, www.frankenmuth-museum.org, 10:30 A.M.–5 P.M. Mon.–Thurs., 10:30 A.M.–8 P.M. Fri., 10 A.M.–8 P.M. Sat., 11 A.M.–7 P.M. Sun., $2 adults, $1 children) traces the city's rich past through possessions and letters from the original settlers. Displays explore the city's connections to logging, Prohibition, the rise of the chicken-dinner phenomenon, and the Frankenmuth brewery. The museum shop is a pleasant surprise among all the cookie-cutter shops along Main Street, with vintage-style toys, sophisticated crafts, and an excellent selection of books regarding the city and surrounding area. Note that the museum has shorter hours in winter and bilingual tours are available.

◖ Bronner's CHRISTmas Wonderland

Check any cynicism at the door when visiting Bronner's CHRISTmas Wonderland (25 Christmas Lane, 989/652-9931 or 800/255-9327, www.bronners.com, 9 A.M.–9 P.M. Mon.–Sat., noon–7 P.M. Sun., free), truly a phenomenon. Prepare yourself for a building that encompasses almost 100,000 square feet—that's nearly two football fields—filled with more than 350 decorated Christmas trees, 800 animated figures, 500 styles of Nativity scenes from 75 countries, 6,000 kinds of glass ornaments, Bibles in more than 30 languages, Advent calendars, lighted villages, and nutcrackers. Many of the offerings are from Eastern Europe, but the staff has worked hard in recent years to add diversity to the store's offerings. These days, you can find books on Hanukkah and Kwanzaa, as well as non-Caucasian Santas and Nativity characters. The complex, which encompasses 27 acres, also contains the Silent Night Memorial Chapel, a replica of the Austrian church that was built where "Silent Night" was first sung in 1818. Note that hours are shorter January–May; the store is closed on New Year's Day, Easter, Thanksgiving, and Christmas.

Bronner's CHRISTmas Wonderland in Frankenmuth

Grandpa Tiny's Farm

A historical 45-acre working farm founded by William "Tiny" Zehnder, Grandpa Tiny's Farm (7775 Weiss St., 989/652-5437 Apr.–Oct. or 989/871-2937 Nov.–Mar., www.grandpatinysfarm.com, 10 A.M.–5 P.M. Mon.–Sat., noon–5 P.M. Sun. Apr.–Oct., $5) invites visitors, especially children, to interact with bunnies, lambs, goats, and other farm animals. Guides give personal tours through the farm, where plowing and wool-spinning demonstrations, narrated horse-drawn wagon rides, and other activities highlight the importance of the area's agricultural history.

Other Attractions

St. Julian Winery (127 S. Main St., 989/652-3281, www.stjulian.com, 9 A.M.–6 P.M. Mon.–Sat., noon–6 P.M. Sun., free tours), the state's largest wine company (based in Paw Paw), has a free tasting room here that showcases the company's many wines and sparkling juices. There's also a small winery on-site, where solera cream sherry is aged.

Michigan's Own Military and Space Museum (1250 Weiss St., 989/652-8005, www.michigansmilitarymuseum.com, 10 A.M.–5 P.M. Mon.–Sat. and 11 A.M.–5 P.M. Sun. Mar.–Sept., closed Jan.–Feb., $5 adults, $2 children 6–18) features exhibits about Michigan governors, astronauts, and veterans of several foreign wars.

FESTIVALS

As one of Michigan's top tourist destinations, Frankenmuth hosts its share of annual events, including a music festival in August and a holiday celebration in November. Every January, **Zehnder's Snowfest** (800/863-7999, www.zehnders.com, outdoor events free) honors winter with fireworks, live entertainment, ice-carving competitions, and cozy treats.

In May, the **World Expo of Beer** ($5 adults, children under 16 free), Michigan's largest beer sampling event, brings together over 150 beers from breweries around the world; during the two-day event, visitors can enjoy live bands, watch brewing demonstrations, and vote for their favorite beer. The following month, the four-day **Frankenmuth Bavarian Festival** ($7 adults, children under 16 free) highlights German culture with traditional music and food. Of course, what German town would be complete without its very own Oktoberfest? The **Frankenmuth Oktoberfest** ($8 adults, children under 16 free), which takes place in late September, showcases all things German, including music and dance performers brought directly from the mother country. For more information about these and other events, call 800/386-3378 or visit www.frankenmuthfestivals.com.

SHOPPING
Main Street

Unlike Flint, Frankenmuth is definitely a popular spot for shopaholics. Main Street alone offers a plethora of quaint emporiums, including toy stores, fudge shops, and German-inspired boutiques like the **Frankenmuth Clock Company** (966 S. Main St., 989/652-2933, www.frankenmuthclock.com, 9 A.M.–6:30 P.M. daily), an importer of genuine, ornately crafted Black Forest cuckoo clocks. Also along this stretch, you'll find specialty food shops such as **Willi's Sausage Company** (316 S. Main St., 989/652-9041, www.willissausages.com, 9 A.M.–5 P.M. Sun.–Wed., 9 A.M.–6 P.M. Thurs.–Sat.) and the **Frankenmuth Cheese Haus** (561 S. Main St., 989/652-6727, www.frankenmuthcheesehaus.com, 9:30 A.M.–9:30 P.M. daily).

For a more unique experience, stop by Michigan's oldest woolen mill. Established in 1894, **McClellan's Frankenmuth Woolen Mill** (570 S. Main St., 989/652-6555, www.thewoolenmill.com, 10 A.M.–8 P.M. Sun.–Thurs., 10 A.M.–9 P.M. Fri.–Sat.) invites visitors to watch the working mill in action; afterwards, feel free to peruse the merchandise, a variety of warm sweaters and comforters.

Resembling a European village—albeit newer-looking than most—**Frankenmuth River Place** (925 S. Main St., 989/652-9043, www.frankenmuth-riverplace.com, 10 A.M.–9 P.M. daily, shorter hours Sept.–June) is Frankenmuth's only mall. Among its more than 30 shops and attractions, you'll find a quilt store, a glass art gallery,

THE THUMB

an incredible mirror maze, and Michigan's largest bead store. From May to October, River Place is also the launching point for one-hour narrated tours on the **Bavarian Belle** Riverboat (866/808-2628, www.bavarianbelle.com, departure times posted daily).

Birch Run

Once just an obscure village eight miles southwest of Frankenmuth, Birch Run is now the state's discount shopping capital, with more than 140 stores within its famed **outlet mall** (12240 S. Beyer Rd., 989/624-6226, www.primeoutlets.com, 10 A.M.–9 P.M. Mon.–Sat., 11 A.M.–7 P.M. Sun., closed Easter, Thanksgiving, and Christmas), the second largest in the world. Plunder the offerings of Nike, Ann Taylor, Columbia Sportswear, Polo/Ralph Lauren, Liz Claiborne, J. Crew, Eddie Bauer, Easy Spirit, American Eagle, Pottery Barn, and more. Situated at the second busiest exit on I-75 (the first being Orlando, Florida), Birch Run now contains a movie palace and a motor speedway—improvements designed to make the town a true weekend destination for the shopping set.

GOLF

For golfers, there are three options near Frankenmuth. Zehnder's, probably the town's most famous restaurant and hotel, offers **The Fortress Golf Course** (950 Flint St., 800/863-7999, www.zehnders.com, daily May–Oct., $35–65 w/cart), an 18-hole championship course not far from Main Street. If you find yourself overwhelmed by Frankenmuth's Bavarian vibe, head five miles west of town to the **Green Acres Golf Course** (7323 Dixie Hwy., Bridgeport, 989/777-3510, www.greenacresgc.com, daily Apr.–Oct., $26–39 w/cart). As an alternative, you can also visit **The Timbers Golf Club** (7300 Bray Rd., Vassar, 989/871-4884, www.timbersgolfclub.com, daily Apr.–Oct., $22–45 w/cart), a wooded course situated about five miles east of Frankenmuth.

ACCOMMODATIONS

Frankenmuth has several bed-and-breakfast inns such as the **Wren Haus Bed and Breakfast** (718 Wren Rd., 989/652-4992, www.wrenhausbedandbreakfast.com, $100 d). In addition, there's no shortage of chain hotels in the area, including **Drury Inn & Suites** (260 S. Main St., 989/652-2800, www.druryhotels.com, $100–140 d) and **Fairfield Inn by Marriott** (430 S. Main St., 989/652-5000, www.fairfieldinn.com, $130–160 d).

In downtown Frankenmuth, you can also opt for the ◖ **Bavarian Inn Lodge** (1 Covered Bridge Lane, 888/775-6343, www.bavarianinn.com, $105–255 d), set back behind the restaurant and shops along the Cass River. The 360 rooms are clean and bright, with balconies and Bavarian touches. Each is named in honor of one of the town's early inhabitants, complete with family pictures. The lodge is especially popular with kids, who flock here to hang out at the indoor water park, mini-golf course, and Family Fun Center, which includes video games and more.

Camping

Despite the plethora of tourist-oriented hotels and inns in Frankenmuth, there is an option for those who enjoy sleeping amid the great outdoors. Not far from Bronner's Christmas store, the year-round **Frankenmuth Jellystone Park** (1339 Weiss St., 989/652-6668, www.frankenmuthjellystone.com, $40–150) offers tent sites, full RV hookups, a laundry, heated restrooms, an indoor pool, a playground and mini-golf course, and free wireless Internet access.

FOOD

No visit to Frankenmuth would be complete without a meal at ◖ **Zehnder's of Frankenmuth** (730 S. Main St., 800/863-7999, www.zehnders.com, 11 A.M.–9:30 P.M. daily, $15–22), a historic complex that comprises a marketplace and America's largest family restaurant. With nine dining rooms, the restaurant can seat more than 1,500 guests at any given time. The full-service menu includes seafood, steaks, European desserts, and all-you-can-eat, family-style chicken dinners. South of the downtown area, Zehnder's also offers a whimsical hotel and water park and an 18-hole golf course.

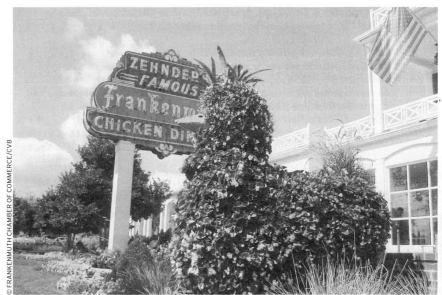

the topiary chicken outside Zehnder's, a restaurant known for its poultry dinners

Thousands of chicken dinners are also sold annually at the vast ◖ **Bavarian Inn Restaurant** (713 S. Main St., 989/652-9941, www.bavarianinn.com, 11 A.M.–9 P.M. Sun.–Thurs., 11 A.M.–9:30 P.M. Fri.–Sat., $20–23), which seats 1,200. If you'd rather skip the poultry, the Bavarian Inn Restaurant also offers German specialties such as *sauerbraten* and strudel. Skip the restaurant itself if you like your food spicy, however; Frankenmuth caters to a largely senior citizen crowd, and many diners find the food a bit bland.

Like any good tourist mecca, Frankenmuth and Birch Run have plenty of restaurants, including the usual rash of fast-food places and chains. Across from Birch Run's discount mall, **Tony's** (8781 Main St., 989/624-5860, 6 A.M.–10 P.M. Sun.–Thurs., 6 A.M.–11 P.M. Fri.–Sat., $8–12) is a long-standing local eatery that started in downtown Saginaw and is still known for its huge, overstuffed sandwiches and thick shakes. Lines can be long, so plan on a wait or visit during off-hours.

INFORMATION AND SERVICES

For more information about Frankenmuth, contact the **Frankenmuth Chamber of Commerce and Convention & Visitors Bureau** (635 S. Main St., 800/386-8696, www.frankenmuth.org, 8 A.M.–6 P.M. Mon.–Wed., 8 A.M.–8 P.M. Thurs.–Fri., 10 A.M.–8 P.M. Sat., noon–6 P.M. Sun., shorter hours Jan.–May and Sept.–Dec.). For city-related issues, contact **City Hall** (240 W. Genesee St., www.frankenmuthcity.com). For local news, pick up a copy of *Frankenmuth News* (www.frankenmuthnews.com).

As a tourist town, Frankenmuth offers a variety of necessary services. For mailing needs, visit the area **post office** (119 N. Main St., 989/652-6751, 8:30 A.M.–5 P.M. Mon.–Fri., 9 A.M.–noon Sat.). In case of an emergency, contact the **Frankenmuth Police Department** (240 W. Genesee St., 989/652-8371). For medical emergencies, dial **911** or contact the **Mobile Medical Response** (989/758-2900, www.mobilemedical.org).

GETTING THERE AND AROUND

While you won't be able to take a plane or train to Frankenmuth, getting there by car is a relative snap. From the south, take northbound I-75/U.S. 23 to Exit #136 (Birch Run/Frankenmuth), drive three miles east on Birch Run Road, and head north on M-83 for four miles, where the route becomes Main Street. From the north, take southbound I-75/U.S. 23 to Exit #144 (Bridgeport/Frankenmuth), drive 2.5 miles

southeast on Dixie Highway, and head east on Junction Road for four miles, where the route becomes Genesee Street. Once within the city limits, you can drive to most places, walk through the downtown area, or board a carriage ride by contacting the **Fantasy Carriage Company** (780 S. Mill St., 989/777-4757, noon–9 P.M. Mon.–Fri., 11 A.M.–10 P.M. Sat., 11 A.M.–9 P.M. Sun.) or the **Frankenmuth Carriage Company** (4520 S. Gera Rd., 989/652-3101, noon–9 P.M. daily).

Saginaw

Saginaw, the industrial heart of east-central Michigan, stretches for four miles along both banks of the Saginaw River. Formerly a logging and agricultural center, all that remains of the city's logging era are scores of old wooden houses built with money gained from the felling of the city's forests.

Saginaw Bay appears variously on 17th- and 18th-century French maps as "Sikonam," "Sakonam," "Saaguinam," and "Saquinam." Southeastern Michigan was generally described as "Saquinam Country" as early as 1688. Later, when lumber camp raconteurs told of Paul Bunyan's legendary feat of "logging off the Saginaw Country," the reference included the entire Lower Peninsula.

Native Americans lived peacefully on these lands for centuries. The earliest whites to penetrate the Saginaw Valley were Canadians. In 1816, Louis Campau built a fur-trading post near downtown. Two years later, at the request of Governor Lewis Cass, he built a council house and helped Cass negotiate the Treaty of 1819 with the Ojibwa. Sensing growing friction, the white settlers stationed troops at Fort Saginaw in 1822. The following year, a harsh winter, disastrous floods, and a summer fever epidemic prompted the garrison's commander to inform the War Department that "nothing but Indians, muskrats, and bullfrogs could possibly exist here." To the delight of the

area's Native Americans, the post was abandoned in 1823.

Although that early pessimism stalled the development of Saginaw, the white man didn't stay away long. By the 1850s, the lumberjacks moved in, bringing with them 14 busy, buzzing sawmills by 1857. Their prey: the heavily forested land around the city. That lasted until about the late 1880s, when timber was replaced by coal as the city's principal industry.

Remnants of those years can still be seen. One example is the stunning Montague Inn, which houses an elegant inn and restaurant in the Georgian-style mansion of a former sugar beet magnate.

SIGHTS
Museums and Other Cultural Sites

Easily dismissed as an aging industrial center, Saginaw is a city of surprises. One of the most delightful is the **Japanese Cultural Center and Tea House** (527 Ezra Rust Dr., 989/759-1648, www.japaneseculturalcenter.org, noon–4 P.M. Tues.–Sat. Apr.–Oct., free, $3 tours, $6 tea ceremony), an authentic Japanese teahouse and garden. The traditional 16th-century-style teahouse was built in 1985, designed to resemble a Zen monastery. It is one of the few places in the United States where visitors can see a formal Japanese tea ceremony performed in an authentic setting. Behind the teahouse, the Friendship Garden is a variation of a traditional Japanese garden, with delicate plantings and an arched footbridge over a stream. Many of the garden's trees, bridges, and stones came directly from Japan. Saginaw was chosen as the center's unlikely site because of its relationship with the city of Tokushima, Japan, Saginaw's sister city.

The serene formal tea ceremony, designed to promote inner tranquility, is performed at 2 P.M. on the second Saturday of each month year-round. At other times, visitors can tour the teahouse and garden, learn more about the ancient Zen ritual of tea, and contemplate its importance in Japanese architecture, politics, and religion. Admission to the ceremony includes a cup of tea and a traditional Japanese sweet.

Another surprise is the **Marshall M. Fredericks Sculpture Museum** at Saginaw Valley State University (7400 Bay Rd., 989/964-7125, www.svsu.edu/mfsm, noon–5 P.M. Mon.–Sat., free). The Scandinavian-American artist who became one of the state's most renowned sculptors studied under famous Swedish artist Carl Milles and is best known for his elegant bronze gazelles in Detroit's Belle Isle conservatory and for the Coleman A. Young Municipal Center's symbolic *Spirit of Detroit*. The gallery features original works, more than 200 original plaster models, photos of pieces installed around the world, a collection of bronze casts in the nearby sculpture garden, and original sketches. The Sculptor's Studio, a space created in 2003 to showcase the casting process, contains over 300 of Fredericks's clay models, molds, tools, and sculptures.

The **Saginaw Art Museum** (1126 N. Michigan Ave., 989/754-2491, www.saginawartmuseum.org, 10 A.M.–5 P.M. Tues.–Sat., 1–5 P.M. Sun., $5 adults, children under 16 free) features local and international artists, displaying their works in a 1904 Georgian Revival mansion. Highlights include a research library, fine collections of 19th- and 20th-century American art,

THE THUMB

© SAGINAW COUNTY CHAMBER OF COMMERCE

the studio space in the Marshall M. Fredericks Sculpture Museum

and a garden restored to reflect the home's original plantings.

The **Castle Museum** (500 Federal Ave., 989/752-2861, www.castlemuseum.org, 10 A.M.–4:30 P.M. Tues.–Sat., 1–4:30 P.M. Sun., $1 adults, $0.50 children) is one of the city's most recognizable landmarks. Constructed in 1898 by architect William Aiken, the limestone building, originally a U.S. post office, was intended to replicate a French chateau. Today, the museum chronicles the region's rich heritage, with artifacts and dioramas that explore the area's former fur trading, logging, farming, and manufacturing industries.

Saginaw Children's Zoo

The Children's Zoo at Celebration Square (1730 S. Washington Ave., 989/759-1408, www.saginawzoo.com, 10 A.M.–5 P.M. Mon.–Sat., 11 A.M.–6 P.M. Sun., $7) is a bargain-priced zoo at a manageable size. It features more than 130 animals, most native to the region. The timber wolves and bald eagles are especially popular with kids.

ENTERTAINMENT AND EVENTS
The Arts

The Dow Event Center (303 Johnson St., 989/759-1330, www.doweventcenter.com, show times and ticket prices vary), home to the Saginaw Spirit Hockey Club, hosts various concerts and Broadway musicals year-round. In addition to classic films, the **Temple Theatre** (203 N. Washington Ave., 989/754-7469, www.templetheatre.com, show times and ticket prices vary), a grand 1927 performance venue, presents performances by the Saginaw Choral Society (www.saginawchoralsociety.com) and Saginaw Bay Symphony Orchestra (www.saginawbayorchestra.com).

Festivals

Saginaw is home to a large Hispanic community, many of whom initially settled here to work on the construction of the state's railroads. Many of their descendants stayed on to work at area sugar beet refineries. Saginaw and Bay City's sugar beet industry makes Michigan the fifth-largest sugar beet producer in the

THE THUMB

LOUIS CAMPAU: FATHER OF TWO MICHIGAN TOWNS

Born in Detroit in 1791, Louis Campau, a French explorer and the nephew of trader Joseph Campau, was a key figure in the settlement of two modern Michigan cities. In 1815, after fighting in the War of 1812, he established a fur-trading post near what would eventually become downtown Saginaw.

Soon after, at the request of Governor Lewis Cass, he built a council house, where he helped Cass negotiate the Treaty of Saginaw in 1819 with the Native American tribes of the Great Lakes region, including the Ojibwa, Ottawa, Potawatomi, and Chippewa. In effect, the Native Americans ceded more than six million acres in the central portion of the Lower Peninsula to the white settlers, who benefited from the region's bountiful timber, salt, and fisheries. In 1822, troops were stationed at Fort Saginaw to monitor the growing tension between the settlers and the Native Americans. The following year, Campau plotted the town.

In 1826, Campau moved southwest and established a trading post at the convergence of several important Ottawa Indian trails in what is now Grand Rapids. Although other permanent white settlers, including Rix Robinson and Baptist minister Isaac McCoy, had arrived before him, Campau is credited as the "father" of Grand Rapids, a distinction solidified by his 1831 purchase of the entire downtown business district from the U.S. government. For the rest of his life, he helped to build and promote Grand Rapids, where he died in 1871 at the age of 79.

country. In May, the Saginaw area is home to the state's largest **Cinco de Mayo** festival and parade, held on Ojibway Island behind the teahouse in Rust Park.

Southwest of Saginaw, in the community of Chesaning, the annual **Chesaning Showboat Music Festival** (989/845-3055, www.chesaningshowboat.org, ticket prices vary) takes place in mid-July. For an entire week, music lovers can hop aboard the Chesaning Showboat, float down the Shiawassee River, and listen to a host of performers in an outdoor amphitheater. Recent acts have included Weird Al Yankovic and Three Dog Night. In late July, Chesaning also hosts the **Saginaw County Fair** (989/845-2143, www.saginawcountyfair. org), a family-friendly event that stages everything from rodeos to scavenger hunts.

SHOPPING

While not a shoppers' paradise like Frankenmuth and Birch Run, Saginaw is an ideal place to look for antiques. Situated within the historic district, you'll find **Adomaitis Antiques & Theatrics** (412 Court St., 989/790-7469, www.adomaitis. com, 10:30 A.M.–5 P.M. Mon.–Sat.), a repository of vintage clothing and costumes. Watch for their occasional estate sales, too. If you can't find what you need at Adomaitis, head to **The Antique Warehouse** (1122 Tittabawassee, 989/755-4343, www.theantiquewarehouse.net, 10 A.M.–6 P.M. Mon.–Sat., noon–6 P.M. Sun.), one of Michigan's largest antique malls. Housing 70 antique dealers, 12 specialty shops, and a café, you could conceivably spend an entire day perusing its inventory, including toys, jewelry, furniture, and more.

The Saginaw area also boasts Michigan's largest village of country "shoppes," the **Pride and Country Village** (5965 Holland Rd., 989/754-5807, www.prideandcountry.com, 10 A.M.–6 P.M. Mon.–Sat., 11 A.M.–5 P.M. Sun.). Consisting of several renovated historic structures, with over 40,000 square feet of shopping possibilities, this unique complex offers a variety of country-style treasures, from candles in the 1899 schoolhouse to handcrafted furnishings in the five-level 1904 farmhouse.

RECREATION

◖ Bird-Watching near Saginaw

Nature takes center stage at the **Shiawassee National Wildlife Refuge** (6975 Mower Rd., 989/777-5930, www.fws.gov/midwest/shiawassee, 7:30 A.M.–4 P.M. Mon.–Fri.), just southwest of Saginaw. The refuge and the nearby **Green Point Environmental Learning Center** (3010 Maple St., 989/759-1669) share a location near the union of four rivers—the Flint, the Tittabawassee, the Cass, and the Shiawassee—all of which converge to form the Saginaw River.

Covering more than 9,500 acres, the refuge was established in 1953 as a wetland for migrating waterfowl, and is now widely regarded as one of the top 25 birding sites in the United States. A checklist available at the headquarters lists more than 270 species that frequent the refuge. In October, some 30,000 ducks and 25,000 geese converge on the area, as well as songbirds, wading birds, owls, hawks, and even bald eagles. About 500 tundra swans migrate through annually.

An observation deck and a wheelchair-accessible blind are strategically placed for prime viewing. The refuge has more than 13 miles of hiking trails, open dawn to dusk, including a 4.5-mile Woodland Trail that loops through bottomland hardwoods and skirts the Tittabawassee River. The adjacent Green Point is operated under a co-op agreement with the U.S. Fish and Wildlife Service, with 76 acres of diverse habitat and an interpretive center. Because it lies in the floodplain of the Tittabawassee River, the Green Point trail system is often under water. It can be a magnet for mosquitoes, so be sure to bring repellent.

Crow Island State Game Area

Each year, thousands drive over one of the state's best bird-watching areas without realizing it's there. The Crow Island State Game Area stretches along the Saginaw River from the foot of the Zilwaukee Bridge to Bay City and covers more than 1,000 acres. The area serves as a giant overflow basin for Michigan's largest watershed. M-13 runs along the Saginaw River's east bank and splits the preserve into east and west. It, too, is an excellent bird-watching area for waterfowl, ospreys, bald eagles, night herons, great egrets, and more. For more information, contact the **Michigan Department of Natural Resources Saginaw Bay District Office** (503 N. Euclid Ave., 989/684-9141, www.michigan.gov/dnr).

Hiking

The Saginaw County Parks and Recreation Commission manages the secluded 186-acre **Price Nature Center** (6685 Sheridan Rd., 989/790-5280, www.saginawcounty.com/parks, 8 A.M.–sunset daily), located five miles south of Saginaw, near the Bridgeport exit on I-75. A good spot for day hikes, the center features a 200-year-old beech and maple forest, three miles of hiking and cross-country skiing trails, a picnic pavilion, and a rustic campground.

ACCOMMODATIONS AND FOOD

Plenty of chain hotels can be found along the I-75 corridor and beside I-675, including the **Hampton Inn** (2222 Tittabawassee Rd., 989/792-7666, www.hamptoninn.com, $90–100 d) and the **Super 8** (4848 Towne Centre Rd., 989/791-3003, www.super8.com, $60–75 d).

Saginaw's most distinctive lodging choice is the ◖ **Montague Inn** (1581 S. Washington Ave., 989/752-3939, www.montagueinn.com, $60–160 d), an elegantly restored three-story brick Georgian mansion with a library, sitting rooms, and a gracious dining room that is open to the public. All of the 17 guest rooms have private baths, and all are furnished with period pieces, including four-poster beds, wing chairs, and other antiques. Rates include a lavish breakfast.

If you're not in the mood for escargot, chicken Florentine, or other equally tempting dishes at the Montague Inn, there are indeed more casual options in the Saginaw area. For just a quick bite, try **Crumbs Gourmet Cookie Café** (4882 Gratiot Rd., 989/498-4010, www.

crumbscafe.com, 6:30 A.M.–9 P.M. Mon.–Thurs., 6:30 A.M.–10 P.M. Fri., 7 A.M.–5 P.M. Sat.–Sun., $2–9), where you'll find coffee, smoothies, soups, salads, wraps, and, of course, chocolate chip cookies on the menu. For a more rowdy alternative, stop by **6 Shooters** (8845 Gratiot Rd., 989/781-6333, www.6shooters. com, 4 P.M.–2 A.M. Thurs.–Sun., $6–14), a country-style bar that offers pool tables, a dance floor, live country acts, several TV screens for sports-viewing, and a menu that includes some of the best pizza in town. Before you pack it in for the night, try your luck on the mechanical bull.

INFORMATION AND SERVICES

For more information about Saginaw, contact the **Saginaw County Chamber of Commerce** (515 N. Washington Ave., 2nd floor, 989/752-7161, www.saginawchamber.org, 8 A.M.–4:30 P.M. Mon.–Fri.) or the **Saginaw Valley Convention & Visitors Bureau** (515 N. Washington Ave., 3rd floor, 989/752-7164 or 800/444-9979, www.visitsaginawvalley.com, 8 A.M.–4:30 P.M. Mon.–Fri.). For city-related issues, contact **City Hall** (www.saginaw-mi. com). For local news, pick up a copy of *The Saginaw News* (www.saginaw-news.com or www.mlive.com).

Saginaw offers the kind of services necessary for any mid-sized town. For mailing needs, visit one of several area **post offices** (1300 Cumberland St., 989/771-5738, www.usps. com, 8:30 A.M.–5 P.M. Mon.–Fri., 9 A.M.–noon Sat.). In case of medical, safety, or fire emergencies, you can dial **911** at any time; for non-emergencies, contact the **Police Department** (612 Federal St., 989/759-1229) or the **Fire Department** (801 Federal St., 989/759-1376). For medical treatment, contact **St. Mary's of Michigan** (800 S. Washington Ave., 989/907-8000, www.stmarysofmichigan.org). Prescriptions can be filled at any one of several pharmacies, including a 24-hour **Walgreens** (4989 State St., 989/791-3088, www.walgreens.com).

GETTING THERE AND AROUND

The closest airport to Saginaw is the **MBS International Airport** (8500 Garfield Rd., Freeland, www.mbsairport.org), which also serves Bay City and Midland. Most travelers, however, reach Saginaw via I-75. If you're headed north from Flint, you can either take Exit #149-AB to M-46 or Exit #150 to I-675. From Bay City, you can take I-75 southbound to Exit #155, where the I-675 bypass will guide you to the northern edge of Saginaw.

Once you reach Saginaw, you can opt to drive through town or hop a bus. For information about routes and schedules, contact the **Saginaw Transit Authority Regional Services** (615 Johnson St., 989/907-4000, www.saginaw-stars.com).

Bay City

Lying three miles upstream from the point where the Saginaw River enters Saginaw Bay, Bay City today bears no resemblance to the rip-roaring mill town it was at the end of the 19th century. Little remains of the color and flavor of the days when bawdy Bay City attracted thousands of lumberjacks who came in with the spring log drives to work in the mills after months of toiling in the surrounding woods.

The first white settlers came here to trade with the Indians, founding Bay City in 1831. After 1860, however, the once-quiet community became the center of the area logging industry. By 1872, there were 36 mills buzzing along the banks of the river, some of which were among the largest in the country. The whine of saws biting into logs could be heard 10 hours each day, and the smell of fresh lumber was said to be strong enough to flavor food.

Logs waiting to be milled lined the banks of the river. With the logs came the lumberjacks who patronized the saloons along the city's Water Street, looking for liquor and women. Around 1890, Bay City reached the height of its boom and the peak of its population—then declined about as quickly as it grew. The city's logging industry abruptly ceased after the stands of timber in Saginaw Valley were depleted and a Canadian export duty caused the abandonment of many mills. Bay City narrowly missed becoming one of the state's ghost towns by smartly developing industries revolving around soft-coal mining, commercial fishing, and beet sugar.

The last of the sawmills that once lined both banks of the Saginaw River were leveled in the late 1930s. Today, large freighters navigate the channel that was once filled with logs driven down from the river's upper reaches. The logging period of what is now the state's second largest port is still reflected in the city's many wood-framed houses, as well as the opulent mansions built by the lumber barons.

In recent decades, Bay City gained notoriety as the birthplace of Madonna. The native daughter is persona non grata these days, though, after a few less-than-flattering comments about her hometown (referring to it as the "armpit" of the United States) that made their way into the national media. Today, Bay City is a vibrant place, with terrific bird-watching spots, historic architecture, maritime attractions, and a host of other recreational and cultural diversions.

SIGHTS
Maritime Legacy

Bay City has other claims to fame besides the Material Girl. With roughly 35,000 residents, it's the state's second largest port. Many of those residents can be found enjoying the city's well-maintained parks system, including the five-mile **Riverwalk,** which follows the west bank of the Saginaw River, accessing an 820-foot pier and passing through **Veterans Memorial Park** and the **Liberty Harbor Marina.** Walkers, cyclists, in-line skaters, and passing freighters from all over the world make for a colorful scene.

Historic Sites

On the east side of town, lumber magnates built grand homes along Center Avenue and the surrounding streets. Center Avenue is the heart of the historic district, with more than 250 structures listed on the national and state historic registers. A few, including the **Keswick Manor** (1800 Center Ave.) have been opened to the public as bed-and-breakfasts.

Even more impressive than the grand homes is Bay City's **City Hall** (301 Washington Ave., 989/894-8147, 8 A.M.–5 P.M. Mon.–Fri., free), completed in 1897 and listed on the National Register of Historic Places. A $3.1-million restoration in 1980 earned it mention by the Smithsonian Institution as one of the 10 most outstanding historic restorations in the United States. The Romanesque-style stone building dominates the city skyline with a 125-foot clock tower. Visitors are welcome to take a self-guided tour and climb the 68 steps in the clock tower, which affords impressive views of Bay City, the Saginaw River, and the surrounding countryside. The Bay County Historical Museum also offers guided tours.

Bay County Historical Museum

The Bay County Historical Museum (321 Washington Ave., 989/893-5733, www.bchsmuseum.org, 10 A.M.–5 P.M. Mon.–Fri., noon–4 P.M. Sat.–Sun., free, donations welcome) traces the development of the county from pre-Columbian times through the 20th century. Displays include period rooms, Native American artifacts, and exhibits on the fur trade, logging, and shipbuilding.

ENTERTAINMENT AND EVENTS
The Arts

Bay City is home to the oldest continuously operating community theater, **Bay City Players** (1214 Columbus Ave., 989/893-5555, www.baycityplayers.com, show times and ticket prices vary), which presents several plays, musicals, and youth programs annually. Recent shows have included *Twelve Angry Men* and *Chicago*.

HARRY DEFOE: FROM PRINCIPAL TO SHIPBUILDER

Given that his father, Joseph, was a Great Lakes sailor and his uncle, John, was a local boat builder, it's no surprise that Harry Defoe, born in 1875, had shipbuilding in his blood. As a child, the Bay City native enjoyed whittling toy boats and watching them float down the Saginaw River. Eventually, he used wood and scrap metal to build working steamboats. Although Defoe became a teacher and later a school principal, the river stayed on his mind.

So, in 1905, with the assistance of his brother, Frederic, a New York-based attorney and his brother-in-law George Whitehouse, a fish merchant, he established the Defoe Boat & Motor Works. By 1917, the company had begun producing torpedo chasers and steam-powered vessels for the U.S. Navy. After World War I, Defoe built self-starting speedboats and pleasure yachts, one of which was later purchased by President John F. Kennedy.

Following the Great Depression, the U.S. government tried to help the entire shipping industry, including Defoe's company; World War II resulted in even more government contracts. Defoe's unique timesaving method — whereby workers started the vessel in an upside-down position and then righted it for completion — allowed him to craft numerous sub-chasers, infantry landing craft, destroyer escorts, freight carriers, troop transports, and rescue tugs for the U.S. Navy, making his company, with more than 4,000 workers, one of Bay City's largest employers.

Even after the war, Defoe's company prospered, building pleasure yachts and harbor tugs. One Defoe ship, the *R.V. Knorr*, even discovered the wreck of the *Titanic*. Despite Defoe's death in 1957, during a business trip to Washington, D.C., his company continued under the supervision of his sons Thomas and William. The Bay City yard saw the creation of enormous war ships and guided missile destroyers, and the company was incorporated in 1956.

By the mid-1960s, however, the firm was beginning to suffer. Shipyards on the East and West Coasts had fewer delivery dilemmas; aging equipment and federal cutbacks in domestic shipbuilding didn't help matters either. In 1976, with fewer than 100 workers, Defoe's company finally closed its doors, but many of its well-crafted vessels continue to sail the open sea.

THE THUMB

Festivals

Every July, the **Munger Potato Festival** (www. mungerpotatofest.com, free) lures visitors to the town of Munger, southeast of Bay City, for figure-eight auto derbies, potato giveaways, and more. In early August, Bay City hosts two family-friendly events: the **Labadie Pig Gig** (Veterans Memorial Park, 989/684-0452, www. piggig.com, $10), offering live concerts and rib cook-offs, and the **Bay County Fair** (www.bay-countyfair.com, ticket prices vary), where you'll see clowns, mud truck races, and horse shows.

SHOPPING

Not surprising, given Bay City's rich history, the city's downtown district can be a fruitful spot for antiquing, with **Bay City Antiques Center** (1020 N. Water St., 989/893-1116, www.antiquecenteronline.com, 10 A.M.–5 P.M. Mon.–Thurs. and Sat., 10 A.M.–8 P.M. Fri., noon–5 P.M. Sun.) claiming the better part of a city block. In 1999, it was named the state's best antique mall by readers of *AAA Michigan Living* magazine, and it's even bigger today. A large showroom includes more than 400 booths overflowing with furniture, kitchen items, and more.

For a change of pace, head five miles west of Bay City to **Warmbier Farms** (5300 Garfield Rd., Auburn, 989/662-7002, www.warm-bierfarms.com, 9 A.M.–6 P.M. Mon.–Thurs., 9 A.M.–5 P.M. Fri.–Sat., 11 A.M.–3 P.M. Sun.), which specializes in home and garden decor, from wreaths to pond floats, and presents a variety of seasonal activities, including wreath-making classes.

THE THUMB

RECREATION

The 2,800-acre **Bay City State Recreation Area** (3582 State Park Dr., 989/667-0717, www.michigan.gov/dnr, 8 A.M.–10 P.M. daily, state park vehicle permit required) connects the Frank N. Andersen Trail, the Bay City State Park, and the Tobico Marsh. Together, they offer a sandy beach along Saginaw Bay, two 32-foot observation towers, a fishing pier, a variety of hiking, biking, and cross-country skiing trails, and a boardwalk with fixed spotting scopes for watching waterfowl and shorebirds like herons, gulls, and egrets.

The paved 1.6-mile Frank N. Andersen Trail follows an abandoned rail grade to Tobico Marsh, an 1,800-acre refuge that is one of the largest coastal marshes on the Great Lakes. The Saginaw Bay Visitor Center (10 A.M.–6 P.M. Mon.–Sat., noon–6 P.M. Sun. Memorial Day–Labor Day, noon–4 P.M. Tues.–Sun. Sept.–May) contains permanent and changing exhibits depicting life in the wetlands, a 15-minute multimedia presentation on wetlands development, and a bird observation room and wet lab. Although the recreation area is open all year, bird-watching is especially enjoyable during the spring and fall migratory seasons.

ACCOMMODATIONS

The **Bay Valley Resort** (2470 Old Bridge Rd., 989/686-3500, www.bayvalley.com, $75–150 d) comprises nice grounds, a lobby full of antiques, and an 18-hole championship Jack Nicklaus/Desmond Muirhead golf course. Opened in 1973, the resort offers nearly 150 spacious rooms and suites, plus live entertainment and weekly drink specials in the Players Lounge.

Perhaps more intriguing, a 19th-century lumber baron's mansion is now the **Keswick Manor** (1800 Center Ave., 989/893-6598, www.keswickmanor.com, $75–200 d). It's been updated with plenty of modern comforts, even whirlpool tubs. Amenities include lush breakfasts, exquisite linens and towels, landscaped grounds, and 24-hour tea and coffee service.

Camping

Depending on the weather, the Bay City State Recreation Area can be a delightful place to camp during spring, summer, and fall, especially if you're interested in hiking, biking, fishing, or bird-watching. The on-site campground offers nearly 200 sites at $16 per night. For reservations, contact the Saginaw Bay Visitor Center (989/667-0717).

FOOD

Try **Krzysiak's House Restaurant** (1605 Michigan Ave., 989/894-5531, www.krzysiaks.com, 6:30 A.M.–9 P.M. Mon.–Thurs., 6:30 A.M.–10 P.M. Fri.–Sat., 6:30 A.M.–8 P.M. Sun., $6–26) for Polish dishes and a popular weekend seafood buffet. A swankier option is the **Lumber Barons' Charcoal Grill** (804 E. Midland St., 989/891-0100, www.lumberbaronsgrill.com, 4–9 P.M. Tues.–Thurs., noon–2 A.M. Fri.–Sat., pub only noon–8 P.M. Sun., $7–24), a brewpub and restaurant featuring a variety of handcrafted beers, salads, pastas, pizzas, steaks, and seafood dishes. Behind the pub, you'll find **The Stables** (989/891-0717, www.thestablesinbaycity.com, 4 P.M.–2 A.M. Mon.–Sat.), an upscale martini and cigar lounge housed in the district's former horse stables.

INFORMATION AND SERVICES

For more information about Bay City, contact the **Bay City Convention and Visitors Bureau** (901 Saginaw St., 989/893-1222 or 888/229-8696, www.tourbaycitymi.org, 8:30 A.M.–5 P.M. Mon.–Fri.) or the **Bay Area Chamber of Commerce** (901 Saginaw St., 989/893-4567, www.baycityarea.com, 8:30 A.M.–5 P.M. Mon.–Fri.). For city-related issues, contact **City Hall** (301 Washington Ave., www.baycitymi.org). For local news, pick up a copy of *The Bay City Times* (www.bctimes.com or www.mlive.com).

In addition, Bay City offers a variety of services that travelers might require. To mail a package or postcard, visit one of several area **post offices** (1000 Washington Ave., 989/895-5555, www.usps.com, 8:30 A.M.–5:45 P.M. Mon.–Fri.). In case of medical, safety, or fire emergencies, you can dial **911** at any time; for nonemergencies, contact the **Bay City Police Department** (501 3rd St., 989/892-8571). For medical treatment, contact the **Bay Regional Medical Center** (1900 Columbus Ave., 989/894-3000, www.bayregional.org).

GETTING THERE AND AROUND

The closest airport to Bay City is the **MBS International Airport** (8500 Garfield Rd., Freeland, www.mbsairport.org), which also serves Saginaw and Midland. Most travelers, however, reach Bay City via I-75, U.S. 10, or M-25. If you're headed north from Flint, you can take I-75 to Exit #160. From Midland, take U.S. 10 east to Bay City. From Port Austin, follow M-25 southwest along the coast.

Once you reach Bay City, you can opt to drive through town or tour the area via bus. For information about routes and schedules, contact the **Bay Metro Transit Authority** (1510 N. Johnson St., 989/894-2900, www.baymetro.com).

Sebewaing to Port Austin

From Bay City, M-25 meanders east along Saginaw Bay and Lake Huron. Along the way is a chain of small fishing ports, including Sebewaing, Bay Port, and Caseville, popular places for cottages but with little to stop most passing travelers. Caseville, originally known as Port Elizabeth, was once an important terminal for lake and rail shipping, with a prosperous salt well and ironworks. Today, most only find the area remarkable for its small, quiet towns; large, prosperous farms; and tabletop flat landscape punctuated by long stretches of blue water.

Still, these coastal towns offer a few diversions en route to Port Austin and the rest of the Lake Huron shore. Most notable are their annual summertime events, including the curiously named Cheeseburger in Caseville.

Port Austin, meanwhile, is known as the "tip of the Thumb." Bob Talbert, a columnist for the *Detroit Free Press,* calls it "the best spot in Michigan to view the sunrise and sunset." Downtown Port Austin is a comfortable, simple place, full of old-fashioned dime stores, soda fountains, collectible shops, and halls run by local legions, and the surrounding waters are popular among deep-sea anglers.

The city was first visited in 1837 by a fugitive of the Canadian Patriotic War, who found an excellent hiding place on this stretch of shore. Others soon followed, with a permanent settlement established not long after. Port Austin later became well known for Pointe aux Barques, a point that extended north into Lake Huron and became a wealthy resort enclave of prominent Detroiters. The point is named for the large rocks offshore, many of which resemble the prows of ships.

SIGHTS

In Sebewaing, regional artists are showcased at the **Burns Gallery** (27 N. Center St., 1–4 P.M. Sat.–Sun.). Recent exhibits have featured colorful quilts, watercolor paintings, and local photography. For information about upcoming events, contact the Lake Huron Community Arts Council (989/883-2450).

Halfway between Caseville and Port Austin, south of M-25, lies the **Huron County Nature Center Wilderness Arboretum** (800/358-4862, www.huronnaturecenter.org, 24 hours daily, free). This 280-acre nature center has rolling sand ridges and shallow, wet depressions known as swales that are traversed by an interpretive trail system, including one suitable for wheelchairs. Trees, plants, vines, and wildflowers are protected here for educational and scientific purposes.

Three miles of sugary sand beach and banks of dunes (unusual in this part of the state) are the highlights of the 565-acre **Port Crescent**

State Park (1775 Port Austin Rd., 989/738-8663, www.michigan.gov/dnr, 24 hours daily, state park vehicle permit required). A three-mile trail winds through wooded dunes and above the banks of the Pinnebog River, climbing up to provide some great views of Saginaw Bay, not to mention birds and other wildlife. The park's east side has a modern RV and tent campground near what was the village of Port Crescent, which disappeared in the 1930s. The stack from a sawmill is all that remains of this old industrial town; an interpretive display at the site chronicles its rise and fall.

FESTIVALS

While not as active as other Thumb-area towns, Sebewaing and Caseville each celebrate their culture with a handful of annual events. In June, Sebewaing's **Michigan Sugar Festival** (http://main.sebewaingchamber.com) offers standard festival fare, including sidewalk sales, tractor pulls, a petting zoo, midway games, and fireworks. Caseville, meanwhile, hosts two curious events: **Shanty Days,** which celebrates February's winter chill with polar bear dips and ice-fishing contests, and **Cheeseburger in Caseville,** a 10-day festival in August inspired by Jimmy Buffet's laid-back vibe and featuring sand sculptures, cheeseburger-eating contests, steel drum performances, and Caribbean jewelry making, among other tropical-themed activities. For more information, contact the Caseville Chamber of Commerce (www.casevillechamber.com).

SHOPPING

Port Austin's limited shopping options are clustered along a two-block stretch of Lake Street in the downtown area. Here, and on surrounding streets, you can expect to find an assortment of antiques and collectibles. Housed in a historic 19th-century brick building, **Heins Hardware** (8735 Lake St., 989/738-7311, www.heinshardware.com, 8:30 A.M.–5:30 P.M. Mon.–Sat.) satisfies a wide array of everyday needs; above the shop is **Lisa's Loft,** the place to go for cards and gifts.

RECREATION
Hiking and Biking

Near Caseville, **Albert E. Sleeper State Park** (6573 State Park Rd., 989/856-4411, www.michigan.gov/dnr, 24 hours daily, state park vehicle permit required) draws most of its visitors because of its half-mile arc of wide sand beach on Saginaw Bay. Sleeper (once called Huron State Park and renamed in 1944 for the governor who created the state park system) is popular with suburbanites looking for that "up north" escape without the long drive. The 723-acre park is quite heavily wooded, mostly with oak and other hardwoods. Nearly five miles of hiking/biking trails wind through the lightly developed park. Pick up a self-guiding brochure at the park office to identify native trees, shrubs, and wildflowers, and learn how Native Americans used them. Trails are groomed for cross-country skiing in winter.

Canoeing and Kayaking

Quiet-water paddlers can spend an entire day exploring the Pinnebog, a river that seems to tie itself in knots as it searches for an outlet to Saginaw Bay. Nearly four miles of river run through the Port Crescent State Park and attract anglers for trout, walleye, salmon, and perch. A private livery, **Tip-A-Thumb Canoe Rental** (2471 Port Austin Rd., 989/738-7656, May–Oct., $20), rents canoes and kayaks for leisurely paddles down the winding river. To explore the Lake Huron shore, rent a kayak from **Port Austin Kayak & Bike Rental** (95 W. Spring St., 989/550-6651, www.thumb-kayak.com, May–Sept., $12/hour, $30/day). Guided tours take you to intriguing rock formations and secluded beaches. Bike rentals and yoga classes are also available.

Fishing

"Deep-sea" fishing is popular throughout the Great Lakes, and the waters around the tip of the Thumb are considered some of the best. Charter boats operate out of many Thumb communities; the **Thumb Area Charter Boat Association** (www.thumbareacharterboats.

com) is a good clearinghouse of information about fishing opportunities in the area. Just remember that a valid state fishing license is required for anyone over 17. Visit www.mdnr-elicense.com for more information about obtaining a license from the Michigan Department of Natural Resources.

ACCOMMODATIONS AND FOOD

The area around Sebewaing and Caseville offers only a handful of overnight options. One such place is the **Fish Point Lodge** (4130 Miller Ave., Unionville, 989/674-2631, www.fishpointlodge.com, $30–65 d), a century-old inn located near the marshes of Saginaw Bay, making it an ideal locale for waterfowl hunters and, in winter, ice fishermen. Besides the main lodge, there are cabins and RV sites for rent. A boat launch as well as guided hunting and fishing tours are also available.

Another option is the **Bella Vista Inn & Sunset Bay Resort** (6024 Port Austin Rd., Caseville, 989/856-2500, www.bella-caseville.com, $70–95 d, $140–220 for cabins and cottages). If you get hungry, the waterfront resort offers **Hersel's on the Bay Grill & Lounge** (2 P.M.–2 A.M. Tues.–Fri., 9 A.M.–2 A.M. Sat.–Sun. July–Aug., 2 P.M.–2 A.M. Fri.–Sat. Sept.–June, $6–18), an ideal spot to watch the sunset over a steak dinner.

The 150-year-old **◖ Garfield Inn** (8544 Lake St., Port Austin, 989/738-5254, www.the-garfieldinn.com, $100–125 d), a national historic site, is named for President James Garfield, who once stayed in this former home of a gentleman farmer and industrialist. Today, its elegant Victorian setting greets guests with six B&B-style rooms, an English-style pub, a lovely garden, and an excellent restaurant (5:30–9 P.M. Thurs., 5–9 P.M. Fri., 11:30 A.M.–9 P.M. Sat., 8:30 A.M.–7 P.M. Sun., $13–20). The menu features dishes like prime rib, BBQ ribs, shepherd's pie, fish and chips, and cranberry orange bread pudding. The inn is open daily; with advance notice, nonguests are welcome to tour the building and grounds.

◖ The Bank 1884 Food & Spirits (8646 Lake St., Port Austin, 989/738-5353, www.thebank1884.com, 8 A.M.–3 P.M. and 5–9 P.M. daily May–Oct., 5–9 P.M. Sat.–Sun. Nov.–Dec., closed Jan.–Apr., $5–27), also a national historic site, is considered by many to offer the finest dining in the Thumb. The 1884 red-washed brick building, formerly a bank, opened as a restaurant in 1982, decorated with the original first-floor teller's cage, stained glass, and oversized historic photographs of Huron County. It has attracted a loyal crowd and high praise ever since, including a review from *The New York Times* speculating that The Bank "would give big city restaurants a run for the gold card." The menu changes regularly; two long-standing specialties have been the lake perch fillets and the broiled walleye. Reservations are recommended.

Camping

Albert E. Sleeper State Park includes a 226-site campground that's quite popular on summer weekends. It's located on the south side of M-25, but there's a pedestrian bridge over the highway that safely links it to the beach. The campsites are equipped with electrical service; modern restrooms and rental cabins are also available. For campground reservations, contact the **Michigan Department of Natural Resources** (800/447-2757, www.michigan.gov/dnr, $25–80).

In addition, **Port Crescent State Park,** closer to Port Austin, has a modern 137-unit RV and tent campground. It's very popular in summer—especially the sites right next to the beach. Make reservations by contacting the **Michigan Department of Natural Resources** (800/447-2757, www.michigan.gov/dnr, $27).

INFORMATION AND SERVICES

For more information about Sebewaing and Caseville, contact the **Sebewaing Chamber of Commerce** (222 N. Center St., http://main.sebewaingchamber.com) or the **Caseville Chamber of Commerce** (6632 Main St.,

THE THUMB

989/856-3818, www.casevillechamber.com, 10 A.M.–4 P.M. Mon.–Sat.). Also, if you need a **post office** while visiting the area, you're in luck; there's one in each town (49 N. Center St., Sebewaing, 989/883-3550, or 7060 Main St., Caseville, 989/856-2273).

For more information about the Port Austin area, contact the **Greater Port Austin Area Chamber of Commerce** (2 W. Spring St., 989/738-7600, www.portaustinarea.com, 9 A.M.–1 P.M. Mon., Wed., Fri., and Sat.). For local news, pick up a copy of the *Huron Daily Tribune* (www.michigansthumb.com) or *The Lakeshore Guardian* (www.lakeshoreguardian.com), a monthly publication.

Although not an enormous town, Port Austin does have its share of necessary services. For banking needs, visit the **Port Austin State Bank** (62 E. State St., 989/738-5235). To mail a letter, head to the town's only **post office** (8710 North St., 989/738-5264, 8 A.M.–4:30 P.M. Mon.–Fri., 8–11:30 A.M. Sat.). For medical services, contact the **Huron Medical Center** (1100 S. Van Dyke Rd., Bad Axe, 989/269-9521, www.huron-medical-center.org). To report a crime or emergency, contact

the **Police Department** (17 W. State St., 989/738-5180).

GETTING THERE AND AROUND

While Sebewaing and Caseville can both be reached via boat, the easiest way for most travelers to visit these two fishing ports is via car. If not driving your own, you'll have to rent a vehicle in a larger town like Flint or Saginaw. Either way, you can head northeast on M-25 from Bay City to Sebewaing; from Port Austin, you can drive southwest on M-25 to Caseville.

As with all of the towns along the Thumb's Lake Huron shore, Port Austin is easy to reach via car. From Bay City to the southwest or Port Huron to the southeast, you can follow M-25 along the shore to Port Austin, at the tip of the Thumb. From Flint, you can take I-69 east to Exit #168 and head north on M-53. Once in Port Austin, you can drive, walk, or hop a bus. For route information, contact the **Thumb Area Transit** (1513 Bad Axe Rd., Bad Axe, 989/269-2121 or 800/322-1125, www.tatbus.com).

Bad Axe and Interior

Definitely the least visited part of the Thumb, the interior towns and counties promise an even more laidback experience than some of the coastal areas. Family-owned farms, 19th-century homes, quaint shopping districts, and slow-moving villages like Caro and Lapeer transport visitors back to a simpler time. Ancient petroglyphs south of Bad Axe can take you back even further.

SIGHTS
C Sanilac Petroglyphs Historic State Park

One of the state's great mysteries is the Sanilac Petroglyphs Historic State Park (2501 Germania Rd., Cass City, www.michigan.gov/dnr, 10 A.M.–5 P.M. Wed.–Sun. Memorial

Day–Labor Day, state park vehicle permit required), a historic site about 13 miles south of Bad Axe via M-53 and Germania Road. The Michigan Archaeological Society raised private funds to purchase the 240-acre site and eventually transferred the land to the State of Michigan, which now maintains it.

The park holds the only known petroglyphs in the state. The petroglyphs are aboriginal rock carvings that were chipped into exposed sandstone up to 1,000 years ago. Fires that swept through the area in the late 1800s cleared the vegetation that once protected sandstone slabs near the Cass River. Once the fires burned out, astonished locals were surprised to discover newly exposed carvings of animals and hunters. Some claim that they were created as recordings of dreams, visions, or significant events during hunting or religious rituals. Far off the beaten tourist path, they receive few visitors, which has undoubtedly helped protect these fragile treasures.

A 1.5-mile interpretive trail weaves through the park and educates visitors about its many historical facets, including the petroglyphs, Indian villages, and remains of Holbrook, a logging town that vanished nearly a century ago. This pleasant trail also cuts across the Cass River twice, weaving through woods and open meadows. The rest of the park is undeveloped with no staff or services, including restrooms. For information, contact Albert E. Sleeper State Park (989/856-4411).

Thumb Octagon Barn

In the midst of rural Tuscola County lies an impressive, eight-sided structure, called the "round barn" by local residents. Designed by James Purdy, former owner of the surrounding acreage, and completed in 1924, the oddly-shaped

Thumb Octagon Barn (989/665-0081, www.thumboctagonbarn.org, 9 A.M.–sunset daily, free) resembled a structure that Purdy had once seen on a trip to Iowa. At the time, it was believed that such a barn would increase productivity, combining livestock pens, granaries, and other agricultural buildings in one spot; ultimately, however, farmers recognized the expense and ineffectiveness of such eight-sided barns.

After Purdy sold the farm in 1942, the 520-acre property swapped hands many times before Michigan's Department of Natural Resources (DNR) purchased the barn, house, and 80 remaining acres in 1991. Unfortunately, the DNR had no intention of preserving the buildings; only the land was of interest. So, in 1993, a group of locals campaigned to preserve the Thumb Octagon Barn as a key landmark. Today, as restoration efforts continue, visitors can learn more about America's agricultural heritage in the early 20th century by touring the farm May–October or attending Fall Family Days just after Labor Day. Donations are appreciated.

THE THUMB

© FRIENDS OF THE OCTAGON BARN

the Thumb Octagon Barn in Tuscola County

PETROGLYPHS SHROUDED IN CONTROVERSY

Situated within the center of Michigan's Thumb area, the ancient sandstone carvings that now comprise **Sanilac Petroglyphs Historic State Park** have been the subject of controversy ever since their discovery in the late 19th century. Although most paleontologists, cryptozoologists, and evolutionists agree that the petroglyphs provide a glimpse into the lives of early Native American artists in what is now Michigan's Lower Peninsula, they cannot concur on the meaning behind the images, even after years of intense study.

For instance, one of the faded etchings depicts the legendary "underwater panther," a spiny, horned mountain lion that supposedly dwelled in lakes and was, according to Native Americans, the cause of storms. Some scientists insist that this creature resembles the long-extinct stegosaurus, lending credence to their belief that dinosaurs might have lived long enough to interact with ancient peoples.

Equally strange are the religious symbols that appear amid these ancient carvings, such as Christian crosses and Jewish menorahs. These, along with the presence of Roman numerals and letters, provide possible proof that Christopher Columbus was not the first representative of the Old World to step foot on the North American continent and make a lasting impression.

While creationists have embraced the validity of such interpretations, evolutionists could just as easily attribute the petroglyphs to less mysterious sources, including Indian mythology or human imagination, the kind that could transform an elk into a dinosaur-like creature. No matter what you believe about the petroglyphs of Sanilac County, however, one thing is certain: Although scientists and explorers will probably never fully understand the origin of these ancient carvings, the wonder lies in the possibilities.

To reach the barn, take M-53 south of Bad Axe and head west on Bay City–Forestville Road; the barn is situated just one mile east of Gagetown.

Lapeer County Courthouse and Vicinity

Built in 1946, the Lapeer County Courthouse (287 W. Nepessing St., www.ci.lapeer.mi.us) is Michigan's oldest active courthouse. With its four fluted Doric columns and three-tiered rear tower, it's also a terrific example of Greek Revival–style architecture, which justifies its inclusion on the National Register of Historic Places.

Lapeer, in fact, boasts several entries on the National Register, including many within the **Piety Hill Historic District,** an irregularly shaped area west of the downtown business district. These restored houses represent an array of architectural styles, from Romanesque and Italianate to Gothic Revival and Queen Anne. Take a moment to stroll through this well-preserved neighborhood, roughly bordered by Cramton, Calhoun, Park, and Main Streets.

Balloon Rides

An ideal way to explore the Thumb is via hot air balloon. **Bad Axe Balloon Adventures** (989/269-8001, www.badaxeballoon.com, $199 adults, children under 7 not allowed) offers one-hour flights at sunrise and sunset every day, weather permitting. From high in the air, you'll spy forests, lakes, Saginaw Bay, and assorted wildlife, from sprinting deer to soaring raptors. Tours include a champagne toast.

FESTIVALS

The Thumb's interior plays host to numerous annual events, including the three-day **Bad Axe Hatchet Festival** (989/269-2630, www.badaxehatchetfestival.com, free), a mid-June event that presents a variety of family-friendly activities, from pony wagon rides to chainsaw carving. Every August, the **Huron County Fair** (Huron County Fairgrounds, 501 Fair St., Bad Axe, 989/883-3997, $3) offers livestock shows, harness racing, and demolition derbies, among other rustic diversions, while Imlay City's

Blueberry Festival (810/724-1361, www.imlaycitymich.com, free) celebrates the berry season with car shows and, of course, pie-eating contests. Imlay City, "gateway to the Thumb," is also home to the **Eastern Michigan Fair** (Eastern Michigan Fairgrounds, 810/724-4145, www.easternmichiganfair.com, $12–15), another August event that offers midway games, amusement rides, and tractor pulls.

While most events take place during the summer, a few honor cold-weather holidays. Each October, Caro hosts the **Tuscola County Pumpkin Festival** (989/673-2511, www.tuscolapumpkinfest.com, free), a four-day event that celebrates autumn with pumpkin pie sales, pumpkin decorating contests, and a grand parade.

RECREATION

South of Lapeer, the 723-acre **Metamora-Hadley Recreation Area** (3871 Herd Rd., Metamora, 810/797-4439 or 800/447-2757, www.michigan.gov/dnr, 8 A.M.–10 P.M. daily, $6 per car) lures a variety of outdoor enthusiasts. Hikers and cross-country skiers appreciate the six miles of groomed trails, while boaters, canoeists, and anglers flock to the 80-acre Lake Minnewanna in the park's center. The property also includes a swimming beach, fishing pier, picnic area, and 214-site campground with a camp store and modern restrooms.

ACCOMMODATIONS AND FOOD

Although the Thumb presents better overnight options along the shore, there are in fact possibilities if you decide to stay within the interior. In Sandusky, the **Thumb Heritage Inn** (405 W. Sanilac Ave., 810/648-4811, www.thumbheritage.com, $50–85 d) provides clean, comfortable rooms, including suites with hot tubs. For slightly nicer accommodations, try the **Days Inn** in Imlay City (6692 Newark Rd., 810/724-8005, www.imlaycitydaysinn.com, $70–120 d); here, you'll find free high-speed Internet access and a heated indoor pool.

If you get hungry during your trek through the Thumb's interior, grab some home-style comfort food at **Apple Tree Family Dining**

(845 S. Main St., Lapeer, 810/664-5200, 7 A.M.–10 P.M. daily, $5–14). You can also try **Brian's Family Restaurant** (281 S. Main St., Lapeer, 810/667-3911, 6 A.M.–midnight daily, closed Christmas, $6–10), which, in addition to sandwiches, steak, and the like, serves breakfast anytime.

INFORMATION AND SERVICES

For more information about the Thumb's interior, contact the **Bad Axe Chamber of Commerce** (989/269-6936, www.badaxemich.com), the **Village of Caro** (317 S. State St., 989/673-2226, www.carovillage.net, 8 A.M.–5 P.M. Mon.–Fri.), the **Sandusky Chamber of Commerce** (26 W. Speaker St., 810/648-4445, www.misandusky.us), the **Sanilac Economic Alliance** (810/648-7000, www.sanilaccounty.org), the **Imlay City Area Chamber of Commerce** (150 N. Main St., 810/724-1361, www.imlaycitymich.com), and the **Lapeer Area Chamber of Commerce** (108 W. Park St., 810/664-6641, http://lapeerareachamber.org, 9 A.M.–5 P.M. Mon.–Fri.).

For county-related issues, contact the **Huron County Building** (250 E. Huron Ave., Bad Axe, www.co.huron.mi.us), **Tuscola County** (www.tuscolacounty.org), **Sanilac County** (www.sanilaccounty.net), and **Lapeer County** (www.lapeercountyweb.org). For area news, pick up a copy of *The County Press* (www.countypress.com).

Although the interior towns are fairly small, you'll definitely find a few services here and there. For medical issues, contact the **Huron Medical Center** (1100 S. Van Dyke Rd., Bad Axe, 989/269-9521, www.huron-medical-center.org) or the **Lapeer Regional Medical Center** (1375 N. Main, Lapeer, 810/667-5500, www.lapeerregional.org). For mailing needs, there are **post offices** in Bad Axe, Sandusky, Imlay City, and Lapeer (www.usps.com).

GETTING THERE AND AROUND

If you have a vehicle, the towns within the Thumb's interior are easy to reach and, given their relatively small size, easy to navigate. From Port Austin, you can drive south on M-53 through Bad Axe, to Imlay City. Along the way, you can drive west on M-81 to Caro, or head east on M-46 to Sandusky. From Imlay City, you can reach Lapeer by driving south to I-69 and taking the interstate west to Exit 155.

It's also possible to reach Lapeer via train. **Amtrak** (800/872-7245, www.amtrak.com) offers a route from Chicago, with stops across Michigan, including Kalamazoo, Battle Creek, East Lansing, and Flint. For schedule information, visit the **Lapeer station** (73 Howard St.).

Although most people travel through the Thumb's interior via car, Huron County also has a bus service. For route information, contact the **Thumb Area Transit** (1513 Bad Axe Rd., Bad Axe, 989/269-2121 or 800/322-1125, www.tatbus.com).

Grindstone City to Lakeport

Along the Lake Huron shore lies a string of coastal villages, including Harbor Beach and Port Sanilac. While some are little more than ghost towns, all are rich in history, culture, and natural delights, including several well-preserved 19th-century buildings and two underwater preserves.

GRINDSTONE CITY

For more than a century, this village took advantage of its plentiful supply of abrasive rock and produced some of the finest grindstones in the world, exporting them to England and other markets around the globe. Two factories operated until World War I, when the development of Carborundum quickly made grindstone quarrying unprofitable. Almost overnight, the town's greatest asset went from being highly prized to virtually worthless. Huge stones, many up to six feet in diameter, were left behind to litter the beach. Also left behind were old docks, stores, houses, mills, and office buildings. Many a grindstone can still be spotted as local lawn art.

HURON CITY

Just four miles south of Grindstone City lies the ghost of Huron City. Though not quite a ghost town, it certainly is a faded image of its past. Langdon Hubbard had big plans for Huron City when he arrived here from Connecticut in the 1870s, buying up thousands of acres of woodland and building sawmills that churned out thousands of feet of lumber a day. But his grand plans were dashed in 1881, when a huge fire—not uncommon in logging regions where dry clear-cut land easily ignited—roared across the Thumb and destroyed his young empire.

Huron City was partially rebuilt—Hubbard even contributed a public roller rink. But the area's water had been contaminated by salt-making, a secondary industry in the area. By 1884, the population had dwindled from 1,500 to about 15.

Huron City's quick demise makes its most dominant building all the more fascinating. The Italianate **House of Seven Gables** (989/428-4123, www.huroncitymuseums.com, 10 A.M.–6 P.M. Mon. and Sat., 11 A.M.–6 P.M. Sun. May–June and Sept., 10 A.M.–6 P.M. Thurs.–Mon. July–Aug., $10 adults, including mansion and village, $5 children 10–15) was rebuilt by Langdon Hubbard after the 1881 fire. It later became the summer residence of Hubbard's son-in-law, William Lyon Phelps, a wildly popular Yale English teacher dubbed "America's favorite college professor" by *Life* magazine during the 1930s. The Hubbard family lived in the house from 1881 until 1987, when it was turned into an informal house museum.

As a result, the house offers an almost unparalleled glimpse into a past era, not someone's interpretation of what life must have been like. The family's books lie piled on tables, the ornate 1886 pool table looks ready for a match, the walls are lined with campy portraits of the beloved Hubbard dogs and cats, and the "state-of-the-art" 1915 kitchen even shows off its fancy and strange-looking dishwasher. Along with the House of Seven Gables, the public can visit the other remaining buildings of Historic Huron City, including the general store, inn, church, and barns.

Port Hope

From Huron City, M-25 curves south along Lake Huron. About seven miles south lies the lakeshore town of Port Hope. The 1857 Pointe aux Barques Lighthouse guards the coastline here. It's surrounded by the pleasant **Lighthouse County Park** (7320 Lighthouse Rd., 989/428-4749, www.huroncountyparks. com, May–Oct., free), which is located between Huron City and Port Hope. The park includes a 110-site campground, picnic area, beach, and small lighthouse museum.

HARBOR BEACH

From Port Hope, M-25 continues south toward Harbor Beach, home to the largest man-made freshwater harbor in the world. The need to improve on the natural harbor was prompted by Michigan's busy logging industry in the 1870s. More and more ships were plying the waters up and down the Lake Huron shore and across Saginaw Bay; in stormy weather, they needed a safe refuge from strong currents and heavy seas. The federal government began work on a harbor in 1873, and worked on the gargantuan project for more than two decades. When completed, the breakwall stretched 8,000 feet! It continues to do duty today, along with the 1881 Coast Guard Station and 1885 lighthouse.

Originally named Sand Beach, Harbor Beach was once notorious as the site of an illegal money factory. In the mid-19th century, counterfeit U.S. currency and Mexican dollars were made here and distributed throughout the Americas.

Frank Murphy ranks as Harbor Beach's most famous son, the Michigan governor who is best known for collective bargaining during the 1937 Flint sit-down strike, paving the way for the rise of the United Auto Workers (UAW). He went on to become U.S. Attorney General, and U.S. Supreme Court Justice. The 1910 **Frank Murphy Birthplace** (142 S. Huron Ave., 989/479-3363, noon–4 P.M. Tues.–Fri. and by appointment Sat.–Sun. Memorial Day–Labor Day, $2 adults, $1 children) serves as a repository for Murphy's personal memorabilia. While the contents prove interesting, the house itself is plain in comparison with the Hubbards' mansion.

PORT SANILAC

Until the mid-1850s, the Port Sanilac area was known as Bark Shanty Point, a name that was heatedly defended in an issue of the village's alternative newspaper, the *Bark Shanty Times*. The *Times* was produced by placing a sheet of newsprint on the counter of the town's general store; townsfolk simply wrote news or commentary on a sheet of paper until it was filled up.

Port Sanilac's past is preserved at the **Sanilac County Historical Museum** (228 S. Ridge St., 810/622-9946, www.sanilaccountymuseum. org, 11 A.M.–4 P.M. Wed.–Fri., noon–4 P.M. Sat.–Sun. May–Dec., $6 adults, $5 children 5–12). Housed in a nicely restored Victorian mansion, the 1872 Loop-Harrison House, the museum contains most of its original furnishings, as well as old-fashioned medical instruments, antique glassware, military and American Indian artifacts, and an original Bark Shanty post office stamp. The grounds also include a dairy museum, a restored late-19th-century cabin, a general store, and a barn with exhibits relating to the fishing, logging, and blacksmithing trades.

LAKEPORT STATE PARK

About 20 miles south of Port Sanilac on M-25, Lakeport State Park (7605 Lakeshore Rd., 810/327-6224, 8 A.M.–10 P.M. daily, $6 per car) preserves more than a mile of fine sand beach on southern Lake Huron. The 556-acre park was established in 1936, one of Michigan's oldest state parks. A couple of miles to the north

THE THUMB

in a separate unit of the park, a popular campground offers 315 modern sites that are just a short walk from another beach and some lakeside bluffs. From the park's low bluffs, you can see distant views of freighter traffic heading in and out of the gateway to the upper Great Lakes. Other park amenities include a picnic shelter, beach house, and playground. For campground reservations, contact the **Michigan Department of Natural Resources** (800/447-2757, www.michigan.gov/dnr).

FESTIVALS

The towns alongside Lake Huron celebrate with a variety of annual events. In mid-July, the **Maritime Festival** (www.harborbeachchamber.com) presents activities throughout Harbor Beach, including historic tours and fireworks displays. Also in July, the **Bark Shanty Days Festival** (www.portsanilac.net) lights up Port Sanilac with an array of competitions, from horseshoe tournaments to sandcastle contests. In mid-September, Lexington offers its own dose of culture with the **Bach and Friends Festival** (www.lexarts.com, ticket prices vary), a four-day musical extravaganza.

SHOPPING

While the Lake Huron shore isn't a hotbed of shopping potential, there's at least one noteworthy stop. **Angel's Garden** (7260 Huron Ave., Lexington, 810/359-2496, www.angelsgardengifts.com, daily Apr.–Dec.), a former harness shop built in the 1840s, now houses a massive collection of angel sculptures, garden accessories, and other unique gifts.

RECREATION
Boating and Fishing

Lake Huron is a wonderful place to explore via boat, whether you're a pleasure cruiser or a die-hard angler. Grindstone City has an artificially constructed harbor and a state-owned boat launch, ideal for private boaters and anglers who want to experience this quiet coast on their own.

If you don't have a boat, however, never fear. Charter boats operate out of many Thumb communities; just contact the **Thumb Area Charter Boat Association** (www.thumbareacharterboats.com) for a list of accredited boat captains and fishing guides. Before heading out, remember to purchase a valid state fishing license for anyone over 17; visit www.mdnr-elicense.com for more information.

(Diving

Two of Michigan's excellent underwater preserves lie off this stretch of Lake Huron shoreline. Situated between Port Austin and Harbor Beach, 19 major shipwrecks lie within the 276-square-mile **Thumb Area Bottomland Preserve.** Most sites are 100 feet deep or more, accessible only to advanced divers. An exception is the popular *Chickamauga,* a 322-foot turn-of-the-century schooner—it was built in the late 1890s, only to founder in 1919. Resting in just 35 feet of water, it's in a relatively protected area about a half-mile east of Harbor Beach.

Farther south, the **Sanilac Shores Underwater Preserve** near Port Sanilac contains some recent shipwreck finds, including the 250-foot *Regina,* a freighter that sank in 1913 but wasn't discovered until 1986. Sanilac Shores shipwrecks tend to be in a little shallower water, and many are in excellent condition. For information on both preserves and a listing of dive shops and charters, contact the **Huron County Economic Development Corporation** (800/358-4862, www.huroncounty.com) or the **Michigan Underwater Preserve Council** (800/970-8717, www.michiganpreserves.org).

ACCOMMODATIONS AND FOOD

Perched just 500 feet from Lake Huron in Port Sanilac, the **Raymond House Inn** (111 S. Ridge St., 810/622-8800, $75–110 d) is an impressive 1871 home that's been converted to an inn. The inn has seven bedrooms on the second floor, an on-site art gallery and gift shop, and free wireless Internet access. Across the street from the Raymond House Inn, the family-owned **Bellaire Motel** (120 S. Ridge

St., 810/622-9981, $45–65 d) offers simple, inexpensive motel rooms.

In Lexington, you might get more than a delicious burger or steak at **The Cadillac House** (5502 Main St., 810/359-7201, www.cadillachouse.com, 11:30 A.M.–9 P.M. Mon.–Thurs., 11:30 A.M.–11 P.M. Fri., 9 A.M.–11:30 P.M. Sat., 9 A.M.–9 P.M. Sun., pub open till 2 A.M. daily, $10–25), built in 1860 and supposedly haunted by a former hotel guest.

INFORMATION AND SERVICES

For more information about Grindstone City and Huron City, contact the **Greater Port Austin Area Chamber of Commerce** (2 W. Spring St., 989/738-7600, www.portaustinarea.com, 9 A.M.–1 P.M. Mon., Wed., Fri., and Sat.). For more information about the Lake Huron shore, contact the **Harbor Beach Chamber of Commerce** (www.harborbeachchamber.com), the **Village of Port Sanilac** (56 N. Ridge St., 810/622-9963, www.portsanilac.net), and the **Lexington Business Association** (810/359-7774, www.lexingtonmichigan.org).

For local and regional news, consult the *Huron Daily Tribune* (www.michigansthumb.com), *The Lakeshore Guardian* (www.lakeshoreguardian.com), or the *Sanilac County News* (www.sanilaccountynews.com).

Despite the small size of these coastal towns, travelers will find many of the services they require. For mailing needs, there are at least three nearby **post offices** (110 School St., Harbor Beach, 989/479-3429; 34 N. Ridge St., Port Sanilac, 810/622-8295; and 5204 Main St., Lexington, 810/359-8591). If you run into any trouble along the coast, dial **911** or contact the **police** in Port Sanilac (810/622-9131).

GETTING THERE AND AROUND

As with all of the Thumb's coastal towns, Grindstone City, Huron City, Harbor Beach, and Port Sanilac are easy to reach via car. Whether you're coming from Bay City or Port Huron, you can simply follow M-25 along the shore to each of these destinations. Given their relatively small size, you can drive or walk within each locale. For bus route information, contact the **Thumb Area Transit** (1513 Bad Axe Rd., Bad Axe, 989/269-2121 or 800/322-1125, www.tatbus.com).

Port Huron

At the southern end of M-25, Port Huron sits at the juncture of Lake Huron and the St. Clair River, which is part of a vital shipping route that links Lake Huron and Lake Erie. Port Huron stretches some eight miles along the lake and this international river boundary, opposite Sarnia, Ontario.

On any given day, visitors can watch as a steady procession of pleasure craft, oil tankers, and bulk freighters file past the city. The most dramatic vantage point is from the crest of the **Blue Water Bridge,** which rises 152 feet over the water and looks down to where Lake Huron meets the St. Clair River. Walk across for the best views.

Due to its strategic geographical position,

Port Huron is one of the oldest settlements in Michigan and, in fact, one of the earliest outposts in the American interior. The French built Fort St. Joseph here in 1686, mainly to seal off the entranceway to the upper Great Lakes from the rival English. The first permanent settlement was established in 1790. In 1814, the Americans built Fort Gratiot on the Fort Joseph site, also an attempt to repel the British. The fort was occupied off and on after the Civil War when it served as a recruiting station.

In the late 1800s, four local villages—Peru, Desmond, Huron, and Gratiot—united to form Port Huron and helped develop the area into a lumber center. When the big trees ran out, Port Huron weathered the industry's demise better than most Michigan cities, since it had already diversified into shipbuilding, railroading, and oil and natural gas distribution. Despite these early industries, the city rejected the bids of chemical companies to build plants here, fearing environmental and safety problems. The plants instead found a home on the Sarnia side of the river, and today make up the 20-mile-long "chemical valley"—Canada's greatest concentration of chemical companies and the creator of most of the pollution in the lower St. Clair River.

SIGHTS
Lighthouses

Just north of the Blue Water Bridge, Michigan's oldest lighthouse, the **Fort Gratiot Light** (800/852-4242, 11 A.M.–5 P.M. Fri.–Mon. May–Oct.), stands 86 feet tall over **Lighthouse Park.** The original tower was poorly constructed in 1825 and crumbled just four years later. It was replaced in 1829 by the much sturdier brick structure that stands today. That still

© CINDY LINDOW

the Fort Gratiot Light

makes it the state's oldest light and older than even Michigan itself, which wasn't admitted to the Union until 1837. The lighthouse was automated in 1933, and it continues to flash a warning to mariners coming south from Lake Huron. Call for tour information.

At nearby **Pine Grove Park,** you can take a self-guided tour of the 1921 *Huron* **Lightship** (810/982-0891, www.phmuseum.org, daily in summer, Thurs.–Mon. Sept.–Dec and Apr.–May, included with museum admission), operated by the Port Huron Museum. This 97-foot vessel served as a floating lighthouse visible from 14 miles away. Retired in 1970, the *Huron* Lightship was the last to operate on the Great Lakes. The park also offers a view of the bridge and passing boat traffic on the St. Clair River, and is an interesting place to watch fishermen scoop up walleye and steelhead.

Edison Memorial

Port Huron's most famous resident was no doubt native son Thomas Alva Edison (1847–1931), who was born here and stayed until adulthood. He is honored at **Thomas Edison Park,** located under the enormous Blue Water Bridge. In the bridge's shadow is the restored **1858 Grand Trunk Depot,** where Edison boarded the Detroit-bound train daily to sell fruits, nuts, magazines, and newspapers. He used much of his earnings to buy chemicals for the small laboratory he had set up in the train's baggage car. The depot now houses a museum dedicated to Edison; it contains historical photos and displays, including artifacts excavated from the site of Edison's boyhood home. For more information, contact the Port Huron Museum (810/982-0891, www.phmuseum.org, included with museum admission), which now oversees the Thomas Edison Depot Museum.

◖ Port Huron Museum

You can check out more nautical history at the Port Huron Museum (1115 6th St., 810/982-0891, www.phmuseum.org, 11 A.M.–5 P.M. daily, all four sites $15 adults, children under 5 free). Housed in a former library that dates to 1904, the two-story museum includes a

THE THUMB

L. DIGGS, PICTURE THIS...

Port Huron's Edison statue near the Blue Water Bridge

restored freighter pilothouse (you can even work the wheel, signal the alarm horn, and ring the engine bell), marine-related items, and objects recovered from Lake Huron shipwrecks. The museum has something for everyone, from Indian artifacts to contemporary paintings by local artists. One of the most interesting exhibits displays objects recovered from digs on the site of Edison's boyhood home, which include evidence of an early laboratory. Currently, the museum oversees three other sites as well: the Thomas Edison Depot, the *Huron* Lightship, and the USCG Cutter *Bramble*.

Tours

For a closer look at the St. Clair River, sign on for a two-hour trip on the *Huron Lady II* (810/984-1500, www.huronlady.com, $15 adults, $8 children 5–12), a 65-foot excursion boat that cruises under the Blue Water Bridge and heads out onto Lake Huron, where it treats passengers to views of giant freighters as they load and unload their cargo. Call for reservations.

EVENTS

Port Huron and its surrounding communities hold a variety of events throughout the year, from fishing tournaments to arts and crafts shows. One intriguing option is the **St. Clair Flats Historical Encampment** (Algonac State Park, Algonac, 810/765-5605, www.clairflats. org) in mid-September. During the two-day event, historical interpreters demonstrate the crafts, skills, and games of the different peoples, both Europeans and Native Americans that inhabited the Great Lakes region during the mid-1700s.

Of course, the Blue Water Area hosts its biggest annual event in mid-July, the **Port Huron to Mackinac Race.** The race attracts some 300 sailboats for the trip up the Huron shore to Mackinac Island; in preceding days, sailors and spectators pack the area's restaurants and hotels. Don't plan to show up without reservations. Contact the Bayview Yacht Club (www. byc.com) for more information.

SHOPPING

For crafters, a visit to **Mary Maxim** (2001 Holland Ave., 810/987-2000, www.mary-maxim.com, 10 A.M.–6 P.M. Mon.–Sat., 11 A.M.–5 P.M. Sun.), an enormous emporium of needlework and home decor, is a must. Others will relish Port Huron's downtown district (888/305-8696, www.mainstreetph.com), where you'll find jewelry boutiques, furniture stores, and more.

GOLF

The Port Huron area boasts a dozen golf courses, including the **Holly Meadows Golf Course** (4855 Capac Rd., Capac, 810/395-4653, www.hollymeadows.com, daily Mar.–Nov., $25–36 w/cart), **Rattle Run Golf Course** (7163 St. Clair Hwy., St. Clair, 810/329-2070, www.rattlerun.com, daily Mar.–Nov., $25–49 w/cart), and **Black River Country Club** (3300 Country Club Dr., Port Huron, 810/982-9595, www.blackrivergolfclub.com, daily Apr.–Oct., $25–48), an 18-hole championship course founded in 1926 that offers stunning views of the Black River.

ACCOMMODATIONS AND FOOD

Located just south of the Grand Trunk Depot and near the former Fort Gratiot site, the **❰ Thomas Edison Inn** (500 Thomas Edison Pkwy., 810/984-8000, www.thomasedisoninn.com, $90–125 d, $165–395 suites) is the city's nicest and largest hotel. It has some wonderful bridge and water views, which anyone can enjoy from the hotel's elegant dining room.

The **❰ Fogcutter** (511 Fort St., 810/987-3300, www.fogcutterrestaurant.com, $12–33) is another fine-dining restaurant with water views and a menu that features classic continental favorites and fresh fish. Other menu highlights include lobster, king crab legs, and herb-encrusted rack of lamb. A more laid-back dining option along the waterfront is the **Quay Street Brewing Company** (330 Quay St., 810/982-4100, www.quaybrewing.com, 11:30 A.M.–9 P.M. Mon.–Thurs., 11:30 A.M.–10 P.M. Fri.–Sat., noon–8 P.M. Sun., $7–17), a spacious, multilevel restaurant, bar, and brewery that serves up salads, sandwiches, steak, seafood, and handcrafted beers in a family-friendly atmosphere.

INFORMATION AND SERVICES

For more information about the Port Huron area, contact the **Blue Water Area Convention and Visitors Bureau** (520 Thomas Edison Pkwy., 800/852-4242, www.bluewater.org, 8 A.M.–5 P.M. Mon.–Fri., 10 A.M.–3 P.M. Sat.) and the **Blue Water Area Chamber of Commerce** (920 Pine Grove Ave., 810/985-7101, www.bluewaterchamber.com, 8:30 A.M.–4:30 P.M. Mon.–Fri.). If you're interested in Port Huron's maritime heritage, visit www.maritimecapitalgl.com.

For city-related issues, contact the **Municipal Office Center** (100 McMorran Blvd., www.porthuron.org). For county-related issues, visit the official St. Clair County website: www.stclaircounty.org. For local news, pick up a daily copy of **The Times Herald** (www.thetimesherald.com).

As one of the largest cities in the Thumb, Port Huron provides travelers with everything they might need during their trip. For mailing issues, visit the **post office** located at 1300 Military St. (810/989-7900). In case of a medical emergency, you can contact the **Port Huron Hospital** (1221 Pine Grove Ave., 810/987-5000, www.porthuronhospital.org). A 24-hour pharmacy is available for all your prescription needs: **Rite Aid** (2910 Pine Grove Ave., 810/987-3663, www.riteaid.com). For all other emergencies, dial **911** at any time. In a non-emergency situation, you can also contact the **Port Huron Police Department** (810/984-8415).

GETTING THERE AND AROUND

Although the closest airport is a few hours southwest, in the Detroit area, travelers can easily reach Port Huron via train. **Amtrak** (800/872-7245, www.amtrak.com) offers a route from Chicago, with stops across Michigan, including East Lansing and Flint. For schedule information, visit the **Port Huron station** (2223 16th St.).

Still, the most likely access is via car; there are three major routes to and from Port Huron. From Detroit, you can take I-94 North. From Flint, I-69 heads east toward the St. Clair River. Those who choose the long scenic route will find themselves traveling along the Thumb's coastline, from Bay City to Port Austin to Port Huron. Of course, the town can also be reached from Ontario, Canada, across the Blue Water Bridge; just remember that motorists often experience a delay when traversing the international border crossing.

ANN ARBOR AND THE HEARTLAND

From any point in the Great Lakes State, at least one of the five Great Lakes (all but Lake Ontario) is never more than 90 miles away. That's auspicious news for Michigan's Heartland—also known as Central Michigan—the only region that doesn't sit astride the coast. Stretching from the southern state line to the middle of the Lower Peninsula, this wide swath of rolling prairies, scenic lakes, weathered barns, and abundant farmland contains some of the state's finest educational institutions and largest cities, including Grand Rapids, Kalamazoo, Midland, and Lansing, the state capital since 1847.

As with the Thumb, travelers often overlook Michigan's Heartland. Early settlers of the 19th century, however, recognized the appeal of this centralized region. A surge of eager,

frontier-bound settlers resulted in the creation of some of Michigan's most picturesque towns, including Marshall, which has been designated a National Historic Landmark District for its varied 19th-century architecture. Migrating Easterners were also responsible for the establishment of many of the Heartland's private colleges, in towns such as Hillsdale, Albion, Alma, and Olivet. A hotbed of academia, the Heartland also has its share of major universities—most notably, the University of Michigan in Ann Arbor, with other standouts nearby, including Western Michigan University in Kalamazoo, Michigan State University in East Lansing, and Central Michigan University in Mount Pleasant.

Besides strolling through the well-groomed campuses and well-preserved villages that

© L. DIGGS, PICTURE THIS...

HIGHLIGHTS

◖ **University of Michigan:** U of M is one of America's finest institutions, with a long list of famous alumni. Even if you're not a student, you can still appreciate the school's wide array of diversions, including museums, art galleries, gardens, live theaters, and, of course, football (page 109).

◖ **Purple Rose Theatre Company:** Founded by award-winning actor Jeff Daniels, this Chelsea-based playhouse was named in honor of the Woody Allen film *The Purple Rose of Cairo* (1985). Audiences travel far and wide to catch the latest play at this renowned theater (page 115).

◖ **Historic Homes:** Picturesque Marshall contains over 850 19th-century homes and businesses, representing a variety of architectural styles. In 1991, the town was designated a National Historic Landmark District (page 121).

◖ **Bird-Watching:** The W. K. Kellogg Bird Sanctuary is one of America's pioneer wildlife conservation centers. Here, nature lovers can hike amid 180 acres of diverse habitats, which nurture hundreds of waterfowl, raptor, and game bird species (page 125).

◖ **Air Zoo:** Devoted to aviation and space exploration, this enormous complex invites visitors to explore an incredible assortment of interactive exhibits and historic displays, including flight simulators, aircraft carrier models, astronaut artifacts, and a pseudo-space walk (page 131).

◖ **Gerald R. Ford Presidential Museum:** Unlike most presidential libraries, President Ford's is divided into two separate components: an extensive library in Ann Arbor and a museum in Grand Rapids. In addition to celebrating the lives of President Ford and his wife, the museum offers temporary exhibits from the Smithsonian Institution and the National Archives (page 135).

◖ **Michigan State University:** MSU has been in operation since 1855. Today, visitors can stroll through several lovely gardens, attend Big

10 football games, view an assortment of art and science exhibits, and catch a wide array of live performances at the Wharton Center (page 138).

◖ **Soaring Eagle Casino & Resort:** The Soaring Eagle is one of the Midwest's largest casinos, offering thousands of slot machines and table games, several restaurants, over 500 luxurious rooms, a four-diamond spa, and live entertainment. Even if gaming isn't your hobby, it's worth a look while you're in Mount Pleasant (page 144).

◖ **Saginaw Chippewa Tribal Powwow:** In early August, the Saginaw Chippewa Indian Tribe hosts a gathering of the clans in Mount Pleasant. For over two decades, this annual event has showcased traditional dancing, drumming, chanting, and cuisine (page 144).

LOOK FOR ◖ TO FIND RECOMMENDED SIGHTS, ACTIVITIES, DINING, AND LODGING.

THE HEARTLAND

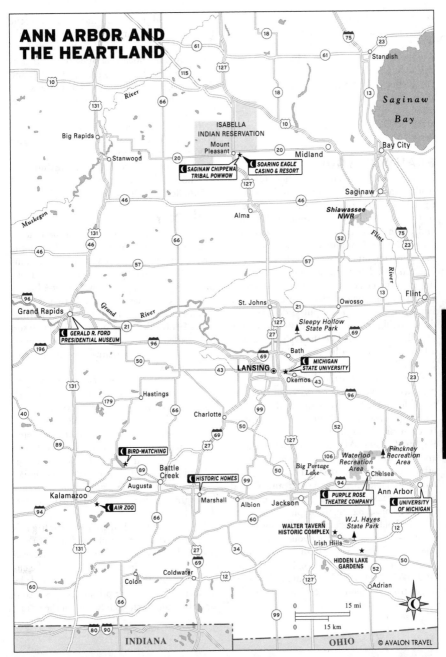

comprise Michigan's Heartland, travelers will find a myriad of other outdoor and cultural pursuits here as well. Whether exploring the Gerald R. Ford Presidential Museum, marveling at Kalamazoo's Air Zoo, hiking through the Kellogg Bird Sanctuary, or watching a show at the Purple Rose Theatre Company (established by Chelsea native and Hollywood actor Jeff Daniels), coast-conscious visitors will be grateful for the inland detour.

PLANNING YOUR TIME

Michigan's Heartland is an enormous place, extending from the Indiana border to M-20, near the center of the Lower Peninsula; it's bordered on the eastern side by Ann Arbor and Midland, and on the western side by Kalamazoo and Grand Rapids. Given its size, what you're able to see depends on your schedule; likewise, your interests will determine how long you plan to linger in the Heartland. If you only intend to visit the area's major cities, like Lansing and Battle Creek, you should put aside about five days. You'll need at least 10 days, however, if you also want to explore the region's outdoor attractions and smaller towns like Chelsea, Marshall, and Mount Pleasant.

Reaching the Heartland is easy. Given the presence of several major towns and cities, it's possible to get here by plane, train, or bus. The region has several commercial airports, in or near places like Kalamazoo, Grand Rapids, Lansing, Midland, and nearby Flint and Detroit. Amtrak and Greyhound both offer routes to Kalamazoo, Battle Creek, East Lansing, Jackson, Ann Arbor, and Grand Rapids. Needless to say, though, the Heartland is not a compact region, so, despite the presence of several public transit systems, having a car is a must—whether you bring your own or rent one at an airport. Major highways and interstates—such as U.S. 23, U.S. 127, U.S. 131, I-69, I-75, I-94, and I-96—make it a snap to get from one end of the Heartland to the other—if you have the time.

The good news is that, save for the Heartland's major museums, annual festivals, and college football games, this centralized region isn't as much of a draw for tourists as coastal locales like Saugatuck, Holland, and Traverse City. So, crowds are often less of a problem here—unless, of course, you simply hate big cities in general.

For more information about Michigan's Heartland, consult **Travel Michigan** (800/644-2489, www.michigan.org) or the **West Michigan Tourist Association** (741 Kenmoor Ave., Ste. E, Grand Rapids, MI 49546, 800/442-2084, www.wmta.org).

HISTORY

By the 1830s, Michigan fever had become an epidemic. Pioneer families from all over the East Coast headed west via the newly completed Erie Canal, passed through Detroit, and continued along the new Detroit-Chicago Road, which cut across the southern half of the state's Lower Peninsula. Their final destination: Michigan's rolling prairies, with rich soil and fertile land that the federal government was selling for the bargain-basement price of $1.25 an acre.

Many of the early settlers were Easterners, leaving already-overwhelming cities to seek better opportunities for themselves and their families. The onrush between 1825 and 1855 spurred the settlement of some of Michigan's largest towns, including Battle Creek and Jackson. That early growth was soon augmented by the railroad; by 1849, Michigan Central began making regular state crossings, disgorging thousands of optimistic settlers along the way.

In the region known as Michigan's Heartland, the most visible evidence of these early settlers can be found in the Greek Revival homes and clean-lined architecture of the cities and villages they built. They also founded a number of Eastern-style private colleges, a concentration unmatched elsewhere in the state.

Ann Arbor and Vicinity

Few would dispute the claim that Ann Arbor, with its population of 113,200, is one of the most interesting cities in the state—if not the country. Home to the well-reputed University of Michigan, part of the Big Ten Conference, it transcends the typical college-town atmosphere with its unique blend of large-city verve and small-town friendliness. Located about 40 miles west of Detroit, Ann Arbor is now a regional research center as well as the suburb of choice for Detroit intelligentsia. Popular with all demographic groups, the city has been awarded the title "quintessentially cool college town" by *Seventeen,* rated the second most "Woman Friendly City in America" by *Ladies Home Journal,* and ranked #27 on *Money* magazine's 2008 list of the "best places to live" in America.

The media continues to heap accolades on the city, in part because of its appealing blend of big city vitality and small-town Midwestern friendliness. This is Michigan, after all. While

THE HEARTLAND

© AVALON TRAVEL

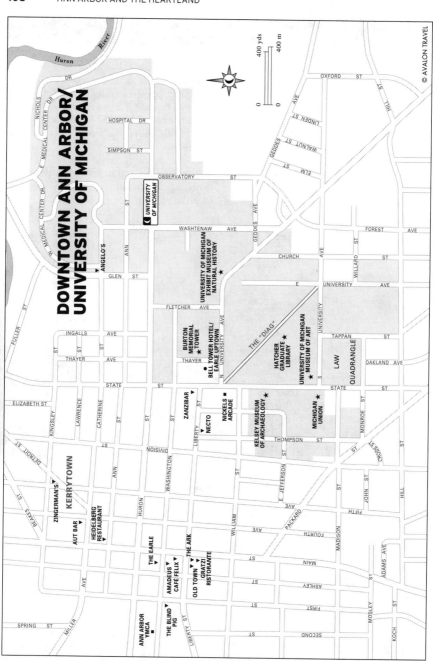

DOWNTOWN ANN ARBOR/ UNIVERSITY OF MICHIGAN

THE HEARTLAND

there's plenty of typical college-town angst, folks are genuinely helpful when you ask for directions and are always ready to recommend a favorite restaurant.

The city is dominated by the well-known university, which occupies most of the area just east of downtown. Historic U of M, founded in 1817, is one of the nation's great public institutions, with a long reputation for excellence in academics and athletics. The university is proud of its statistics, including having the largest pre-law and pre-med programs in the country; graduates that include eight NASA astronauts, one president, numerous actors and filmmakers, and several Pulitzer Prize and Nobel Prize winners; and a diverse student body that represents all 50 states and more than 100 foreign countries.

SIGHTS
◖ University of Michigan

A campus tour of the University of Michigan (www.umich.edu) reveals the expected and the less expected—both backpacked and Birkenstocked students and a quirky collection of 2,500 rare musical instruments. The heart of it all is the **"Diag,"** the diagonal walkway crossing the original 40-acre campus between State Street, North University, and South University. Many of the buildings house classrooms, and on many days this is the site of student protest demonstrations and outdoor concerts. Ann Arbor, while still politically aware these days, is not the hotbed of activism it was in the 1960s, when an ongoing campaign began here to legalize marijuana.

For a terrific view, climb the eight floors to the map room in the **Hatcher Graduate Library.** Afterward, cross State Street, where you'll find the venerable **Michigan Union** (530 S. State St., 734/763-5750, 7 A.M.–2 A.M. Mon.–Sat., 9 A.M.–2 A.M. Sun. fall/winter, 7 A.M.–midnight Mon.–Thurs., 7 A.M.–2 A.M. Fri.–Sat., 9 A.M.–midnight Sun. spring/summer), built in the 1920s and site of President Kennedy's announcement to form the Peace Corps. Just north of the Diag, you'll find another historic student union, the **Michigan**

League (911 N. University Ave., 734/764-0446, 7 A.M.–11 P.M. daily), opened in 1929 as a center for women's social and cultural activities on campus; today, it houses a gift shop, an information center, a 640-seat theater, and a small inn for visitors.

Across from the League is the **Burton Memorial Tower,** a campus landmark that's capped by one of the world's heaviest carillons, containing 43 tons of bells. Another campus favorite is the **Law Quadrangle,** home of U of M's respected law school. Built 1923–1933, the picturesque quad was modeled after Britain's Cambridge University. The level of workmanship in the Gothic building was rare even in the arts-and-crafts inspired 1920s. Rest your feet in the library's hushed reading room, where blue and gold plaster medallions decorate the ceiling.

No visit to Wolverine territory would be complete without a stop at **Michigan Stadium** on Stadium Street and Main. The largest collegiate stadium in the United States, it draws more than 105,000 screaming fans for home

the Burton Memorial Tower at the University of Michigan

© ANN ARBOR AREA CVB

THE HEARTLAND

games and post-game tailgating marathons. Constructed in 1927, this historic stadium remains open and active, even as it undergoes much-needed renovations.

Campus Museums

Established in 1817, U of M has long been a leading research institution; over the years, it's developed extensive collections. Most are housed in the university's exceptional museums. The **University of Michigan Exhibit Museum of Natural History** (1109 Geddes Ave., 734/764-0480, www.lsa.umich.edu/exhibitmuseum, 9 A.M.–5 P.M. Mon.–Sat., noon–5 P.M. Sun., donation suggested) is one of the best natural science museums in the country, with displays on prehistoric life, dinosaurs, anthropology, Native Americans, Michigan wildlife, and geology. Most of the highlights—especially the dinosaur dioramas—are on the second floor.

Among the top 10 U.S. university art museums, the **University of Michigan Museum of Art** (525 S. State St., 734/764-0395, www.umma.umich.edu, 11 A.M.–6 P.M. Tues. and Fri.–Sun., 11 A.M.–9 P.M. Wed.–Thurs., free) has a permanent collection of more than 15,000 regularly rotated pieces, including works by big names like Picasso, Miró, Cézanne, and more. Masterpieces include Max Beckmann's *Begin the Beguine,* Monet's *The Break-up of the Ice,* and the especially strong collection of Whistler prints. The knowledgeable staff works hard to make art more accessible and relevant to the general public, with a high-caliber museum shop, enthusiastic docents, and a weekly series of gallery talks, art videos, and slide lectures. Since 2006, the museum's historic home, Alumni Memorial Hall, has undergone extensive renovations, expected to be completed by 2009. During the renovation, a smaller version of the museum is operating in a temporary exhibition space (1301 S. University).

Other intriguing museums include the **Gerald R. Ford Presidential Library** (1000 Beal Ave., 734/205-0555, www.ford.utexas.edu, 8:45 A.M.–4:45 P.M. Mon.–Fri., free), an enormous collection of letters, reports, photographs,

televised campaign commercials, audiotapes of speeches, and other archival materials, and the **Sindecuse Museum of Dentistry** (Kellogg Building, 1011 N. University Ave., www.dent.umich.edu/museum, 8 A.M.–6 P.M. Mon.–Fri., free), a rare collection of over 10,000 objects focused on the history of dentistry from the 18th century to the present. In addition, the **Stearns Collection of Musical Instruments** (1100 Baits Dr., 734/764-0583, www.music.umich.edu, 10 A.M.–5 P.M. Mon.–Fri., free) is a fascinatingly quirky repository of over 2,500 musical instruments collected by drug manufacturer Fred Stearns. The collection features permanent and occasional displays throughout the Earl V. Moore Building of the School of Music, Theatre & Dance in the North Campus area.

University Gardens

If you enjoy perusing collections of a more natural kind, then take some time to stroll through the University of Michigan's lovely gardens. The **Matthaei Botanical Gardens** (1800 N. Dixboro Rd., 734/647-7600, www.lsa.umich.edu/mbg, grounds 8 A.M.–dusk daily, conservatory 10 A.M.–4:30 P.M. Tues. and Thurs.–Sun., 10 A.M.–8 P.M. Wed., $3 adults, $1 students, grounds free) is an ideal place for a nature walk. In addition to an expansive conservatory of tropical, warm-temperate, and desert plants, you'll find picturesque gardens, several nature trails, and a re-created prairie.

The **Nichols Arboretum** (1610 Washington Heights Rd., 734/647-7600, www.lsa.umich.edu/mbg, 8 A.M.–dusk daily, free) offers some of the area's best hiking trails and a natural area that serves as an education and research facility for the university. It's located next to the central campus and offers more than 400 identified tree species, a variety of plant collections, as well as a lush peony garden, which blooms in early summer.

ENTERTAINMENT AND EVENTS
Nightlife

Like many college towns, Ann Arbor offers up some eclectic nightlife. The **Blind Pig** (208

S. 1st St., 734/996-8555, www.blindpigmusic.com, Wed.–Mon., show times and ticket prices vary) was one of the first clubs outside of Seattle to give Nirvana a boost; besides rock 'n' roll, the hip space features reggae and blues artists. The city's gay community convenes Friday night at the New York–style **Necto** (516 E. Liberty, 734/994-5436, www.necto.com, 9 P.M.–2 A.M. Mon. and Thurs.–Sat., cover charges vary), a dance club that features a different theme each night, including industrial, top 40, and gay.

One of the best known of Ann Arbor's clubs is **The Ark** (316 S. Main St., 734/761-1451, www.a2ark.org, show times and ticket prices vary), a 400-seat venue that has been hosting local, national, and international acoustic performers since 1965. The club moved to larger digs on South Main in the former Kline's Department Store several years ago, but the philosophy is the same: Book the best of folk and roots musicians. Period.

The Arts

The University of Michigan is a hotbed of live music and other performing arts. If you're interested in such cultural pursuits, contact the **University Musical Society (UMS)** (734/764-2538, www.ums.org, show times and ticket prices vary), which oversees a wide assortment of choral and chamber concerts, dance and theatrical performances, jazz and piano series, even family-friendly shows. Performance venues are situated throughout the campus, including the Lydia Mendelssohn Theatre (911 N. University Ave.), the Hill Auditorium (825 N. University Ave.), and the Power Center for the Performing Arts (121 Fletcher St.), among others.

Ann Arbor Summer Festival

For three weeks each summer (usually mid-June–early July), the Ann Arbor Summer Festival (734/994-5999, www.annarborsummerfestival.com) presents a dizzying array of concerts, dance performances, films, exhibitions, parties, and other activities throughout Ann Arbor. The festival, a beloved community event for over 25 years, features an eclectic mix of performers, which, in recent years, has included Mandy Patinkin, Garrison Keillor, Willie Nelson, and the Funk Brothers.

SHOPPING

The area along State Street remains the main campus commercial strip, with a funky mix of coffeehouses, bookstores, and urbane boutiques. A standout is the historic 1915 **Nickels Arcade,** a small, European-style arcade filled with ever-changing boutiques and galleries between State and Maynard. One longtime favorite is **Bivouac** (336 S. State St., 734/761-6207, www.bivouacannarbor.com, hours vary), the resource for Ann Arbor–area campers, hikers, climbers, and skiers.

More shopping is concentrated on and around Main Street (www.mainstreetannarbor.org) in the city's vintage downtown. Once a mainstay of longtime German businesses, it has since become a stylish place for browsing, people-watching, and noshing. The **Selo/Shevel Gallery** (301 S. Main St., 734/761-4620, www.seloshevelgallery.com, 11 A.M.–7 P.M. Mon.–Thurs. and Sat., 11 A.M.–10 P.M. Fri., noon–6 P.M. Sun.) has one of the state's best collections of handmade contemporary jewelry as well as a nice selection of art glass. Try **Falling Water Books & Collectables** (213 S. Main St., 734/747-9810, www.fallingwatermi.com, 10 A.M.–9 P.M. Mon.–Thurs., 10 A.M.–10 P.M. Fri.–Sat., 11 A.M.–7 P.M. Sun.) for arty gifts, journals, jewelry, candles, and other New Age goodies.

Kerrytown District

Once forlorn and forgotten, this old commercial strip north of downtown is enjoying its second go-round as a retail district, boasting the impressive **Peoples Food Co-op** (216 N. 4th Ave., 734/994-9174, www.peoplesfood.coop, 8 A.M.–10 P.M. Mon.–Sat., 9 A.M.–10 P.M. Sun.), Ann Arbor's only community-owned grocery store. Two other popular shopping options are the colorful (if pricey) open-air **Ann Arbor Farmer's Market** (315 Detroit St., 734/994-3276, 7 A.M.–3 P.M. Wed. and Sat.), where early risers will find the finest flowers and produce, and the **Ann Arbor Artisan Market** (315 Detroit St., 734/913-9622, www.artisanmarket.org, 11 A.M.–4 P.M. Sun.), a find for arts-and-crafts lovers.

Top restaurants and interesting indoor shops also lure visitors into the **Kerrytown Market & Shops** (415 N. 5th Ave., 734/662-5008, www.kerrytown.com, shop hours vary), where you can browse through boutiques such as **Mudpuddles,** a kid's store featuring puppets, wildlife mobiles, award-winning games, and other delights; the gourmet-inspired **Everyday Cook;** the 5,000-square-foot **Hollander's,** the premier place for decorative paper and bookbinding supplies; and **Mathilde's Imports,** offering a unique selection of women's apparel from Latin America, Europe, and Southeast Asia. For more information about this one-of-a-kind shopping district, contact the **Kerrytown District Association** (www.kerrytown.org).

COLLEGE SPORTS

If you're a sports fan, visiting Ann Arbor during the fall football season, you might consider catching a U of M Wolverines game, which can be a rousing all-day affair. For information about tickets and schedules—or for details about any university sporting event, from baseball to ice hockey—contact the **University of Michigan Athletics Ticket Office** (1000 S. State St., 734/764-0247, www.mgoblue.com, 8:30 A.M.–5 P.M. Mon.–Fri., ticket prices vary).

ACCOMMODATIONS
$50-150

Lodgings in Ann Arbor aren't as varied as the entertainment or dining options. Most are chain hotels that can't be missed on your way into town. The 223-room **Holiday Inn** (3600 Plymouth Rd., 734/769-9800, www.crowneplaza.com, $126–189 d), for instance, has an indoor pool, a fitness center, a beauty salon, laundry facilities, and high-speed Internet access, plus convenient in-room coffee makers and irons. A more affordable option is the pet-friendly **Comfort Inn & Suites** (2376

Carpenter Rd., 734/477-9977, www.comfortinn.com, $80–157 d), which offers 50 comfortable rooms, an indoor pool and exercise room, free wireless Internet access, and other basic amenities.

On the eastern edge of town, the **Best Western Executive Plaza** (2900 Jackson Rd., 734/665-4444, www.bestwesternmichigan.com, $80–130 d), a full-service, pet-friendly hotel, provides an indoor/outdoor pool, a sauna, a fitness center, a restaurant and lounge, cable television, complimentary Internet access, and abundant free parking. To the south lies the elegant 【 **Four Points by Sheraton Ann Arbor** (3200 Boardwalk, 734/996-0600, www.fourpointsannarbor.com, $109–163 d), with its fitness center, sauna, heated pool, gift shop, excellent steakhouse, and 197 tasteful guestrooms.

Budget-conscious travelers will appreciate the **Lamp Post Inn** (2424 E. Stadium Blvd., 734/971-8000, www.lamppostinn.com, $45–140 d), which offers a free continental breakfast, comfortable rooms with complimentary wireless Internet access, and convenient shopping at the adjacent Lamp Post Plaza.

For history buffs, the restored 【 **Vitosha Guest Haus** (1917 Washtenaw Ave., 734/741-4969, www.vitosha.org, $75–149 d) promises more than just 11 old-fashioned rooms, Internet access, a deluxe breakfast, afternoon tea, English-style gardens, and a pet-friendly policy; the stone chalet was built by Dr. Dean Meyer in 1917 and occupied by Unitarians before becoming a sophisticated cultural retreat, a favorite among artists and scholars.

$150-300

For a unique option, consider the intimate 【 **Bell Tower Hotel** (300 S. Thayer, 734/769-3010, www.belltowerhotel.com, $169–210 d), which offers 66 rooms and suites, right in the middle of campus. It's a surprisingly elegant place, with accommodations decorated in a crisp, traditional English style, as well as the on-site Earle Uptown, one of the city's finest French restaurants.

If you prefer the coziness of a bed-and-breakfast, the **Ann Arbor Bed & Breakfast** (921 E. Huron St., 734/994-9100, www.annarborbedandbreakfast.com, $169–189 d) might suit your needs. Just steps from some of the university's finest performance venues, the inn features hearty breakfasts, wireless Internet access, and free covered parking. Two of the guest studios even come with kitchenettes.

FOOD

Ann Arbor and surrounding Washtenaw County is home to more than 275 restaurants, a number seldom found in comparably sized cities.

Downtown

Reliable choices in downtown Ann Arbor include **Afternoon Delight** (251 E. Liberty, 734/665-7513, www.afternoondelightcafe.com, 8 A.M.–3 P.M. Mon.–Sat., 8:30 A.M.–3 P.M. Sun., $5–9), an ideal spot for homemade soups, deli sandwiches, and scrumptious desserts, and **Amadeus Restaurant** (122 E. Washington,

alfresco dining at Ann Arbor's Gratzi Ristorante

734/665-8767, www.amadeusrestaurant.com, 11:30 A.M.–2:30 P.M. and 5–10 P.M. Tues.–Thurs., 11:30 A.M.–2:30 P.M. and 5–11 P.M.Fri., 11:30 A.M.–11 P.M. Sat., 11 A.M.–3 P.M. Sun., $7–16), a cozy European-inspired café and patisserie that features hearty Polish, central European, and vegetarian entrées.

Another nearby favorite is **Gratzi Ristorante** (326 S. Main St., 734/663-6387, www.gratzirestaurant.com, 11:30 A.M.–10 P.M. Mon.–Thurs., 11:30 A.M.–11 P.M. Fri.–Sat., 4–9 P.M. Sun., $9–30), serving up Northern Italian fare in a vintage 1920s theater. For the best view of the large, Bacchanalian murals, sit in the balcony. If you'd prefer lighter fare, such as terrific coffee, pastries, and gourmet sandwiches, head for **Café Felix** (204 S. Main St., 734/662-8650, www.cafefelix.com, 9 A.M.–close daily, $7–18), a pleasant European-style bistro and Ann Arbor's first full-menu tapas bar.

North of Downtown

To the north, you'll find the three-story **Heidelberg Restaurant** (215 N. Main St., 734/663-7758, www.heidelbergrestaurant.net, 11 A.M.–10 P.M. Mon.–Thurs., 11 A.M.–midnight Fri.–Sat., 3 P.M.–2 A.M. Sun., $9–18), an integral part of Ann Arbor's fine dining tradition since the early 1960s. The basement level, Rathskeller, serves as a traditional German bar; the main dining room presents German specialties like *sauerbrauten* and *wiener schnitzel;* and the top floor, The Club Above, offers live entertainment seven nights a week.

Kerrytown District

Head a few blocks into the Kerrytown District, where you shouldn't miss **Zingerman's Delicatessen** (422 Detroit St., 734/663-3354, www.zingermans.com, 7 A.M.–10 P.M. daily, $5–19), a story in itself. Gastronomes and food critics alike consider this New York–style deli the best deli in the Midwest—maybe the nation. Most head for the deli counter, offering more than 100 sandwiches, side salads, and fragrant imported cheeses. The grocery side of the store has homemade breads and surrounding shelves stocked with the best of everything,

THE HEARTLAND

© ANN ARBOR AREA CVB

from jams to olive oils. The grocery counter is busiest on weekday mornings, after work, and all day on weekends; the sandwich area is mobbed for lunch and dinner. Consider calling ahead, to have your order waiting, and plan on eating at the relaxed Zingerman's Next Door, where you can linger as long as you want over a meal.

Around the University of Michigan

Closer to the University of Michigan campus, you'll encounter **Zanzibar** (216 S. State St., 734/994-7777, www.zanzibarannarbor.com, 11:30 A.M.–9 P.M. Mon.–Thurs., 11:30 A.M.–10 P.M. Fri., 5–10 P.M. Sat., 10:30 A.M.–2 P.M. and 5–9 P.M. Sun., $10–29), which looks like a drug-induced dream of the tropics—lots of bright, neon colors and fake palm trees. Equally colorful food choices include Caribbean seafood stew and fizzy Polynesian cocktails, plus a wide selection of beer and wine. If you're looking for a decent breakfast spot near campus, consider **Angelo's** (1100 E. Catherine, 734/761-8996, www.angelosa2.com, 6 A.M.–3 P.M. Mon.–Sat., 7 A.M.–2 P.M. Sun., $5–10), the hands-down favorite for their famous deep-fried French toast, made with homemade raisin bread and loaded with fresh berries.

For a more sophisticated dining experience, reserve a table at the ◖ **Gandy Dancer** (401 Depot St., 734/769-0592, www.muer.com, 11 A.M.–10 P.M. Mon.–Thurs., 11 A.M.–11 P.M. Fri., 4:30–11 P.M. Sat., 10 A.M.–9 P.M. Sun., $22–50), part of the Muer seafood restaurant chain. Housed inside the restored 1886 Michigan Central Depot, this elegant restaurant showcases creative seafood dishes like wasabi pea–encrusted tuna and pan-seared jumbo sea scallops with smoked bacon and asparagus. The delectable Sunday brunch features live jazz. Another fine-dining favorite is **The Earle Uptown** (300 S. Thayer, 734/994-0222, www. theearleuptown.com, 5–10 P.M. Tues.–Thurs., 5–11 P.M. Fri.–Sat., $22–42), a follow-up to the popular Earle Restaurant in downtown Ann Arbor. Situated in the Bell Tower Hotel

on the university campus, this well-appointed restaurant presents traditional and modern French cuisine, plus an extensive wine list.

INFORMATION AND SERVICES

For more information about Ann Arbor, contact the **Ann Arbor Area Convention & Visitors Bureau** (120 W. Huron St., 734/995-7281, www.annarbor.org, 8:30 A.M.–5 P.M. Mon.–Fri.) or the **Ann Arbor Area Chamber of Commerce** (115 W. Huron St., 3rd Floor, 734/665-4433, www.annarborchamber.org, 9 A.M.–5 P.M. Mon.–Fri.). For information about Washtenaw County, visit www.ewashtenaw.org. For local news and entertainment, consult *The Ann Arbor News* (www.mlive. com/annarbornews) or **WCBN** (88.3 FM, www. wcbn.org), the University of Michigan's student-run radio station.

Sizable Ann Arbor offers all the services required by travelers, from grocery stores to banks to pharmacies. For mailing needs, stop by one of Ann Arbor's many **post offices** (200 E. Liberty St., 734/662-2009, www.usps. com). As a college town, Ann Arbor is also a terrific place to snag free wireless Internet access, so find a coffee shop, such as **Café Verde** (734/994-9174, www.peoplesfood.coop, daily), and start surfing.

In case of an emergency that requires police, fire, or ambulance services, dial **911** from any cell or public phone. For medical assistance, consult the **University of Michigan Health System** (1500 E. Medical Center Dr., 734/936-4000, www.med.umich.edu).

GETTING THERE AND AROUND

Reaching Ann Arbor is a snap. Both **Amtrak** (800/872-7245, www.amtrak.com) and **Greyhound** (800/231-2222, www.greyhound.com) serve the city. In addition, you can fly into the **Detroit Metropolitan-Wayne County Airport (DTW)** (734/247-7678 or 800/642-1978, www.metroairport.com), rent a vehicle from one of seven national car rental agencies, and head west on I-94 to Ann Arbor.

Of course, most travelers probably reach Ann Arbor by car, whether headed from Flint on U.S. 23 or from Jackson on I-94.

Ann Arbor is a walking town. Those who don't have cars (and the majority of the students) use foot power or zip around town on bikes or in-line skates. There's a reliable public bus system, the **Ann Arbor Transportation Authority** (734/973-6500, www.theride.org), which delivers passengers around the main campus as well as farther afield. If you've brought your car, watch for the easy-access parking garages spread throughout the city. There's also plenty of parking on the street, but beware that the city has very thorough parking enforcement officers. Bring plenty of change.

CHELSEA

Considered by many to be little more than a trendy suburb of neighboring Ann Arbor, Chelsea has begun to make a name for itself, thanks to a big-name Hollywood star who still resides in this picturesque little town, and a big swath of public land just west of town.

◖ Purple Rose Theatre Company

When he's not off making movies, actor Jeff Daniels eschews the Tinseltown glitz for his hometown of Chelsea. Despite a crammed film schedule, Daniels keeps busy running the Purple Rose Theatre Company (137 Park St., 734/433-7673, www.purplerosetheatre.org, box office 10 A.M.–6 P.M. Mon.–Fri., show days noon–10 P.M. Sat., noon–4 P.M. Sun., $13–38), which he founded in 1991, naming it after the Woody Allen film *The Purple Rose of Cairo,* in which he'd starred six years prior. This critically acclaimed regional playhouse features classic plays such as *A Streetcar Named Desire* as well as modern works, even plays written by Daniels himself.

After catching a show at this landmark theater, head to the town's other big-name attraction: **The Common Grill** (112 S. Main St., 734/475-0470, www.commongrill.com, 11 A.M.–10 P.M. Tues.–Thurs., 11 A.M.–11 P.M. Fri.–Sat., 11 A.M.–9 P.M. Sun., $10–30), a superb restaurant founded in 1991 by former employees of Detroit's Chuck Muer restaurant

Chelsea's Purple Rose Theatre Company, founded by actor Jeff Daniels

JEFF DANIELS: MICHIGAN'S TOP PROMOTER

Certainly one of the more recognizable faces in Michigan, actor Jeff Daniels has been gracing movie screens for nearly three decades. In recent years, he's also appeared in several television commercials, part of a national campaign to promote Michigan's tourism and business opportunities.

Born in Athens, Georgia, in 1955, Jeffrey Warren Daniels grew up in Chelsea, Michigan, where his family has owned a lumber company since the 1920s. After marrying his high school sweetheart in 1979, he began to pursue an acting career. Some of his early films included *Terms of Endearment* (1983), *The Purple Rose of Cairo* (1985), and *Arachnophobia* (1990).

In 1991, he founded the Purple Rose Theatre Company in his hometown of Chelsea. Although he, his wife, and his three children still consider Michigan home, Daniels has continued to work in Hollywood, turning in memorable performances in films like *Gettysburg* (1993), *Speed* (1994), *Pleasantville* (1998), *Blood Work* (2002), *Imaginary Heroes* (2004), *The Lookout* (2007), and *Howl* (2009).

Even with such success, Daniels has never forgotten his Midwestern roots. In 2001, he wrote, directed, and starred in *Escanaba in da Moonlight,* a quirky comedy about deer-hunting season in the Upper Peninsula.

Jeff Daniels

PHOTO BY PR PHOTOS

Today, despite an incredibly busy film schedule, Daniels continues to do his part to support his home state, lending his voice to radio spots that promote Michigan tourism and using his well-known persona to lure businesses here. While some residents find it hard to be hopeful in times of downsizing auto factories and an uncertain economy, many appreciate his sincerity and commitment. It's admirable, after all, that a movie star as famous as Jeff Daniels would eschew the Hollywood scene and use his celebrity status to help the people of the Midwest.

chain. The Grill helped put sleepy Chelsea on the map, and waits easily reach two hours on weekends. Folks come for the signature fish dishes and the chic yet comfortable atmosphere, which includes painted Hopperesque scenes of old Chelsea (including the Jiffy Baking Company's tower) on the exposed brick walls.

Waterloo Recreation Area

Sprawling across two counties and some 20,000 acres, the Waterloo Recreation Area (16345 McClure Rd., 734/475-8307, www.michigan.gov/dnr, daily, state park vehicle permit required) counts as the largest park in the Lower Peninsula. The park's landscape clearly shows evidence of the glaciers that once blanketed this part of the state. Waterloo is located at the intersection of the Kalamazoo and the Missaukee moraine systems, where two glaciers collided thousands of years ago. The ice sheets ripped apart massive mountains of rock from the Canadian shield to the north, carrying fragments with them as the ice moved across this part of the state—a journey one park interpreter has described as "the movement of pancake batter on a hot griddle."

The area is a pleasing patchwork of field, forest, and lake. Pick up a map at park headquarters to help navigate you around this expansive place, which contains 11 fishing lakes, several beaches and picnic areas, and miles of hiking, biking, equestrian, and cross-country skiing trails. Here, you'll also find the year-round **Gerald E. Eddy Discovery Center,** which offers engaging exhibits about Michigan's geologic features, and the 1,000-acre **Haehnle Audubon Sanctuary,** a favorite fall hangout of sandhill cranes.

Waterloo maintains four campgrounds in all ($12–24). Equestrian (for campers with horses) and Green Lake are rustic areas, with nice wooded sites. Portage Lake and Sugarloaf are large, modern campgrounds, with sites near (but not on) their namesake lakes.

Information

For more information about Chelsea, consult the **Chelsea Area Chamber of Commerce** (310 N. Main St., Suite 120, 734/475-1145, www.chelseamichamber.org, 10 A.M.–4 P.M. Mon.–Fri.).

Getting There and Around

Chelsea is situated between Ann Arbor and Jackson, easily accessible via car, motorcycle, or RV. From Ann Arbor, take I-94 west to Exit #159 and head north on M-52 to Chelsea. From Jackson, take I-94 East. Once here, you can park the car and take a stroll through the downtown area.

Jackson and Vicinity

If you're looking for Michigan's liberal stronghold, don't look in Jackson. The Republican Party was founded in this small city of 36,300 back in 1854. More than a thousand Free Soilers, Whigs, and Democrats gathered here, where they adopted the Republican name, issued a platform, and nominated candidates for state office. A tablet still marks the site at the corner of Franklin and 2nd Streets. The Jackson area has also been home to several astronauts. Moreover, it has often claimed fame as "Nuge Country," a nod to Ted Nugent, rocker and bow hunter extraordinaire, who lives nearby. As if that isn't enough, Jackson holds the Midwest's largest and oldest Civil War muster each August, attracting more than 1,200 costumed reenactors from across the country who gather here for battle, balls, and ballistics.

Like many once-booming industrial cities in mid-Michigan, downtown Jackson was hit hard by unemployment and the "malling" of America. Few shops still occupy the city's stately Victorian and art deco storefronts. Even Jacobson's—the posh department store chain founded in Jackson, with stores that once stretched to Florida—closed its downtown store here and eventually filed for bankruptcy in 2002.

But even a flat economy can't affect the wealth of wonderful lakes in surrounding Jackson County. Hundreds of natural lakes dot the countryside, keeping the Jackson area near the top of the list for those in southern Michigan and northern Indiana looking for an easy weekend getaway. Area golf courses, museums, antique shops, and vineyards only sweeten the deal for many vacationers.

SIGHTS
Museums and Waterfalls

Trace the development of the Jackson area at the **Ella Sharp Museum of Art and History** (3225 4th St., 517/787-2320, www. ellasharp.org, 10 A.M.–4 P.M. Tues.–Fri., 11 A.M.–4 P.M. Sat., $5 adults, $3 children 5–12). Sharp's mother was a rich expatriate who had invested in western Michigan land in the 1800s and later came to live on it—a rarity, since most investors were absentee landlords. Ella, born in Jackson, grew into a successful reformer who worked to improve rural life through good government, women's associations, and conservation. She also was a pack rat, so plenty of 19th-century artifacts and memorabilia fill this museum complex, which includes Ella Sharp's 1857 farmhouse, an 1840 log cabin, a one-room schoolhouse, and the Midwest's finest wildlife art collection.

THE HEARTLAND

Perhaps in response to the awe-inspiring waterfalls of the Upper Peninsula, Jackson has created one of the largest man-made waterfalls in North America. Better known as **The Cascades** (1992 Warren Ave., 517/788-4320, 11 A.M.–11 P.M. daily May–Sept., $3, children under 6 free), they were a creation of "Captain" William Sparks, a well-known area industrialist, philanthropist, and former mayor. This is truly an amazing slice of Americana: 18 separate falls up to 500 feet high, six fountains of various heights and patterns, 1,200 colored lights, and choreographed show tunes. Kids especially love it. The falls and surrounding 465-acre Sparks County Park date back to the early 1930s, when Sparks, a three-time mayor and chamber of commerce president, developed the whole shebang and presented it as a gift to his beloved city. You can make a day of it here, since the falls are augmented by a golf course, a picnic area, fishing ponds, tennis courts, and paddleboat rentals.

Southeast Michigan Pioneer Wine Trail

While the winemaking region of southeastern Michigan is no match for the wineries that line the Southwest Coast and surround Grand Traverse Bay, connoisseurs will still appreciate the selections that constitute the Southeast Michigan Pioneer Wine Trail (www.pioneerwinetrail.com). In Jackson, you'll find **Sandhill Crane Vineyards** (4724 Walz Rd., 517/764-0679, www.sandhillcranevineyards.com, 11 A.M.–6 P.M. Mon.–Sat., noon–6 P.M. Sun.), an award-winning, family-owned winery with a year-round tasting room. Other area wineries include the **Lone Oak Vineyard Estate** (8400 Ann Arbor Rd., Grass Lake, 517/522-8167, www.loneoakvineyards.com, noon–7 P.M. daily), established in 1997 and offering complimentary tastings, and the **Pentamere Winery** (131 E. Chicago Blvd., Tecumseh, 517/423-9000, www.pentamerewinery.com, 11 A.M.–7 P.M. Tues.–Fri., 10 A.M.–7 P.M. Sat., noon–5 P.M. Sun.), where you can even take classes on the techniques of tasting and evaluating wines.

FESTIVALS AND EVENTS

The Ella Sharp Museum of Art and History (3225 4th St., 517/787-2320, www.ellasharp.org) holds three interesting annual events: the **Sugar & Shearing Festival,** a late March event that celebrates the arrival of springtime with sheep-shearing and maple sugar demonstrations; the **Art & Wine Festival,** which invites visitors to the museum grounds in early June for the chance to sample area wines and peruse regional artwork; and the **Fall Harvest Festival,** an October event that celebrates autumn with pumpkin painting, a farmers market, and an antique tractor trade. For something completely different, plan a trip around the annual **Hot Air Jubilee** (Jackson County Airport, 3606 Wildwood Ave., 517/782-1515, www.hotairjubilee.com, $10 adults, $5 children 6–12) in mid-July. Watching nearly 70 colorful hot air balloons take to the sky at once is quite a dazzling sight to see. Besides the balloons, the weekend features an arts-and-crafts show, stunt kite demonstrations, carnival rides, aircraft and antique military displays, and live entertainment. Stick around until dusk for the Balloon Night Glow, a spectacular light show of tethered balloons.

SPORTS AND RECREATION
Michigan International Speedway

For fans of auto racing, the Michigan International Speedway (12626 U.S. 12, Brooklyn, 517/592-6666, www.mispeedway.com, racing times and ticket prices vary), which opened in 1968, offers one of the country's premier racing facilities. Featuring over 80,000 seats and a large RV campground, the track presents NASCAR races (for the Truck, Sprint Cup, and Nationwide series) from mid-June to mid-August. In addition, the speedway often presents official driving schools during the warmer months, so if you have a lead foot, perhaps you should try some legal speeding instead.

Golf

The Jackson area is nuts for golf and hides a number of high-quality public courses. Two good choices are the **Arbor Hills Golf Club** (1426 Arbor Hills Rd., 517/750-2290, www.arborhillsgolf.com, daily Apr.–Oct., $15–35 w/cart), formerly a private club for over 80 years, and the **Cascades Golf Course** (1992 Warren Ave., 517/788-4323, www.cascadesgolfcourse.com, daily Apr.–Oct., $18–35 w/cart), established in 1929 and voted Jackson's best golf course in 2007.

ACCOMMODATIONS AND FOOD

You'll find a range of reasonably-priced chain hotels clustered near the I-94 interchange in Jackson. Three include the **Hampton Inn** (2225 Shirley Dr., 517/789-5151, www.hamptoninn.com, $119–139 d), the **Fairfield Inn** (2395 Shirley Dr., 517/784-7877, www.marriott.com, $94–149 d), and the **Country Hearth Inn** (1111 Boardman Rd., 517/783-6404, www.countryhearth.com, $63–83 d).

Not far from the Cascades, you'll find **⊄ The Parlour** (1401 Daniel St., 517/783-1581, 11 A.M.–9 P.M. Sun.–Thurs., 11 A.M.–10 P.M. Fri.–Sat., $3–20), an ice-cream emporium that has been dishing it out for more than 50 years. Choose from 35 flavors and dozens of sundaes, parfaits, malts, and shakes, including the always-popular tin roof sundae and the towering banana split, nearly a foot high. The diner-style menu also offers salads, burgers, sandwiches, and pizza—just in case you didn't actually come for dessert.

This is meat-and-potatoes country, and you're going to have a tough time beating it. If you're happy to join it, try **Steve's Ranch** (311 Louis Glick Hwy., 517/787-4367, www.stevesranch.com, 6 A.M.–10 P.M. Mon.–Sat., 6 A.M.–8 P.M. Sun., $10–30), a longtime favorite for omelets, burgers, and, of course, steaks.

INFORMATION AND SERVICES

For more information about Jackson, contact the **Jackson County Convention & Visitors Bureau** (141 S. Jackson St., 517/764-4440, www.visitjacksonmi.com, 8 A.M.–5 P.M. Mon.–Fri.) or the **Greater Jackson Chamber of Commerce** (141 S. Jackson St., 517/782-8221, www.gjcc.org, 8 A.M.–5 P.M. Mon.–Fri.). For local news and events, consult the *Jackson Citizen Patriot* (www.mlive.com/citpat).

For groceries and prescriptions, stop by **Meijer** (3333 E. Michigan Ave., 517/787-8722, www.meijer.com), part of an enormous regional chain. For mailing needs, visit one of Jackson's many **post offices** (113 W. Michigan Ave., 517/768-0611, www.usps.com), and for banking assistance, consult **Flagstar** (www.flagstar.com), which has several branches in town.

In case of an emergency, dial **911** from any cell or public phone. For medical services, consult **Allegiance Health** (205 N. East Ave., 517/788-4800, www.allegiancehealth.org).

GETTING THERE AND AROUND

Both **Amtrak** (501 E. Michigan Ave., 800/872-7245, www.amtrak.com) and **Greyhound** (127 W. Cortland, 800/231-2222, www.greyhound.com) serve Jackson. In addition, the town is situated halfway between the **Detroit Metropolitan-Wayne County Airport (DTW)** (734/247-7678 or 800/642-1978, www.metroairport.com) and the **Kalamazoo/Battle Creek International Airport (AZO)** (5235 Portage Rd., Kalamazoo, 269/388-3668, www.azoairport.com), from which you can rent a vehicle and head to Jackson via I-94.

Of course, if you've driven to Michigan, there are a number of ways to reach Jackson. From Lansing, for instance, you can simply head south on U.S. 127 and bypass the interstate altogether.

THE IRISH HILLS AND LENAWEE COUNTY

Just a few miles southeast of Jackson via U.S. 127 and U.S. 12, the lovely Irish Hills have long been a popular family getaway, dotted with summer cottages owned by residents of Michigan, Indiana, and Ohio. The area was formed during the last Ice Age, when huge ice chunks swept across the land, leaving behind a varied landscape of round kettle-hole lakes, steep valleys, and picturesque sweeping meadows. It got its name from Irish settlers who thought the region resembled their homeland.

You can enjoy the area's natural state at **W. J. Hayes State Park** (1220 Wamplers Lake Rd., Onsted, 517/467-7401, daily, state park vehicle permit required). The 654-acre park, which isn't far from the Michigan International Speedway, features two popular fishing lakes tucked amid gentle rolling hills. Facilities include a sandy swimming beach, a boat launch, a picnic area, and 185 modern campsites.

Nearby, the **Cambridge Junction Historic State Park** (13220 M-50, Brooklyn, 517/467-4414, hours vary, free) features the 1832 **Walker Tavern,** which tells the story of the spine-crunching Chicago Road, the chief route of settlement during the 1830s pioneer boom. Now a fine small state historical museum, it illustrates how travelers once piled into the tavern's few sleeping rooms, shared beds, and passed much of their time in the first-floor bar and dining room. Daniel Webster and James Fenimore Cooper stayed here on expeditions west.

Information

For more information about the Irish Hills, contact the **Lenawee County Conference & Visitors Bureau** (209 N. Main St., Adrian, 517/263-7747, www.visitlenawee.com).

Marshall

When Lansing was chosen as the seat of the state government in 1847, no city was more surprised and more disappointed than Marshall, located 31 miles west of Jackson. The State Senate originally passed a bill designating Marshall the capital, a measure defeated by just one vote in the House. Marshall was so sure of its upcoming role as the capital city that it set aside a site known as Capitol Hill. It even built a governor's mansion, which still exists today.

Being spurned by the Legislature, though, gave Marshall a reprieve from rampant development, and today it ranks as one of the country's best preserved 19th-century towns, with just under 7,500 residents. Lined by large shade trees and an outstanding collection of 1840s and 1850s Greek and Gothic Revival–style homes, house-proud Marshall has become a poster child for historic preservation, an example of what can be done when businesses and homeowners work together. It has been featured in dozens of travel articles and architectural magazines. "Marshall's small-town pride is a genteel descendant of the boosterism that Sinclair Lewis savaged in *Main Street* and *Babbitt,*" once declared *The New York Times.*

Before Marshall was old enough to turn heads for its architecture, it was carving out a niche as a center of the patent medicine boom in the early 1900s, producer of such classic tonics as Lydia Pinkham's Pink Pills for Pale People. It wasn't until the 1920s that a savvy mayor, Harold Brooks, first recognized the city's fine architecture and led a crusade to maintain it. The first home tour was held in 1964 and remains a large and popular annual event more than 45 years later. Marshall's designated National Historic Landmark District includes over 850 homes and businesses, the country's largest district in the "small urban" category. One National Park Service manager called Marshall "a textbook of 19th-century small-town architecture."

There's a rich and controversial history hiding behind those pretty 19th-century facades, too. Marshall drew nationwide attention in 1846 when Adam Crosswhite, a slave who had escaped from Kentucky and lived in Marshall for two years, was seized by slave hunters. The whole town rose up in his support. Local abolitionists helped Crosswhite and his family escape to Canada, arrested the slave hunters, and tried them in Federal District Court. Although the Marshall abolitionists lost in court, the Crosswhite case was instrumental in the creation of the 1850 Fugitive Slave Act, which in turn contributed to the tensions that later caused the Civil War.

SIGHTS
◖ Historic Homes

The best way to see the area's historic homes is on the annual home tour held the weekend after Labor Day. At other times, you can still enjoy the city's architecture with the help of an excellent (and free) walking-tour brochure available at the chamber of commerce and a number of local shops and inns.

One of the first stops should be the lavishly quirky **Honolulu House** (107 N. Kalamazoo Ave., 269/781-8544, www.marshallhistoricalsociety.org, noon–5 P.M. daily May–Sept., noon–5 P.M. Thurs.–Sun. Oct., $5 adults, $4 children 12–18 and seniors, children under 12 free), home to the Marshall Historical Society and described by *The New York Times* as "the architectural equivalent of a four-rum cocktail served in a coconut." Featuring a pagoda-shaped tower and decorative pineapple trim, the Polynesian-style home was built in 1860 by State Supreme Court Judge Abner Pratt, who served as U.S. consul to the Sandwich Islands (now Hawaii) 1857–1859. His wife's poor health forced the couple to return to Marshall, where they brought back their love of the tropics. Pratt's wife died shortly upon their return, and Pratt himself succumbed to pneumonia soon afterward—perhaps because of his stubborn habit of wearing tropical-weight clothing during the long and cold Midwestern winters.

Inside, the house features 1880s replicas of Pratt's original tropical murals, a riot of purples, pinks, and dozens of other rich colors, and several exquisite fireplaces. Many of the other furnishings did not belong to the Pratts, but represent Marshall history, such as the Marshall Folding Bathtub in the basement. Disguised as a cabinet, it's a rare reminder of the city's patent medicine boom.

Other fine examples of early Marshall architecture can be found two blocks north of the Honolulu House on Kalamazoo Street.

They include the home of Mayor Harold Brooks, who spurred the city's revival; the 1857 Italianate Adams-Schuyler-Umphrey House, built on land once owned by James Fenimore Cooper; the 1907 Sears-Osborne House, ordered from the Sears catalog at the turn of the 20th century for just $1,995; the 1886 Queen Anne–style Cronin-Lapietra House, one of the city's most ornate, designed by the Detroit firm best known for the city's Michigan Central Railroad Terminal; and the 1843 Greek Revival Camp-Vernor-Riser House, once home to the founder of Vernor's Ginger Ale.

American Museum of Magic

Renowned magician David Copperfield has called the American Museum of Magic (107 E. Michigan Ave., 269/781-7570, www.americanmuseumofmagic.org, by appointment 2nd weekend of each month, $5 adults, $3.50 seniors and children, children under 5 free) one of his "favorite places on earth" and, if you believe the local rumor mill, wants to purchase the museum and move it to Las Vegas. For now, anyway, this fascinating attraction remains in Marshall, housed in a historic 1868 building.

The late Robert Lund, a retired automotive writer, and his wife, Elaine, opened the American Museum of Magic in 1978, after spending years collecting "notional whimsies, cabalistic surprises, phantasmagorical bewilderments, and unparalleled splendors." Roughly translated, that means anything and everything remotely related to the practice of magic. Spanning six continents and over four centuries, this extensive collection of more than 87,000 artifacts and memorabilia includes showbills, programs, books, magazines, photographs, and antique props (even the milk can used by Harry Houdini for a popular escape stunt).

FESTIVALS AND EVENTS

Marshall's must-see event is, of course, the **Annual Historic Home Tour** (800/877-5163, www.marshallhistoricalsociety.org, $15–20), which usually occurs the weekend after Labor Day and is a wonderful way to view hundreds

THE HEARTLAND

of historic buildings. While strolling along the shady streets of Marshall, visitors can listen to choirs, quartets, and brass bands, the nostalgic sounds of the 19th century.

If you happen to be in town in mid-October, you may be able to check out one of the most unique festivals, **Marshall Scarecrow Days** (800/877-5163, www.scarecrowfestival.com). As the name suggests, this weeklong event focuses on scarecrows, scarecrows, and more scarecrows. You'll see a variety of scarecrows in gardens and yards throughout Marshall. There's even a parade that features costumed children and "live" scarecrows.

Southwest of Marshall, Colon's **Magic Get Together** is worth a look, even if you're not a magician. Begun in 1934 as a sales incentive, this annual August gathering of magicians has lured some of the best names in the business, from Harry Blackstone to Lance Burton. For more information, contact **Abbott's Magic Company** (124 St. Joseph St., Colon, 269/432-3235, www.magicgettogether.com, 9 A.M.–5 P.M. Mon.–Fri., 9 A.M.–4 P.M. Sat.), with its enormous inventory of magic books and supplies.

ANTIQUE SHOPPING

Modern Marshall, with a downtown full of lacy Victorian homes and storefronts, has become an immensely popular weekend getaway for Detroit and Chicago metro–area residents. They come to ogle the architecture, shop at a number of well-stocked (if somewhat expensive) antique stores and malls, and stay in one of the town's historic bed-and-breakfast inns.

You'll find most of the best shops along several blocks of Michigan Avenue and its cross streets. For antiques, try the **Marshall Antique Center** (119 W. Michigan Ave., 269/789-0077, 11 A.M.–5 P.M. Tues.–Sat., noon–4 P.M. Sun.), which houses quality dealers in a historic home, or **Keystone Architectural and General Antiques** (110 E. Michigan Ave., 269/789-1355, www.keystoneantiques.com, 1–5 P.M. Wed.–Fri. and Sun., 10 A.M.–5 P.M. Sat.), with an outstanding

collection of vintage furniture, leaded glass, old light fixtures, hand-knotted Persian rugs, and other antique furnishings.

ACCOMMODATIONS AND FOOD

Established in 1835, ◖ **The National House Inn** (102 Parkview, 269/781-7374, www.nationalhouseinn.com, $85–160 d) is the oldest operating inn in the state. This former stagecoach stop along the Chicago Road once served as a station on the Underground Railroad. Guest rooms range from the elegant Victorian-style Ketchum Suite to smaller, pleasant country-style rooms with folk art portraits on the walls. A tip: The old road in front of the inn is now a busy intersection. Ask for a room overlooking the garden if you desire peace and quiet.

Your best budget bet is the **Arbor Inn** (15435 W. Michigan Ave., 269/781-7772, www.arborinnmarshall.com, $45–69 d), a comfortable hotel with an outdoor pool, situated along a strip of fast-food restaurants beyond the historic downtown. For cheap eats, head to **Louie's Bakery** (144 W. Michigan Ave., 269/781-3542, 5:30 A.M.–5 P.M. Mon.–Fri., 5:30 A.M.–3:30 P.M. Sat.), the kind of old-fashioned bakery you might remember from childhood, with gooey cakes, pies, and sweet rolls galore.

Wayne and Marjorie Cornwell introduced their first turkey sandwich at a county fair over 40 years ago. Today, their campy, country-style restaurant and turkey farm just north of Marshall is known as ◖ **Cornwell's Turkeyville U.S.A.** (18935 15-1/2 Mile Rd., 269/781-4293, www.turkeyville.com, 11 A.M.–8 P.M. daily, $4–9). The menu includes everything from a classic buttered turkey sandwich to a piled-high turkey Reuben to a turkey stir-fry. An adjacent 170-seat dinner theater presents afternoon and evening performances of family favorites.

INFORMATION AND SERVICES

For more information about Marshall, contact the **Marshall Area Chamber** of Commerce (424 E. Michigan Ave., 269/781-5163, www.marshallmi.org, 8:30 A.M.–4:30 P.M. Mon.–Fri. year-round, 10 A.M.–3 P.M. Sat. seasonally). If you require more than just information, you'll find everything you need in surrounding towns like Battle Creek and Jackson, including groceries, pharmacies, gas stations, laundries, and banks. Marshall, too, has its share of businesses, including two post offices; consult www.usps.com for locations and hours. In case of an emergency, dial **911** from any cell or public phone. For medical services, visit **Oaklawn Hospital** (200 N. Madison Ave., 269/781-4271, www.oaklawnhospital.org).

GETTING THERE AND AROUND

Marshall is surrounded by major towns, all of which have bus and train stations. In addition, it's not far from the **Kalamazoo/Battle Creek International Airport (AZO)** (5235 Portage Rd., Kalamazoo, 269/388-3668, www.azoairport.com) and the **Capital Region International Airport (LAN)** (4100 Capital City Blvd., Lansing, 517/321-6121, www.flylansing.com), from which you can rent a vehicle and head to Marshall via I-94 and I-69, respectively. Of course, if you've driven to Michigan, there are a number of ways to reach Marshall, such as taking I-94 west from Jackson or heading north on I-69 from Indiana.

Battle Creek

To generations of American youngsters, Battle Creek was the home of Tony the Tiger, that g-r-r-r-e-a-t and magical place where they sent their cereal box tops in exchange for free gifts and toys. For decades before that, however, Battle Creek was known as the home of the Church of Seventh-Day Adventists and for the work done at the church's sanitarium, the Western Health Reform Institute, which opened in 1866. John Harvey Kellogg joined the founders in 1876 and spent the next 25 years developing the sanitarium into an institution recognized around the world for its regimen of hydrotherapy, exercise, and vegetarian diet.

Part of that regimen was a new, healthy grain-based flaked breakfast that Kellogg cooked up in 1894. An alternative to traditional breakfast foods such as grits, bacon, and eggs, Kellogg's creation went on to revolutionize the breakfast-foods industry and to fuel the economy of this former settlement. From 1901 to 1905, more than 1,500 new homes cropped up to house the workers and others who converged on Battle Creek, hoping to capitalize on its renown as the "Health City." (This bizarre tale was the basis for *The Road to Wellville,* a 1994 Hollywood film starring Anthony Hopkins,

which painted a not-too-positive portrait of the Kellogg family and phenomenon.)

Today, Battle Creek is still home to the Kellogg Company as well as Post Cereals (recently transferred from Kraft Foods to Ralcorp). It's also home to the World's Longest Breakfast Table, a downtown event held as part of the annual Battle Creek Cereal Festival in June.

SIGHTS
Historic Sites and Museums

If you're curious about the Kelloggs, you can visit the sanitarium, now the **Battle Creek Federal Center** (74 N. Washington Ave., 269/961-7015, www.dlis.dla.m.il). Recognized on the National Register of Historic Places, the building now houses governmental and military offices, though there are still artifacts and other items on display about the Kellogg era.

If you're looking for an engaging place to take the kids, try the **Kingman Museum** (175 Limit St., 269/965-5117, www.kingmanmuseum.org, 9 A.M.–5 P.M. Tues.–Fri., 1–5 P.M. Sat., $5 adults, $4 seniors 65 and over, $3 children 3–18). The museum, which has been undergoing extensive renovations since

THE HEARTLAND

SOJOURNER TRUTH

Described by one biographer as a "riveting preacher and spellbinding singer who dazzled listeners with her wit and originality," Sojourner Truth was born around 1797 as Isabella Baumfree. She spent her childhood and early adulthood as a slave, suffering abuse at the hands of her masters and giving birth to several children. Towering more than six feet, she gained her freedom in New York state in the late 1820s, dropped her given name, and moved west on a "sojourn to preach truth." Her antislavery crusade took her into both small rural churches and the office of President Abraham Lincoln.

She settled in Battle Creek, an abolitionist stronghold, in 1857 and continued to help her people along the Underground Railroad to Canada. While revisionist history has claimed she never physically assisted runaway slaves, she no doubt inspired many of them with her fiery oratories, which preached economic competence, self-improvement, and social tolerance. A few days before she died in 1883, she said, "I isn't goin' to die, honey, I'se goin' home like a shootin' star." Her funeral was described as the biggest that Battle Creek had ever seen. She is buried in Oak Hill Cemetery by a simple old-fashioned square monument – still a popular pilgrimage spot – just steps away from the ornate marble mausoleum of cereal pioneer C. W. Post.

2006, offers a wide array of paleontological and anthropological artifacts, from fossils and skulls to Native American war shields. Visitors can also catch a star show in the new planetarium.

Binder Park Zoo

More modern species can be found at the Binder Park Zoo (7400 Division Dr., 269/979-1351, www.binderparkzoo.org, 9 A.M.–5 P.M. Mon.–Fri., 9 A.M.–6 P.M. Sat., 11 A.M.–6 P.M. Sun. late Apr.–mid-Oct., $7 Mon.–Thurs., $8 Fri.–Sun.), a small but choice zoo that houses exotic and domestic animals in natural settings. Highlights include the **Swamp Adventure,** a boardwalk that takes you over bird-filled bogs, marshes, and swamps, and **Wild Africa,** a pseudo-savannah with giraffes, zebras, ostriches, antelope, and other animals of the region.

Parks and Gardens

The Kelloggs preached plenty of fresh air as part of their health regimen. Battle Creek, therefore, excels in its number of parks and recreational opportunities. Among the most unusual is the **Battle Creek Linear Park** (269/966-3431, www.bcparks.org, dawn–dusk daily), a 17-mile system that links wooded areas, open fields, and parks with a continuous paved pathway. It's a favorite of local cyclists, skaters, and joggers. Walkers and other nature lovers, in particular, head to the **Leila Arboretum** (928 W. Michigan Ave., 269/969-0270, www.leilaarboretumsociety.org, dawn–dusk daily, free), part of Linear Park. This excellent 72-acre botanical garden is one of the best reasons to visit Battle Creek. The gift of Mrs. Leila Post Montgomery, it contains more than 3,000 species of trees and shrubs (many dating back to the 1920s), laid out in the manner of famous European gardens. Highlights include a rhododendron garden, a breathtaking flowering tree collection, and a children's garden.

FESTIVALS AND EVENTS

Battle Creek hosts several celebrations throughout the year. For over five decades, the **Battle Creek Cereal Festival** has celebrated the city's most famous industry in mid-June with a parade, live entertainment, and the world's longest breakfast table, offering complimentary cereals, fruit juice, and other Kellogg's breakfast foods. Started in 1956 as part of the Kellogg Company's Golden Jubilee, it has become a beloved annual tradition in downtown Battle Creek. Another popular event is the **International Festival of Lights,** during which Linear Park is decorated with lighted holiday displays from late November to New Year's Eve. For more information about both events, visit www.bcfestivals.com.

SPORTS AND RECREATION
Golf
If you're visiting Battle Creek during the warmer months and game for a round of golf, take a drive out to **Gull Lake View Golf Club & Resort** (7417 N. 38th St., Augusta, 269/731-4149 or 800/432-7971, www.gulllakeview. com, daily Apr.–Oct., $30–56), the oldest and largest golf resort in southwestern Michigan. En route from Battle Creek to Kalamazoo, this long-standing, family-operated resort offers top-notch lodging and dining, plus five championship golf courses: Gull Lake View East, Gull Lake View West, Stonehedge North, Stonehedge South, and Bedford Valley.

Hiking and Skiing
Naturalists will appreciate the **Kellogg Forest** (7060 N. 42nd St., Augusta, 269/731-4597, 8 A.M.–8 P.M. in summer, 8 A.M.–dusk in winter, free), begun by cereal king W. K. Kellogg as a demonstration project for reforesting abandoned farms. Michigan State University maintains the 716-acre property as an experimental forest, which includes more than 200 species of trees, 2.5 miles of road, and 35 miles of hiking and cross-country skiing trails. Hikers and skiers also use the forest's 25 miles of ungroomed firebreaks separating experimental stands of trees, and picnickers favor the forest, too.

◖ Bird-Watching
Ornithologists and other bird lovers flock to the experimental **W. K. Kellogg Bird Sanctuary** (12685 E. C Ave., Augusta, 269/671-2510, www.kbs.msu.edu, 9 A.M.–7 P.M. daily May–Oct., 9 A.M.–5 P.M. daily Nov.–Apr., $4 adults, $2 seniors, $1 children 2–12), one of North America's pioneer wildlife conservation centers. W. K. Kellogg started the sanctuary in 1928 as a refuge for Canada geese, which were then threatened by a loss of habitat to agriculture and urbanization. Today, Canada geese thrive at the 180-acre sanctuary, now part of MSU's W. K. Kellogg Biological Station, along with other native waterfowl, including ducks and swans that stay year-round. Also present are several species of raptors and game birds, from red-tailed hawks to pheasants, which you can view from several observation areas on the grounds. Many other species migrate through the region in spring and fall.

Situated along the waterfront of Wintergreen Lake, the grounds can be explored year-round on self-guided trails. A bookstore on-site includes information on how to transform your backyard into a bird sanctuary following the same principles and planting guidelines used in the refuge.

ACCOMMODATIONS AND FOOD
Situated amid rolling meadows, ◖ **Greencrest Manor** (6174 Halbert Rd., 269/962-8633, www.greencrestmanor.com, $105–200 d) is an unlikely find—a French chateau in the middle of the Midwestern prairie. Eight rooms, including six suites, are decorated with lots of chintz and antiques. For something less expensive, try the **Baymont Inn & Suites** (4725 Beckley Rd., 269/979-5400, www.baymontinns.com, $69–79 d), which includes free breakfast, high-speed Internet access, and access to a pool.

Battle Creek offers plenty of dining options, from fast-food establishments to fancier fare. One solid choice is the **Arcadia Brewing Company** (103 W. Michigan Ave., 269/963-9690, www.arcadiabrewingcompany.com, 11 A.M.–9 P.M. Mon.–Thurs., 11 A.M.–10 P.M. Fri., noon–10 P.M. Sat.,

THE HEARTLAND

RETURN OF THE TRUMPETER SWAN

The trumpeter swan, the world's largest waterfowl, can weigh up to 35 pounds when fully grown, with a wingspan of nearly eight feet. Similar in appearance to other white swans, its distinguishing characteristic is its all-black bill. Trumpeter swans typically create large nests in marshy areas, among cattails and other aquatic plants.

Centuries ago, trumpeter swans were abundant throughout the Great Lakes region, even in southern Michigan. In fact, Antoine de la Mothe Cadillac, founder of Detroit, noted their presence along the Detroit River in 1701. As European settlers spread throughout the state, however, the swan population plummeted. During the late 19th century, hunters captured swans for their fine down, while settlers drained crucial marsh habitat. By 1933, only 66 trumpeter swans remained in the continental United States, mainly in remote parts of Alaska and the Rocky Mountains.

During the mid-1980s, Michigan initiated a reintroduction program, intended to establish three self-sustaining populations of at least 200 swans by the year 2000. Despite early failures, biologists were able to incubate eggs collected from zoos and rear the cygnets for two years before releasing them into prime wetland habitat. In 1989, biologists from the Michigan Department of Natural Resources and the Kellogg Bird Sanctuary traveled to Alaska to collect eggs from wild populations as well.

By 2000, the program was considered a success. At the time, more than 400 trumpeter swans dwelled in Michigan: in the southwestern and northeastern parts of the Lower Peninsula, and in the U.P.'s Seney National Wildlife Refuge.

In recent years, the Kellogg Bird Sanctuary, which today nurtures over 20 year-round trumpeter swans, has continued reintroduction efforts. Since 2003, the sanctuary has released 28 swans in order to establish breeding populations elsewhere, including six that were transported to Sleeping Bear Dunes in 2007. In 2004, Michigan State University conducted a population survey throughout the state; the findings revealed that 655 trumpeter swans were then living in Michigan: roughly 45 percent in the U.P., 26 percent in northeastern Michigan, and 29 percent in the L.P.'s southern portion.

For more information about conservation efforts, consult the **Michigan Department of Natural Resources** (www.michigan.gov/dnr) or the **Kellogg Bird Sanctuary** (www.kbs.msu.edu).

$7–18), a microbrewery that specializes in British-style ales and offers an adjacent restaurant and tavern called TC's Wood-Fired Fare. For hearty all-American cuisine, consider **Finley's American Grill** (140 E. Columbia, 269/968-3938, www.finleys-rcfc.com, 11 A.M.–10 P.M. Sun.–Thurs., 11 A.M.–11 P.M. Fri.–Sat., $6–17), part of a popular southern Michigan chain, with locations in Jackson, Kalamazoo, and Lansing. If you're in the mood for Italian dishes, stop by **Fazoli's** (5445 Beckley Rd., 269/979-8662, www.fazolis.com, 11 A.M.–9 P.M. daily, $6–14), part of a nationwide chain that offers pasta bowls, panini sandwiches, pizzas, and tasty favorites like fettuccine alfredo and meat lasagna.

INFORMATION AND SERVICES

For more information about Battle Creek, contact the **Battle Creek/Calhoun County Convention & Visitors Bureau** (77 E. Michigan Ave., Ste. 100, 269/962-2240, www.battlecreekvisitors.org, 8:30 A.M.–5 P.M. Mon.–Fri.). For local news, entertainment, and sports, consult the *Battle Creek Enquirer* (www.battlecreekenquirer.com) or watch **WWMT** (www.wwmt.com), the CBS television affiliate that serves Battle Creek, Kalamazoo, and Grand Rapids.

Battle Creek offers all the services necessary for travelers, including groceries, pharmacies, gas stations, laundries, banks, and post offices.

In case of an emergency, dial **911** from any cell or public phone. For medical assistance, consult the **Battle Creek Health System** (300 North Ave., 269/966-8000, www.bchealth.com).

GETTING THERE AND AROUND

Battle Creek is accessible via plane, train, bus, and, naturally, car. The **Kalamazoo/Battle Creek International Airport (AZO)** (5235 Portage Rd., Kalamazoo, 269/388-3668, www.azoairport.com) is situated about 25 miles to the west. Both **Amtrak** (800/872-7245, www.amtrak.com) and **Greyhound** (800/231-2222, www.greyhound.com) serve the same station (104 Capital Ave. SW). If you have a car, you can reach Battle Creek via I-94, I-69, and several state highways. Once here, you can either stick with your car, opt for a bicycle, or use **Battle Creek Transit** (269/966-3474).

Kalamazoo and Vicinity

Yes, there really is a city named Kalamazoo. In reference to the area's bubbling natural springs, the name is derived from an Indian word meaning "place where the water boils." Its notoriety came later, when it inspired the Big Band–era song, "I Gotta Gal in Kalamazoo," as well as Carl Sandburg's poem.

From Grand Rapids, Kalamazoo is a straight shot south on U.S. 131. Produce from the nearby vegetable-growing region, pharmaceutical industries, and several papermaking plants form the foundation of the city's diverse economy. Academia provides steady employment, too: Kalamazoo is home to Western Michigan University and a number of respected private schools, including the academically renowned Kalamazoo College, site of a popular annual Bach festival and internationally known for its K-Plan, which includes international study and required internships.

Kalamazoo's population of 72,600 comprises a sizable gay community, a substantial African-American community, a burgeoning alternative music scene, a number of big-city refugees, and an almost even split between liberals and conservatives. Kalamazoo's balanced economy and population represent such a slice of the American pie that *The Wall Street Journal* featured the city as a focus group during the 1992 presidential election.

While the poet Carl Sandburg didn't think much of Kalamazoo, its downtown streets reveal many of the vanishing pleasures of small-town life: quaint paths perfect for walking, a gracious downtown park, vintage architecture, interesting shops (including a number of antique outlets), and several top-of-the-line bed-and-breakfasts. There's a great sense of civic pride and an active population that truly gets involved in city affairs. While not really a final destination, Kalamazoo makes a great stop en route to Harbor Country to the south or Lake Michigan's well-known resort communities in the north.

SIGHTS

Built in 1927, the opulent Spanish-style **Kalamazoo State Theatre** (404 S. Burdick St., 269/345-6500, www.kazoostate.com, show times and ticket prices vary) now showcases rock, blues, country, and folk concerts. The interior is a rare example of the work of famed architect John Eberson, who re-created an exotic Mediterranean town with a working cloud machine and stars that really twinkle.

Unlike many other Michigan towns, Kalamazoo experienced few boom-and-bust cycles in the last century, thanks to its plentiful and diversified industry. Houses were well maintained, and many stayed in families for generations. You can see the results of that care in the **South Street Historic District.** Impressive houses went up here between 1847 and World War I, in architectural styles ranging from Greek and Gothic Revival to Georgian and Tudor. Just north of Kalamazoo College,

THE HEARTLAND

THE HEARTLAND

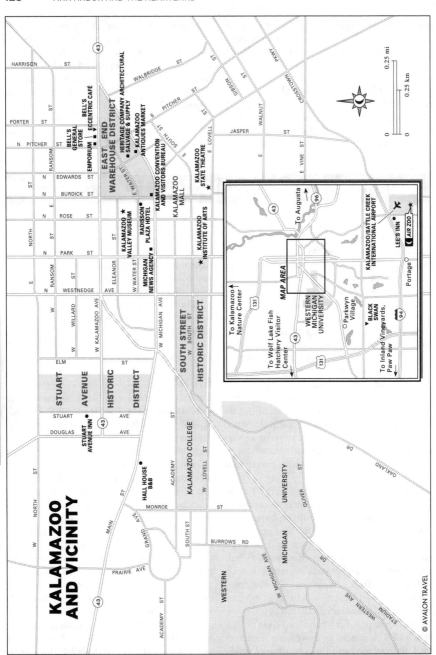

KALAMAZOO AND VICINITY

© AVALON TRAVEL

along Stuart and Woodward between West Michigan and North, business owners built large suburban homes in what is now known as the **Stuart Avenue Historic District** to display the wealth they amassed after the Civil War. You'll find a variety of elaborate Queen Anne, Italianate, and Eastlake homes here, including the meticulously restored **Stuart Avenue Inn** bed-and-breakfast.

If you appreciate Frank Lloyd Wright's architecture, the city's **Parkwyn Village,** at Taliesin and Parkwyn Drives in southwest Kalamazoo, was designed as a cooperative neighborhood by the famed architect in the late 1940s and includes examples of his Usonian style. You can view more Wright homes in the 11000 block of Hawthorne, south of the city of Galesburg.

SHOPPING

Downtown Kalamazoo, which is known as "Central City," offer six distinct shopping districts: Kalamazoo Mall, East End, South Town, Haymarket, Arcadia, and Bronson Park. The streets around the Kalamazoo State Theatre constitute **Kalamazoo Mall** (www.central-city.net), home to coffeehouses, galleries, restaurants, bakeries, and a diverse selection of resale and vintage clothing shops. Stretching from Lovell to Eleanor Streets, it was the first open-air downtown pedestrian mall created by blocking a city street to car traffic. Like many downtown shopping districts, it's suffered from the encroachment of suburban malls, but still offers popular cafés, funky stores that cater to the college crowd, and a gourmet market, among other delights.

If you haven't tired of shopping for antiques in Michigan, head for the **Kalamazoo Antiques Market** (130 N. Edwards St., 269/226-9788), which represents more than 30 quality dealers selling vintage clothing, unique jewelry, vinyl records, pottery, and lots of household stuff. You might also consider the **Emporium** (313 E. Kalamazoo Ave., 269/381-0998, 7–9 P.M. Mon.–Fri., 2–6 P.M. Sat.–Sun.), worth seeking out for its vintage furniture, despite its unusual hours.

To explore a vintage newsstand, visit the **Michigan News Agency** (308 W. Michigan Ave., 269/343-5958, www.michigannews.biz, 6 A.M.–8 P.M. daily), which dates to the 1940s. Inside, you'll find everything from the everyday to the truly eclectic: the usual maps, tobaccos, comics, and newspapers, as well as more than 6,000 magazine titles and 15,000 paperbacks. The friendly and knowledgeable owners don't seem to mind if you spend the better half of the day perusing their publications. There's also a small selection of books by local writers.

SPORTS AND RECREATION
Spectator Sports

While Kalamazoo might not boast the professional teams of, say, Detroit, sports fans will still find several seasonal options here. If you'd like to catch an IHL hockey game, consider visiting the city October–April, when the **Kalamazoo Wings** (3600 Vanrick Dr., 269/345-1125, www.wingsstadium.com, game times and ticket prices vary) thrash across the ice of Wings Stadium. For family-friendly Frontier League baseball games, come in late May–early September, when the **Kalamazoo Kings** (251 Mills St., 269/388-8326, www.kalamazookings.com, game times and ticket prices vary) are in full swing at Homer Stryker Field. Of course, if that's not enough, consider the full roster of men's and women's sports at Western Michigan University, where the **WMU Broncos** (1903 W. Michigan Ave., 269/387-8092, www.wmubroncos.com, game times and ticket prices vary) play everything from basketball to soccer to football.

Hiking and Bird-Watching

Nature lovers won't find a much better spot than the **Kalamazoo Nature Center** (7000 N. Westnedge Ave., 269/381-1574, www.nature-center.org, 9 A.M.–5 P.M. Mon.–Sat., 1–5 P.M. Sun., $6 adults, $5 seniors 55 and over, $4 children 4–13). At 1,100 acres, it ranks as one of the largest nature centers in the Midwest, with over 11 miles of trails, an arboretum, an herb garden, a restored 1858 homestead housing crafts and local artifacts, and a peaceful glen that was the favorite stomping ground of author James Fenimore Cooper. Other exhibits include a free-flying butterfly zone, an indoor bird-watching area that looks out over the trees and grounds, and a re-created 1830s settlers' farm.

ACCOMMODATIONS

Lee's Inn (2615 Fairfield Rd., 269/382-6100, www.leesinn.com, $77–125 d) is one of the more affordable lodgings in town, with an indoor pool, high-speed wireless Internet access, and a bright, airy breakfast room. For other reasonable deals, Kalamazoo offers a wide assortment of chain hotels and motels, including **Comfort Inn** (739 W. Michigan Ave., 269/384-2800, www.comfortinn.com, $110–140 d), an ideal location for exploring the downtown area.

For a more unique experience, consider the (**Stuart Avenue Inn** (229 Stuart Ave., 269/342-0230, www.stuartavenueinn.com, $75–100 d), widely regarded as the city's best B&B. It comprises three adjacent 19th-century homes (including the Bartlett-Upjohn House of pharmaceutical fame) and lovely perennial gardens. The present owners furnished the inn's well-appointed rooms with many of their own antiques as well as goodies collected on shopping sprees around the state. The **Hall House Bed and Breakfast** (106 Thompson St., 269/343-2500, www.hallhouse.com, $105–180 d) offers six rooms in a restored 1923 home. Just steps away from private Kalamazoo College, it's popular with families of students and visiting professors.

FOOD

You can't leave Kalamazoo without stopping by the highly touted (**Bell's Eccentric Café** (355 E. Kalamazoo Ave., 269/382-2332, www.bellsbeer.com, 11 A.M.–midnight Mon.–Wed., 11 A.M.–1 A.M. Thurs.–Sat., noon–midnight Sun., $3–7), part of Bell's Brewery, formerly known as the Kalamazoo Brewing Company, a forerunner of the brewpub craze. Owner Larry Bell's more than 20 acclaimed brews, including Amber Ale, Kalamazoo Stout, and Cherry

Stout, have won a loyal following in Chicago, where much of his output is sold. While you're downing a few pints, nibble on some munchies in the smoke-free eatery. This appealing spot has board games scattered around the tables, table tennis, and live acoustic music on Friday and Saturday nights. In warm weather, casual crowds congregate on the outdoor "beer garden" patio.

Just a few minutes from downtown lies **The Black Swan** (3501 Greenleaf Blvd., 269/375-2105, www.millenniumrestaurants.com, 11:30 A.M.–close Mon.–Sat., 5–9 P.M. Sun., $20–34). This large, light-filled restaurant overlooks manicured grounds and a lovely fountain. The signature menu features specialties like pecan-crusted walleye, coconut shrimp, and wood-grilled pork and butternut squash ravioli in sage cream sauce.

INFORMATION AND SERVICES

For more information about the Kalamazoo area, contact the **Kalamazoo County Convention & Visitors Bureau** (141 E. Michigan Ave., Ste. 100, 269/488-9000, www.discoverkalamazoo.com, 8 A.M.–5 P.M. Mon.–Fri.). For local news, entertainment, and sports, consult the *Kalamazoo Gazette* (www.mlive.com/kzgazette) or watch **WWMT** (www.wwmt.com), the CBS television affiliate that serves Battle Creek, Kalamazoo, and Grand Rapids.

With its assortment of groceries, pharmacies, gas stations, laundries, banks, and other helpful establishments, Kalamazoo can fulfill most travelers' needs. For mailing issues, you'll find over a dozen post offices in and around Kalamazoo; visit www.usps.com for locations and hours.

In case of an emergency, dial **911** from any cell or public phone. For medical assistance, consult **Borgess Health** (1521 Gull Rd., 269/226-7000, www.borgess.com).

GETTING THERE AND AROUND

Kalamazoo is accessible via plane, train, bus, and, naturally, car. The **Kalamazoo/**

Battle Creek International Airport (AZO) (5235 Portage Rd., 269/388-3668, www.azoairport.com) is just south of town. Both **Amtrak** (800/872-7245, www.amtrak.com) and **Greyhound** (800/231-2222, www.greyhound.com) serve the same station (459 N. Burdick St.). If you have a car, you can reach Kalamazoo via I-94, U.S. 131, and several state highways. Once here, you can either stick with your car or use **Kalamazoo Metro Transit** (269/337-8222).

GREATER KALAMAZOO
◖ Air Zoo

Just south of the Kalamazoo/Battle Creek International Airport, you'll spy the excellent Air Zoo (6151 Portage Rd., 269/382-6555, www.airzoo.org, 9 A.M.–5 P.M. Mon.–Sat., noon–5 P.M. Sun., $19.50 adults, $17.50 seniors 60 and over, $15.50 children 5–15). Considered the nation's premier museum of military aircraft, the three-campus Air Zoo stands out because of its emphasis on education. Not only can visitors examine vintage planes, like the Curtiss P-40 Warhawk or Grumman F-14A Tomcat, they can also sit at the controls of state-of-the-art flight simulators and get a small taste of what fighter pilots experience.

This enormous museum also features educational flight-related displays, such as a 2,000-square-foot exhibit chronicling the history of aircraft carriers (complete with over 400 archival photographs and three large models). In addition, the Air Zoo's original facility (now its East Campus) houses the Michigan Space Science Center, a 17,000-square-foot repository of space artifacts, from a Gemini crew-training simulator to a full-size replica of a Mercury space capsule. This impressive facility, much of which was once located near Jackson, offers an interactive exhibit as well. The International Space Station Exhibit uses hands-on demonstrations, simulations, models, theaters, and other experiences to illustrate the history and everyday operations of the largest international peacetime project in the world.

THE HEARTLAND

© AIR ZOO

Historic planes hover above visitors to Kalamazoo's Air Zoo.

© GILMORE CAR MUSEUM

vintage vehicles at the Gilmore Car Museum

Gilmore Car Museum

While in the Kalamazoo area, you simply must put aside a few hours for the Gilmore Car Museum (6865 Hickory Rd., Hickory Corners, 269/671-5089, www.gilmore-carmuseum.org, 9 A.M.–5 P.M. Mon.–Fri., 9 A.M.–6 P.M. Sat.–Sun. May–Oct., $9 adults, $8 seniors 62 and over, $7 children 7–15), considered one of the top five car museums in the United States. Situated on 90 landscaped acres northeast of Kalamazoo, not far from Gull Lake, the Gilmore Car Museum houses nearly 200 vintage automobiles in several restored historic barns. Exhibits range from an 1899 locomotive to the infamous 1948 Tucker to muscle cars of the 1970s. Other treats include a new miniature museum and an authentic 1941 diner, a great place for an afternoon snack. All buildings are wheelchair-accessible.

Grand Rapids

Grand Rapids—the state's second largest city, with a population of 193,000—owes its development and name to the rapids of the free-flowing Grand River, a place of gathering and exchange since Louis Campau established a trading post here in 1826. The power and transportation afforded by the river, coupled with the abundance of wood from the neighboring forests, made the growth of the city's furniture industry a natural.

By 1854, logging had become an important industry, and Grand Rapids entered the most vigorous phase of its development. Huge quantities of logs were floated down the Grand to Grand Rapids' mills. Upstream mill owners,

seeing the valuable timber floating unattended past their mills, often stole the logs and cut them into lumber. This practice, known as "hogging," precipitated fierce brawls along the Flat, Rogue, Grand, and other area rivers and caused the birth of the "river driver," a colorful character who rode the logs downstream to ensure they reached their final destination safely.

Grand Rapids was not always the Calvinist stronghold it is today. During the 1860s, Campau Square was notorious for its brothels, gambling houses, and basement bars. It became better known for its furniture making in 1876, when the city's wares were

© AVALON TRAVEL

THE HEARTLAND

displayed at America's centennial celebration in Philadelphia. In 1880, the incorporation of the Wolverine Chair and Furniture Company helped solidify that reputation; by 1900, Grand Rapids was nicknamed "Furniture City." The moniker still sticks today, since the area serves as headquarters for Herman Miller and Steelcase, two of the largest office furniture companies in the country.

Grand Rapids went through a decline in the early 1980s, but somehow managed to reinvent itself as a thriving showcase for the arts, local history, and business. Today, the downtown sparkles with busy hotels, shopping areas, pedestrian malls, and public artworks. One of the most striking downtown sights is Alexander Calder's dramatic sculpture, *La Grande Vitesse,* a 42-ton strawberry-red sculpture that pays homage to the rapids that built the city. Controversial at first, it has since become a symbol of Grand Rapids. More recent city improvements include a new eco-friendly Grand Rapids Art Museum and the addition of one of the nation's largest lion exhibits at the John Ball Zoo.

Much of the redevelopment can be attributed to the area's loyal and exceedingly generous business community, a group that includes the headquarters for the Meijer Corporation (pioneers of the dual grocery/discount store phenomenon) and Amway, that genius of direct marketing, which racks up annual sales in the billions. The names DeVos and Van Andel—the founding families of Amway— seem to top the list of every charitable cause in town. Most of the business and civic leaders are alumni of nearby Holland's Hope College (part of the Reformed Church in America) or of Grand Rapids' Calvin College, run by the Christian Reformed Church. Grand Rapids, by the way, is the epicenter of religious publishing in the United States.

Hardworking Grand Rapids may be known for its Protestant work ethic, but a surprising amount of diversity hides beneath the city's Calvinist veneer. Yes, it's a Republican stronghold, but Grand Rapids is also home to an active alternative press and one of the state's largest Native American populations. The city's older neighborhoods celebrate a mix of cultures, comprising Asian, Latino, African American, Lithuanian, Ukrainian, German, and Polish communities.

SIGHTS
Heritage Hill Historic District

As a manufacturing city with many locally owned businesses, Grand Rapids housed early residents who earned considerable riches and weren't shy about displaying them. Prominent families, including those who owned the city's famed furniture factories, built their mansions on the city's hillside where they could overlook their domain, from far above the smoke and soot their factories generated. Heritage Hill (616/459-8950, www.heritagehillweb.org) was their neighborhood of choice from roughly 1840 through 1920. Located just east of downtown, it displays the wealth of Grand Rapids' lumber boom, with more than 60 architectural styles reflected in its 1,300 residences. Considered the city's first neighborhood, Heritage Hill is now one of the largest urban historic districts in the country.

As in most of America's urban areas, today's Heritage Hill residents are more economically and racially diverse. The neighborhood is overseen by the Heritage Hill Association, an active group of organizers who work hard at maintaining both their property and the area's sense of community. Among the most spectacular homes are those built by the city's one-time lumber barons, plus a few others designed or inspired by Frank Lloyd Wright.

The highlight has to be the **Meyer May House** (450 Madison Ave., 616/246-4821, 10 A.M.–1 P.M. Tues. and Thurs., 1–4 P.M. Sun., free), an anomaly in this predominantly Victorian neighborhood. It was designed in 1906 by Frank Lloyd Wright for a prominent local clothier, founder of the May's clothing store chain. Vincent Scully, an architectural historian, has called the Meyer May House the most beautifully and completely restored of Wright's Prairie houses. "To come suddenly into that interior . . . is to be wholly caught up and carried along by something rarely experienced: absolute peace, integral order, deep quiet grandeur and calm—all of it achieved in a house of no more than moderate size," he has said. Through the generous funding of Steelcase, the nationally famous Grand Rapids office furniture maker, the house has since been restored to reflect Wright's original organic building concept, with custom-made furniture, art glass, carpets, light fixtures, even linens.

Gerald R. Ford Presidential Museum

The Gerald R. Ford Presidential Museum (303 Pearl St. NW, 616/254-0400, www.ford.utexas.edu, 9 A.M.–5 P.M. daily, closed on major holidays, $7 adults, $6 seniors, $3 children 6–18) honors Michigan's only native-born president in this triangular building on the west bank of the Grand River. The nation's 38th president—named to the post on August 9, 1974, after the infamous resignation of Richard Nixon—Ford grew up in Grand Rapids and represented the Fifth Congressional District in Michigan from 1948 to 1973, when he became the nation's vice president.

Renovated in 1997, the museum portrays both the private life and public challenges of Ford, president for just two years. The most popular attraction is the full-size replica of the Oval Office as it looked while Ford was president and the holographic tour of the White House. Other exhibits include a surprisingly moving section on Nixon's resignation and Ford's subsequent pardon, the events surrounding the fall of Saigon, and a multimedia recreation of 1970s pop culture. Visitors can also see President Ford's burial site.

Other Museums

In 2007, the long-standing **Grand Rapids Art Museum (GRAM)** (101 Monroe Center, 616/831-1000, www.artmuseumgr.org, 10 A.M.–5 P.M. Tues.–Thurs. and Sat., 10 A.M.–9 P.M. Fri., noon–5 P.M. Sun., $8 adults, $7 seniors and students, $5 children 6–17) was moved from its original spot and reborn within an environmentally-friendly building that has been hailed by architectural critics throughout the world. Inside, extensive collections include fine 19th- and 20th-century prints, paintings, photographs, sculptures, and decorative arts with an emphasis on—surprise!—furniture.

The art museum's major competition for the dollars and time of museum-goers is the **Public Museum** (272 Pearl St. NW, 616/456-3977, www.grmuseum.org, 9 A.M.–5 P.M. Mon.–Sat., noon–5 P.M. Sun., closed on major holidays, $8 adults, $3 children 3–17). Arguably the city's best museum, the Public is housed in a spectacular structure and ranks as the largest general museum in the state. It cost $35 million to build in 1995, much of it a gift from Amway co-founder Jay Van Andel.

The Public Museum holds an outstanding permanent collection of incredible size and scope. Here, you can witness the massive flywheel of a 1905 Corliss-type steam engine that once powered the city's furniture factories in "The Furniture City" exhibit, walk through a re-creation of 1890s Grand Rapids, take a turn aboard a restored 1928 Spillman carousel, or see stars at the Roger B. Chaffee Planetarium. The groundbreaking exhibit "Anishinabek: The People of This Place" sensitively explores the culture and artifacts of the Anishinabe people, western Michigan's Native Americans. An illuminating explanation of the state's indigenous Ottawa, Chippewa, and Potawatomi peoples, it includes video interviews that trace the modern challenges of Native Americans and the stereotypes that continue to haunt them.

Frederik Meijer Gardens and Sculpture Park

Another local benefactor—Fred Meijer, owner and founder of the Meijer grocery/discount stores—has given back to his hometown with the spectacular Frederik Meijer Gardens & Sculpture Park (1000 E. Beltline Ave. NE, 616/957-1580, www.meijergardens.org, 9 A.M.–5 P.M. Mon. and Wed.–Sat., 9 A.M.–9 P.M. Tues., noon–5 P.M. Sun.,

THE HEARTLAND

$12 adults, $9 seniors and students, $6 children 5–13, $4 children 3–4), which opened its doors in 1995. Its 125 acres encompass a 15,000-square-foot tropical conservatory (the state's largest), an outdoor area of colorful flower gardens complemented by ponds, woods, and wetlands, and an extensive collection of sculpture—including works by Auguste Rodin, Henry Moore, Claes Oldenburg, and Coosje van Bruggen. Quotations throughout the gardens by Michigan poets, such as Theodore Roethke and Jim Harrison, connect people to the plants.

THE ARTS

Grand Rapids' performing arts scene is rich and diverse, offering everything from Michigan's only professional ballet company to summertime concerts at the outdoor amphitheater in Frederik Meijer Gardens. One must-see is the **Grand Rapids Civic Theatre** (30 Division Ave., 616/222-6650, www.grct. org, show times and ticket prices vary), which represents a grand piece of the city's architecture. The largest community theater in Grand Rapids and one of the largest in the United States, this impressive landmark offers six main-stage and two children's productions annually in a restored 1903 theater once known as The Majestic.

ACCOMMODATIONS AND FOOD

For one of the best downtown values, consider the **Days Hotel** (310 Pearl St. NW, 616/235-7611, www.daysinn.com, $69–129 d), centrally located near the Gerald Ford and other public museums, with high-speed Internet access, a pool, a fitness center, a restaurant, and clean, attractive rooms. Pets are allowed.

At the other end of the spectrum, the ◖ **Amway Grand Plaza Hotel** (187 Monroe NW, 616/774-2000, www.amwaygrand. com, $170–275 d) ranks as the finest lodging in Grand Rapids and one of Michigan's top hotels. Two hotels actually make up the complex: the original 1913 Pantlind, and the newer Glass Tower, completed in 1981.

Depending on your mood, you can choose from a lush traditional or cool contemporary room. In all, the two house more than 680 rooms, nine restaurants and coffee shops, several elegant boutiques, and a state-of-the-art fitness center.

The city's oldest operating bar and restaurant, **The Cottage Bar & Restaurant** (18 LaGrave Ave., 616/454-9088, www.cottagebar. biz, 11 A.M.–midnight Mon.–Thurs., 11 A.M.–12:30 A.M. Fri.–Sat., $4–8), concocts Grand Rapids' best burgers and three different styles of chili. The outside café is a popular meeting place in good weather.

Tapas, paella, and other specialties of the Iberian peninsula draw crowds tired of the all-too-common prime rib and pasta to sunny ◖ **San Chez** (38 W. Fulton, 616/774-8272, www.sanchezbistro.com, 11:30 A.M.–10 P.M. Mon.–Thurs., 11:30 A.M.–11 P.M. Fri., noon–11 P.M. Sat., 4–10 P.M. Sun., $4–20). Lively and fun, it draws an eclectic crowd with entrées such as spiced Moroccan meatballs and lamb ribs with raspberry chili sauce.

Charley's Crab (63 Market Ave. SE, 616/459-2500, www.muer.com, hours vary daily, $12–35) is part of Chuck Muer's well-loved, nationwide chain of seafood restaurants. Try one of the fresh catches or one of the always-tasty pastas, or load up on carbs at the Sunday brunch. The signature rolls have been copied by a number of restaurants across the state. In good weather, ask for an outside table overlooking the Grand River.

INFORMATION AND SERVICES

For more information about the Grand Rapids area, contact the **Grand Rapids/Kent County Convention & Visitors Bureau** (171 Monroe Ave. NW, Suite 700, 616/459-8287, www. visitgrandrapids.org, 9 A.M.–5 P.M. Mon.–Fri.) or the **Grand Rapids Area Chamber of Commerce** (111 Pearl St. NW, 616/771-0300, www.grandrapids.org, 8:30 A.M.–5 P.M. Mon.–Fri.). For official city-related information, visit www.grand-rapids.mi.us. For local news, entertainment, and sports, consult *The Grand*

Rapids Press (www.mlive.com/grpress) or watch **WOOD** (www.woodtv.com), the NBC television affiliate.

Grand Rapids offers all the services you might require, including gas stations, laundries, and banks. For groceries, prescriptions, and other supplies, stop by a **Meijer** superstore (www.meijer.com); there are several in the area. For mailing needs, you'll find over a dozen post offices in and around Grand Rapids; visit www.usps.com for locations and hours.

In case of an emergency, dial **911** from any cell or public phone. For medical assistance, consult **Spectrum Health** (866/989-7999, www.spectrum-health.org), which oversees several hospitals and medical centers in the region.

GETTING THERE AND AROUND

Grand Rapids is accessible via plane, train, bus, and, naturally, car. The **Gerald R. Ford International Airport (GFIA)** (5500 44th St. SE, 616/233-6000, www.grr.org) is southeast of town. Both **Amtrak** (431 Wealthy St. SW, 800/872-7245, www.amtrak.com) and **Greyhound** (250 Grandville SW, 800/231-2222, www.greyhound.com) serve the city. Of course, if you have a vehicle, you can reach Grand Rapids via I-96, I-196, U.S. 131, and several state highways. Once here, you can either stick with your car or hop aboard **The Rapid** (www.ridetherapid.org), an outstanding public transit system that even links Grand Rapids to surrounding towns, from Kentwood to Grandville.

Lansing and East Lansing

In the 1940s, the WPA *Guide to Michigan* described Lansing as a place where "the political activity of a State capital, the rumbling tempo of an industrial city, and the even temper of a farming community are curiously blended." Over 60 years later, it's still an apt description.

Curiously, Lansing was developed by a legislative prank. Until 1847, Detroit was the state's capital, as mandated in a provision in the 1835 constitution. When the provision expired, legislators (two of whom had been burned in effigy by Detroit rowdies) decided that the Detroit border was in constant danger of invasion and voted to move the capital. Where to put it, however, posed a problem. After months of wrangling and debating just about every settlement in lower Michigan, someone jokingly suggested Lansing, a wide spot in the road that consisted of one log house and a sawmill. Amid laughs and for want of a better solution, it won the vote. The state's seat of government was moved in 1847.

Even the name was a lark. The original

the state capitol building in Lansing

THE HEARTLAND

© AVALON TRAVEL

settlement was named after Lansing, New York, and a New York chancellor. When it became the new capital, many wanted to rename the tiny town Michigan or Michigamme. But the legislature once again became bogged down in political infighting. Lansing it remained.

Once the decision was made and the place had a name, it began to grow. By the time the city was incorporated in 1859, it had 4,000 residents, a number of small businesses, a new capitol building, and two newspapers to cover it all. The city received another economic boost in the early 1900s, when R. E. Olds began making his "merry Oldsmobile" here.

Today, Lansing is the state's governmental seat, headquarters for many trade and professional associations, and home to heavy industry. East Lansing, a neighboring community that is part of the capital city in all respects except government, is the home of Michigan State University, part of the Big Ten conference.

Ironically, the powers-that-be also selected the university site by default.

Urban decay and rampant freeway construction have bruised downtown Lansing, and the city is often all but empty after five o'clock. While it has been described as a city in search of a center, it has a surprising amount to offer once you find it: good museums, a full plate of MSU events, some of the state's loveliest and most accessible gardens, even a minor league baseball team, the Lansing Lugnuts.

SIGHTS
◖ Michigan State University

Dubbed "Moo U," Michigan State University was established in 1855 as the country's first agricultural college and the forerunner of the nationwide land-grant university system. Despite its nicknames and rather well-known reputation as a party school, the campus has a long, rich history and an excellent reputation

LANSING/ MSU CAMPUS

To Bath

COOLIDGE RD
SAGINAW
ABBOTT RD
ALTON RD
HARRISON RD
BURCHAM DR
GRAND RIVER AVE
43
GUNSON RD
EL AZTECO
BEGGAR'S BANQUET
MACKEREL SKY GALLERY OF CONTEMPORARY CRAFT
ALBERT AVE
THE PEANUT BARREL
To Okemos, Nokomis Learning Center
BEAUMONT TOWER
BEAL BOTANICAL GARDEN
M.S.U. MUSEUM
MICHIGAN STATE UNIVERSITY
BESSEY HALL
KRESGE ART MUSEUM
ABRAMS PLANETARIUM
MARIGOLD
SHAW
LN
WHARTON CENTER
HARRISON RD
WILSON RD
SCIENCE RD
BOGUE ST
PLANT SCIENCE GREENHOUSES
TROWBRIDGE
HORTICULTURAL DEMONSTRATION GARDENS
SOUTH SERVICE RD
AMTRAK/ GREYHOUND
AZALEA AND RHODODENDRON GARDEN
FARM LN
496
127

The campus has long been regarded as one giant outdoor laboratory. Very few planted environments in the Midwest have enjoyed such sustained commitment for more than 150 years. At one point, a school policy expected three hours per day of manual labor from all students, part of the hands-on laboratory approach that helped the university maintain the campus and also enabled poor students to afford a college education. Today, both students and professional landscapers maintain the university's impressive collection of gardens.

Campus Gardens

Among MSU's extensive plantings are the **Horticulture Gardens** (B-110 Plant and Soil Sciences Building, 517/353-3770, www.hrt. msu.edu/gardens, dawn–dusk daily, free). The gardens are responsible for transforming a bleak-looking, post-1960 section of campus into a dramatic environment. Once as flat and bare as the newest subdivision, the 14-acre area is now full of pergolas, gazebos, arbors, and topiary. The entrance is off Bogue Street, south of Wilson Road, not far from the Wharton Center. Before venturing into the gardens, pick up a map at the Plant and Soil Sciences Building.

South of the Horticulture Gardens is the year-round **Clarence E. Lewis Landscape Arboretum** (517/355-5191, www.hrt.msu. edu/cella, dawn–dusk daily, free), dedicated in 1984 as an instructional arboretum for students interested in landscape development. The ever-growing collection of demonstration gardens experiment with vegetables, fruit, herbs, conifers, and native plants. You'll also be able to walk through a water garden, a sculpture garden, a Japanese garden, and a topiary garden, among other displays. Another campus area worth a special stop is the **W. J. Beal Botanical Garden** (www.cpa.m.su.edu/beal), founded in 1873 and believed to be the oldest continuously operated garden of its type in the country. Situated between Red Cedar River and West Circle Drive, this outdoor museum of living plants includes more than 2,000 species arranged by family and economic use, as

in many fields of study—especially agricultural ones, of course. Credit for its founding goes to a group of enlightened Michigan farmers who began lobbying in 1849 for a state college to promote modern agriculture. They chose the 677 acres of forest five miles east of the new state capital, in part because they wanted the school to be autonomous and not tied to an existing university.

Today, the MSU campus has grown to more than 5,000 beautifully landscaped acres, home to more than 7,000 different species and varieties of trees, shrubs, and vines. In the older part of the campus, curving drives and Gothic buildings create a park-like setting, shaded by huge beeches and some gnarled white oaks that date back more than 200 years. Students walk to class through what has become a true arboretum with the passing of time, home to more than 5,000 varieties of woodsy plants and trees.

THE HEARTLAND

©GREATER LANSING CVB

Sparty the Spartan, MSU's official mascot

well as exotic flowering landscape specimens and an enlightening section on endangered plants.

Campus Museums

With a collection of more than one million items, the 150-year-old **Michigan State University Museum** (W. Circle Dr., 517/355-7474, www.museum.msu.edu, 9 A.M.–5 P.M. Mon.–Fri., 10 A.M.–5 P.M. Sat., 1–5 P.M. Sun., donation suggested), situated east of Beaumont Tower, has been called one of the Midwest's best-kept secrets. In 2001, Michigan's leading public natural and cultural history museum also became the state's first museum to receive Smithsonian affiliate status. Three floors of exhibits concentrate on the history of the Great Lakes region; on display are numerous tools, quilts, folk art pieces, and other archaeological artifacts. Popular stops include the fur-trader's cabin and the life-size dinosaur dioramas.

Also on campus, at the intersection of Auditorium and Physics Roads, **Kresge Art Museum** (517/355-7631, www.artmuseum.

msu.edu, 10 A.M.–5 P.M. Mon.–Wed. and Fri., 10 A.M.–8 P.M. Thurs., noon–5 P.M. Sat.–Sun. Sept.–May, 11 A.M.–5 P.M. Tues.–Fri., noon–5 P.M. Sat.–Sun. June–July, closed on major holidays, free) houses a permanent collection that spans the centuries from the prehistoric to the contemporary. Founded in 1959, the museum contains over 7,000 works of art, from Egyptian artifacts to Renaissance illuminations. Wide-ranging highlights include a dramatic *Vision of St. Anthony of Padua* by Francisco Zurburán, Andy Warhol's *Marilyn,* and a solid collection of art from the 1960s and 1970s, an era often overlooked by other museums.

Other Museums

Part of the huge Michigan Library and Historical Center, the **Michigan Historical Museum** (702 W. Kalamazoo St., Lansing, 517/373-3559, www.michigan.gov/museum, 9 A.M.–4:30 P.M. Mon.–Fri., 10 A.M.–4 P.M. Sat., 1–5 P.M. Sun., free) has become a pilgrimage for many history buffs. With three floors and more than 30 permanent galleries, it tells a detailed story of Michigan's rise from wilderness to industrial powerhouse. Unlike many self-serving state museums, however, the narrative here is frank and intelligent. Placards explain how within a few generations of contact with European settlers, the state's Native American cultures transformed from self-sufficient lifestyles to those with a dependence on manufactured goods. The museum also contains an excellent and detailed copper-mining exhibit that's probably better than any found in the U.P. today. It features a walk-through copper mine and videos on life in the mining camps.

The third floor chronicles more recent history, including the dawn of the automobile age and the Great Depression. On the lower level, a small but choice museum store offers lighthouse prints, jewelry crafted from Petoskey stones, and one of the state's best selections of books relating to the history of African Americans. The Michigan Library and Historical Center complex also houses the state archives and state

THE HEARTLAND

FAMOUS SPARTANS AND WOLVERINES

Established during the 19th century, both Michigan State University and the University of Michigan have long, rich histories, with an even longer list of attendees and graduates. Some of their more notable alumni include:

- Selma Blair, actress
- Tom Brady, NFL football player
- James Caan, actor
- Jim Cash, screenwriter
- John Engler, Michigan governor
- Gerald R. Ford, U.S. president
- David Alan Grier, actor/comedian

- Jim Harrison, novelist
- Earvin "Magic" Johnson, NBA basketball player
- James Earl Jones, actor
- Lawrence Kasdan, writer/director
- Lucy Liu, actress
- Arthur Miller, playwright
- David Paymer, actor
- Robert Urich, actor
- Mike Wallace, journalist

library, a popular pilgrimage spot for genealogists from around the country. The building itself is of interest, too, designed by prominent Detroit architect William Kessler, who relied largely on native building materials.

Not far from downtown Lansing, **The Michigan Women's Historical Center & Hall of Fame** (213 W. Main St., 517/484-1880, www.michiganwomenshalloffame.org, noon–5 P.M. Wed.–Fri., noon–4 P.M. Sat., 2–4 P.M. Sun., $2.50 adults, $2 seniors, $1 children 5–18) honors the mostly unsung achievements of the state's native daughters through changing and permanent exhibitions. It celebrates the lives and contributions of Michigan women such as Sojourner Truth, a former slave and crusader for human rights; Laura Smith Haviland, an organizer of one of the state's first Underground Railroad stations; Anne Howard Shaw, a minister and physician whose dynamic leadership resulted in the passage of the 19th Amendment; and Gilda Radner, a courageous Detroit-born actress and comedienne.

Adado Riverfront Park

Lansing's Louis F. Adado Riverfront Park and Trail System ranks as one of the finest urban green spaces in the state. This greenbelt stretches on both sides of the Grand River from Kalamazoo Avenue just north of I-496 to North Street, three miles downstream. A riverwalk, popular with joggers and in-line skaters, runs along the entire east side of the river.

ENTERTAINMENT
Nightlife

East Lansing's best club is arguably **Rick's American Café** (224 Abbot Rd., 517/351-2288, www.ricksamericancafe.com, 6:30 P.M.–close Mon.–Sat., 8 P.M.–close Sun., cover charges vary), with great live acts, topline DJs, and drink specials every night. Things tend to get loud, so be prepared. If you're a jazz and blues aficionado, **The Green Door Blues Bar & Grill** (2005 E. Michigan Ave., Lansing, 517/482-6376, www.greendoorlive.com, 3 P.M.–2 A.M. Mon.–Sat., 7 P.M.–2 A.M. Sun., no cover) features some top-notch acts and dynamite drink specials, while offering the kind of moody lounge atmosphere you might find in a bigger city.

The Arts

BoarsHead Theater (425 S. Grand Ave., Lansing, 517/484-7805, www.boarshead.org, show times and ticket prices vary), central

THE HEARTLAND

Michigan's oldest professional theater, offers a season of dynamic productions at the city's Center for the Arts. This talented troupe performs October–May, and tries especially hard to make theater accessible to everyone.

Lovers of Broadway musicals, dance, comedy routines, and other special events can get their fill at the **Wharton Center** (517/353-1982, www.whartoncenter.com, show times and ticket prices vary) on the MSU campus. This renowned venue boasts four unique stages—the Pasant Theatre, the MSU Concert Auditorium, the Fairchild Theatre, and Cobb Great Hall, where the Lansing Symphony Orchestra regularly performs.

SHOPPING

Not far from Adado Riverfront Park is the **Lansing City Market** (333 N. Cedar St., 517/483-7460, www.lansingcitymarket. com, 9 A.M.–6 P.M. Tues. and Thurs.–Fri., 8 A.M.–5 P.M. Sat.). Established in 1909 and relocated to its current spot in 1938, this year-round market attracts plenty of vendors offering fruit, vegetables, sandwiches, baked goods, and more. After making your purchases, eat at a picnic area near the river.

SPORTS AND RECREATION
Spectator Sports

MSU has a spectator sport for everyone, from football to basketball, hockey to baseball. For scheduling and ticket information on Spartan sporting events, contact the **MSU Athletic Ticket Office** (Jenison Field House, 517/355-1610, http://msuspartans.cstv. com, 10 A.M.–6 P.M. Mon.–Fri. Aug.–Apr., 10 A.M.–5 P.M. Mon.–Fri. May–July).

Golf

Although northern Michigan boasts even more award-winning golf courses, the Heartland has its share of eye-catchers. **Eagle Eye Golf Club** (15500 Chandler Rd., Bath, 517/641-4570, www.hawkhollow.com, daily Apr.–Oct., $50–89) is one such place, located about 10 miles northeast of Lansing on I-69. Even better, this exceptional course is part of a spread

that includes three others: the 9-hole Falcon, the 27-hole Hawk Hollow, and the Little Hawk putting course.

ACCOMMODATIONS AND FOOD

There's no lack of lodging in the Lansing area, thanks to Big Ten fans and business travelers. You'll find a long list of reliable franchise options, including the **Hampton Inn** (525 N. Canal Rd., Lansing, 517/627-8381, www. hamptoninn.com, $69–129 d), with well-maintained rooms and a free breakfast bar—an affordable spot for your football-weekend accommodations. For a bit more luxury, try the **Kellogg Hotel & Conference Center** (55 S. Harrison Rd., East Lansing, 517/432-4000, www.hfs.msu.edu/kellogg, $114–369 d), the only four-star hotel on MSU's campus.

Housed in a restored Victorian-style train station, **Clara's Lansing Station** (637 E. Michigan Ave., 517/372-7120, www.claras. com, 11 A.M.–10 P.M. Mon.–Thurs., 11 A.M.– midnight Fri.–Sat., 10 A.M.–10 P.M. Sun., $9–24) is chock-full of vintage memorabilia, from old train schedules to antique sheet music. The enormous menu is equally eclectic, with a full range of salads, sandwiches, pizzas, pastas, hefty entrées, and ice cream drinks. If you're in the mood for seafood, check out **Mitchell's Fish Market** (2975 Preyde Blvd., Lansing, 517/482-3474, www.mitchellsfish-market.com, 11:30 A.M.–10 P.M. Mon.–Thurs., 11:30 A.M.–11 P.M. Fri.–Sat., 11:30 A.M.–9 P.M. Sun., $15–32), where you'll find everything from exotic seafood to local catches.

You can't beat the combination of good burgers, friendly service, inexpensive prices, and cold beer at (**The Peanut Barrel** (521 E. Grand River, East Lansing, 517/351-0608, www.peanutbarrel.com, 10 A.M.–midnight daily, $4–6). The olive burger is simply to-die-for. For some good ol' Mexican cuisine, stop by **El Azteco** (225 Ann St., East Lansing, 517/351-9111, 11 A.M.–midnight Tues.–Sat., 11 A.M.–11 P.M. Sun.–Mon., $5–12), where the atmosphere isn't as dank as it once was, but the food still screams of fine dive cuisine.

INFORMATION AND SERVICES

For more information about Lansing and East Lansing, contact the **Greater Lansing Convention & Visitors Bureau** (1223 Turner St., Ste. 200, Lansing, 888/252-6746, www.lansing.org, 8:30 A.M.–5 P.M. Mon.–Fri.). For official city-related information, visit www.cityoflansingmi.com. For local news, entertainment, and sports, consult the *Lansing State Journal* (www.lansingstatejournal.com) or watch **WLNS** (www.wlns.com), the CBS television affiliate that serves Lansing and Jackson.

Between Lansing and East Lansing, you'll surely find everything you need during your trip, from gas stations to banks. For groceries, prescriptions, and other supplies, stop by a **Meijer** superstore (www.meijer.com); there are several in the area. For mailing needs, you'll find over a dozen post offices in the Lansing/East Lansing area; visit www.usps.com for locations and hours.

In case of an emergency, dial **911** from any cell or public phone. For medical services, stop by **Sparrow Hospital** (1215 E. Michigan Ave., Lansing, 517/364-1000, www.sparrow.org).

GETTING THERE AND AROUND

To reach Lansing, travelers can fly into the **Capital Region International Airport (LAN)** (4100 Capital City Blvd., 517/321-6121, www.flylansing.com), take an **Amtrak** train (800/872-7245, www.amtrak.com) or **Greyhound** bus (800/231-2222, www.greyhound.com) to the East Lansing station (1240 S. Harrison Rd.), or drive into town via I-69, I-96, U.S. 127, and several state highways. Once here, you can either stick with your car or hop aboard a bus operated by the well-regarded **Capital Area Transportation Authority** (517/394-1000, www.cata.org).

Mount Pleasant

As exemplified by the city seal, Mount Pleasant's history was indelibly shaped by four elements—its Native American heritage as well as agriculture, education, and the discovery of oil. Native Americans, who had been promised lands in an 1855 treaty, began settling within Isabella County the following year. When a timber scout named David Ward purchased the land on the southern side of the Chippewa River, directly opposite what is today the Isabella Indian Reservation, he decided to call the fledgling village Mount Pleasant. Soon, merchants, artisans, and farmers flocked to the area.

The town gradually expanded, and by 1892, there was even a community college, the Central Michigan Normal School and Business Institute, which would eventually become today's Central Michigan University. The discovery of oil in 1928 changed the fortunes of the burgeoning town, which soon boasted hotels, restaurants, oil companies, and plenty of new residents. During the oil boom, many other industries left the area, but oil production kept Mount Pleasant from becoming a ghost town.

Today, Mount Pleasant (with a population of 26,200) is a more laid-back town, celebrated for its rich Chippewa heritage. Its two biggest attractions are, in fact, an Indian-owned casino and an annual powwow. Of course, the area's numerous golf courses, military memorials, recreational parks, and CMU football games also entice visitors.

ZIIBIWING CENTER

The Midwest's premier Native American museum, the Ziibiwing Center of Anishinabe Culture & Lifeways (6650 E. Broadway, 989/775-4750, www.sagchip.org/ziibiwing, 10 A.M.–6 P.M. Mon.–Sat., $7 adults, $4 seniors 60 and over, $4 children 5–17) demonstrates the rich culture and history of the Great Lakes's Anishinabek tribe. The

THE HEARTLAND

THE HEARTLAND

a permanent exhibit at the Ziibiwing Center

permanent "Diba Jimooyung" exhibit illustrates the amazing history of the original inhabitants of the Great Lakes, including their prophecies and their struggle to preserve their land, language, and culture. At different times during the year, the museum often hosts traveling exhibits about tribes from other parts of Michigan and elsewhere in the United States.

ENTERTAINMENT AND EVENTS
◖ Soaring Eagle Casino & Resort

You might not think that one of the Midwest's largest casinos would be situated in the Mount Pleasant area—instead of in a more tourist-centric place along the coast—but it might make more sense when you consider that the Indian-owned Soaring Eagle Casino & Resort (6800 Soaring Eagle Blvd., 888/732-4537, www.soaringeaglecasino.com, 24 hours daily, prices vary) is located next to the state's largest Native American reservation, the Isabella Indian Reservation, home to the Saginaw

Chippewa tribe. With its enormous gaming area, six restaurants, and more than 500 well-appointed rooms, the resort can pack in a ton of partygoers at any given moment. Even if you don't like gaming, you can still relax in one of the on-site pools or spend the day at the spa. After dining in one of the resort's eateries or fine restaurants, catch a show at the concert hall, where big-name entertainment often takes to the stage.

◖ Saginaw Chippewa Tribal Powwow

For over 20 years, the annual Saginaw Chippewa Tribal Powwow (7070 E. Broadway, 989/775-4000, www.sagchip.org, free) has offered visitors the opportunity to observe and experience traditional Native American dress, dancing, drumming, chanting, cuisine, and crafts. The competition, held in early August, attracts performers from all over the United States, making it one of the biggest events in the Indian Nation—and a terrific place for outsiders to learn about Native American culture.

SPORTS AND RECREATION
College Sports

Throughout the year, the Central Michigan University Chippewas stage a wide range of sporting events, from football to women's basketball. If you're interested in catching a game while you're in Mount Pleasant, contact the **CMU Athletics Ticket Office** (989/774-3045, www.cmuchippewas.com).

Golf

The Mount Pleasant area offers several decent golf courses. Two options include **Bucks Run Golf Club** (1559 S. Chippewa Rd., 989/773-6830, www.bucksrun.com, daily Apr.–Nov., $40–80 w/cart), situated on 290 gorgeous acres that include wetlands, three lakes, and the Chippewa River, and **Riverwood Resort** (1313 E. Broomfield Rd., 989/772-5726, www.riverwoodresort.com, daily Apr.–Oct., $12–48), which offers 27 classic holes, a spacious clubhouse, several deluxe villas, and two dozen bowling lanes.

ACCOMMODATIONS AND FOOD

If you're looking for lodgings beyond the casino, check out **The Green Suites** (1900 S. Summerton Rd., 989/772-1703, www.greensuites.net, $140–200 d), Mount Pleasant's only all-suite hotel. With its proximity to the Soaring Eagle Inn and several nearby golf courses, it's an ideal spot for those visiting the Mount Pleasant area. Suites range in size, from 995-square-foot one-bedroom suites to spacious 1,687-square-foot chambers, but all contain a living room, a dining area, and a kitchen.

The Soaring Eagle Casino isn't the only game in town for food either. **The Brass Cafe and Saloon** (128 S. Main St., 989/772-0864, www.thebrasscafe.com, 11 A.M.–10 P.M.

Tues.–Sat., $8–16) offers a wide range of menu choices, featuring innovative American and global cuisine. Set within two turn-of-the-20-th-century shopfronts, this popular eatery offers an intimate setting for relaxing after a hard day of golf or gambling.

INFORMATION AND SERVICES

For more information about Mount Pleasant, consult the **Mount Pleasant Area Convention and Visitors Bureau** (114 E. Broadway, 989/772-4433, www.mountpleasantwow.com, 8 A.M.–5 P.M. Mon.–Fri.). For local and regional news, consult *The Morning Sun* (www.themorningsun.com).

Mount Pleasant might not be as large as other Heartland cities, but it still has its share of groceries, banks, gas stations, and the like. In fact, there's a **Meijer** superstore (www.meijer.com) and a **post office** (www.usps.com) at the same location (1015 E. Pickard St., 989/772-4700).

In case of an emergency, dial **911** from any phone. For medical services, head to **Central Michigan Community Hospital** (1221 South Dr., 989/772-6700, www.cmch.org).

GETTING THERE AND AROUND

To reach Mount Pleasant, situated in the middle of the Lower Peninsula, visitors can fly into **MBS International Airport** (8500 Garfield Rd., Freeland, www.mbsairport.org), rent a car, and head west on M-20. **Greyhound** (1608 N. Fancher Rd., 800/231-2222, www.greyhound.com) also offers a bus route into the area. Most folks, of course, will likely be driving from elsewhere in Michigan. Luckily, M-20 and U.S. 127 pass directly through the Mount Pleasant area.

THE HEARTLAND

Midland

THE HEARTLAND

When the lumbermen withdrew from Midland to follow the green frontier north, the city might have become just another ghost town if it weren't for Herbert H. Dow. In 1890, Dow began a series of experiments to extract chemicals from the common salt brine that was below the surface of most of central Michigan, eventually founding Dow Chemical Company.

Although the 24-year-old was called "Crazy Dow" by the locals when he arrived in town with little but a good idea, he was a surprisingly farsighted inventor and humanitarian who founded a well-planned city of neat streets and good architecture. Today, this city of 41,000 continues to benefit from Dow's influence, and many of the city's attractions—from sports to cultural activities—bear his fingerprints.

SIGHTS

If your schedule's tight, and you have time for only one attraction in Midland, make it the **Dow Gardens** (1809 Eastman Ave., 800/362-4874, www.dowgardens.org, 9 A.M.–8:30 P.M. daily mid-Apr.–Labor Day, 9 A.M.–6:30 P.M. daily Labor Day–Oct., 9 A.M.–4:15 P.M. daily Nov.–mid-Apr., $5 adults, $1 children 6–17) and the buildings designed by Alden B. Dow, Herbert's son. Alden Dow was one of Frank Lloyd Wright's original Taliesin fellows, and he had a long and distinguished architectural

© AVALON TRAVEL

career. Like Wright, he tried to merge architecture and nature, insisting that "gardens never end and buildings never begin."

Developed by Herbert and Alden Dow over the course of more than 70 years, the garden's lovely landscape began as Herbert Dow's extended 10-acre backyard. When he arrived in Midland, the town was a barren landscape of sad stumps left behind by the lumber industry. In 1899, Dow began to landscape the space around his house to show his fellow townsfolk what they could do with their yards. He took his hobby seriously, and corresponded with Luther Burbank and other leading horticulturists of his era. During his lifetime, Dow planted 5,000 fruit trees, including 40 varieties of plums.

Unlike other historic American gardens, which owe a design debt to the formal gardens of Europe, the Dow Gardens are original, an unusual place of unfolding environments often likened to Japanese or Oriental styles. Always an enthusiastic traveler, Dow traveled to Japan frequently and became friends with a noted designer of Tokyo parks.

Texture, form, and contrast are as important here as more obvious displays of blooms. The gardens were renovated in the 1970s by Alden Dow as a retirement project, and more than a thousand trees and shrubs were added. Fantasy environments, including a jungle walk and a yew maze, reveal Dow's gentle, playful spirit. Don't miss the wheelchair-accessible sensory trail, the herb garden, and the extensive garden of perennials.

The **Midland Center for the Arts** (1801 W. St. Andrews Rd., 989/631-5930, www.mcfta.org, hours and prices vary daily) is another Alden Dow building. Inside the anthropomorphic, Guggenheim-style structure is a wide range of art and science displays, including a hands-on Hall of Ideas and a ferocious-looking mastodon that's especially popular with kids.

RECREATION

In Midland, cyclists favor the **Pere Marquette Rail-Trail** (989/832-6870), a 30-mile-long asphalt trail that's also a hit for those on foot, in-line skates, or with wheelchairs or strollers. It begins in downtown Midland near the **Tridge,** a three-way pedestrian footbridge spanning the confluence of the Tittabawassee and Chippewa Rivers. The Tridge is a local landmark, and a gathering spot for picnics, concerts, festivals, and more. From there, the rail-trail follows Saginaw Road to Coleman, passing by the Dow Historical Museum and Bradley Home before reaching the towns of Averill and Sanford.

Hikers have another option in Midland. After a visit in the 1970s, the vice president of the National Audubon Society called the **Chippewa Nature Center** (400 S. Badour Rd., 989/631-0830, www.chippewanaturecenter.com, visitor center 8 A.M.–5 P.M. Mon.–Fri., 9 A.M.–5 P.M. Sat., 1–5 P.M. Sun., free) "one of the finest—if not *the* finest—private nature centers in the world." More recently, the National Park Service cited the center for its outstanding educational accomplishments and designated it a National Environmental Study Area. The 1,200-acre

a log homestead at the Chippewa Nature Center

center sits along the Pine River and was designed (not surprisingly) by Alden Dow to merge with the living world around it. Its most striking feature is the River Overlook, a 60-foot-long, glass-walled room cantilevered over the Pine River, with great views of the center's birdlife and wildlife.

The center offers an unusually rich mix of things to see, including an authentic log homestead, items discovered from on-site archaeological digs, and a display that's a good all-around introduction to the area's natural history. Other highlights include well-executed dioramas that show Michigan geology and scenes from the Saginaw Valley Indian culture. Despite the wide range of attractions, the center's hallmark is the seclusion, peace, and beauty of its surroundings. A map available at the visitors center guides visitors through the 13-mile trail system that parallels the Chippewa River. Popular with hikers and cross-country skiers, the trails include artificially created wetlands, begun in 1990 to compensate for a wetlands destroyed to build a nearby shopping mall.

ACCOMMODATIONS AND FOOD

Although Midland is no mecca of lodging and dining options, you'll find a variety of dependable chain motels clustered near the intersection of Wackerly and Eastman. Try the 90-room **Fairview Inn** (2200 W. Wackerly St., 989/631-0070, www.fairviewinnmidland.com, $79–109 d).

Not far from the hotel is **Bamboo Garden** (721 S. Saginaw Rd., 989/832-7967, 11 A.M.–10 P.M. Mon.–Sat., 1–7 P.M. Sun., $9–16), a classy Chinese restaurant with a relaxing atmosphere and reliably good food, including sizzling steak, Buddha duck, and moo shu pork with Mandarin pancakes.

Camping

For campers, **Black Creek State Forest Campground** (220 W. Ellsworth, 989/275-5151, daily mid-Apr.–Nov., $20) offers 23 semi-modern sites (as in no electricity or showers), which can accommodate tents or RVs. Sites are available on a first-come, first-served basis. Campers can enjoy nearby hiking trails, bird-watching opportunities, a boat launch, and access to several lakes and rivers ideal for anglers.

INFORMATION AND SERVICES

For more information about the Midland area, contact the **Midland County Convention and Visitors Bureau** (300 Rodd St., 989/839-9522, www.midlandcvb.org). For other services, you'll have no trouble finding groceries, banks, post offices, and the like. If you need help in an emergency situation, dial **911** from any cell or public phone. For medical assistance, head to the **MidMichigan Medical Center** (4005 Orchard Dr., 989/839-3000, www.midmichigan.org).

GETTING THERE AND AROUND

Travelers can fly directly into the **MBS International Airport** (8500 Garfield Rd., Freeland, www.mbsairport.org), rent a car, and head to Midland via M-20/U.S. 10. Those driving from elsewhere in Michigan can take M-20 from Mount Pleasant or I-75 to Bay City, which is linked to the Midland area via U.S. 10.

THE SOUTHWEST COAST

Celebrated for its dramatic sand dunes and glorious sunsets, Michigan's Southwest Coast attracts thousands of tourists annually. The westerly winds that blow across Lake Michigan are responsible for pushing sun-warmed, surface waters closer to shore, making the beaches here perfect for swimming during the summer months. Over the last century, wealthy tourists from Detroit, Grand Rapids, and Chicago flocked to the sunny shores of southwestern Michigan and helped to transform a string of coastal villages into the posh resort towns of today. This 130-mile stretch of picturesque coastline, extending from the Indiana border to just north of Muskegon, offers a wide array of diversions, including golf courses, bike paths, Saugatuck's art galleries, fishing and boating charters, several state parks, and annual events like Holland's Tulip Time Festival.

The same temperate climate that lures beach-loving visitors to this part of Michigan is also responsible for the inland abundance of agriculture: ever-flourishing fields, orchards, and vineyards. Popular mild-weather pastimes in this area include touring one of the Midwest's finest wine-growing regions and plucking bushels of fresh produce at several U-pick farms. At such seasonal establishments, visitors are also welcome to sample other gourmet delicacies, including homemade jams, honey, maple syrup, salsa, and baked goods.

Such diversity has earned the Southwest Coast a variety of monikers over the years, including "Michigan's Gold Coast," "The Art Coast of Michigan," and "The Riviera of the

© JEFF GREENBERG

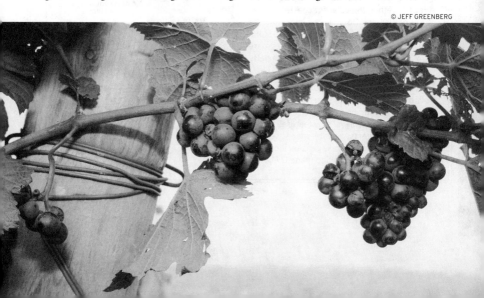

HIGHLIGHTS

◖ Warren Dunes State Park: Situated along the Lake Michigan shore, just north of Sawyer, this impressive, year-round park offers a three-mile stretch of beaches, several hiking and cross-country skiing trails, numerous modern and rustic campsites, and stupendous views from atop rugged 240-foot-high sand dunes (page 154).

◖ Lake Michigan Shore Wine Trail: Several wineries and tasting rooms, extending from Union Pier to Fennville, have long lured wine connoisseurs to the southwestern corner of Michigan's Lower Peninsula. Award-winners include the Tabor Hill Winery near Buchanan, The Round Barn Winery in Baroda, and Warner Vineyards in Paw Paw (page 160).

◖ Blossomtime Festival: Save for a decade-long period during and after World War II, this annual celebration of blossoming fruit trees has, since 1923, spotlighted the agricultural splendor of southwestern Michigan, a region known for its flavorful peaches, apples, grapes, tomatoes, cherries, melons, and more (page 164).

◖ Art Galleries of the Saugatuck Area: Together, the adjacent coastal villages of Saugatuck and Douglas are known as the "Art Coast of Michigan" – a place that, along with the nearby town of Fennville, boasts more than 30 fine art, studio, craft, and specialty galleries (page 172).

◖ Tulip Time Festival: For over 80 years, Holland has honored its Dutch heritage with this annual springtime event, which, in addition to colorful tulip displays, now features trolley tours, free concerts, variety shows, several parades, fireworks extravaganzas, local artwork, and traditional dancing (page 177).

◖ Michigan's Adventure Amusement Park: Children and teenagers (not to mention their parents) are especially fond of this Muskegon-area amusement and water park, where you'll find over 60 rides and attractions, including several gigantic waterslides, plus one of the nation's highest wooden roller coasters (page 185).

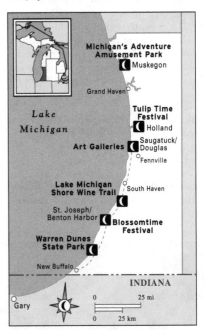

LOOK FOR ◖ TO FIND RECOMMENDED SIGHTS, ACTIVITIES, DINING, AND LODGING.

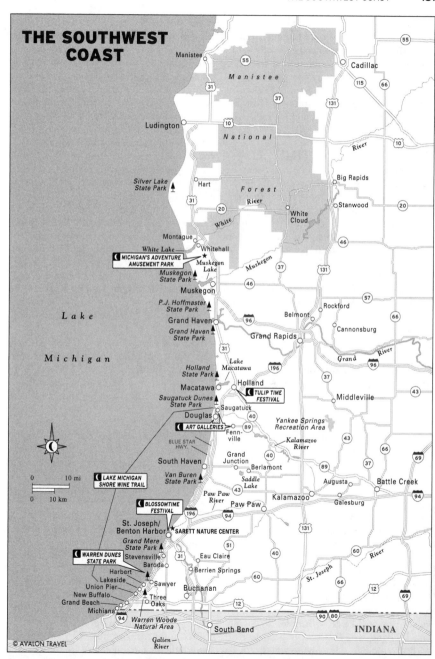

THE SOUTHWEST COAST

Midwest." But, no matter what it's called, the Southwest Coast is an understandably popular destination for vacationers, especially in the summertime, when the vibrant blue waters of Lake Michigan, formed by enormous glaciers during the last Great Ice Age, entice weary travelers and residents to put aside day-to-day worries for a while and simply contemplate the magnificence of nature.

PLANNING YOUR TIME

Practically the entire western coast of Michigan's Lower Peninsula—including the resort towns and incredible beaches that dot the southern half—is a major tourist draw, especially during the state's traditionally mild summers. So, if you're not fond of crowds, you might want to avoid places like Saugatuck and Warren Dunes State Park during the popular months of July and August. Even during the off-season, however, the area will appeal to art lovers, golfing enthusiasts, beachcombers, wine connoisseurs, and many other fun-seekers.

Unlike many of the state's other regions, the Southwest Coast is fairly easy to explore. Save for a few inland vineyards and villages, most of the area's most popular destinations lie close to the coast, accessible via I-94, I-196, and U.S. 31. It's literally a snap to drive from Michiana to Montague, a journey requiring less than three hours. Of course, to really enjoy this coastal trip, you should allow yourself at least five days, making sure to see South Haven, Saugatuck, Holland, Grand Haven, and Muskegon along the way. Double the time, and you'll be able to linger in Saugatuck's art galleries, catch a few annual events, play a few rounds of award-winning golf, take a bike ride on the Kal-Haven Trail, and explore some of the vineyards and U-pick farms in the region's interior.

Despite the presence of a commercial airport and a superb public transit system in Muskegon (arguably the largest town on the Southwest Coast) as well as Amtrak train services to towns like New Buffalo, St. Joseph, and Holland, you'll probably be better off with a vehicle of your own—whether it's a motorcycle, an RV, or a rental car. You'll benefit, too, from smart packing. As with the rest of Michigan, the Southwest Coast is a seasonal place. Bring warm clothes in winter, bathing suits in summer, and always be prepared for surprises—even in August, rain and cool temperatures are indeed possible. In addition, you should pack according to your interests; although you can procure most goods (from batteries to toiletries) in all the coastal towns, you'll usually need to bring specialty items, such as your own golf clubs, along for the ride. So, it's important to consider your plans before embarking on your trip.

For more information about the Southwest Coast, consult the **Michigan Beachtowns Association** (www.beachtowns.org), the **Southwestern Michigan Tourist Council** (2300 Pipestone Rd., Benton Harbor, MI 49022, 269/925-6301, www.swmichigan.org), or the **West Michigan Tourist Association** (741 Kenmoor Ave., Ste. E, Grand Rapids, MI 49546, 800/442-2084, www.wmta.org).

HISTORY

The history of the Southwest Coast is steeped in stories of Indians, French explorers, lumber, and agriculture. Many area towns still bear Indian names, like Paw Paw and Muskegon. With several rivers, such as the Grand near what is today Grand Haven, emptying into Lake Michigan—the perfect transportation system for logs—southwestern Michigan prospered during the logging era. After the Civil War, a growing number of sawmills buzzed along its shoreline, and the state soon became one of the leading lumber-producing regions in the country. Most of the lumber used to rebuild Chicago after the Great Fire in 1871 was felled in the forests of southwestern Michigan.

Once the forests were plucked nearly bare, the region became better known for its shipping ports and bountiful produce, luring settlers from places as far afield as America's East Coast and the Netherlands. By the late 19th century, the main mode of transportation shifted from rivers to railroads, and then to roads built for automobiles. With the car came

CITIZEN POTAWATOMI NATION

Michigan's earliest inhabitants were, of course, Native Americans, and while some of their descendants still dwell here, many others have long since departed the Great Lakes State. One such tribe was the Potawatomi, one of several Algonquian-speaking peoples who occupied the Great Lakes region from prehistoric times through the early 19th century. Once part of a larger group that included the Chippewa and Ottawa, the autonomous Potawatomi lived in southwestern Michigan over 500 years ago.

Following the Beaver Wars of the mid-1600s, many Potawatomi moved to Wisconsin, where they became trappers for French fur traders. Soon, the Potawatomi began hiring other local tribesmen to collect and trap furs, which they would sell or trade to the French, thus expanding their tribal control over a five million-acre estate that comprised Wisconsin, Illinois, Michigan, Indiana, and part of Ohio.

For most of the 1700s, the Potawatomi thrived. Adapting well to their environs, they traveled by canoe, fished in area lakes and streams, hunted waterfowl and larger game, harvested wild rice and berries, and cultivated an assortment of crops. The Potawatomi wore distinctive clothing, dwelled in birch-bark wigwams, and embraced communal events like the springtime tapping of sugar maple trees.

Unfortunately, the Potawatomi did not escape the fate of many other Native Americans; by 1800, white settlements had begun to displace tribal villages. In the fall of 1838, one group of the Potawatomi, the Mission Band, was forced to leave Indiana and march over 660 miles to a reserve in Kansas. Several members died along the way, inspiring the event's name: the Potawatomi Trail of Death.

For over 20 years, the Mission Potawatomi remained in Kansas, eventually settling small farms, many of which were later taken by white settlers and traders. In 1867, Mission Potawatomi members signed a treaty that allowed them to sell their Kansas lands and purchase new lands in present-day Oklahoma. After adopting U.S. citizenship, the Mission Band became known as the Citizen Potawatomi.

By the 1870s, the Citizen Potawatomi had formed several communities near present-day Shawnee. The Dawes Act of 1887, however, forced them to accept individual allotments again, and half of their reservation was lost during the 1891 government-sanctioned land run. Although many tribal members left for places like California and Texas, many stayed in Oklahoma. Now the ninth largest tribe in America, the Citizen Potawatomi Nation (www.potawatomi.org) owns several grocery stores and banks, not to mention a casino resort.

Luckily, though, that's not the end of the Potawatomi story in Michigan. In 1994, President Clinton restored tribal recognition to the **Pokagon Band** (www.pokagon.com), which currently services over 3,600 members in a 10-county area, including four counties in southwestern Michigan. In fact, the Pokagon Band has a casino of their own: the **Four Winds Casino Resort** (11111 Wilson Rd., 866/494-6371, www.fourwindscasino.com) in New Buffalo.

the tourists and southwestern Michigan's nickname, "Michigan's Gold Coast." Today, a string of resort towns stretch north from the Indiana border, serving as base camps for exploring the region's wealth of hiking trails, antique shops, wineries, and remnants of the Southwest Coast's prosperous agricultural and shipping history, such as the Morton House, built by one of the founding families of Benton Harbor.

Harbor Country

Eight lakefront resort communities cluster north of the Indiana border: Michiana, Grand Beach, New Buffalo, Union Pier, Lakeside, Harbert, Sawyer, and, just a few miles inland, Three Oaks. Known collectively as Harbor Country, they've also been dubbed the "Riviera on Lake Michigan" and the "Hamptons of the Midwest." Perhaps that's an exaggeration, but with a kernel of truth. Just an hour from Chicago's Loop, Harbor Country has indeed become the summer escape of choice for well-heeled Windy City expatriates—including film critic Roger Ebert, novelist Andrew Greeley, architect Stanley Tigerman, and scores of others. The well-to-do weekend at a chorus line of glass-fronted luxury homes and condos lining Lake Michigan, shopping, dining, and driving from town to town. (A few words to the wise: Skip the area in summer if you loathe crowds and hate to shop.)

Behind the area's silver-spoon facade, however, are vestiges of the area's original sleepy charm. Tony shops and art galleries may line the main streets, but the legendary sand, surf, and sunsets are still famous, and, for the most part, still free. Hotels, inns, and restaurants exist in all price ranges. While travelers can easily drop $200 for a steak dinner for two at the Four Winds Casino Resort, they can just as easily chow down on a huge breakfast of eggs, bacon, and thick French toast at Rosie's in downtown New Buffalo for less than $10.

SIGHTS
◖ Warren Dunes State Park

Raised in nearby Three Oaks, E. K. Warren was a well-known inventor, entrepreneur, philanthropist, conservationist, and community leader, but perhaps the most celebrated legacy of his fortitude and foresight is Warren Dunes State Park (12032 Red Arrow Hwy., Sawyer, 269/426-4013, daily, state park vehicle permit required). On hot summer weekends, an exodus from Chicago descends on the southern end of the park, jamming a stretch of beach

and crunching up the 240-foot Tower Hill dune, with views all the way to the Chicago skyline. It's also a favorite of weekend hang gliders. To get away from the crowds, explore the back dunes farther from the water (but stay off fragile dune grasses!) or head for the northern two-thirds of the park—largely ignored by the weekend crowds and undeveloped save for six miles of hiking and skiing trails. The Yellow Birch nature trail includes a wheelchair-accessible, bird-watching boardwalk at its north end, frequented by more than 100 bird species.

The ecology of the dunes is a fascinating study in biodiversity. Because of the way dunes form, plant communities can change drastically as you move inland. Closest to the water are the newest "active" dunes, still ever-changing piles of windswept sand. Farther inland, vegetation like marram grass takes hold and begins to stabilize the dunes. Even farther back from the water, older dunes have established larger plant communities that include jack pine, black oak, and a variety of shrubs. In between the dunes, swales filled with bogs and fens harbor water-loving plants like leatherleaf and carnivorous pitcher plants. The result is a staggering array of plants, including many not often seen in northern climates.

Grand Mere State Park

For years, Grand Mere State Park near Stevensville (269/426-4013, daily, state park vehicle permit required) was the well-kept secret of locals and summer residents. Although the area has since been discovered by out-of-towners, it remains remarkably natural (though still within earshot of the interstate). The 985-acre park preserves a valuable habitat of three interdunal lakes, scooped out by glaciers and once part of a larger bay. Shoreline currents carrying sediments have built sandbars and spits across the bay mouth, creating the small inland lakes. Two more lakes once existed south of the current three, now filled in as wooded swamps and remnant bogs.

The diverse ecological community supports a distinctive array of birds, including yellow-throated warblers, mockingbirds, summer tanagers, and Bell's vireos. Grand Mere is one of only a dozen Michigan areas listed as national natural landmarks. Several trails wind among the open sand dunes, and it's a half-mile walk to reach the park's one mile of Lake Michigan shoreline—happily, a far enough distance to deter many beachgoers.

Museums and Gardens

Established in 1989, the **New Buffalo Railroad Museum** (530 S. Whittaker St., 269/469-5409, www.newbuffalo.com/museums.shtml) celebrates the area's history with an interesting collection of artifacts, documents, and photographs. The museum—which is housed inside a replica of the original Pere Marquette Railroad Depot, alongside the railroad tracks just one mile north of I-94—even has a working miniature train display that depicts the 1920s-era Pere Marquette Railroad Yards.

Situated in downtown Three Oaks, roughly 10 miles east of Lake Michigan, is the delightful **Three Oaks Spokes Bicycle Museum and Information Center** (1 Oak St., 269/756-3361, www.applecidercentury.com/museum.htm, 9 A.M.–5 P.M. daily, free, donation welcome). Housed inside the historic 1898 Michigan Central Railroad Depot, the museum offers a collection of bicycles from the 1860s through the present, including a spine-crunching 1870s model known as the Boneshaker and an unusual chainless bike from the 1890s. The museum also provides information about the history of cycling and the town of Three Oaks, plus area maps and brochures.

In 1941, a Chicago schoolteacher, Kay Boydston, and her husband, Walter, bought 12.5 acres between Berrien Springs and Buchanan, to serve as their country home. There, Kay began experimenting with horticulture and, over the next 20 years, created perennial and lilac gardens, a boxwood garden, a fern trail, and an enchanting rock garden. With the help of philanthropists Lawrence and Mary Plym, the property gradually became the 105-acre **Fernwood Botanical Garden & Nature Preserve** (13988 Range Line Rd., Niles, 269/695-6491, www.fernwoodbotanical.org, 10 A.M.–6 P.M. Tues.–Sat., noon–6 P.M. Sun. May–Oct., shorter hours Nov.–Apr., $6 adults, $5 seniors 65 and over, $4 children 13–18, $3 children 6–12).

Today, highlights include the arboretum, which was added in the 1970s, a reconstructed tallgrass prairie (in bloom May–Aug.), a fern conservatory, an art gallery, and a nature center, which comprises an outdoor bird-feeding station and evolving nature exhibits. Near the visitors center, which contains a gift shop and a library, is a charming herb and sensory garden grouped by use, including culinary, medicinal, and pest-repellent qualities. Music lovers will also appreciate these lovely environs; outdoor music festivals and chamber concerts occur throughout the year.

ENTERTAINMENT AND EVENTS
Four Winds Casino Resort

Opened in 2007 by the Pokagon Band of Potawatomi Indians, the Four Winds Casino Resort (11111 Wilson Rd., New Buffalo, 866/494-6371, www.fourwindscasino.com, 24 hours daily) is the only land-based casino in southwestern Michigan. In addition to the 130,000-square-foot casino, which offers over 3,000 slot machines and gaming tables, the Four Winds houses a luxurious hotel, six restaurants, four bars, and live entertainment.

Festivals and Events

In the fall, many of the communities in Harbor Country celebrate **Harvest Days** (269/469-5409, www.harborcountry.org/harvestdays), a four-day event in mid-October that honors the autumn harvest with hay rides, pumpkin patches, a scarecrow contest, and a farmers market. In addition, many of the shops, galleries, and restaurants in New Buffalo, Union Pier, Lakeside, and other nearby villages host events like open houses, artist receptions, culinary demonstrations, and family activities.

Inland from the coast, the town of Three

Oaks has fewer than 1,700 residents most of the year, but in late September, three times that number converge on the area for the **Apple Cider Century** (269/756-3361, www.applecidercentury.com, fees vary), a one-day cycling event that winds amid orchards, forests, vineyards, and a handful of area towns. Since it began in 1974, the event has grown into the Midwest's largest one-day, 100-mile ride. It's sponsored by the Three Oaks Spokes Bicycle Club, and all proceeds help to finance organizations like the Rails-to-Trails Conservancy as well as the Backroads Bikeway, a lovely system of 12 self-guided biking trails.

Farther east, the town of Niles hosts three annual events worth attending. In early June, the **Niles Bluegrass Festival** (www.nilesbluegrass.com, free) presents four days of food, crafts, and traditional bluegrass performances at the town's Riverfront Park, which is also host to free Sunday concerts throughout the summer. In late July, the **Niles Riverfest** (www.nilesriverfest.net, free) invites people of all ages to celebrate the St. Joseph River with raft races, live entertainment, car shows, and more. In early fall, the four-day **Four Flags Area Apple Festival** (269/683-8870, www.fourflagsapplefestival.org, prices vary) promotes the apple harvest with plenty of food, crafts, carnival rides, parades, contests, and free entertainment.

SHOPPING

In Harbor Country, there are as many clothing boutiques, furniture stores, and other shops as you and your credit card can handle. For something unique, bypass the tony downtown emporiums and head out on the highway. The offbeat galleries and antique shops that have sprouted up along the **Red Arrow Highway,** from Union Pier to Sawyer, are one of the area's chief charms. Everything from "serious" art to campy Popsicle stick lamps can be found here, and it's easy to spend the day wandering, stopping to rest and refuel along the way. In between shops, the highway passes old cottage compounds, ramshackle resorts, and elegant lakefront estates that grew like weeds in the 1910s and 1920s.

Galleries seem to dominate at the southern end of Harbor Country. **Courtyard Gallery** (813 E. Buffalo St., New Buffalo, 269/469-4110, www.courtyardfineart.com, 11 A.M.–6 P.M. Mon., 11 A.M.–6 P.M. Wed.–Sat., 11 A.M.–5 P.M. Sun.) showcases a broad array of oils, watercolors, bronzes, and sculptured glass. Local artists dominate at **Local Color Gallery** (16187 Red Arrow Hwy., Union Pier, 269/469-5332, noon–5 P.M. daily). In Lakeside, visitors can purchase jewelry, pottery, paintings, and sculpture at the long-standing **Lakeside Gallery/Studio** (15486 Red Arrow Hwy., 269/469-3022, www.lakesidegalleries.com, by appointment) or rustic furniture made of tree trunks, branches, and twigs at **Hearthwoods Cottage Design** (15310 Red Arrow Hwy., 269/469-5551, www.hearthwoods.com, 10 A.M.–6 P.M. daily in summer, shorter hours in winter).

Farther north, roadside antiquing haunts fill former cottages, old brick storefronts, and cavernous warehouses. In Sawyer, hunt away at **Dunes Antique Center** (12825 Red Arrow Hwy., 269/426-4043, www.dunesantiques.com). In Harbert, try **Harbert Antique Mall** (13887 Red Arrow Hwy., 269/469-0977, 10 A.M.–6 P.M. daily).

While in a shopping mood, don't forget that you're in one of Michigan's leading agricultural regions. During summer and fall, you'll find many produce stands and farmers markets in and around Harbor Country. So, take a quick trip to **Shelton Farms** (1832 S. 11th St., Niles, 269/684-3230, www.sheltonfarms.com, 8:30 A.M.–7 P.M. Mon.–Thurs. and Sat., 8:30 A.M.–8 P.M. Fri., 9 A.M.–6 P.M. Sun.), where you'll find grapes, strawberries, apples, flowers, even Christmas trees.

SPORTS AND RECREATION
Golf

Although Harbor Country isn't known for its amazing golf, you'll find several courses open to the public. The **Whittaker Woods Golf Community** (12578 Wilson Rd., New Buffalo, 269/469-3400, www.golfwhittaker.com, daily Mar.–Nov., $55–85 w/cart), for instance, presents an 18-hole championship golf course amid 400 acres of woods and wetlands. The clubhouse, a renovated 1920s-era farmhouse, contains a pro golf shop, full locker rooms, and a restaurant that overlooks the course and offers weekend entertainment.

Hiking and Bird-Watching

If all this conspicuous consumption wears you out, you can find plenty of simpler pleasures in Harbor Country, too. Situated three miles north of Three Oaks, the **Warren Woods Natural Area** (269/426-4013, daily, state park vehicle permit required) protects 312 acres, including the state's last remaining virgin beech-maple forest. Along the banks of the twisting Galien River, beeches, maples, and hemlocks grow so large that two people can't link their arms around them. A 3.5-mile trail circles through the woods and along the Galien. Warren Woods is known far and wide among bird-watchers, due partly to its location on the Lake Michigan shoreline and the forest's abundant deadwood, perfect for nesting. Warbler sightings can be particularly good here.

E. K. Warren, a Three Oaks shopkeeper who made his fortune by inventing an affordable corset crafted from turkey feathers, bought the property in 1879, determined to preserve the land at a time when other businessmen were looking only to exploit it. Today, the area is designated a national natural landmark. The only concessions to human visitors are pit toilets, a wooden footbridge spanning the Galien River, a small parking lot, and one picnic table. In spring, you may notice an abundance of wildflowers and morel mushrooms, but keep in mind all plants are protected in this area. To reach Warren Woods, take the Red Arrow Highway to Union Pier, turn east on Elm Valley, and follow it five miles.

Biking

Harbor Country is an incredibly scenic place for a bike ride, especially during September and October, when the changing leaves are particularly vibrant. The **Backroads Bikeway** is a picturesque system that includes a dozen self-guided trails on paved roads, varying 5–60 miles in length. The routes cross gurgling streams and rolling hills, traverse meadows and farmland, and provide access to Warren Dunes and Warren Woods. For trail brochures, regional bike touring information, and bicycle rentals, consult the **Three Oaks Spokes Bicycle Museum and Information Center** (1 Oak St., 269/756-3361, www.applecidercentury.com/museum.htm).

ACCOMMODATIONS

The eight communities of Harbor Country offer as many lodging choices as a mid-sized city, with prices to match. Though you won't find many bargains among the bunch, it would be a shame to visit Harbor Country and not stay at one of its distinctive small inns. For budget accommodations, your best bet is to stick with franchises along I-94.

In New Buffalo, you'll find at least two unique options. **The Harbor Grand** (111 W. Water St., 888/605-6800, www.harborgrand.com, $109–349 d) is a waterfront inn featuring an indoor pool, a massage therapy center, complimentary high-speed Internet access, and luxurious rooms with fireplaces, spa showers, and harbor views. It's also just a short walk from downtown New Buffalo and a Lake Michigan beach. Meanwhile, 50 acres of spring-fed lakes, wildflower meadows, and whispering pines stretch behind the gates of **Sans Souci Euro Inn & Cottages** (19265 S. Lakeside Rd., 269/756-3141, www.sans-souci.com, $165–225 d), the perfect retreat for a romantic getaway. Choose from two luxury suites, two vacation homes, or two lakeside cottages, all featuring European-style decor and wireless Internet access.

A little farther north, Union Pier offers a wealth of lodging choices. *Chicago* magazine voted [C] **The Inn at Union Pier** (9708 Berrien St., 269/469-4700, www.innatunionpier.com, $155–230 d) one of the region's "best small inns." With a primo location just "200 steps" from Lake Michigan, this inn features an outdoor hot tub, gourmet breakfasts, and 16 spacious rooms, many decorated with antique Swedish ceramic fireplaces—according to the owners, the largest private collection in the country. The **Pine Garth Inn** (15790 Lakeshore Rd., 269/469-1642, www. pinegarth.com, $160–210 d) was built in 1905 as a private summer home. It opened its doors to guests in 1989 and has been a favorite ever since. The unique building is constructed so that the lake and its often-magnificent sunsets can be seen from every room. A more retro option is the **(Fire Fly Resort** (15657 Lakeshore Rd., 269/469-0245, www.fireflyresort.com, $130–220 d) a complex of private cottages built in the 1930s as an escape for city dwellers. Guests will enjoy comfortable furnishings, outdoor grills, picnic nooks, perennial gardens, and proximity to the beach.

Nature lovers should opt for the **Lakeside Inn** (15251 Lakeshore Rd., Lakeside, 269/469-0600, www.lakesideinns.com, $75–210 d), a historic resort built in the late 19th century, completed in 1915, and designated a state historic landmark in 2004. Today, the inn offers over 30 rooms, a cozy lobby, an exercise room, and picturesque surroundings, including a garden, a shady grove, and a nearby beach, the ideal spot to watch the sunset.

Camping

Camping may be your best bet if you're looking to travel cheaply through pricey Harbor Country. **Warren Dunes State Park** (12032 Red Arrow Hwy., Sawyer, 269/426-4013, daily Mar.–Oct., state park vehicle permit required) offers 182 modern and 36 semi-modern (no electricity or showers) sites for $16–27 per night, as well as three mini-cabins with woodstoves and bunks for $45 a night. For reservations—which are recommended May–September, especially on weekends—contact the **Michigan Department of Natural Resources** (800/447-2757, www.michigan. gov/dnr).

To the north, the town of Bridgman maintains the **Weko Beach Campground** (5239 Lake St., 269/465-3406 Apr.–mid-Oct. or 269/465-5407 mid-Oct.–Mar., www.bridgman.org), which offers developed (water and electricity) and semi-developed sites for $25–30 per night, as well as cabins for $45 per night. Situated along the sunny shores of Lake Michigan, this campground welcomes tents and RVs; amenities include hot showers, outdoor grills, picnic areas, a playground, a concession stand, and a dump station.

FOOD

In New Buffalo, you'll find two winning eateries. **Hannah's Restaurant** (115 S. Whittaker St., 269/469-1440, www.hannahsrestaurant. com, 11 A.M.–10 P.M. daily, $15–45) features old-world specialties such as pot roast and pork chops, plus a children's menu. **Redamak's** (616 E. Buffalo St., 269/469-4522, www.redamaks.com, noon–10:30 P.M. Mon.–Sat., noon–10 P.M. Sun. June–Aug., shorter hours Mar.–early June and late Aug.–Oct., closed Nov.–Feb., $4.50–12) is known for the "hamburger that made New Buffalo famous," as well as its casual, friendly dining.

In Union Pier, **Red Arrow Roadhouse** (15710 Red Arrow Hwy., 269/469-3939, www. redarrowroadhouse.com, 5–10 P.M. Mon.–Thurs., 5–11 P.M. Fri., noon–10 P.M. Sat.–Sun., $8–21) offers inexpensive, homestyle fare in a casual, lodge-style atmosphere. Features include an enclosed patio and weeknight discounts September–May. Up in Harbert, the delectable, old-fashioned **Harbert Swedish Bakery** (13698 Red Arrow Hwy., 269/469-1777, 7 A.M.–3 P.M. Fri.–Mon.) has been here since poet Carl Sandburg ran a goat farm nearby. It still specializes in traditional Swedish breads and cakes.

INFORMATION AND SERVICES

For more information about Harbor Country and the surrounding area, contact the **Harbor Country Chamber of Commerce** (530 S. Whittaker St., Ste. F, New Buffalo,

269/469-5409, www.harborcountry.org, 9 A.M.–5 P.M. Mon.–Fri.) or the **Four Flags Area Council on Tourism** (321 E. Main St., Niles, 269/684-7444, www.fourflagsarea.org, 10 A.M.–3 P.M. Tues. and Thurs.). For local news, consult the *Harbor Country News* (www.harborcountry-news.com).

If you have any mailing needs, you'll find post offices in New Buffalo, Union Pier, Lakeside, Harbert, Sawyer, and Three Oaks. Refer to www.usps.com for **post office** locations and hours. Despite the small size of these lakeside communities, many have necessary services like auto shops, groceries, and banks, including several branches of **Fifth Third Bank** (www.53.com) and **Horizon Bank** (www.accesshorizon.com).

In case of an emergency that requires police, fire, or ambulance services, dial **911** from any cell or public phone. For medical services, visit the **Lakeland Regional Medical Center** (1234 Napier Ave., St. Joseph, 269/983-8300, www.lakelandhealth.org) or the **Lakeland Community Hospital** (31 N. St. Joseph Ave., Niles, 269/683-5510, www.lakelandhealth.org).

GETTING THERE AND AROUND

Although **Amtrak** (800/872-7245, www.amtrak.com) has train stations in New Buffalo (517 S. Whittaker St.) and Niles (598 Dey St.), reaching Harbor Country is much easier if you have a rental car or a vehicle of your own. From Indiana, you can simply drive north along the coast, either on U.S. 12 or I-94. U.S. 12 also gives you easy access to the Four Flags Area, where you'll find the festivals of Niles and the wineries of Buchanan and Berrien Springs. From Muskegon, you can head south on U.S. 31 to Benton Harbor and take I-94 to Harbor Country.

St. Joseph and Benton Harbor

Once called Newberryport, the area now known as St. Joseph grew as a rest stop for travelers between Detroit and Chicago. Set on a bluff overlooking Lake Michigan, "St. Joe" is a pleasant city of 8,500 people with attractive historic buildings and a vibrant downtown shopping district, lined with art galleries, trendy boutiques, and charming coffeehouses. Ship captains and lumber barons built many of the town's 19th-century Victorians; today, vacationers and second-home owners enjoy the bluff-top views of the area's lovely beaches and parks.

Home to the Whirlpool world headquarters and one of the country's oldest Christian communities, Benton Harbor, St. Joseph's slightly larger northern neighbor, has a burgeoning arts community of its own. Together, the two towns present the well-attended Blossomtime Festival, the state's oldest multi-community festival, every spring, and not far away lies a string of wineries that comprise the Lake Michigan Shore Wine Trail.

SIGHTS
Beaches

Many visitors need no more entertainment than the **Silver Beach County Park,** the lovely municipal beach that skirts downtown St. Joseph, a favorite spot for anglers and anyone wishing for a front-row seat to watch the sunset. From here—and from **Tiscornia Beach,** situated near the northern bank of the St. Joseph River—you'll spy the North Pier, a long cement breakwater jutting 1,000 feet into the lake, leading to twin lighthouses that guard the harbor. The farthest light is cylindrical, while the other is perched atop an octagonal, red-roofed structure, a replica of the 1859 lighthouse that once stood on the bluff. The well-photographed North Pierhead Lighthouse was once featured on a U.S. postal stamp commemorating Great Lakes–area lighthouses. When lined up, these two lights guide mariners to St. Joseph's harbor. They remain as one of only two range-light systems in the Great Lakes region; the other is in Grand Haven, farther north.

THE SOUTHWEST COAST

Museums and Historic Sites

Housed in an old brick four-square house above Lake Michigan, St. Joseph's clever **Curious Kids' Museum** (415 Lake Blvd., 269/983-2543, www.curiouskidsmuseum.org, 10 A.M.–5 P.M. Mon.–Thurs. and Sat., 10 A.M.–7 P.M. Fri., noon–5 P.M. Sun., shorter hours Sept.–May, $4–6) ranks as one of the best museums of its kind in the state. From the minute they walk in the door, kids (and adults) are treated to bright, colorful displays—including the lobby murals by eccentric Niles cartoonist/artist Nancy Drew—that are both engaging and playful. Excellent exhibits teach but don't preach: Kids can explore a rainforest, navigate a ship through the Great Lakes, experience what it's like to be handicapped, or follow an apple crop through autumn processing and sell the results at a farm stand.

Down the street at the **Krasl Art Center** (707 Lake Blvd., 269/983-0271, www.krasl. org, 10 A.M.–4 P.M. Mon.–Wed. and Fri.–Sat., 10 A.M.–9 P.M. Thurs., 1–4 P.M. Sun., donation suggested), visitors find both energetic volunteers and a schedule of well-chosen changing exhibits. Four galleries display fine art, contemporary works, folk arts and crafts, creations by regional artists, and occasional traveling exhibitions. A gallery shop offers art-related gifts and other goodies, and the center encourages patrons to take a SculpTour, a self-guided tour of outdoor sculptures in St. Joseph and Benton Harbor.

For history buffs, **The Heritage Museum and Cultural Center** (601 Main St., St. Joseph, 269/983-1191, www.theheritagemcc. org, 10 A.M.–4 P.M. Tues.–Sat., noon–4 P.M. Sun., shorter hours Oct.–May, free, prices vary for special exhibits and events) explores the area's culture and history with exhibits, lectures, walking tours, and extensive archives. Recent exhibits have explored St. Joseph's lighthouses and southwestern Michigan's fruit belt.

While St. Joseph's history harkens back to the 1670s, Benton Harbor's origins began in 1835, when Eleazar Morton and his family became the first white settlers on the northern side of the St. Joseph River. By 1849, they owned 500 acres of farmland, including a peach orchard and a hilltop house overlooking what would become Benton Harbor, founded in part by Eleazar's son Henry. Today, the **Morton House Museum** (501 Territorial Rd., 269/925-7011, www.mortonhousemuseum. com, tours offered 10 A.M.–4 P.M. Mon.–Wed., noon–5 P.M. Sun. May–Sept., $5 adults, $3 seniors 62 and over, $3 children 6–15), the oldest standing home in Benton Harbor, educates visitors about life in the 19th century.

Box Factory for the Arts

Until 1989, the Williams Brothers Box Factory, built near the turn of the 20th century, served as a manufacturing plant for various decorative and specialty boxes. Since 1995, the historic building has been used as an arts facility for local artists and residents. Today, the Box Factory for the Arts (1101 Broad St., St. Joseph, 269/983-3688, www.boxfactoryforthearts.org, 10 A.M.–4 P.M. Mon.–Sat., 1–4 P.M. Sun., free) houses a gift shop, a café, three art galleries, and 37 artists' studios. The center also offers art classes and workshops, presents films on Friday night, and holds concerts every Saturday evening.

◖ Lake Michigan Shore Wine Trail

Thanks to the moderating effects of nearby Lake Michigan, a pocket of southwestern Michigan from Buchanan to Fennville basks in a microclimate surprisingly good for growing grapes. With its sandy soils, gently rolling terrain, and dependable snow cover needed to protect the fragile vines, it has been compared to the wine-producing areas of northern Europe, including France's renowned Champagne region.

While that may be wishful thinking, the state is indeed becoming more and more recognized for its winemaking. (Southwest Michigan is one of two recognized wine regions in the state; the other is farther north, in the Traverse City area.) Early on, wineries experimented with hardy but overly sweet grapes such as Concord and Catawba.

As tastes grew more sophisticated and drier wines became the vogue, French hybrids were introduced, including vidal blanc, from white grapes, and chancellor and chambourcin, from red.

In recent years, Michigan's award-winning wines have become genuine competition for California's crop. Now, Michigan winemakers are building on their growing success by developing their marketing sense along with their grapes. Like California, Michigan works aggressively to promote the picturesque vineyards as a tourist attraction. On weekends, busloads of tourists pour into the St. Julian Winery in Paw Paw for tours. Tabor Hill has a restaurant overlooking its gorgeous vineyards. Warner Vineyards has an elegant tasting room and a charming patio.

Each of the 11 vineyards in this part of the state indeed makes a pleasant warm-weather pilgrimage. You may wish to plan your visit for the weekend after Labor Day, when the three-day Paw Paw Wine & Harvest Festival features free wine-tastings. For more information about Michigan wines, contact the **Lake Michigan Shore Wine Trail** (www.miwinetrail.com) or the **Michigan Grape and Wine Industry Council** (517/241-4468, www.michiganwines.com).

DOMAINE BERRIEN CELLARS AND WINERY

Established in 2001 on part of a family-owned 80-acre fruit farm six miles east of Lake Michigan, Domaine Berrien Cellars and Winery (398 E. Lemon Creek Rd., Berrien Springs, 269/473-9463, www.domaineberrien.com, noon–5 P.M. Wed.–Mon. May–Dec., noon–5 P.M. Fri.–Sun. Jan.–Apr.) is one of the first vineyards you'll encounter on the road from St. Joseph. Although relatively new to the scene, Domaine Berrien has already garnered a reputation for excellent hand-crafted wines, including their award-winning selections like pinot noir, cabernet franc, Syrah, pinot grigio, and traminette. Visitors can tour the winemaking area and enjoy a glass of wine with locally-made cheeses and

sausages on an outside patio overlooking the scenic vineyards.

LEMON CREEK WINERY

Just down the road from Domaine Berrien lies the Lemon Creek Winery and Fruit Farm (533 E. Lemon Creek Rd., Berrien Springs, 269/471-1321, www.lemoncreekwinery.com, 10 A.M.–6 P.M. Mon.–Sat., noon–6 P.M. Sun., shorter hours in winter). The vineyards are part of a 150-year-old, 200-acre fruit farm that has been in the Lemon family for more than a century. The farm began growing grapes in the early 1980s as a way of diversifying crops. The winery opened in 1984, eventually drawing more than 100 awards. Well-known varietals include ruby rose and the full-bodied meritage.

Visitors are welcome to wander among the neatly labeled vines outside the tasting room and picnic at the nearby tables. Afterward, sign on for one of the informal tours that give an overview of wine production, from grape growing through bottling. If the tour inspires you to try your hand at winemaking at home, you can purchase pre-picked grapes or head out to the fields to pluck your own. U-pick options also include raspberries, sweet cherries, nectarines, plums, peaches, and a variety of apples.

FREE RUN CELLARS

Chris and Matt Moersch, the current general manager and winemaker/brewer of the family-run Round Barn Winery, have recently opened a sister winery, Free Run Cellars (10062 Burgoyne Rd., Berrien Springs, 269/471-1737, www.freeruncellars.com, noon–6 P.M. Thurs.–Mon., closed in winter). Hailing from a family with over 25 years of grape-growing and wine-producing experience, the brothers claim they're using this new venture to enhance their family's legacy, "with a reverence to tradition, the desire to explore new ideas, and the free run to find our own style of winemaking." Although no tours are offered, wine connoisseurs can sample wines in the on-site tasting room or visit the year-round tasting room in Union Pier.

THE SOUTHWEST COAST

TABOR HILL WINERY AND RESTAURANT

Today's Tabor Hill (185 Mount Tabor Rd., Buchanan, 269/422-1161 or 800/283-3363, www.taborhill.com, 10 A.M.–5 P.M. Mon.–Tues., 10 A.M.–9 P.M. Wed.–Sat., noon–6 P.M. Sun., tours noon–4:30 P.M. daily May–Oct. and noon–4:30 P.M. Sat.–Sun. Nov.–Apr.) is a far cry from the winery's early commune-like days under visionary founder and salesman Len Olson. David Upton, an heir to the Whirlpool fortune, rescued the ailing operation in the late 1970s, eventually turning it into one of the state's largest producing wineries, best known for its mid-priced wines made from French hybrid grapes, including the classic demi-sec, known as the "President's Wine" because it has been served at the White House, the dry riesling, and the grand mark—all award-winners.

If you're lucky, you'll catch winemaker Michael Merchant giving a tour. After a tour or tasting, consider a stop at Tabor Hill's glass-walled, year-round restaurant, where you can watch workers tending the vines and songbirds crowding the feeders. Views sometimes stretch to the distant Lake Michigan dunes. Entrées such as New Zealand elk chop and macadamia nut–crusted tilapia are always first-rate and feature homemade breads and fresh-from-the-field ingredients. Tabor Hill also has tasting rooms in Bridgman, Benton Harbor, and Saugatuck.

THE ROUND BARN WINERY

Nestled in the rolling hills of the Southwest Coast's countryside, The Round Barn Winery (10983 Hills Rd., Baroda, 800/716-9463, www.roundbarnwinery.com, 11 A.M.–6 P.M. Mon.–Sat., noon–6 P.M. Sun., slightly shorter hours Jan.–Mar.) is a family-owned winery, distillery, and brewery. Once known as the Heart of the Vineyard, it was opened in 1992 by Rick Moersch, formerly a winemaker at Tabor Hill, and specializes in handcrafted wines, fruit brandies, vodka, and microbrews.

An 1880s post-and-beam farmhouse serves as the tasting room, where you can learn about the winery's unique winemaking style, which incorporates techniques pioneered at Michigan State University. A former science teacher, Moersch is more than willing to explain the winery's unique characteristics, including its choice of the French-influenced Alsatian style of winemaking, the unusual vine-trellising system introduced by Michigan State University, and the necessity of yeast in making complex wines. The winery hosts winemaking classes and holiday events throughout the year; there's also an additional tasting room in Union Pier.

HICKORY CREEK WINERY

The southernmost winery along the Lake Michigan Shore Wine Trail, Hickory Creek (750 Browntown Rd., Buchanan, 269/422-1100, www.hickorycreekwinery.com, 11 A.M.–6 P.M. Fri.–Sat., noon–6 P.M. Sun., by appointment Mon.–Thurs.) is the product of three distinct perspectives; the winery's trio of owners, all of whom share a lifelong passion for winemaking, hail from three premier

The Round Barn Winery in Baroda

wine-growing nations: America, Australia, and Germany. Hickory Creek specializes in crafting world-class wines from grapes grown exclusively along Lake Michigan's eastern shore. Current selections include riesling, chardonnay, pinot noir, gewürztraminer, and apple wine.

CONTESSA WINE CELLARS

Between Benton Harbor and Paw Paw, you'll find Contessa Wine Cellars (3235 Friday Rd., Coloma, 269/468-5534, www.contessawinecellars.com, noon–5 P.M. daily), the brainchild of third-generation winemaker Tony Peterson, who longed to blend traditional winemaking practices with old-world ambience. Here, visitors are treated to an enormous selection of wines, from a full-bodied merlot to a dry white divino, served in an elegant tasting room that's reminiscent of an Italian villa. The view's not bad either; from the winery's European-style terrace, you can look across acres of stunning orchards, nestled in the verdant Coloma Valley.

KARMA VISTA
VINEYARDS AND WINERY

Just a little farther east, on the road to Paw Paw, you'll encounter Karma Vista (6991 Ryno Rd., Coloma, 269/468-9463, www.karmavista.com, 11 A.M.–5 P.M. Mon. and Wed.–Sat., noon–5 P.M. Sun., shorter hours in winter), which prides itself on being "one of Michigan's newest wineries from one of the state's oldest farm families." Situated on a serene hillside above the town of Coloma, Karma Vista promises a relaxing experience for wine connoisseurs. Those with a sense of humor will also appreciate this quirky winery, where the colorful wine labels will elicit a chuckle. Who, after all, can resist sampling selections like Cha Cha Chardonnay, Watusi Red, Stone Temple Pinot, and Moondance Merlot?

ST. JULIAN WINERY

Family-owned St. Julian (716 S. Kalamazoo St., Paw Paw, 269/657-5568, www.stjulian.com, 9 A.M.–6 P.M. Mon.–Sat., noon–6 P.M.

Sun.) has always prided itself on making good wines that are accessible to a wide variety of tastes and budgets. The winery is located on a busy commercial strip and is heavily marketed to tour buses and groups, so it isn't exactly on par with the personalized attention given by smaller boutique wineries. What the oldest and largest winery in the state does well is wine education and wine-related tourism: Its year-round tours include an informative audiovisual show, and a visit to the bottling line and fermenting room. Visitors in late August and September can watch grapes being delivered and crushed. The winery and its Union Pier, Dundee, and Frankenmuth tasting rooms are open year-round.

WARNER VINEYARDS

Next to St. Julian's, Warner Vineyards (706 S. Kalamazoo St., Paw Paw, 269/657-3165 or 800/756-5357, www.warnerwines.com, 10 A.M.–5 P.M. Mon.–Sat., noon–5 P.M. Sun.), the state's second oldest winery, operates out of an appealing 1898 waterworks building. Founded in 1938, Warner boasts one of the Midwest's only champagne cellars, which realistically simulates the chalk storage vaults of the Champagne region of France. Visitors can take a short, self-guided tour, then relax afterward over a glass of bubbly (or any of the other Warner wines) on the charming wine deck. Warner's specialties include their award-winning dry champagne and the popular *liebestrauben* and holiberry. Warner also offers a tasting room in South Haven.

FENN VALLEY VINEYARDS
AND WINE CELLAR

The northernmost winery on the Lake Michigan Shore Wine Trail, Fenn Valley (6130 122nd Ave., Fennville, 269/561-2396, www.fennvalley.com, 11 A.M.–5 P.M. Mon.–Sat., 1–5 P.M. Sun.) isn't far from the art galleries of Saugatuck and Douglas. Since 1973, this family-operated winery has been producing award-winning handcrafted wines that benefit from the combination of a favorable climate, traditional winemaking techniques, and

THE SOUTHWEST COAST

modern technology. Vineyard tours are offered on weekends August–October; tastings are included for a nominal fee. Cellar tours and special events are offered year-round. Fenn Valley also has a tasting room in nearby Saugatuck.

FESTIVALS AND EVENTS
◖ Blossomtime Festival

Among southwestern Michigan's many warm-weather events, one highlight is the Blossomtime Festival, usually held in early May in the neighboring communities of St. Joseph and Benton Harbor. Begun in 1923 to promote the area's agricultural industry, the Blossomtime Festival (269/926-7397, www.blossomtimefestival.org) celebrates the coming of spring with a Grand Floral Parade featuring more than 125 floats, tractors, antique cars, bands, and costumed performers from several surrounding communities. As the oldest and largest multi-community festival in Michigan, Blossomtime also fills the weeklong celebration with children's events, food tents, pageants, and more.

Venetian Festival

Held in late July on Silver Beach and the St. Joseph River, the Venetian Festival has, for over three decades, celebrated St. Joseph's sunny shores and waterfront culture with boat rides and love songs. For four days, the Venetian Festival (269/983-7917, www.venetian.org) brings the community together with wine-tastings, food vendors, sand-sculpture competitions, marathon swims, classic car shows, fireworks displays, big-name entertainment, and, of course, the famous lighted boat parade.

Other Area Festivals

Given the Southwest Coast's notoriety as a significant wine-producing region, it's no surprise that the **Paw Paw Wine & Harvest Festival** (269/655-1111, www.wineandharvestfestival.com) takes place every September, the weekend after Labor Day. During the three-day event, festival-goers can enjoy live music, carnival rides, car shows, turtle derbies, and grape-stomping contests. Meanwhile, wine connoisseurs are treated to free winery tours and wine-tastings at St. Julian Winery and Warner Vineyards, all weekend long.

To the southeast, in nearby Cass County, you'll find at least two other fun-filled events. In late July or early August, the six-day **Cass County Fair** (Cassopolis, 269/445-8265, www.casscountyfair.com, $6 adults, $1 children 6–12) invites revelers to watch or participate in dog shows, livestock competitions, demolition derbies, tractor pulls, parades, and other farm-related activities. In mid-May, the **Dogwood Fine Arts Festival** (Dowagiac, 269/782-1115, www.dogwoodfinearts.org) entices lovers of art, music, dance, and literature with a week of lectures, concerts, performances, and readings from regional artists.

SHOPPING

While St. Joseph's State Street shopping district contains a myriad of bookstores, gift shops, clothing boutiques, and jewelry emporiums, perhaps the highlight of this region is its bountiful produce. Nature's fruits can be enjoyed at two of the area's largest growers: **Fruit Acres Farm Market & U-Pick** (3390 Friday Rd., Coloma, 269/468-5076, www.fruitacresfarms.com, 9 A.M.–7 P.M. daily June–Oct.) and **Tree-Mendus Fruit Farm** (9351 E. Eureka Rd., Eau Claire, 269/782-7101, www.treemendus-fruit.com, 10 A.M.–6 P.M. Wed.–Mon. June–Aug., 10 A.M.–6 P.M. Fri.–Mon. Sept.–Oct.).

Since 1964, the family-operated Fruit Acres has provided area communities with a wide range of fresh produce and products. Today, the 230-acre orchard boasts seasonal crops of plums, peaches, black cherries, tree-ripened apricots, and crisp apples. The market also sells apple cider; flowers, fruit, and vegetables from other area farmers; and locally-made jams, jellies, salsas, and other condiments. During the season, visitors can pick their own fruit every Saturday and Sunday. Leashed dogs are welcome.

Tree-Mendus is one of the area's best U-pick farms, with acres upon acres of apples, pears, cherries, nectarines, peaches, plums, and more. Don't miss the chance to bite into one of the special heritage apples, a hobby of Tree-Mendus's curator. Besides the full fields, there's also a full roster of special events such as pony rides, harvest-time activities, and the International Cherry Pit–Spitting Championship.

SPORTS AND RECREATION
Golf

Near the intersection of I-94 and I-196, **Lake Michigan Hills Golf Club** (2520 Kerlikowske Rd., Benton Harbor, 269/849-4653, www.lakemichiganhills.com, daily Apr.–Oct., $35–55 w/cart) has been voted one of the best public golf courses in southwestern Michigan by *Michigan Golfer* magazine. Farther inland, you'll find several other well-favored courses, including **Paw Paw Lake Golf Course** (4548 Forest Beach Rd., Watervliet, 269/463-3831, www.pawpawlakegolfcourse.com, daily Apr.–Oct., $24–29 w/o cart) and **Indian Lake Hills Golf Course** (55321 Brush Lake Rd., Eau Claire, 269/782-2540, www.indianlakehills.com, daily Apr.–Oct., $20–39 w/cart).

Bird-Watching

Those who seek sanctuary find it at the **Sarett Nature Center** (2300 Benton Center Rd., Benton Harbor, 269/927-4832, www.sarett.com, 9 A.M.–5 P.M. Tues.–Fri., 10 A.M.–5 P.M. Sat., 1–5 P.M. Sun., donation suggested). These 800 acres along the Paw Paw River northeast of Benton Harbor comprise a number of natural habitats, including upland meadows, swamp forests, and lowland marshes. As a nod to bird-watchers, the property contains many benches, elevated towers, and five miles of trails, which are open dawn to dusk every day. A naturalist is usually on hand to answer questions. Ask about the full schedule of demonstrations, nature walks, workshops, and classes.

Boating and Fishing

As with most of the towns along the Southwest Coast, St. Joseph and Benton Harbor share both a shipping past and a modern-day boating fever, as evidenced by the 30 colorful boat

sculptures throughout downtown St. Joseph and by the full-service **Pier 1000 Marina** (1000 Riverview Dr., 269/927-4471, www.pier1000.com) in adjacent Benton Harbor. There's nothing quite like sailing off across the blue expanse of Lake Michigan on a cloudless summer day.

But, even if you don't have your own boat, you can still enjoy venturing out on the water. **Headhunter Charters** (10034 Painter School Rd., Berrien Center, 269/461-0034, www.headhuntersportfishing.com, rates vary) specializes in year-round, open-water sportfishing charters on Lake Michigan and guided river trips for salmon and steelhead on the St. Joseph River.

ACCOMMODATIONS AND FOOD

Overlooking Lake Michigan, **◖ The Boulevard Hotel Inn & Bistro** (521 Lake Blvd., St. Joseph, 269/983-6600, www.theboulevardinn.com, $100–200 d) provides spacious suites, a genteel decor, and a super restaurant (269/983-3882, $8–31) that offers breakfast, lunch, and dinner daily. Dinner can be especially wonderful here; take a seat on the lovely outdoor terrace, order the chef's three-course special, select from one of the world's most outstanding restaurant wine lists, and enjoy the incredible lake views below. As a bonus, the Boulevard is within easy walking distance of shops, restaurants, and beaches.

The **South Cliff Inn** (1900 Lakeshore Dr., St. Joseph, 269/983-4881, www.southcliffinn.com, $85–229 d) is a gracious English-inspired bed-and-breakfast with seven sun-filled rooms that also overlook the big lake. It's run by charming Bill Swisher, who left behind a 10-year career as director of a probate court to open the inn.

If you'd feel more comfortable in a chain hotel, you'll find several in the area. Benton Harbor has at least two options: **Howard Johnson** (798 Ferguson Dr., 269/927-1172, www.hojo.com, $60–150 d) and **Courtyard St. Joseph/Benton Harbor** (1592 Mall Dr., 269/925-3000, www.marriott.com, $120–200 d).

THE SOUTHWEST COAST

Comfort Inn & Suites (153 Ampey Rd., Paw Paw, 269/655-0303, www.comfortinn.com, $85–100 d) is located in the heart of southwestern Michigan's wine country.

As for area vittles, **Schu's Grill & Bar** (501 Pleasant St., 269/983-7248, www.schus.com, 11 A.M.–10 P.M. Mon.–Thurs., 11 A.M.–11 P.M. Fri.–Sat., 11 A.M.–9 P.M. Sun., $8–22) has quickly become a St. Joseph institution, with great sandwiches, soups, and brews in a pub-style setting above the waterfront. For morning coffee and baked goods, head for **Caffe Tosi** (516 Pleasant St., St. Joseph, 269/983-3354, www.caffetosi.com, 7 A.M.–8 P.M. Mon.–Fri., 8 A.M.–8 P.M. Sat., 8 A.M.–4 P.M. Sun., $4–9).

Camping

For a real bargain, there are two excellent campgrounds in the vicinity. The **Dune Lake Campground** (80855 Country Road 376, Coloma, 269/764-8941, www.dunelake-campground.com, $24–28) welcomes RVs and tents to a picturesque area not far from Lake Michigan. Farther inland, **Shamrock Park** (9385 Old U.S. 31 S. Berrien Springs, 269/473-5691, www.shamrockpark.net, $15–25), a year-round camping and fishing park in the heart of wine country, provides easy access to several of the wineries along the Lake Michigan Shore Wine Trail. For those without a tent or an RV, both campgrounds also offer rental cabins.

INFORMATION AND SERVICES

For more information about St. Joseph, Benton Harbor, and the surrounding area, contact the **Southwestern Michigan Tourist Council** (2300 Pipestone Rd., Benton Harbor, 269/925-6301, www.swmichigan.org, 8:30 A.M.–5 P.M. Mon.–Fri.), the **Coloma-Watervliet Area Chamber of Commerce** (209 N. Paw Paw St., Coloma, 269/468-9160, www.coloma-watervliet.org, 9 A.M.–5 P.M. Mon.–Fri.), or

the **Four Flags Area Council on Tourism** (321 E. Main St., Niles, 269/684-7444, www.fourflagsarea.org, 10 A.M.–3 P.M. Tues. and Thurs.). For local news and weather, consult *The Herald-Palladium* (www.heraldpalladium.com). For county information, contact the **Berrien County Administration** (www.berriencounty.org).

For mailing needs, visit the **St. Joseph post office** (205 Main St., 269/983-1579, www.usps.com); Benton Harbor has several locations, too. Both towns also have necessary services like groceries, dentists, and banks, including a few branches of **Fifth Third Bank** (www.53.com).

In case of an emergency, dial **911** from any cell or public phone. For medical services, visit the **Lakeland Regional Medical Center** (1234 Napier Ave., St. Joseph, 269/983-8300, www.lakelandhealth.org). If necessary, you can fill prescriptions at **Rite Aid** in Benton Harbor (1701 S. M-139, 269/927-3101, www.riteaid.com).

GETTING THERE AND AROUND

Amtrak (800/872-7245, www.amtrak.com) offers rail service between Chicago and St. Joseph (410½ Vine St.), **Greyhound** provides bus service to Benton Harbor (2412 M-139, 269/925-1121, www.greyhound.com), and the **Kalamazoo/Battle Creek International Airport (AZO)** (5235 Portage Rd., Kalamazoo, 269/388-3668, www.azoairport.com) isn't too far east via I-94. Still, exploring St. Joseph, Benton Harbor, and the surrounding wine country is infinitely easier with a vehicle. Whether you're coming from Indiana or Kalamazoo, you can take I-94 directly to the St. Joseph/Benton Harbor area. From here, I-94, I-196, and U.S. 31 provide easy access to the wineries and tasting rooms along the Lake Michigan Shore Wine Trail.

South Haven

Once the center of Michigan's "fruit belt," the South Haven area is still a leading producer of blueberries and peaches. Lake Michigan can take credit for the area's well-drained soil and the moderating temperature effects of the prevailing west winds. Southwest Michigan's fruit belt had its origins in the 1850s, when St. Joseph and Benton Harbor farmers noticed that their peaches survived the severe winters that killed off other crops in the rest of the state. Fresh fruit was in high demand in bustling Chicago, and by the 1860s, crops were being shipped across the lake almost as fast as they could be picked.

Eventually, fruit farming and fruit-related industries spread throughout much of Van Buren and Berrien Counties. South Haven became famous for its peach crop; at the turn of the 20th century, some 144,000 acres were devoted to peaches, more than all the other fruit crops combined. But freezes during the 1920s led many farmers to abandon peaches in favor of heartier apples. More recently, blueberries have gained popularity, with the area around South Haven emerging as the world's leading blueberry producer. In July (National Blueberry Month), you'll spot blueberry stands along rural roadsides.

South Haven proper is known for its beautiful beaches and scenic fishing port, which prompted the *London Financial Times* to call it "one of the most picturesque and charming small fishing ports you could hope to find." In summer, the population of this lakeside town swells from 5,000 to nearly 20,000, as visitors fill the historic inns that line North Shore Drive, stroll along the walks and shops that parallel the Black River near its mouth, and sunbathe on the long arc of sand beach that rims the town's northwestern edge. The town also offers its share of museums, festivals, golf courses, and other outdoor pleasures, including the trailhead of the Kal-Haven Trail, popular among hikers and bikers.

SIGHTS

Beaches

Seven lovely beaches line the Lake Michigan shore, north and south of where the Black River opens into the great lake. **North Beach,** situated on the northern bank of the river, is a hot spot for summertime beachgoers, with its volleyball courts and concession stand. For swimmers who enjoy a few less people and a little more quiet, **Packard Park Beach** farther north might be your best bet. But, for those eager to sunbathe, watch passing boats, and take a stroll toward the vibrant red-and-black **South Haven South Pierhead Light, South Beach** is definitely the place for you. Established in 1903 at the end of the South Pier and accessible via a sturdy catwalk, the cylindrical lighthouse is still active today; of course, most visitors just enjoy walking along the picturesque pier for an up-close glimpse.

Museums

The **Michigan Maritime Museum** (260 Dyckman Ave., 269/637-8078, www.michiganmaritimemuseum.org, 10 A.M.–5 P.M. daily, $5 adults, $4 seniors, $3.50 students, children under 6 free) features a variety of maritime displays, some of which chronicle the U.S. Coast Guard and the commercial fishermen who plied the local waters. Another intriguing attraction is the **Michigan Flywheelers Museum** (06285 68th St., 269/639-2010, www.michiganflywheelers.org, 10 A.M.–3 P.M. Wed. and Sat.–Sun. Memorial Day–Labor Day), dedicated to the preservation of antique gas engines, steam engines, and tractors. In early September, the museum hosts its annual Antique Engine and Tractor Show, which includes historic demonstrations and a flea market as well as the usual parades, games, and crafts.

Van Buren State Park

South of South Haven, Van Buren State Park (23960 Ruggles Rd., 269/637-2788, daily, state park vehicle permit required) boasts some of the best water views in this part of the state. The high, wooded sand dunes of the 400-acre park hide a narrow opening that leads to the property's main attraction: the limitless blue waters of Lake Michigan, edged by a broad sweep of fine, black-speckled sand. "No Trespassing" signs on the huge barrier dunes hopefully prevent human erosion from adding to the natural wear of the fragile sand mountains.

ENTERTAINMENT AND EVENTS
The Arts
In addition to displaying a wide array of visual arts, the **South Haven Center for the Arts** (600 Phoenix St., 269/637-1041, www.southhavenarts.org, 10 A.M.–5 P.M. Tues.–Thurs., 10 A.M.–4 P.M. Fri., 1–4 P.M. Sat.–Sun., event prices vary) hosts numerous concerts each year, showcasing styles as varied as Brazilian jazz, Celtic and classical music, blues, and folk.

National Blueberry Festival
South Haven hosts several different events during the year, but the town's probably best known for its long-standing National Blueberry Festival (www.blueberryfestival.com), which takes place in early August. Besides standard fare like raffles, pageants, parades, and the like, this four-day event does its best to celebrate the blessed fruit with blueberry pie–eating contests, blueberry pancake breakfasts, and blueberry-related cooking demonstrations.

SHOPPING
While South Haven has a few whimsical shops—such as **Decadent Dogs** (505 Phoenix St., 269/639-0716, www.decadentdogs.com, 10 A.M.–9 P.M. daily in summer, shorter hours in winter), a terrific place to pamper your pooch with glitzy collars, fancy treat jars, and the like—shopping in these parts is all about the fruit. For blueberries and blueberry products—including everything from jellies to plush toys—check out the **Blueberry Store** (525 Phoenix St., 269/637-6322, www.theblueberrystore.com, 9 A.M.–9 P.M. Mon.–Sat.,

9 A.M.–5 P.M. Sun. in spring/summer, shorter hours in fall/winter).

In addition, there are several farms, markets, and orchards in the vicinity, including the **South Haven Farmers' Market** (546 Phoenix St., 8 A.M.–2 P.M. Sat. May–mid-Oct.), a smorgasbord of locally-grown seasonal produce behind Dyckman Park. Northeast of South Haven, you'll find **McIntosh Apple Orchards** (6431 107th Ave., 708/878-3734, www.mcintoshorchards.com, Fri.–Sun. Apr.–June, daily July–Aug., Wed.–Sun. Sept.–Dec.), a 76-acre orchard and winery that's home to 26 different apple varieties. Here, you can purchase a myriad of homegrown products, including traditional hard cider.

SPORTS AND RECREATION
Golf
Golfers shouldn't miss playing a round at **HawksHead** (523 HawksNest Dr., 269/639-2121, www.hawksheadlinks.com, daily Apr.–Oct., $30–70), once an asparagus farm that has now become one of the state's highest-ranked resorts, with a fine restaurant, a luxurious inn, and a championship course overlooking Lake Michigan. Another excellent choice is **Beeches Golf Club** (09601 68th St., 269/637-2600, www.beechesgolfclub.com, daily Apr.–Oct., $44–49 w/cart), which offers five sets of tee boxes, sandy waste areas on the front nine holes, and water hazards on the back nine—a challenge for almost any player.

Hiking and Biking
The **Kal-Haven Trail** (www.kalhaventrail.org), open to hiking and biking, stretches from South Haven to Kalamazoo, along the abandoned Kalamazoo & South Haven Railroad, which existed from 1870 to 1970. There are several access points along the 34-mile route, which passes through the towns of Grand Junction, Bloomingdale, Gobles, and Kendall. The trail is also popular among bird-watchers, cross-country skiers, and snowmobilers. Trail passes ($3 individuals or $7 families daily, $15 individuals or $35 families yearly) are required for use of the trail; they can be purchased at

various stores, restaurants, and museums, as well as the South Haven Visitors Bureau.

Diving

Given the shipping histories of the towns along the Southwest Coast, including St. Joseph, South Haven, Saugatuck, Holland, and Grand Haven, it's no surprise that underwater shipwrecks line the Lake Michigan shore. Established in 1999, the **Southwest Michigan Underwater Preserve** comprises at least 15 shipwrecks and geological formations between New Buffalo and Holland, with the greatest concentration of sites near South Haven. Some of the more popular ones include the *Rockaway,* a 107-foot schooner lost in a storm while transporting lumber from Ludington to Benton Harbor, and the *Havana,* a 92-foot yacht that sank in heavy seas en route from Chicago to Holland. Divers are welcome to explore these and other fascinating relics, though it's strongly advised that they bring along a compass, tow a warning flag, and watch out for obstacles that could cause entanglement. For more information, contact the **Michigan Underwater Preserve Council** (800/970-8717, www.michiganpreserves.org).

ACCOMMODATIONS AND FOOD

South Haven has no shortage of lodgings, from campgrounds to luxurious resorts. The **Old Harbor Inn** (515 Williams St., 269/637-8480, www.oldharborinn.com, $90–300 d) is part of a New England–style waterfront shopping village, on the banks of the Black River—a great location, with extras like a friendly bar. **The Last Resort B&B Inn** (86 N. Shore Dr., 269/637-8943, www.lastresortinn.com, $100–225 d) was, ironically, South Haven's first resort. A few rooms have been updated with whirlpool suites, but the place has a funky, laid-back feel to it, largely due to its artist/owner Mary Hammer. All rooms and suites offer views of Lake Michigan or the garden. It's open from early May through October. **Lake Bluff Inn & Suites** (76648 11th Ave., 269/637-8531,

www.lakebluffinnandsuites.com, $53–227 d) is a well-kept waterfront resort that has been expanded over the years. It sits on a lovely bluff-top site south of South Haven, with outdoor pools, an indoor hot tub, a playground, and wireless Internet access.

Clementine's (500 Phoenix St., 269/637-4755, www.ohmydarling.com, 11 A.M.–10 P.M. Mon.–Thurs., 11 A.M.–11 P.M. Fri.–Sat., noon–10 P.M. Sun., $8–19), originally a bank, is now a beloved family-owned restaurant. Don't miss the old pictures of Lake Michigan steamers and their captains and crews on the walls. The magnificently carved bar spent its first life on one of the many steamboats that once frequented the city. Almost everything on the menu has a clever, countrified moniker, but specialties include the Golden Garter (a fried pork sandwich) and the Tugboat Annie (charbroiled steak smothered with mushrooms, crab, shrimp, and mozzarella).

Camping

Like the area's other waterfront state parks, **Van Buren State Park** (23960 Ruggles Rd., 269/637-2788, daily, state park vehicle permit required) draws visitors because it offers a beach as well as the wooded dunes of Lake Michigan. Its 220 modern sites ($16–23 per night) are a five-minute walk from the beach and frequently fill on summer weekends. For reservations, which are highly recommended, call 800/447-2757 or visit www.michigan.gov/dnr.

For fancier environs, you can opt for the **Sunny Brook RV Resort** (68300 County Road 388, 888/499-5253, www.sunnybrookrvresort.com, $35–45), which includes a pool, a laundry and bathhouse, hiking trails, and a fishing lake. The resort is open mid-April–October.

INFORMATION AND SERVICES

For more information about South Haven, contact the **South Haven Visitors Bureau** (546 Phoenix St., 269/637-5252 or 800/764-2836, www.southhaven.org, 9 A.M.–5 P.M. Mon.–Fri., 10 A.M.–5 P.M. Sat., 11 A.M.–4 P.M. Sun., shorter hours in winter) or the **Greater South Haven Chamber of Commerce** (606 Phillips St., 269/637-5171, www.southhavenmi.com, 9 A.M.–5 P.M. Mon.–Fri.). For county information, contact the **Van Buren County Community Center** (www.vbco.org).

For mailing needs, visit the **South Haven post office** (336 Broadway St., 269/637-1283, www.usps.com). If you need an ATM, you'll find several branches of **Fifth Third Bank** (www.53.com) in the area, including one in South Haven and another in nearby Bangor.

In case of an emergency, dial **911** from any cell or public phone. For medical services, visit the **South Haven Community Hospital** (955 S. Bailey Ave., 269/637-5271, www.shch.org); prescriptions can be filled at the **Wal-Mart Supercenter** (201 73rd St., 269/637-7802, www.walmart.com).

GETTING THERE AND AROUND

Although there are no direct flights to South Haven, you can get pretty close by flying into the **Kalamazoo/Battle Creek International Airport (AZO)** (5235 Portage Rd., Kalamazoo, 269/388-3668, www.azoairport.com), where you can rent a car and head west on M-43 toward Lake Michigan. **Amtrak** (800/872-7245, www.amtrak.com), meanwhile, offers rail service between Chicago and Bangor (541 Railroad St.), about 10 miles southeast of South Haven. To reach South Haven directly, you can either hop a **Greyhound** bus (1210 Phoenix Rd., 269/637-2944, www.greyhound.com) or take a road trip. If you're driving from elsewhere along the coast, you'll more than likely take I-196/U.S. 31—whether you're coming from Benton Harbor or Saugatuck.

Saugatuck and Douglas

Some claim success has spoiled Saugatuck. Visit on a summer weekend, and you may be inclined to agree, when the city's narrow streets fill with much of what urban refugees are looking to escape: long lines in restaurants, shops overstuffed with designer threads, and beaches clogged with humanity. But come in any other season—or even midweek in summer—and Saugatuck reveals its real charm. The streets quiet down; you can linger over the excellent local cuisine and rich arts scene. And the folks who run the village's many fine B&Bs kick back and remember why they originally got into the business.

Saugatuck ("river's mouth" in the parlance of the Potawatomi tribe that settled the area) grew up in a fine natural setting—near the mouth of the wide Kalamazoo River, tucked between steep, rolling Lake Michigan dunes immediately west and lush, green orchards immediately east. Lumber interests discovered the region in the mid-1800s. Soon, it was home to a thriving mix of sawmills, factories, and the people to support them. Saugatuck, in fact,

produced the majority of the lumber used to rebuild Chicago after the Great Fire in 1871.

When the trees inevitably disappeared, so did much of the city. The lack of trees proved especially fateful to a neighboring village known as Singapore. Without the windbreak the trees provided, blowing sand carried by the prevailing western winds eventually buried the city. Today, this ghost town lives on in local lore and in stories told by area tour guides.

While Singapore became the stuff of legend, Saugatuck survived and found new life as an art colony. In 1911, artists from the Art Institute of Chicago, less than two hours away, began sponsoring a summer art camp. Lured by the warm breezes and picturesque location, other creative types soon followed, earning Saugatuck an early reputation as Michigan's "Art Coast." Today, the Ox-Bow School of the Arts is still open to the public from June through August and includes galleries, demonstrations, and changing exhibitions.

Douglas, Saugatuck's nearest neighbor, has also evolved over the years. Established in 1851

SAUGATUCK AND DOUGLAS

To Saugatuck Dunes State Park

LUCY ST

SAUGATUCK BOAT CRUISES/ ★
STAR OF SAUGATUCK II

SPEAR ST

BLUE STAR HWY

MAPLE ST

IDA RED'S
COTTAGE

FRANCIS ST

CHAIN FERRY ●
WICKWOOD COUNTRY INN ●

MARY ST

MAPLEWOOD HOTEL ●

Saugatuck

LINCOLN RD

To Oval Beach

MAIN ST

SINGAPORE BANK BOOKSTORE
AMERICAN SPOON FOODS

MOTHER MOON ●

HOFFMAN ST

PUMPERNICKEL'S EATERY

GOOD GOODS ★

TWIN OAKS INN

SAUGATUCK DRUG STORE

CHEMICAL BANK

MASON ST

CHEQUERS ▼▼

SAUGATUCK CENTER
FOR THE ARTS

CULVER ST

ALLEGAN ST

132ND AVE

RESTAURANT
TOULOUSE

CAPTAIN'S
QUARTERS MOTEL ●

RIVER RD

LAKE ST

PLEASANT ST

STATE ST

FERRY ST

Kalamazoo

Harbor

BRADLEY RD

River
Bluff
Park

196

KEEWATIN MARITIME MUSEUM ★

Douglas

BLUE STAR HWY

BUTTON GALLERY/ ★
CONSTANCE PETTER
GALLERY

HAMILTON ST

THE PINES
MOTOR LODGE ●

UNION ST

MAIN ST

WASHINGTON ST

0   300 yds

0   300 m

CENTER ST

© AVALON TRAVEL

as a port for ships carrying lumber and produce to Chicago and other cities in the Great Lakes area, this small village-by-the-sea is now a popular vacation spot. Together, Saugatuck and Douglas have become two of the state's premier resort towns, boasting historic homes, quaint eateries, unique shops, and, of course, art galleries galore.

SIGHTS
The Keewatin Maritime Museum

The S.S. *Keewatin* (Blue Star Hwy. at Union St., 269/857-2464, www.keewatinmaritimemuseum.com, 10:30 A.M.–4 P.M. daily Memorial Day–Labor Day, $12–25 adults, $6–12 children 6–12) is hard to miss. Docked near the bridge that separates Saugatuck from neighboring Douglas, the 350-foot-long cruise ship had to be cut in half to fit through the narrow channel linking Lake Michigan and the Kalamazoo River. Now reassembled as a tourist attraction, it's a fascinating tribute to a lost era. The *Keewatin* was built in 1907, one of the last of the steamships that plied the Great Lakes. Informative tours show off its ornate mahogany interior, and allow you to relive the elegant era when passengers toured the lakes to revel in their beauty, fresh air, and fine beaches.

THE SOUTHWEST COAST

◖ Art Galleries

The area's reputation as an "Art Coast" has attracted over 30 galleries within Saugatuck, Douglas, and Fennville. Notable stops include the **Button Gallery** (161 Blue Star Hwy., Douglas, 269/857-2175, 11 A.M.–5 P.M. Mon.–Sat., noon–5 P.M. Sun., shorter hours in winter), with its spectacular outdoor sculpture garden, and the eclectic **Good Goods** (106 Mason St., Saugatuck, 269/857-1557, www.goodgoods.com, 10 A.M.–6 P.M. Sun.–Wed., 10 A.M.–7 P.M. Thurs., 10 A.M.–10 P.M. Fri.–Sat.), housed in a restored Victorian boardinghouse. Good Goods is the only place in town where you can pick up a one-of-a-kind piece by one of the area's founding artists, Sylvia Randolph, amazingly prolific into her 90s. The **Constance Petter Gallery** (161 Blue Star Hwy., Douglas, 269/857-7861, www.constancepettergallery.com, 11 A.M.–5 P.M. daily) has been western Michigan's largest fine art marketplace for more than 20 years. Between South Haven and Saugatuck, you'll also encounter the **Blue Coast Artists** (www.bluecoastartists.com, locations and hours vary), a group of six artists who allow visitors a behind-the-scenes look into their studios and galleries every spring, summer, and fall; some are even open year-round by appointment.

Beaches and Parks

If you're seeking a little more solitude, head instead for 1,000-acre **Saugatuck Dunes State Park** (269/637-2788, daily, state park vehicle permit required). Despite 2.5 miles of undeveloped beach and dunes, and 14 miles of well-marked trails (some winding to the top of the dunes for fantastic views), only about 40,000 visit annually—the least-visited park along this popular shoreline. Just a few miles north of Saugatuck, the park, which has no office or campground, offers easy-to-reach serenity in stark contrast to the downtown district.

Just a few steps from the shop-lined streets of Saugatuck, the frilly gingerbread **Chain Ferry** (269/857-2603, www.saugatuck.com, Memorial Day–Labor Day) shuttles visitors across the Kalamazoo River to the sandy Lake Michigan shore at **Oval Beach.** Families flock to this popular beach, filling the broad ribbon of sand and scaling Mount Baldhead, the steep dune that rises between town and the beach.

Tours

The two-level sternwheeler docked on the riverfront, the **Star of Saugatuck II,** offers cruises along the Kalamazoo River. Along the way, she passes beautiful homes, including one that once belonged to gangster Al Capone. (Keep in mind that in the Midwest, Capone apparently lived in as many places as Lincoln slept.) It operates May–October. For schedules, contact **Saugatuck Boat Cruises** (269/857-4261, www.saugatuckboatcruises.com, $16 adults, $8 children 6–12, $5 children 3–5, children under 3 free).

If you prefer land-based tours, consider **Saugatuck Dune Rides** (269/857-2253, www.saugatuckduneride.com, hours vary, $16 adults, $10 children 3–10). Expert guides lead small groups on 40-minute rides through the area's impressive dunes, sharing tales of the lost town of Singapore and educating visitors about local vegetation and wildlife.

ENTERTAINMENT AND EVENTS
The Arts

Visual arts are not Saugatuck's only creative claim to fame. The **Saugatuck Center for the Arts** (400 Culver St., 269/857-2399, www.sc4a.org, hours and prices vary) has, in addition to paintings and other artistic exhibitions, two theater spaces that present a variety of concerts, films, and comedy shows.

Festivals and Events

If possible, try to visit Saugatuck during one of its summertime festivals and art fairs. One that you should definitely not miss is the **Waterfront Film Festival** (various venues, 269/857-8351, www.waterfrontfilm.org, $10 per film). In mid-June, this well-respected film fest brings a bit of Hollywood to Saugatuck. For one weekend, filmgoers, actors, producers, and directors converge for outstanding independent films from around the country, all screened in a casual setting.

CLAES OLDENBURG: AN OX-BOW ALUMNUS

Founded in 1910 along the shores of Lake Michigan, Saugatuck's **Ox-Bow School of the Arts** (3435 Rupprecht Way, 269/857-5811, www.ox-bow.org), a summer art school and artists' residency, has long inspired visual artists with its 115-acre campus of pristine forests, dunes, marshes, and historic buildings. Affiliated with the School of the Art Institute of Chicago, Ox-Bow offers courses in ceramics, glass, painting, drawing, papermaking, print, and metals. Not surprisingly, this prestigious school has lured many distinguished students, teachers, visiting artists, and board members over the years, from painter/sculptor Max Kahn to puppeteer Jim Henson – who, according to author Kit Lane (in her 1997 book *Painting the Town: A History of Art in Saugatuck and Douglas*), supposedly created an early version of his Kermit the Frog character amid Ox-Bow's pastoral splendor.

Claes Oldenburg, perhaps Ox-Bow's most famous alumnus, arrived in 1953 as a student. The son of a diplomat, Oldenburg was born in Sweden in 1929. As a child, he immigrated with his family to America, where he lived in New York and Chicago, and eventually studied literature and art history at Yale University. Back in the Windy City, he worked as a newspaper reporter, while taking lessons at the Art Institute of Chicago. By 1953, he'd become a naturalized U.S. citizen and opened his own art studio.

During his summer at Ox-Bow, he further honed his artistic skills, dabbling in oil painting and staging his first "happening" – a choreographed combination of music, dance, dramatics, and poetry for which he and other artists became famous during the late 1950s and early 1960s. At Ox-Bow's annual end-of-summer farewell, Oldenburg planned a series of sulphur bomb explosions over the lagoon to illuminate a barge carrying students dressed as priests and scantily-clad maidens.

Following his Ox-Bow experience, Oldenburg sold his first art pieces at Chicago's annual 57th Street Art Fair. In 1956, he returned to New York and met numerous fellow artists, including Allan Kaprow and Robert Whitman, who introduced him to the world of interactive, performance-art "happenings." His first wife, model Pat Muschinski, frequently performed in his shows.

Of course, Oldenburg is probably best known as a pop-art sculptor, famous for his soft oversized sculptures of food, such as apple cores, and public art installations featuring large replicas of everyday objects, including clothespins. Although initially dismissed as ridiculous, Oldenburg's colossal creations have since gained appreciation for their whimsy and insight.

Since 1976, Oldenburg has collaborated with his second wife, Dutch-American pop sculptor Coosje van Bruggen. Together, they have created more than 40 colorful, large-scale projects, for urban environments as varied as Miami, Los Angeles, Barcelona, and Tokyo. For more information, visit www.oldenburg-vanbruggen.com.

© OX-BOW PHOTO ARCHIVE

Students gather on the front porch at the Ox-Bow School.

SHOPPING

The Saugatuck/Douglas area offers some of the best shopping in western Michigan, with an eclectic mix of more than 70 stores and 30 art galleries, most housed in well-kept 19th-century storefronts. The stylish merchandise ranges from high-brow antiques and trendy housewares to more campy fare.

Most of Saugatuck's shops are clustered along Butler, the main street. Two highlights include **American Spoon Foods** (308 Butler St., 269/857-3084, www.spoon.com, 10 A.M.–6 P.M. Mon.–Thurs., 10 A.M.–8 P.M. Fri.–Sat., 11 A.M.–5 P.M. Sun.), a Petoskey-based operation that specializes in fruit spreads and other gourmet foodstuffs, and the **Singapore Bank Bookstore** (317 Butler St., 269/857-3785, 10 A.M.–6 P.M. daily), saved from the sands when it was moved here. Incense, jewelry, and metaphysical books are the specialty at **Mother Moon** (127 Hoffman St., 269/857-4407, hours vary). If trendiness threatens to overwhelm you, head for a breather at the **Saugatuck Drug Store** (201 Butler St., 269/857-2300, 9 A.M.–6 P.M. Mon.–Sat., 10 A.M.–5 P.M. Sun.), which has lured parched tourists and locals since 1913 with phosphates and other authentic treats.

For fresh produce, head to nearby Fennville, where family-operated **Crane Orchards** (6054 124th Ave., 269/561-8651, www.craneorchards.com, 10 A.M.–6 P.M. daily) offers an outstanding U-pick orchard, boasting sweet cherries in June, peaches in July, and apples in the fall. On-site diversions include a pumpkin barn, hay rides, and a 15-acre corn maze. Almost more popular is **Crane's Pie Pantry Restaurant** (6054 124th Ave., 269/561-2297, www.cranespiepantry.com, 9 A.M.–8 P.M. Mon.–Sat., 11 A.M.–8 P.M. Sun. May–Oct., shorter hours Nov.–Apr., $4–10), which serves up thick sandwiches on homemade bread and Lue Crane's signature pies.

SPORTS AND RECREATION
Golf

For golfers, there are few nicer courses than **The Ravines Golf Club** (3520 Palmer Dr., Saugatuck, 269/857-1616, www.ravinesgolfclub.com, daily Apr.–Oct., $39–95 w/cart). In 2008, *Golf Digest* rated this Arnold Palmer–designed signature golf course, which opened to the public in 1999, as one of the "Best Places to Play" and as "The Best Conditioned Course in the State."

Horseback Riding

If golf isn't your thing, you might enjoy a pleasant horseback ride at the **Wild West Ranch** (2855 36th St., Allegan, 269/673-3539, www.4horserides.com, daily, $25–50 adults, $20–40 children), which offers a one-hour trip past a natural wetland, a 1.5-hour trip through the woods, or a two-hour trip across scenic hills. If you or your children need something a little tamer, you can always opt for a pony ride, a hay ride, or, in winter, a sleigh ride.

ACCOMMODATIONS

With at least 30 bed-and-breakfasts in the area, Saugatuck has fast become one of the B&B capitals of the Midwest. The 1860 Victorian-style **Twin Oaks Inn** (227 Griffith St., Saugatuck, 269/857-1600, $110–150 d) is among the friendliest of the inns, with spacious rooms, portable cribs, and pull-out beds for families.

An 1860s Greek Revival building adjacent to the village square has served as a luxury resort hotel for more than 135 years. Today, it does business as the **Maplewood Hotel** (428 Butler St., Saugatuck, 269/857-1771, www.maplewoodhotel.com, $140–275 d) with 15 antique-filled bedrooms in the heart of the city's shops, galleries, and restaurants. Some suites have amenities like double whirlpool tubs and fireplaces. Breakfast is served in the Burr Tillstrom Dining Room, named for former Saugatuck resident and the creator of *Kukla, Fran, and Ollie* (a once-popular children's puppet show).

The **Wickwood Country Inn** (510 Butler St., Saugatuck, 800/385-1174, www.wickwoodinn.com, $175–385 d) is owned by Julee Rosso, co-author of *The Silver Palate* cookbook series, who treats guests at her bed-and-breakfast with seasonal menus she created herself. But that's not the only special touch at this art-filled inn, recognized by numerous magazines. The 11 guest rooms are lavishly decorated with English and French country antiques, featherbeds, and antique linens.

For more economical options, head away from the water and toward the Blue Star Highway, where you'll find simple motels like the **Captain's Quarters Motel** (3242 Blue Star Hwy., Saugatuck, 269/857-2525, www.captainsmotel. com, $50–125 d) or **The Pines Motor Lodge** (56 Blue Star Hwy., Douglas, 269/857-5211, www. thepinesmotorlodge.com, $70–205 d).

FOOD

Locals flock to **Ida Red's Cottage** (645 Water St., Saugatuck, 269/857-5803, 8 A.M.–2 P.M. Wed.–Sun., $5–12) for the best breakfast in town, served all day. Specialties include dishes with a Greek or Italian flair, like the delectable Italian sausage omelets. Pick up an overstuffed sandwich and a few pastries for a carryout picnic at **Pumpernickel's Eatery** (202 Butler St., Saugatuck, 269/857-1196, www.pumpernickelssaugatuck.com, 8 A.M.–4 P.M. daily, $6–9), though you may want to eat there when you spot the restaurant's great patio and sun deck.

C Chequers (220 Culver St., Saugatuck, 269/857-1868, www.chequersofsaugatuck.com, 11:30 A.M.–9 P.M. Mon.–Thurs., 11:30 A.M.–10 P.M. Fri.–Sat., noon–9 P.M. Sun., $12–24) is a bit of London in western Michigan, with a pubby atmosphere of dark paneled walls, stained glass, and lots of leather. Classic Brit-inspired grub includes shepherd's pie, fish and chips, and bangers and mash. There's also a good variety of ales and beer. Reservations are not accepted, so expect a wait at peak hours.

The **Restaurant Toulouse** (248 Culver St., Saugatuck, 269/857-1561, www.restauranttoulouse.com, hours vary, $16–26) features French country cuisine in a Provençal-inspired setting, complete with tableside fireplaces and live jazz on Saturday. Specialties include escargot, cassoulet, rack of lamb, and a killer chocolate fondue.

INFORMATION AND SERVICES

For more information about Saugatuck, Douglas, and surrounding towns, contact the **Saugatuck/Douglas Convention & Visitors Bureau** (2902 Blue Star Hwy., Saugatuck, 269/857-1701, www.saugatuck.com, 9 A.M.–5 P.M. Mon.–Fri.), the **Saugatuck/Douglas Area Business Association** (269/857-1620, www.saugatuckdouglas.com), the **Greater Fennville Chamber of Commerce** (www.greaterfennville.com), or the **Allegan County Tourist Council** (888/425-5342, www.visitallegancounty.com). For local or county news, refer to *The Commercial Record* or *The Allegan County News* (both accessible at www.allegannews.com). For gay-related events and businesses in the area, visit www.gaysaugatuckdouglas.com.

Despite their small size, Saugatuck and Douglas offer plenty of practical services, from pharmacies to post offices. You'll find several banks in the area, too, including **Chemical Bank** (249 Mason St., Saugatuck, 269/857-2116, www.chemicalbankmi.com).

In case of an emergency, dial **911** from any cell or public phone. For medical services, head 10 miles north to the **Holland Hospital** (602 Michigan Ave., Holland, 616/392-5141, www.hollandhospital.org).

GETTING THERE AND AROUND

There are three major airports near Saugatuck and Douglas: the **Kalamazoo/Battle Creek International Airport (AZO)** (5235 Portage Rd., Kalamazoo, 269/388-3668, www.azoairport.com), the **Gerald R. Ford International Airport (GFIA)** (5500 44th St. SE, Grand Rapids, 616/233-6000, www.grr.org), and the **Muskegon County Airport (MKG)** (99 Sinclair Dr., Muskegon, 231/798-4596, www.muskegonairport.com). All offer reputable rental car services, so reaching the "Art Coast" is a snap, even for those without their own vehicle. From Kalamazoo, you can take I-94 west to I-196, which traces the coast north to Douglas. From Grand Rapids, follow I-196 southwest to Saugatuck. From Muskegon, head south on U.S. 31, through Grand Haven, Holland, and the Saugatuck/Douglas area.

THE SOUTHWEST COAST

Holland

For years, people of Dutch ancestry dominated the city of Holland, just north of Saugatuck. In fact, the city remained 90 percent Dutch for more than a century—an impressive demographic in today's melting-pot world. While the ethnic makeup is a bit more varied today (Holland is also home to the state's largest Hispanic community, a fact that gets noticeably less press), many local families can still trace their roots back to the 1840s, when Dutch separatists settled in this part of the Midwest. Whatever their original heritage, however, Holland's residents know it's the Dutch touch that brings thousands of visitors each year, and they are quick to roll out the "welkom" mat for out-of-towners.

The city hits its stride in early May, when the annual Tulip Time Festival is in full bloom. Then, the almost-too-quaint downtown streets are a rainbow of flowers (and a jam of tour buses) as well as costumed *klompen* dancers, local bands, and parades.

SIGHTS
Dutch Experience

Holland clings proudly to its Dutch heritage at spots like **Veldheer Tulip Gardens** (12755 Quincy St., 616/399-1900, www.veldheer.com, 8 A.M.–5:30 P.M. Mon.–Fri., 9 A.M.–5 P.M. Sat.–Sun., shorter hours in winter, $7 adults, $4 children 3–13). Even if you find parts of town overly commercial, you'll be charmed by the sheer spectacle of this rainbow of blooms that take center stage in the spring, followed by more perennials such as lilies, then annuals from June through October. Beds are numbered to correspond with mail-order catalogs, so visitors can place orders for bulbs and flowering plants after seeing the real thing. Locals recommend visiting the gardens at dusk, when the tour buses are gone and sunset casts a warm glow on the thousands of beautiful blooms.

Adjacent to the gardens, the **De Klomp Wooden Shoe & Delftware Factory** (12755

Quincy St., 616/399-1803, same hours as gardens) remains the only working Delft production factory in the United States. Strategically placed windows allow visitors to watch the crisp blue-and-white china being made by hand and see craftsmen carve wooden shoes on well-worn Dutch machinery. A gift shop sells the goods produced here.

Holland's treasure presides over Windmill Island on the east end of town. The 240-year-old **De Zwaan** (The Swan) was shipped to Michigan in 1964, the last authentic windmill the Dutch government allowed to leave the Netherlands. Guides today give careful and thorough tours of the wooden windmill, lovingly reconstructed and still operating, its massive 40-foot blades spinning in the wind and grinding wheat into flour.

De Zwaan serves as the centerpiece of a variety of Dutch displays in **Windmill Island Gardens** (1 Lincoln Ave., 616/355-1030, www.windmillisland.org, 9:30 A.M.–5 P.M. daily mid-April–Oct., $7 adults, $4 children 5–15), including reconstructed buildings like the tile-roofed 14th-century Posthouse, an authentic Dutch carousel, and **Little Netherlands,** a 50-foot-long model village, complete with canals, farms, a cheese market, and, naturally, windmills.

If you still haven't gotten your fill of Dutch culture, head north on U.S. 31 to **Nelis' Dutch Village** (12350 James St., 616/396-1475, www.dutchvillage.com, hours vary seasonally, $6–12 adults, $5–10 seniors, $3–6 children 4–15), a theme park that's essentially a replica of a typical 19th-century community in the Netherlands. Here, you'll encounter Dutch dancing; wooden shoe–carving demonstrations; Dutch products like pottery, lace, and cheese; and a museum dedicated to Dutch culture, including tulip farming.

Museums

City residents are justly proud of three neat-as-a-pin local museums: **The Holland**

Holland's iconic windmill and tulip field at Windmill Island Gardens

Museum (31 W. 10th St., 616/392-9084, www.hollandmuseum.org, 10 A.M.–5 P.M. Mon. and Wed.–Sat., 2–5 P.M. Sun., $7 adults, $6 seniors, $4 students, children under 6 free) and the **Cappon and Settlers House Museums** (226 W. 9th St., 616/392-6740, www.hollandmuseum.org, 1–5 P.M. Wed.–Sat. June–Oct., 1–5 P.M. Fri.–Sat. Nov.–May, $7 adults, $6 seniors, $4 students, children under 6 free). Together, they contain more than 400 years of Dutch and American heritage, with displays that cover the city's 160-year history.

Beaches and Parks

The long, broad beach at **Holland State Park** (2215 Ottawa Beach Rd., 616/399-9390, daily, state park vehicle permit required) is one of the most accessible and beautiful in the Lower Peninsula. Like the other state parks along this stretch of the Lake Michigan shore, it attracts sunbathers by the hundreds on weekends. Facilities include a bathhouse, a dozen or so well-used sand volleyball courts, and two large campgrounds. Lake Michigan

fishing can be quite good from shore. As a bonus, the Holland State Park offers a clear view of a staunch red lighthouse. The **Holland Harbor Light** (called "Big Red" by the locals) was established in 1872 on the southern pier, which partially separates Lake Michigan from Lake Macatawa.

If you'd like to do more than swim, sunbathe, and sightsee, never fear. Just a couple of miles away, on Lake Macatawa, **Holland Water Sports** (1810 Ottawa Beach Rd., 616/399-6672, www.hollandwatersports.com, $100–425) rents Jet Skis for up to three hours, plus powerboats, pontoon boats, and sailboats.

◖ TULIP TIME FESTIVAL

In early May, Holland's world-famous Tulip Time Festival (800/822-2770, www.tuliptime.com) features, naturally, millions of vivid tulip bulbs, quite a thrilling sight to see. During the weeklong celebration of Dutch heritage and culture, visitors will encounter traditional arts and *klompen* dancing, in addition to free concerts, fireworks displays, carnival rides, and three rousing parades.

THE SOUTHWEST COAST

VANRAALTE'S DETOUR

The founding of Holland, one of Michigan's most popular sightseeing destinations, was essentially a fluke. In 1846, Reverend Albertus Christiaan VanRaalte (1811-1876), seeking religious freedom and economic prosperity, led a group of 60 Dutch Calvinists on a seven-week trip from the Netherlands to New York. Despite a plan to head west and purchase land in Wisconsin, travel delays and early winter weather forced the group to stop in Detroit. When VanRaalte heard about available lands in southwestern Michigan, he decided to scout the territory. By January 1847, he'd reached the banks of present-day Lake Macatawa, and the initial group of settlers arrived about a month later.

While subsequent Dutch immigrants were dismayed to find a dense forest, an insect-infested swamp, and a scarce food supply, the settlers persevered, recognizing the value of the surrounding woods and lakes. Without government aid, they dug a channel to Lake Michigan and created a centralized market square. In 1851, VanRaalte helped to establish the Pioneer School, which soon evolved into Hope College.

When two railroads extended spurs to Holland in the early 1870s, it seemed the town was poised for a booming future. Then disaster struck. In October 1871, a fire swept through Holland, bankrupting its citizens. With the aid of surrounding communities, the villagers began a steady revival, and by the end of the 19th century, Holland had utility systems, paved streets, mail delivery, transportation facilities, manufacturing plants, a thriving agricultural market, and several resort hotels.

As the 20th century dawned, Holland continued to prosper — as both a manufacturing center and a tourist destination. During the 1920s, thousands of vacationers flocked to Holland, for its gorgeous beaches, burgeoning resorts, Tulip Time Festival, and other attractions. The Great Depression caused the closure of many of Holland's furniture factories, and yet the town survived. Farmers worked together, and new businesses replaced old ones, especially during World War II.

Despite an influx of varied ethnic groups — such as Latino farm workers in the 1940s and Southeast Asian refugees in the 1960s — Holland continued to honor its Dutch heritage. The 1947 centennial celebration included an exhibition of Dutch artwork and a play about the Dutch pioneers. Fourteen years later, a local businessman successfully transplanted an authentic windmill from the Netherlands.

Since then, Holland has undergone many changes. During the 1980s, the area witnessed a deteriorating downtown core and an increase in the number of housing developments, fast-food restaurants, outlet stores, and shopping malls, but preservation efforts prevailed, even through the 1990s. The historic Tower Clock building was saved, three downtown parks were added, the old post office became the Holland Museum, and Hope College was expanded.

Today, Holland continues to thrive, with Dutch-inspired sites, outdoor concerts, bountiful harvests, holiday festivities, and vibrant annual events like the ever-popular Tulip Time Festival. How could Holland's stout-hearted founders have guessed that the little settlement plagued by bugs, harsh winters, and a cataclysmic fire would, in 2002, be named a "Distinctive Destination" by the National Trust for Historic Preservation? Thank goodness for VanRaalte's accidental detour.

SHOPPING

Like many other towns along the coast, Holland has its share of shopping options. Besides two malls and plenty of retail centers along U.S. 31, the downtown area offers unique establishments, including several art galleries. Inspired by its coastal environment, the **Lake Effect Gallery** (29 W. 8th St., Ste. 100, 616/395-3025, www.lakeeffectgallery. com, hours vary year-round) presents paintings, jewelry, and fine crafts from over 20 of western Michigan's finest artists. A couple of blocks away, **The Nines Gallery** (17 W. 10th St., Ste. 130, 616/392-3239, www.theninesgallery.com, 10 A.M.–5:30 P.M. Mon.–Fri.,

10 A.M.–3 P.M. Sat.) is one of Holland's most adventuresome galleries, specializing in emerging painters, sculptors, and printmakers.

ACCOMMODATIONS

The **Dutch Colonial Inn** (560 Central Ave., 616/396-3664, www.dutchcolonialinn.com, $109–169 d) has five nonsmoking rooms and a complimentary full breakfast in a restored 1928 home. Whirlpools, free wireless Internet access, and warm Dutch hospitality make this inn a safe bet. **Bonnie's Parsonage 1908** (6 E. 24th St., 616/396-1316, $100–135 d) is housed in a former Dutch parsonage built in 1908. It offers four guest rooms, a conservatory/porch, and an outdoor patio. Away from downtown but near Nelis' Dutch Village, try the reliable and affordable **Country Inn by Carlson** (12260 James St., 616/396-6677, www.countryinns.com, $79–115 d). Like many places in town, it's decorated with Delft tiles and country decor. Of its 116 guest rooms, 24 have in-room whirlpools.

Camping

Holland State Park (2215 Ottawa Beach Rd., 616/399-9390, daily, state park vehicle permit required, $27–33) has 309 RV and tent sites in two units, one near Lake Michigan, the other near inland Lake Macatawa. Most sites are quite close together with little shade. Of course, chances are you'll be spending most of your time by the water anyway.

FOOD

Housed in a gray batten-board structure, **Piper Restaurant** (2225 S. Shore Dr., Macatawa, 616/335-5866, www.piperrestaurant.com, 5–9:30 P.M. daily, shorter hours in winter, $6.50–28) overlooks Lake Macatawa and is known for its extensive seafood selection. Save room for the signature dessert, a rum vanilla caramel flan. Reservations are recommended.

In downtown Holland, the **New Holland Brewing Company** (66 E. 8th St., 616/355-6422, www.newhollandbrew.com, 11 A.M.–close daily, $8–18) is a microbrewery, distillery, and lively restaurant and pub all rolled into one; in addition to handcrafted beers and

other spirits, the menu includes soups, salads, sandwiches, pizza, and enormous desserts. **Butch's Dry Dock** (44 E. 8th St., 616/396-8227, www.butchs.net, hours vary, $6–22) serves up great New York–style deli sandwiches to eat on-site or pack for a picnic, along with specialty cheeses, wines, and more. The **(Alpen Rose Restaurant & Café** (4 E. 8th St., 616/393-2111, www.alpenroserestaurant.com, 7:30 A.M.–9 P.M. Mon.–Sat., 10 A.M.–2 P.M. Sun., $7–32) specializes in Wiener schnitzel, goulash, and other German and Austrian dishes in an authentic old-world atmosphere, complete with carvings by master German woodworkers adorning the ceilings and paneling. European pastries are a popular menu item, also available for carryout.

INFORMATION AND SERVICES

For more information about the Holland area, contact the **Holland Area Convention & Visitors Bureau** (76 E. 8th St., 616/394-0000, www.holland.org, 8 A.M.–5:30 P.M. Mon.–Fri. year-round, 10 A.M.–5 P.M. Sat. mid-Apr.–Nov.). For local news, pick up a copy of *The Holland Sentinel* (www.hollandsentinel.com). For county information, visit www.co.ottawa.mi.us.

If you have any mailing needs during your stay, you'll be pleased to know that Holland has several post offices, including a **downtown location** (190 E. 8th St., 616/396-5201, www.usps.com). To pick up supplies or fill a prescription, stop by **Meijer** (746 E. 16th St., 616/355-4864, www.meijer.com), part of a statewide superstore chain that sells groceries, pharmaceuticals, electronics, toys, furniture, and other necessities.

In case of an emergency, dial **911** from any cell or public phone. For medical services, head to the **Holland Hospital** (602 Michigan Ave., Holland, 616/392-5141, www.hollandhospital.org).

GETTING THERE AND AROUND

Travelers can reach Holland directly via bus or train. Both **Greyhound** (616/396-8664, www.greyhound.com) and **Amtrak** (800/872-7245, www.amtrak.com) offer service to the same station (171 Lincoln Ave.). Two airports are situated in nearby towns—the **Gerald R. Ford International Airport (GFIA)** (5500 44th St. SE, Grand Rapids, 616/233-6000, www.grr.org) and the **Muskegon County Airport (MKG)** (99 Sinclair Dr., Muskegon, 231/798-4596, www.muskegonairport.com)—so it's also possible to fly into the area and rent a car. For those driving to Holland, you'll find the highways easy to navigate, whether you're headed from Grand Rapids via I-196 or Muskegon via U.S. 31.

Grand Haven

Just a few miles south of Muskegon lies the lakeside town of Grand Haven, whose history dates back to 1833, when fur trapper and trader Rix Robinson purchased the area from the U.S. government and established a trading post at the mouth of the Grand River. By the spring of 1835, Grand Haven's first white settlers—Reverend William Montague Ferry and his family and friends, had erected permanent dwellings and the town's first sawmill. As the town grew, other nearby settlements followed, and for the next six decades, the area's lumbering industry flourished. Before the state's white pine forests had been virtually depleted, Grand Haven had already begun evolving into an important manufacturing town and shipping port, assisted by the arrival of the railroad in 1858.

During the mid-19th-century, Grand Haven also became a respite for affluent middle-class families, seeking rest, relaxation, and recreation along the shores of the Grand River, Spring Lake, and Lake Michigan. Today, this town of 10,500 residents continues to be a vacation destination, offering a variety of diversions, from art galleries and a historic shopping district to well-favored beaches and the world's largest musical fountain. Adjacent Lake Michigan is popular among deep-sea anglers, and the town's surrounding countryside is ideal for long-distance hikers and bikers.

SIGHTS
Tri-Cities Historical Museum
Grand Haven focuses its attention on the waterfront—in particular, the boardwalk that traces the Grand River's south bank from downtown to the river's mouth at Lake Michigan. The 2.5-mile waterfront boardwalk is full of places to shop, eat, and stroll. The walk wanders past the city's vintage railroad station, now the Tri-Cities Historical Museum (200 Washington Ave., 616/842-0700, www.tri-citiesmuseum.org, 9:30 A.M.–7:30 P.M. Tues.–Fri., 12:30–7:30 P.M. Sat.–Sun., shorter hours in winter), where a "puffer belly" steam locomotive and three rail cars sit idle. It ends at **Chinook Pier**, where many of the area's Great Lakes fishing boats dock and display the day's catch.

Musical Fountain
Across the street, shops fill the **Harbourfront Place,** a renovated Story & Clark Piano Company factory. Hang around the harbor at dusk, and you'll be treated to a burst of music and a revolving blast of colored lights, as Grand Haven's musical fountain begins to spray and dance in a choreographed half-hour show. The fountain is a beloved tradition in this resort town and plays every summer evening.

Beaches and Parks
Connected to downtown by the city's popular boardwalk, you won't find solitude at **Grand Haven State Park** (1001 Harbor Ave., 616/847-1309, daily, state park vehicle permit required), but you will find a sandy swimming beach, a convenient campground, a fishing pier, and, of course, the **Grand Haven South Pier Lighthouses.** These two vivid red lighthouses—the outer light built in 1875 and moved to the end of the breakwater in 1905, and the inner 51-foot light fabricated

THE SOUTHWEST COAST

© L. DIGGS, PICTURE THIS...

the range lights of Grand Haven

in 1905—are still operational and constitute one of only two range-light systems in the Great Lakes region; the other is in St. Joseph, farther south. It's no surprise that Grand Haven's lighthouses are popular among photographers and sightseers. Just be careful on the breakwater when the winds blow across Lake Michigan.

Coopersville and Marne Railway

About 17 miles east of Grand Haven lies Coopersville, a small town that celebrates its agricultural heritage and wholesome vibe with a number of annual events and historic sites—from the **Outhouse 500,** a late-February race of decorated outhouses, to the **Coopersville Farm Museum** (www.coopersvillefarmmuseum.org), which showcases a tractor exhibit, a feed sack collection, and more. Of course, one of the most popular area attractions is the Coopersville & Marne Railway (311 Danforth St., Coopersville, 616/997-7000, www.coopersvilleandmarne.org, 11 A.M. and 1 P.M. Wed. and Sat. May–Oct., 11 A.M. and 1 P.M. Sat. Apr. and Nov.–Dec., theme train hours vary,

$10.50–14.50 adults, $9.50–13.50 seniors 60 and over, $6.50–11.50 children 2–12), a train of antique passenger cars that travels over farmlands, creeks, and bridges, from Coopersville to Marne and back again. For well over an hour, this 14-mile journey transports passengers back to a simpler time, before the rise of the automobile. Throughout the year, the railway also offers thematic rides, including "The Great Train Robbery" and the "Santa Train."

FESTIVALS AND EVENTS

For two decades, Grand Haven has hosted the annual **Great Lakes Kite Festival** (Grand Haven State Park, 616/847-1309), the state's biggest kite festival. During the mid-May event, experts from across the country display a wide array of giant kites. The impressive festival, the proceeds of which benefit the Children's Leukemia Foundation of Michigan, features everything from free kite seminars to nighttime flying. For more information, contact **Mackinaw Kites & Toys** (800/622-4655, www.mackite.com/glskc.htm).

To honor the men and women of the United

States Coast Guard, Grand Haven also holds an annual **Grand Haven Coast Guard Festival** (113 N. 2nd St., 616/846-5940, www.coastguardfest.org, most events free), usually from the end of July to the beginning of August. Highlights include a grand parade, a downtown carnival, and ship tours on two USCGC ice-breaker vessels, the *Mackinaw* and the *Biscayne Bay.*

SHOPPING

If you do plan to attend Grand Haven's kite festival, there's no better place to pick up your own highflier than **Mackinaw Kites & Toys** (106 Washington Ave., 800/622-4655, www.mackite.com, hours vary by season). This whimsical store, a sponsor of the festival, has a wide assortment of amazing kites, as well as kiteboarding and kitesurfing gear.

But kites aren't the only things for sale in Grand Haven. If you're looking for some gourmet Italian goodies, look no further than **Fortino's** (114 Washington St., 616/842-0880, www.fortinos-gourmet.com, hours vary), not far from the kite shop. Here, you'll find a superb selection of fine wines, gourmet meats, and excellent cheeses. Take your pick, then head to the beach for a stylish picnic.

SPORTS AND RECREATION
Golf

With all that Grand Haven has to offer, you still might want to set aside some time to play a round of golf on what *Golf Digest* considers one of America's best public courses. The **Grand Haven Golf Club** (17000 Lincoln St., 616/842-4040, www.grandhavengolfclub.com, daily Apr.–Oct., $28–65) was designed in 1965 by legendary golf architect Bruce Matthews, Sr., who carved through the rolling sand dunes and towering pines of the Southwest Coast, creating a real stunner.

Biking

Grand Haven and surrounding Ottawa County claim more than 100 miles of bicycle paths. (Most are also open to in-line skates, roller skis, and other recreational uses.) The 15-mile

Lakeside Trail circles inland Spring Lake, a lovely ride. The **Lakeshore Connector Path** links Grand Haven to Holland, 30 miles south, utilizing some sidewalks but mostly a paved off-road route near the Lake Michigan shore. For more information about bike trails, contact the **Grand Haven Area Convention & Visitors Bureau** (1 S. Harbor Dr., 800/303-4092, www.visitgrandhaven.com, 9:30 A.M.–5 P.M. Mon., 8 A.M.–5 P.M. Tues.–Fri. year-round, 10 A.M.–2 P.M. Sat. summer only).

ACCOMMODATIONS AND FOOD

While the accommodations in Grand Haven used to be a bit slim, that's changed in recent years. You'll find a few chain hotels along U.S. 31, such as the **Best Western Beacon Inn** (1525 S. Beacon Blvd., 616/842-4720, www.bestwesternmichigan.com, $75–120 d) for basic motel rooms with coffeemakers and free movies. On the waterfront, you'll spy the charming **Harbor House Inn** (114 S. Harbor Drive, 616/846-0610, www.harborhousegh.com, $95–275 d), a spacious Victorian-style manor offering both comfortable guest rooms as well as the quaint Harbor Cottage, for even more privacy.

For dining, try **◖ The Kirby House** (2 Washington St., 616/846-3299, www.thegilmorecollection.com, 11 A.M.–10 P.M. Sun.–Thurs., 11 A.M.–11 P.M. Fri.–Sat., $10–32), situated within a historic 1873 building in the heart of downtown. It's actually three restaurants in one: The Kirby Grill, a casual eatery; The Grill Room, a stylish chophouse; and K2, an authentic pizzeria with a wood-fired oven.

If you're looking for one of western Michigan's best watering holes, stop by the **Rosebud Bar & Grill** (100 Washington St., 616/846-7788, www.rosebudgrill.com, 11 A.M.–2 A.M. daily, $13–40), known for scrumptious steaks, seafood, and pasta dishes.

Camping

Grand Haven State Park (1001 Harbor Ave., 616/847-1309, daily, state park vehicle permit required, $16–29) offers a spacious campground. There are 174 modern sites, mostly in an open area near the water, as well as clean restrooms. For reservations, which are highly recommended, call 800/447-2757 or visit www.michigan.gov/dnr.

INFORMATION AND SERVICES

For more information about the Grand Haven area, contact the **Grand Haven Area Convention & Visitors Bureau** (1 S. Harbor Dr., 800/303-4092, www.visitgrandhaven.com, 9:30 A.M.–5 P.M. Mon., 8 A.M.–5 P.M. Tues.–Fri. year-round, 10 A.M.–2 P.M. Sat. summer only) or the **Grand Haven Chamber of Commerce** (1 S. Harbor Dr., 616/842-4910, www.grandhavenchamber.org, 9:30 A.M.–5 P.M. Mon., 8 A.M.–5 P.M. Tues.–Fri. year-round, 10 A.M.–2 P.M. Sat. summer only). For local news and events, pick up a copy of *The Grand Haven Tribune* (www.grandhaventribune.com).

The Grand Haven area offers a wide range of services necessary to travelers, including groceries, pharmacies, banks, and post offices. In case of an emergency, dial **911** from any cell or public phone. For medical services, consult the **North Ottawa Community Hospital** (1309 Sheldon Rd., 616/842-3600, www.noch.org).

GETTING THERE AND AROUND

Grand Haven is situated on the Lake Michigan coast, accessible via private boat. Visitors can also reach the town by flying into one of two nearby airports—the **Gerald R. Ford International Airport (GFIA)** (5500 44th St. SE, Grand Rapids, 616/233-6000, www.grr.org) or the **Muskegon County Airport (MKG)** (99 Sinclair Dr., Muskegon, 231/798-4596, www.muskegonairport.com). Whether you rent a car or drive your own, it's easy to reach Grand Haven via U.S. 31, a route that traces the entire western coast of the Lower Peninsula, from the Indiana border to just north of Petoskey.

Muskegon and Vicinity

The largest town along this stretch of Lake Michigan shoreline, with more than 39,000 year-round residents, Muskegon has its roots in white pine. The deep Muskegon River that flows through town, into Lake Muskegon, and toward Lake Michigan proved the perfect route for transporting timber from the rich inland pine forests to the city's sawmills.

Muskegon's first sawmill went up in 1837. In the following 50 years, the frontier town grew at a feverish pace. By the 1880s, it was known throughout the world as a lumber metropolis, home to 47 sawmills and at least as many saloons, dance halls, and gambling joints—earning the city nicknames that ranged from "Lumber Queen of the North" to the more unsavory "Red Light Queen."

Muskegon was unprepared for the day just a decade or so later when the area's timber was tapped. Mills soon closed or were mysteriously torched. By the 1890s, the region's lumber industry and population declined steadily. By the 1950s, the city teetered on the brink of ruin—until tourists took over where timber left. After decades of decline in industry and self-image, Muskegon has finally risen from the sawdust. While many parts of the city still have a tattered feel, visitors to Muskegon focus on its benefits, which include more than 26 miles of Lake Michigan shoreline, western Michigan's most extensive lakeshore park system, outstanding cultural and historical resources, a popular amusement park, and a lively multiethnic population—perhaps refreshing in a part of the state so dominated by the Dutch.

SIGHTS
Historic Sites

The lumber barons in Muskegon left behind grand homes—since lovingly restored—that

© MUSKEGON COUNTY CVB

Muskegon's Hackley & Hume Historic Site

preservationists point to as some of the finest Queen Annes in North America. The **Hackley & Hume Historic Site** (W. Webster at 6th St., 231/722-0278, www.muskegonmuseum.org, noon–4 P.M. Wed.–Sun. May–Oct., $3 adults, children under 13 free) includes two mansions built by lumber magnates Charles Hackley and Thomas Hume in the late 1800s. These flamboyant homes, administered by the Muskegon County Museum, feature some 28 shades of paint, lavish woodcarving, stained glass, and high Victorian furnishings.

The **Great Lakes Naval Memorial and Museum** (1346 Bluff St., 231/755-1230, www. glnmm.org, hours vary Apr.–Oct., $10 adults, $8 seniors and students, $7 children 5–11, children under 5 free) has two historic ships, the USS *Silversides,* and the USCGC *McLane,* which commemorate life at sea during World War II. Completed just after the attack on Pearl Harbor in 1942, *Silversides* went on to sink 23 ships, the third highest total of all U.S. submarines that served in the second World War. Now a national historic landmark, *Silversides* remains in excellent condition, with original

furnishings including bunks, sonar equipment, radios, and furniture. The tour gives a good feel of what it was like to venture out on a 45-day tour deep into enemy territory.

Museums

Charles Hackley also donated to Muskegon one of the finest art museums in the state. The **Muskegon Museum of Art** (296 W. Webster Ave., 231/720-2570, www.muskegonartmuseum.org, 10 A.M.–4:30 P.M. Tues.–Wed. and Fri.–Sat., 10 A.M.–8 P.M. Thurs., noon–4:30 P.M. Sun., $5 adults, students and children under 18 free) is a surprise for a city of this size, with a permanent collection that includes the well-known *Tornado Over Kansas* by John Steuart Curry and works by Winslow Homer, Edward Hopper, and Andrew Wyeth. Another surprise is the largest collection of works by painter Françoise Gilot, best known as Picasso's mistress and mother to their daughter, Paloma.

The **Muskegon County Museum** (430 W. Clay Ave., 231/722-0278, www.muskegonmuseum.org, 9:30 A.M.–4:30 P.M. Mon.–Fri., noon–4 P.M. Sat.–Sun., free) recounts the city's colorful logging past, including details about the dangers of living in the city's lumber camps. Don't miss the murals of Muskegon's history, done for the National Lumberman's Bank in 1929. Other exhibits explore the area's geology, early Native Americans, and the wildlife of various habitats.

Beaches and Parks

Almost a half million swimmers, beachcombers, surfers, sailboarders, boaters, campers, and picnickers descend each year upon **Muskegon State Park** (3560 Memorial Dr., North Muskegon, 231/744-3480, daily, state park vehicle permit required). Despite the large numbers, most visitors head for the beach, leaving the rest of the park rather uncrowded. Its 1,165 acres actually feel more like several small parks, divided into swimming, fishing, and hiking areas. From the coast, you might be able to spot the 53-foot-tall **Muskegon South Pierhead Lighthouse,** established in 1903, still active today, and often called the Pere Marquette Lighthouse, given its position on the south side of the Muskegon Lake Channel, near Pere Marquette Beach.

In winter, the Muskegon State Park is best known for its **Muskegon Winter Sports Complex** (231/744-9629, www.msports.org, 10 A.M.–10 P.M. daily in winter, prices vary), which offers ski and snowshoe rentals, houses an ice-skating rink, and includes one of the only luge runs in the nation. On winter weekends, you can reserve a spot for a quick lesson and give it a try yourself. Speeds reach up to 40 miles per hour, careening down the ice-covered wooden chute—and seem terribly faster on a sled made of wood, metal, and canvas. The luge is open on weekends only, beginning in mid-December; a day's pass includes a sled, helmet, and coach. First-timers are fully supervised. The park is also a favorite among cross-country skiers, who find some of the longest lighted trails in the state. The area usually enjoys a long season, thanks to reliable lake effect snows.

The **Gillette Sand Dune Visitor Center**

at **P. J. Hoffmaster State Park** (6585 Lake Harbor Rd., Muskegon, 231/798-3711, daily, state park vehicle permit required) gives an excellent introduction to dune history and ecology. Slide shows, dioramas, and colorful displays demonstrate the natural forces that shaped and continue to shape the face of these majestic mountains of sand. Besides the center, the 1,200-acre park contains two miles of shoreline, towering dunes that stand guard over a sandy beach, deep forests, interdunal valleys, 10 miles of hiking and cross-country trails (also popular with snowshoers in winter), and a very good campground.

Michigan's Adventure Amusement Park

Muskegon also has plenty to offer for those looking for more commercial amusements. Together, Michigan's Adventure Amusement Park and Wild Water Adventure Water Park (4750 Whitehall Rd., 231/766-3377, www.miadventure.com, times vary seasonally, $25 plus parking) make up the state's largest amusement and water park, with more than 60 rides and attractions, including seven roller coasters and several pools and waterslides. The newest roller coaster, Thunderhawk, is the state's first and only suspended coaster; it's the steel complement to the park's long-time favorite, Shivering Timbers, a 125-foot-tall wooden coaster that's routinely considered one of the best in America.

FAIRS AND FESTIVALS

In late June, the **Taste of Muskegon** (Western Ave., www.tasteofmuskegon.com, 11 A.M.–8 P.M. Sat., 11 A.M.–6 P.M. Sun., free to enter, $1–5 for food items), a relatively new diversion, offers a two-day celebration of the region's cuisine, with the area's best restaurants and bakeries serving their specialties to crowds of willing gourmands. Since all the proceeds benefit the Muskegon Main Street organization and Make a Wish Foundation of Michigan, you can fill your belly while knowing you're helping two good causes.

MICHIGAN'S MAPLE SYRUP

Centuries before European settlers discovered the undeniable sweetness of maple syrup, Native Americans were using it to flavor their meat and fish. Several legends exist about how various tribes first embraced distilled maple sap as a cooking ingredient. In one such tale – as recounted by the Chippewa and Ottawa natives of Michigan – a god named Nenawbozhoo supposedly cast a spell on the sugar maple tree, turning the sweet pure syrup into colorless sap. His justification? Apparently, he feared that his people would become lazy and ungrateful if nature's gifts were so readily available.

Though the legends varied from tribe to tribe, the original freezing and boiling methods of turning sap into syrup were pretty universal – and fairly time-consuming. As early 17th-century settlers discovered, 40 gallons of sap might be required to produce one gallon of syrup. Following the invention of the tin can during the mid-1800s, however, maple syrup production – the nation's oldest agricultural enterprise – became easier for the self-sufficient farmers that comprised the burgeoning industry.

By the 1970s, large companies had taken over the maple industry, using advancements like tubing systems, vacuum pumps, preheaters, reverse-osmosis filters, desalinization machines, and better storage containers to increase production. Today, Michigan ranks sixth in the nation for maple syrup production; each year, roughly 2,500 commercial and home-use producers throughout the state utilize a mere 1 percent of Michigan's maple forests to yield an estimated total of 90,000 gallons of syrup. Harvested February–April, Michigan's maple syrup is used to enhance everything from popcorn to pork ribs to ice cream. There's even a maple cocktail that blends maple syrup with gin, bourbon, and lemon juice.

For maple-related recipes and statistics, as well as information about seasonal events, consult the **Michigan Maple Syrup Association** (www.mi-maplesyrup.com). To purchase pure Michigan maple syrup, stop by one of the Southwest Coast's many roadside markets and farms.

Another not-to-miss event is the **Muskegon Film Festival** (425 W. Western Ave., www.muskegonfilmfestival.com, $8 adults, $6 students), which takes place in late January or early February at the Frauenthal Center for the Performing Arts. During the weekend-long festival, filmgoers are treated to a variety of films, from high school, college, and professional filmmakers.

SPORTS AND RECREATION
Golf
If you're hankering to play a casual round of golf in a gorgeous setting, visit the **Stonegate Golf Club** (4100 Sweeter Rd., Twin Lake, 231/744-7200, www.stonegategolfclub.com, daily Apr.–Oct., $30–59 w/o cart). In addition to a round of golf, Stonegate provides golf training and a beautiful bar and grill, popular for its famous fish fry every Friday night.

Hiking and Biking
The 25-mile-long **Musketawa Trail** (www.musketawatrail.com) is a multiuse recreational pathway that links Marne in eastern Ottawa County to Muskegon. Passing amid a myriad of farmlands, wetlands, creeks, and villages, it offers hikers and biking enthusiasts a marvelous scenic tour of the area. Horseback riders, in-line skaters, and nature lovers frequent the Musketawa, too, and in winter, it's popular among cross-country skiers and snowmobilers.

ACCOMMODATIONS
Overlooking Muskegon Lake, the **(C Port City Victorian Inn** (1259 Lakeshore Dr., 231/759-0205, www.portcityinn.com, $125–225 d), a Queen Anne–style bed-and-breakfast built in 1877, has five guest rooms and a rooftop balcony with terrific views of the lake. It's open year-round. If you'd prefer staying

in a chain establishment, the **Holiday Inn Muskegon Harbor** (939 3rd St., 231/722-0100 or 877/863-4780, www.ichotelsgroup.com, $100–125 d) offers a convenient location in the heart of Muskegon. Amenities include an indoor pool and sauna.

Camping

Muskegon State Park (3560 Memorial Dr., North Muskegon, 231/744-3480, daily, state park vehicle permit required) has three campgrounds with a total of 252 sites. Tents and RV campers are welcome here; the campsites are equipped with 50-amp electricity, and there are modern restrooms available. The Lake Michigan Campground is especially nice. While not on the water, it's protected by tall maples and beaches and tucked behind dunes, with an easy walk to the beach. For reservations, which are definitely recommended in summer, call 800/447-2757 or visit www.michigan.gov/dnr.

FOOD

Adjacent to Muskegon's Shoreline Inn at Terrace Point, **Rafferty's Dockside Restaurant** (750 Terrace Point Blvd., 231/722-4461, www.shorelineinn.com, 11:30 A.M.–9:30 P.M. Mon.–Thurs., 11:30 A.M.–10 P.M. Fri.–Sat., 10:30 A.M.–8 P.M. Sun., shorter hours in winter, $14–35) on the shores of Muskegon Lake, offers casual dining in the restaurant, in the lounge, or on the patio. With an extensive wine list and some amazing house specials, you'll be hard-pressed to find a better dining experience. While in town, stop by **Tony's Bistro** (211 S. Seaway Dr., 231/739-7196, www.tonysbistro.net, 11 A.M.–midnight Mon.–Thurs., 11 A.M.–1 A.M. Fri., 4 P.M.–1 A.M. Sat., 4–10 P.M. Sun., $8–22), a family-operated establishment since 1969, specializing in steaks, seafood, pasta, pizza, and Greek specialties.

INFORMATION AND SERVICES

For more information about the Muskegon area, contact the **Muskegon County Convention & Visitors Bureau** (610 W. Western Ave., 231/724-3100, www.visitmuskegon.org, 8 A.M.–5 P.M. Mon.–Fri.) or the **Muskegon Area Chamber of Commerce** (380 W. Western Ave., 231/722-3751, www.muskegon.org, 8:30 A.M.–5 P.M. Mon.–Fri.). For government information, visit www.co.muskegon.mi.us. For local news, pick up a copy of the **Muskegon Chronicle** (www.mlive.com/chronicle).

As the Southwest Coast's largest city, Muskegon has no shortage of services for travelers. **Meijer** (www.meijer.com), a Midwestern superstore chain, offers three locations in the Muskegon area; here, you can fill prescriptions, get film processed, and pick up all manner of supplies. For mailing needs, you'll find several **post offices** in Muskegon; consult www.usps.com for locations and hours. If you're looking for an ATM, you'll find plenty here; consult **Comerica Bank** (www.comerica.com) or **National City** (www.nationalcity.com) for locations.

In case of an emergency, dial **911** from any cell or public phone. For medical services, consult the **Mercy Health Partners** (231/672-2000, www.mghp.com), which has two campuses in Muskegon.

GETTING THERE AND AROUND

Travelers can reach Muskegon via boat, bus, plane, or vehicle. Since 2004, the **Lake Express** (1918 Lakeshore Dr., 866/914-1010, www.lake-express.com), the first high-speed ferry to operate on the Great Lakes, has transported passengers and vehicles across Lake Michigan, between Milwaukee and Muskegon. **Greyhound** (351 Morris Ave., 231/722-6048, www.greyhound.com) also provides bus service to Muskegon, and Northwest Airlines offers flights from Detroit to **Muskegon County Airport (MKG)** (99 Sinclair Dr., Muskegon, 231/798-4596, www.muskegonairport.com).

Once in town, you'll be pleased to know that Muskegon has decent public transportation, provided by the **Muskegon Area Transit System (MATS)** (231/724-6420, www.

THE SOUTHWEST COAST

matsbus.com). Of course, as with the rest of the Southwest Coast, having a car is essential. Whether you're coming from Traverse City to the north or Benton Harbor to the south, U.S. 31 is one of the most convenient routes to the Muskegon area. From Lansing and Grand Rapids, simply take I-96 west.

WHITEHALL AND MONTAGUE

About 12 miles north of Muskegon, the sleepy twin towns of Whitehall and Montague are friendly rivals. Both sit on U.S. 31 at the head of White Lake, both have hospitable inns and old-fashioned general stores, and both fill up with summer people during the high season. Friendly and unfussy, they're good places to wander in and out of nautical- and country-themed stores, watch the swans in the White River marsh, enjoy a root beer at the Dog 'n' Suds, and take in the sunsets and sailboats at the marinas that ring White Lake.

Sights

Operated by the administration of Muskegon State Park farther south, **Duck Lake State Park** (3560 Memorial Dr., North Muskegon, 231/744-3480, daily, state park vehicle permit required) is a 728-acre day-use property, stretching along the northern shore of Duck Lake, adjacent to Lake Michigan. Swimmers, anglers, hikers, cross-country skiers, and snowmobilers all favor this less-traveled place. Besides a picnic area, a restroom building, and a boat launch, there are few amenities here, but it's still worth a look if you're in the White Lake area.

Another interesting attraction is the **White River Light Station Museum** (6199 Murray Rd., Whitehall, 231/894-8265, www.whiteriverlightstation.org, 11 A.M.–5 P.M. Tues.–Fri., noon–6 P.M. Sat.–Sun. June–Aug., shorter hours in fall and winter, $2 adults, $1 children 10–18, children under 10 free). Visitors can climb the spiral staircase to the top of the 1875 lighthouse (deactivated in 1960), where spectacular views of Lake Michigan and the White Lake Channel await. Down below, the museum features stories, artifacts, photographs,

and paintings that depict western Michigan's fascinating maritime heritage.

Recreation and Camping

The **Hart-Montague Trail** stretches 22 miles along the former C&O Railroad route between Hart and Montague. The smooth paved surface is popular for hiking, biking, and in-line skating. It leads north from Montague, passing through high sandy hills and orchards between Muskegon and Ludington, an area renowned as one of America's top producers of apples, tart cherries, and Christmas trees. Small towns along the trail have a rural 1940s feel; a map available at trailheads lists area restaurants, B&Bs, and bike rentals. For more information about the trail, contact **Silver Lake State Park** (9679 W. State Park Rd., Mears, 231/873-3083).

Famous as a logging river, the **White River** offers some wonderful paddling—the river feels more remote than many of the longer and better-known rivers farther north. On early morning and late afternoon floats, you'll share the waters with blue herons, sandhill cranes, and an occasional beaver. The narrow river winds between steep, forested banks, across marshy flats, and through the Manistee National Forest, a hardwood and conifer forest that hasn't seen a logger since the 19th century. Access points to the river can be hard to find; one of the easiest solutions is to arrange for a rental through the **Happy Mohawk Canoe Livery** (735 Fruitvale Rd., Montague, 231/894-4209, www.happymohawk.com, hours vary, $30–71 canoes, $23–77 kayaks, $69 rafts, $11 tubes), the only full-service provider of watercraft on the White River. The livery rents canoes, kayaks, inner tubes, and rafts for trips ranging 1–7 hours in length. Happy Mohawk also owns the nearby ◖ **White River RV Park & Campground** (735 Fruitvale Rd., Montague, 231/894-4708, www.whiterivercampground.com, May–mid-Oct., $26–43 sites, $64–74 cabins) in a heavily wooded valley near little Sand Creek. In addition to 235 premium and rustic campsites, the facility includes camping cabins along the creek, a heated pool, a wading creek, hiking trails, basketball and volleyball courts, and several playgrounds.

Information and Services

For more information about Whitehall and Montague, contact the **White Lake Area Chamber of Commerce & Visitors Bureau** (124 Hanson St., Whitehall, 231/893-4585, www.whitelake.org, 9 A.M.–5 P.M. Mon.–Fri., 9 A.M.–3 P.M. Sat., noon–2 P.M. Sun.). For local news and events, consult the *White Lake Beacon* (www.whitelakebeacon.com).

If you require postal, banking, dental, medical, automotive repair, or other services during your stay, you'll find several friendly businesses in these adjacent towns, not to mention in nearby Muskegon. In case of an emergency, dial **911** from any cell or public phone.

Getting There and Around

Whitehall and Montague lie just a mile west of U.S. 31, so you can easily reach them via car—whether you're traveling south from Traverse City or north from Indiana. Since Muskegon is only 12 miles south of the White Lake area, you can also arrive by plane, bus, or ferry, rent a car at the Muskegon County Airport, and head north on U.S. 31.

TRAVERSE CITY AND NORTHWEST MICHIGAN

Although the entire state is defined by water, perhaps no region is more dramatically contoured by lakes, bays, and rivers than the northwestern corner of Michigan's Lower Peninsula, especially the coast surrounding Traverse City, the area's largest town and the self-proclaimed "cherry capital of the world." The aquamarine waters of Lake Michigan mingle with two stunning coastal bays: Grand Traverse Bay, a majestic, 32-mile-long inlet partially bisected by the slender Old Mission Peninsula, and Little Traverse Bay, situated farther north near Petoskey, a town famous for its high concentration of Petoskey stones, the fossilized coral rock that was named Michigan's state stone in 1965.

On summer weekends, the lakeside towns of Traverse City, Charlevoix, and Petoskey seem to grow exponentially. While some fear the overdevelopment that's encroached upon this area in recent years, visitors continue to flock to the coast, embracing a wide array of diversions, including windsurfing, fishing charters, bike trails, chic restaurants and galleries, golf and ski resorts, and old-fashioned downtown shopping districts. Along the coast, visitors can also admire a number of historic lighthouses, from the 1858 Beaver Head Lighthouse on Beaver Island to the picture-perfect 1870 Old Mission Point Lighthouse amid Grand Traverse Bay. Beyond the many islands and breezy shores of Lake Michigan, numerous inland lakes pepper this diverse region, too.

Outdoor enthusiasts embrace the pristine beaches and clear waters of Northwest Michigan, a breathtaking area that's also

HIGHLIGHTS

◖ National Cherry Festival: First held in 1926, this annual celebration of Michigan's booming cherry industry attracts over 500,000 participants every July. Activities include parades, fireworks displays, live entertainment, turtle races, cherry pie-eating contests, a grand buffet, and a cherry farmers market (page 197).

◖ Traverse City Film Festival: Since 2005, Michigan's premier film festival – cofounded by filmmaker Michael Moore – has lured thousands upon thousands of filmmakers and cinema lovers to Traverse City in midsummer, for a week of eclectic screenings, panel discussions, parties, and musical performances (page 197).

◖ Interlochen Center for the Arts: Situated on an inspiring 1,200-acre campus, Interlochen has, for over 80 years, cultivated a passion for the arts. Besides offering a summer camp for young artists and year-round programs for adults, this renowned institute invites visitors to attend concerts, readings, theatrical performances, film screenings, art exhibitions, and more (page 202).

◖ Sleeping Bear Dunes National Lakeshore: Established in 1977, this one-of-a-kind national park features some of the largest freshwater dunes in the world, not to mention two isolated islands in Lake Michigan. Visitors can climb the dunes, explore historic buildings, and pursue a wide array of outdoor activities, from hiking to kayaking to scuba diving (page 203).

◖ Wineries of Grand Traverse Bay: Sandy soils and lake-effect snows have helped to nurture one of the finest winemaking regions in the country: the shores surrounding Michigan's Grand Traverse Bay. Wineries and

tasting rooms pepper the Leelanau and Old Mission Peninsulas, the destinations of choice for countless connoisseurs (page 209).

◖ Loda Lake Wildflower Sanctuary: Nestled within the Manistee National Forest, north of White Cloud, this is the only wildflower sanctuary ever established in a U.S. national forest. Nature lovers can stroll through oak-maple woodlands, old pine plantations, and a shrub swamp, boasting a slew of plant species, from columbine to witch hazel to huckleberries (page 214).

LOOK FOR ◖ TO FIND RECOMMENDED SIGHTS, ACTIVITIES, DINING, AND LODGING.

NORTHWEST MICHIGAN

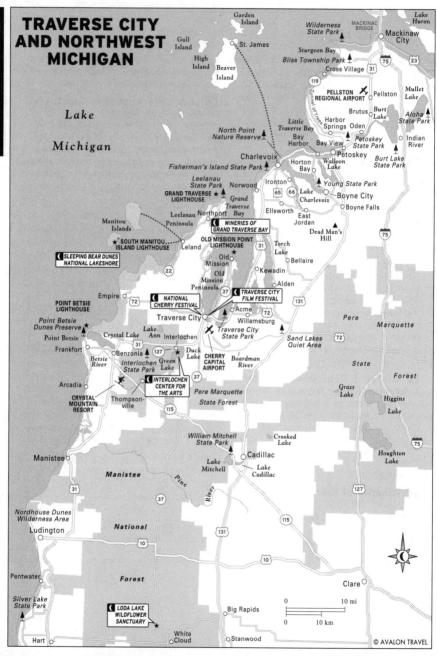

TRAVERSE CITY AND NORTHWEST MICHIGAN

Lake Michigan

Garden Island
Gull Island
High Island
Beaver Island
St. James

Wilderness State Park
MACKINAC BRIDGE
Mackinaw City
Lake Huron
Sturgeon Bay
Bliss Township Park
Cross Village
PELLSTON REGIONAL AIRPORT
Pellston
Mullet Lake
Brutus
Burt Lake
Aloha State Park
Harbor Springs
Oden
Indian River
Little Traverse Bay
Bay Harbor
Bay View
Petoskey State Park
Petoskey
Burt Lake State Park
North Point Nature Reserve
Charlevoix
Fisherman's Island State Park
Horton Bay
Walloon Lake
Leelanau State Park
Norwood
Ironton
Lake Charlevoix
Young State Park
Boyne City
GRAND TRAVERSE LIGHTHOUSE
Grand Traverse Bay
Ellsworth
Boyne Falls
Leelanau Peninsula
Northport
East Jordan
Manitou Islands
SOUTH MANITOU ISLAND LIGHTHOUSE
WINERIES OF GRAND TRAVERSE BAY
Dead Man's Hill
SLEEPING BEAR DUNES NATIONAL LAKESHORE
Leland
OLD MISSION POINT LIGHTHOUSE
Old Mission
Torch Lake
Bellaire
Kewadin
Old Mission Peninsula
Alden
Empire
NATIONAL CHERRY FESTIVAL
TRAVERSE CITY FILM FESTIVAL
Acme
Willamsburg
Pere Marquette
POINT BETSIE LIGHTHOUSE
Traverse City
Traverse City State Park
Point Betsie Dunes Preserve
Lake Ann
Interlochen
Sand Lakes Quiet Area
State
Point Betsie
Crystal Lake
Frankfort
Benzonia
Duck Lake
CHERRY CAPITAL AIRPORT
Boardman River
Forest
Betsie River
Interlochen State Park
Green Lake
Grass Lake
Higgins Lake
Arcadia
INTERLOCHEN CENTER FOR THE ARTS
Pere Marquette State Forest
CRYSTAL MOUNTAIN RESORT
Thompsonville
Houghton Lake
William Mitchell State Park
Crooked Lake
Manistee
Cadillac
Lake Mitchell
Lake Cadillac
Manistee
Nordhouse Dunes Wilderness Area
Pine
River
National
Ludington
Forest
Pentwater
Silver Lake State Park
LODA LAKE WILDFLOWER SANCTUARY
Clare
Big Rapids
Hart
White Cloud
Stanwood

0   10 mi
0   10 km

© AVALON TRAVEL

home to many state parks, several state forests, and the expansive Manistee National Forest. Located along the western edge of the Leelanau Peninsula—known for its scenic, award-winning wineries—lies another natural wonder, the Sleeping Bear Dunes National Lakeshore, one of the Midwest's finest natural escapes and a popular destination for cyclists, anglers, hikers, skiers, kayakers, and amateur geologists. While there's plenty to keep anyone occupied, the most eye-catching features are the pyramidal dunes themselves, some of which rise over 400 feet high, constituting the largest freshwater dunes in the world and offering an unparalleled view of Glen Lake and the surrounding hills.

PLANNING YOUR TIME

Extending from the southern edge of Manistee National Forest to the Mackinac Bridge, Northwest Michigan is a sprawling region. Although you can reach the area via boat, bus, or plane, you'll find it easier to navigate with a vehicle—whether your own or a rented one. By car, you can get here via U.S. 31 from Muskegon, U.S. 131 from Grand Rapids, U.S. 10 from Midland, and I-75 from the U.P.

If your schedule's tight, plan a weekend getaway to Traverse City. Two weeks, however, will ensure time to experience more than just the Cherry Capital, including Sleeping Bear Dunes, the Leelanau Peninsula, Manistee National Forest, Beaver Island, and several coastal towns, beaches, and golf resorts.

Summer is exceedingly popular in Northwest Michigan, especially in the resort towns and during the area's annual festivals. So, if you aren't a fan of crowds, try to come in spring, fall, or winter.

For more details about Northwest Michigan, contact the **West Michigan Tourist Association** (741 Kenmoor Ave., Ste. E, Grand Rapids, MI 49546, 800/442-2084, www.wmta.org).

HISTORY

Traverse City has been hosting visitors ever since the French explorers and fur traders passed through in the 1600s, soon spreading word of the treacherous canoe passage across the gaping mouth of the bay, *la grande traversée*. The Traverse region has attracted everyone from James Jesse Strang, a self-proclaimed king who set his sights on ruling Beaver Island, to a family called the Hemingways, who summered for decades on the shores of Walloon Lake.

But it was the Victorian "resorters" who left an indelible mark. Summer visitors began trickling in around the 1860s, escaping hot and sticky Midwestern cities for the lake's crisp breezes and gentle shores. Soon, they were flooding into communities like Charlevoix and Petoskey, by steamship and by train. The "old money" of Chicago, Detroit, and Cleveland built exclusive summer homes. The simply rich stayed in grand pastel-painted hotels. Good Christians came to the church-run camps, which soon evolved from canvas tents to frilly Victorian cottages that remain well preserved today. Decade after decade, they attended Sousa concerts in the park, sailed dinghies across the harbor, and sipped lemonade on verandas overlooking the beautiful blue-green bays.

Today, the two bays anchor one of the state's most popular vacation areas, where the air is still crisp and clean, and the waters are still clear and accessible. Like elsewhere, development is a hot-button issue, as slick developments for urban visitors push aside the quaint cottages and small-town life that made everyone want to visit here in the first place. The populations of lakeside Traverse City, Charlevoix, and Petoskey can grow severalfold on a good July weekend. Legions of "designer" golf resorts, blue-ribbon fly-fishing rivers, back-road cycling routes, and some of the Midwest's largest ski resorts have drawn visitors inland, too.

But for all this activity, the region's past still weaves into the scene—the lyrical French names, the proud old lighthouses, the industrialists' homes, the century-old family farms. Like the great dunes that ignore park boundaries and drift across the newly paved park roads, past and present jumble together here, some parts planned, other parts as wild as the wind.

Nowhere does that seem more apparent than on Beaver Island. Irish immigrants arrived here in the 1840s, fleeing the potato famine and looking for new opportunity. They built Beaver Island into one of the premier commercial fisheries on the Great Lakes, ringing the hooked harbor at St. James with docks, net sheds, and icehouses. At about the same time, a man named Jesse Strang arrived. A New Yorker who challenged Brigham Young and claimed to be the leader of the Mormons, brought his faithful to Beaver Island, where he proclaimed himself king, took five wives, began a newspaper, pushed the Irish off their land, and eventually was assassinated by two of his followers.

The Irish reclaimed their island, the population soared to nearly 2,000 by the turn of the 20th century, and today, more than a third of the island's 500 year-round residents are descendants of the original Irish immigrant families. The St. Patrick's Day celebration lasts for the better part of a week.

The parasitic lamprey eel and overfishing pretty much ruined the commercial fishing trade, and the island's other main industry, logging, disappeared when ships converted from wood-burning engines to fossil fuels. Today, residents earn their living coaxing a few crops out of the rocky, sandy soil or, more commonly, by running service businesses that make a lion's share of their annual wages in July and August. By and large, residents encourage the summer tourist trade and the business visitors bring to the island. There's more of a battle regarding those who build summer cottages. While the building trades are a mainstay of the island economy and many welcome the jobs new construction provides, plenty of others oppose development. It's the universal controversy, fought in rural areas all over the continent.

Traverse City and Vicinity

Traverse City sits at the foot of Grand Traverse Bay, a body of water with incredible color and clarity. From blue to green to aquamarine, it shifts hues like a chameleon warming in the sun. The bay, not surprisingly, remains the top vacation draw in Traverse City. In summer months, this water lover's playground hums with activity—filled with kayaks, fishing boats, Jet Skis, sailboards, cruising sailboats, and twin-masted tall ships—and the sand beaches fill up with sunbathers and volleyball players.

Though its population swells from 14,400 to nearly 300,000 in summer months—especially during the National Cherry Festival—Traverse City has managed to accomplish what few "vacation towns" have: It remains a real community, where services like hardware stores and quick-print shops still operate alongside the gift shops and galleries. Locals actually use their pretty downtown area, and peaceful neighborhoods still thrive just a few blocks away. Traverse City, the self-proclaimed

"cherry capital of the world," has style *and* substance. Oh, there's no doubt tourism drives the economy here, but Traverse City's strong sense of place makes it all the more appealing to residents and visitors alike.

SIGHTS
Historic Sites and Museums

Downtown Traverse City abounds in Victorian architecture and historic buildings. One must-see is the 1892 red-brick **City Opera House** (106 E. Front St., 231/941-8082, www.cityoperahouse.org), which is currently being restored to its Victorian splendor. Visitors can better appreciate the lovely theater by attending one of its regularly scheduled concerts, comedy shows, and other events.

On the campus of Northwestern Michigan College, the **Dennos Museum Center** (1701 E. Front St., 231/995-1055, www.dennosmuseum.org, 10 A.M.–5 P.M. Mon.–Sat., 1–5 P.M. Sun., $4 adults, $2 children) is a wonderful find. It houses one of the nation's finest collections of

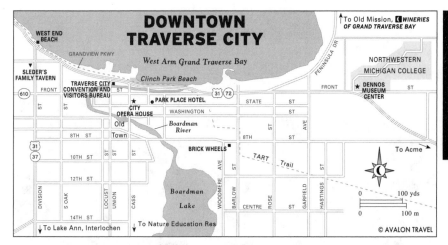

Inuit art, along with interactive exhibits in the Discovery Gallery that combine art, science, and technology.

In nearby Acme, the **Music House Museum** (7377 U.S. 31 N, 231/938-9300, www.musichouse.org, 10 A.M.–4 P.M. Mon.–Sat., noon–4 P.M. Sun. May–Oct., 10 A.M.–4 P.M. Fri.–Sat., noon–4 P.M. Sun. Nov.–Dec., $10 adults, $3 children 6–15) is another surprise, showcasing a vast array of rare antique musical instruments, from 1870 to 1930. Its collection includes music boxes, jukeboxes, nickelodeons, pipe organs, and a hard-carved Belgian dance organ.

Old Mission Peninsula

The Old Mission Peninsula pierces north from Traverse City, a narrow sliver of land that neatly divides Grand Traverse Bay in two. This whale-back ridge stretches 22 miles, a quiet agrarian landscape cross-hatched with cherry orchards and vineyards. Nowhere else on earth grows more cherries per acre than the Old Mission Peninsula, where the surrounding waters, insulating snows, and cool summer air form the perfect microclimate for raising fruit. Veer off M-37 onto almost any country road to wander past the pretty, peaceful orchards.

Grapes also thrive on the Old Mission Peninsula, creating a burgeoning winemaking

industry (www.wineriesofoldmission.com). (Though locals like to tell you it's because the peninsula sits at the same latitude as Bordeaux, France, they really should thank the moderating effects of the lake.) Most of the seven wineries here offer tours and tastings, and visiting them brings an extra benefit: The ridge-top roads of the Old Mission Peninsula come with incredible views that often take in both arms of Grand Traverse Bay.

Chateau Grand Traverse Winery (12239 Center Rd., 231/223-7355, www.cgtwines. com, 10 A.M.–7 P.M. Mon.–Sat., noon–6 P.M. Sun. June–Aug., shorter hours Sept.–May), located nine miles north of Traverse City on M-37, was a pioneer in bringing European Vinifera wines to the Midwest. It has a beautiful tasting room, with wonderful bay views, for tasting its internationally award-winning rieslings and ice wines. In addition, the winery offers tours as well as luxurious accommodations in its hilltop inn.

Just east of Bowers Harbor, **Bowers Harbor Vineyards** (2896 Bowers Harbor Rd., 231/223-7615, www.bowersharbor.com, 10:30 A.M.–6 P.M. Mon.–Sat., noon–6 P.M. Sun. May–Oct., 10:30 A.M.–5 P.M. Mon.–Sat., noon–5 P.M. Sun. Nov.–Apr.) is a small, friendly, family-run winery, with a year-round tasting room. **Chateau Chantal** (15900 Rue

© CHATEAU CHANTAL

the year-round Chateau Chantal winery on the Old Mission Peninsula

de Vin, 231/223-4110, www.chateauchantal. com, 11 A.M.–8 P.M. Mon.–Sat., noon–5 P.M. Sun. mid-June–Aug., shorter hours Sept.–mid-June) includes both a tasting room and a B&B in a French chateau–inspired winery high on a hill. Winery tours are offered during the summer months; complimentary wine-tastings are available all year. **Peninsula Cellars** (11480 Center Rd., 231/933-9787, www.peninsulacellars.com, 10 A.M.–6 P.M. Mon.–Sat., noon–6 P.M. Sun.) is one of the peninsula's newer wineries, with a tasting room in a converted 1896 schoolhouse.

The peninsula was named for the mission first built near its tip in 1829 by a Presbyterian minister who came from Mackinac to convert the Ojibwa and Ottawa. The **Mission Church** on M-37 in Old Mission is a replica, but it houses the original bell. A few displays tell the peninsula's early history and evolution into a fruit-growing region. Nearby, the 1842 **Dougherty House** is the real thing. Curve east around Old Mission Harbor to **Haserot Beach,** a curve of sand near the small protected harbor.

The **Old Mission Point Lighthouse** stands sentinel over the point, a pretty structure dating to 1870, along with its white clapboard keeper's home (now privately owned). The state has acquired several hundred acres around the lighthouse, including much of the rocky beach, land set aside for a possible future state park.

Beaches and Tours

The Old Mission Peninsula divides Grand Traverse Bay into two "arms." The West Arm (or West Bay) is the larger and deeper of the two, home to marinas, the bay's tall ship cruises, and a few commercial enterprises. The East Arm (or East Bay) is shallower, warmer, and ringed with sugary sand at its south end— prompting lodging and water-sports ventures along its shores.

Along with all the wonderful beaches on the Leelanau Peninsula, Traverse City has several right downtown. Most popular is **Clinch Park Beach** on West Bay, east of Union Street. A little farther west, at the foot of Division, **West End Beach** is the place to head for volleyball. On East Bay, **Bayside Park** has 600 feet of

MICHAEL MOORE'S SALUTE TO FILM

Perhaps Michigan's most infamous son, Michael Francis Moore was born in Flint in 1954. Years after studying journalism at the University of Michigan-Flint, Moore turned to filmmaking. His first film, *Roger & Me* (1989), was lauded by some as a biting indictment of the automotive industry, and has been considered by others as the start of Moore's truth-bending, politically-charged style of filmmaking. In equal measure, he's been called a documentary filmmaker and a propaganda artist. Some of his films include *The Big One* (1997), another exposé about greedy executives and callous politicians; the Oscar-winning *Bowling for Columbine* (2002), an exploration of America's violent culture; *Fahrenheit 9/11* (2004), Moore's take on how the Bush administration used the tragic 9/11 event to push its war agenda; and *Sicko* (2007), a comparison of America's healthcare industry to others around the world.

No matter what you might think of Moore's controversial films, his contribution to Michigan's modern culture is undeniable. In 2005, Moore – along with photographer John Robert Williams and author Doug Stanton – established the **Traverse City Film Festival,** a charitable, educational organization whose sole purpose is to preserve one of America's few native art forms: cinema. The festival, which owns and operates a year-round arthouse movie theater in the Cherry Capital, also lures filmmakers and cinema buffs from around the world to its annual film festival in late July. This event, which has quickly become one of the state's biggest attractions, features panel discussions about the film industry in addition to screenings that include foreign films, American independent films, documentaries, and classic movies. For more information about the Traverse City Film Festival, visit www.traversecityfilmfest.org.

---

sand beach and a bathhouse, just off U.S. 31 near the Acme turnoff.

The **Nauti-Cat** (231/947-1730, www. nauti-cat.com) offers varied cruises on West Bay aboard a 47-foot catamaran. The open-deck arrangement allows for up to 43 guests. Prices range from $15 for a 90-minute kids cruise, to $35 for a champagne sunset cruise. Reservations are recommended, but walk-ons are accepted if there's space. An authentic replica of an 18th-century wooden schooner, the **Tall Ship Manitou** (Dockside Plaza, 13390 S. West Bay Shore Dr., 231/941-2000, www. tallshipsailing.com, $34–42 adults, $18–26 children) sets sail three times daily in July and August, cruising West Bay.

FESTIVALS AND EVENTS
◖ National Cherry Festival
Without question, Traverse City's largest event is the National Cherry Festival (800/968-3380, www.cherryfestival.org, prices vary), which takes place every July in various locations throughout downtown Traverse City. First held in 1926, this annual celebration of Michigan's cherry industry attracts over 500,000 participants, who come for the parades and fireworks, live entertainment, turtle races, cherry pie–eating contests, a grand cherry-themed buffet, and a cherry farmers market. Participants will be able to taste a wide array of cherry-enhanced cuisine and cherry wines, produced by local wineries.

One of the busiest days, but well worth the fuss, is the first Sunday of every festival, when an air show features the astonishing flying skills of the U.S. Navy Blue Angels. Get there early, and plan to be camped out in the same spot for much of the day. If you're feeling really lucky, try entering the cherry pit–spitting contest, always a crowd pleaser.

◖ Traverse City Film Festival
The state's premier film event, the Traverse City Film Festival (various venues, 231/392-1134, www.traversecityfilmfest.org, tickets $9–50), brings a bit of Hollywood to northern Michigan. Founded in 2005 by Academy Award–winning filmmaker Michael Moore,

the festival lures more and more celebrities, filmmakers, and cinema buffs every summer (usually at the end of July or beginning of August). For an entire week, the festival showcases eclectic film screenings, informative panel discussions, various parties, and live musical performances; it also offers a terrific opportunity to see a few of your favorite movie stars in person.

SHOPPING

Traverse City's main east-west avenue, **Front Street,** is lined with dozens of cafés, galleries, and shops, offering everything from nautical home furnishings to cherry pies. Cobblestone **Union Street** marks Old Town, a growing area of arts and antiques.

If you have a desire for produce, you can always browse the **farmers market,** held every Saturday morning from spring through fall along the banks of the Boardman River, between Union and Cass Streets. Depending on the season, you'll find all manner of veggies, fruits, and flowers—and you can always count on the reliable muffin crop.

SPORTS AND RECREATION
Golf

Award-winning golf courses abound in the Traverse region, just a few minutes away from Traverse City. About three miles from town, **Elmbrook Golf Course** (1750 Townline Rd., 231/946-9180, www.elmbrookgolf.com, daily Apr.–Oct., $39 w/cart) is an older, unpretentious course, with lots of hills, valleys, and views of Grand Traverse Bay.

In Acme, about five minutes east of Traverse City on U.S. 31, you'll find one of the state's finest golfing destinations. The 900-acre **Grand Traverse Resort and Spa** (100 Grand Traverse Village Blvd., 231/534-6000, www. grandtraverseresort.com, daily Apr.–Oct., $35–140) features two signature courses: The Bear, a famously humbling course designed by Jack Nicklaus, with minute greens and deep, deep bunkers, and the Gary Player–designed Wolverine, a watery course with views of Grand Traverse Bay. Both tend to overshadow

Spruce Run, the resort's other fine championship course, which, though less challenging, is equally stunning. Set amid an evergreen forest, Spruce Run can even be appreciated by bird-watchers; ducks, swans, and blue herons abound here. In addition to the courses, the resort provides luxurious accommodations, excellent dining, a top-notch spa, an indoor water park, and a 24-hour dog care facility.

East of Acme, the rolling pine forests and old orchards of **High Pointe Golf Club** (5555 Arnold Rd., Williamsburg, 231/267-9900, www. highpointegolf.com, daily Apr.–Oct., $30–79 w/cart) once earned it a spot among *GOLF Magazine*'s 100 favorites. Meanwhile, the views of picturesque Torch Lake add an extra challenge to keeping your head down at the **A-Ga-Ming Golf Resort** (627 A-Ga-Ming Dr., Kewadin, 231/264-5081, www.a-ga-ming.com, daily Apr.–Oct., $44–84), which is situated north of Acme via U.S. 31 and offers two 18-hole courses: Torch and the relatively new Sundance.

Perhaps you'll find it surprising that the quiet countryside southwest of Traverse City is home to one of the best public golf courses in the state, but it's indeed true. Situated alongside a gorgeous stretch of Lake Michigan shoreline and accessible via M-22, the 18-hole **Arcadia Bluffs Golf Course** (14710 Northwood Hwy., Arcadia, 231/889-3001, www.arcadiabluffs. com, daily Apr.–Nov., $50–180) promises incredible views of the glistening lake, plus a pro shop and seasonal restaurant in the Nantucket-style clubhouse.

For those who enjoy a somewhat less challenging golf game, stop by **Pirate's Cove Adventure Park** (1710 U.S. 31 N, 231/938-9599, www.piratescove.net, 10 A.M.–11 P.M. daily Apr.–Oct., $7.95 adults, $7.50 children), where families can play at one of the finest miniature-golf chains in the country. At this award-winning theme park, players can learn about infamous pirates while navigating their way through caves, over footbridges, beneath cascading waterfalls, and alongside wrecked pirate ships. The complex offers two 18-hole courses in addition to bumper boats, racing go-carts, and a water coaster.

Hiking and Biking

Here's the happy general rule about the Traverse Bay region: Downhill ski resorts seem to morph into golf resorts, and cross-country skiing trails often become mountain-biking trails.

As proof, the **Pere Marquette State Forest** has a couple of "pathways" in the Traverse City area that double as cross-country and mountain-biking trails. You may hike them, too, of course. Most widely known is the 15.6-mile **North American VASA Trail** (www.vasa.org). The VASA (named after Swedish King Gustav Vasa) has challenging climbs and descents. Take U.S. 31 toward Acme, turn right onto Bunker Hill Road, drive 1.5 miles, then turn right again onto Bartlett to reach the trailhead.

The **Sand Lakes Quiet Area** is a classic north-woods area of small lakes, forest, and meadow about 10 miles east of Traverse City. Ten miles of trails loop through the 2,500 acres of terrain, which is moderately hilly—pleasant, but nothing extreme. For more information on biking, hiking, and camping in the Pere Marquette State Forest, call or stop by the **Michigan Department of Natural Resources** district office (970 Emerson Rd., 231/922-5280).

For getting around Traverse City and reaching various trailheads on your bike, you can avoid busy U.S. 31 by using the 10.5-mile **Traverse Area Recreation Trail (TART)** (www.traversetrails.org). This off-road path shares a railroad right-of-way. It currently extends from U.S. 72 at the West Bay beach to the Acme area, with plans to continue expanding it eastward.

The entire Traverse region offers fantastic back-road cycling. The **Cherry Capital Cycling Club** (231/941-2453, www.cherry-capitalcyclingclub.org) has mapped out zillions of options on its *Bicycle Map of Northwest Michigan,* printed on coated stock that can take a lot of abuse. It's available for $7 at local bike shops like **Brick Wheels** (736 E. 8th St., 231/947-4274, www.brickwheels.com, daily). This full-service shop has knowledgeable employees and rents road bikes, mountain bikes, and in-line skates.

Bird-Watching

A few miles south of Traverse City on Cass Road, the **Nature Education Reserve** maintains 435 acres along the Boardman River and the Sabin and Boardman Ponds. Though just outside of town, this surprisingly peaceful area includes five miles of self-guided nature trails (no bikes) that wind along the river and cross through marshes and grasslands. The Traverse Bay region attracts particularly large populations of mute swans, and a pair frequently nests here, gliding gracefully across the glassy ponds. Farther upstream on the Boardman, large stands of oak crown a steep bluff climbing up from the river and another small flowage, **Brown Bridge Pond.** Stairs and trails lead out to observation platforms and down to the water's edge.

Canoeing and Fishing

What's that island in the West Arm, you ask? It's **Power Island,** a 200-acre nature preserve owned by the city, with beaches and five miles of hiking trails. For paddlers and other boaters, it's a fun destination for an afternoon picnic, but on weekends, it often becomes a local party spot.

Grand Traverse Bay isn't the only show in town. The beautiful **Boardman River** twists gently through Grand Traverse County before melting into the West Arm at Traverse City. The Boardman offers excellent fly-fishing and canoeing. Generally, its upper stretches run deeper and are better for paddling.

Skiing

West of Thompsonville on M-115, **Crystal Mountain Resort** (12500 Crystal Mountain Dr., 231/378-2623, www.crystalmountain. com) began as a downhill skiing destination but has evolved into much more. While it still offers plenty of downhill—45 runs on two camel-humped slopes—it really shines in the cross-country department. Nordic skiers ride a chairlift from the Nordic Center to the top of the downhill slopes, where a trailhead leads to 25 miles of impeccably groomed cross-country terrain—a combination of gentle pathways and roller-coaster rides that weave all over the resort's 1,500 acres of land. The network is truly one of the finest in the Midwest.

Crystal Mountain invested wisely in its architecture, with pretty villas and tasteful condos scattered all around the property. Rates begin at about $120, but vary widely depending on unit and time of visit. Ski or golf packages are usually your best deal. In summer, Crystal's 36 holes of golf are the main draw, but it also offers clay tennis courts, indoor and outdoor pools, and other resort amenities. Some of those great cross-country trails welcome mountain bikes in spring—more than 10 miles of intermediate and advanced terrain overlooking the Betsie River Valley, along with 13 more miles in the nearby state forest.

ACCOMMODATIONS

The Traverse City area has more than 5,000 rooms, everything from inexpensive motels to deluxe resorts. The **Traverse City Convention & Visitors Bureau** (101 W. Grandview Pkwy., 231/947-1120, www.mytraversecity.com) has a good directory and can help you narrow down your choices. In summer months, you'd be wise to show up with a reservation.

Lots of mom-and-pop motels and chain operations line U.S. 31 along East Bay, Traverse City's original tourist stretch, known as the "miracle mile." Some newer ones have nudged onto this desirable real estate, like the **Pointes North Beachfront Resort Hotel** (2211 U.S. 31 N, 800/968-3422, www.pointesnorth.com, $150–250 d). It has 300 feet of private beach, a waterfront pool, balconies, and in-room mini-kitchens. You'll save money by staying on the other side of U.S. 31, of course, and plenty of public beaches mean you can still get to the water easily enough. The **Traverse Bay Inn** (2300 U.S. 31 N, 800/968-2646, www.traversebayhotels.com, $39–125 d) is a tidy and pleasant older motel, with an outdoor hot tub and pool, and some fancier new suites with kitchens and fireplaces. It gets bonus points for allowing dogs.

It's not on the water, but the upper floors of the ◖ **Park Place Hotel** (300 E. State St., 231/946-5000, www.park-place-hotel.com, $105–200 d) come with incredible views of Grand Traverse Bay. This 1870s downtown landmark was in sad disrepair in 1989, when the local Rotary club purchased it and poured $10 million into renovations. The Traverse City Rotary is believed to be the wealthiest in the nation, after it discovered oil on property it owned. The club did a fabulous job restoring the Park Place to its turn-of-the-20th-century opulence.

Outside of town, the **Ellis Lake Resort** (8440 U.S. 31 S, Interlochen, 231/276-9502, www.ellislakeresort.com, $63–240 d) has cute waterfront cabins and an outdoor hot tub just 10 minutes from Traverse City. Pets are permitted. **Ranch Rudolf** (6841 Brown Bridge Rd., Traverse City, 231/947-9529, www.ranchrudolf.com, $68–150 d) has motel units and a lodge with fireplaces, but the draw here is the location: 12 miles from Traverse City in the Pere Marquette State Forest on the shores of the Boardman River. There's paddling and fly-fishing right outside the door. Tent and RV sites are also available.

Camping

You won't find a quiet nature retreat, but if you're looking for clean and convenient camping, then **Traverse City State Park** (1132 U.S. 31 N, 231/922-5270, state park vehicle permit required, $27) fits the bill. Just two miles east of downtown, the park has 343 modern sites in a suburbanish setting, grassy with shade trees. A pedestrian overpass will get you across busy U.S. 31 to the main feature of the park: a grassy picnic area and a quarter-mile of beach on Grand Traverse Bay. Though pretty, the stretch of sand can quickly become unpleasantly jammed on a summer weekend. Camp here for convenience, maybe, but head elsewhere for a day at the beach—the region has plenty of better choices. For reservations at the state park campground, contact the **Michigan Department of Natural Resources** (800/447-2757, www.michigan.gov/dnr).

You'll find more peace and seclusion at the many rustic campgrounds in the **Pere Marquette State Forest** just a few miles east of town. One to consider is **Arbutus Lake 4** (231/922-5280, $15), with 50 sites on a pretty chain of lakes. From U.S. 31 near the state park, take Four Mile Road south to North Arbutus Road.

FOOD

Traverse City is thick with good restaurants, from simple to elegant. **Apache Trout Grill** (13671 S. West Bayshore Dr., 231/947-7079, www.apachetroutgrill.com, 10 A.M.–10 P.M. daily, $8.50–28) is a casual spot overlooking the West Arm, featuring "northern waters" fish specialties partnered with distinctive sauces. **Sleder's Family Tavern** (717 Randolph St., 231/947-9213, www.sleders. com, 11 A.M.–11 P.M. Mon.–Thurs., 11 A.M.– midnight Fri.–Sat., noon–9 P.M. Sun., $8–17) has been around since 1882, an institution known for its burgers and ribs, and its gorgeous original mahogany and cherry bar.

On the Old Mission Peninsula, the **Boathouse** (14039 Peninsula Dr., 231/223-4030, www.boathouseonwestbay.com, 5 P.M.– close daily, $26–42) is one of the region's most highly touted restaurants, with fine, diverse cuisine in a nautical atmosphere overlooking the Bowers Harbor marina. The nearby **❰ Bowers Harbor Inn** (13512 Peninsula Dr., 231/223-4222, www.bowersharborinn.net, 5 P.M.–10 P.M. Sun.–Thurs., 5 P.M.–11 P.M. Fri.–Sat., $20–36) offers elegant dining in an 1880s mansion, complete with a resident ghost and an excellent wine list. Specialties include fish-in-a-bag and rack of lamb. Try the fried ice cream with bananas Foster sauce for dessert. For something quite different, try the Asian-inspired **Red Ginger** (237 E. Front St., 231/944-1733, www.eatatginger.com, 5 P.M.– 10 P.M. Mon.–Thurs., 5 P.M.–11 P.M. Fri.–Sat., $9–32). Featuring flavors from Chinese, Thai, Vietnamese, Japanese, and other Asian cuisines, the Red Ginger is easily the best Asian restaurant in northern Michigan. If you go on a Monday, you can enjoy some live jazz, while dining on Red Ginger dragon rolls and sake-glazed sea bass.

INFORMATION AND SERVICES

For more information about Traverse City, contact the **Traverse City Convention & Visitors Bureau** (101 W. Grandview Pkwy., 231/947-1120, www.mytraversecity.com, 8 A.M.–9 P.M. Mon.–Fri., 9 A.M.–5 P.M. Sat., noon–6 P.M. Sun.). Stop by the visitors center to pick up maps and brochures, talk to a volunteer staff member about area activities, and check out rotating exhibits that feature the area's culture, history, and environment. You can also consult the **Traverse City Area Chamber of Commerce** (202 E. Grandview Pkwy., 231/947-5075, www.tcchamber.org). For regional news and events, pick up a copy of the **Traverse City Record-Eagle** (www.record-eagle.com) or **Traverse** magazine (www.traversemagazine.com).

To learn more about the Old Mission Peninsula, visit www.oldmission.com. For details about Benzie County, contact the **Benzie County Visitors Bureau** (826 Michigan Ave., Benzonia, 800/882-5801, www.visitbenzie. com, 9 A.M.–5 P.M. Mon.–Fri.).

As Northwest Michigan's largest town, Traverse City offers an assortment of necessary services, including groceries, laundries, banks, and post offices. In case of an emergency requiring police, fire, or ambulance services, dial **911** from any cell or public phone. For medical assistance, consult **Munson Healthcare** (www.munsonhealthcare.org), which offers several locations in the area, including **Munson Medical Center** (1105 6th St., Traverse City, 231/935-5000).

GETTING THERE AND AROUND

Traverse City is 256 miles from Detroit and 318 miles from Chicago, via major routes such as I-94, I-75, U.S. 31, and M-72. If you're not driving, you can take a **Greyhound** bus (107 Hall St., 800/231-2222, www.greyhound. com) to Traverse City or fly into Traverse City's **Cherry Capital Airport (TVC)** (727

Fly Don't Dr., 231/947-2250, www.tvcairport.com), which offers service from Detroit and Minneapolis on Northwest Airlines and from Chicago on American Eagle and United Express. Five rental car companies are available.

Once in Traverse City, you can eschew the car in favor of public transit. The **Bay Area Transportation Authority** (231/941-2355, www.bata.net) offers year-round service throughout Grand Traverse and Leelanau Counties.

◖ INTERLOCHEN CENTER FOR THE ARTS

South of town, the summertime bustle of Traverse City quickly fades into rolling farmland and woodlots. Incongruously tucked within this rural landscape, 14 miles southwest of Traverse City on M-137, the Interlochen Center for the Arts (4000 M-137, Interlochen, 231/276-7200, www.interlochen.org) operates a renowned school on a 1,200-acre campus under a tall canopy of pines. For over 80 years, Interlochen has cultivated a passion for the arts, with year-round programs for adults and a yearly summer camp for young artists, during which nearly 2,500 gifted students come to explore music, dance, theater, film, literature, and visual arts. Audiences can also appreciate Interlochen; throughout the year, this acclaimed institute offers hundreds of concerts, readings, dance and theatrical performances, film screenings, and art exhibitions. Its lineup of musicians and entertainers has always been diverse and impressive, ranging from Itzhak Perlman to the Neville Brothers.

INTERLOCHEN STATE PARK

Not far from the Interlochen school, 187-acre Interlochen State Park (M-137, 231/276-9511, state park vehicle permit required) fans out between Green Lake and Duck Lake, preserving one of the area's few remaining stands of virgin white pine. Thanks to the park's location near Traverse City and Interlochen, its campsites are the main draw. They're very nice ones, too, clustered around the lakeshores with many nice lake views. The modern campground, with the bulk of the park's 480 campsites, is on Duck Lake. Several dozen rustic sites are across the park on Green Lake. Both fill up in summer, so reserve a site ahead of time. For reservations, call 800/447-2757 or visit www.michigan.gov/dnr.

BENZIE COUNTY

Unspoiled Benzie County stretches from west of Traverse City to the port of Frankfort, a hilly region dotted with lakes and bisected by two pristine rivers, the Platte and the Betsie.

The six miles of trails in the **Lake Ann Pathway** offer plenty to see, taking you past Lake Ann, some smaller lakes, a stretch of the Platte River, bogs, and natural springs. The hilly terrain is pleasant for hiking, mountain biking, or cross-country skiing. Part of the Pere Marquette State Forest, it also has a very nice rustic campground with 30 shady, grass-covered sites and a swimming beach on Lake Ann. Follow U.S. 31 west from Traverse City to Reynolds Road (4.5 miles past the turnoff to Interlochen). Turn right and drive four miles to the campground and trailheads.

The **Betsie River** wanders across Benzie County, eventually growing into a broad bay at Frankfort. Popular among anglers for trout and lake salmon, it is also a pretty paddling spot. From a put-in at Grass Lake, it's a 44-mile float to Betsie Lake near the Lake Michigan shore, largely through undeveloped state forest. There are several other public launches for a shorter trip.

West of Benzonia, the Betsie passes through the private wildlife sanctuary of **Gwen Frostic Prints** (231/882-5505, www.gwenfrostic.com, 9 A.M.–4:30 P.M. Mon.–Sat., 10 A.M.–4 P.M. Sun., free). Frostic's studio is an eclectic building of wood, stone, glass, and cement, where a dozen old Heidelberg presses clank away, cranking out Frostic's woodblock prints and poetry. Frostic, who died in 2001, was a woman of bold spirit, whose works paid homage to nature and independence. This intriguing shop has note cards, books, and more.

At Frankfort, the Betsie River flows into Betsie Lake, which forms a remarkably well-protected harbor in Lake Michigan. A crude wooden cross at the river's mouth marks the site of French explorer Père Jacques Marquette's death in 1675. Researchers now believe that the French voyageurs who wrote in their journals of the "Rivière du Père Marquette" were describing the Betsie. From here, you might be able to spot the offshore **Frankfort North Breakwater Light.**

North of Frankfort at Point Betsie, the 1858

Point Betsie Lighthouse (231/352-4915, www.pointbetsie.org, 10:30 A.M.–4:30 P.M. Sat., 12:30 P.M.–4:30 P.M. Sun., $2 adults, $1 children) perches atop a dune, with waves practically lapping at its base, a tenuous but highly scenic setting. The lighthouse was automated in 1984. The **Point Betsie Dunes Preserve** stretches south from the lighthouse, 71 acres of wonderfully undeveloped duneland, with barren sand beach, scrubby pines, and low-lying dunes.

The Leelanau Peninsula

A ragged land of hills, lakes, and scribbled shoreline straggling northward between Lake Michigan and Grand Traverse Bay, the Leelanau Peninsula has long held a grip on writers and artists (novelist Jim Harrison, among others, also makes his home here). Maybe it's the dramatic dichotomy of the place: On its western shore, the oh-so-grand dunes, rising directly up from the lake's surface; inland, a soft and pretty landscape, a muted watercolor of red barns, white farmhouses, and Queen Anne's lace waving in the roadside ditches.

All kinds of people will tell you that Leelanau is an Indian word meaning "land of delights," a description that certainly fits this varied peninsula. The only problem is, the word never existed in the language of the area's Ottawa Indians; they never even used the letter *l.* Henry Schoolcraft, the white man who explored the Lake Michigan coast in the 1820s, most likely named it, giving it an "Indian-sounding" name. "Leelanau" can be anything you want it to be—just like your time here.

Leelanau County begins just west of Traverse City, and the county line stretches 30 miles straight west to the Sleeping Bear Dunes and Lake Michigan. Everything above that line is the Leelanau, a 28-mile-long peninsula that includes 98 miles of Great Lakes shoreline, 142 inland lakes and ponds, 58 miles of streams, and numerous award-winning wineries. Roads twist along with the contours of the hills, luring you toward farm stands and onto dirt roads

that can't possibly go anywhere you intended to go.

As local author Bill Mulligan has noted, "The meandering expanse of water, woods, and sand of Leelanau is a nice counterweight to the exuberance of Traverse City." So meander.

◖ SLEEPING BEAR DUNES NATIONAL LAKESHORE

Glaciers and a millennium of wind and water sculpted the Sleeping Bear Dunes, rimming this corner of Michigan with a crust of sand and gravel, like salt on a margarita glass. Beach dunes line the southern part of the national seashore, the classic hillocks of sand you might picture when you think of dunes, created by the prevailing west winds carrying sand to low-lying shores.

But it's the perched dunes that claim center stage here, immense pyramids of sand spiking up from the very edge of Lake Michigan and climbing at an impossible angle toward the sky. Glaciers first carried these mountains of sand and gravel to what is now the shoreline; nature continues the process, with waves eroding the great dunes and westerlies building them up again. At their highest, the perched dunes once topped out at about 600 feet. Today, Sleeping Bear measures closer to 400 feet, still the largest freshwater dune in the world.

To borrow an old cliché, words really *can't* describe the Sleeping Bear Dunes. They can be a sunny, friendly playground, with squealing

LEGEND OF THE SLEEPING BEAR

According to the Ojibwa Indians that formerly inhabited the Great Lakes region, a terrible forest fire once raged in what is now Wisconsin, along the shores of Lake Michigan. In an effort to flee the conflagration, a mother bear and her two cubs tried to swim across the enormous lake, toward present-day Michigan. When the mother reached the far shore, she climbed to the top of a bluff to await her cubs, who had grown tired and lagged behind. As she waited, the sands collected around her, creating Sleeping Bear Dune, the largest in what eventually became **Sleeping Bear Dunes National Lakeshore** in 1977. Though the cubs sadly drowned in the lake, the Great Spirit took pity on the grieving mother and raised her children from the depths as North and South Manitou Islands, which lie offshore and are also part of the national park.

© TRAVERSE CITY CVB

a pebble-strewn beach at Sleeping Bear Dunes National Lakeshore

children tumbling down the Dune Climb. They can be lunar-like and desolate, a bleak desert on a January day. They can be pale and white-hot at noon, then glow in peaches and pinks like white zinfandel at sunset.

But they are always spectacular. Today, the Sleeping Bear Dunes National Lakeshore (9922 Front St., Empire, 231/326-5134, www.nps.gov/slbe, visitors center 8 A.M.–6 P.M. daily in summer, shorter hours off-season, dunes 24 hours daily, $10 vehicles, $5 individuals), established in 1977, encompasses nearly 72,000 acres, including 35 miles of Lake Michigan shoreline, North and South Manitou Islands, lakes, rivers, beech and maple forest, waving dune grasses, and those unforgettable dunes. It's truly a magnificent landscape, unlike anything else on the continent.

Empire Area

Situated beside Lake Michigan, Empire is home to the state's newest lighthouse, the cylindrical **Robert Manning Memorial Lighthouse,** erected in 1991 to honor a longtime resident. South of Empire, the **Empire Bluff Trail** winds

through forest before erupting into a clearing, for a dramatic vantage point of the big dunes some five miles north. In 0.75 mile, the trail dead-ends at a high bluff overlooking the water, so clear you can often see schools of big lake trout. Farther south, **Platte River Point** improves on a great day at the beach with a perfect setting, a sandy spit bordered by Lake Michigan and the mouth of the Platte River. Rent an inner tube from **Riverside Canoe Trips** (5042 Scenic Hwy., Honor, 231/325-5622 or 231/882-4072, www.canoemichigan.com, 8 A.M.–7 P.M. daily) on M-22 at the Platte River Bridge and enjoy the popular sport of launching in the river and shooting out into the lake.

Pierce Stocking Scenic Drive

"When I lived in Manhattan in the 1970s, I used to have a recurrent nightmare that there was a big highway across the top of the dunes and at the topmost point, a Holiday Inn," writes Kathleen Stocking in *Letters from the Leelanau*. "Now, except for the Holiday Inn, that prescient dream has materialized."

Ironically, the drive is named for Stocking's

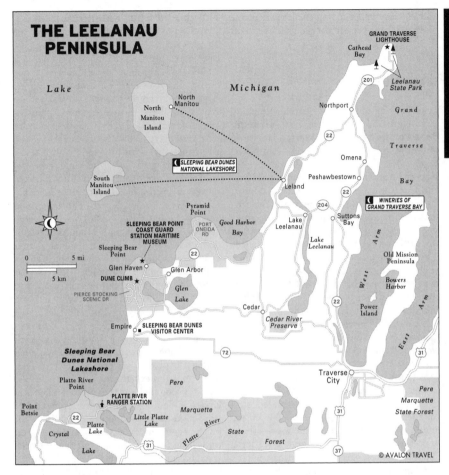

THE LEELANAU
PENINSULA

Lake

Michigan

GRAND TRAVERSE
LIGHTHOUSE

Cathead
Bay

Leelanau
State Park

(201)

North
Manitou

North
Manitou
Island

Northport

Grand

Traverse

Omena

SLEEPING BEAR DUNES
NATIONAL LAKESHORE

Peshawbestown

Bay

South
Manitou
Island

Leland

(22)

WINERIES OF
GRAND TRAVERSE BAY

Pyramid
Point

(204)

Lake
Leelanau

Suttons
Bay

SLEEPING BEAR POINT
COAST GUARD
STATION MARITIME
MUSEUM

PORT
ONEIDA
RD

Good Harbor
Bay

Lake
Leelanau

Arm

Old Mission
Peninsula

Sleeping Bear
Point

(22)

0   5 mi

0   5 km

Glen Haven

DUNE CLIMB

Glen Arbor

West

Bowers
Harbor

PIERCE STOCKING
SCENIC DR

Glen
Lake

Cedar

Cedar River
Preserve

Power
Island

East

Arm

Empire

SLEEPING BEAR DUNES
VISITOR CENTER

(22)

**Sleeping Bear
Dunes National
Lakeshore**

(72)

Platte River
Point

Pere

Traverse
City

Point
Betsie

PLATTE RIVER
RANGER STATION

Pere

(22)

Marquette

(31)

Marquette
State Forest

Platte
Lake

Little Platte
Lake

Platte

River

Crystal

(31)

State

Forest

Lake

(37)

© AVALON TRAVEL

father, a lumberman who owned much of the land that is now a national park. For those of us who didn't grow up with the dunes as our backyard, this 7.4-mile paved loop that winds through the woods and atop a stretch of dune is less offensive. In fact, it could be argued that it keeps people from traipsing over fragile dune plants for views. Either way, the extremely popular route *is* there, with scenic overlooks of Glen Lake, the dunes, and Lake Michigan.

The drive offers access to the **Cottonwood Trail,** a 1.5-mile sandy, self-guided walk that educates visitors about the ecology and diverse plant life in the dunes. The drive also leads you to the **Lake Michigan Overlook,** a platform 450 feet above the water with views stretching to Point Betsie, 15 miles south, and 54 miles across to Wisconsin. Though the park service discourages it—having seen too many sprained ankles, broken arms, and close cardiac calls—you can slide your way down the dune here, though it's a steep, long, exhausting climb back up, about an hour's worth of crawling.

That's why the park service points visitors instead to the nearby **Dune Climb,** a more manageable 130-foot dune that Mother Nature conveniently deposited on the lee side of the plateau. It's the perfect place to let kids run off their energy, or to climb up for a fine view of shimmering Glen Lake.

Glen Haven Area

In sleepy Glen Haven, the Park Service operates a nifty museum in the old lifesaving station. In summer months, the **Sleeping Bear Point Coast Guard Station Maritime Museum** (11 A.M.–5 P.M. daily mid-May–Sept., noon–5 P.M. Sat.–Sun. Oct., free) depicts the work of the U.S. Lifesaving Service, the forerunner of the U.S. Coast Guard. Exhibits include lifesaving boats and the cannon used to shoot lifelines out to the sinking vessels, while video programs illustrate the drill and the rigorous life the crews led. They got a regular workout: Some 50 ships wrecked along this passage between the mainland and the nearby Manitou Islands, one of the busiest routes on the Great Lakes in the mid-19th century, since it offered a convenient shortcut between Mackinac Island and Chicago. The station originally sat a few miles west at Sleeping Bear Point, but was moved here in 1931 when the ever-omnipotent dunes threatened to bury it.

East on M-109, **Glen Arbor** occupies a small patch of private real estate completely surrounded by the national park, Lake Michigan, and Glen Lake. It caters to the tourist trade with mostly tasteful galleries and craft shops, and also has a grocery for reloading the picnic supplies. Cherry lovers shouldn't miss **Cherry Republic** (6026 Lake St., 800/206-6949, www.cherryrepublic.com, 9 A.M.–9 P.M. daily), which bills itself as "the largest exclusive retailer of cherry products in the United States." You'll find cherry baked goods, cherry sodas, chocolate-covered cherries, cherry salsas, cherry jam . . . well, you get the idea.

Near Glen Arbor, the **Pyramid Point** hiking trail is a hilly 2.7-mile loop that leads to the park's northernmost point, with a high lookout over Lake Michigan and Sleeping Bear Bay. To reach the trailhead, take M-22 three miles east of Glen Arbor to Port Oneida Road.

North and South Manitou Islands

Lying about 17 miles off the mainland, the Manitous comprise more than 20,000 acres of once-developed land that has largely been reclaimed by nature and now is managed as part of Sleeping Bear Dunes National Lakeshore. South Manitou is the smaller (5,260 acres) and more accessible of the two, serviced by passenger ferry from Leland daily in summer months. The same ferry also stops at North Manitou five times a week in July and August, fewer times in spring and fall. The trip to either island takes about 90 minutes. No cars, bicycles, or pets are permitted. For schedule information and reservations, contact **Manitou Island Transit** (Leland, 231/256-9061, www.leelanau.com/manitou, round-trip $30 adults, $16 children under 13). The islands have potable water at a few locations, but no other services. Even day hikers should pack a lunch.

South Manitou Island was first settled in the 1830s. Islanders made a living by farming and logging, supplying food and fuel to the wood-burning steamers that traveled through the busy Manitou Passage. Farming was exceptional on South Manitou. Isolated from alien pollens, it proved the perfect place to produce crops and experiment with hybrid seeds, and was soon highly respected in agricultural circles. A South Manitou rye crop won first prize in an international exposition in 1920; by the 1940s, most of Michigan's bean crop came from South Manitou seed. By the 1960s, though, the island had become mostly a summer cottage getaway and, a decade later, the National Park Service began condemning and buying up the land for a national lakeshore.

Today, visitors can arrange for a tour ($8 adults, $5 children) through the ferry company, a 90-minute trip in an open-air truck that follows abandoned roads to farmsteads, a schoolhouse, and a cemetery. Near the ferry dock, a small visitors center in the old village post office has displays on island history. Nearby, the 1872 **South Manitou Island Lighthouse** is open on summer afternoons, allowing you to scale the 100-foot tower.

Hikers and backpackers will want to get

farther afield, though. The island has 10 miles of marked hiking trails that lead to some interesting sights. Day hikers will have to move right along, but they can make the six-mile round-trip to check out the wreck of the *Francisco Morazan* and still make it back in time for the afternoon ferry. Like many ships that failed to navigate the tricky Manitou Passage, this Liberian freighter ran aground in 1960. Its battered skeleton lies largely above the water's surface, just a few hundred yards offshore.

Nearby, a side trail winds through a grove of virgin cedars, some more than 500 years old. Deemed too isolated to log, the slow-growing trees are the largest of their kind left in North America, some measuring more than 15 feet around and nearly 90 feet tall. Another half-mile west, the state's most remote dunes tower over the western shore, 300-foot perched dunes similar to those on the mainland.

To properly enjoy all the island has to offer, of course, you need to spend more than an afternoon. Camping is permitted only at three rustic campsites; reservations are required.

Like South Manitou, **North Manitou Island** was once a farming and logging community, then a summer getaway. Acquired by the National Park Service in 1984, it still has some patches of private property. But otherwise, this large island is even less developed than its southern neighbor. Those who come here do so to camp, hike, and explore the abandoned buildings.

North Manitou receives far fewer visitors than South Manitou—until fall hunting season, anyway. Nine deer were introduced in the 1920s in the hopes of developing a herd large enough to hunt. Boy, did that work! In 1981, more than 2,000 deer roamed the island, decimating the vegetation so much that the island's forests had an "open park-like appearance," according to the Park Service. Today, it manages the herd by issuing hunting permits.

North Manitou has only one water source and one small rustic campground near the ferry dock; backcountry camping is permitted throughout the island's public property. Backcountry permits, though free, are required.

For camping permits and more information on the Manitous, contact **Sleeping Bear Dunes National Lakeshore** (231/326-5134, www.nps.gov/slbe).

LELAND TO NORTHPORT

The restored **"Fishtown"** at Leland's harbor is probably one of the most photographed spots in all of Michigan, a collection of 19th-century weathered gray fish shanties lined up on the docks. Whether you find it charming or obnoxious pretty much pegs your feelings about development—or reveals you as a local who remembers what the harbor looked like before the gift shops came to town. For many Leelanau residents, slicked-up Leland is a sad commentary on how tourism is erasing a simpler lifestyle.

Leland was a diverse industrial center in the mid-1800s, with two sawmills, a gristmill, an iron smelter, and a flourishing commercial fishing trade. By the early 1900s, eight fisheries were operating out of Leland. Where the Carp River spills into Lake Michigan, they built shanties along the docks, which they used to store ice, repair nets, and house equipment. Once common in ports all over the Great Lakes, most of these complexes completely disappeared when commercial fishing declined in the mid-1900s.

In Leland, the shanties happily remain, lined up on the docks right out of a historical photo. **Carlson's Fisheries** (231/256-9801, 9 A.M.–6 P.M. daily) still operates here, with its sturdy snub-nosed boats tied up to the pier and a shop that sells fresh fillets and smoked trout out of a long deli case. Most of the other shanties, though, now house gift shops and galleries, and the fishnets dry in the sun solely for the benefit of the summer tourist trade.

Though it's undeniably touristy, Leland is also undeniably attractive. The Carp River rolls by, where you can gaze down at the steelhead schooling in the waters. And whether or not you care for the shops, appreciate the fact that no one tore down these neat old buildings.

East of Leland lies lengthy Lake Leelanau. Popular with anglers, the lake is also a good quintessential view of Leland's historic "Fishtown" district

spot for paddlers, especially at the **Cedar River Preserve** (Leelanau Conservancy, 231/256-9665, www.theconservancy.com) along its southern shore, part of the Pere Marquette State Forest. Launch a canoe partway up the eastern shore, where Lake Leelanau Road intersects Bingham Road.

North of Leland, handsome **Peterson Park** sits high atop a bluff overlooking Lake Michigan, with picnic tables, a playground, and a great vantage point for the area's renowned sunsets. A steep staircase leads to a rocky beach, a good spot to hunt for Petoskey stones. Take M-201 to Peterson Park Road and turn left. For swimming, **Christmas Cove** offers a perfect arc of sugar-sand beach near the tip of the peninsula. To find it, follow M-201 north from Northport; just after it joins County Road 640, turn left on Kilcherman Road, which leads to Christmas Cove Road.

With a fine horseshoe harbor in the protected waters of Grand Traverse Bay, it's not surprising that Northport was one of the first spots settled on the Leelanau. Catholic missionaries established a village there in 1849, bringing with them several area Ottawa families that they had successfully converted to Christianity. Within 20 years, Northport was the county seat, overseeing a population of 2,500, and had a thriving commercial fishing industry. At the turn of the 20th century, it built a fancy resort hotel with room for 250 guests; within five years, the uninsured building burned to the ground. Today, Northport is popular with pleasure boaters, who still appreciate its snug harbor, and shoppers, who cruise its cute little downtown, a row of revamped 1860s buildings filled with eclectic antique and clothing shops.

LEELANAU STATE PARK

Split into two units at the tip of the Leelanau Peninsula, this 1,350-acre state park (15310 N. Lighthouse Point Rd., Northport, 231/386-5422 in summer or 231/922-5270 in winter, state park vehicle permit required) is a wonderful surprise: While the northern unit, with its lighthouse and campground, is very popular, most visitors seem to ignore its southern portion—meaning you can often have its lovely beaches and trails all to yourself.

In the southern unit, low dunes and more than a mile of sand beach curve along Cathead Bay. It's a mile walk from the parking area through maple and beech forest to get to the water, so it rarely draws a crowd. The park's 8.5 miles of walking trails radiate out from the same parking area. The **Mud Lake Tour** circles a wetland area and small lake, a good choice in spring and fall when waterfowl migrate through the area. The **Lake Michigan Trail** leads to the water, but don't skip the short side trail to the overlook—a stairway climbs up a dune for a breathtaking view of North Manitou Island. To reach the southern unit, follow County Road 629 north and turn left just after Woolsey Airport.

Five miles north, the **Grand Traverse Lighthouse** (15500 N. Lighthouse Point Rd., Northport, 231/386-7195, www.grandtraverse-lighthouse.com, 10 A.M.–6 P.M. daily June–Aug., noon–4 P.M. daily May and Sept.–Oct., $4 adults, $2 children) presides over the park's northern unit at the peninsula's tip. Built in 1858, the pretty white brick tower looks woefully small for the huge expanse of water that surrounds it. (The Coast Guard thought so, too; the light was decommissioned in 1972, replaced by a more pedestrian—but taller—steel tower churning away down on the beach.) Today, visitors can stroll through the on-site museum or climb the tower when the lighthouse is open.

SUTTONS BAY

Once a town largely inhabited by immigrant laborers from the fruit orchards, Suttons Bay has gotten fancier and wealthier along with the rest of the Leelanau Peninsula. With mechanization, there simply aren't that many laborers anymore, and the desirable real estate—on Grand Traverse Bay, just 12 miles from Traverse City, with views of the cross-hatched orchards of the Old Mission Peninsula—was just too good to leave alone. These days, Suttons Bay has almost become a suburb of Traverse City. Residents have worked hard to maintain the community's own personality, though, with colorfully painted storefronts and old-fashioned red telephone booths along St. Joseph's Avenue (M-22). Suttons Bay's downtown boasts a restored movie theater, all manner of galleries and boutiques, and some of the best restaurants in the Grand Traverse region.

█ WINERIES OF GRAND TRAVERSE BAY

As on the Old Mission Peninsula, the surrounding waters of Lake Michigan have a moderating effect on the Leelanau Peninsula, providing a surprisingly fruitful climate for growing cherries, apples, peaches, and wine grapes. Slow-changing lake temperatures keep things nice and cool during the growing season; come winter, they insulate the delicate trees and vines from killing deep freezes.

Michigan leads the nation in cherry production, and the Leelanau accounts for a quarter of that crop. And while Michigan's grape harvest isn't yet ready to challenge California's, a few of its wines have been. Leelanau (and Old Mission Peninsula) wineries regularly produce award-winning vintages, especially rieslings, which do particularly well in this climate, and chardonnays. Sure, you can still find some overly sweet cherry wines, but serious vintners are letting their wines do the talking, and winning over new converts every year. Some 18 wineries now make their home on the Leelanau Peninsula, and most offer both tours and tastings. For the latest information about this winemaking region, consult the **Leelanau Peninsula Vintner's Association** (www.lpwines.com).

Leelanau Cellars

Leelanau Cellars (7161 N. West Bay Shore Dr., Omena, 231/386-5201, www.leelanaucellars.com, noon–5 P.M. daily, June–Oct.) is the largest winery on the peninsula, producing 65,000 gallons of vinifera, hybrid, and fruit wines each year. Highest honors go to its Tall Ship chardonnay.

L. Mawby Vineyards

L. Mawby Vineyards (4519 S. Elm Valley Rd., Suttons Bay, 231/271-3522, www.lmawby.com, noon–6 P.M. Thurs.–Sat.), on the other hand, is one of the region's smallest wineries—with a big reputation, especially for its sparkling wines and oak-barrel-fermented dry whites. Larry Mawby produces about 3,000 cases a year, with a goal to "keep things small enough to do what I want to do—make great wine with minimal intervention." He brings a creative flair to the winemaking business, evidenced in the artful wine labels designed by his wife, artist Peggy Core. From Suttons Bay, follow County Road 633 south to Elm Valley Road.

Boskydel Vineyard

Boskydel Vineyard (7501 E. Otto Rd., Lake Leelanau, 231/256-7272, www.boskydel.com, noon–6 P.M. daily) was the first vineyard in the Grand Traverse region, with French hybrid grapes first planted in 1964. Today, the winery produces about 2,500 cases a year—mostly semi-dry red and white table wines—from its vineyards sloping down toward Lake Michigan. The winery is located two miles south of Lake Leelanau on County Road 641.

Good Harbor Vineyards

Some consider Bruce Simpson's dry white chardonnay and pinot gris the finest wines to come out of the Traverse Bay region. An informative self-guided tour at Good Harbor Vineyards (34 S. Manitou Trail, 231/256-7165, www.goodharbor.com, 11 A.M.–5 P.M. Mon.–Sat., noon–5 P.M. Sun. May–Nov.), three miles south of Leland on M-22 in Lake Leelanau, explains how he's done it.

Chateau Fontaine Vineyards & Winery

If you have a little more time, stop by Chateau Fontaine Vineyards & Winery (2290 S. French Rd., Lake Leelanau, 231/256-0000, www.chateaufontaine.com, noon–5 P.M. Wed.–Sun. June–Oct., noon–5 P.M. Sat.–Sun. May and Nov.–Dec.), a long-ago potato farm and cow pasture now transformed into 22 acres of grapevines. Head east to Suttons Bay, where you'll find **Black Star Farms** (10844 E. Revold Rd., 231/944-1271, www.blackstarfarms.com, 10 A.M.–6 P.M. Mon.–Sat., noon–5 P.M.

Sun. May–Nov., 11 A.M.–5 P.M. Mon.–Sat., noon–5 P.M. Sun. Dec.–Apr.), billed as "an agricultural destination." This fascinating winery, distillery, creamery, and farmers market also offers a welcoming tasting room and a luxurious bed-and-breakfast.

More Wineries

Take special note of several other locales in Suttons Bay, including **Raftshol Vineyards** (1865 N. West Bay Shore Dr., 231/271-5650, www.raftsholvineyards.com, noon–5 P.M. daily), a former dairy enterprise and cherry orchard that now produces over 1,000 cases of bordeaux varietal red wines annually. Owned by a cardiologist, with a special interest in Michigan's agriculture, **Chateau de Leelanau Vineyard & Winery** (5048 S. West Bayshore Dr., 231/271-8888, www.chateaudeleelanau.com, 11 A.M.–6 P.M. Mon.–Sat., noon–5 P.M. Sun. May–Oct., shorter hours Nov.–Apr.) presents a tasting room and retail store not far from Grand Traverse Bay, as well as one in Frankenmuth. Established in 1995, the **Ciccone Vineyard and Winery** (10343 E. Hilltop Rd., 231/271-5553, www.cicconevineyards.com, noon–6 P.M. daily June–Oct., shorter hours Nov.–May), curiously owned by Madonna's father, is a Tuscan-inspired winery and tasting room. For a $5 fee, you can purchase a Ciccone wine glass and up to six tastings of the vintner's choice.

FESTIVALS AND EVENTS

The Leelanau Peninsula is home to a myriad of art festivals, culinary events, and seasonal gatherings. One curious event occurs in late September, the annual **Harvest Stompede Vineyard Run & Walk**, which features a race through Leelanau's vineyards as well as a tour of area wineries. During the weekend, visitors are able to sample wines, gourmet pastas, and other culinary delights. For more information, consult the **Leelanau Peninsula Vintner's Association** (www.lpwines.com).

DIVING

The waters around North Manitou Island, South Manitou Island, and the Sleeping Bear Dunes are rife with historic dock ruins and shipwrecks, making the **Manitou Passage Underwater Preserve** a fascinating place for scuba divers. Besides the popular *Francisco Morazan* wreck near the south end of South Manitou Island, divers enjoy exploring the artifacts that abound on the *Walter L. Frost,* a wooden steamer that ran aground in 1905, only to be further wrecked in 1960 when the *Morazan* landed on top of it. For more information, contact the **Michigan Underwater Preserve Council** (800/970-8717, www.michiganpreserves.org).

ACCOMMODATIONS AND FOOD

If your budget won't allow a stay at **(€ Black Star Farms** (10844 E. Revold Rd., Suttons Bay, 231/944-1271, www.blackstarfarms.com, $215– 395 d)—a winery, creamery, market, and luxurious B&B—you'll be happy to know that the region also accommodates campers. The rustic campground at **Leelanau State Park** (15310 N. Lighthouse Point Rd., Northport, 231/386-5422 in summer or 231/922-5270 in winter, state park vehicle permit required, $15) has 52 wonderful sites, with several right along the water and several more with water views. Though the campground is extremely popular in summer, most sites offer a fair amount of seclusion.

In Leland, a couple of restaurants overlook the river and Fishtown, including **(€ The Cove** (111 River St., 231/256-9834, www.thecoveleland. com, 11:30 A.M.–9 P.M. daily, $9–26), featuring seafood chowder, fish stew, and fresh fish specials. A block or two farther upstream, across M-22 (the main drag), **The Bluebird Restaurant & Bar** (102 River St., 231/256-9081, www.leelanau.com/bluebird, 11:30 A.M.–9 P.M. Tues.– Sun., $6–14) is a well-known dinner spot, with reasonably priced seafood dishes, homemade soups, and a decent wine list.

Meanwhile, in Suttons Bay, **Samuel's** (111 St. Joseph Ave., 231/271-6222, 5 P.M.–close Tues.–Sat., $12–23) has a particularly good wine list and an "upscale regional" menu that features gingersnap–encrusted walleye and Leelanau County's "most outrageous burger." For more casual dining, try **Dick's Pour House**

(103 Philip, Lake Leelanau, 231/256-9912, www.dickspourhouse.com, 11:30 A.M.–10 P.M. Sun.–Thurs., 11:30 A.M.–11 P.M. Fri.–Sat., shorter hours in winter, $7–16) for pizza, sandwiches, soups, pies, and a Friday fish fry.

INFORMATION AND SERVICES

For more information about the Leelanau Peninsula, contact the **Traverse City Convention & Visitors Bureau** (101 W. Grandview Pkwy., 231/947-1120, www. mytraversecity.com, 8 A.M.–9 P.M. Mon.–Fri., 9 A.M.–5 P.M. Sat., noon–6 P.M. Sun.). You can also consult the **Leelanau Peninsula Chamber of Commerce** (5046 S. West Bay Shore Dr., Ste. G, Suttons Bay, 231/271-9895, www.leelanauchamber.com), **Leelanau Communications** (113 N. Main, Leland, 231/256-2829, www.leelanau.com), the **Leland Michigan Chamber of Commerce** (231/256-0079, www.lelandmi.com), the **Suttons Bay Area Chamber of Commerce** (231/271-5077, www.suttonsbayarea.com), and **The Third Coast Traveler** (www.thetctraveler.com).

If you require other services while traveling across the Leelanau Peninsula, remember that nearby Traverse City offers everything you might need, from groceries to hospitals. If an emergency occurs, don't hesitate to dial **911** from any phone.

GETTING THERE AND AROUND

To reach the Leelanau Peninsula, you can take a **Greyhound** bus (107 Hall St., 800/231-2222, www.greyhound.com) to Traverse City or fly into **Cherry Capital Airport (TVC)** (727 Fly Don't Dr., 231/947-2250, www.tvcairport.com), where you'll find five major rental car companies. If you're driving through Michigan, you can also reach the peninsula via U.S. 31, whether you're coming from Muskegon or Petoskey. To navigate the peninsula itself, you can either rely on the **Bay Area Transportation Authority** (231/941-2355, www.bata.net) or drive yourself from village to village, using M-72 and M-22.

Manistee to Cadillac

As you continue south along the Lake Michigan shoreline, towns grow sparser, summer crowds thin, and beaches climb into windswept dunes. If you're looking for a quiet beach walk or a mellow waterfront town without a full parade of activities and attractions, this may be the stretch of shore for you. Even farther south lies the Manistee National Forest, which is surrounded by towns like Ludington and Pentwater and contains several inland lakes, miles of hiking possibilities, and a wildflower sanctuary.

MANISTEE

Manistee's slogan is "Manistee: A Great Place to Be." While the city's downtown is a charming mix of historic logging buildings and ornate Victorian mansions, much of the credit for that claim goes to the wonderful Manistee National Forest that lies just outside the city limits. In fact, the national forest is such a part of Manistee's psyche that the city honors it with the annual **Manistee National Forest Festival** each July. Manistee serves as a good base camp for exploring the forest, as well as an exceptionally lovely and untouched stretch of Lake Michigan shoreline. Before you head south, though, stop by the **Manistee North Pierhead Light,** erected in 1927 and still active today.

LUDINGTON

Because of its midpoint position on Lake Michigan and its ample supply of lumber, Ludington enjoyed a boom as a busy port during the latter half of the 19th century. (Originally named Père Marquette in honor of the missionary explorer who died here in 1675, the city later changed it's name to reflect the influence of its more recent founder, James Ludington, a lumber baron.) Today, visitors are drawn to its enormous expanse of sugar-sand

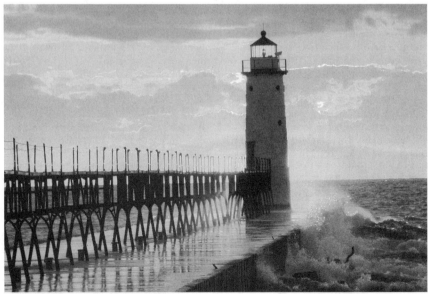

© MONTE SPANIER

the Manistee North Pierhead Light

beach. As you'll see from the busy marina in the heart of town, fishing and boating are the pulse of this appealing community. Take special note of the white pyramidal lighthouse, the 1924 **Ludington North Pierhead Light,** which replaced a much older lighthouse at the end of the breakwater.

Historic White Pine Village

Opened in 1976, the Historic White Pine Village (1687 S. Lakeshore Dr., 231/843-4808, www.historicwhitepinevillage.org, 10 A.M.–5 P.M. Tues.–Sat., 1–5 P.M. Sun. Memorial Day–Labor Day, shorter hours off-season, $7 adults, $5 children 6–17) presents over 25 buildings and historic sites, dedicated to preserving Mason County's past. It's worth bringing the whole family for this educational, yet fun-filled, tour. The old-fashioned ice cream parlor is an especially big hit with young travelers.

Ludington State Park

Ludington State Park (8800 W. M-116, 231/843-8671, www.ludingtonfriends.com, state park vehicle permit required) is one of the state's finest outdoor playgrounds and one of the largest state parks in the Lower Peninsula. Attendance ranks in the top 10 of all Michigan state parks, with good reason. The park encompasses more than 5,300 acres of beautiful beaches, almost six miles of Lake Michigan shoreline, dunes and forests that wrap around picnic areas, biking and hiking paths, three campgrounds, an interesting interpretive center, an inland lake, and a canoe trail.

The park occupies a wide strip of land between Lake Michigan and Hamlin Lake, straddling the Big Sable River, which connects them. The numerous trails that lace the park's interior are among the finest foot paths in the Lower Peninsula. They offer everything from a leisurely half-hour stroll to a rather strenuous six-mile round-trip trek to the 1867 **Big Sable Point Lighthouse** (www.bigsablelighthouse. org, 10 A.M.–5 P.M. daily May–Oct., $2 adults, $1 children 12–18), painted in tiers of black and white, and standing guard over Big Sable

Point. Trudging through sand is tiring on the calves, but the view from the top of the tower makes it all worth it.

PENTWATER AND SILVER LAKE

Once considered a sleepy town along the Lake Michigan shore, the Victorian logging town of Pentwater ticks along at a pleasant—but not frantic—summer pace. On Hancock Street, Pentwater's main drag, visitors prowl through a growing number of antique shops, searching for turn-of-the-20th-century treasures and nautical artifacts. A parade of pleasure boats purr through the boat channel that links Pentwater Lake and Lake Michigan, accompanied by folks strolling along the Channel Lane Park walkway. On the north side of the boat channel, **Charles Mears State Park** (400 W. Lowell St., 231/869-2051, state park vehicle permit required) seems more like a city beach than a state park.

Between Silver Lake and Lake Michigan lie more than 2,000 acres of unspoiled and ever-shifting sand dunes, remnants of the glaciers that once scrubbed this landscape. They are one of the largest deposits of dunes on the shores of Lake Michigan, acre after acre of ridges and valleys of wind-blown sand that are void of trees, scrub, or, in many places, even dune grass. Most of the dunes are protected as **Silver Lake State Park** (9679 W. State Park Rd., 231/873-3083, state park vehicle permit required), with hiking trails that climb high sand hills and weave through grasses and stunted trees. The park and dunes are located on one of the westernmost spots of the state's shoreline, a broad point that extends more than seven miles out from the main shore. From here, you can visit the 1874 **Little Sable Point Light,** a tall brick conical structure preserved by the park.

The Wood family once owned most of this land, and sold it to the state in 1973. They retained the right to use about 700 acres at the park's south end to operate **Mac Wood's Dune Rides** (629 N. 18th Ave., Mears, 231/873-2817, www.macwoodsduneridres.com, daily mid-

May–Oct., $15 adults, $10 children 3–11). Visitors load into hybrid buggy/trucks for a seven-mile drive through the dunes, roaring up and down hills and splashing along the Lake Michigan surf line. While it's easy to question this kind of use of the dunes, the operation does make an effort to help visitors understand and appreciate the region's unique ecology.

MANISTEE NATIONAL FOREST

Manistee National Forest (231/775-2421) stretches from Manistee south to Muskegon, over a half-million acres of woods, beaches, dunes, and two fine paddling rivers, the Pine and Pere Marquette. Most notable of the national forest's many attractions is the **Nordhouse Dunes Wilderness Area,** a 3,450-acre swath of untouched dunes and dune forest. It is the only federally designated wilderness in Michigan's Lower Peninsula, and the only federal dune wilderness in the nation.

The wilderness area includes three miles of isolated Lake Michigan beach, where dunes reach more than 140 feet. From the beach, 10 miles of hiking trails spin inland. Because they are minimally signed, bring a map and compass, along with plenty of water. Backcountry camping is permitted in the wilderness more than 200 feet from the waterline. The adjacent Nordhouse Dunes Recreation Area offers a modern campground with potable water.

Hikers should seek out the **Manistee River Trail,** a 10-mile route that follows the east bank of the Manistee River. The trail offers plenty of diversity, scaling steep slopes, meandering through pine and hardwood forest, dipping through ferny glades and crossing several creeks. It is open to foot traffic only. The north trailhead is near the south end of the Hodenpyl Dam, which lies east of Manistee. Pick up a map at the ranger office (412 Red Apple Rd., Manistee, 231/723-2211).

For paddlers, the **Pine National Scenic River** serves up lots of twists and turns, and some Class II rapids as well. There are four access sites within the national forest, each with toilets, water, grills, and parking areas. Rent canoes from **Horina Canoe & Kayak Rental** (9889 M-37, Wellston, 231/862-3470, www. horinacanoe.com, $42/day). The wonderfully clear **Pere Marquette River,** also a National Scenic River, is great for both canoeing and fishing, with healthy populations of brown trout, steelhead, and salmon. The navigable stretch within the national forest is more than 43 miles long, with several access points.

Loda Lake Wildflower Sanctuary

Nestled within the Manistee National Forest, between the towns of Brohman and White Cloud, the Loda Lake Wildflower Sanctuary (www.fs.fed.us/r9/hmnf/Loda/Loda.htm) is the only sanctuary of its kind ever established in a U.S. national forest. Nature lovers can take a self-guided tour through oak-maple woodlands, old pine plantations, and a shrub swamp, boasting a slew of wildflowers and other plant species, from columbine to witch hazel to huckleberries. A detailed brochure is available from the Baldwin/White Cloud Ranger District (650 N. Michigan Ave., Baldwin). To reach the sanctuary, head north from White Cloud on M-37 for 6.8 miles; the sanctuary will be on your left.

CADILLAC

It may share a name with the luxury car maker, but snowmobiles, not Caddies, are the preferred means of transportation in the forest and lake country surrounding Cadillac. An intricate web of trails links the city with routes through the Manistee National Forest. In summer, much of the same crowd turns to fishing. The city of 10,000 sits on the shore of large 1,150-acre Lake Cadillac, which is linked by canal to even larger Lake Mitchell. Both are known for excellent northern pike and walleye fishing. The canal was originally built by loggers, who grew tired of the twisting, shallow river that originally traversed the wetlands between the two lakes.

Situated between the two lakes, **William Mitchell State Park** (6093 E. M-115, Cadillac, 231/775-7911) is a dream come true for anglers and pleasure boaters. Some of its 221 modern campsites ($27–29) are in fact on the canal itself, where boats can be tied up right next to your tent or RV. The park maintains a boat launch on Lake Cadillac, as well as swimming beaches on both lakes. There's a short nature trail skirting a wetlands area with an observation tower. Visit early in the morning to observe the active birds here. Though pretty, be aware that this park and both of its lakes tend to be extremely busy throughout the summer. Those looking for a peaceful retreat will likely be disappointed by the buzz of activity.

GOLF

Situated in Mecosta County, east of Manistee National Forest and accessible via U.S. 131, the **St. Ives Resort** (9900 St. Ives Dr., Stanwood, 231/972-4837, www.stivesgolf.com, daily Apr.–Oct., $40–125) is popular among golfers of all skill levels. This fine resort, which you'll find on the road between Grand Rapids and Cadillac, offers two marvelous 18-hole courses, an Irish pub, and two fine restaurants.

ACCOMMODATIONS

In Manistee, the **Days Inn** (1462 U.S. 31 S, 231/723-8385, www.daysinn.com, $55–79 d) offers an indoor pool and spa, and a nice location at the south end of town near the scenic riverwalk. The mom-and-pop **Hillside Motel** (1675 U.S. 31 S, 231/723-2584, $50–125 d) offers clean, simple rooms.

Just steps from Lake Michigan and downtown Ludington, **Snyder's Shoreline Inn** (903 W. Ludington Ave., 231/845-1261, www.snydersshoreinn.com, mid-May–Oct., $69–309 d) offers a variety of rooms and cottages. Also in Ludington, **The Lamplighter Bed & Breakfast** (602 E. Ludington Ave., 231/843-9792, www.ludington-michigan.com, $125–170 d) is a Victorian-inspired inn housed within an 1894 home, with five guest rooms and original paintings, lithographs, and antiques throughout. On Hamlin Lake, **Sauble Resort** (3343 N. Stearns, 231/843-8497, www.saubleresort.com, $67–165 d) presents housekeeping cottages overlooking the dunes, not far from Ludington State Park.

Camping

Ludington State Park (8800 W. M-116, 231/843-8671, state park vehicle permit required, $16–29) offers 354 sites in four campgrounds, as well as three rustic mini cabins; call 800/447-2757 for reservations. The **Mason County Campground** (5906 W. Chauvez Rd., Ludington, 231/845-7609, $35) has 50 modern sites and a wooded picnic area set among tall trees. A paved path leads visitors to Vista Point, a scenic overlook above Lake Michigan.

FOOD

While in Manistee, stop by **Four Forty West** (440 W. River St., 231/723-6248, $7–18), which has a great Sunday brunch, prime rib specials on Wednesday, fresh seafood in season, a salad bar, and more in a casual, riverfront atmosphere. In Ludington, the **Jamesport Brewing Company** (410 S. James St., 231/845-2522, www.jamesportbrewing-company.com, 11:30 A.M.–9 P.M. Sun.–Thurs., 11:30 A.M.–10 P.M. Fri.–Sat., $6–24) offers a wide array of salads, burgers, and other bar favorites, along with handcrafted beers.

INFORMATION AND SERVICES

For more information about this area, contact the **Manistee Convention & Visitors Bureau** (www.visitmanisteecounty.com), the **Manistee Area Chamber of Commerce** (11 Cypress St., Manistee, 800/288-2286, www.manisteecountychamber.com), the **Ludington Area Convention and Visitors Bureau** (5300 W. U.S. 10, Ludington, 877/420-6618, www.ludingtoncvb.com), the **Pentwater Chamber of Commerce** (231/869-4150, www.pentwater.org), the **Hart-Silver Lake/Mears Chamber & Visitors Bureau** (2388 N. Comfort Dr., Hart, 231/873-2247, www.thinkdunes.com), the **Newaygo County Convention & Visitors Bureau** (4686 S. Evergreen, Newaygo, 231/652-9298, www.newaygocountytourism.com), the **Mecosta County Area Convention & Visitors Bureau** (246 N. State, Big Rapids, 231/796-7640, www.bigrapids.org), and the **Cadillac Area**

Visitors Bureau (222 Lake St., Cadillac, 231/775-0657, www.cadillacmichigan.com).

The towns along this route offer a limited number of services. For a bit more, head north to Traverse City, which offers everything from groceries to banks. If an emergency occurs, don't hesitate to dial **911** from any phone or visit **Mercy Hospital Cadillac** (400 Hobart St., 231/876-7200, www.munsonhealthcare.org).

GETTING THERE AND AROUND

To reach the towns and counties south of Traverse City, you can travel via **Greyhound** (107 Hall St., 800/231-2222, www.greyhound.com) or fly into **Cherry Capital Airport (TVC)** (727 Fly Don't Dr., 231/947-2250, www.tvcairport.com), then rent a car and head south. From Traverse City, you can reach Manistee, Ludington, and the Pentwater area via U.S. 31, cut through the Manistee National Forest on M-20, and drive north to Cadillac via U.S. 131.

Lake Michigan Carferry

Ludington is also home to the Great Lakes' only authentic passenger steamship, offering two round-trip sailings each day in summer between Ludington and Manitowoc, Wisconsin. This historic car ferry, the 410-foot S.S. *Badger* (701 Maritime Dr., Ludington, 231/845-5555, www.ssbadger.com) is the sole survivor of the fleet of auto/train/passenger ferries that once plowed across Lake Michigan, linking Midwestern cities like Chicago, Muskegon, and Milwaukee. The first steamer, the *Pere Marquette,* was hailed as a "titan of size and power." These hard-working vessels were owned by the railroads, and were even equipped with rails in their holds, so they could load box cars as well as automobiles and passengers. The *Badger* operates daily from mid-May through mid-October.

Charlevoix and Vicinity

Woodland Indians were likely the first to settle in present-day Charlevoix (SHAR-luh-voy), summering along the Lake Michigan shores some 4,000 years ago. But it was a French missionary who gave the town its name. Pierre François-Xavier de Charlevoix traveled through the region in the early 1700s, surreptitiously searching for the fabled Northwest Passage without tipping off the British. He never found a passage, of course, but that hasn't stopped boats from gathering in this yachter's paradise.

Nestled between Grand Traverse Bay and Little Traverse Bay, Charlevoix was practically destined to become a vacation spot. Along with the inherent appeal of Lake Michigan, Charlevoix also sidles up against lovely Lake Charlevoix, a clear, wishbone-shaped lake that draws anglers and pleasure boaters.

Inland, along the north arm of Lake Charlevoix toward Horton Bay, the land crumples like a fallen soufflé. This is lake country, river country, trout-fishing country, the boyhood backyard of a young Ernest Hemingway, whose family spent summers on nearby Walloon Lake. Just a few miles from the summer throngs that can descend on Charlevoix, much of Charlevoix County ticks along at a much mellower pace, the kind of place that inspires you to drift downstream in a canoe, make a few casts from a quiet bank, or pedal the two lanes that twist through the region.

Or really get away from it all on Beaver Island, which you can reach by ferry or plane from Charlevoix. Originally settled by the Irish, it became a Mormon stronghold in the 1840s, ruled by a self-proclaimed king who was eventually assassinated by two of his followers. Things are considerably tamer on the island today, a sandy, wooded retreat with an Irish flavor and a decidedly somnolent air. Like much of the region, it's just the kind of place to spark creativity, maybe even inspire prose. Hey, it worked for Hemingway.

SIGHTS
Downtown

"Charlevoix the Beautiful," they call this nautical town of 3,000, wedged on an isthmus between Lake Michigan and Round Lake, which opens to large Lake Charlevoix. With flowers flanking Bridge Street (U.S. 31), a walkway along the Pine River linking the lakes, gleaming yachts with clanging halyards, screeching gulls, and yacht shops, Charlevoix *is* pretty beautiful.

Downtown Charlevoix also can be crammed on a summer weekend, so do yourself a favor: If you don't arrive by boat (as many do), leave the car at your hotel or on the edge of town and walk. This is a town meant for strolling, and you can enjoy nearly all of its sights on foot.

Bridge Street is Charlevoix's main drag, lined with restaurants, galleries, gift shops, and 50,000 petunias (planted by volunteers each spring, watered by volunteers with a donated tank truck). For a free directory, stop by the Charlevoix Area Convention & Visitors Bureau.

Toward the north end of the shopping district, a lift bridge rises on the half-hour to allow tall-masted boats to travel the **Pine River Channel** from Lake Michigan to Round Lake, essentially a yacht basin that connects to much larger Lake Charlevoix. A lovely walkway lit with Victorian-style lamps lines both sides of the channel between Bridge Street and Lake Michigan. Follow the north side to reach the long pier that extends far out into Lake Michigan. To your right, Michigan Avenue parallels the lakeshore, where stately old homes preside over the waterfront.

Follow the south side of the walkway to the **South Pierhead Lighthouse** and **Lake Michigan Beach,** with fine white sand, changing rooms, a playground, and a picnic area. The woods behind the beach have some short walking trails. Cross the street that parallels the beach, Park Avenue, to check out the weird elfin architecture of **Earl Young** scattered throughout this pleasant neighborhood. Young, a local real estate agent and self-taught home designer, constructed or remodeled two

© CHARLEVOIX AREA CVB

Earl Young's elfin architecture in downtown Charlevoix

dozen homes in the 1930s and 1940s, many in the triangular block bordered by Park, Clinton, and Grant. Young used natural materials like enormous lake boulders to build his odd mushroom-shaped homes, topping them with curved cedar shake roofs. Tucked amid Victorians, it looks like Smurfs have invaded the neighborhood.

Young was also selected to design the Weathervane Terrace Inn and Stafford's Weathervane restaurant along the channel. Rock walls and massive fireplaces characterize the designs; the restaurant's fireplace features a nine-ton keystone shaped like the state of Michigan. The local convention and visitors bureau has a map that directs you to Charlevoix's Young homes.

On the east side of Bridge Street, **East Park** fronts the bustling marina and city docks on Round Lake. This is a fun spot to grab a sandwich and watch the comings and goings of all the boat business. Even better, pick up some smoked fish from **John Cross Fisheries** (209 Belvedere Ave., 231/547-2532). One of the last commercial fisheries left in the area, it sells fresh walleye, perch, lake trout, and whitefish, which it also supplies to local restaurants. You can also buy smoked whitefish or trout by the chunk.

Northern Charlevoix

Around the southern end of Round Lake, the grounds of the century-old **Belvedere Club** spread across a high hill, overlooking both Round Lake and Lake Charlevoix. Founded by Baptists from Kalamazoo in the 1870s, the Belvedere Club was planned as a summer resort community, mirroring the Methodists' successful Bay View near Petoskey. Wealthy summer folk built homes in the opulent fashion of the day, with verandas, dormers, and gabled roofs. Today, many of the homes are occupied in summer by the grandchildren and great-grandchildren of the original owners. Though the streets through still-private Belvedere are closed in July and August, you can get a glimpse of the neighborhood from Ferry Avenue along Lake Charlevoix.

Inspired by the Belvedere Club, the First Congregational Church of Chicago formed a similar community on the north side of the Pine River Channel. As with the Belvedere, the **Chicago Club** is closed to the public. Check out its fancy Victorians from East Dixon Avenue. As a bonus, this road also leads you to **Depot Beach,** a popular swimming beach, playground, and picnic area on Lake Charlevoix.

About a half-mile north of the city pier lies the **Mt. McSauba Recreation Area** (231/547-3267), one of the state's few municipal ski facilities. Overlooking Lake Michigan, it lures downhill and cross-country skiers. Other popular wintertime activities include snowboarding, snowshoeing, sledding, and ice-skating. The groomed 1.2-mile cross-country trail is even lit at night.

At its northern end, Mt. McSauba shares a boundary with the **North Point Nature Preserve.** The 27-acre preserve was purchased with funds raised by the people of Charlevoix, with help from the Michigan Natural Resources Trust Fund. Today, it offers several steep nature trails through hardwood forest and a pretty stretch of fairly secluded sand, home to threatened plant species like Pitcher's thistle. To reach the preserve, take U.S. 31 north to Mercer Road, turn left onto Mt. McSauba, and turn right before the dirt road. The preserve will be on your left.

CHARLEVOIX VENETIAN FESTIVAL

As with several other communities along the Lake Michigan coast, Charlevoix presents its own Venetian Festival (231/547-3253, www.venetianfestival.com, free) in summer. Begun in 1930 as a simple candlelit boat parade, Charlevoix's version has grown to be the highlight of the season. Usually occurring in late July, the weeklong Charlevoix Venetian Festival offers daily events, from live concerts to athletic competitions, within the town's waterfront parks, in Round Lake Harbor, and on Lake Charlevoix, attracting tens of thousands of visitors each year. The annual event culminates in a beautiful Venetian Boat Parade on

Round Lake, followed by a terrific fireworks display.

SHOPPING

Charlevoix's quaint downtown district offers its share of equally quaint shops. For unique children's clothing, check out **Ga Ga For Kids** (323 Bridge St., 231/547-1600, 9 A.M.–6 P.M. daily). Another fine clothing store is just down the street at the **Claymore Shop** (411 Bridge St., 231/237-0400, 9 A.M.–6 P.M. daily). Exuding a "shop around the corner" vibe, the **Round Lake Bookstore** (107 Mason St., 231/547-2699, 10 A.M.–7 P.M. daily) offers a great sampling of works by regional authors.

RECREATION
Hiking and Biking

The **Little Traverse Wheelway** extends for approximately 29 miles from Charlevoix to Harbor Springs. The trail is ideal for hiking, jogging, bicycling, and in-line skating. Horses and snowmobiles, however, are not permitted. The trail begins at the intersection of Division and Mt. McSauba Roads on the north side of Charlevoix.

Boating

Situated between Lake Michigan and several other inland lakes, Charlevoix is truly a boater's paradise. In fact, the area has three principal centers for boating: the Jordan River, Lake Charlevoix, and, of course, Lake Michigan, which has several access sites along the coast. Boaters and canoeists can access the Jordan River in East Jordan, at Old State Road, Webster's Bridge, and Roger's Bridge. Lake Charlevoix, meanwhile, presents lovely swimming beaches and several access points for boaters and anglers. Pleasure cruisers can view several sights along the Lake Charlevoix shoreline, from some of the area's most beautiful homes to an old shipwreck at Oyster Bay.

ACCOMMODATIONS AND FOOD

Charlevoix can get pretty busy, especially during the summer months, so make reservations

early before coming into town. That said, Charlevoix has loads of lodging possibilities, from basic motels on U.S. 31 to swanky condos along the waterfront.

The **Edgewater Inn** (100 Michigan Ave., 231/547-6044, www.edgewater-charlevoix. com, $89–359 d) has suites on Round Lake and amenities like an indoor/outdoor pool and full kitchen facilities. The (**Weathervane Terrace Inn & Suites** (111 Pie River Lane, 231/547-9955, www.weathervane-chx.com, $59–299 d) sits directly on the channel, offering an outdoor pool and hot tub as well as views of Lake Michigan and Round Lake. The **Charlevoix Inn & Suites** (800 Petoskey Ave., 231/547-0300, www.charlevoixinn.org, $50–150 d) offers less expensive accommodations, with an indoor pool and proximity to Lake Charlevoix beaches.

The (**Weathervane Restaurant** (106 Pine River Lane, 231/547-4311, www.staffords.com, 11 A.M.–10 P.M. Tues.–Sat., 10:30 A.M.–9 P.M. Sun., $10–25) is one of Charlevoix's best restaurants, in terms of both food and location. Affiliated with the Stafford restaurants of Petoskey, it specializes in planked whitefish and steaks, and overlooks the Pine River Channel. Outside seating is available for lunch and dinner. **Terry's Place** (101 Antrim St., 231/547-2799, www.terrysofcharlevoix.com, 5 P.M.–close daily, $20–36) is frequented for its fresh walleye and whitefish.

INFORMATION AND SERVICES

For more information about the Charlevoix area, contact the **Charlevoix Area Chamber of Commerce** (109 Mason St., 231/547-2101, www.charlevoix.org, 9 A.M.–5 P.M. Mon.–Fri.), the **Charlevoix Area Convention & Visitors Bureau** (100 Michigan Ave., 231/237-0920, www.charlevoixlodging.com), or the **Petoskey Area Visitors Bureau** (401 E. Mitchell St., 231/348-2755, www.boynecountry.com, 8 A.M.–4 P.M. Mon.–Fri.). For local news and events, consult the *Charlevoix Courier* (www. charlevoixcourier.com).

Charlevoix may be a small town, but it still

has its share of necessary services, such as beauty salons, pharmacies, and banks. There are even several **post offices** in the area, including one near downtown Charlevoix (6700 M-66 N., 231/547-2631, www.usps.com). For medical services, consult the **Charlevoix Area Hospital** (14700 Lakeshore Dr., 231/547-4024, www.cah.org). If an emergency occurs, don't hesitate to call **911** from any phone.

GETTING THERE AND AROUND

Travelers can fly into the **Cherry Capital Airport (TVC)** (727 Fly Don't Dr., Traverse City, 231/947-2250, www.tvcairport.com) or the **Pellston Regional Airport (PLN)** (Pellston, 231/539-8441, www.pellstonairport.com), rent a vehicle, and take U.S. 31 to Charlevoix. With several marinas in the area, it's also possible to arrive in Charlevoix by boat. Of course, most visitors come via car, which is an ideal way to explore the surrounding towns and lakes.

FISHERMAN'S ISLAND STATE PARK

Five miles south of Charlevoix off U.S. 31, Fisherman's Island State Park (16480 Bells Bay Rd., 231/547-6641, state park vehicle permit required) does indeed encompass a little 10-acre offshore island, but most visitors come to enjoy its five miles of lakeshore and wooded dunes. With long stretches of soft sand and exceptionally clear water, it's a particularly good spot to hunt for Petoskey stones.

There's evidence that Woodland Indians inhabited Fisherman's Island more than 1,000 years ago. In the early 1900s, one enterprising Charlevoix innkeeper planned a casino for the site. But those plans died with the property owner, and the state eventually acquired the island and nearby shoreline, naming it a state park in 1978. Today, the small island is inhabited only by birds and insects. Wading or swimming to it is not recommended, since a strong current often rushes between the island and mainland.

The park is nearly divided in two by a parcel of private property in its middle. The northern portion is the more popular of the two state park sections, with five miles of hiking trails, a pretty day-use area, and 81 rustic campsites. Most are nice, private sites in the woods near the water; if you're really lucky, you'll snag one of the dozen or so sites right on the beach.

To reach the day-use area, hike the marked trail along the dune ridge, or drive south on the park road past the campgrounds. It has grills, picnic tables, outhouses, and a trail leading across bubbling Inwood Creek to the beach. On a clear day, you can see the tip of the Leelanau Peninsula from this fine stretch of beach, and you'll often be treated to a spectacular sunset. For real solitude, access the southern end of the park from the town of Norwood, 11 miles south on U.S. 31. Follow signs to Norwood Township Park on the shoreline, then trace the double track into the state park. (Driving is not recommended if it's wet.) You're likely to have the beach and old truck trails all to yourself.

LAKE CHARLEVOIX
Horton Bay

Several authors and artists have roots in northern Michigan, but none as celebrated as Ernest Hemingway. Hemingway spent his childhood summers at the family cottage on nearby Walloon Lake, fished the waters of Lake Charlevoix, hunted on the point at Horton Bay, and once escaped a game warden by fleeing across the lake's north arm to the point between the arms, now known as Hemingway Point.

The tiny town of Horton Bay, on Boyne City Road about 10 miles east of Charlevoix, played a special role in Hemingway's life. He whiled away summer afternoons on the front steps of the classic false-front, white-clapboard general store, which he describes in his short story "Up in Michigan." (He drew on many of his surroundings, in fact, for his Nick Adams short stories.) Later, he married his first wife, Hadley Richardson, at Horton Bay's Congregational church.

Today, the **Horton Bay General Store** (5115 Boyne City Rd., 231/582-7827, www.

hortonbaygeneralstore.com, 9 A.M.–5 P.M. daily, $9–18) is preserved more as a shrine to Hemingway than a store and eatery—light on foodstuffs but heavy on Hemingway nostalgia. Built in 1876, the cavernous building is filled with Hemingway photos, novels, even a copy of his 1922 marriage certificate. There's a small lunch counter and a few assorted groceries. But it's the charming old building itself that draws you in. Steeped in literary history, its inviting front porch is still a great place to while away a summer afternoon.

Boyne City

At the foot of Lake Charlevoix, pleasant and relaxing Boyne City was once a loud industrial town. In the 19th century, Boyne City thrived as a regional logging center, with 90 miles of railroad track and several hundred logging cars linking the town to the surrounding logging camps and feeding its hungry sawmills. Tanneries also became big business at the turn of the 20th century, using bark from the hemlock tree to tan leather. One Boyne City tannery produced 6 million pounds of shoe leather annually.

Boyne City has done a fine job preserving some of its historic buildings, with a main street that looks like it could be in the Wild West. The best example is the **Wolverine-Dilworth Inn** (300 Water St., 231/582-7388, www.wolverinedilworthinn.com, $89–299 d), a 1911 brick hotel with a spacious veranda, a terrazzo tile lobby with fireplace, and a saloon dining room. This landmark is open for dining and lodging.

Boyne Mountain

Six miles southeast of Boyne City in Boyne Falls, Everett Kircher carved out his own piece of history at Boyne Mountain (800/462-6963, www.boyne.com). A Studebaker dealer from the Detroit area, Kircher figured out that Detroit's booming auto industry would make for a lot of wealthy Michigan residents, many of whom would be looking for a place to vacation. He obtained some farmland near Boyne Falls and proceeded to develop the area's first downhill ski resort. Boyne Mountain opened in 1947.

Over the years, the visionary Kircher became known for "firsts"—the Midwest's first chairlift in 1948, the nation's first freestyle skiing exhibition in 1961, the world's first quad chairlift in 1967, the state's first high-speed quad in 1990, and the nation's first six-person chair in 1992. Kircher was the first to perfect artificial snowmaking, and Boyne's patented snowguns are used at resorts all over the world. Olympic ski planners still contact Boyne for snowmaking consultation.

Even in his 80s, Everett Kircher would come to Boyne headquarters in Boyne Falls nearly every day, overseeing a privately held ski/golf enterprise that seems to grow exponentially every year. In the tightly consolidated ski industry, Boyne is a player: It owns three impressive ski resorts in Michigan. The company's not doing too badly in the golf industry department either, with its spectacular Bay Harbor development near Petoskey.

By those standards, Boyne Mountain seems almost quaint, but is an extremely popular resort in summer and winter. The ski area offers over 40 runs, including the Disciples Ridge area, which features some of the steepest pitches in the state. The property also has over 20 miles of groomed and tracked trails for cross-country skiing, which double as mountain-biking trails. Come summer, two 18-hole golf courses help fill Boyne Mountain's 600-plus rooms (and its jumbo 30-person outdoor hot tub).

Jordan River

You'll better understand Ernest Hemingway's love for this land after passing a little time along the Jordan River, which empties into Lake Charlevoix's south arm. Look for the small wooden canoe signs that signify access points, like the one along Alba Road near the Charlevoix-Antrim county line. Here, the Jordan rolls silently northward, the pale brown of hospital coffee, framed by weeping willows and grassy banks. Though anglers hate to advertise it, the Jordan is one of the finest trout streams in the state.

The Jordan River valley cuts a wide swath through the landscape south of Lake Charlevoix, and nowhere is the view more dramatic than from **Dead Man's Hill,** off U.S. 131 south of Boyne Falls. Two miles south of M-32 west, watch for Dead Man's Hill Road; turn west and travel 1.5 miles or so to the end. Here, the flat country lane suddenly falls away to reveal a marvelous valley more than 1,000 feet below: The Jordan straggles through a woodland of pines interspersed with beech and maple, reaching out across the lowlands like spider veins.

The morbid name is in reference to Stanley Graczyk, a 21-year-old logger who, in 1910, mistakenly drove his team of horses up the hill and right over the edge. Whoops. Dead Man's Hill is also the trailhead for the **Jordan River Pathway,** which loops 18 miles through the valley floor. There's a marked three-mile loop, too. Maps are available at the trailhead.

Ironton Ferry

Up M-66, the tiny Ironton Ferry (6:30 A.M.–10 P.M. daily, $3.25 vehicles, $0.50 pedestrians) chugs its way from Ironton across the narrows of Lake Charlevoix's south arm to Hemingway Point—a distance of about 100 yards. The U.S. flag flies gallantly from the *Charlevoix*'s white steel pilothouse; a sign sternly warns auto passengers—all three of them—that "We will not be responsible for vehicles left unattended," a difficult task, considering you can't even open the car door wide enough to get out. The funky little ferry even made the "Ripley's Believe It or Not" newspaper feature, noting that its captain traveled more than 15,000 miles without ever being more than 1,000 feet from home.

It is efficient. The *Charlevoix* takes just two minutes to follow its cable to the far shore, and just a little over four minutes to unload, reload, and be back again—but saves a 15-mile trip around the south arm of the lake. People have found it to be a worthwhile service since 1876. Its "1884 Rates for Ferriage" are still posted: "Double Teams, .30; Single Teams, .20; Beast, .10 except sheep; Sheep, .10 up to 6, .05 over 6; footmen, .05 without beast."

ELLSWORTH AND BELLAIRE

Eleven miles south of Charlevoix on County Road 65, Ellsworth wouldn't be much more than a wide spot in the road but for a couple of very notable exceptions: The Rowe Inn and Tapawingo. These two restaurants have put unlikely Ellsworth on the map, with rave reviews in national publications like *Gourmet* and *Wine Spectator.*

With a warm farmhouse exterior and chic, modern interior, **Tapawingo** (9502 Lake St., 866/588-7881, www.tapawingo. net, 11:30 A.M.–close Tues.–Sun., $27–42), features Midwestern ingredients, like its renowned morel mushroom dishes, presented with a nouvelle artistic flair. It was named one of "America's Top Tables" by *Gourmet.*

A scant half-mile away, **The Rowe Inn** (6303 E. Jordan Rd., Ellsworth, 231/588-7351, www. roweinn.com, 5 P.M.–close daily, $20–39), has a more rustic decor and one-of-a-kind entrées like duck Magret with port-cinnamon sauce. Its distinctive menu—thick with rich local ingredients like duck, veal, trout, morels, and fresh berries—along with the largest and most outstanding wine cellar in Michigan have earned it a spot among the nation's top restaurants.

Shanty Creek

If you're looking for a year-round destination that accommodates a yen for golf, hiking, biking, winter sports, and much more, consider visiting **Shanty Creek Resorts** (1 Shanty Creek Rd., Bellaire, 800/678-4111, www. shantycreek.com), a half-hour's drive south of Charlevoix. Separated into three villages—Cedar River, Schuss, and Summit—this enormous 4,500-acre swath of land features several dining, lodging, and spa options, three award-winning golf courses, numerous downhill skiing runs, and a fantastic trail network for cross-country skiers and mountain bikers.

The main draw here is golfing ($20–99), which is usually available April–October, weather depending. Summit Village, which offers a newly renovated hotel and conference center, also presents two favored courses: **The Legend,** designed by Arnold Palmer and named the best course in the Midwest by readers of *GOLF Magazine,* and the more wide-open **Summit Golf Course,** the resort's original course. In addition, Summit Village boasts heated indoor and outdoor pools, a spa and fitness center, and a downhill ski area with a dozen slopes.

Five minutes away, Schuss Mountain offers more advanced skiing, with 37 runs, three terrain parks, and seven lifts. Its Bavarian-style base area is smaller, with a scattering of villas and condos. This village also has its share of other diversions, including the challenging **Schuss Mountain Golf Course,** set amid abundant wetlands and rolling hills.

The newest resort, Cedar River Village, houses 14 condos, over 70 luxurious suites, two restaurants, and **Cedar River Golf Course,**

situated amid verdant hills and peaceful waters. Between the three resorts, over 13 miles of groomed and tracked cross-country trails wind through hilly terrain and hardwood forest. In summer, many of those same trails become prime mountain-biking terrain. The network includes beginner to expert trails, some made even more difficult by the area's sandy terrain.

BEAVER ISLAND

Traveling to Beaver Island is kind of slow, rather expensive, and there isn't much to do when you get there. There is no must-see attraction and no particularly spectacular scenery on this flat, wooded island. Nope, Beaver Island ticks along at a rather sleepy, predictable pace: The bank opens every Tuesday 9 A.M.–1 P.M. The ferry brings the mail. When Island Airways arrives from Charlevoix, everybody leaving pretty much knows everybody arriving.

If this sounds hopelessly dull, then don't go

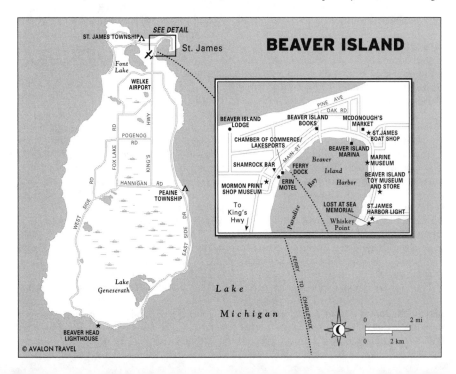

© AVALON TRAVEL

to Beaver Island. There is precious little in the way of formal entertainment on Beaver, save for some occasional Irish music and beer drinking at the Shamrock Bar. Though it ranks as the largest island in Michigan—13 miles long and six miles wide—you won't find any towns outside the port of St. James, just simple cottages and 100 miles of sandy roads.

On the other hand, if the inherent isolation and somnolent pace appeal to you, then by all means, go. Stranded 18 miles from the nearest Lower Peninsula shoreline, Beaver Island is the most remote inhabited island in the Great Lakes, offering what may be a quintessential glimpse of island life: unhurried, unbothered, unaffected by whim and fashion. You make your own entertainment here, and it can be delightful. Bike a quiet road to an even quieter beach. Explore the island's quirky history at a couple of terrific little museums. Buy a local a cup of coffee and talk island politics. Paddle a kayak to another island in the Beaver archipelago. Take off your watch.

Sights

Beaver Island activity centers around St. James on hook-shaped Beaver Harbor, which many locals still call by its 19th-century name, Paradise Bay. This is where the ferry lands, and where you'll find the sum of the island's commercial development. Everything in St. James is within walking distance.

You can pick up much of the island's colorful history and character without ever leaving the harbor. The **Shamrock Bar** (26245 Main St., 231/448-2278, 11 A.M.–9 P.M. daily, $12–19), is the most popular spot in town for a burger, beer, and island news. At the **St. James Boat Shop** (38230 Michigan, 231/448-2810), Bill Freese builds gorgeous wood-strip canoes and kayaks, along with beautiful handmade wooden buckets.

From the boat shop, it's just a short walk to Whiskey Point, the **Lost at Sea memorial,** and the **St. James Harbor Light,** marking the entrance to this well-protected natural harbor. The 19th-century light was "manned" for years by Beaver Island native Elizabeth Whitney Williams, the only woman light keeper on the Great Lakes.

The southern half of the island has far more public land than the northern half, much of it a state wildlife research area. It has several small lakes, bogs, unimproved roads, and trails that are fun to explore, especially if you have a mountain bike. Fish in **Lake Geneserath,** swim at several sandy beaches on the southern shore, or check out the **Beaver Head Lighthouse** near the island's southern tip, a pretty cream-brick house and tower built in 1858, one of the oldest on all the Great Lakes. Back in the 1920s, thrill-seekers from Charlevoix drove across the thick lake ice, headed for Beaver Island. When a thick fog left them completely disoriented, the keeper guided them to safety with the light's fog signal.

If you plan to explore Beaver Island on your own, pick up two maps in St. James first: the comprehensive island map available at **McDonough's Market** (38240 Michigan Ave., 231/448-2736, www.mcdonoughsmarket.com) and a small history map, available at the chamber of commerce. It points out several noteworthy attractions that you can seek out on your own.

Kayaking

Eleven other islands scatter around Beaver's northern half, an inviting archipelago for sea kayakers. The islands range in distance from Garden (2 miles away) to Gull (11 miles). Garden, practically due north from St. James, is probably the most intriguing for paddlers, with several protected bays and inlets. High Island, four miles west, has bluffs along the western shore rising to 240 feet. Most of High and Garden are public land, part of the **Beaver Islands State Wildlife Research Area.** Some of the smaller islands are privately owned or otherwise off-limits to preserve nesting sites.

The **Inland Seas School of Kayaking** (231/448-2221, www.inlandseaskayaking.com) offers instruction and guided tours. If you plan to do any inter-island paddling, observe all the usual safety precautions, watch the weather, and make sure you have a good nautical chart.

The open waters of the Great Lakes are not for amateurs.

Accommodations

There are several motels, lodges, B&Bs, and cabins for rent on the island. Near the ferry dock, the **Erin Motel** (231/448-2240, $69–99 d) overlooks the water with a sand beach. The **Beaver Island Lodge** (231/448-2396, $79–149 d) sits along a secluded stretch of beach west of town, with nice rooms and an on-site restaurant.

The island has two rustic campgrounds (with pit toilets and water), both on the lakeshore. The **St. James Township Campground** is on the north side of the island one mile from town, and has 12 sites. The **Bill Wagner Memorial Campground,** with 22 sites, is along the east shore, seven miles south of town. Both are $10 per night (no reservations). There are two grocery stores and a handful of restaurants on the island.

Information and Services

For information about Beaver Island's services, businesses, and lodging options, contact the **Beaver Island Chamber of Commerce** (231/448-2505, www.beaverisland.org). For local news and events, consult the monthly *Beaver Beacon* (www.beaverisland.net).

Getting There and Around

Commercial transportation to Beaver Island is available only from Charlevoix, 32 miles away. The **Beaver Island Boat Company** (103 Bridge Park Dr., 231/547-2311 or 888/446-4095, www.bibco.com, one-way $21–23 adults, $11–13 children 5–12, $9 bicycles, rates vary for pets and vehicles) makes scheduled trips April–December, with two trips daily most of the summer. It takes a little over two hours each way, and the 95-foot *Beaver Islander* or 130-foot *Emerald Isle* can be a bit of a rough ride in choppy waters. Reservations are recommended for passengers and required for autos. If you take the first ferry in the morning, you can make Beaver Island a day trip of six hours or so, returning on the late afternoon ferry. Of course, the time constraints will limit you to exploring just a small portion of the island.

Island Airways (111 Airport Dr., 800/524-6895, www.islandairways.com, one-way $43 adults, $29 children under 10, $21 pets, $10 bicycles) provides daily air service from Charlevoix in a little 10-seater. The flight takes about 20 minutes, and reservations are required.

It's probably not necessary to have a car on Beaver Island. Though the island is quite large and has more than 100 miles of roads, downtown St. James is ideal for walking and biking. Many accommodations provide transportation from the dock or airport; if there's something specific you want to see (the lighthouse on the southern shore, for example), you can rent a vehicle for less than $60 a day from **Gordon's Auto Rentals and Clinic** (231/448-2438). Reserve ahead of time.

Petoskey and Vicinity

Petoskey (puh-TOS-kee) was originally settled by the Ottawa Indians in the 1700s and takes its name from a local Native American, Petosega. With bountiful fishing and hunting, the region was a desirable place to live, and Ottawa and Ojibwa tribes thrived here. In the 1800s, the federal government negotiated more equitably with local tribes than it did elsewhere in the young nation; tribes were given the first choice of land (albeit their land!) until 1875.

White settlers began arriving in the 1850s, establishing logging operations along the Bear River, the name the town used until 1873. With a sawmill, a lime quarry, and other enterprises along the river and Little Traverse Bay, Bear River quickly became an industrial town of buzzing saws and belching smoke.

But the town began changing with the arrival of the railroad in 1873. Lured north by the beautiful Lake Michigan waters and cool northern air, residents from southern Great Lakes cities like Chicago and Detroit began migrating to Petoskey, gradually converting its industrial squalor to an elegant summer getaway. The artesian springs that bubbled throughout town and their "health-giving waters" only encouraged Petoskey's growth.

By the turn of the 20th century, Petoskey's downtown was filled with fine shops and 13 grand resort hotels like the Arlington, with its imposing columns, dance hall, and 24-foot-wide veranda. At its heyday in 1900, three trains a day stopped at the Arlington, which could sleep 800—surpassed only by the rival Grand Hotel on Mackinac Island. Unfortunately, the Arlington burned to the ground in 1915, the same fate that met almost every single one of Petoskey's grand resorts—The Jewel, The Imperial, the City Hotel. Only the Perry Hotel, made of expensive brick, still stands.

Thankfully, plenty of other historic buildings still stand in the Petoskey area, a city that wisely realized early the value of protecting them. From its well-preserved Gaslight District to the entire Victorian neighborhood of Bay View, Petoskey maintains the charm of the grand resort era, along with the natural resources that brought summer visitors here in the first place. Equally appealing to anglers, boaters, shoppers, golfers, and skiers, the town has so far been able to balance its need for tourism with its desire for preservation, but only time and resolve will determine if it will last. In 1996, the National Trust for Historic Preservation listed Petoskey as one of 10 national historic treasures most worthy of fighting for, warning that "retail, roadway, and residential sprawl threaten the town's historic character and pastoral setting."

SIGHTS

Though growth indeed threatens Petoskey—busy U.S. 31 slices right between downtown and the waterfront—it remains a charming city for vacationers, with a downtown made for strolling. The **Gaslight District** anchors the downtown, an eight-block area of well-preserved Victorian brick storefronts filled with shops and restaurants that has drawn shoppers since the early 1900s. A low-interest loan program sponsored by the regional chamber of commerce encourages their preservation and renovation. Centered around Lake and Howard Streets, the district mixes high-brow boutiques with bookstores, galleries, antique haunts, and homegrown souvenir shops.

Near the intersection of Petoskey and Bay Streets, follow the pedestrian tunnel under U.S. 31 to **Bayfront Park,** which merges with **Sunset Park** to the east, offering a vast green space along the waterfront. Once the center of Petoskey's sawmill operations, now this beautifully renovated area comprises a marina, a walkway along the Bear River, one of the area's historic mineral springs, and the fine **Little Traverse History Museum** (231/347-2620, www.petoskeymuseum. org, 10 A.M.–4 P.M. Mon.–Sat. Memorial

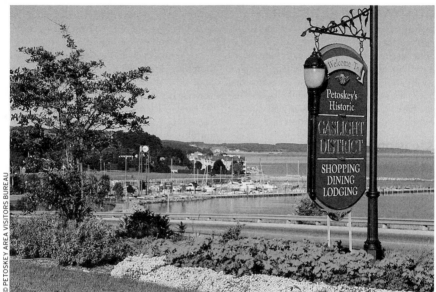

© PETOSKEY AREA VISITORS BUREAU

Petoskey's Gaslight District

Day–mid-Oct., $2 adults, $1 children 5–17) in the restored rail depot.

The museum is crammed full of interesting displays, including a photo collection of Petoskey's old hotels and an exhibit detailing the sad tale of the passenger pigeon, which migrated to the Little Traverse Bay area by the billions (yes, *billions*) in the 1870s. Accounts tell of the skies blackening when the birds were in flight, with individual flocks stretching for miles and miles. Alas, the nesting habits and docile nature of the pigeons made them easy to hunt by simply clubbing them to death in their nests. Entrepreneurs did so with glee, since their meat was considered a delicacy. By the 1870s, entire steamships were loaded with pigeons for delivery to urban restaurants in the southern Great Lakes. In less than 25 years, the passenger pigeon had completely disappeared from the region; by 1914, it became officially extinct.

Probably the museum's most popular display is the collection of Ernest Hemingway memorabilia. Hemingway's family began vacationing on nearby Walloon Lake when Hemingway was just a boy, and the family still owns a couple of acres of land there. After he was injured in World War I, Hemingway recuperated in Petoskey, living in a rooming house at the corner of State and Woodland Streets in 1919–1920. Here, he gathered material and began drafting *Torrents of Spring,* which alludes to several Petoskey locations. The museum's display includes first editions of that classic novel as well as *For Whom the Bell Tolls* and *A Farewell to Arms.*

Hemingway overshadows Petoskey's other famous author, Bruce Catton, who won a Pulitzer Prize in 1954 for his Civil War account *A Stillness at Appomattox.* The Little Traverse History Museum gives him his due.

Near the museum, you can pick up the **Top of Michigan trail,** a 15-mile paved, off-road path that stretches from Bay Harbor through Petoskey to Harbor Springs. Several other trails radiate off this route, creating a network of 180 miles of multiuse recreation pathways between Charlevoix to Mackinaw City. Trails maps are available at the Petoskey Area Visitors Bureau.

ODAWA CASINO RESORT

Just outside town, the Odawa Casino Resort (1760 Lears Rd., 877/442-6464, www. odawacasino.com, 24 hours daily) provides a 300,000-square-foot entertainment complex, with gaming, restaurants, and a theater that books big-name talent on a regular basis. They also have O zone, a state-of-the-art nightclub that compares to many of the hot spots in Vegas.

SHOPPING

Petoskey's delightful Gaslight District offers a wide assortment of shops. **American Spoon Foods** (1668 Clarion Ave., 231/347-9030, www. spoon.com, 9 A.M.–7 P.M. daily) offers an assortment of delicious jams, sauces, and more, all made from local produce and other fresh ingredients. Check out the adjacent café, for delicious sandwiches made with their sauces. The **McLean & Eakin Booksellers** (307 E. Lake St., 231/347-1180, 9 A.M.–8 P.M. Mon.–Sat., 10 A.M.–5 P.M. Sun.) offers an eclectic assortment of titles and regularly hosts educational and literary events. If antiques are more your style, stop in at **Longton Hall Antiques** (329 Bay St., 231/347-9672, 9 A.M.–7 P.M. Mon.–Sat., 11 A.M.–5 P.M. Sun.).

SPORTS AND RECREATION
Golf

While the area around Traverse City and Charlevoix boasts several terrific courses, the Petoskey/Harbor Springs area has no shortage of great golf either. Several lodgings even offer packages and will reserve tee times.

Best known are the four courses at **Boyne Highlands Resort** (600 Highland Dr., 231/526-3000 or 800/462-6963, www.boyne. com, daily May–Oct., $25–134), a ski/golf resort a few miles north of Harbor Springs: The Moor, the Donald Ross Memorial, The Heather, and the Arthur Hills. *GOLF Magazine* considers The Heather course, designed by Robert Trent Jones, one of the top courses in the country, with lots of sculpted bunkers and water hazards (and cool global positioning systems on the carts to feed you yardage information). The Ross Memorial course is a perennial favorite. It re-creates several of the

most famous holes throughout the world designed by Ross, considered by many to be the "father of golf course architecture."

Boyne also operates the **Crooked Tree Golf Club** (Bay Harbor, 231/439-4030, www.boyne. com), a British-style course overlooking Little Traverse Bay near Petoskey. In Harbor Springs, the **Harbor Point Golf Course** (8475 S. Lake Shore Dr., 231/526-2951, www.harborpoint-golfclub.com, daily late Apr.–mid-Oct., $45–65 w/cart) had been an exclusive private club since 1896; it's now open to the public and considered a favorite walking course by *Golf Digest*. Near Burt Lake in Brutus, **Hidden River Golf & Casting Club** (7688 Maple River Rd., 231/529-4653, www.hiddenriver.com, daily Apr.–Oct., $32–89) offers classic "up north" scenery, with tall stands of pine and hardwoods and the meandering Maple River; this resort is also popular for fly-fishing.

Winter Activities

Nub's Nob (500 Nubs Nob Rd., Harbor Springs, 231/526-2131, www.nubsnob.com,

a lakeside golf course in Bay Harbor

© PETOSKEY AREA VISITORS BUREAU

lift tickets $47–58) often gets overshadowed by the Boynes, but has its own loyal following. The well-protected, wooded slopes (blocked from cold winter winds) are best known for short and steep faces like Twilight Zone and Scarface, but its 23 trails and 427-foot vertical drop have plenty of beginner and intermediate terrain, too. If Boyne Highlands gets crowded, this is the place to escape.

ACCOMMODATIONS AND FOOD

Petoskey offers an enormous array of lodging, from basic motels along U.S. 31 to resort complexes to condo units that are especially convenient for families or groups.

Unless you're on a tight budget, opt for a stay at the lemon chiffon–colored **Stafford's Perry Hotel** (100 Lewis St., 231/347-4000, www.staffords.com, $69–299 d), which overlooks Little Traverse Bay and dates back to 1899. Today, it's run by successful local innkeeper/restaurateur Stafford Smith, who has done a wonderful job of updating the venerable old building while retaining every bit of its charm. Rates are reasonable for such a treasure. The Perry also features three separate dining choices, if you just want to relax and don't feel like wandering around town.

The **Terrace Inn** (1549 Glendale, 800/530-9898, www.theterraceinn.com, $259–469 d) provides an elegant bed-and-breakfast experience in a turn-of-the-20th-century building. If you're on a tighter budget, try the **Econo Lodge South** (1859 U.S. 131 S, 231/348-3324, www.econolodge.com, $59–89 d).

Petoskey also offers a superb array of dining options, especially in the downtown area. Since 1875, the historic **City Park Grill** (432 E. Lake St., 231/347-0101, www.cityparkgrill.com, 11:30 a.m.–9 p.m. Mon.–Thurs., 11:30 a.m.–10 p.m. Fri.–Sat., 11:30 a.m.–9 p.m. Sun., extended bar hours, $7–24) has lured residents and visitors alike, despite several transformations over the years. Today, patrons come for the happy-hour specials and live weekend music in the adjacent bar, plus an eclectic restaurant menu that includes shellfish chowder,

jambalaya, almond-crusted whitefish, and filet mignon with blue cheese sauce. Another delectable downtown eatery is **Grand Traverse Pie Company** (316 E. Mitchell St., 231/348-4060, www.gtpie.com, 7 a.m.–6:30 p.m. Mon.–Sat., $4–13), part of a statewide chain that offers scrumptious soups, salads, sandwiches, quiches, and, naturally, pies—from the Suttons Bay Blueberry to the Glen Haven Peach Crumb.

INFORMATION AND SERVICES

For more information about the Petoskey area, contact the **Petoskey Area Visitors Bureau** (401 E. Mitchell St., 231/348-2755, www.boynecountry.com, 8 a.m.–4 p.m. Mon.–Fri.) or the **Petoskey Regional Chamber of Commerce** (401 E. Mitchell St., 231/347-4150, www.petoskey.com). For local news and events, consult the **Petoskey News-Review** (www.petoskeynews.com).

Though a relatively small town, Petoskey still has its share of necessary services, from post offices to pharmacies. For banking needs, contact **Chase** (www.chase.com) and **Fifth Third Bank** (www.53.com), both of which have several branches in Petoskey. To stock up on supplies, stop by one of three **Glen's Markets** (www.glensmarket.com) in and around town. For medical services, consult the **Northern Michigan Regional Hospital** (416 Connable Ave., 800/248-6777, www.northernhealth.org). If an emergency occurs, don't hesitate to call **911** from any phone.

GETTING THERE AND AROUND

North of Petoskey, the **Pellston Regional Airport (PLN)** (231/539-8441, www.pellstonairport.com) offers commuter service from Detroit via Northwest Airlink. From there, you can rent a vehicle and take U.S. 31 to Petoskey. Given its position beside Little Traverse Bay, Petoskey is also accessible via boat. In addition, visitors can reach Petoskey via **Greyhound** bus (301 W. Mitchell St., 800/231-2222, www.greyhound.com). Of course, most visitors come by car, which is an ideal way to explore the surrounding towns and lakes.

LITTLE TRAVERSE BAY

North of the Leelanau Peninsula and just a half-hour south of the Straits of Mackinac, Little Traverse Bay delves due east nine miles, forming a picture-perfect bay ringed by bluffs, fine sand, and well-protected harbors. Well-known Petoskey, with its historic downtown Gaslight District, sits at the foot of the bay, justifiably drawing many of the area's visitors. But golfers, skiers, anglers, and wanderers will find plenty to enjoy in this appealing and compact region, too.

LAKE MICHIGAN SHORE
Bay Harbor

A couple of miles west of downtown Petoskey, Bay Harbor represents the nation's largest land reclamation project, a stunning example of what foresight and $100 million can accomplish. Stretching five miles along the shore of Little Traverse Bay and encompassing more than 1,100 acres, this beautiful chunk of real estate spent its last life as, of all things, a cement plant. When the plant closed in 1981, it left behind a scarred, barren landscape that sat untouched for a decade.

But from industrial squalor comes impressive luxury. With the combined resources of CMS Energy (the Jackson, Michigan, parent company of a large utility) and ski-industry giant Boyne, Bay Harbor has shaped up into one of the nation's most spectacular resort communities. The **Bay Harbor Yacht Club**, with little touches like a compass rose made of inlaid cherrywood, overlooks a deepwater port (the old quarry) with nearly 500 slips, including 120 for public transient use. An equestrian club entertains the horsy set. Multimillion-dollar homes dot the property, at a low density that maintains a breezy, resort feel. Public parks buffer Bay Harbor on both sides.

Acclaimed golf designer Arthur Hills has created **The Links, The Preserve,** and **The Quarry golf courses** (5800 Coastal Ridge Dr., 231/439-4085, www.bayharborgolf.com,

$79–199), 27 holes that ramble atop 160-foot bluffs, over natural sand dunes and along the shoreline for more than two miles. Eight holes hug the water—more, Boyne developers like to tell you, than at Pebble Beach. Completed in 1998, it was almost immediately named the eighth-best public course in the nation by *GOLF Magazine.*

Bay View

Adjacent to Petoskey on the east side of town, Bay View looks like a Hollywood set for a Victorian romance. This amazing community includes 430 Victorian homes, most built before the 1900s, a riot of gingerbread trim and cotton-candy colors. All are on the National Historic Register, and represent the largest single collection of historic homes in the country.

Bay View was founded by the Methodist Church in 1875, a summer-only religious retreat that took some inspiration from the Chautaqua movement in the East. Summers at Bay View were filled with lectures, recitals, craft classes, and religious programs. Over the years, speakers included such notable names as Booker T. Washington, Helen Keller, and William Jennings Bryan.

Originally a tent community, Bay View's canvas lodgings were slowly replaced by Victorian cottages, many with grand views of Little Traverse Bay. Bay View residents were not an extremely wealthy lot; the homes come in all shapes and sizes, lined up in tidy rows in a shady, park-like campus. Residents own their cottages but lease the land from the Methodist Church.

Today, Bay View remains a quiet enclave, still hosting a full roster of courses, concerts, and other events. While many residents are descendants of Bay View's founding families, the strict religious focus has been diluted. The biggest emphasis now, it seems, is on carefully preserving Bay View's slice of history. (Even minor renovations require approval by the Bay View Association.) Plan a stroll or a bike ride through this calm, gentle place for a true taste of another era.

PETOSKEY STONES

Michigan's official state stone isn't really a stone at all, but a chunk of fossilized coral more than 350 million years old. Coral reefs once thrived in the warm-water seas that covered northern Michigan from Grand Traverse Bay to Alpena on present-day Lake Huron. They are characterized by the distinct honeycomb pattern that covers them. Petoskey stones are common enough that they don't have much real value, but are prized nonetheless by rockhounds and anyone looking for a true local souvenir.

When dry, Petoskey stones often look like, well, ordinary stones. Usually a dusty gray-brown color, their pattern becomes more ap-

parent when wet and especially when polished. The stones are quite soft; locals suggest polishing them by hand with 220-grit wet sandpaper, then repeating the process with 400-grit and 600-grit sandpaper. Rock tumblers are not recommended.

Hunt for Petoskey stones along public beaches almost anywhere in the Traverse Bay region. Some of the more productive spots include Fisherman's Island State Park south of Charlevoix and Petoskey State Park beside Little Traverse Bay. You also can find Petoskey stones at gift shops throughout northwestern Michigan, polished up and often crafted into jewelry.

©TRAVERSE CITY CVB/WMTA

pendants crafted from polished Petoskey stones

Petoskey State Park

Just beyond Bay View, Petoskey State Park (2475 M-119, Petoskey, 231/347-2311, state park vehicle permit required), bends along the east end of Little Traverse Bay. Though quite small at 300 acres, the park nonetheless offers a nice dose of nature right smack between the summertime bustle of Petoskey and Harbor Springs. Its main attraction is its mile-long

beach, with soft sand and enough rocks to keep people on the hunt for Petoskey stones. (The coral pattern appears most clearly when wet, so dip a promising-looking stone in the water.) Try to look up occasionally; the beach has great views of Petoskey and Harbor Springs, and can serve up some terrific sunsets.

Climb the 0.7-mile **Old Baldy Trail** for an even better view from the top of a dune. The park's only other hiking trail, the **Portage Trail,** is an easy 2.8-mile loop that winds south to a little inland lake. It's groomed in winter for cross-country skiing.

Nearly 200 modern campsites are tucked behind some small dunes, mostly wooded sites with good privacy. Sites along the southern loop are closer to the bay, with a few prime (though more public) sites right on the water.

Harbor Springs

Just before Petoskey State Park, U.S. 31 veers inland toward Mackinaw City and the Straits. To stay along the water, turn west on M-119, which follows the curve of Little Traverse Bay and traces the Lower Peninsula's final stretch of Lake Michigan shoreline.

If you were to imagine the quintessential summer resort getaway, it might look a lot like genteel Harbor Springs on the north side of Little Traverse Bay: a deep clear harbor tucked against a high, wooded bluff, ringed with grand estates and white church spires and, for good measure, gleaming yachts bobbing at anchor.

Harbor Springs, in fact, has the deepest natural harbor on all of the Great Lakes, which made it a natural stopping point for the large passenger steamers in the early 1900s. Several artesian wells added to its appeal, making it a popular destination for those seeking healthful air and water. Families like the Fords and the Gambles (of "Proctor and" fame) decided Harbor Springs looked pretty good and helped create exclusive resort communities like Harbor Point and Wequetonsing, where crisp white mansions line up across crisp emerald lawns.

Those "old money" communities still thrive, now inhabited largely by younger generations of Fords and Gambles. Harbor Point remains the more exclusive of the two, with homes topping $10 million hidden away behind gates. The only way in and out is by foot or carriage; even cars are banned from the point. You can walk, bike, or drive through Wequetonsing (WEE-kwee to the locals), where homes have wonderfully nostalgic names like Summer Set and Brookside, and long lines of Adirondack

chairs line up on porches, just in case 10 or 12 friends drop by for gin and tonics.

It all makes for an interesting diversity, where ultra-wealthy Old Guard, younger trustfunders, vacationing families, and hired help all commingle easily in the delightfully tidy downtown. No one begrudges the wealthy their lot in life ("Old money," after all, always has exhibited finer manners than the nouveau riche), and everyone seems to appreciate the civility and gentle grace that is Harbor Springs—a welcoming enclave of continuity in a world that seems so hell-bent on change. Of course, Harbor Springs has no strip malls, no sprawl, no ugly franchise signs. Of course, Thursday is "Maid's Day Out." It *always* has been.

Shopping is a popular sport in Harbor Springs, which hosts an appealing mix of galleries, tony boutiques, and distinctive handmade crafts. Start your exploring at Main and State. Also check out the **Andrew Blackbird Museum** (368 E. Main, 231/526-7731, www.harborspringsareahistoricalsociety.org, 9 A.M.–5 P.M. daily, free) named for an Ottawa chief who lived here in the mid-1800s. The town's first postmaster, Blackbird wrote books about Indian language, legends, and adapting to white civilization. Run by the local Ottawa tribe, the museum shares Native American history and artifacts like elaborate birchbark quill boxes.

The harbor-front is a natural for strolling, with ample benches and a swimming beach at **Zorn Park** near the west end. (Hardy bathers only—the harbor's water is *cold*.) For a more natural beach, the **Thorne Swift Nature Preserve** offers a quiet 300-foot sand beach and dune observation deck with a wonderful bay view. Other trails wind through cedar lowlands, with trees canted and curved at crazy angles, and are marked with interpretive signs. A protected holding of the very active Little Traverse Conservancy, Thorne Swift has a naturalist on duty daily from Memorial Day to Labor Day. Pick a breezy day to visit, since bugs can be zealous here in summer months. The preserve is off M-119 on Lower Shore Drive, just west of downtown.

Tunnel of Trees

The stretch of M-119 from Harbor Springs to Cross Village is considered one of the prettiest drives in Michigan, and deserves the distinction. The narrow lane twists and turns as it follows Lake Michigan from high atop a bluff, with furtive views of the water and the Beaver Island archipelago. Yet it is the trees that take top billing, arching overhead to form a sun-dappled tunnel. The effect is spectacular on autumn afternoons, when the fiery oranges and bronzes glow in the angled sunlight like hot coals.

In spring, trilliums form a blanket of white on the forest floor. Spring also offers a few more deep blue glimpses of the lake, since the trees usually are not fully leafed out until late May. And any season is a good time to spot wildlife. One trip up the corkscrewy road tallied five deer, 15 wild turkeys, and countless grouse.

Try to bike or drive this road during the week, or at least early or late in the day, when traffic should be lighter. The combination of narrow blacktop, blind curves, no shoulders, and lots of wildlife means you'll need to keep a close eye on the road. The more cars there are, the less scenery you can enjoy.

Legs Inn

Even if you've traveled far and wide, it's doubtful you've ever encountered anything like the Legs Inn (6425 N. Lake Shore Dr., 231/526-2281, www.legsinn.com, 11 A.M.–9 P.M. daily, $14–25). Part ethnic restaurant, part eclectic folk art display, this is a weird and fascinating place to explore. Outside is strange enough, a roadside building with a facade of fieldstones, accented with bizarre-looking totems and carved wooden legs spiking up from the roof (hence, the "legs" name).

But that's nothing compared with the interior, where the bar is a dark and mysterious den crammed with twisted driftwood, roots, and stumps-turned-cocktail tables. Seemingly every square inch has been carved into fanciful shapes, weird faces, and indescribable animals—and more and more seem to appear as your eyes adjust to the darkness. The theme carries through to the dining rooms, though

not with such intensity. These areas are brighter and warmer, with picture windows overlooking gardens and distant views of Lake Michigan.

Legs Inn was created by Stanley Smolak, a Polish immigrant who moved to Cross Village from Chicago in the 1920s. He became enamored with the local land and its native people. He befriended the local Ottawa tribes, still thriving here in the 1920s, and was accepted enough into their culture that they gave him an Indian name, Chief White Cloud. Inspired by their art, he began carving. Soon, word of his restaurant and his relations with the Indians made Smolak a celebrity back in Poland.

With its eccentric decor, it's almost easy to overlook the food at the Legs Inn, but you shouldn't. It offers a wonderful array of Polish cooking, with rich soups, thick stews, and popular Polish specialties like pierogies. Even the drink menu offers Polish vodkas and Polish meads, made from honey and fruit juices. This is authentic stuff—many of the cook staff are immigrants themselves. They'll smile and nod and feed you like long-lost relatives.

Sturgeon Bay

M-119 ends at Cross Village, but continue northeast on Scenic Route 1 along Sturgeon Bay to reach **Bliss Township Park,** with low dunes and a pretty sand beach, great for swimming and sunsets. Far enough away from Petoskey and the Straits, it rarely draws a crowd.

Sturgeon Bay also offers the best big-water windsurfing in the area, with easy shore-break and generally warmer water than Little Traverse Bay. Bliss Township Park is a wonderful launch in southwest through north winds. A second launch is about a mile north of the township beach, just where the road makes a hard right. Watch for poison ivy. Advanced sailors looking for big waves should check out the boat launch in Cross Village—good in west through north winds.

Wilderness State Park

North of Cross Village near the top of the "mitten," Waugoshance Point stretches west out into Lake Michigan and dribbles off into a series of islands. This is the spectacular setting for Wilderness State Park (903 Wilderness Park Dr., Carp Lake, 231/436-5381, state park vehicle permit required), the second largest state park in the Lower Peninsula. Aptly named, it occupies more than 7,500 acres of largely undeveloped land, including more than 26 miles of Lake Michigan shoreline. Considering that it sits just 15 minutes away from the Straits of Mackinac, it offers remarkable solitude.

As proof, this is one of the nesting sites of the endangered piping plover. (When the birds are nesting in late spring and early summer, part of the point is closed to visitors.) About 100 other bird species also nest or migrate through Wilderness State Park, making it a favorite of bird-watchers. Anglers also gather here, with notable bass fishing especially in the grassy beds along the southern shore of the point. The park has a boat launch near the campgrounds and day-use area.

The park offers a wide range of topography, with sandy beaches and rocky limestone ledges along the shore. Inland, 12 miles of trails (mostly old truck trails) wind through cedars, pines, and birches. A gravel road leads toward the end of the point, open to autos. To hike there, you can follow the northern shoreline for two miles, unless the endangered piping plovers are nesting. Depending on weather conditions and water depths, it's often possible to wade to Temperance Island—a fun mini-adventure.

Wilderness State Park has two large campgrounds with 250 sites, five rustic cabins, and 24-bunk lodges for rent ($12–69). The Lakeshore Campground sits on Big Stone Bay in an open, grassy setting, with several sites right along the water. Just across the park road, the Pines Campground has more shaded, private sites in the, uh, pines.

MACKINAC ISLAND AND NORTHEAST MICHIGAN

Commonly called the Sunrise Side, the northeastern part of Michigan's Lower Peninsula is perhaps the L.P.'s most underappreciated region—a shame given the untamed beauty that abounds here. Of course, year-round residents and seasonal vacationers value the tranquility of this less-traveled place, so most are grateful that development has been slower here than in other parts of Michigan.

The area's remarkable woods—including sizable Hartwick Pines State Park—lure a wide array of recreationists, from hikers in summer to hunters in winter, while the region's many lakes, such as Higgins Lake south of Grayling, attract numerous anglers, boaters, and canoeists. Wildlife enthusiasts relish Northeast Michigan, too—it's common to spot scurrying foxes amid the underbrush, curious deer along country roads, bald eagles circling above the coves, and majestic elk stalking through the Pigeon River Country State Forest, home to the largest free-roaming elk herd east of the Mississippi River.

Although many locals live here all year long—even during the splendid, if bitter-cold, winters—more come during the summer months, escaping humid places like Chicago and Florida. Dwelling in vacation cottages that line the roads and encircle the area's idyllic lakes, these seasonal residents spend their summers playing golf, shopping for antiques, fishing for walleye, and picking wild blueberries.

A superb way to experience the hinterlands of Northeast Michigan is, ironically, via the road. The 22-mile River Road Scenic Byway showcases the high cliffs, white pines, and wooded

HIGHLIGHTS

◖ **Colonial Michilimackinac State Historic Park:** Just south of the Mackinac Bridge lies this reconstruction of the original Fort Michilimackinac, a French fur-trading village and military outpost established in 1715. Visitors can tour over a dozen historic buildings, where costumed soldiers, traders, and colonial ladies demonstrate skills of the late 18th century (page 240).

◖ **Grand Hotel:** Opened in 1887, this gorgeous hotel is a timeless piece of American history, boasting the world's longest porch and a guest list that's included at least five U.S. presidents. Nonguests can stroll amid the flower-filled grounds or enjoy a meal in the stylish main dining room (page 245).

◖ **Diving in Thunder Bay:** Scuba divers will discover a wealth of artifacts in the 448-square-mile Thunder Bay National Marine Sanctuary and Underwater Preserve, east of Alpena. Fog banks, sudden gales, and rocky shoals made this region, known as "Shipwreck Alley," the unfortunate resting place of more than 100 historic vessels (page 255).

◖ **Canoeing on the Au Sable River:** Home to North America's longest nonstop canoe marathon, the Au Sable is one of the most picturesque rivers in Michigan, stretching from Grayling to Oscoda. Several resorts offer canoe rentals for visitors during the spring and summer months (page 259).

◖ **Houghton and Higgins Lakes:** Between West Branch and Grayling, these sizable inland lakes, two of the state's largest, offer five swimming beaches, a dozen access sites for boaters and anglers in summer, and the possibility of ice fishing for walleye, pike, bass, and bluegill (page 261).

◖ **Hartwick Pines State Park:** The largest state park in Michigan's northern Lower Peninsula also preserves the largest stand of virgin white pines remaining in the L.P. Visitors can view forestry exhibits, experience a former logging camp, explore several hiking and skiing trails, and observe a variety of wildlife, from woodpeckers to black bears (page 266).

◖ **Golfing in Gaylord:** Golfers will find a wide assortment of options in the northern half of the Lower Peninsula, especially in the area around Gaylord, which offers a high concentration of championship golf courses, with challenging holes, scenic views, and fine lodgings (page 268).

LOOK FOR ◖ TO FIND RECOMMENDED SIGHTS, ACTIVITIES, DINING, AND LODGING.

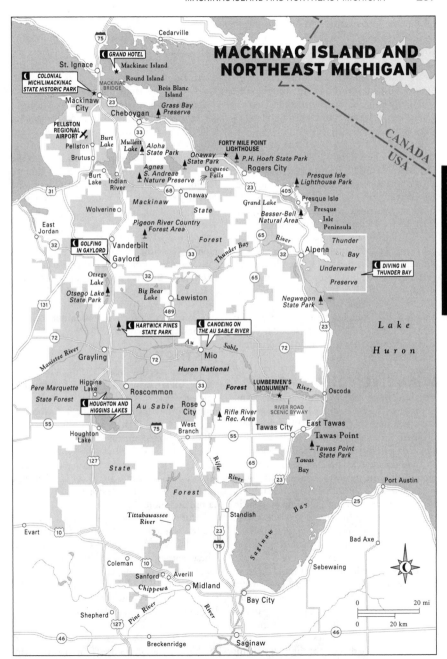

MACKINAC ISLAND AND NORTHEAST MICHIGAN

Cedarville

🌙 **GRAND HOTEL**

St. Ignace
Mackinac Island

🌙 **COLONIAL MICHILIMACKINAC STATE HISTORIC PARK**

Round Island

MACKINAC BRIDGE

Bois Blanc Island

Mackinaw City

Cheboygan

Grass Bay Preserve

PELLSTON REGIONAL AIRPORT ✈

Pellston

Brutus

Burt Lake

Mullett Lake

Aloha State Park

FORTY MILE POINT LIGHTHOUSE

Onaway State Park

P.H. Hoeft State Park

Agnes S. Andreae Nature Preserve

Ocqueoc Falls

Rogers City

Presque Isle Lighthouse Park

Burt Lake

Indian River

Onaway

Grand Lake

Presque Isle

Wolverine

Mackinaw

State

Besser-Bell Natural Area

Presque Isle Peninsula

East Jordan

Pigeon River Country Forest Area

Forest

🌙 **GOLFING IN GAYLORD**

Vanderbilt

Gaylord

Thunder Bay River

Alpena

Thunder Bay

Underwater Preserve

🌙 **DIVING IN THUNDER BAY**

Otsego Lake

Otsego Lake State Park

Big Bear Lake

Lewiston

Negwegon State Park

🌙 **HARTWICK PINES STATE PARK**

🌙 **CANOEING ON THE AU SABLE RIVER**

Au

Sable

L a k e

Grayling

Mio

H u r o n

Manistee River

Huron National

Higgins Lake

Pere Marquette State Forest

Roscommon

Au Sable

Rose City

Forest

LUMBERMEN'S MONUMENT

River

Oscoda

🌙 **HOUGHTON AND HIGGINS LAKES**

Rifle River Rec. Area

RIVER ROAD SCENIC BYWAY

East Tawas

Houghton Lake

West Branch

Tawas City

Tawas Point

Tawas Point State Park

State

Rifle River

Tawas Bay

Port Austin

Forest

Tittabawassee River

Standish

Saginaw Bay

Bad Axe

Evart

Coleman

Sanford Averill

Chippewa

Midland

Sebewaing

Shepherd

Pine River

River

Bay City

Breckenridge

Saginaw

0   20 mi

0   20 km

NORTHEAST MICHIGAN

lakes of the Au Sable River Valley. Meanwhile, the Sunrise Side Coastal Highway (U.S. 23) stretches for 200 miles along the Lake Huron shoreline, from Standish to the Mackinac Bridge. Along the way, motorists can experience quaint coastal towns, inviting beaches, and lovely lighthouses. These stunning drives are especially wonderful in the fall, when the trees are ablaze with spectacular colors.

Situated just north of the mainland lies Mackinac Island, a nostalgic destination claimed by both the Upper and Lower Peninsulas. Although most of the island is preserved as a state park, about 20 percent of it has become a year-round tourist mecca, offering boat docks, historic sites, enchanting hotels, and intriguing attractions like the Original Mackinac Island Butterfly House. Since automobiles are banned here, bicycles, horses, and carriages are the preferred modes of transportation—just another facet of the island's yesteryear vibe. Mackinac Island might be, at times, teeming with "fudgies" (a local term for tourists), but its charms are unmistakable, worth a look after exploring the wilds of Northeast Michigan.

PLANNING YOUR TIME

For those who prefer small towns, the solitude of the great outdoors, and winter activities like snowmobiling, Northeast Michigan is an ideal precursor to visiting the even wilder and more isolated U.P. In summer, it's also a good spot to avoid the crowded beaches and resort towns along Lake Michigan. Of course, that doesn't mean you won't encounter plenty of folks on the area's championship golf courses, near inland lakes during summer weekends, and on Mackinac Island throughout the year. You will, however, likely avoid crowds during the off-season, from November to March.

To hit the highlights of Northeast Michigan, you'll need a minimum of three days, including a day trip to Mackinac Island. A whole week will allow you more opportunity to tour the historic coastline and explore the interior's impressive forests and lakes.

Two main roads cut through the Huron shore region. U.S. 23 hugs the coastline from Standish to the Straits of Mackinac, offering vistas and villages along the way. I-75 is the quicker, though less scenic, route, heading north from Bay City, through Grayling and Gaylord, to the Mackinac Bridge.

For those not driving to Northeast Michigan (or arriving via private boat), consider taking a Greyhound bus to towns like Cheboygan, Rogers City, Alpena, Tawas City, Grayling, and Gaylord. It's also possible to fly into the Pellston Regional Airport and Alpena County Regional Airport, both of which are served by Northwest Airlines. If you plan on exploring several areas in this spread-out region, it's advisable to rent a vehicle as soon as you arrive.

Tourism folks market the Huron shore region as the state's "Sunrise Side." For more information about Northeast Michigan, contact **Michigan's Sunrise Side Travel Association** (1361 Fletcher St., National City, MI 48748, 800/424-3022, www.visitmichigansunriseside.com) or the **Northern Michigan Tourist Association** (www.travelnorth.org).

HISTORY

In appearance, Northeast Michigan has come nearly full circle in 200 years. Its first inhabitants were Native Americans, who left the land much as they found it, until the Europeans arrived in the 17th century. By the mid-1800s, logging companies that had exhausted the nation's eastern forests had moved on to Michigan's fertile ground, making it the largest lumber-producing state in the country between 1850 and 1910, with an estimated 700 logging camps and more than 2,000 mills.

Before the rush of settlers to Michigan in the 1830s, more than 13 million of the state's 37 million acres were covered with white pine. These majestic trees thrived in sandy soil, grew up to 200 feet tall, and could live an incredible 500 years. By 1900, however, all that was left of these once awe-inspiring forests were stumps. Logging had devastated the terrain, leaving behind a wasteland.

In 1909, the federal government established the Huron National Forest, the first of many such preserves that sought to repair years of damage. A century later, much of this region is once again forested, and it's possible to hike for miles through towering, whispering pines. While the impenetrable white pine forests that once characterized this part of the state are a thing of the past, one 49-acre stand of old-growth white pine remains, a glimpse of the grandeur that once blanketed this landscape.

Mackinac Island, of course, has its own unique history. The Ojibwa and Ottawa peoples called it Michilimackinac, which some scholars claim means "The Great Turtle," an apt description for this hump of limestone. The Indians summered here, hunting, fishing, and trading some of their catch for grains and produce from other tribes.

French missionaries were the first Europeans to settle in the area, erecting a mission in nearby St. Ignace in 1671. The French were also the first whites to exploit the rich fur harvest, establishing a trading post in St. Ignace in the late 1600s. In 1715, they erected Fort Michilimackinac in Mackinaw City. The British, meanwhile, were also eager to expand their territory. They regularly skirmished with the French, and Fort Michilimackinac traded hands more than once—that is, until the 1763 Treaty of Paris gave all French land east of the Mississippi to Great Britain.

Upstart colonists became the new enemy. In 1780, the British commander abandoned Fort Michilimackinac in favor of Mackinac Island, where the high limestone bluffs offered better protection from attack. Though American troops never came, they won the fort anyway, gaining title to the northern territory after the American Revolution. Still, the British refused to turn over the fort until 1796.

During the War of 1812, British troops landed at the northern end of the island in early morning darkness, dragged a couple of cannons up the bluff and aimed them at Fort Mackinac below. The surprised Americans surrendered without firing a single shot. The British once again controlled Fort Mackinac until 1814, when the Treaty of Ghent passed the land back to the United States once and for all.

In 1817, John Jacob Astor set up the American Fur Company here, bartering with the Indians for beaver pelts and storing them in warehouses on the island. Until overhunting decimated the fur industry and commercial fishing became the area's mainstay, Astor ranked as the richest man in the United States.

By the second half of the 19th century, Mackinac Island had evolved from a battleground to a gracious getaway. Wealthy Midwesterners, who had heard about the island's lovely waters and clean air, began arriving by lake steamer to summer here. Hotels sprang up, soon followed by private homes along the bluffs—30-room Victorian "cottages," complete with carriage houses, stables, and servants' quarters.

To minimize its potentially destructive impact, the automobile was banned from Mackinac Island as quickly as it arrived. Today, roughly 600 horses are stabled on the island in summer, used for hauling freight, pulling carriages, and private recreation. The horses, carts, carriages, bicycle fleets, and well-preserved Victorians all blend to give Mackinac the magical, frozen-in-time feel that has turned it into one of the most popular vacation spots in the Midwest.

NORTHEAST MICHIGAN

Mackinaw City

Although some may consider it a tourist trap, Mackinaw City offers more than just strip malls and souvenir shops. Despite overdevelopment, the town has several things to recommend it—namely, a maritime museum, a lighthouse, two excellent historic parks, several fudge shops, numerous hotel rooms, terrific views of the Great Lakes, and, of course, ferry service to Mackinac Island.

SIGHTS
◖ Colonial Michilimackinac State Historic Park

Archaeologists have been uncovering treasures since 1959 on the site of this 18th-century fur-trading post, believed to be the nation's longest-running archaeological dig. Long a well-traveled Indian hunting and trading ground, the French built a post here in 1715. The French exploited the Indians, bribing them with gifts and alcohol, and encouraging them to work in the fur trade. Though the unfortunate relationship led many Indians to abandon their traditional way of life, the two groups rarely fought. Instead, the French feuded with the British, who sought to expand their landholdings in the region. For the next 65 years, the fort along the Straits alternately fell under French and British control.

The fort's most violent episode occurred while it was under British rule. In 1763, Pontiac, the Ottawa war chief, ordered an attack on British posts all over Michigan, an attempt to drive the growing British population out of their native land. While Pontiac laid siege to Detroit, local Ojibwa stormed the fort, killing all but 13 soldiers. In the end, though, it was the feisty colonists who sent the British fleeing from Fort Michilimackinac. They dismantled what they could and burned the rest to the ground in 1780, opting for a new, more-defensible post on nearby Mackinac Island.

a period gardener at Colonial Michilimackinac

Today, Colonial Michilimackinac State Historic Park (102 W. Straits Ave., 231/436-4100, www.mackinacparks.com, 9 A.M.–6 P.M. daily June–Aug., 9 A.M.–4 P.M. daily May and Sept.–mid-Oct., $10 adults, $6.25 children 5–17), located just west of the Mackinac Bridge, portrays the lives of both the Indians and European settlers, with costumed interpreters reenacting daily life at an Indian encampment and a stockaded fort. Displays include many of the artifacts unearthed by archaeologists. Interpreters demonstrate various crafts and skills, from cooking and weaving to cleaning weapons. Interpreters are quite knowledgeable and able to answer most visitors' questions. Don't miss the underground archaeological tunnel exhibit, "Treasures from the Sand."

Historic Mill Creek Discovery Park

Today, this exceptionally pretty glen and rushing stream creates a pleasant oasis for visitors, but it once was an innovative industrial site. When the British made plans to move from Fort Michilimackinac to Mackinac Island, Scotsman Robert Campbell recognized their imminent need for lumber. He purchased 640 acres of the land around the only waterway in the area with enough flow to power a sawmill. He built the mill in 1790 and later added a blacksmith shop and gristmill.

The site was no longer profitable when the fort ceased operation, so it was abandoned in the mid-1800s. Since the 1970s, archaeologists and historians have worked together to re-create the water-powered sawmill on its original site. Today, visitors to the 625-acre Historic Mill Creek Discovery Park (9001 U.S. 23, 231/436-4100, www.mackinacparks.com, 9 A.M.–5 P.M. daily June–Aug., 9 A.M.–4 P.M. daily May and Sept.–mid-Oct., $7.50 adults, $4.50 children 5–17) can see the splashing waterwheel in action and visit the Orientation Center, which has an audiovisual presentation and displays on other artifacts uncovered during the dig. Make sure to walk the park's 1.5 miles of trails, which wind along the creek and mill pond, rising up to scenic overlooks with views of the Straits and Mackinac Island.

Old Mackinac Point Lighthouse

Old Mackinac Point Lighthouse

Located on a point just east of the Mackinac Bridge, this 1892 cream-brick light guided ships through the busy Straits of Mackinac for nearly 70 years. When the Mackinac Bridge was completed in 1957, it became obsolete, since vessels could range on the bridge's high lights instead of the diminutive 40-foot tower. Today, this charming lighthouse (9 A.M.–5 P.M. daily June–Aug., 9 A.M.–4 P.M. daily May and Sept.–mid-Oct., $6 adults, $3.50 children 5–17), topped with a cherry-red roof, houses a maritime museum, part of Colonial Michilimackinac State Historic Park. A schooner and other ships are docked and on display. The lighthouse grounds serve as their own delightful little park, with impressive views of the Mackinac Bridge as well as picnic tables scattered around a tidy lawn.

From here, you can reach several island and offshore reef lights via boat—though you should take care in these potentially dangerous waters. Two of the most interesting are the 1874 **Spectacle Reef Light,** an impressive example of a monolithic stone lighthouse, and the 1895 **Round Island Light** in the Straits of Mackinac.

Mackinac Bridgemen Museum

It's not slick or fancy, but this small museum (231 E. Central, 231/436-8751, www.mackinacbridgemenmuseum.com, 8 A.M.–midnight daily May–Oct., free) above Mama Mia's Pizza is loaded with tidbits and artifacts on the construction of the $100 million Mackinac Bridge. A very well-done video documents the bridge's design and construction. For more information about the bridge itself, consult the **Mackinac Bridge Authority** (www.mackinacbridge.org).

Lighthouse Tours

Although a self-guided tour of Michigan's lighthouses can be a delightful way to pass a few days in the Great Lakes State, the experience can be even more enlightening with a well-informed guide. Besides shuttling tourists to and from Mackinac Island, **Shepler's Mackinac Island Ferry** (800/828-6157, www.sheplersferry.com) also offers lighthouse cruises ($49.50 adults, $37.50 children 5–12). Departing from Mackinaw City, these trips guide passengers amid lighthouses and shipwrecks that would be difficult for most people to reach otherwise. Along the way, passengers are treated to historical tales that provide an informative context for the lighthouses that still stand today. The eastbound cruise features offshore lights like Round Island Light and the privately owned Bois Blanc Island Light, while the westbound cruise highlights structures such as the red-and-white striped White Shoal Light and the 1873 St. Helena Island Lighthouse.

SHOPPING

Although Mackinaw City isn't as high on shoppers' lists as, for instance, the resort towns along Lake Michigan, it does have its share of decent shops. Of course, no area is quite as pleasant as **Mackinaw Crossings** (248 S. Huron Ave., 231/436-5030, www.mackinawcrossings.com, shop hours vary), a tidy open-

air collection of restaurants and stores. Here, you can find everything from **To Bead or Not to Bead,** which offers handmade jewelry and beads for creating your own accessories, to the **Great Lakes Bear Factory,** where children (and adults) can customize their very own stuffed teddy bears.

ACCOMMODATIONS AND FOOD

With the Straits a major tourism draw, Mackinaw City alone has more than 3,000 rooms. For a variety of amenities, check out the **Comfort Inn Lakeside** (611 S. Huron Ave., 231/436-5057, www.comfortinn.com, $75–108 d) or the **Ramada Inn Waterfront** (723 S. Huron Ave., 231/436-5055, www.ramadainn.com, $48–278 d).

In between sightseeing and shopping, grab a bite to eat at one of the numerous area restaurants. Step back a couple of centuries at the **Dixie Saloon** (401 E. Central Ave., 231/436-5449, www.dixiesaloon.com, hours vary, $6–24), a historic landmark. Try the potato-encrusted walleye or the fried perch, both of which are locally caught. For something a little more elegant, stop by **The Lighthouse Restaurant** (618 S. Huron Ave., 231/436-5191, 11 A.M.–9 P.M. daily, $10–42), with its prime rib, lobster, and excellent wine list.

INFORMATION AND SERVICES

For more information about Mackinaw City, contact the **Mackinaw Area Visitors Bureau** (231/436-5664, www.mackinawcity.com). While you won't find a ton of services here, there is indeed a small grocery, a post office, and a 24-hour ATM at **Citizens National Bank** (580 S. Nicolet St., 231/436-5271, www.cnbismybank.com). In case of a police-related or medical emergency, dial **911** from any cell or public phone.

GETTING THERE AND AROUND

Pellston Regional Airport (PLN) (231/539-8441, www.pellstonairport.com) offers commuter service from Detroit via Northwest Airlink. From there, you can rent a vehicle, take U.S. 31 to I-75, and head north to Mackinaw City. Of course, many visitors come to Michigan by car, usually heading for Mackinaw City via I-75 or U.S. 23. Once in town, you can park your vehicle and walk to the shops and eateries.

Mackinac Island

Linking Lakes Huron and Michigan, the Straits of Mackinac (MAK-i-naw) have been a crossroads of the Great Lakes for hundreds of years, a key waterway for hunting, fishing, trading, and transportation. The four-mile-wide Straits also sever Michigan in two, both emotionally and geographically. Until the 1950s, the only way across was by ferry, effectively blocking the development of the Upper Peninsula and creating half-day backups at the ferry dock during prime hunting and fishing season.

Today, the magnificent five-mile-long Mackinac Bridge stitches the state together, allowing a free flow between the Upper and Lower Peninsulas. But the Straits, now a key vacation area for much of the Midwest, continue to lure people, and many come specifically for Mackinac Island.

No place name in Michigan conjures up as much history, attention, and affection as the tiny parcel known as Mackinac Island. Over the centuries, the 2,200-acre island has been a sacred ground for the Native Americans who summered here, an important base for French fur trappers, a fort for British soldiers, and a gilded summer retreat for the wealthiest of Victorian-era industrialists.

It is the Victorian era that Mackinac chose to preserve, from the exquisite 1887 Grand Hotel, with its 660-foot-long porch stretching across the hillside, to the clopping of the horse-drawn carriages down the vehicle-free streets. Yes, it can seem touristy at first blush. Yes, it can be crowded. But Mackinac Island can also be irrepressibly charming, all buffed up and neatly packaged, the state's heirloom jewel.

Some of the criticism lobbed at Mackinac is based on misconception, anyway. For starters, Mackinac is more than the tangle of fudge and souvenir shops that greet you at the ferry dock. A full 80 percent of the island is a state park, comprising a restored 18th-century fort, undeveloped woodlands, crisscrossing trails, rare wildflowers, and sculpted limestone outcroppings.

Secondly, Mackinac Island has far more lodging choices than the famous Grand Hotel. Many are moderately priced. Plan to spend at least one night, so you have a little time to wander around and get past the cliché. Mackinac doesn't lend itself well to a cursory glance. Like those wealthy resorters knew, it's a wonderful place to retreat from the pulls of the real world.

SIGHTS
Downtown

Everyone wants to wander among the four blocks of shops and restaurants on Main Street. The ferry docks themselves are particularly interesting. At the Arnold Transit dock, you can sneak a peek at the day-to-day grunt work of Mackinac, like workers unloading carton after carton of vegetables from the ferry and reloading them by hand onto drays (wagons) for horse-drawn delivery to area restaurants. Even the UPS man does his route on bicycle, pulling a cart loaded with packages.

Once you've done the Main Street stroll and nibbled your requisite hunk of fudge (there's a reason tourists are known as "fudgies"), make the most of your visit by getting off the main drag. You can get a good taste of what the island has to offer on a carriage tour with **Mackinac Island Carriage Tours** (906/847-3307, www.mict.com, 9 A.M.–4 P.M. daily May–Oct., $23.50 adults, $9 children 5–12), located across from the Arnold Transit ferry

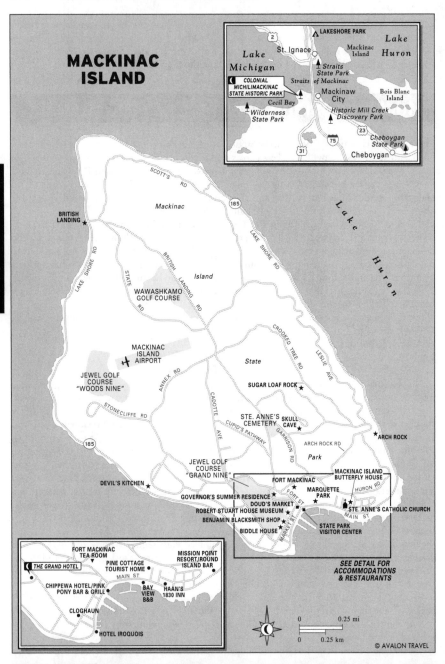

MACKINAC ISLAND

LAKESHORE PARK
Lake Huron
Lake Michigan
St. Ignace
Mackinac Island
Straits State Park
Straits of Mackinac
COLONIAL MICHILIMACKINAC STATE HISTORIC PARK
Mackinaw City
Bois Blanc Island
Cecil Bay
Historic Mill Creek Discovery Park
Wilderness State Park
Cheboygan State Park
Cheboygan

SCOTT'S RD
Mackinac
BRITISH LANDING
LAKE SHORE RD
BRITISH LANDING RD
STATE RD
Island
WAWASHKAMO GOLF COURSE
LAKE SHORE RD
Lake Huron
MACKINAC ISLAND AIRPORT
CROOKED TREE RD
JEWEL GOLF COURSE "WOODS NINE"
State
LESLIE AVE
ANNEX RD
STONECLIFFE RD
SUGAR LOAF ROCK ★
CADOTTE AVE
STE. ANNE'S CEMETERY
SKULL CAVE ★
CUPID'S PATHWAY
GARRISON RD
ARCH ROCK RD
ARCH ROCK ★
JEWEL GOLF COURSE "GRAND NINE"
Park
MACKINAC ISLAND BUTTERFLY HOUSE
DEVIL'S KITCHEN ★
FORT MACKINAC ★
MARQUETTE PARK
GOVERNOR'S SUMMER RESIDENCE ★
HURON RD
DOUD'S MARKET
ROBERT STUART HOUSE MUSEUM ★
STE. ANNE'S CATHOLIC CHURCH
BENJAMIN BLACKSMITH SHOP ★
MAIN ST
BIDDLE HOUSE ★
MARKET ST
STATE PARK VISITOR CENTER

SEE DETAIL FOR ACCOMMODATIONS & RESTAURANTS

FORT MACKINAC TEA ROOM
MISSION POINT RESORT/ROUND ISLAND BAR
THE GRAND HOTEL
PINE COTTAGE TOURIST HOME
MAIN ST
CHIPPEWA HOTEL/PINK PONY BAR & GRILL
BAY VIEW B&B
HAAN'S 1830 INN
CLOGHAUN
HOTEL IROQUOIS

0   0.25 mi
0   0.25 km

© AVALON TRAVEL

dock. The pleasant narrated tour takes about two hours, rambling along at a relaxing pace past the Grand Hotel, Arch Rock, Skull Cave, Fort Mackinac, and most of the island's other key sights. This locally owned business is the world's largest horse and buggy livery, with more than 300 horses, mostly crosses of beefy Percherons, Belgians, and Clydesdales.

One block inland from Main, some of Mackinac's original residences line up on **Market Street.** Much quieter than frenetic Main, Market has several interesting stops for visitors. The headquarters of the American Fur Company, John Jacob Astor's empire, is now the **Robert Stuart House Museum** (9 A.M.–4 P.M. daily May–late Oct.). The 1817 building retains much of its original decor, including fur company ledgers, fur weighing scales, and other artifacts. The museum is operated by the City of Mackinac Island.

A block west, knowledgeable interpreters demonstrate spinning at **Biddle House** and blacksmithing at the **Benjamin Blacksmith Shop** (both 11 A.M.–4 P.M. daily mid-May–late Oct.). These and other historic buildings are part of the state park, and are included with the admission ticket to Fort Mackinac. For current information, stop by the park visitors center across from Marquette Park on Huron Street, or contact **Mackinac State Historic Parks** (213/436-4100, www.mackinacparks.com, 11 A.M.–4 P.M. daily).

From Marquette Park, follow Fort Street up the hill to the **Governor's Residence** at the corner of Fort and East Bluff Road. The state purchased the "cottage" in the 1940s. It is the official summer residence of the governor, though the amount of time actually spent here varies from governor to governor. The house is open for tours on Wednesday mornings.

Some of the island's more impressive "cottages" line up along **East Bluff.** Wander east from the governor's mansion to see some of these Victorian marvels. Happily, most survived the Depression era—when they could be purchased for pennies on the dollar, of course. Today, they're well cared for and worth $1 million plus. (And remember, most are summer homes only!)

Work your way down one of the sets of public steps to the lakefront. Main Street has become Huron Street here. Continue your walk east, passing smaller but no less appealing cottages and homes. Many are skirted with geraniums and lilacs, the island's signature flowers. Behind Ste. Anne's Catholic Church, seek out the **Original Mackinac Island Butterfly House & Insect World** (906/847-3972, www.originalbutterflyhouse. com, 10 A.M.–7 P.M. daily Memorial Day–Labor Day, $7.50 adults, $4 children 5–12), tucked away on McGulpin Street.

Owner Doug Beardsley used to use his greenhouses to grow thousands of geraniums for the Grand Hotel and others. He relied on biodynamic growing methods, releasing beneficial insects to care for his plants rather than chemical sprays. When economics made his small greenhouse less viable, he stuck with his insects. After hearing about a butterfly house in Europe, Beardsley added some different host plants and began ordering pupa from around the world. Now hundreds of butterflies fly freely in his greenhouse/atrium, some nearly six inches long. You can observe them up close on walls and plants, or sit still long enough and they'll land on you.

The engaging Beardsley hopes his attraction will help convince gardeners to wean themselves off herbicides and pesticides. He sells helpful insects to control garden pests like aphids and will give you ideas for attracting butterflies to your own garden. (Host plants like milkweed and cabbage, where butterflies like to lay their eggs, will work best. "Think of it as planting a caterpillar garden, not a butterfly garden," he says.)

(Grand Hotel

The Grand Hotel (906/847-3331, www.grand-hotel.com) has become practically synonymous with Mackinac Island, a gracious edifice built on a truly grand scale. It is the largest summer resort in the world, operating from early May through late October. Its famous 660-foot-long covered front porch gets decked out each spring with 2,000 geraniums planted in seven *tons* of

NORTHEAST MICHIGAN

© L. DIGGS, PICTURE THIS...

Grand Hotel on Mackinac Island

potting soil. Its 11 restaurants and bars serve as many as 4,000 meals a day. Its impeccable grounds offer guests every amenity, from saddle horses to designer golf to swimming in the outdoor pool made famous by the 1940s swimming actress Esther Williams, who filmed *This Time for Keeps* here.

But opulence is what the railroads and steamships were after when they formed a consortium and built the Grand Hotel in 1887, dragging construction materials across the frozen waters by horse and mule. The wealthiest of all Mackinac Island visitors stayed here, of course, high on the hill.

Yet unlike other turn-of-the-20th-century resorts that burned to the ground or grew dog-eared and faded, the Grand Hotel has managed to maintain its grace and dignity over the years. It still hosts all manner of celebrities and politicians—five U.S. presidents to date—and still offers a sip of the Gilded Age, with high tea in the parlor each afternoon and demitasse served after dinner each evening. Room rates still include a five-course dinner in the soaring main dining room, and jackets/ties and skirts/dresses are still the required attire.

The Grand Hotel's time-capsule setting prompted director Jeannot Szwarc to choose it as the location for the 1980 film *Somewhere in Time,* starring Christopher Reeve, Jane Seymour, and Christopher Plummer. Curiously, the movie has developed a huge following; its fan club reunites at the hotel each year in late October.

While room rates can get outright astronomical, they can be a worthwhile splurge if you enjoy this kind of thing. What the heck—take high tea, loll in the beautifully landscaped pool, or dance to the swing orchestra in the Terrace Room. Nonguests can sneak a peek at the hotel's public areas and grounds for a not-unreasonable $10. (It's needed to thin the sightseers more than anything.) Highly recommended are a stroll through the grounds, filled with Victorian gardens—24,000 tulips in spring!—and a visit to the snazzy Cupola Bar, with views halfway to Wisconsin.

Fort Mackinac

Located at the crest of the bluff, whitewashed Fort Mackinac (231/436-4100, 9 A.M.–5 P.M. daily mid-May–mid-Oct., $10 adults, $6.25 children 6–17) is worth a visit for the views alone, presiding over—as forts do—the downtown, the marina, and Lake Huron. But there's also plenty to see at this military outpost, which the British and Americans haggled over for nearly 40 years.

Along with peering over the parapets, you can wander in and out of 14 buildings within the fort. The barracks, officers' quarters, post hospital, and others are filled with interpretive displays and decorated in period decor. Costumed guides lead all sorts of reenactments, including musket firings and cannon salutes. A short audiovisual presentation, "The Heritage of Mackinac," does a good job of presenting basic history.

Mackinac Island State Park

Often overshadowed by other visitor attractions, Mackinac Island's natural history has attracted scientific observation for over 200 years. In the early 19th century, botanists discovered several species completely new to science, including the dwarf lake iris, still found predominantly in the Straits of Mackinac region.

Early scientists also marveled at the island's distinctive geology, mostly brecciated limestone that has been sculpted by eons of wind and waves. The result is some dramatic rock formations, like the giant inland slab of limestone called Sugar Loaf Rock, the lakeside caves of Devil's Kitchen, and impressive Arch Rock, which rises nearly 150 feet above the eastern shore and spans some 50 feet.

In recognition of the park's distinctive "natural curiosities" and growing tourism, the U.S. government created Mackinac National Park in 1875—following Yellowstone as the nation's second national park. Twenty years later, it was returned to Michigan and became Mackinac Island State Park, Michigan's first state park.

SHOPPING

Although shopping isn't a huge activity here, the island does present a few unique browsing options. The **Island Scrimshander** (906/847-3792, www.scrimshanders.com, 9 A.M.–4 P.M. daily May–Oct.), for instance, offers amazing engraved trinkets. You should also check out **La Galerie** (906/847-6311, 9 A.M.–4 P.M. daily May–Oct.), with its line of Pandora Jewelry and Christopher Radko Ornaments.

RECREATION

Walk, run, bike, or ride a horse, but make sure you get out of downtown to really see Mackinac Island. You'll be surprised how quickly you can leave any crowds behind as you set out on the paved eight-mile path that circles the island. The trail never wanders far from the pleasant shoreline and passes many of the island's natural features, which are well marked. Traveling clockwise, the first you'll reach is Devil's Kitchen; heading in the opposite direction, you'll arrive first at Arch Rock, the most dramatic of all Mackinac limestone oddities.

About halfway around, on the island's northwestern side lies **British Landing,** where British soldiers sneaked onto the island in 1812. They hiked across Mackinac's interior, totally surprising the American garrison stationed at the fort (and apparently looking the other way), and recaptured the island. Today, the landing is a good spot for a picnic or short break (water and restrooms available). There's a small **nature center** here, staffed in summer months by a helpful naturalist. Hike the short nature trail, which has several interpretive signs as it weaves up a bluff.

British Landing is also a good spot from which to head inland and explore the island's interior. British Landing Road bisects the island and links up with Garrison Road near Skull Cave, leading to the fort. It's a hilly, three-mile trip from shore to shore. British Landing Road is considered a "major road" by Mackinac standards, meaning you'll share it with carriages. On bike or foot, you'll have endless other options—at last count, Mackinac had some 140 miles of trails and footpaths.

Pick up a free *Mackinac Island Map,* available all over town, and venture off. The map marks the location of old cemeteries, rock formations, and such, but it's even more appealing to just

MACKINAC'S MIGRANT VISITORS

While the Straits of Mackinac usually serve as a mighty barrier for many of the mammals that dwell on Mackinac Island, Michigan winters can indeed alter the situation, allowing some of the larger mammals, such as wolves, bears, and deer, to reach the mainland via an ice bridge. So, unlike the isolated isles of warmer climates, this 2,200-acre island is less of a biological vacuum. In fact, many of its seasonal visitors are migrant birds, who use this popular migration spot as a resort habitat in the spring, while en route to summer homes in the north.

Although Mackinac Island also attracts seasonal recreationists, such as hikers and bikers, bird-watchers are especially fond of this enchanted place. In late April and early May, you'll spot golden eagles, bald eagles, red-tailed hawks, and broad-winged hawks flying above. Yellow warblers, American redstarts, and indigo buntings arrive in summer. Along the shoreline, you might also see herrings, cormorants, great blue herons, loons, and Canadian geese. Even wintertime guests will be treated to bird sightings: Beautiful snowy owls and great gray owls often fly south from the Arctic to savor the comparatively warmer climate of Mackinac Island.

Of course, some bird species stay here year-round, including cardinals, blue jays, black-capped chickadees, and large red-crested woodpeckers. The difference between them and many other native inhabitants is that they're here by choice. They can spread their wings and leave at any time – unlike coyotes, for instance, which must wait for an ice bridge to form before making their escape.

explore the smaller trails on your own and discover pretty, peaceful Mackinac. Everything's well marked, and you can't really get lost anyway—you're on a small island, after all.

ACCOMMODATIONS

Along with the 【 **Grand Hotel** (906/847-3331, www.grandhotel.com, $450–750 d), there are plenty of grand and graceful places to stay on Mackinac Island. Yes, rates can be high, but don't dismiss staying on Mackinac; you can find reasonable rates at smaller B&Bs and apartments, the latter of which often have good deals for weeklong stays. The options below tip both ends of the scale.

The **Chippewa Hotel** (250 Main St., 906/847-6494, www.chippewahotel.com, $95–545 d) is a venerable old Mackinac Hotel that had a $3 million renovation several years back. The result is a classy and comfortable place to stay, with a location in the heart of the island, on Main Street, overlooking the marina. The 24-person lakeside hot tub alone may be worth the stay.

The **Mission Point Resort** (6633 Main St., 906/847-3312, www.missionpoint.com, $149–599 d) may have the island's very best location,

spread across 18 acres at the island's southeastern tip. Though not from the Victorian era—it was built in the 1950s by the Moral Rearmament Movement, a post–World War II patriotic group—the sprawling, bright-white resort is attractive and well kept, with beautiful lawns lined with Adirondack chairs. Amenities include an outdoor pool, tennis and volleyball courts, and loads of children's activities.

The **Pine Cottage Tourist Home** (906/847-3820, $79–129 d), just three blocks from Main Street, offers one of the island's most economical lodging options.

FOOD

One of the best dining deals on the island is the 【 **Fort Mackinac Tea Room** (906/847-3328, 10 A.M.–4 P.M. daily June–Sept., $9–18), located in the lower level of the Officer's Stone Quarters within the fort. Surrounded by thick masonry walls, the tearoom serves up both a great atmosphere and delicious food, with good soups, salads, and sandwiches prepared by Grand Hotel chefs. Opt for a spot on the terrace since the high setting is outstanding, and forts were not exactly designed for expansive views.

Everyone has to hit the **Pink Pony Bar & Grill** (906/847-3341, 10 A.M.–1:30 A.M. daily, $9–32) at least sometime during a Mackinac visit. Located in the Chippewa Hotel overlooking the marina, this is *the* party place following the famed Chicago-to-Mac yacht race. The food's great, too, with good burgers, whitefish sandwiches and such on the lunch menu, and steaks, seafood, and ribs for dinner.

Sooner or later, you'll succumb to fudge. A visitor treat since Victorian tourism days, shops line Main Street. One of the oldest, **Murdick's Fudge** (www.murdicks.com), established in 1887, has a Main Street location (as well as one in Mackinaw City). You can buy a sizable slab to take or mail home, or just a small sliver to nibble. (A little goes a long way—it's very rich stuff.)

INFORMATION AND SERVICES

For more information about Mackinac Island, contact the helpful **Mackinac Island Tourism Bureau** (7274 Main St., 877/847-0086, www.mackinacisland.org, 9 A.M.–5 P.M. daily), which is located across from the Arnold Transit ferry dock. For further information, consult www.mackinac.com or pick up a copy of the weekly *Mackinac Island Town Crier* (www.mackinacislandnews.com).

Mackinac Island offers a limited amount of services, including a couple of groceries, one post office, and a small police department. For banking needs, stop by the **Central Savings Bank** (21 Hoban St., 906/847-3759, www.centralsavingsbank.com). In case of a medical emergency, dial **911** from any phone or consult the **Mackinac Island Medical Center** (906/847-3582), which offers an on-call staff 24 hours daily.

GETTING THERE AND AROUND

A million people visit Mackinac Island every year, so getting there isn't a problem. You can fly into the **Pellston Regional Airport (PLN)** (231/539-8441, www.pellstonairport.com), then either charter a flight to the island through **Great Lakes Air** (906/643-7165, www.greatlakesair.net) or use the **Mackinaw Shuttle**

(888/349-8294, www.mackinawshuttle.com) to reach the ferry docks in Mackinaw City.

There are in fact three ferry services that can zip you across the Straits of Mackinac, from Mackinaw City or St. Ignace, in less than 20 minutes: the **Arnold Transit Company** (800/542-8528, www.arnoldline.com, round-trip $25 adults, $12 children 5–12, $7.50 bicycles), **Shepler's Mackinac Island Ferry** (800/828-6157, www.sheplersferry.com, round-trip $23 adults, $11 children 5–12, $7.50 bicycles), and **Star Line** (800/638-9892, www.mackinacferry.com, round-trip $25 adults, $12 children 5–12, $7.50 bicycles).

During the main tourist season—May–October—they operate several times daily. Only one, the long-standing Arnold Transit, in operation since 1878, offers service in April and November (from St. Ignace only). Since much of the island shuts down for the winter, you'll find it a little more challenging to reach Mackinac December–March.

No matter which ferry you choose, it will deposit you at the southern end of the island, in the heart of the hotels and shops lining Main Street, which follows the curve of the waterfront. It's a wild scene: Dock workers load luggage onto pull-carts and carriages, flocks of bicycles dodge horse-drawn buggies, pedestrians stream up and down the road eating fudge and window-shopping.

Horse-drawn "taxis" are available 24 hours daily from **Mackinac Taxi Service** (906/847-3323) or **Mackinac Island Carriage Tours** (906/847-3307, www.mict.com). If you enjoy walking and hiking, you can easily traverse Mackinac on foot. It's a wonderful place for casual strolls and all-day hikes. The island also is a terrific place for biking. Bike rentals are available all over downtown; the **Mackinac Island Bike Shop** (906/847-6337, www.mackinacislandbikes.com), for instance, rents bicycles for $6–12 per hour or $30–70 per day. Equipment varies, so look before you pay. If you plan to do much biking, you'll be happier with your own bike, since you can transport it on the ferry. You'll want a hybrid or mountain bike to negotiate most interior trails. Be sure to bring your own helmet.

NORTHEAST MICHIGAN

Cheboygan and Vicinity

With a population of 5,000, Cheboygan ranks as one of the largest cities along Lake Huron. While the town offers history buffs a few interesting sites, including a 19th-century opera house, it mainly appeals to outdoor enthusiasts, who venture beyond the city limits to explore surrounding lakes, rivers, and forests. Boaters and anglers especially focus their gaze inland, where a 45-mile-long waterway links Lake Huron with several large inland lakes, ending just shy of Lake Michigan's Little Traverse Bay. Cheboygan sits at the mouth of this popular waterway, welcoming boaters with open arms. Hikers, bird-watchers, and other lovers of the outdoors will find plenty to interest them here, too.

SIGHTS
Historic Sites and Lighthouses

The **Cheboygan County Historical Museum** (404 S. Huron St., 231/627-9597, www.cheboyganmuseum.com, 1–4 P.M. Tues.–Sat. Memorial Day–Sept., $2) was built in 1882 and served as the county jail and local sheriff's home until 1969. The two-story brick structure houses a parlor, kitchen, schoolroom, and bedroom in period style, with an adjacent building that contains logging and marine displays.

The city's **Opera House** (403 N. Huron, 231/627-5841, www.theoperahouse.org, 10 A.M.–4 P.M. daily, $2) once entertained the likes of Mary Pickford and Annie Oakley. Built in 1877 and later rebuilt after an 1888 fire, the Victorian-style theater serves as a stage for local entertainment and is open for tours in summer.

From the boardwalk in **Gordon Turner Park** at the northern end of Huron Street, you can gaze out over one of the largest cattail marshes in the Great Lakes. A nesting ground for more than 50 species, it's a favorite of bird-watchers. From the boardwalk and nearby fisherman's walkway, you also can see the Mackinac Bridge as well as Round and Bois Blanc Islands. Visitors might also appreciate the quaint 1884

Cheboygan Crib Light, an octagonal structure that, when deactivated, was relocated from the mouth of the Cheboygan River to the base of the west breakwater on Lake Huron. Now, the pretty white and red lighthouse is an ideal stop for photographers.

Parks and Preserves

Cheboygan's **Grass Bay Preserve** contains a rare find in the Great Lakes—one of the finest examples of an original interdunal wetland habitat, characterized by beach pools, marshes, flats, and wetlands, all separated by low dunes. Owned by the Nature Conservancy, this delicate ecosystem comprises a great diversity of plants, including more than 25 species of orchids and 11 types of conifers. Four of the species—dwarf lake iris, Lake Huron tansy, Pitcher's thistle, and Houghton's goldenrod—grow only on the Lake Huron and Lake Michigan shores.

The Nature Conservancy considers Grass Bay its best property in Michigan. The preserve's original 80 acres have grown to more than 400, including a one-mile stretch of Lake Huron shore. From May to September, Grass Bay is noted for its carpet of wildflowers, including lady's slipper, Indian paintbrush, blue harebell, and sundews. The best way to take them all in is from one of the park's two short trails, which wander through an aspen/birch forest and across old shoreline ridges to the beach. Note, however, that this is private—and very fragile—land. Parking can be hard to find, too—most visitors use lots on U.S. 23 (ask first).

HIKING

For hikers and cross-country skiers, the **Wildwood Hills Pathway** on Wildwood Road in nearby Indian River offers almost complete isolation. Three well-marked trails—ranging 4–9 miles in length—take visitors deep into the heart of a northern Michigan second-growth forest and cross high, rolling hills in the Mackinac State Forest just a few miles south of Burt Lake.

Two trailheads on Wildwood Road provide access to the pathway, leading into a dense forest of hardwoods and evergreens. Along the way, the only companion you'll likely have is the wind through the trees, an occasional bird-call, and a curious chipmunk or two. Trail system maps are located at the trailheads and most major intersections.

The swift and turbulent Pigeon River, designated by the state as a natural river, is the highlight of the **Agnes S. Andreae Nature Preserve.** Located in Indian River, the beautifully secluded 27-acre preserve includes 2,000 feet of Pigeon River frontage. On the river's west side, a lowland stand of cedar bordering the riverbank rises to high bluffs covered with conifers and dense hardwoods. There are no designated trails, but hikers and cross-country skiers find well-worn tracks to follow and other trails that border the river. Like many other tracts in this undeveloped part of the state, the preserve is owned by the Little Traverse Conservancy.

ACCOMMODATIONS AND FOOD

There are several decent motels in the Cheboygan area, such as the **Best Western River Terrace Motel** (847 S. Main St., 231/627-5688, www.bestwesternmichigan. com, $79–129 d), with most rooms overlooking the Cheboygan River. You can also camp at **Cheboygan State Park** (4490 Beach Rd., 616/627-2811, state park vehicle permit required, $12–27), at one of 78 modern sites along Lake Huron's Duncan Bay. The area is a favorite among anglers, but there's not much in the way of swimming at the campground; instead, head for the park's day-use area, four miles away, which has a sandy beach and bathhouse.

For good food served up with interesting history, try **The Boathouse** (106 Pine St., 231/627-4316, 11 A.M.–8 P.M. daily, $7–19), the former boathouse of the infamous Purple Gang, part of Detroit's 1920s underworld;

or the **Hack-Ma-Tack Inn** (8131 Beebe Rd., 231/625-2919, www.hackmatackinn.com, 5 P.M.–close daily May–mid-Oct., $18–50), housed in a rustic 1894 lodge overlooking the Cheboygan River. Whitefish is the specialty.

INFORMATION AND SERVICES

For more information about Cheboygan, contact the **Cheboygan Area Chamber of Commerce** (124 N. Main St., 231/627-7183, www.cheboygan.com, 9 A.M.–5 P.M. Mon.–Fri.). For local news and events, consult the *Cheboygan Daily Tribune* (www.cheboygannews.com).

Cheboygan offers most of the services that travelers might require. Here, you'll find groceries, banks, even a **post office** (200 N. Main St., 231/627-9898, www.usps.com). In case of a police-related or medical emergency, dial **911** from any phone. For medical assistance, visit the **Cheboygan Memorial Hospital** (748 S. Main St., 231/627-5601, www.cheboyganhospital.org).

GETTING THERE AND AROUND

From **Pellston Regional Airport (PLN)** (231/539-8441, www.pellstonairport.com), you can rent a car, head north on U.S. 31, and take County Road 66 east to Cheboygan. In addition, you can take a bus via **Greyhound** (300 Mill St., 800/231-2222, www.greyhound. com). If you're already traversing Michigan by car, you can reach Cheboygan via M-27, M-33, or U.S. 23.

THE INLAND WATERWAY

The geography of this region was kind to the early Indians and French voyageurs traversing the Lower Peninsula: A chain of lakes and rivers forms a 45-mile water route, very nearly linking Lakes Michigan and Huron. The route was safer and faster than traveling on the big lakes, and certainly beat the heck out of portaging. Today, the inland waterway remains extremely popular, mostly for fishing and recreational boating. Narrower portions are dredged to a depth of five feet and a width of 30 feet. Boats up to 30 feet long can join in on what sometimes looks like a nautical parade.

Burt Lake State Park

Big Burt Lake is the focus of its namesake state park (6635 State Dr., Indian River, 231/238-9392, state park vehicle permit required), located at the lake's southern end. Anglers flock to this 10-mile-long lake, known as one of the best fisheries in the state for walleye, panfish, and bass—but especially walleye. Swimmers seek it out, too, since a soft sand beach runs the entire length of the park. The park has two boat launches, one located next to a popular campground with 375 modern sites ($22). The park offers little in the way of hiking, but does have a nifty observation tower that gives you a great view of the lake.

Mullett Lake

Popular with anglers, Mullett Lake also has a lesser-known claim to fame: the origin of the term *kemosabe,* used by Tonto in *The Lone Ranger.* Yep, it's true—according to the diehard research of Cecil Adams, anyway, who authors "The Straight Dope," a quirky factfinding column that began in the *Chicago Reader* and has appeared in alternative weeklies around the country.

Here's what Cecil's research turned up: "The term *kemosabe* . . . seems to have been the contribution of Jim Jewell, who directed *The Lone Ranger* until 1938. In an interview, Jewell said he'd lifted the term from the name of a boys' camp at Mullett Lake, just south of Mackinac, Michigan, called Kamp Kee-Mo-Sah-Bee. The camp had been established in 1911 by Jewell's father-in-law, Charles Yeager, and operated until about 1940. Translation of kee-mo-sah-bee, according to Jewell: 'trusty scout.' While Indian language experts scoff at the spelling, they agree that the pronunciation roughly jibes with the Ottawa word for "scout." Now there's some trivia to throw out at your next party.

Speaking of name mysteries, no one really knows why a small town on the east end of Mullett Lake was originally named Aloha Depot. Today, it's the site of **Aloha State Park** (231/625-2522, state park vehicle permit required), a small 100-acre state park that primarily consists of a boat launch and 295-site campground ($14). Not particularly picturesque by Michigan standards, most sites sit in a relatively open setting, with just a handful directly on the water.

Along with neighboring Burt Lake, pretty Mullett Lake is one of the most popular and productive fishing lakes in the state. Anglers vie for walleye and northern pike, but larger stuff lurks down there as well: In 1974, Mullett produced a 193-pound sturgeon, a scaly, longnosed creature that hasn't evolved much since prehistoric times. Think about that while you're taking a dip.

Rogers City to Alpena

Driving along the picturesque Lake Huron shore, you'll encounter several slow-moving communities, including Rogers City, home to lovely lighthouses, parks, and beaches, and Alpena, a larger city favored by outdoor enthusiasts for its wildlife sanctuary and underwater preserve.

Despite its beautiful beaches, few travelers visit Rogers City, a quiet town of 3,300, better known as home to the world's largest limestone quarry. The Huron shore's limestone was formed by ancient seas that once covered most of the state. Full of coral-forming organisms, they eventually created large limestone deposits, one of which nears the earth's surface in Rogers City. In 1907, tests found that the limestone was unusually pure, ideal for making steel and many chemicals. The Michigan Limestone and Chemical Company was formed a year later, and subsequently purchased by U.S. Steel. Nearly four miles long and roughly three miles wide, the quarry is expected to produce well into the 21st century.

Alpena, protected by the deep curve of Thunder Bay, is the largest city north of Bay City on the Lake Huron shore, yet has always been tinged by a lack of respect. When surveyed in 1839, a deed to the land was offered to anyone in the survey party in lieu of summer wages, but few took the offer. At the time, the area was considered mostly a desolate cedar swamp.

Not long after, however, the intrepid Daniel Carter arrived with his wife and young daughter and built a log cabin, becoming the town's first white settler. By 1857, a store and boardinghouse had popped up, and in 1859, Alpena became the site of the county's first steam-powered sawmill. Before long, some 20 lumber and shingle mills buzzed life into the growing town.

Today, the town's economy relies on a large cement industry. But for visitors, it also offers the chance to enjoy the natural beauty of the Great Lakes without the trendy development and gentrification that have taken over so many of the old resort towns on the opposite side of the state.

Part of the reason visitors have overlooked Alpena is because it's not that easy to reach. More than 70 miles from the nearest interstate, it remains an unpretentious working-class town of corner bars and friendly residents. For decades, diversified industries, including paper mills, cement plants, and an Air Force base, meant that the area didn't have to seek out the tourist trade the way other areas have.

But with its bread-and-butter industries gone, Alpena has learned to promote its assets. And there's plenty worth promoting, including two lightly visited state parks with several miles of Lake Huron shoreline, a handsome marina, an impressive museum, northern Michigan's only year-round professional theater, and a fascinating underwater preserve with more than 80 shipwrecks.

SIGHTS
Jesse Besser Museum and Planetarium
The excellent Jesse Besser Museum and Planetarium (491 Johnson St., Alpena, 989/356-2202, www.bessermuseum.org, 10 A.M.–5 P.M. daily, $5 adults, $3 children) combines art, history, and science on two levels. The museum's highlight is the "Gallery of Early Man," a collection of Great Lakes Native American artifacts considered one of the finest in the country. To the probable dismay of archaeologists, the collection, which numbers more than 60,000 pieces, was gathered by Gerald Haltiner, a local state highway worker, and his museum-curator son, Robert.

The museum purchased the collection from the Haltiners in the 1970s and is working closely with local Native American tribes to review the collection with repatriation in mind. Some of its most intriguing artifacts are the copper items that date back more than 7,000 years, made by a people known only as the Copper Culture. The museum's Sky Theater Planetarium puts on changing shows, many with Native American themes, throughout the year.

Alpena Wildlife Sanctuary
Alpena Wildlife Sanctuary, on U.S. 23 within the Alpena city limits, has been a favorite sanctuary of hikers, paddlers, anglers, and nature lovers since it was established in 1938 by the Michigan Conservation Department. The 500-acre refuge bordering the Thunder Bay River contains a large expanse of wetlands, an island with fishing platforms, and a viewing platform that overlooks the river. According to the Thunder Bay Audubon Society, more than 130 different species of birds have been spotted here. Year-round residents include Canada geese and mute swans; spring migration brings others, including buffleheads, canvasbacks, whistling swans, and more.

Lighthouses
Travelers who find the Huron shore lacking in comparison with the state's Lake Michigan

shore change their minds after a visit to the **Forty Mile Point Light.** Seven miles north of Rogers City on U.S. 23, a limitless expanse of blue water sweeps in a 180-degree arc to the horizon. A gently sloping beach proves just right for wading, sandcastle building, and swimming. The 52-foot-tall lighthouse, built in 1897, stands guard as a reminder that Huron can, and does, turn dangerous. Though not open to the public, it is a favorite of photographers.

Other lighthouses along this stretch include the 1905 **Middle Island Lighthouse** and the 1832 **Thunder Bay Island Light,** both accessible via boat. In Alpena, you won't need a vessel to view the 1914 **Alpena Light,** a skeletal red structure near the Thunder Bay River.

Beaches and Parks

Many rate **P. H. Hoeft State Park** (U.S. 23 N, Rogers City, 989/734-2543, state park vehicle permit required) as the most beautiful state park along Michigan's Lake Huron shore. It's easy to see why. With a mile-long swath of soft, white sand, low rolling dunes, and a mixed hardwood/conifer forest, it offers a breathtaking, simple beauty. Surprisingly, it's also one of the least visited state parks in the Lower Peninsula. Even the 144-site modern campground ($22), set against mature pines and hardwoods with lots of shade and privacy, sits half empty most of the time. Head directly for sites 1–33, located just a few steps from the beach. One cabin and four rent-a-tents are also available.

Behind the park's picnic area lies an almost totally undeveloped area, with dunes and woods that abound in wildlife and vegetation. Naturalists can search for the more than 40 species of wildflowers that grow here, including many orchids and irises rare in the state and North America. More than four miles of trails loop through the area for hikers and cross-country skiers.

From Rogers City, it's just 11 miles west on M-68 to the Lower Peninsula's only major waterfall. **Ocqueoc (sacred water) Falls** cascades over a series of two- to six-foot drops.

The picturesque site is a favorite of picnickers, sunbathers, and swimmers. A seven-mile trail for hikers and cross-country skiers starts next to the falls.

Just a few hundreds yards away, the **Bicentennial Pathway** (created in 1976) loops through the deep woods and over the gently rolling hills of the Mackinaw State Forest. The pathway's three loops measure 3, 4, and 6.5 miles and are well used by area hikers. Bed down at the **Ocqueoc Falls State Forest Campground** across M-68.

Just north of Rogers City on U.S. 23, **Seagull Point Park** (193 E. Michigan Ave.) draws visitors to its beautiful beach, curved like a scimitar. A wide band of soft sand and a gradual slope into Lake Huron create a perfect spot for beachcombers, sunbathers, and families. Behind the beach, a two-mile interpretive trail winds through a series of low dunes, with signs along the route that identify the area's natural history and accompanying flora and fauna. Near the park, the **Herman Vogler Conservation Area** (240 W. Erie St., Rogers City, 989/734-4000) provides a quiet, car-free area on the Trout River. Five miles of nature trails are open to cross-country skiing in the winter.

Negwegon State Park (Ossineke, 989/724-5126, state park vehicle permit required) is the carefully guarded secret of a number of outdoor lovers. What exactly are they hiding? Some of the most beautiful and most isolated beaches on Lake Huron. The 2,469-acre park's shoreline stretches for more than six miles, a lovely string of bays and coves.

Named after Chippewa chief Negwegon, the park also offers three hiking trails named after Native American tribes: the Algonquin, Chippewa, and Potawatomi. The 10 miles of trails skirt the shoreline and loop through a heavily wooded interior. A serene retreat, this isolated park offers natural beauty to hikers and backpackers willing to trade conveniences for quiet, contemplative walks along eight miles of Lake Huron shoreline. Note: There are no camping or picnic facilities here.

Between this park and the considerably smaller **Harrisville State Park** (248 State Park Rd., Harrisville, 989/724-5126, state park vehicle permit required) is one of several lighthouses along the Lake Huron shore. The gleaming white **Sturgeon Point Lighthouse,** built in 1869, is still active today—as both a lighthouse and a maritime museum (daily Memorial Day–mid-Sept.). The grounds are open to the public year-round.

◖ DIVING IN THUNDER BAY

Divers have their own sanctuary just off the Alpena shore. Here, the **Thunder Bay National Marine Sanctuary and Underwater Preserve** thrills divers with its clear waters, interesting underwater limestone formations, and shipwrecks. Rocky islands and hazardous shoals proved treacherous for mariners; the preserve protects some 80 shipwrecks, 14 of which can be explored with the help of a wreck-diving charter. Among the most popular are the *Nordmeer,* a German steel steamer that sank in 1966, and the *Montana,* a 235-foot steamer that burned and sank in 1914. **Thunder Bay Scuba** (413 S. Ripley Blvd., Alpena, 989/356-6228, www.tbscuba.com, 9 A.M.–5:30 P.M. Mon.–Fri., 10 A.M.–2 P.M. Sat.–Sun.) offers charter diving services for about $44 per day, departing from Alpena's city marina.

The state established the Thunder Bay National Marine Sanctuary and Underwater Preserve—more than 288 protected miles in all—in 1981, largely to prohibit divers from removing artifacts from the site. In October 2000, the state preserve was also designated a national marine sanctuary, a status that grants it federal funding and additional resources for scientific and archaeological study. For more information, contact the **Michigan Underwater Preserve Council** (800/970-8717, www.michiganpreserves.org).

ACCOMMODATIONS AND FOOD

Lodging choices are pretty limited in Rogers City. The best place in town (and the only place with an indoor pool) is the 43-room **Driftwood Motel** (540 W. 3rd St., 989/734-4777, $49–99 d), which overlooks Lake Huron. Adjacent to the motel, the **Buoy Restaurant** (530 N. 3rd St., 989/734-4747, 11 A.M.–7 P.M. daily, $7–19) serves up Lake Huron views and fish dishes.

Hotels and restaurants in Alpena have a funky, nostalgic vibe, as if you've been transported back to the 1950s or '60s. Chief among them are the **40 Winks Motel** (1021 State St., 989/354-5622, $49–69 d), with simple rooms opposite Lake Huron.

INFORMATION AND SERVICES

For more information about this area, contact the **Rogers City Chamber of Commerce** (292 S. Bradley Hwy., Rogers City, 989/734-2535, www.rogerscity.com) or the **Alpena Area Convention & Visitors Bureau** (235 W. Chisholm St., Alpena, 800/425-7362, www.alpenacvb.com). For local news, consult the *Presque Isle County Advance* (www.piadvance.com) or *The Alpena News* (www.thealpenanews.com).

Between Rogers City and Alpena, you're likely to find the services you need, from groceries and pharmacies to banks and post offices. In case of a medical emergency, dial **911** from any phone or consult **Alpena Regional Medical Center** (1501 W. Chisholm St., Alpena, 989/356-7000, www.alpenaregionalmedicalcenter.org).

GETTING THERE AND AROUND

Northwest offers commuter service to the **Alpena County Regional Airport (APN)** (1617 Airport Rd., Alpena, 989/354-2907, www.alpenaairport.com), and **Greyhound** (800/231-2222, www.greyhound.com) provides bus service to both Rogers City (409 N. Bradley) and Alpena (1235 State St.). But it's probably easier (and cheaper) to reach this area via car. From I-75, take M-68 to Rogers City or M-32 to Alpena. Both towns can also be accessed via U.S. 23 along the coast.

PRESQUE ISLE

It would be easy to pass the Presque Isle peninsula and never know it was there. Easy, but a mistake. This almost completely undiscovered resort area off the beaten path between Rogers City and Alpena features two of the jewels in the region's crown. Both are well worth driving out of the way to see.

On a map, the peninsula looks like a beckoning finger (*presqu'île* means "peninsula"—"almost an island"—in French). Two classic lighthouses perch at the tip of the strangely shaped peninsula, including the tallest lighthouse on the Great Lakes.

Inside the **Old Presque Isle Lighthouse Park,** exhibits and displays relate the history of Great Lakes shipping and light keeping, with artifacts and antiques that range from wooden doors from a shipwreck to an old pump organ that visitors can play. Built in 1840, the lighthouse was used for 30 years until it was replaced by a new light a mile north. But no automatic light can provide the view you'll get from the parapet surrounding the lantern room, reached by a trip up the two-story tower's winding steps.

The **New Presque Isle Lighthouse and Museum** (4500 E. Grand Lake Rd., 989/595-9917, 9 a.m.–6 p.m. daily May–Oct., free) dates to 1871. Trees had grown to obscure the older, shorter lighthouse; the "new" one stretches to 113 feet, the tallest on all the Great Lakes. Situated in the middle of 100-acre **Presque Isle Lighthouse Park,** the tower and restored light keeper's house look much as they did more than a century ago. Inside, a caretaker—a descendant of generations of Great Lakes sailors—plays the part of turn-of-the-20th-century light keeper on special occasions.

The park's fine nature trails begin at the lighthouse and circle the peninsula's tip. The trails border rugged shoreline, then weave in and out of evergreens and hardwoods, before reaching the peninsula's tip and a sweeping view of Lake Huron from a rocky beach.

Presque Isle's **Besser-Bell Natural Area** offers an intriguing mix of attractions: nearly a mile of wild, undeveloped Lake Huron shoreline, a ghost town, a sunken ship, and one of the few remaining stands of virgin white pine left in the state. Reach the 137-acre preserve from U.S. 23 south of Grand Lake.

The boom-and-bust logging industry both created and destroyed the ghost town of Bell, which once included a school, a sawmill, a store, a saloon, and several houses during the 1880s. A one-mile self-guided trail leads through a magnificent stand of virgin white pine and passes the ghost town and a tiny inland lagoon, the graveyard for an unnamed small vessel. Halfway along the trail, a plaque honors Jesse Besser, who donated this land to the state in 1966 as a memorial to Michigan's lumbermen. The trail continues through a dark cedar forest before emerging on Lake Huron's shore.

Oscoda to West Branch

Farther along the Lake Huron shore, several towns serve as gateways to incredible outdoor delights, including Oscoda, popular among canoeists, and Tawas City, a favorite among bird-watchers.

Oscoda sits at the mouth of the Au Sable River, famed as a trout stream and navigable by canoe as far as Grayling and Roscommon. The waterway played a prominent part in the state's early pine-logging days. At its most populous, the city's population numbered more than 23,000, and the river was filled with pine logs on their way to the sawmills. While the logs were plentiful, Oscoda grew unchecked. With the depletion of the resource, though, its population began to shrink. Finally, nature put an abrupt end to the city's logging boom: A forest fire swept through in 1911, reducing the city's heyday to ashes. The current population is less than 1,000.

As for Tawas City, its name derives from Otawas, the name of an important Chippewa chief. He's honored in this stretch of Lake Huron shore many times over. The twin cities of Tawas City and East Tawas straddle the Tawas River, which empties into Tawas Bay, formed by a crooked finger of land called—you guessed it—Tawas Point.

Today, local festivals, such as February's Perchville U.S.A., reveal the area's popularity with anglers. Visitors can watch the boat-filled bay in Tawas Point State Park, which occupies the fishhook-shaped Tawas Point. It's a favorite of naturalists, as much for the ever-changing landscape created by wind and waves during annual winter storms as for some of the best bird-watching in the state.

West of Tawas City, West Branch is a small town with quaint Victorian-style architecture, a downtown shopping district, and an outlet mall. It's also not far from a popular recreation area, the Huron National Forest, and the road to Houghton and Higgins Lakes.

SIGHTS
Beaches
Opposite the large beach on the shore of Tawas Bay, part of 183-acre **Tawas Point State Park** (686 Tawas Beach Rd., East Tawas, 989/362-5041, daily, state park vehicle permit required), the white Victorian-style 1876 **Tawas Point Lighthouse** is undoubtedly the park's most-photographed feature and a favorite among lovers of these classic lights. One of the state's most well-maintained lighthouses, it is often open to the public for self-guided tours. Not far away, bird-watchers gather at the day-use area and nature trail. A checklist of birds spotted in the park lists more than 250, with 31 species of warblers and 17 species of waterfowl.

In summer, swimmers favor this park for its white sand and warm, shallow waters. Anglers and hikers appreciate Tawas Point, too. Here, you'll also find a playground, a picnic area, public restrooms, a spacious campground, and gorgeous sunsets.

From the state park, history buffs can take a self-guided 68-mile driving tour amid key historical, natural, and cultural features west of the park, including the site of a 1984 forest fire, a 1,000-acre marsh that nurtures deer and other wildlife, the 1917 Foote Dam, a former Air Force base, and the Lumbermen's Monument, a bronze statue erected in 1931 on the high scenic banks of the Au Sable River. Dedicated to the pioneer spirit and efforts of Michigan lumbermen, the monument isn't far from a visitors center, whose exhibits relate to Michigan's logging era. For more information, pick up brochures at the park office.

Rifle River Recreation Area
Inner tubes seem to be the transportation option of choice on the slower-moving Rifle River, which meanders from the Rifle River Recreation Area (2550 E. Rose City Rd., Lupton, 989/473-2258, $12–19), about 15

NORTHEAST MICHIGAN

miles northeast of West Branch, to Saginaw Bay, some 90 miles south. Paddlers shouldn't overlook the Rifle, though, since it flows through Devoe Lake, one of five paddle-only lakes in this spacious preserve.

The 4,449 acres that now make up the Rifle River Recreation Area were once part of the private hunting preserve of H. M. Jewett, an early auto-industry tycoon. Today, most of the visitors who are hoping to leave with a catch are bagging bass and other varieties of fish, not four-legged game.

The recreation area includes several miles of paved and packed dirt trails that travel across one-lane bridges, past forest-fringed lakes, and up several high hills that reveal vistas of tangled stands of cedar. For a great view, head for **Ridge Road,** a dirt track that passes over the park's highest elevations. Those who like to hike can follow 14 miles of picturesque trails that cut through some of the park's most breathtaking terrain.

Visitors can stay at a choice of on-site accommodations, including both rustic and modern campsites as well as five "frontier-style" cabins, all located in secluded areas far from campgrounds and day-trippers. They have vault toilets, hand pumps, and only basic furnishings. In winter, the park is a popular spot for cross-country skiing, ice fishing, and snowmobiling.

SHOPPING

Needless to say, shopping isn't why most people come to the southern reaches of Northeast Michigan. But not all the attractions in this area are of the natural kind. In a seemingly unlikely place, the **Tanger Outlets Center** (2990 Cook Rd., West Branch, 989/345-2594, www.tangeroutlet.com, 9 A.M.–9 P.M. Mon.–Sat.,

OMER IN THE NEWS

Located along the Sunrise Side Coastal Highway (U.S. 23), Omer is one of the smallest cities in Michigan. Founded as a logging town in the mid-1860s and originally called Rifle River Mills, the town was renamed by the first postmaster, who wanted to call it Homer. When, however, he discovered that Michigan already had a town named Homer – south of Marshall – he dropped the H, and the town of Omer was incorporated as a city in the early 20th century.

With a population of around 300, Omer has little to recommend it to travelers – except, perhaps, its proximity to the Rifle River. Still, the town is curious for at least one reason. It was near here that, in 1998, Timothy Joseph Boomer was canoeing with friends when he fell into the water and began yelling a long string of expletives, in the presence of a man, his wife, and their two young children. A sheriff's deputy, who heard the shouts downstream, ticketed Boomer for violating an 1897 law that claimed anyone using immoral or obscene language within earshot of a woman or child could be charged with a misdemeanor.

An Arenac County jury found Boomer guilty of the charge, and though a district judge ruled the ban on cursing in front of women unconstitutional, he left intact the provision concerning children. Boomer was fined $75 and ordered to work in a child-care program, but the sentence was postponed during the appeals process.

The case of the "cussing canoeist" sparked a nationwide debate about free speech and public behavior. While some protested the vague nature of the law – which could leave the question of what constitutes "indecent" language up for interpretation – others defended the need to regulate improper conduct, especially in front of children. Needless to say, the American Civil Liberties Union (ACLU) was only too quick to handle the case, and in 2002, the Michigan Court of Appeals successfully overturned the 105-year-old law. Afterward, the "cussing canoeist," who had initially admitted to using only a few choice words (not the alleged string of them), decided to be more careful about what he said in public.

10 A.M.–7 P.M. Sun.) offers an enormous variety of mainstream shopping choices, everything from a Gap Outlet to a Bath & Body Works store. The outlet mall lies east of I-75.

🜂 CANOEING ON THE AU SABLE RIVER

While anglers often try their luck on the Au Sable, paddlers may appreciate the river even more. The **Au Sable River Canoe Marathon** (www.ausablecanoemarathon.org) starts in Grayling and ends here. For canoe rentals, try **Oscoda Canoe Rental** (678 W River Rd., Oscoda, 989/739-9040, www.oscodacanoe.com, 8 A.M.–4 P.M. daily, $20–40) or **Hunts Canoe & Mini Golf** (711 Lake St., Oscoda, 989/739-4408, $18–40).

Trips on the *Au Sable River Queen* (1775 W. River Rd., Oscoda, 989/739-7351, www.ausableriverqueen.net, 10 A.M.–5 P.M. daily, $8.50) depart from Foote Dam daily in season. The tours are especially popular during fall color tours, and reservations are recommended.

ACCOMMODATIONS AND FOOD

The **Redwood Motor Lodge** (3111 N. U.S. 23, Oscoda, 989/739-2021, www.redwoodmotorlodge.com, $54–127 d) offers both standard motel rooms as well as cottages near Lake Huron. Also on Lake Huron, the **Rest-All Inn** (4270 N. U.S. 23, Oscoda, 989/739-8822, www.restallinn-oscoda.com, $59–109 d) has clean motel rooms (some with microwaves and refrigerators), a beach, and a playground.

In West Branch, stay at the **LogHaven Bed, Breakfast, and Barn** (1550 McGregor Rd., 989/685-3527, www.loghavenbbb.com), where you'll find comfortable rooms, private baths, hearty country-style breakfasts, and a place to stable horses. It's a perfect home base for exploring the area's hiking, horseback-riding, snowmobiling, and cross-country skiing trails.

Michigan's state parks offer consistently good campgrounds. **Tawas Point State Park** (686 Tawas Beach Rd., East Tawas, 989/362-5041, state park vehicle permit required, $27)

is no exception, with 210 campsites and a large sand beach.

Order up a homemade brew at **Wiltse's Brew Pub and Family Restaurant** (5606 N. F-41, Oscoda, 989/739-2231, www.wiltsebrewpub.com, 8 A.M.–12:30 A.M. Mon.–Sat., 8 A.M.–9 P.M. Sun., $12–27) to wash down the chicken dishes and steaks cut to order.

While you won't find any gourmet hideaways in the area, restaurants offer good, stick-to-the-ribs food in generous portions. They tend to be family-style, including **Genie's Fine Foods** (601 W. Bay, 989/362-5913), a lakefront spot that serves up a country-style breakfast and a gluttonous evening buffet. **Champs Food and Spirits** (444 W. Lake St., Tawas City, 989/362-8080, 11 A.M.–10:30 P.M. daily, $7–18) offers steaks, seafood, and lighter fare with fine views of Tawas Bay.

INFORMATION AND SERVICES

For more information about the area, contact the **Oscoda Area Convention and Visitor's Bureau** (Oscoda, 989/739-0900, www.oscoda.com), the **Oscoda-AuSable Chamber of Commerce** (4440 N. U.S. 23, Oscoda, 800/235-4625, www.oscodachamber.com), the **Tawas Bay Tourist and Convention Bureau** (877/868-2927, www.tawasbay.com), the **Tawas Area Chamber of Commerce** (402 E. Lake St., Tawas City, 800/558-2927, www.tawas.com), or the **West Branch-Ogemaw County Travelers & Visitors Bureau** (422 W. Houghton Ave., West Branch, 989/345-2821, www.visitwestbranch.com).

Although you won't find a ton of services in these smaller towns, basics like groceries, banks, and post offices won't be too hard to find. If an emergency occurs, dial **911** or consult **St. Joseph Health System** (200 Hemlock, Tawas City, 800/362-9404, www.sjhsys.org).

GETTING THERE AND AROUND

Given that the closest airports are located in Alpena and Freeland, your best bet for reaching the area will be to drive here yourself. West

Branch is situated just east of I-75. From there, you can take M-55 to Tawas City or U.S. 23 to Oscoda. In addition, **Greyhound** (800/231-2222, www.greyhound.com) provides bus service to Tawas City.

HURON NATIONAL FOREST

Oscoda also is known as the gateway to the Huron National Forest (Huron Shores Ranger Station, 5761 N. Skeel Rd., 989/739-0728), which covers most of the acreage between Oscoda to the east and Grayling to the west. Together, the Manistee National Forest in the western part of the state and the Huron National Forest cover more than 950,000 acres in the northern part of the Lower Peninsula. The scenic Au Sable River flows through the Huron National Forest and was once used to float logs to the sawmills in East Tawas and Oscoda; now, of course, it's more popular with paddlers.

The national forest is favored by a wide range of outdoor enthusiasts, including morel hunters who visit in the spring, backpackers, swimmers, and cross-country skiers. Trout fishing is a good bet in most lakes and streams, as well as in the legendary Au Sable River.

The forest's famous **River Road Scenic Byway** runs 22 miles along the southern bank of the Au Sable. The byway passes some of the most spectacular scenery in the eastern Lower Peninsula and provides stunning vistas of tree-banked reservoirs and views of wildlife that include everything from bald eagles to spawning salmon. Along the way, you'll also pass the **Lumbermen's Monument,** a nine-foot bronze statue that depicts the area's early loggers and overlooks the river valley 10 miles northwest of East Tawas. A visitors center here houses interpretive displays that explore the logging legacy. Just a short walk away, a cliff plummets in a near-vertical 160-foot drop to the Au Sable River below. It offers jaw-dropping views of the valley and marks the beginning of the **Stairway to Discovery,** an unusual interpretive nature trail that descends 260 steps to the river and earns distinction as the nation's only nature trail located entirely on a staircase.

Also in the national forest, the **Tuttle Marsh Wildlife Management Area,** about seven miles west of Au Sable, was created in the spring of 1990 as a cooperative effort by the U.S. Forest Service, the state's Department of Natural Resources, and Ducks Unlimited. Once an area filled with sad-looking shrubs and scattered patches of grass, the wetlands now attract a significant number of migrating waterfowl, shorebirds, and sandhill cranes, as well as muskrats, mink, beaver, and bald eagles.

Backpackers looking for a wilderness camping experience should try the **Hoist Lakes Trail System.** Backcountry camping is allowed just about anywhere in this large rugged area of more than 10,000 acres. Nearly 20 miles of trails (hiking only) wander through second-growth forest over gently rolling wooded terrain, around marshes, past beaver floodings, and across streams. The forest teems with deer, bear, coyote, fox, owls, hawks, and songbirds, along with turkey, woodcock, grouse, and other game birds. Fishing includes good numbers of bass and panfish. The 6.1-mile **Reid Lake Foot Travel Area** marks another great hiking area surrounded by some of the forest's most imposing hardwoods.

About 10 miles west of East Tawas, the **Corsair Trail System** bills itself as "Michigan's Cross-Country Ski Capital," but is equally popular with hikers and backpackers. Also part of the Huron National Forest, the well-marked trail system (groomed in winter) includes more than 15 loops totaling 44 miles. One writer described this sprawling complex as "a web spun by a spider high on LSD." Choose-your-own adventures range from a short jaunt along Silver Creek to a two-day trek through the entire system.

Full of rolling hills, deep glacial potholes, and a beautiful hardwood forest, the **Island Lake Recreation Area** offers a quiet and beautiful alternative to the more heavily used recreation areas. You'll find it seven miles north of Rose City via M-33 and County Road 486. Out of the way and relatively small, it hides a swimming beach, a 17-site campground, and a 65-acre lake that supports perch, bluegills, and large- and smallmouth bass. A self-guiding

THE TINY BIRD WITH THE HUGE FOLLOWING

To call **Kirtland's warbler** endangered is an understatement – save for parts of Wisconsin and Canada, 14 counties in Michigan, especially the region around the Au Sable River between Grayling and Mio, are the only places in the world where the bird is known to breed today. The world population is estimated at less than 1,400 pairs.

A tiny blue-gray bird with a yellow breast, Kirtland's warbler winters in the Bahamas, then returns to the Au Sable River area, where it searches for the proper habitat to suit its picky nesting requirements: young stands of jack pine with small grassy clearings. It builds nests on the low-lying branches of jack pines between 5 and 20 feet high; when the trees get much higher, the warbler seeks out younger trees.

The bird's precarious plight is a classic case of habitat loss. When forest fires occur naturally, jack pines are one of the first trees to regenerate in burned areas. But decades of logging and fire suppression led to fewer forest fires, which in turn led to fewer young jack pines. To help the warbler, the U.S. Forest Service, the U.S. Fish and Wildlife Service, and other government agencies now do nature's job, cultivating, harvesting, and replanting acres of jack pines in the Kirtland's Warbler Wildlife Management Area, in order to keep an ample supply of young trees suitable for the warbler's nesting needs.

The bird's breeding grounds are off-limits to the public during the May–August nesting season. From mid-May through June, however, guided tours are led by the U.S. Forest Service (daily, $5) and U.S. Fish and Wildlife Service (daily, free). Of course, actual sightings aren't guaranteed. For information on the tours, contact the **Forest Service's Mio Ranger Station** (989/826-3252) or the **Seney National Wildlife Refuge** (906/586-9851).

nature trail explains the area's natural history and notes points of interest along the way.

◖ HOUGHTON AND HIGGINS LAKES

Near the southern end of Northeast Michigan, in Roscommon County, lie two of the state's largest inland lakes—22,000-acre Houghton Lake and 10,200-acre Higgins Lake—both of which entice plenty of anglers, boaters, canoeists, swimmers, hikers, and campers during the summer months. In winter, this area is also popular among hunters, ice fishermen, and cross-country skiers.

Beaches

Both lakes present a number of terrific beaches. On Higgins Lake, you'll find the **North Higgins Lake State Park Day Use Area,** situated on North Higgins Lake Drive, and the **South Higgins Lake State Park Day Use Area,** located on County Road 100. Each offers a sandy swimming beach, a bathhouse, a playground, picnic shelters, and a boat launch. You'll need a state park vehicle permit in order to utilize either of these beaches.

Meanwhile, on Houghton Lake, you'll discover the **Roscommon Township Beach** (Sanford St.), which has a pleasant sandy beach on the south shore, ideal for swimmers of all ages. The area also offers a sheltered picnic area, a small playground, and restrooms.

Boating and Fishing

Houghton and Higgins Lakes are both well known among boaters, canoeists, and anglers. Together, the two enormous lakes offer a dozen launch sites and tons of water to explore. Although Houghton and Higgins are particularly ideal for those with their own canoes, kayaks, and fishing boats, several facilities do rent boats as well. For more information about renting pontoon and fishing boats, check out **Houghton Lake Marina** (13710 W. Shore Dr., 989/422-7257). It's a terrific way for those without boats of their own to enjoy drifting around the lake, savoring the sunshine, or trying their luck at snagging bass, bluegill, walleye, and pike.

Of course, if you'd rather have someone else at the helm, consider taking a 2.5-hour lunchtime or dinnertime cruise aboard the **Cumberland Princess** (6560 W. Houghton Lake Dr.). The boat operates out of the Comfort Suites Lakeside (989/422-4000) on Houghton Lake.

Accommodations and Food

You'll find a decent variety of lodgings in the area, including chain hotels. The **Holiday Inn Express Houghton Lake** (200 Cloverleaf Ln., 877/863-4780, www.hiexpress.com, $63–149 d) and the **Comfort Suites Lakeside** (100 Clearview Dr., Houghton Lake, 989/422-4000, www.comfortsuites.com, $80–180 d) each offer terrific access to the lakes as well as numerous water-related amenities, such as canoeing packages and watercraft rentals. Comfort Suites also features a 9,000-square-foot water park, a boat dock, and the Blue Bayou Restaurant and Lounge, with a deck bar that overlooks the majestic lake.

Houghton and Higgins Lakes both have numerous campgrounds, too, some catering to RVs, others allowing both tent and RV camping. On Houghton Lake, you'll find the **Houghton Lake Travel Park** (370 Cloverleaf

Ln., 989/422-3931, www.michcampgrounds. com/hnlktpk, Apr.–Oct., $28–41), which has something for everyone. On Higgins Lake, check out the **Higgins Lake KOA** (3800 W. Federal Hwy., 989/275-8151, www.koa.com, $28–34).

Coyles Restaurant (9074 Old U.S. 27, 989/422-3812, www.coylesrestaurant.com, 8 A.M.–9 P.M. daily, $5–13) offers breakfast, a lunch buffet, and a huge dinner buffet, for those hungry after a long day of boating. **Buccilli's Pizza** (2949 W. Houghton Lake Dr., 989/366-5374, www.buccillispizza.com, 11 A.M.–10 P.M. daily, $5–19) offers good pizza for dine-in, take-out, or delivery.

Information and Services

For more information about Houghton and Higgins Lakes, contact the **Houghton Lake Tourism Bureau** (989/366-8474, www.visithoughtonlake.com). If you require other services, such as banks and groceries, your best bet would probably be to drive north on I-75 to Grayling or Gaylord.

Getting There and Around

The easiest way to reach the lakes is via car. From West Branch, take I-75 to M-55, which hugs the southern shore of Houghton Lake. From Grayling, head south on I-75 and take U.S. 127 to Higgins Lake. Once you reach the lakes, you can explore the area via boat, bicycle, or foot.

Grayling Area

From Bay City, I-75 cuts across the northeastern part of the state until it bisects the North Country near Grayling. Several clean, clear, and immensely popular rivers—most notably, the Au Sable and the Manistee—corkscrew their way through the region, making Grayling the hub of one of the Lower Peninsula's leading recreational areas.

First classified in 1884, the grayling once was the only game fish to inhabit the upper Au Sable system. Related to trout and salmon and characterized by a long, wavy dorsal fin, grayling were considered both a fine sporting fish and a delicious eating fish—a fatal combination. The thrill of landing one drew the attention of sportsmen near and far, who came by railroad to Grayling, soon a bustling center of fishing trips. With no regulations at the time, anglers snatched grayling from area rivers by the thousands. The wanton fishing, combined with the declining water quality caused by riverbank erosion from logging, put a quick end to the species. Grayling were rare in Grayling by 1900 and extinct by 1930.

Alas, the town's namesake fish may be gone, but we've learned a few lessons about protecting species and their habitat along the way. Today, Grayling offers some of the finest trout fishing in the Midwest—even the nation—and is a key destination for anglers, canoeists, hunters, hikers, mountain bikers, cross-country skiing enthusiasts, and snowmobilers.

RECREATION
Hiking and Biking

Popular with equestrians, hikers, cross-country skiers, and snowshoers, the 220-mile **Michigan Shore-to-Shore Riding and Hiking Trail** traverses the entire Lower Peninsula. In this area, it skirts the north end of the George Mason River Retreat Area, passing through pine plantations, stands of hardwood, and along the gentle Au Sable. Other good area access points include the McKinley Trail Camp in Oscoda and across from the Curtisville Store in Glennie.

The rolling terrain of Crawford County makes for some great mountain biking, and even better, the local tourism council actually encourages it—a rare thing in the Midwest. The Grayling Visitors Bureau recommends the following near Grayling: **Michigan Cross Country Cycle Trail,** a great technical single track that "goes for miles and miles." Access it where it crosses Military Road, 0.5 mile north of the North Higgins Lake State Park exit off U.S. 27. Also check out **Hanson Hills,** a recreation area just outside Grayling, with challenging terrain that includes some sandy stretches, and **Wakely Lake,** with three loops of 4.5, 5, and 7 miles near this lovely lake.

Canoeing

Scenic streams crisscross the forests around Grayling. The Boardman, Manistee, Pine, Rifle, and Au Sable Rivers meander through wetlands, across dunes, and past tree-covered hills. Canoeing ranks among the area's most popular pastimes, with a number of liveries offering adventures on the Au Sable and other area rivers. Even novice paddlers can handle the easygoing currents of these waterways as they scan the shoreline for deer, beaver, black bear, and winsome river otters. The area's canoe liveries are concentrated in Grayling.

Flowing east out of Grayling, the Au Sable coils through the **Au Sable State Forest.** Designated a state natural river with stretches of the main stream protected as a national wild and scenic river, the Au Sable flows past wooded islands and stretches of white sand. At night, weary paddlers can bed down at one of several state and national forest campgrounds along the river's shore. For day-trippers, the most popular take-outs are at Stephan Landing (about a four-hour leisurely paddle from Grayling) and Wakely Landing, a 5.5-hour trip at a similar pace.

Recognized for its excellent trout fishing and often overlooked by paddlers, you can also launch a boat in the Au Sable's South Branch.

You'll find landings at Chase Bridge on the south end and at Smith Bridge, 11 miles to the north.

The Au Sable can be a victim of its own success, though, with raucous crowds sometimes floating the river en masse on hot summer weekends. If you're looking for a party, this is the place, but be aware that local authorities watch for intoxication carefully and fine liberally. (Glass containers, kegs, and Styrofoam coolers are prohibited on the Au Sable to keep down the partying and the littering.) If you're looking for a more peaceful experience, avoid the party set by departing during the week or arranging to paddle a stretch farther outside Grayling, if you can talk an outfitter into it. Alternately, many paddlers find the Manistee River less of a scene. For a complete list of liveries in the Grayling region, contact the Grayling Visitors Bureau.

As a testament to its paddling popularity, Grayling is the site of one of the country's only canoeing festivals, the **AuSable River Canoe Marathon** (www.ausablecanoemarathon.org). Held in late July, the 120-mile route runs from Grayling to Oscoda on Lake Huron and ranks as North America's longest and most difficult nonstop canoe race. An estimated 30,000 fans turn out, many following the world-class athletes in the 120-mile nonstop race down the river, which requires some 55,000 paddle strokes and more than 14 hours to complete. It's worth going just to watch the thrilling 9 A.M. shotgun start, when more than 50 teams carrying canoes on their heads race through downtown Grayling to the launch site.

Fishing

Fly fishers from all over the country make the pilgrimage to the Au Sable, where the combination of spring-fed waters, clean gravel river bottoms, and all the right insect hatches make for stellar trout fishing. "There are more than 100 miles of prime trout water in the Au Sable system," says Rusty Gates, who operates a simple lodge and Orvis-endorsed fly-fishing school (989/348-8462). "If you designed a river to fly-fish in, this would be it."

All along the area's rivers, you'll spot anglers plying their sport, standing midstream in hip waders, unfurling a long arc of lemon-colored line across the river with their fly rods, or casting from a flat-bottom Au Sable riverboat specifically designed for drifting these shallow waters. Many congregate just east of town in a 10-mile catch-and-release area known as "the holy waters."

While the Grayling Visitors Bureau will help you link up with fishing guides, you also can try your luck from shore. (Obtain a license—available at local shops and gas stations—and check fishing regulations first.) Both the Manistee and Au Sable pass through several miles of state and federal lands, so you won't have much trouble finding public access.

Farther southeast, the Rifle River and its upper tributaries have earned reputations for yielding good catches of brown, rainbow, and brook trout. Some steelhead and chinook salmon are caught on the river's upper reaches, and pike, bass, and panfish are pulled from the park's 10 lakes and ponds, many of which have public access sites.

ACCOMMODATIONS AND FOOD

For paddlers, you can't do better than **Penrod's Au Sable River Resort** (100 Maple St., 888/467-4837, www.penrodscanoe.com, $60–96 d), where cute cabins line a peaceful bend in the river. Penrod's adjacent paddle-sport center rents canoes, kayaks, and mountain bikes, and offers shuttle service for river trips. If you care more about location than amenities and are coming to fish, **Gates Au Sable Lodge** (471 Stephan Bridge Rd., 989/348-8462, www.gateslodge.com, $90 d) has motel-style rooms with a perfect setting right on the banks of the Au Sable. Also right on the Au Sable, **Borchers Au Sable Canoe Livery with Bed & Breakfast** (101 Maple St., 989/348-4921, www.canoeborchers.com, $75–95 d) invites you to slow to the pace of the river on its wraparound porch.

Hungry hunters, paddlers, and bird-watchers head to **Spikes Keg O Nails** (301 N. James

REBUILDING AMERICA: THE CIVILIAN CONSERVATION CORPS

By 1933, the United States was cracked deeply by the Great Depression. One after another, factories and businesses had shut down. Lines at soup kitchens straggled around city blocks. Nearly 14 million Americans were unemployed.

Along with an economy in ruin, President Franklin D. Roosevelt saw an environment in ruin as well. While virgin forests had once covered 800 million acres of the United States, old growth had dwindled to just 100 million acres. Erosion had ruined more than 100 million acres of the nation's tillable land, and more was eroding at an alarming rate.

In March 1933, President Roosevelt asked Congress for the power to create the Civilian Conservation Corps (CCC). A New Deal program, the proposed corps would recruit 250,000 unemployed young men to work on federal- and state-owned land for "the prevention of forest fires, floods, and soil erosion, plant, pest and disease control."

As proposed, the War Department would run the program, housing, clothing, and feeding the men in work camps, and paying them a monthly stipend of $30 – $25 of which had to be sent home to their families. The Department of Agriculture and Interior planned the work projects, which included reforesting cutover land, preventing fires, developing state parks, and building dams, bridges, and roads. Along with the field work, education was a hallmark of the CCC. Camps helped members obtain their high school diplomas, and provided supplemental training in at least 30 different vocations.

The program was not without controversy. Some criticized the cost; others balked at the idea of military control over labor, comparing it to fascism and Hitlerism. Still others contended young men should be with their families, or, as Michigan Congressman Fred Crawford suggested, at work in farm fields rather than in "some camp in the woods to participate in a face-lifting operation on Mother Earth."

But Roosevelt saw it differently. Through the CCC, he believed two invaluable and impoverished resources – the nation's young men and its land – could be brought together in an attempt to save both. In his message to Congress, Roosevelt declared that "we face a future of soil erosion and timber famine" and that the CCC would "conserve our precious national resources" and "pay dividends to the present and future generations."

The measure was easily passed, and so was Roosevelt's goal of 250,000 workers. On April 17, 1933, the nation's first CCC camp opened in the George Washington National Forest in Virginia. By July 1, 250,000 men were at work in more than 1,300 camps – the fastest large-scale mobilization of men (including World War I) in U.S. history. By 1935, "Roosevelt's Tree Army" had ballooned to more than 500,000 workers.

Evidence of the CCC's work remains apparent throughout the Great Lakes region. CCC workers eradicated white pine blister rust in Minnesota, built fire towers and fire roads in Wisconsin, and improved hundreds of miles of fishing streams in Michigan. They built park shelters in Ohio, campgrounds in Indiana, and trails in Illinois. They planted thousands of acres of trees, fought countless wildfires, and built hundreds of bridges and buildings. They even moved moose from Isle Royale to the Upper Peninsula for wildlife studies.

By 1936, the CCC was above reproach, supported by more than 80 percent of Americans and even endorsed by Roosevelt's political opponents. With the bombing of Pearl Harbor in 1941, however, the nation soon had a more pressing duty for its young men. The nation's entry into World War II, along with an improving economy, meant the end of the CCC. But its legacy, like the trees it planted, continues to grow in our nation's parks and forests.

The **Civilian Conservation Corps Museum** (11747 N. Higgins Lake Dr., Roscommon, 989/821-6125, mid-June-Labor Day, state park vehicle permit required), in North Higgins Lake State Park, tells the story of Michigan's CCC crews, through various photographs and artifacts.

St., 989/348-7113, www.spikes-grayling.
com, 10 A.M.–1:30 A.M. Mon.–Sat., noon–
1:30 A.M. Sun., $6–19) for a burger. Try the
"World Famous Spikeburger," topped with
everything.

Camping

You'll find plenty of good, inexpensive public
campgrounds in the Grayling area. **Hartwick
Pines State Park** (4216 Ranger Rd., 989/348-
7068, state park vehicle permit required,
$16–33) in Grayling offers clean, modern sites
that fill up fast. You might find a little more
solitude (and fewer RVs) at the **Au Sable State
Forest** (5.5 miles east of Grayling via N. Down
River Rd., 989/826-3211, $15), with 10 camp-
grounds and more than 260 campsites. The
Grayling-area brochure lists a number of other
public campgrounds in the area.

INFORMATION
AND SERVICES

For more information, contact the **Grayling
Visitors Bureau** (213 N. James St., 800/937-
8837, www.grayling-mi.com). Grayling has a
limited number of services; if necessary, you
can always head north to Gaylord to stock up
on supplies prior to an outing in the great outdoors. If an emergency occurs, dial **911** from
any cell or public phone.

GETTING THERE
AND AROUND

While **Greyhound** (800/231-2222, www.grey-
hound.com) provides bus service to Grayling,
most visitors come via car, motorcycle, or RV.
Given that the town sits at the junction of I-75
and M-72, it's easy to reach whether you're
headed from Bay City to the south, Traverse
City to the west, or Mackinaw City to the
north.

GEORGE MASON RIVER
RETREAT AREA

George Mason, an area industrialist, so loved
this area that he bequeathed 1,500 acres to
the state for its preservation in 1954. Located
about 15 miles east of Grayling on Canoe

Harbor Campground Road, the George Mason
River Retreat Area is considered part of the
Au Sable State Forest. Subsequent land acquisi-
tions have nearly doubled the size of this natural area, which provides ample opportunity to
fish, canoe, or hike along a stretch of the South
Branch of the Au Sable River.

◖ HARTWICK PINES
STATE PARK

The majestic white pine may be the state tree,
but few virgin stands remain today. One of the
last can be seen at the Hartwick Pines State
Park (4216 Ranger Rd., 989/348-7068, state
park vehicle permit required), one of the largest parks in the state. A century ago, more than
13 million of the state's 38 million acres were
covered with the majestic trees, but by the
early 1900s more than 160 billion board feet
of timber had been harvested. By the 1920s,
these once majestic forests were denuded
wastelands.

More than 250,000 visitors stroll through
the pines annually, marveling at trees that
have been here since before the Revolutionary
War. Long a popular stop for vacationers heading north, the state park has been improved
over the years, with a superb visitors center, a
walkway to the pines that's accessible to both
wheelchairs and strollers, and a steam sawmill
that's part of an extensive logging museum
area. The park is also the site of the **Hartwick
Pines State Forest Festivals:** four different
events held throughout the summer, including
Sawdust Days, Wood Shaving Days, Black Iron
Days, and Old Time Days.

The park's **Michigan Forest Visitors
Center** boasts a 100-seat auditorium; a 14-
minute audiovisual show on "The Forest:
Michigan's Renewable Resource," which is
presented every 30 minutes; and an exhibit
hall that concentrates on forest management.
Ironically, many of the displays were funded by
forestry products companies, so don't expect to
see explorations of the negative environmental
effects of logging.

The 49-acre virgin tract of white and red
pines is the main attraction. Reaching as high

© HARTWICK PINES LOGGING MUSEUM

Black Iron Days, Michigan's largest annual gathering of blacksmiths, at Hartwick Pines State Park

as 10 stories, the majestic trees were slated for cutting in the mid-1890s. Fortunately for us, the logging company charged with felling the trees was forced to suspend operations due to economic problems. In 1927, the trees and the surrounding 8,000 acres were purchased from the lumber company and donated to the state for a park.

The self-guided **Old Growth Forest Trail** connects the pines with the visitors center, a 1.25-mile blacktopped path that weaves among the regal giants, including the Monarch. Once the tract's largest specimen at 155 feet, a windstorm destroyed the top 40 feet of the now-diseased and dying tree. Part of nature's cycle, several other immense white pines tower nearby, ready to take its place in the record books.

The pines and museums overshadow the rest of the park, but don't overlook it yourself. With more than 9,600 acres, it offers plenty to do besides admire tall trees. Signs and other displays

mark the eight-mile **Scenic Drive,** about two miles north of the main entrance, encouraging visitors to explore the woods and natural world around them. Hiking and biking trails include 17 miles of easy trails open to mountain bikes in summer and cross-country skiers in winter. The Au Sable River Trail (no bikes) is one of the loveliest. It crosses the East Branch of the legendary river and passes a rare forest of virgin hemlock, saved from the saw by a sudden drop in the price of its bark, which was once used for tanning leather. The two-mile Mertz Grade Nature Trail loops through the park and past an old logging railroad grade before linking up with the Virgin Pines Trail behind the visitors center.

Open year-round, the park is especially popular in the spring, when wildflowers bloom, and in the early fall, when the colorful hardwoods explode in a riot of fiery reds, yellows, and oranges.

Gaylord Area

North of Grayling on I-75, Gaylord was officially organized in 1875 as "Otsego," an Indian word that means "beautiful lake." Located at the north end of long, skinny Otsego Lake, Gaylord remains a basically rural village with a year-round population of less than 3,700. But its topography lures vacationers by the thousands.

Gaylord sits on the highest point in southern Michigan, which inspired the town to morph itself into "the Alpine Village." Its Main Street is decorated with balconies, blossoming window boxes, even a glockenspiel on the Glen's Market grocery store. And while more Polish and German descendants reside here than Swiss, the townspeople happily don dirndls and lederhosen each July during the annual Alpenfest. Some visitors come for the culture, but Gaylord offers plenty of outdoor attractions as well—from world-class golf to accessible lakes to bugling elk.

SIGHTS
Call of the Wild Museum
While this unassuming museum has been around for decades (during which the displays haven't changed all that much), the Call of the Wild Museum (850 S. Wisconsin Ave., 989/732-4336, www.gocallofthewild. com, 9 A.M.–9 P.M. daily June 15–Labor Day, 9:30 A.M.–6 P.M. Mon.–Sat. in winter, $7 adults, $4.50 children 5–13) is still a terrific place to take your children for a little while. Many of its wildlife displays come packed with audio features, bringing the animals to life. Creepy, yet fascinating, the two projected images of Joseph Bailly help to educate visitors about what life was like in the early 1800s, when he (one of the area's first trappers) initially ventured into the Michigan area.

Otsego Lake State Park
Established in 1920, Otsego Lake State Park (7136 Old 27 S, 989/732-5485) is a boating enthusiast's dream. The lake itself is long and wide, allowing ample room for boats and all manner of other water sports. This park has been a popular, family-friendly destination for nine decades.

ALPENFEST
Every July, Gaylord's Main Street is blocked off for the annual Alpenfest (989/732-6333, www.gaylordalpenfest.com), a five-day event that offers live music, great food and beer, and an assortment of craft booths from Michigan artists. The town even makes room for several amusement park rides.

SPORTS AND RECREATION
Golfing
But Gaylord is best known for its golf, boasting the largest number of courses in the state: more than 20, with more on the drawing board all the time. The area around Gaylord, in fact, has emerged as America's premier golf mecca, with the thickest concentration of designer courses anywhere in the United States, including those by well-known designers such as Robert Trent Jones, Sr., Tom Fazio, and Al Watrous.

If you have the time, consider visiting at least three of the area's favored golf clubs. Head first to Onaway, on M-68, where you'll find the **Black Lake Golf Club** (2800 Maxon Rd., 989/733-4653, www.blacklakegolf.com, daily Apr.–Oct., $40–85). Operated by the UAW, this magnificent golf course is part of the union's 1,000-acre family center that sits astride picturesque Black Lake. Another winning choice is **Garland Resort** (4700 N. Red Oak Rd., Lewiston, 989/786-2211 or 877/442-7526, www.garlandusa.com, daily May–Oct., $30–120). Considered one of the state's most beautiful resorts, this family-owned destination presents four magnificent golf courses amid the woods of northeastern Michigan. Lastly, schedule a tee time at the lovely **Treetops Resort** (3962 Wilkinson Rd., Gaylord, 989/732-6711 or 888/873-3867, www.treetops.com, daily Apr.–Oct., $30–135). This year-round resort keeps visitors busy with downhill skiing in winter, activities like tennis and biking in summer, and, of course, five stunning golf courses.

Hiking

The Shingle Mill Pathway links up with the **High Country Pathway,** an 80-mile route that snakes east through state land in four counties, passing through a wilderness of rolling hills and several creeks feeding the Black River. A side trail leads to Shoepac Lake and the Sinkholes Pathway, where the land is pitted with dry sinkholes and sinkhole lakes, formed when underground limestone caves collapsed.

Elk may be the main attraction at Pigeon River, but beavers bring visitors to the **Big Bear Lake Nature Pathway,** 17 miles east of Gaylord. Part of the Mackinaw State Forest trail, the pathway's two loops total just over two miles and lead through a variety of landscape and habitats home to deer, porcupine, woodcock, waterfowl, and beaver. The shorter, 0.8-mile Beaver Lodge Loop circles a pond with an active beaver colony. The longer Eagles Roost Trail carves a wide, two-mile loop that threads its way through upland hardwoods and through a dense stand of aspen and an open area carpeted with wildflowers in the summer. Both trails begin and end at a large state forest campground on the north shore of Big Bear Lake.

Snowmobiling

Gaylord is the crossroads of many snowmobiling trails (www.visitgaylord.com/snowmobile). With over 150 inches of average snowfall a year, Gaylord is a snowmobiler's dream. Many of the state's best trails either start or pass through the area. If you're looking for a great ride, the **Gaylord-Frederic-Grayling-BlueBear Loop** will give you a 2–4-day adventure.

ACCOMMODATIONS AND FOOD

The Gaylord area is best known for its golf resorts, and they can offer some good package deals, especially for families. **C** Garland

snowmobiling in the woods between Grayling and Gaylord

© WOODLAND MOTEL

NORTHEAST MICHIGAN

MICHIGAN'S ELK

Once a common sight in the Lower Peninsula, the eastern elk disappeared from Michigan in the late 1870s. Biologists made several attempts to reintroduce the animal to the state throughout the early 1900s, but it wasn't until the successful release of seven Rocky Mountain elk in 1918 that the mammals once again were seen regularly in northeastern Michigan.

Wildlife biologists today believe that the region's elk are descendants of those early animals. They roam a 600-square-mile area primarily east and north of Gaylord in Otsego, Cheboygan, Presque Isle, and Montmorency Counties. The heaviest concentration is north of Gaylord in the 98,000-acre **Pigeon River Country State Forest** (9966 Twin Lakes Rd., Vanderbilt, 989/983-4101).

The best way to plan a visit is to stop by the Pigeon River forestry field office off Sturgeon Valley Road. Staff will provide maps and suggest good areas and times to view the elk. Fall rutting season proves most spectacular, when the bulls throw their heads back and fill the forests with eerie bugling sounds, their distinctive mating call.

Resort (4700 N. Red Oak Rd., Lewiston, 989/786-2211, www.garlandusa.com, $99–499 d) has a lot of stay-and-play deals where golf is included in the price. If you're just looking for a simple motel room, you'll find several of the usual chains—Super 8, Days Inn, Comfort Inn, etc.—near I-75.

The same Greek American family has been running the **Sugar Bowl** (216 W. Main St., 989/732-5524, 7 A.M.–11 P.M. daily, $6–22) since 1919. Specialties include Lake Superior whitefish, scampi, Athenian chicken, and other favorite ethnic dishes, all prepared on an open hearth. Tip: They serve morel mushroom dishes in season, usually May. Don't miss the vintage photos of historic Gaylord on the walls.

Gobbler's Famous Turkey Dinners (900 S. Otsego, 989/732-9005, 10 A.M.–9 P.M. daily, $5–14) prepares more than 80,000 pounds of bird annually, all from scratch and served with mashed potatoes, biscuits, gravy, and dressing. The portion sizes are legendary. There are also hand-breaded fresh fish and barbecued ribs if you don't do turkey.

Between Gaylord and Lewiston is the single traffic light town of Johannesburg, where you'll find **Paul's Pub** (10757 M-32 E, 989/732-5005, 10 A.M.–midnight Mon.–Thurs., 10 A.M.–2 A.M. Fri.–Sat., 8 A.M.–midnight Sun., $6–28), with its wide assortment

of beers and the best fried perch in Michigan. They also have quite the Sunday brunch, but get here early. This local favorite can get pretty busy on the weekends.

Camping

Pigeon River Country State Forest (off Sturgeon Valley Rd., 989/983-4101, $15) offers 29 rustic sites in a nice secluded setting. For waterfront sites, try **Otsego Lake State Park** (7136 Old 27 S, 989/732-5485, state park vehicle permit required, $16–26) with 206 sites on or near Otsego Lake.

INFORMATION AND SERVICES

For more information about the Gaylord area, contact the **Gaylord Area Convention & Tourism Bureau** (101 W. Main St., 989/732-4000, www.gaylordmichigan.net). For local news, consult the *Gaylord Herald Times* (www.gaylordheraldtimes.com).

Despite its relatively small size, Gaylord offers a wide range of services, including a post office, several banks and gas stations, and numerous stores, from Wal-Mart to Home Depot to Glen's Market. If a medical emergency occurs during your visit, dial **911** or consult **Otsego Memorial Hospital** (825 N. Center Ave., 989/731-2100, www.goodhealthstartshere.com).

GETTING THERE AND AROUND

While **Greyhound** (800/231-2222, www.greyhound.com) provides bus service to Gaylord, most visitors come via car, motorcycle, or RV. Given that the town sits at the junction of I-75 and M-32, it's easy to reach whether you're coming from Saginaw, Charlevoix, or the U.P.

PIGEON RIVER COUNTRY STATE FOREST

With a shaggy chocolate mane and a crown of showy antlers, the eastern elk may be Michigan's most spectacular mammal, sometimes weighing in at close to 1,000 pounds. Elk are rare in the Midwest, but about 1,000 of them—the largest free-roaming elk herd east of the Mississippi River—populate this state forest and the surrounding countryside.

Although its primary draw is the opportunity to spot the elk herd, this 97,000-acre state forest north of Gaylord has miles of hiking trails, good fishing, and scenic rustic campgrounds. The **Shingle Mill Pathway** passes through deep woods and across rolling, hilly terrain. Keep an eye out for the forest's "other" wildlife, which includes bear, coyote, bobcat, beaver, otter, woodcock, turkey, bald eagle, osprey, loon, and blue heron. For more information on the state forest, stop by the **Pigeon River forestry field office** (off Sturgeon Valley Rd., 989/983-4101).

NORTHEAST MICHIGAN

THE EASTERN UPPER PENINSULA

A short drive across the Mackinac Bridge, from the Lower to the Upper Peninsula, can feel like a journey between two very disparate countries. Despite the presence of sizable towns like St. Ignace and Sault Ste. Marie, the eclectic eastern half of this enormous, sparsely populated peninsula epitomizes the very definition of "wilderness," illustrated by its rushing rivers, thunderous cascades, dramatic cliffs, deserted beaches, and vast tracts of forested terrain.

Although there are several ways to reach the U.P., most travelers utilize "Big Mac," the only link between the northern and southern parts of Michigan. From the south, the first stop is St. Ignace, a former fur-trading town that now offers a variety of attractions, from an Ojibwa history museum to a casino. Via I-75, the eastern U.P.'s largest city, Sault Ste. Marie, lies only 50 miles north. Here, travelers will find a unique maritime attraction: the Soo Locks, an engineering marvel that has allowed safe passage between Lake Superior and the other Great Lakes for more than 150 years.

Those seeking a more untamed landscape should head west, where over a million acres of protected state and federal land—including the enormous Hiawatha National Forest—await. From the highway, many of these coniferous woods look the same—the "real" peninsula is accessible via more challenging routes. Of course, the difficulty of reaching such breathtaking places is part of the reward. Every season, adventure seekers are lured to these remote forests and wetlands to share the open space with native deer, foxes, black bears, and bald eagles—the true "locals" of these parts.

© GREGG BRUFF, NATIONAL PARK SERVICE

HIGHLIGHTS

◖ Mackinac Bridge: Once you've crossed the "Mighty Mac," make a quick stop in lovely Bridge View Park, where you can snap pictures of this engineering marvel, the third longest suspension bridge in the world. The eight-acre grounds include an observation building and several picnic pavilions (page 277).

◖ Seul Choix Point Lighthouse: Michigan's lengthy coastline is dotted with dozens of historic lighthouses, some of which are open to the public. If you only have time to visit one in the U.P., head to Seul Choix Point southeast of Gulliver, where you'll find a seasonal museum and a supposedly haunted lighthouse (page 282).

◖ Grand Island National Recreation Area: For those who aren't ready to brave the isolation of Isle Royale, Grand Island offers its own treasures, including sandy beaches, sandstone cliffs, historic lighthouses, and clear Lake Superior waters. Better yet, it's only a half-mile from the mainland (page 288).

◖ Miners Castle: Less visited than the Lower Peninsula's Sleeping Bear Dunes, lovely Pictured Rocks National Lakeshore presents windswept beaches, gorgeous waterfalls,

wooded trails, and tall sandstone cliffs, including the park's most famous formation, which overlooks frigid Lake Superior (page 290).

◖ Great Lakes Shipwreck Museum: Housed within a historic building near the Whitefish Point Light Station – the oldest active lighthouse on Lake Superior – this is the only museum dedicated to the dangers of maritime transport on the Great Lakes. Exhibits include a bronze bell recovered from the famous *Edmund Fitzgerald* shipwreck (page 296).

◖ Tahquamenon Falls: South of Whitefish Point lies a 52,000-acre, year-round state park that preserves the second largest waterfalls east of the Mississippi River. Visitors can take a scenic train ride and narrated riverboat cruise to these impressive cascades (page 297).

◖ Soo Locks: Situated in the St. Mary's River, between Sault Ste. Marie and its Canadian sister city, this marvelous structure allows the passage of massive freighters between Lake Superior and the other Great Lakes, the world's largest waterway traffic system. Boat tours guide visitors along this international shoreline (page 301).

EASTERN UPPER PENINSULA

LOOK FOR ◖ TO FIND RECOMMENDED SIGHTS, ACTIVITIES, DINING, AND LODGING.

The peninsula's wild interior, once depleted by the 19th-century logging industry, also contains a variety of stunning lakes and waterways. In summer, boaters and anglers flock to the Manistique Lakes, while paddlers relish exploring serpentine rivers like the Two Hearted.

Of course, the most well-visited areas lie along the perimeter. The southern shore, beside Lake Michigan, contains nostalgic towns, sheltered harbors, and historic sites like the haunted Seul Choix Point Lighthouse. While the northern shore, along Lake Superior, contains its share of man-made highlights, its most well-known destinations are of the natural variety, such as Pictured Rocks National Lakeshore and Tahquamenon Falls, one of the largest waterfalls east of the Mississippi River.

Sadly, the rugged shoreline along Lake Superior is also known as the "Graveyard of the Great Lakes"—an 80-mile stretch that has witnessed the wreckage of more than 300 ships, the memories of which are preserved within the Great Lakes Shipwreck Museum and the Alger Underwater Preserve.

PLANNING YOUR TIME

Airports, bus stations, and public transit systems are few and far between in the Upper Peninsula, so while it's possible to reach the eastern half by flying into Escanaba, Marquette, or Sault Ste. Marie, Ontario, you'll definitely require a car to explore much of the area. Though not a compact region, the eastern U.P. is relatively easy to navigate via its main routes, such as I-75 between St. Ignace and Canada, U.S. 2 along Lake Michigan, M-28 from I-75 to Munising, and M-123 between Paradise and Newberry.

At minimum, you'll need at least four days to visit St. Ignace, Sault Ste. Marie, Pictured Rocks, and the attractions near Whitefish Bay. A week or more will be necessary for die-hard outdoor enthusiasts or those interested in exploring the Lake Michigan shoreline and inland lakes. Although you don't have to worry about crowds in much of this region, you do have to bear the seasons in mind. In general, the U.P. is much harsher than Michigan's lower half. Summer

here is cooler, especially in the evening, and winter tends to come faster and stay longer.

Pictured Rocks' tourist season, for instance, is short. Most of the park's 440,000 annual visitors come in July and August when they're most likely to enjoy daytime temperatures in the 70s. Visit in June and you'll share the park with fewer people, but the black flies and mosquitoes often aren't worth the trade-off. May and September may be the park's finest months. No matter when you go, pack plenty of warm clothes, just in case—and try to avoid swimming in Lake Superior, which is bone-numbing all year.

For more information about the communities and attractions within the eastern U.P., consult the **Upper Peninsula Travel & Recreation Association** (P.O. Box 400, Iron Mountain, MI 49801, 906/774-5480, www.uptravel.com).

HISTORY

As with other parts of Michigan, the history of the eastern U.P. was defined by its Native American cultures, the 19th-century logging industry, and the Great Lakes' use as a major shipping route. Names like Chippewa County, old logging towns like Blaney Park, and the presence of numerous lighthouses and shipwrecks along the Lake Michigan and Lake Superior shorelines are evidence of this diverse past.

Of course, the two main towns in the eastern U.P. have their own interesting histories. St. Ignace was founded by Father Marquette in 1671 and named for St. Ignatius of Loyola. Once the bustling hub of the 17th-century French fur trade, St. Ignace witnessed even more growth in the 1800s, as the logging and fishing industries prospered. Of course, the lumber industry came to an abrupt halt in the early 20th century, when the U.P.'s forests were nearly depleted of their timber. Although railroad ferries made it easier for travelers to cross the Straits of Mackinac from lower Michigan, it was the opening of the Mackinac Bridge in 1957 that improved the town's fortunes, facilitating the flow of tourists.

Even older is Sault Ste. Marie, which was first settled by the Ojibwa Indians in the

THE EASTERN UPPER PENINSULA

© AVALON TRAVEL

1500s. After discovering a rich supply of white-fish in the turbulent waters, they established a permanent settlement along the shore. The Ojibwa lived here for more than 300 years, but the combination of warring Iroquois—forced west by European immigrants—and the ever-growing European settlement of Sault Ste. Marie (founded in 1668) eventually drove the Ojibwa from the region.

By the early 1800s, Michigan's northern reaches were increasingly being settled, and people were discovering the bounty of natural resources—copper, iron, lumber, grain—ringing the shores of Lake Superior. The only problem was those rapids. For decades, ship cargo had to be unloaded by hand, portaged around the rapids by horses and mules pulling carts, then reloaded onto another boat. In 1839, the American Fur Company built a short railroad line, which eased the job, but it remained back-breaking and exceedingly slow. While shipping was booming on the lower Great Lakes, Superior remained largely isolated, its cargo backed up by the rapids.

Eastern industrialists began lobbying for government-funded locks. Locals, however, opposed such a project, fearing the loss of their portaging business. The town managed to stave off the inevitable until 1852, when President Millard Fillmore signed a bill authorizing the first lock at Sault Ste. Marie. In 1855, the State Lock opened, a system of two 350-feet-long locks. In the first year, nearly 12,000 tons of iron ore passed through the locks; within a decade, that figure grew to more than 120,000 tons. By World War I, the nation's hunger for iron and copper, coupled with the opening of vast iron mines in Minnesota's Mesabi Range, made the Soo Locks the busiest shipping canal in the world.

Soon after the completion of the State Lock, the burgeoning commercial traffic indicated that more locks were needed. The 515-foot Weitzel Lock opened in 1881. Since then, a succession of locks have been built, both to handle the traffic and the increasing size of Great Lakes–area ships. Today, three U.S. locks are in operation (there's a fourth smaller lock on the Canadian side), including the 1,200-foot Poe Lock built in 1968 to accommodate the huge vessels now common on the Great Lakes.

Today, Sault Ste. Marie is inseparable from the locks that shaped its past. Although Lake Superior State University and the Ojibwa-owned Kewadin Casino are two of the area's largest employers, tourism remains a staple of the economy—with many of those visitors coming specifically to see the parade of commerce that incessantly passes through town.

A ship is guided through one of the Soo Locks in Sault Ste. Marie.

St. Ignace and Vicinity

The St. Ignace (IG-nus) economy benefits from two groups of tourists: those stopping by on their way to Upper Peninsula destinations, and those using it as a base for Mackinac Island day trips and area exploration. Along with a large supply of lodgings, restaurants, and services, the city at the north end of the Mackinac Bridge has a few attractions of its own, including museums, parks, even a casino. To the east, you'll also find several islands worth a look.

SIGHTS
◖ Mackinac Bridge
Opened in late 1957, the Mackinac Bridge was built to link Michigan's two disparate peninsulas. Presently, "Mighty Mac" is the third longest suspension bridge in the world. Once you've crossed the five-mile-long bridge, between Mackinaw City and St. Ignace, make a quick stop at lovely **Bridge View Park,** where you can snap pictures of this modern engineering marvel. The eight-acre grounds include an observation building and several picnic pavilions. For more information about the bridge, consult the **Mackinac Bridge Authority** (www.mackinacbridge.org).

Father Marquette National Memorial
High above the Straits of Mackinac, in **Straits State Park** (906/643-8620, state park vehicle permit required), west of I-75 and south of U.S. 2, this open-air site commemorates French explorer and Jesuit missionary Jacques Marquette. In the 1660s and '70s, Marquette paddled through the Great Lakes, founding dozens of cities—including Sault Ste. Marie and St. Ignace—along the way. Next, Marquette linked up with Louis Joliet and paddled another several thousand miles, thus becoming the first white explorers of the Mississippi. Walking trails at the memorial (www.nps.gov/fama, 9:30 A.M.–5 P.M. daily Memorial Day–Labor Day) feature interpretive signs that discuss Marquette's Great Lakes travels and the impact that geography had on the area's settlement.

Museum of Ojibwa Culture
In contrast to the Father Marquette memorial, this excellent museum (500 N. State, 906/643-9161, 10 A.M.–6 P.M. daily, $2 adults, $1 children under 13) tells the story of the Ojibwa and the effect that the European explorers had on their culture. Ironically, the museum is on the presumed site of Father Marquette's grave and the site of his Jesuit mission.

Displays housed in a former Catholic church include artifacts from archaeological digs on the grounds (some dating to 6000 B.C.), explanations of how the Ojibwa adapted and survived in the area's sometimes harsh climate, and a discussion of how they allied with the French fur traders, though it greatly diminished their traditional way of life. The Huron boardwalk follows the shoreline, with interpretive signs explaining the role of the bay in the area's settlement.

ENTERTAINMENT
St. Ignace might not be the hottest nightlife spot in Michigan, but you will find at least one round-the-clock entertainment venue. The **Kewadin Casino** (3015 Mackinac Trail, 800/539-2346, www.kewadin.com) promises Las Vegas–style gaming 24 hours daily and top-notch live entertainment on Friday and Saturday nights. Situated on the shores of Lake Huron, the casino resort also offers an 81-room hotel, with plenty of amenities. Kewadin has four other casinos in the eastern Upper Peninsula, in the towns of Hessel, Manistique, Christmas, and Sault Ste. Marie.

ACCOMMODATIONS AND FOOD
The St. Ignace area offers plenty of lodging, from simple motels to full-service resorts. If you're looking for an inexpensive choice, **America's Best Value Inns** (1074 N. State

EASTERN UPPER PENINSULA

THE BUILDING OF "BIG MAC"

A bridge across the Straits of Mackinac, connecting the Lower and Upper Peninsulas of Michigan, was first proposed in 1884. It remained a point of debate for decades. Detractors believed that such a structure – required to span nearly five miles of open water – was an impossible feat. But "the people of Michigan built the world's greatest bridge," wrote bridge designer David B. Steinman. "They built it in the face of discouragement, of faintheartedness on the part of many of their leaders, of warnings that the rocks in the Straits were too soft, the ice too thick, the winds too strong, the rates of interest on the bonds too high, and the whole concept too big."

Steinman and his supporters proved the detractors wrong. After three years of construction and $99 million, the Mackinac Bridge opened on November 1, 1957. It was, and is, an engineering marvel, the world's third longest suspension bridge. Some 33 underwater foundations support the five-mile-long steel structure. It is designed to withstand anything Mother Nature can dish out, including winds of up to 600 miles per hour!

It can be unnerving to drive across the Mackinac Bridge, which visibly bows as much as 30 feet in strong crosswinds. The 552-foot-high towers are designed to give, too, swaying as much as 15 feet. Not everyone appreciates the engineering show; bridge workers take over the wheel numerous times each year for drivers too terrified to cross the bridge themselves.

But for most, the Mackinac Bridge is Michigan's pride and joy. Not only do hotel rooms with bridge views command premium rates, the bridge opened up the Upper Peninsula to the hundreds of cars that used to form a huge snarl waiting for the ferry. (Especially during fall hunting season, the wait to cross the Straits could stretch to six hours or more.) Today, it's just a matter of handing over $3 and keeping both hands on the wheel – and all of Michigan is yours to explore, linked together as one.

For more information about "Big Mac," which serves over 4 million vehicles annually, contact the **Mackinac Bridge Authority** (www.mackinacbridge.org).

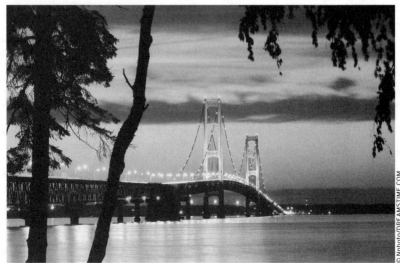

Mackinac Bridge ("Big Mac") at dusk

© Nphoto/DREAMSTIME.COM

St., 906/643-7777, www.americasbestvalueinnstignace.com, $59–76 d) offers basic rooms at a good value. For something a little fancier, stay at the [C] **Kewadin Casino** (3015 Mackinac Trail, 800/539-2346, www.kewadin.com), which offers an 81-room hotel, an indoor pool, a fitness center, and a game room. Unfortunately, pets aren't allowed.

When you're craving a bite to eat, consider the Kewadin's two dining options: the **Horseshoe Bay Restaurant** and the **White Tail Bar & Grill.** You can also stop by the **Mackinac Grille** (251 S. State St., 906/643-7482, 10:30 A.M.–midnight daily, $8–16), where you can sample everything from ribs to burritos.

Camping

The St. Ignace area provides campers lots of options, especially if you want to stay somewhere with some seclusion but still be close to the area's many attractions. Just a couple miles west of the bridge, the **Lakeshore Park Campground** (416 Pointe La Barbe, 906/643-9522, www.lakeshoreparkcampground.com, $25–36) has RV sites, tent spaces, and easy access to Lake Michigan. **Straits State Park** (720 Church St., 906/643-8620, state park vehicle permit required, $16–28) may not be particularly peaceful, but 270 modern and semi-modern sites are clean and convenient. Aim for the nicely wooded sites right on the Straits, which offer great views of the bridge. To reach the park, take I-75 to U.S. 2 and exit at Church Street, then follow Church south for a half-mile. For camping reservations, call 800/447-2757 or visit www.michigan.gov/dnr.

INFORMATION AND SERVICES

For more information about St. Ignace, contact the **St. Ignace Visitors Bureau** (6 Spring St., Ste. 100, 800/338-6660, www.stignace.com) or the **St. Ignace Chamber of Commerce** (560 N. State St., 906/643-8717, www.saintignace.org). St. Ignace offers numerous services for travelers, from groceries to banks. In case of an emergency, dial **911** from any phone, or

Lakeshore Park Campground

© KAREN SMEJA

visit the **Mackinac Straits Hospital & Health Center** (220 Burdette St., 906/643-8585, www.mshosp.org).

GETTING THERE AND AROUND

The easiest way to reach St. Ignace is via car. From the Lower Peninsula, simply cross the Mackinac Bridge; you'll find St. Ignace at the northern end of "Big Mac." If you're already in the U.P., simply head east from Manistique via U.S. 2 or south from Sault Ste. Marie via I-75. If you have no car of your own, take a **Greyhound** bus (800/231-2222, www.greyhound.com) to St. Ignace or fly into **Pellston Regional Airport (PLN)** (231/539-8441, www.pellstonairport.com), rent a vehicle, and head north on U.S. 31, toward the Mackinac Bridge.

LAKE HURON SHORE

East of I-75, the Upper Peninsula narrows and dribbles off into a series of peninsulas, points, and islands. The area has a simple, pretty feel, the kind of place where casual biking, beach-combing, and picnicking set the pace for a summer day, though there are few true "desti-nations." In fact, the whole area is often over-looked by guidebooks—which is just fine with the locals and summer cottage owners.

M-134, between I-75 and Drummond Island, is a lovely stretch. This pretty and un-usually peaceful road skims along the Lake Huron shore, past coastal villages, rocky bays, and pine-studded islands. **DeTour Village** marks the end of the road and the end of the U.P. mainland. This small village has long served an important navigational role for ships heading up and down the St. Mary's. Many ships squeeze through DeTour Passage here, the narrow waterway between the point and Drummond Island. They make a turn, or de-tour, to chart a course from the St. Mary's River to the Straits of Mackinac. When Detroit was still a blank spot on the map, DeTour Village was busy guiding ships, with a navigational light as far back as 1848. It remains a pleasant place to watch the ship traffic.

Les Cheneaux Islands

"The Snows," everyone calls them, though the real name for these islands is Les Cheneaux (lay shen-O), French for "The Channels." And there are channels aplenty. Like shards of glass, 36 long and narrow islands lie splintered just off the U.P.'s southeastern shore, forming a maze of calm channels and protected bays in north-ern Lake Huron. Not surprisingly, this area is a delight for boaters. Tall sailboats, classic cabin cruisers, and simple canoes all share these wa-ters, as they have for more than a century.

The best way to see Les Cheneaux, of course, is to get out on the water. Aside from the pretty wooded islands themselves, part of the fun is eyeing the beautiful old boathouses that dot the shorelines, especially on Marquette Island. If you've got your own craft, you'll find launches in Hessel and Cedarville, the only two towns in the area. Though the waters are protected and normally quite safe, be sure to bring a chart, or at least a map provided by local busi-nesses. The various bays, channels, and points can be confusing for a newcomer.

EASTERN UPPER PENINSULA

© ELIZABETH FELS

Boat docks abound in the waters around Hessel and the Les Cheneaux Islands.

Drummond Island

Few would likely guess that low-key Drummond is, in fact, the largest U.S. island in the Great Lakes. About 66 percent of Drummond Island is state-owned; the rest is largely owned by summer residents, who swell the island's population to about 5,000 in July and August. You'd never know it—life in this fishing-oriented place is focused along the shore, which you can rarely see from the island's few roads.

With sandy beaches, inland lakes, cedar swamps, hardwood forests, and open meadows, Drummond Island boasts remarkably diverse animal and plant habitat. Loons, bobcats, moose, and wolves all roam here, and various orchid species grow wild on the island. Biking is a fun way to explore Drummond, since M-134 dissolves into a variety of double-tracks and, eventually, single-track. Kayaking is even better. The fjord-like bays and 150 miles of ragged shoreline make this a magical place to paddle.

For such a mellow island, you might be surprised to run across **The Rock** (Drummond Island Resort and Conference Center, 800/999-6343, www.drummondisland.com, daily Apr.–Oct., $35–59 w/cart), a spectacular designer golf course completed in 1990 by then-owner Tom Monaghan, owner of the Domino's Pizza chain. The first-rate course makes fine use of the natural environment, its holes weaving through woods and limestone outcroppings.

Accommodations

Along the Lake Huron shore near Cedarville, **The Spring Lodge and Cottages Resort** (916 Park Ave., 906/484-2282, www.springlodge.com, June–Nov.) has a wonderful location in the heart of Les Cheneaux. Large and well-kept grounds house cottages, most overlooking the water. In nearby Hessel, you can stay at year-round **(Hessel on the Lake** (210 Island View Rd., 906/484-2440, www.hesselonthelake.com, $125–235 d), which offers 11 fully-equipped cottages.

On Drummond Island, stay in luxury at the **Drummond Island Resort and Conference Center** (800/999-6343, www.drummondisland.com, $119–155 d), a grandiose retreat with handsome log-lodge rooms and several private cottages. Guests have access to all resort facilities, including tennis courts, a restaurant, and a golf course.

The island's best camping is at **Township Park** (906/493-5245) not far from the ferry dock. This rustic campground has 43 pretty RV and tent sites tucked within the woods on Potagannissing Bay. Amenities include picnic tables, outhouses, a sandy beach, and a boat ramp.

Information and Services

For more information about the Lake Huron shore, contact the **DeTour Area Chamber of Commerce** (DeTour Village, 906/297-5987, www.detourvillage.com), the **Les Cheneaux Islands Tourist Association** (Cedarville, 888/364-7526, www.lescheneaux.org), and the **Drummond Island Tourism Association** (Drummond Island, 906/493-5245, www.drummondislandchamber.com). Services are limited here; head south to St. Ignace for groceries and other needs. In case of an emergency, dial **911** from any phone, or visit the **Mackinac Straits Hospital & Health Center** (220 Burdette St., St. Ignace, 906/643-8585, www.mshosp.org).

Getting There and Around

From St. Ignace, you can drive north on I-75, then east on M-134. You can reach the Les Cheneaux Islands via private boat. To reach Drummond Island, take the **Drummond Island ferry** (906/235-3170, $14), which departs often from DeTour Village May–March.

Manistique Area

Four factors created the logging legacy that once dominated the southern reaches of the U.P.: vast stands of timber, wide rivers for transporting logs, well-protected harbors, and a building frenzy that began in southern Great Lakes–area ports like Chicago and stretched west across the treeless prairie. Devastating clear-cuts and diminished demand ended the region's logging boom by the early 20th century, but those well-protected ports and deep harbors still serve the area well, as busy shipping centers and enviable fishing waters.

These ports can be accessed via U.S. 2, which traces the incomparable Lake Michigan shore west of St. Ignace. One such town, Manistique, sits where the corkscrewing Manistique River, which pours through the sloughs of the Lake Superior State Forest, empties into Lake Michigan. A community of 3,400, Manistique offers proximity to historic sites and good swimming beaches, and it serves as an ideal home base for anglers, boaters, hikers, and other recreationists.

DOWNTOWN MANISTIQUE

Manistique presents a few curiosities for history buffs. The **siphon bridge,** built across the Manistique River in 1919, is a strange engineering feat, partially supported by the water underneath it. In fact, the roadway sits four feet below water level. Its construction was prompted by a paper mill just upstream, which needed to dam the river for its water needs, thus raising the river.

Also interesting is the historic **Manistique Water Tower,** a fancy neoclassical brick structure built in 1922, now serving as the town's landmark. From the boardwalk, strollers can view the vivid red **Manistique East Breakwater Light,** constructed in 1916 and still operational today.

◖ SEUL CHOIX POINT LIGHTHOUSE

East of Gulliver, a road leads you down a point to this 1895 light, a worthwhile detour. Pronounced "sis SHWA" or "sel SHWA"—French for "Only Choice"—the Seul Choix Point Lighthouse (672 N. West Gulliver Lake Rd., 906/283-3183, www. greatlakelighthouse.com, 10 A.M.–6 P.M. daily Memorial Day–mid-Oct., donation suggested) sits at the end of a finger of land that once offered Native Americans and French fur traders the "only choice" for hiding from storms along this stretch of Lake Michigan shoreline.

The Gulliver Historical Society has done a splendid job of restoring the light and creating a maritime museum in the fog signal building. (It includes an admirable scale model of the lighthouse, made by hand with thousands of miniature bricks.) Climb the tower for great views of much of northern Lake Michigan. You have a good chance of seeing ship traffic, since Port Inland, just to the east, is an important commercial port. There's also a chance that you'll have an otherworldly experience while touring the site. Over the years, visitors and employees have reported odd occurrences at the lighthouse complex, such as phantom footsteps, unexplained smells (like cigar smoke), and misplaced items. Some believe that the spirit of a former lighthouse keeper is still in residence.

To reach Seul Choix, head to Gulliver via US-2. From there, go southeast on Country Road 432 about four miles. Turn right onto Country Road 431 (a gravel road) and travel another four miles to the light.

THE BAYS DE NOC

At Green Bay's northern end, two large peninsulas—Stonington and Garden—hang down from the U.P., forming Little Bay de Noc and Big Bay de Noc. More than 200 miles of wonderfully protected and undulating shoreline, combined with the region's temperate climate, make for outstanding fishing for northern pike, perch, lake salmon, rainbow trout, smallmouth bass, and especially tasty walleye.

Stonington Peninsula

The quiet Stonington Peninsula is largely ignored by tourists, lacking accessible sand beaches or commercial attractions. It is a soft and peaceful place, with smooth slabs of bedrock shoreline and sunny meadows that have reclaimed abandoned farmland. To explore the 15-mile-long peninsula, follow U.S. 2 west of Manistique and turn south on County Road 513 or County Road 511. The Hiawatha National Forest manages a nice stretch of shoreline along the peninsula's west side, with numerous hiking trails.

The peninsula preserves several stands of old-growth hemlocks, hardwoods, and pines. One of the most notable examples is now protected as the **Squaw Creek Old Growth Area,** part of the Hiawatha National Forest. Though not virgin timber, loggers in the 19th century practiced selective cutting (quite unusual in those days) and left behind several large trees, now huge. Trails are few—just a couple of abandoned logging roads open only to foot traffic. Walking is easy, however, since the high shade canopy created by the trees crowds out the underbrush usually found in the woods.

The peninsula is also an excellent spot for bird-watchers, since the Stonington is a favorite migration stopping point for songbirds. Watch the water's edge for the great blue herons. These grand birds stand straight and motionless in the water for several minutes, then quickly snatch unsuspecting fish out of the shallows.

Garden Peninsula

Like the Stonington Peninsula, the Garden Peninsula is a quiet, peaceful point of land, filled with little-used blacktopped roads perfect for biking, and a handful of sleepy farms and orchards. The main road down the peninsula is M-183, accessed off U.S. 2. As it traces the east shore of Big Bay de Noc, M-183 passes through the tiny hamlet of Garden. Along with a few shops, it's home to a commercial fishery at the end of Little Harbor Road, where you can buy some fresh catch.

By far the peninsula's most notable attraction—and rightly so—is the 711-acre **Fayette Historic State Park** (13700 13.25 Lane, 906/644-2603, state park vehicle permit required). If you make time for just one stop in this part of the U.P., make it this outstanding state park. Once the site of a large smelting operation, Fayette's limestone furnaces converted raw iron ore from U.P. mines into pig iron that was loaded onto barges bound for Escanaba. In the 1880s, stinky, industrial Fayette boasted a population of 500, and its loud, hot blast furnaces cranked away seven days a week. By 1891, nearby forests that fueled the furnace were all but depleted, and more efficient steelmaking methods came into vogue. The furnace shut down, and the town died with it.

Nearly a century later, Fayette was reborn as a wonderfully restored historic site and state park. Today, Fayette is surely one of the nation's most scenic ghost towns, its dozen limestone buildings tucked along the sheer white bluffs and deep, clear waters of Snail Shell Harbor. Start at the visitors center, which gives a good historical overview and features a helpful scale model of the village. You can wander in and out of the hotel, opera house, homes, and other buildings, some intact, some more decayed.

MANISTIQUE LAKES

At the intersection of H-33 and H-42, the town of Curtis serves as base camp for the Manistique Lakes Recreation Area. Three lakes—North Manistique, Big Manistique, and South Manistique—combine to offer 15,000 acres of shallow, warm waters that are extremely popular with boaters, swimmers, and anglers. Big Manistique, one of the largest lakes in the U.P., is just 5–10 feet deep, and best known for its perch and bass fishing.

THE FOX RIVER

In 1919, Ernest Hemingway stepped off a train in Seney, asked for directions to a good trout stream, and was directed up an old railroad grade to the east branch of the Fox. Where truth meets fiction we'll never know, but Hemingway's U.P. travels resulted in "Big Two-Hearted River," his Nick Adams tale about fishing on what was really the Fox. (The more lyrical Big Two Hearted actually flows about 25 miles to the northeast.) Consequently, the Fox has always carried a special cachet in the U.P. and among trout fishermen.

The **Fox River Pathway** was no doubt prompted by perennial interest in Hemingway's river. The route stretches 27 miles from Seney north to just shy of Pictured Rocks National Lakeshore and, by U.P. standards, is really nothing that special. Its most appealing stretch—especially for anglers looking for fishing access—is the southern end, where the trail parallels the main river for 10 miles. Farther north, it follows the Little Fox and the west branch. Heading north, the trail traverses the Kingston Plains, where loggers left behind "stump prairies." Markers along the route provide information about the area's logging history.

SENEY NATIONAL WILDLIFE REFUGE

Seney was the center of action in the 1880s, both in and out of the woods. Situated along a railroad siding and the shores of the Fox River—used to transport the logs—it became an important transit point. Turns out, the local economy also revolved around drinking, whoring, and gambling. Seney was sensationalized in the national press, right along with Tombstone and other wild towns in the Wild West.

Problem was, Seney never had the huge fertile forests so common elsewhere in Michigan. Glaciers scrubbed this swath of the central U.P. flat, creating a patchwork of rivers, wetlands, and rocky, sandy soil. The red and white pines that did grow here were leveled in just a few short years; soon, loggers were settling for the less valuable hardwoods and small conifers, burning the scrub as they went. Shortly after the turn of the 20th century, they moved on, leaving behind the denuded land and vast "stump prairies."

Optimistic farmers followed the quickly departed loggers. They burned the brush and went to great lengths to drain the wetlands,

THE MOOSE CAPITAL OF MICHIGAN

East of the Manistique Lakes and Seney National Wildlife Refuge lies the village of Newberry, a gateway town to the impressive Tahquamenon Falls. Surrounded by acres of state and national forestland, Newberry also serves as a terrific home base for hikers, anglers, off-road enthusiasts, and snowmobilers.

The town also has another claim to fame. In 2002, Michigan's state legislature designated Newberry the "moose capital" of Michigan. There are, after all, more moose sightings in Luce County than in any other place in the state. So, while the majestic moose tend to be elusive creatures, your chances of seeing one in the wild are fairly high in the Newberry area. Just remember to keep your distance, snap photos from afar, and report any moose sightings to the **Newberry Area Chamber of Commerce** (corner of M-28 and M-123, Newberry, 906/293-5562, www.newberrychamber. net, 9:15 A.M.-5 P.M. Mon.-Fri.).

digging miles of 20-foot ditches. Yet their hopes were quickly buried by the area's poor soils and they, too, departed almost as quickly as they came. But the fires had a more lasting effect, scarring the fragile soil deeply.

Eventually, humans began to help this beleaguered land. The immense Seney National Wildlife Refuge now manages and protects 95,000 acres immediately west of M-77, restoring the wetlands with an intricate series of dikes and control ponds in what began as a Civilian Conservation Corps project in the 1930s. While humans on foot or bicycle can access much of this preserve via an extensive network of maintenance roads, the sanctuary offers plenty of seclusion for its inhabitants. More than 200 species of birds and nearly 50 species of mammals have been recorded here, including bald eagles, trumpeter swans, loons, even the occasional moose or wolf. Whether you're a dedicated bird-watcher or a casual observer, Seney is a wonderful place to get in and among a fascinating array of wildlife.

Start your tour at the **visitors center** (906/586-9851, 9 A.M.–5 P.M. daily mid-May–mid-Oct.), five miles south of the town of Seney on M-77. A 15-minute audiovisual program, interactive exhibits, and printed materials give you a good overview of what you can expect (or at least look for) in the refuge. From the center, the 1.2-mile **Pine Ridge Nature Trail** allows for a quick foray into wetland habitat.

Biking

Many visitors to Seney never get out of their cars and beyond the Marshland Drive, which is a shame. A bicycle is really the way to experience Seney. Bikes are welcome on more than 100 miles of gravel and dirt maintenance roads, which are closed to all motorized traffic except refuge vehicles. Though you won't find any technical rides, a bicycle allows you to cover a lot of ground and is quiet enough not to spook much of the wildlife. Besides, there's something magical about spinning down a gravel road amid chirping and twittering, with nothing but waving grasses and glinting ponds surrounding you for miles. No off-road riding is permitted in the refuge.

ACCOMMODATIONS AND FOOD

Several nice mom-and-pop motels are managing to hang on along U.S. 2, though they're getting more and more competition from chains. Let's hope places like the **Star Motel** (1142 E. Lakeshore Dr., Manistique, 906/341-5363, www.thestarmotel.com, $34–62 d) continue to fend off the big boys. Located a mile east of Manistique on U.S. 2, this tidy, vintage 1950s-era motel has large rooms, meticulous owners, and a nice setting on the lake. It allows well-behaved dogs, too.

The gracious **Celibeth House Bed & Breakfast** (M-77 Rt. 1, Blaney Park, 906/283-3409, $75–125 d), once a lumber baron's home, is a fine out-of-the-way relaxation spot, or a good base for day trips to Pictured Rocks National Lakeshore, Seney National Wildlife Refuge, Lake Michigan beaches, and more. You're welcome to explore the inn's grounds, which cover 85 acres and include a small lake, beaver ponds, woods, and meadows. A hoard of hummingbirds frequenting the backyard birdfeeders practically guarantees a wildlife encounter.

Camping

Camping is readily available at dozens of rustic campgrounds within the **Hiawatha National Forest** (2727 N. Lincoln Rd., Escanaba, 906/786-4062, $12–18). A particularly nice one is the very secluded—and difficult to reach—Portage Bay campground on the Garden Peninsula's eastern shore. It's southeast of Garden, at the end of Portage Bay Road.

INFORMATION AND SERVICES

For more information about the area around Manistique and Seney, contact the **Manistique Tourism Council** (800/342-4282, www.visitmanistique.com), the **Bays de Noc Convention & Visitors Bureau** (230 Ludington St., Escanaba, 906/789-7862, www.travelbaysdenoc.com), and the **Manistique Lakes Area Tourism Bureau** (Curtis, 800/860-3819, www.curtismi.com). For services like banks and groceries, your best bet would be Manistique, though you'll find a better selection in major towns like Marquette and Sault Ste. Marie. If an emergency occurs, dial **911** from any phone. Even in remote areas, help will surely come—though it might take a while.

GETTING THERE AND AROUND

The closest airport to this region is **Delta County Airport (ESC)** (3300 Airport Rd., Escanaba, 906/786-4902, www.deltacountymi.org/airport.php), which offers limited service via Northwest Airlines. Most travelers, however, will find it easier to venture across the U.P. by car. From St. Ignace, you can reach Manistique via U.S. 2, while Seney and the Manistique Lakes are accessible via M-77 or M-28.

EASTERN UPPER PENINSULA

Munising Area

When it comes to enticing visitors, nature dealt Munising, situated on the U.P.'s northern coast, a royal flush. The town of 2,350 curves around the belly of protected Munising Bay. The Grand Island National Recreation Area looms just offshore, in expansive Lake Superior. Pictured Rocks National Lakeshore begins at the edge of town and stretches for over 40 miles east. The Hiawatha National Forest spills across the forests to the south and west. So, obviously, if you're looking for outdoor activities, Munising's got all the right cards. M-28 leads you right to the heart of town, where you'll find restaurants, mom-and-pop motels, and the ferry dock for cruises to Pictured Rocks.

SIGHTS
Historic Sites
If you do just one thing in the Munising area, make it the marvelous two-hour **Glass Bottom Boat Tours** (1204 Commercial St., Munising, 906/387-4477, www.shipwrecktours.com, June–Sept., $20 adults, $8.50 children under 13). Pete Lindquist, an experienced local who also operates a dive charter, came up with the idea of installing viewing wells in the hulls of a couple of tour boats, so even nondivers can marvel at the area's shallow-water shipwrecks.

The view through the 8- to 10-foot-long windows is truly remarkable. The boat glides directly over shipwrecks, some in as little as 28 feet of water. They fill the viewing windows like historic paintings, perfectly visible in the clear water and looking close enough to touch. On the *Bermuda,* you can easily make out deck lines, hatches, even piles of iron ore lying on the deck. Weather permitting, the tour visits three shipwrecks, dating from 1860 to 1926. Along the way, Lindquist's knowledgeable crew also shares history and points out features (including the wooden East Channel Light) along the shore of Grand Island.

Waterfalls
The Munising area is thick with waterfalls, and

many are easy to reach. The **Munising Visitors Bureau** (422 E. Munising Ave., 906/387-2138, www.munising.org) prints a waterfall map that will direct you to most of them. Nearby Pictured Rocks National Lakeshore also has several notable falls.

The Tannery Creek spills over **Memorial Falls** and **Olson Falls** just on the northeast edge of town. Follow H-58 (Washington Street) northeast out of town, and watch for a small wooden staircase on the right side of the road, across from the road to Sand Point and the National Park Service headquarters. (If you've come by car, note that you can't park alongside the road here.) Climb the stairs and follow the trail through a small canyon to Tannery Falls. To reach Memorial Falls, it's easiest to return to H-58, turn right on Nestor Street, and follow the signs.

Right on the outskirts of town, M-28 leads east to **Horseshoe Falls** (turn east on Prospect Street) and **Alger Falls,** which spills down along the highway. The impressive **Wagner Falls** is right in the same area, just off M-94 near the junction of M-94 and M-28. It's a well-marked spot, operated by the state park system as a scenic site. Though it feels secluded, 20-foot Wagner Falls is just a few minutes' walk from the parking area. Continue up the streamside trail past the main falls to a second cascade. About 20 miles west of Munising, wonderful **Laughing Whitefish Falls** has also been protected as a state park scenic site. Here, water plunges 30 feet over hard dolomite rock ledges, then continues rolling and frothing at least twice that far to the bottom of a gorge. To reach Laughing Whitefish Falls, follow M-94 west from Munising to Sundell, then go north on Dorsey Road for 2.5 miles.

SHOPPING
Aluminum snowshoes now dominate the sport, but for beauty and tradition, they simply can't match white-ash-and-rawhide snowshoes. In Shingleton, 25 miles west of Seney on M-28,

workers at **Iversons Snowshoe & Furniture** (E-12559 Mill St., 906/452-6370, www.iversons-snowshoes.com, 10 A.M.–4 P.M. Mon.–Fri.) shape by hand strips of local ash into those classic snowshoe frames. Iverson also makes rustic furniture and trout fishing nets.

DIVING

When loggers were felling the vast stands of pine across the central Upper Peninsula in the 1800s, Munising grew into a busy port, with schooners carrying loads of timber to the growing cities of the southern Great Lakes and iron ore to an ever-growing number of factories. Yet the narrow and shoaly passage between the mainland and Grand Island, and along the Pictured Rocks shoreline, was the downfall of many ships; their skeletons litter the lake floor here.

The **Alger Underwater Preserve** covers 113 square miles, from just west of Grand Island to Au Sable Point near the east end of Pictured Rocks National Lakeshore. Nearly a dozen ships lie here, well preserved in Lake Superior's cold, fresh water. Some wrecks, like the 19th-century *Bermuda* and the 145-foot *Smith Moore,* lie upright and nearly intact. The Alger Underwater Preserve marks many of the dive sites with buoys and helps ensure that they will be protected from poachers—it's a felony to remove or disturb artifacts within any Great Lakes underwater preserve.

Several factors combine to make the Alger Underwater Preserve one of the finest sport-diving locations in the Midwest. There are several wrecks concentrated in one area; the cold, fresh water keeps them from deteriorating; many wrecks are in very shallow water, as little as 20 feet deep; visibility is excellent, usually a minimum of 25 feet and sometimes twice that; and Grand Island helps moderate the cold water temperatures. "It's one of the best wreck diving sites for beginners that I can imagine," notes Pete Lindquist, who operates a dive charter in Munising.

Just offshore from the Munising High School, an **underwater museum** among dock ruins includes underwater signs that interpret large maritime artifacts. The Alger Underwater Preserve also attracts divers for its sea caves in about 20 feet of water, where sandstone cliffs have been eroded by wave action. To arrange a dive charter, contact **Lake Superior Shipwreck Diving** (1204 Commercial St., Munising, 906/387-4477, www.shipwreck-tours.com).

ACCOMMODATIONS AND FOOD

The **Sunset Resort Motel** (1315 E. Bay, 906/387-4574, $59–89 d) has a great location right on Munising Bay at the east end of town. Some rooms have kitchenettes. Unlike most commercial strips, the one along M-28 on Munising's near east side is still within walking distance of downtown and the waterfront. It has some nice chain offerings like the **Days Inn** (420 E. M-28, 906/387-2493, www.daysinn.com, $59–89 d), the best of the chains with a close-in location and an indoor pool.

For a town on the edge of a national park that presumably gets a fair amount of tourist traffic, Munising has surprisingly little in the way of dining. Try **Sydney's** (400 Cedar St., 906/387-4067, www.sydneysfamilyrestaurant.com, 6 A.M.–11 P.M. Mon.–Thurs., 6 A.M.–2 A.M. Fri.–Sat., 6 A.M.–10 P.M. Sun., $6–24) for fresh whitefish and lake trout, as well as steaks and a Friday seafood buffet, served with an Australian touch. **Muldoon's Pasties** (1246 W. M-28, 906/387-5880, 10 A.M.–6 P.M. daily) is the best spot in town for a fresh, authentic taste of this potpie-type meal, a U.P. classic.

Camping

For ultimate convenience but with a sense of seclusion, the Hiawatha National Forest's **Bay Furnace** (906/786-4062, $12–18) is a good choice. Just west of Munising, north of M-28, it offers 50 rustic sites with a very nice setting next to Lake Superior and overlooking Grand Island. Some sites almost have their own private stretch of beach, and a short cross-country ski trail at the campground's north end gives campers a little extra breathing room.

INFORMATION AND SERVICES

For more information about Munising, contact the **Munising Visitors Bureau** (422 E. Munising Ave., 906/387-2138, www.munising.org). Although you'll find a limited amount of supplies in Munising, you might want to head west to Marquette for a wider range of services. In case of an emergency, however, don't hesitate to dial **911** from any cell or public phone.

GETTING THERE AND AROUND

To reach Munising, you can fly into **Sawyer International Airport (SAW)** (125 G Ave., Gwinn, 906/346-3308, www.sawyerairport.com), rent a vehicle from several major car rental agencies, and head west on M-94. If you're already driving through the state, you can take M-28 to Munising, whether you're headed east from Marquette or west from I-75.

◖ GRAND ISLAND NATIONAL RECREATION AREA

Though it's just a 10-minute ferry ride from Munising, the surrounding Lake Superior waters effectively isolate Grand Island. Owned since 1901 by the Cleveland Cliffs Iron Company, the 13,000-acre, largely wooded island was maintained for decades as a private hunting playground for the firm's executives and stockholders. In 1989, the Hiawatha National Forest purchased all but 40 acres of Grand Island and proclaimed it a national recreation area. Except for those few patches of private property, you have the entire island—roughly the size of Manhattan—for hiking, beachcombing, mountain biking, and camping.

With its status as a national recreation area, Grand Island will likely see more development than the rest of the Hiawatha National Forest. Since 1989, the Forest Service has generated mountains of paperwork developing various management plans and putting them out for public comment. Ideas range from leaving the island in its natural state to developing roads, lodges, and other visitor amenities.

So far, a few compromises have been reached. Autos are not allowed on the island except with special permission or those rare few owned by island landholders. Van tours now operate under special permit, bumping along few dirt roads on the island's southern half. ATVs are allowed October–mid-April; mountain bikes are permitted anytime on all public-land trails. Pets are allowed on leash. Note that drinking water is not available anywhere on the island.

Sights and Recreation

About 50 miles of trails crisscross Grand Island, mostly old roadbeds. If you're just visiting for a day, a mountain bike is the only way you'll have time to see the entire island: It's about a 23-mile trip around the perimeter. In fact, it's probably one of the best mountain bike routes in the U.P. for the nontechnical rider, with wide grassy paths cutting through hardwood forests, passing under towering pines, shinnying up against Lake Superior shorelines, and rewarding you with grand views of wilderness bays and the distant Pictured Rocks.

Both hikers and bikers can reach **Murray Bay,** about two miles from the ferry dock at the southern end of the island. Murray Bay has a nice day-use area and sand beach nestled in a grove of pines. There are also two campsites here, but the location near the ferry dock means you'll have less privacy than elsewhere on the island.

Don't miss the nearby **historic cemetery,** where you can pick up a little history and examine the gravestones of various shipwreck victims and the island's first white settlers. Grand Island had long been a summering ground for the Ojibwa when Abraham Williams arrived in the 1840s to establish a trading post. He raised a family and died on the island in 1873 at the rather amazing age of 81. Today, only the descendants of Williams and their spouses can be buried here.

North of Murray Bay, the island sprouts a tombolo off its southeastern corner known as "the thumb." This landmass wraps north and forms **Trout Bay,** a lovely spot ringed with honey-hued beaches and sandstone cliffs. Watch for the low profile of loons bobbing in calm waters. Trout Bay is home to the island's four other developed campsites, and you could camp a long time before finding another site this pretty.

Camping

There are no reservations, fees, or permits required for camping on Grand Island. The island has two designated campgrounds at Murray Bay (two sites) and Trout Bay (four sites), offering the relative luxury of pit toilets and fire rings. Backcountry camping is permitted throughout the island as long as you stay off the tombolo, off private property, and at least 100 feet away from lakes, streams, cliffs, trails, roads, and natural research areas. No ground fires permitted. And remember, there is no drinking water anywhere on the island, so come prepared.

Information

For more information about Grand Island, contact the **Munising Ranger District** (Hiawatha National Forest, 400 E. Munising Ave., 906/387-3700, www.grandislandmi.com).

Getting There and Around

A **passenger ferry** travels from Munising to Grand Island (906/387-3503, www.grandislandmi.com, times vary Memorial Day–early Oct., $15 adults, $10 children 6–12). The ferry's departure point is about two miles west of downtown near Powell Point. Follow M-28 west and watch for the signs. Even if you're planning just a day trip, you'd be wise to pack some warm clothing and a method for purifying water. Rough weather can cancel ferry service at any time; similarly, probably more than one hiker or biker has lost track of time and missed the last ferry. There is a ship-to-shore radio at Williams Landing in the event of an emergency.

Altran Bus Service (530 E. Munising Ave., Munising, 906/387-4845, $16 adults, $8 children) offers two- to three-hour van tours of Grand Island, from June through early October. The tour makes six stops on the southern end of the island, including Echo Lake, the Trout Bay Overlook, and Mather Beach, an excellent swimming beach where Echo Creek empties into Lake Superior.

EASTERN UPPER PENINSULA

Pictured Rocks National Lakeshore

Lake Superior takes center stage at this national park, just three miles wide but spanning more than 40 miles along this magnificent lake from Munising to Grand Marais. Pictured Rocks derives its name from the sandstone bluffs that rise 200 feet directly up from the water's surface. Washed in shades of pink, red, and green due to the mineral-rich water that seeps from the rock, these famous bluffs extend for more than 15 miles, at times sculpted into caves, arches, and castle-like turrets. The national lakeshore also features a lesser-known, but equally spectacular, stretch of shoreline called the Grand Sable Banks, where 200-foot sand dunes are hemmed by a 12-mile ribbon of sand and pebble beach. If that's not enough, you'll also find lakes, forest trails, waterfalls, a lighthouse, and other historic attractions—plenty of reasons to put Pictured Rocks at the top of the list for anyone visiting the eastern U.P.

SIGHTS
Munising Falls

Just inside the park's western boundary, a short trail leads to 50-foot Munising Falls, which spills into a narrow gorge before emptying into Lake Superior's Munising Bay. The highlight of this spot used to be the trail that led hikers behind the falls, but erosion problems prompted its closure. It's still worth a stop here, though, for the falls and the adjacent **interpretive center,** which offers a glimpse of this peaceful area's history, home to a belching pig iron furnace in the 1860s. Munising Falls also marks the west trailhead for the **Lakeshore Trail,** a 43-mile segment of the North Country National Scenic Trail that spans seven states from New York to North Dakota. The Lakeshore Trail runs the length of the Pictured Rocks National Lakeshore—predictably, never far from the water's edge. The park's eastern trailhead lies near Sable Falls.

Past Munising Falls, the paved access road ends at **Sand Point,** home of the national lakeshore headquarters. While the headquarters primarily houses offices (not visitor services), it displays some interesting Coast Guard and shipwreck artifacts on its grounds. Sand Point has a small beach and a boat ramp, a good spot to launch a small craft for exploring nearby Grand Island.

◖ Miners Castle

The sandstone cliffs five miles northeast of Munising Falls are known as Miners Castle, for the turret-like shape caused by wind and wave erosion. The nine-story-high rock formation is impressive and ranks as one of the park's most popular attractions, despite a 2006 collapse of one of the signature "turrets." Boardwalks and steps lead you to two viewing platforms out on the rock, where you can peer down into the gloriously clear waters of Lake Superior. If that entices you to do a little beachcombing and wading, a nearby trail leads down some

Miners Castle at Pictured Rocks National Lakeshore

steps through the pines to inviting **Miners Beach.**

To reach Miners Castle, follow H-58 east from Munising to the well-marked turnoff for Miners Castle Road. Before you reach the Miners Castle formation itself, you'll see another sign on Miners Castle Road directing you to Miners Falls. It's a one-mile walk to this pleasant cascade, where Miners Creek tumbles 40 feet over a rocky escarpment.

Chapel Basin Area

Continuing northeast on H-58, the next auto-accessible route into the heart of the park is at Melstrand, where the gravel/dirt Chapel Road bumps six miles toward the shore and another park highlight, the Chapel Basin area. Park your car here and you'll find plenty to entertain you during a long day hike or a weekend: three waterfalls, a deep inland lake, Superior beaches, and a good hiking loop.

Chapel Falls is the key attraction, as evidenced by the wide paved pathway that leads 1.5 miles to the falls. Amid a pale birch forest, frothing water drops like a horsetail some 90 feet into a deep gorge and Chapel Lake below. Continue past the falls to reach Chapel Beach in another 1.75 miles, where you'll find a backcountry campground. From here, you can turn right to Chapel Rock and follow the Lakeshore Trail 1.5 miles to Spray Falls, one of the least visited and loveliest waterfalls in the park, where Spray Creek drops over the sandstone cliffs right into Lake Superior.

If you turn left instead of right

EASTERN UPPER PENINSULA

at Chapel Beach, you can make a 10-mile loop around Chapel Basin. Along the way, you'll pass Grand Portal Point—another significant Pictured Rocks landmark—before returning to the parking area. Don't leave Chapel Basin without a visit to Mosquito Falls, a little farther inland off Chapel Road. The Mosquito River spills over a series of ledges, creating an accessible and calm enough waterfall for wading and soaking fatigued hiking feet. A trail leads to various sections of the falls and links up with the Lakeshore Trail.

Beaver Lake

Located near the center of the park, 800-acre Beaver Lake is the largest inland lake in Pictured Rocks. Anglers are drawn to the lake and the tributaries that feed it, especially for trout. Little Beaver Lake, connected by a small channel, has a boat launch. Boats are limited to 10 hp or less, making this a pleasant waterway for paddlers. Little Beaver has one of the park's three auto-accessible campgrounds, with eight sites available on a first-come, first-served basis. Be aware that wetlands cover much of the land between Beaver Lake and Lake Superior, so bugs can be a problem here especially in June and early July.

Two good hiking trails leave from the campground. The short and pleasant 0.7-mile **White Pine Trail** is a self-guided nature trail that circles through a 300-year-old pine forest. The five-mile **Beaver Basin Loop Trail** makes a lap around Little Beaver and Big Beaver Lakes, then follows the Lake Superior shore past sea caves cut by the lake's pounding waves. Boardwalks skirt the wetlands before returning you to the trailhead.

Twelvemile Beach

An icon near the Twelvemile Beach campground says it all: Indicating that this is a permitted beach area, it shows a swimmer not in the usual "crawl" position, but with water lapping at the ankles. In other words, the water here is damn *cold*. Swim if you dare, but wading is really more realistic.

Which is what keeps Twelvemile Beach the pristine, stunning ribbon of sand that it is. After all, if such a perfect beach boasted 75° water, it would be overrun with stereos, Jet Skis, and zinc oxide. Instead, it's a beach where you can stroll for hours with only the company of peregrine falcons, bald eagles, deer wandering down for a drink, even the occasional black bear snorting around in the sand.

The **Twelvemile Beach campground** is easy to reach, just a short drive off H-58 through a pretty birch forest. Many of the 37 campsites string out along a bluff over the beach—come midweek (or early on Saturday, often a turnover day) for one of the choice spots. Some are larger than the average house lot and undoubtedly have a better view. Well-placed stairs deposit campers and picnickers at lake level. The campground also has a nice day-use area at its east end.

Just about five miles farther up the beach (or H-58) lies the auto-accessible **Hurricane River campground,** where the Hurricane River spills into Lake Superior.

Au Sable Point

It's a 1.5-mile walk along the Lakeshore Trail from the Hurricane River campground to the **Au Sable Light Station** at Au Sable Point. Built in 1874, the 87-foot brick light and its keepers did yeoman's duty for decades—warning ships away from the rocky shoals that extend out for nearly a mile and create shallows of just 6–30 feet. Nonetheless, at least 10 steamers were wrecked here. As you walk the trail from the campground, look for parts of the shipwrecks just offshore, often poking out of the sand bottom and easily visible in the gin-clear water. The light was automated in 1958 and recently restored.

Grand Sable Dunes

Just east of Au Sable Point, the **Log Slide Overlook** marks the spot of a once-busy logging operation. In the late 1800s, loggers used this high point—some 300 feet above Lake Superior—to send freshly cut logs down to the water's edge where they were loaded on Great Lakes schooners. Today, you can stand on a platform and simply marvel at the view, with the lighthouse to your left, the great dunes to your right, and the brilliant blue of the big lake filling the horizon. If you're in the mood for some exercise, the two-mile stretch of the **North Country National Scenic Trail** from the Log Slide to the Au Sable Light Station is one of the park's most scenic hikes.

The Grand Sable Banks and Dunes (*grand sable* is French for "big sands") stretch for nearly five miles from the overlook, glacial banks of gravel supporting the huge mounds of sand. They are magnificent when viewed from a distance, glowing gold and rising up abruptly from the cobalt waters of Lake Superior. In many areas, especially near the overlook, the dunes are free of grasses and plants, so you can play around on them without fear of damaging fragile plant life or causing erosion. Though park officials discourage it for safety reasons, no one will stop you from flopping on your butt and rocketing down the slope. Be aware, though, that the climb back up takes a lot longer!

Most people, however, choose to explore the dunes from the eastern end. Near the Grand Sable Visitors Center, a trail winds across the top of the dunes, where marram grass, beach pea, and sand cherry cling to the sand for dear life. (Be careful to stay on the trail here.) Interpretive signs discuss the plants' tenuous hold on the environment. The trail to **Sable Falls** also leaves from the visitors center, a half-mile walk largely composed of steps. As you work your way downhill, you'll be treated to several views of this exceptionally pretty cascade, which drops in tiers through a narrow canyon and out to a rocky Lake Superior beach. Across H-58, the sandy shores and often warm waters of **Grand Sable Lake** make this a wonderful spot for a swim or picnic.

Grand Marais

Though not part of Pictured Rocks National Lakeshore, sweet little Grand Marais marks the park's eastern boundary and is an excellent jumping-off point for a visit to the national lakeshore. This sleepy New England–style village is worth a visit of its own for its simple windswept beauty. With an outstanding natural harbor—rather rare on Lake Superior's southern shore—Grand Marais was originally settled by fishermen. Loggers soon followed, when sawmills were built here in the 1860s and '70s to handle the logging that went on just south of here.

Today, commercial fishing remains an economic factor (though an increasingly difficult way to make a living), but a little bit of tourism is what keeps the town slowly ticking along. The downtown huddles around the harbor, which, incidentally is a good spot for kayakers to play in the surf on a north to east wind. The few streets here offer some arts-and-crafts shops and a handful of clean, inexpensive motels and restaurants.

ACCOMMODATIONS AND FOOD

ArborGate Inn (E21795 Randolf St., Grand Marais, 906/494-2681, $59–79 d) has large rooms, each with a view of the water. A block east of H-77 on Randolph, it's within walking distance to everything in town. East of H-77 on Wilson Street, **Voyageur's Motel** (906/494-2389, http://voyageursmotel.grand-maraismichigan.com, $59–129 d) sits atop a ridge overlooking Grand Marais Harbor. Nice rooms with minifridges and a sauna/whirlpool facility make this a good choice.

Grand Marais has a couple of good finds in the food department, both right downtown on H-77. The **Sportsman's Restaurant** (204 Lake St., 906/494-2800, 11 A.M.–close daily, $6–24) is more distinctive than its name suggests, with good fish dishes, salads, and homemade soups, as well as plenty of burgers and steaks. Down the street, **Ⓒ Lake Superior Brewing Company** (N14283 Lake Ave., 906/494-2337, 9 A.M.–2 A.M. daily, $4–18) does the microbrewery tradition proud, with homemade brews like Sandstone Pale Ale and Granite Brown, as well as sandwiches, soups, and great homemade pizzas.

Camping

Having made the case for leaving the car behind, you should also know that Pictured

Rocks has three auto-accessible camp-grounds—Beaver Lake, Twelvemile Beach, and Hurricane River—with water and pit toilets. No reservations are accepted, and fees are $10 per night. Backcountry camping is permitted only at designated hike-in sites, mostly along the Lakeshore Trail. A $15 permit is required, good for 1–6 campers, and for any number of nights. Most sites do not have water or toilets. Camping is also available in Munising, Grand Marais, and the Lake Superior State Forest, which borders Pictured Rocks to the south.

KAYAKING

For paddlers, an even better alternative to really experience the grandeur of this shoreline is in a sea kayak. Safety warnings cannot be over-emphasized, however. Only experienced paddlers should venture out on their own, and only in a closed cockpit (i.e., no canoes) and after scrupulously monitoring weather conditions. Paddlers can get themselves into serious trouble along Pictured Rocks, caught in sudden summer squalls along the 15-mile rock wall with nowhere to hide. Having said that, sea kayaking along Pictured Rocks ranks as one of the finest paddles on all the Great Lakes.

Kayak rentals (and longer trips to Grand Island and Isle Royale) are available. **Great Northern Adventures** (906/225-8687, www.greatnorthernadventures.com) also offers guided paddling trips, from one-day excursions along Pictured Rocks to multi-day trips that combine kayaking with hiking and mountain biking on nearby Grand Island.

INFORMATION AND SERVICES

For general information, contact the **Pictured Rocks National Lakeshore** (906/387-3700, www.nps.gov/piro). Pictured Rocks also operates several visitors centers, including one in Munising and another near the Grand Sable Dunes, just a few miles from Grand Marais. Be sure to stop at one of these centers before beginning your trip—they have on-duty rangers, excellent maps, informative displays, and historical information that will certainly enhance your visit. Both have small but very good bookstores, too. The **Pictured Rocks National Lakeshore/Hiawatha National Forest Interagency Visitor Center** (400 E. Munising Ave., 906/387-3700, 9 A.M.–4:30 P.M. daily in summer, shorter hours in winter) and the **Grand Sable Visitor Center** (E21090 H-58, 906/494-2660, 9 A.M.–5 P.M. daily May–Labor Day) serve both the Pictured Rocks National Lakeshore and the Hiawatha National Forest.

GETTING THERE AND AROUND

H-58 provides access to the park, winding roughly along the park's southern boundary and linking Munising and Grand Marais. A large stretch of the road—from Beaver Lake to the Grand Sable Dunes—is unpaved and can deteriorate into washboard rough enough to jar your dental work loose. Leave the '55 T-bird at home and plan your time accordingly—it's about a 90-minute trip from one end to the other.

Lake Superior Shore

Traveling east from Pictured Rocks National Lakeshore, you leave behind the grand bluffs, enormous dunes, and well-marked attractions for the unknown. Like many U.P. roads, the sometimes paved, often gravel, H-58 winds through the trees, giving few clues as to what lies beyond the pines and hardwoods. The land flattens out here—a far less dramatic landscape than the nearby Pictured Rocks area—so many visitors just pass on by. That's good news for those looking for simple solitude, since these woods hide little-used hiking trails, scenic paddling rivers, undeveloped stretches of Lake Superior shoreline, and all kinds of secluded lakes and campsites known only by regulars. Of course, if you continue along the meandering county roads to Whitefish Bay, you'll find some of the U.P.'s more popular sights, including towering waterfalls and a shipwreck museum.

SIGHTS
Lake Superior State Forest

H-58 passes largely through state forest land, which encompasses much of the Lake Superior shoreline, extends six or seven miles inland in many places, and serves as a buffer zone protecting Pictured Rocks. Several other "truck trails" spin off gravel H-58, sandy roads that are *usually* well marked at intersections and quite navigable. They can be confusing, however, so venture off onto them with a good map or at least a good sense of direction.

Muskallonge Lake State Park

Wedged on a quarter-mile strip of land between Lake Superior and Muskallonge Lake, Muskallonge Lake State Park occupies the site of the old Deer Park township, once home to a sawmill, a hotel, and no doubt a saloon or two. Today, a couple of fishing resorts represent the only commerce in this remote area 18 miles east of Grand Marais.

Water is the draw here. The park's two miles of Lake Superior frontage is wonderfully secluded, with low, grass-covered dunes stretching off to the east and west, and no visible development in either direction. It offers peace, quiet, and good rockhounding, especially for agates. Muskallonge Lake is stocked by the Department of Natural Resources and produces good fishing opportunities for northern pike, walleye, smallmouth bass, and perch. Because the lake is relatively shallow, it warms up enough for comfortable swimming—a rarity in much of the U.P., which accounts for this park's somewhat surprising popularity in summer.

Crisp Point Life Saving Station

If lighthouses are your thing, here's a truly obscure one to add to the list. The 58-foot Crisp Point Light sits on a tiny arc of land 14 miles west of Whitefish Point, an isolated, unbroken stretch of Lake Superior shoreline. Though an automated light took over duty decades ago, the handsome 1904 tower and adjacent home still stand. The buildings definitely need work, but the tower was recently painted, so there's some movement afoot for their preservation. You'll need a map to find the light—and a four-wheel-drive vehicle wouldn't hurt either. (Don't attempt the last couple of miles if the ground is wet.) The light is about nine miles east of the mouth of the Two Hearted. Reach it from the west on Country Road 412, or from the east via the Farm Truck Road truck trail off M-123.

Whitefish Point

"The searchers all say they'd have made Whitefish Bay if they put 15 more miles behind her…" Singer/songwriter Gordon Lightfoot immortalized the ill-fated ore carrier *Edmund Fitzgerald* for the masses, but locals here need no reminders. Less than 20 miles from Whitefish Point and the safety of Whitefish Bay, the huge laker and all 29 hands on board were swallowed up in mere minutes by a fierce November squall in 1975.

On Lake Superior—the largest and fiercest of the Great Lakes—northwest storms can build over 200 miles of cold, open water. They unleash their full fury on the 80-mile stretch of water from Grand Marais to Whitefish Point (hence the nickname, the "Graveyard of the Great Lakes"). Whitefish Point has long served as a beacon for mariners, a narrow finger of land reaching toward Ontario and forming the protected waters of Whitefish Bay, one of the few safe havens on the big lake.

C Great Lakes Shipwreck Museum

To commemorate the many ships that failed to round that point of safety, Whitefish Point is now the proper home of the Great Lakes Shipwreck Museum (18335 N. Whitefish

THE MEMORY AND THE MYSTERY OF THE *EDMUND FITZGERALD*

In early November 1975, the 729-foot lake carrier *Edmund Fitzgerald* departed Superior, Wisconsin, loaded with 26,000 tons of taconite pellets, bound for the port of Detroit and area steel mills. Launched in 1958, the *Fitzgerald* had a long and profitable record for the Columbia Line, the ship's Milwaukee-based owner. This was to be one of the last trips across Lake Superior before the shipping lanes and Soo Locks shut down for the season.

The *Fitzgerald* had rounded the Keweenaw Peninsula when, at dusk on November 10, one of the worst storms in 30 years screamed across Lake Superior. Winds howled at 90 miles an hour, whipping the immense lake into 30-foot seas. The *Fitzgerald* was prepared for bad weather from the northeast; Superior was notorious for her November gales. Like the captain of the 767-foot *Arthur M. Anderson* traveling nearby, the captain of the *Fitzgerald* had chosen to follow a more protected route across the lake, some 20-40 miles farther north than usual.

Just 10 miles apart, the two captains had been in intermittent visual and radio contact, discussing the perilous weather, which had dangerously shifted from northeast to northwest. At 7:10 P.M., the *Fitzgerald* captain radioed, "We are holding our own." Then abruptly at 7:15, radio contact was lost. Turning to his radar, the captain of the *Anderson* stared in disbelief: The *Fitzgerald* had completely disappeared off the screen. A 729-foot lake carrier and all 29 hands simply vanished, without a single distress call, without a trace.

When the storm cleared, the wreck of the *Ed-mund Fitzgerald* was found in 530 feet of water, just 17 miles from the shelter of Whitefish Bay. She lay at the bottom in two pieces, 170 feet apart, with debris scattered over three acres – evidence of the force with which the massive hull hit bottom. Many believe the *Fitzgerald* torpedoed bow first, which would have meant nearly 200 feet of the ship was towering above the water's surface at impact.

But even after over 30 years, an exhaustive Coast Guard investigation, and several dives to the site, no one really knows what happened. Theories abound, of course. The Coast Guard's best deduction is that the ship took on water through leaking hatches, then developed a list and was swamped by the storm's huge waves. Others believe that, outside the normal shipping lane, she scraped bottom on uncharted shoals. Still others believe the warm taconite pellets weakened the structure of the ship, causing it to snap in two when caught between two particularly enormous waves. No doubt books will continue to be written and new theories put forth.

Meanwhile, the *Edmund Fitzgerald* remains in its grave at the bottom of the lake, along with all its victims, whose bodies were never recovered. It ranks as the worst modern-day disaster on the Great Lakes, a constant reminder of the power of these inland seas.

For further details about this tragedy, or to view the bronze bell recovered from the *Fitzgerald* shipwreck, visit the **Great Lakes Shipwreck Museum** (18335 N. Whitefish Point Rd., Paradise, 888/492-3747, www.shipwreckmuseum.com).

Point Rd., Paradise, 888/492-3747, www.shipwreckmuseum.com, 10 A.M.–6 P.M. daily May–Oct., $12 adults, $8 children). With dim lighting and appropriately haunting music, this fine, compact museum traces the history of Great Lakes commerce and the disasters that sometimes accompanied it. Several shipwrecks are chronicled here, each with a scale model, photos or drawings, artifacts from the wreck, and a description of how and why it went down. Most compelling is the *Edmund Fitzgerald* display, complete with a life preserver and the ship's huge bell, recovered in a 1994 expedition led by museum founder Tom Farnquist, an accomplished diver and underwater photographer.

Housed in the former Coast Guard station, the museum also includes the restored light keeper's home, a theater showing an excellent short film about the *Fitzgerald* dive, and an interesting gift shop with nautical charts, prints, books, and more. To reach it, take M-123 to Paradise and follow Whitefish Point Road 11 miles north. The museum alone makes this out-of-the-way point a worthy detour.

Whitefish Point Light Station

Whitefish Point first beamed a warning light in 1849, and has done so ever since, making it the oldest operating light station on all of Lake Superior. Marking the bay's entry, the Whitefish Point Light Station is a utilitarian-looking 80-foot steel structure supported by a framework of steel girders. Though it looks relatively modern, the light actually dates to 1902. The beefy design was considered an extraordinary engineering experiment at the time, but one deemed necessary to withstand the gales that frequently batter this exposed landscape. It was automated in 1970 and continues to do yeoman's duty.

◖ Tahquamenon Falls

West of Newberry, the headwaters of the Tahquamenon bubble up from underground and begin a gentle roll through stands of pine and vast wetlands. Rambling and twisting northeast through Luce County, the river

Tahquamenon Falls

© L. DIGGS, PICTURE THIS...

EASTERN UPPER PENINSULA

grows wide and majestic by the time it enters its namesake state park. Then, with the roar of a freight train and the power of a fire hose, it suddenly plummets over a 50-foot drop, creating a golden fountain of water 200 feet wide.

As much as 50,000 gallons of water per second gush over the Upper Tahquamenon, making it the second largest falls (by volume) east of the Mississippi, outdone only by Niagara. Adding to Tahquamenon's majesty are its distinctive colors—bronze headwaters from the tannic acid of decaying cedars and hemlocks that line its banks, and bright white foam from the water's high salt content.

Accessing Tahquamenon Falls is easy, since both the Upper Falls and Lower Falls lie within **Tahquamenon Falls State Park** (41382 W. M-123, Paradise, 906/492-3415), which has provided short, well-marked paths to prime viewing sites. At the Upper Falls, follow the trail to the right and down the 74 steps to an observation deck, which brings you so close you can feel the fall's thundering power and its cool mist on your face. The view provides a dual glimpse of the placid waters above and the furious frothing below. Four miles downstream, the Lower Falls plunges over a series of cascades. The best vantage point is from a small island mid-river; a state park concessionaire obliges visitors by renting canoes and rowboats to make the short crossing.

With the dramatic centerpiece of Tahquamenon Falls, it's easy to overlook the rest of this 40,000-acre state park, Michigan's second largest. In sharp contrast to the often frenzied crowds at the falls (more than half a million people per year, the greatest of any U.P. state park), the vast majority of the park remains peaceful, etched with 25 miles of little-used hiking trails. From the Upper Falls, the Giant Pines Loop passes through a stand of white pines before crossing M-123. Once on the north side of the highway, link up with the Clark Lake Loop, a 5.6-mile hike that traces the southern shoreline of the shallow lake.

The final 16 miles of the Tahquamenon River wind through the park, spilling into Lake Superior's Whitefish Bay at its eastern end. Fishing for muskie and walleye is usually quite good in the pools below the Lower Falls. Also consider joining the fleet of runabouts and anglers in waders near the mouth of the river, where trout often school.

It's possible to paddle nearly all 94 miles of the Tahquamenon. A popular put-in is off County Road 415 north of McMillan, but you'll start off through several buggy miles of wetlands. A better choice is about 10 miles downstream, off County Road 405 at Dollarville, where you'll also avoid portaging around the Dollarville Dam. Beyond Newberry, you'll be treated to a pristine paddle, since no roads come anywhere near the river. Watch the banks for bear, deer, and other wildlife. Naturally, you'll have to portage around the falls, but then you can follow the river to its mouth without any other interruptions.

Tahquamenon Falls Tours

For another look at the river and falls, you may want to plan a day for the **Toonerville**

Trolley and Riverboat (Soo Junction, 906/876-2311, mid-June–mid-Oct., $42 adults, $26 children 9–15, $17 children 4–8). It's much more appealing than its cheesy name suggests, and a good way to experience a remote stretch of the river. Departing from Soo Junction near Newberry (watch for a sign on M-28), a narrow-gauge train chugs its way five miles along an old logging route, through roadless spruce and maple forest, tamarack lowlands and peat bogs. In about a half-hour, the train sighs to a stop deep in the woods at the Tahquamenon's banks. Here, you'll transfer to a large tour boat and cruise downstream nearly two hours toward the falls. Just as the river begins to roil and boil, the boat docks on the river's south shore, and guests walk the last half-mile to the falls. It's a nifty trip, one that has been in operation since long before there was a state park providing easy access to the falls. Originally, the tour operator—the grandfather of present-day owner Kris Stewart—used a Model T truck with train wheels to reach the river.

Curley Lewis Memorial Highway

This twisting, scenic road (also called Lakeshore Drive) follows the curve of Lake Superior's Whitefish Bay from M-123 east 20 miles or so to Sault Ste. Marie. It's almost an attraction in itself, passing through the Hiawatha National Forest, offering up plenty of water views and a handful of worthwhile stops.

Pendills Creek National Fish Hatchery

Four miles west of tiny Dollar Settlement, this federally run fish hatchery (21990 W. Trout Lane, Brimley, 906/437-5231, 9 A.M.–5 P.M. Mon.–Fri., free) raises thousands of lake trout that grow up to tempt anglers in Lakes Superior, Michigan, and Huron. Visitors can wander around the tanks to peer down at the hundreds of wriggling trout fry (the raceways are covered to keep birds and other predators from helping themselves to a free lunch) and the breeder trout that weigh in at 15 pounds or more.

Point Iroquois
Light Station and Museum

Continuing east, don't miss a chance to climb the tower at the Point Iroquois Light Station (906/437-5272, 9 A.M.–5 P.M. daily mid-May–mid-Oct., free), where Whitefish Bay narrows into the St. Mary's River. Since 1855, a beacon here has helped guide ships through this extremely difficult passage, where reefs lurk near the Canadian shore and the rock walls of Point Iroquois threaten on the Michigan side. In 1871, the original wooden light tower was replaced with the present one, a classic white-painted brick structure. A keeper's home was added in 1902.

With fewer and fewer lighthouses open to the public, it's fun to climb the iron spiral staircase for a freighter-captain's view of the river, the bay, and frequent shipping traffic. Stop in the adjacent light keeper's home, too, where the local historical society has restored some rooms to illustrate the life of a light keeper; other rooms feature displays and old photos. The lighthouse and adjacent beach are now part of the Hiawatha National Forest, which should help ensure continued protection.

Mission Hill Overlook

This is the kind of road where every view is better than the last. As the highway curves south, watch for the turnoff to the west marking this terrific overlook. Drive up the sand and gravel road for grand, sweeping views of the river and bay, Ontario's Laurentian Mountains, the cityscape of Sault Ste. Marie, freighters that look like toy ships, the Point Iroquois light, and just below, Spectacle Lake.

RECREATION
Bird-Watching

A needed resting spot for birds migrating across Lake Superior, **Whitefish Point** is a birdwatcher's dream. Beginning with the hawk migration in April through late fall, the point attracts an amazing variety of birds. Eagles, loons, songbirds, waterfowl, owls, some unusual arctic species like arctic loons and arctic terns, and more all pass through, some 300

© ROSS REINHOLD, SUPERIORTRAILS.COM

the Point Iroquois Light Station and Museum

EASTERN UPPER PENINSULA

species in all. Even if you're not a birding enthusiast, plan to spend some time at this lovely point, where you can wander the sand beaches, watch the birds, and keep an eye out for the big lakers that pass quite close to shore as they round the point. Bring along binoculars and an extra jacket.

Canoeing

The Two Hearted is a fine canoeing river, clean and clear and usually quite mellow—except in spring when, depending on snowmelt, it can crank out some pretty serious white water. A state-designated wilderness river, the Two Hearted winds through pine and hardwood forest; the only signs of civilization you're likely to see are a handful of cottages at the river's mouth. It offers plenty of low banks and sandbars, so picnic spots are easy to find. The Two Hearted is also a widely regarded blue-ribbon trout stream, so be prepared for plenty of anglers when the season opens in April.

Put in at the High Bridge state forest campground on County Road 407 for a 23-mile trip to the mouth. (You'll find two state forest campgrounds and other camping sites along the route.) Alternately, you can hook up with **Two Hearted Canoe Trips** (County Road 423, Newberry, 906/658-3357), a livery based out of the Rainbow Lodge at the river's mouth. It operates trips ranging from a couple of hours to three days. A popular half-day trip departs from the Reed and Green Bridge (east of Muskallonge Lake State Park on County Road 410) and takes out at Lake Superior.

Diving

For experienced divers, the **Whitefish Point Underwater Preserve** offers a fantastic array of wrecks—18 steamers and schooners littered all around the point. (The *Edmund Fitzgerald* is not among them.) Good visibility is a hallmark of this 376-acre preserve. Most wrecks lie in deep water, though—ranging 40–270 feet—and in an area with few protected harbors. Needless to say, only very experienced divers and boaters should consider this spot. For

information on area dive services, contact the **Paradise Area Tourism Council** (906/492-3927, www.paradisemi.org).

ACCOMMODATIONS

While there are plenty of chain hotels from which to choose, the area also has some smaller, more interesting lodgings. **Curley's Paradise Motel** (M-123 at Whitefish Point, 906/492-3445, $49–129 d) has nice standard rooms. Ask about their cottages and home rentals. To the south, you'll find the **Evening Star Motel** (7475 M-123, Newberry, 906/293-8342, www.theeveningstarmotel.com, $49–89 d), which boasts 40 clean rooms, some with kitchenettes. The property also has an indoor heated pool, so bring your swimsuit.

Camping

There are many campgrounds along the Lake Superior shoreline, including the **Mouth of the Two Hearted River Campground** (906/293-3293, $15), where you'll find rustic sites in the state forest. You can also pitch your tent at the **High Bridge State Forest Campground** (906/293-3293, $15), only 10 miles from Pine Stump and 24 miles from Newberry.

INFORMATION AND SERVICES

For more information about the Lake Superior shore, consult the **Upper Peninsula Travel & Recreation Association** (Iron Mountain, 906/774-5480, www.uptravel.com). If you require services like banks, post offices, groceries, and medical care, consider heading to more sizable towns like St. Ignace or Sault Ste. Marie. In an emergency, dial **911** from any phone.

GETTING THERE AND AROUND

The easiest way to navigate this part of the eastern Upper Peninsula is definitely via car. From Munising, head east on H-58, which leads to several county roads. To reach the eastern part of this shoreline, take M-123 from Newberry to Paradise.

Sault Ste. Marie and Vicinity

The second largest city in the Upper Peninsula, Sault Ste. Marie serves as a striking contrast to the surrounding hinterlands of northern Michigan. With a population of 14,300, this historic city is well worth a visit, especially to view the boat traffic through the famous Soo Locks that link Lakes Superior and Huron. At the foot of Whitefish Bay, grand Lake Superior narrows to a close at the St. Mary's River, the sole waterway that connects it to the other Great Lakes. With Superior 21 feet higher than the others, the St. Mary's naturally erupted into a series of falls and rapids near Sault Ste. Marie. Sault, pronounced *SOO* (and often spelled that way as a city nickname), means "falling water," a name given by early French explorers. While in town, you should consider hopping across the river to Canada, where you'll find Sault Ste. Marie's sister city, considerably larger and also known as Sault Ste. Marie.

SIGHTS
◖ Soo Locks

Nearly every visitor to the Soo makes a pilgrimage to the locks, right in the heart of downtown at the end of Ashmun Street (Business I-75). The city has smartly dressed up this area beautifully, with lovely **Brady Park.** Blue freighter signs mark the **Locks Park Walkway,** which wanders along Water Street and is dotted with interpretive plaques that share the city's history.

In the heart of the rather formal park, the U.S. Army Corps of Engineers manages the locks and a **visitors center** (Portage Ave., 906/932-1472, www.soolocksvisitorscenter.com, 9 A.M.–9 P.M.

daily, free), next to a raised **viewing platform** that lets you peer down on the action. Start at the visitors center to make sense of what's happening. Here, a moving model shows how the locks raise and lower ships by opening and closing the gates of a lock chamber and allowing water to rush in or rush out. No pumps are required; the water simply seeks its own level. Other displays explain the construction of the locks. A knowledgeable staff with a P.A. system, along with video cameras upriver, notify you about approaching vessels. In summer months, you can usually count on a ship coming through every hour or so. The visitors center will have the day's shipping schedule, but be aware that times can change depending on weather conditions and other factors.

It's easy to while away an hour or two watching the ships as they slither into the locks with seemingly just inches to spare. Summer evenings are especially pleasant, when you'll likely have the platform to yourself to watch the illuminated ships. If you're lucky, you might see a "saltie," an oceangoing vessel that's likely hauling grain to foreign ports. Overall, the three most plentiful Great Lakes shipments are iron ore (for steelmaking), limestone (a purifying agent for steelmaking, also used in construction and papermaking), and coal (for power plants).

The locks and viewing platform are open throughout the Great Lakes shipping season, which runs March 25–January 15. Those are the official dates when the locks cease operation for maintenance; ice build-up on Superior sometimes affects the length of the shipping season, too. The visitors center is open mid-May–mid-November.

Soo Locks Boat Tours

After viewing the locks, you can "lock through" yourself on one of these extremely popular tours. The two-hour trip takes you through both the American and Canadian locks and travels along both cities' waterfronts. At busy times, you'll be in the midst of freighter traffic, dwarfed by their enormous steel hulls. The large passenger boats have both heated and open deck areas. The Soo Locks Boat Tours (1157 E. Portage Ave. or 515 E. Portage Ave., 906/632-6301, www.soolocks.

com, times vary, $21 adults, $10.50 children 5–12) depart daily from early May to mid-October beginning at 9 A.M.

Other Downtown Attractions

After watching the big Great Lakes boats, the **Museum Ship Valley Camp** (501 E. Water St., 906/632-3658, hours vary, $19 adults, $10 children 6–16) gives you a chance to see what it was like to live and work aboard a giant steamer. This 550-foot steamship logged more than a million miles on the Great Lakes, hauling ore, coal, and stone on the Great Lakes from 1907 to the mid-1970s. Now, it's permanently docked five blocks east of the Soo Locks. Visitors can tour the pilothouse, engine room, main deck, crew quarters, coal bunker, and more. Throughout, the ship has a number of aquariums and maritime displays, some better than others. Most popular: a display on the sinking of the *Edmund Fitzgerald,* including two tattered lifeboats found empty and drifting on the lake. All in all, it's well worth a couple of hours. Make sure to stop at the museum shop, housed in a separate building next to the parking lot. It has an excellent selection of maritime books and videos.

Like most observation towers, the **Tower of History,** four blocks east of the Soo Locks at 326 Portage Avenue, is sort of an ugly blight on the landscape—a 21-story stark concrete monolith—but with a wonderful 360-degree view of the twin Soos, the St. Mary's, Lake Superior, and forests rolling off in the distance. Rather than being stuck behind windows, you get to enjoy the views from an open-air deck. (Bring a jacket!) The tower also includes a few small exhibit areas and a theater showing documentary videos. Yes, there is an elevator to the top. Curiously, the tower was originally built as a bell tower for the neighboring church—a project that went, uh, slightly over budget.

The **River of History Museum** (209 E. Portage Ave.) uses St. Mary's River as the framework for telling the story of the region's history. Life-sized dioramas depict things like Native Americans spearfishing in the rapids and a French fur trapper's cabin. The museum incorporates lots of sound in its displays: dripping ice from melting glaciers, roaring rapids, and Ojibwa elders passing down legends.

I-500 SNOWMOBILE RACE

Founded in 1968, the International 500 Snowmobile Race (906/635-1500, www.i-500.com) has become one of the world's largest and longest snowmobile races. Usually occurring in the beginning of February, this annual event lures thousands of snowmobilers to Sault Ste. Marie, where they speed around a one-mile oval course, competing against one another for an impressive purse, nowadays close to $40,000. Visitors, too, relish this frenzied spectacle, one you're unlikely to see in many places.

ACCOMMODATIONS AND FOOD

Now part of the Ramada chain, the rather plush **☾ Ojibway Hotel** (240 W. Portage Ave., 906/632-4100, www.waterviewhotels.com, $99–179 d) has the nicest accommodations in town, and the best location, too, overlooking the St. Mary's River and the locks. Ask for an upper-level, north-facing room. The elegant 1928 building has been well restored, with large rooms, an indoor pool, a whirlpool, and the Freighters restaurant. Ask about packages for a better deal.

For the same good location but for less money, try the **Longships Motel** (427 W. Portage Ave., 888/690-2422, www.longshipsmotel.net, $59–99 d), a clean and comfortable mom-and-pop-style motel with a fine spot across from Locks Park. There are plenty of chain hotels near I-75, but they are nowhere near the locks or other downtown walking attractions.

Start your day at **Cup of the Day** (406 Ashmun, 906/635-7272, www.cupoftheday.com, 7:15 A.M.–6 P.M. Mon.–Fri., 8:30 A.M.–3 P.M. Sat., $4–6) for good coffee drinks, a juice bar, and sandwiches and salads at lunchtime. In the Ojibway Hotel, **☾ Freighters** (240 W. Portage Ave., 906/632-4100, www.waterviewhotels.com, 8 A.M.–9 P.M. daily, $4–24) offers a wall of glass overlooking the locks and a very nice menu featuring steaks and seafood, especially local fish. This is a great spot for a good breakfast, too.

Camping

Right in Sault Ste. Marie, there's a modern, 65-site municipal campground at **Aune-Osborn Park** (1225 E. Portage Ave., 906/632-3268, mid-May–mid-Oct., $20–22) on the St. Mary's River near the Sugar Island ferry dock. Just east of Brimley, **Brimley State Park** (9200 W. 6 Mile Rd., 906/248-3422, state park vehicle permit required, $16–23) offers about a mile of sandy Lake Superior beach, a large modern campground, and not a whole lot else. Still, it's a good choice for anyone looking for an easy place to set up camp to enjoy the Soo and other nearby attractions. This is a popular park, so consider making reservations (800/447-2757) if you're aiming for a summer weekend.

INFORMATION AND SERVICES

For more information about the Sault Ste. Marie area, contact the **Sault Ste. Marie Convention & Visitors Bureau** (536 Ashmun St., 906/632-3366, www.saultstemarie.com). For local news, consult the *Sault Ste. Marie Evening News* (www.sooeveningnews.com).

The Sault Ste. Marie area offers its share of services, including banks, groceries, post offices, and more. Just ask the locals for directions—they're a friendly bunch. In case of an emergency that requires police, fire, or ambulance services, dial **911** from any cell or public phone.

GETTING THERE AND AROUND

While it's possible to fly into the **Sault Ste. Marie Airport (YAM)** (www.saultairport.com) in Ontario and cross the International Bridge to Sault Ste. Marie, most travelers will reach the Soo from some other part of Michigan. From the Lower Peninsula, head north on I-75. From the western U.P., head east on M-28 or U.S. 2 to I-75.

EASTERN UPPER PENINSULA

© TOURISM SAULT STE. MARIE

the Agawa Canyon Train Tour

SAULT STE. MARIE, ONTARIO

Just across the International Bridge lies the Soo's sister city in Ontario, also named Sault Ste. Marie. With a population of 74,600, it's the larger of the two cities, home to a huge steel plant and paper company. But along with these industries, Sault Ste. Marie, Ontario, also has a lot to offer visitors. Downtown, a lovely **boardwalk** rambles along the river for a mile or so, beginning at the bridge and extending east past fishing platforms, shops, and the MS *Norgoma,* the last passenger cruise ship built for the Great Lakes, now a museum. On Wednesday and Saturday, there's a farmers market near the tented pavilion.

One of the most popular visitor attractions is the **Agawa Canyon Train Tour** (129 Bay St., 800/242-9287, www.agawacanyontourtrain. com, times vary, $65 adults, $56 seniors, $25 children 5–18, $20 children under 5), a seven-hour round-trip through the scenic wooded gorge of the Agawa Canyon. The daylong tour includes a two-hour stopover in the canyon, where you can hike to lookouts, visit waterfalls, wander along the river, or just hang out in the grassy picnic area. The train trip is even more popular in the fall color season, which usually runs mid-September–mid-October, and in winter when it is known as the "Snow Train" (and during which the two-hour layover is eliminated).

Reach Ontario via the three-mile-long **International Bridge** (one-way costs $2 for autos). Nowadays, U.S. citizens need to show either a passport or an official birth certificate with photo identification, such as a driver's license. You can exchange money and pick up maps and other useful area information at the travel center at the foot of the bridge.

Information

For more information about Sault Ste. Marie in Canada, contact **Tourism Sault Ste. Marie** (800/461-6020, www.northernontario.com or www.saulttourism.com).

THE WESTERN UPPER PENINSULA

As with other parts of Michigan, town names found throughout the western half of the Upper Peninsula reveal the region's diverse history. Some monikers, such as Mohawk and Menominee, refer to the Native American tribes that once dwelled amid these remote lands. Other names signify words used by the Chippewa Indians, such as Escanaba ("flat rock"), Negaunee ("pioneer"), and Ishpeming ("high ground"). Many more, however, highlight the area's former mining industries; names like Copper Harbor, Copper City, Ironwood, Iron River, Iron Mountain, and Mineral Hills are nearly all that's left of the copper and iron ore operations that thrived here from the mid-19th to the early 20th centuries.

Following a Copper Rush in 1840, which eventually yielded more mineral wealth than California's better publicized Gold Rush, and the discovery of iron ore four years later, the U.P. flourished, employing thousands of eager Americans and European immigrants, resulting in the construction of numerous cities, and creating millionaires virtually overnight. Timber was also an important commodity in the U.P., but eventually all three industries declined during the 20th century. Nowadays, the only remnants of this mineral-rich past are the aptly named cities, enormous mansions, abandoned mines, ghost towns, and occasional cave-ins that occur beneath homes and streets.

In many respects, the wilderness has reclaimed the land, much of which has been preserved in the form of regional, state, and national parks and forests, including the Porcupine Mountains Wilderness State Park

© MARQUETTE COUNTRY CVB

HIGHLIGHTS

(Isle Royale Boat Tours: For those not ready to venture alone into Isle Royale National Park, the MV *Sandy* offers several boat tours that guide visitors around this isolated archipelago, taking in sights like Rock Harbor Lighthouse, Pine Mountain, and Lookout Louise (page 311).

(Fort Wilkins Historic State Park: Near the tip of the Keweenaw Peninsula, you'll find this historic recreation area, where visitors can stroll, bike, or ski along a four-mile nature trail, explore a restored 1844 military outpost, view one of the oldest lighthouses on Lake Superior, and watch costumed interpreters demonstrate the peninsula's history (page 315).

(Quincy Mine: Now part of the Keweenaw National Historical Park, this former copper mine, once one of the world's richest, offers visitors a fascinating glimpse into a bygone era; informative tours include a visit to the on-site museum and towering shaft house, a guided stroll through the 1894 hoist building, and an expert-led tram ride to the underground mine (page 318).

(Porcupine Mountains Wilderness State Park: This 59,020-acre expanse is one of the few remaining large wilderness areas in the Midwest. Hikers, mountain bikers, anglers, canoeists, and cross-country skiers can explore towering trees, secluded lakes, wild rivers, and sights like the Lake of the Clouds Overlook (page 323).

(Downhill Skiing: The Lower Peninsula may contain several fantastic downhill ski resorts, but so does the U.P. In fact, the mountainous region around Ironwood boasts three

solid choices, all of which offer lessons for first-timers (page 329).

(Iron County Historical Museum: Located at Caspian, not far from Iron River, the U.P.'s largest outdoor museum presents an assortment of exhibits, including wildlife art, early mining equipment, an 80-foot-long miniature logging camp, a former mining site, and several old log cabins (page 331).

LOOK FOR **(** TO FIND RECOMMENDED SIGHTS, ACTIVITIES, DINING, AND LODGING.

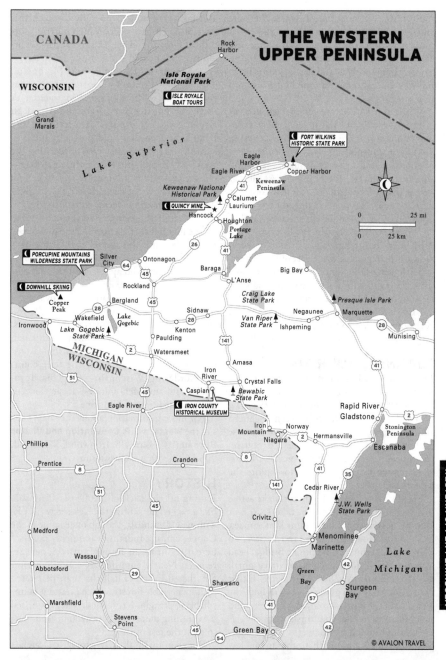

and Ottawa National Forest, where there are miles of hiking, mountain biking, and cross-country skiing trails; where cell phone signals do not exist; where the chance of seeing moose, timber wolves, and black bears is high; and where the summer sun might not set until 11 P.M.

While tourism has never thrived here as in the Lower Peninsula, it seems that every year more and more people are discovering this region's unspoiled beauty and cultural attractions, including several museums in and around Marquette, the U.P.'s largest city, as well as the various heritage sites that comprise the Keweenaw National Historical Park, established in 1992. Outdoor enthusiasts travel to the western U.P. and nearby Isle Royale, an isolated, road-free archipelago in Lake Superior, to savor the region's cornucopia of wild rivers, majestic waterfalls, desolate beaches, remote lakes, downhill ski resorts, and surprisingly tall mountains (by Midwestern standards), including 1,979-foot Mount Arvon east of L'Anse. For those seeking solitude, history, and challenging winters, this is an ideal destination.

PLANNING YOUR TIME

The western U.P. is even less compact than the eastern half, especially when you consider isolated Isle Royale, the protruding Keweenaw Peninsula, and the stretch between Escanaba and Menominee. The easiest way to traverse this vast region is via vehicle. Of course, you'll need to rely on canoes, bicycles, boats, or your own feet if you want to explore the wilderness.

Luckily, several major highways snake across this region. From Wisconsin, take U.S. 2 or U.S. 51 to Ironwood, U.S. 45 to Watersmeet, U.S. 141 to Iron Mountain, and U.S. 41 to Menominee. From the Mackinac Bridge, head west on U.S. 2 to Escanaba, or drive north on I-75 and take M-28 to Marquette. Either U.S. 41 or M-26 can guide you north onto the Keweenaw Peninsula, from which ferries and small planes can take you to Isle Royale.

Although much of the western U.P. comprises untamed land, with sizable towns few and far between, it is possible to reach this part of Michigan via commercial transportation. Greyhound serves several towns, including Hancock, Ironwood, Iron River, Iron Mountain, Escanaba, and Marquette. The region's primary airport is the Sawyer International Airport, south of Marquette; it's served by Northwest Airlines and American Eagle. Smaller airports also exist in the Houghton, Ironwood, and Escanaba areas.

Still, the relative difficulty of reaching the western U.P. promises fewer tourists throughout the year—which is ideal for those seeking solitude. So, your seasonal interests will likely determine when you decide to visit this region and how long you plan to stay. If you intend to hit the highlights of Isle Royale, the Keweenaw Peninsula, and Marquette, then three days should be sufficient. A week or more is necessary for those who appreciate the great outdoors; after all, average visitors can spend at least three days just exploring Isle Royale.

During your visit to the western U.P., you should keep in mind the matter of time zones. While most of the Upper Peninsula is situated, as with the Lower Peninsula, in the eastern standard time (EST) zone, the four counties bordering Wisconsin—Gogebic, Iron, Dickinson, and Menominee—are in the central standard time (CST) zone.

For more information about this area, consult the **Western U.P. Convention and Visitor Bureau** (P.O. Box 706, Ironwood, MI 49938, 906/932-4850, www.westernup.info).

HISTORY

Raking off the back of the Upper Peninsula like a ragged dorsal fin, the Keweenaw (KEE-wuh-naw) Peninsula, though once home to the Copper Culture Indians, was quickly shunned by early European immigrants: Hopelessly remote. Nearly engulfed by Lake Superior. Smothered in snows half the year. Blanketed by impenetrable forests, which grew out of untillable rock and infertile sand. They dismissed it as nothing more than a wasteland, even more so than the rest of the U.P.

But then in 1840, state geologist Douglass

Houghton confirmed the presence of copper. Vast deposits of pure, native copper, much of it right near the surface, there for the taking. The young United States had an insatiable appetite for the metal, first for new industrial machinery, and later, for Civil War hardware, electrical wiring, and other innovations. Houghton's find was as good as gold. Actually, it was even better than gold.

The Copper Rush began almost overnight, first with prospectors, then large mining enterprises flooding the "wasteland" of the Keweenaw. It was the nation's first mineral rush. Copper employed thousands of immigrant laborers, built cities, made millionaires, and prompted extravagant luxuries like opera houses and "copper baron" mansions. Before it was over, King Copper generated more than $9.6 billion—10 times more money than the California gold rush.

The Keweenaw's copper legacy still looms large, but in the form of abandoned mines, ghost towns buried in the forest, and the odd juxtaposition of lavish buildings in almost-forgotten towns. Neglected for most of the 20th century, a slow pull finally began in the 1970s to preserve the Keweenaw's copper heritage. The result is the Keweenaw National Historical Park, established in 1992 (and still very much in development). To be sure, a lot of rich history has been demolished, thrown away, or crushed under the weight of winter snows. But an astounding amount remains, too.

The Keweenaw Peninsula might have its roots in veins of copper, but much of the rest of the western Upper Peninsula traces its heritage to iron. You can read it in the town names—Iron Mountain, Iron River, National Mine, Mineral Hills—and see it on the faces of the residents, an ethnically diverse mix descended from the melting pot of immigrant mine workers. The U.P.'s iron industry stretched from the western border east some 150 miles

to the Lake Superior port of Marquette and the Lake Michigan port of Escanaba. It comprised three major ranges: the Gogebic Range, with operations centered around Ironwood; the Menominee Range, based largely around the Iron River and Iron Mountain areas; and the Marquette Range, encompassing Marquette and the Ishpeming/Negaunee area.

Federal surveyors first discovered iron ore in 1844, near present-day Iron River. As workers systematically surveyed this strange landmass recently acquired by Michigan, their compasses swung wildly near Negaunee, where iron ore was so plentiful it was visible even on the surface, intertwined in the roots of a fallen tree. The tree is the official symbol of the city of Negaunee, which itself became completely intertwined with the rise and fall of the iron industry.

Aside from a handful of small mining operations, the unfathomable wealth of the Upper Peninsula's iron remained largely untapped for several decades, until the ever-expanding web of railroad lines reached the area. In the 1870s, the arrival of the railroad prompted the development of the first major mines in the Menominee Range. A few years later, the Gogebic Range opened. Many of the early mines were open-pit affairs, but soon the need for iron ore drove miners deeper and deeper underground. Today, communities like Ishpeming sit atop a swiss-cheese patch of earth riddled with mine shafts; occasionally, tracts of land sink, leaving behind tilted and abandoned houses.

World War II and its insatiable demand for iron drove area mines to peak production, eventually depleting some of them. By the 1960s and '70s, the western U.P. iron ranges grew quiet after shipping out nearly two billion tons of ore. All underground iron mines in the U.P. closed by 1978, hurt by foreign steelmakers and the use of more and more plastics in manufacturing.

WESTERN UPPER PENINSULA

Isle Royale National Park

Stranded in the vast waters of Lake Superior, Isle Royale is perhaps the model of what a national park is supposed to be—wild, rugged, and remote. No roads touch the 45-mile-long island, and its only contact with the outside world remains ship-to-shore radio. One of the least-visited parks in the National Park Service system, Isle Royale's yearly attendance is less than a single weekend's worth at Yellowstone.

Civilization on Isle Royale (ROY-al) is concentrated in two small developments at opposite ends of the island. Windigo, on the southwest end, includes an information center, a grocery, and a marina. Rock Harbor, near the northeast end, offers the same, plus a no-frills lodge and restaurant across from the ferry dock, and a handful of cabins overlooking fingerlike Tobin Harbor. The rest of the island is backcountry, 210 square miles of forested foot trails, rocky bluffs, quiet lakes, and wilderness campsites.

Those who make the trek by boat or seaplane to Isle Royale come primarily to hike its 165 miles of trails, fish its 46 inland lakes, and paddle its saw-toothed shoreline. Wildlife viewing is popular, too, especially for the moose that swam across from Ontario several decades back, and the eastern timber wolves that later followed their prey across on the pack ice. Though the wolves are notoriously elusive, you can pretty much bet that your wildlife sightings will outnumber your human ones on Isle Royale.

The geography of Isle Royale is inseparable from the water that surrounds it. Along with its namesake island—the largest in Lake Superior—Isle Royale National Park actually consists of an archipelago of some 400 islands, all of them remnants of the same landmass. More than 80 percent of the national park lies underwater, beneath shallow ponds, bogs, inland lakes, and the clear, cold water of Lake Superior. And here's some trivia: Ryan Island, located on Isle Royale's Siskiwit Lake, is the largest island in the largest lake on the largest island in the largest freshwater lake in the world.

The islands' wildlife, especially the moose and wolf populations, have been a draw for many naturalists and tourists alike. Populations for both animals have fluctuated rather dramatically over the decades. Moose, which numbered more than a 1,000 in 2002, have plummeted to less than 400, mainly due to increasingly warm summers, which have caused the moose to eat less and fatal ticks to thrive.

Still, hikers have a decent chance of spotting the 1,000-pound mammals, which often feed in ponds and lowlands or along inland lakeshores. Hidden Lake, across Tobin Harbor south of Lookout Louise, is an exceptionally good spot, since moose have a taste for its mineral licks. If you're lucky enough to come upon a moose, give it very, very wide berth. Although they look cartoonish and friendly, moose can be exceptionally dangerous if approached too closely—especially cows with calves or males during the fall rutting season—capable of inflicting lethal blows with their hooves.

The wolf population, too, has dwindled, in part because of the hot summers and the lessening of their food supply. The wolves, which numbered around 21 in 2007, tend to hide out in the remote southwestern corner of the island. Only the rare backpacker ever spots one of the shy and stealthy creatures, and many a wolf howl heard at night is probably the haunting call of a loon. But the notion that wolves are there, somewhere—perhaps even watching from deep in the forest—is compelling enough for most, especially those lucky enough to spot a paw print across the trail.

While many national parks struggle with their fate as islands of wilderness surrounded by a more developed world, Isle Royale has the advantage of a much larger buffer zone protecting it from outside encroachment and influence. As a result, it is one of the most closely managed holdings in the national park system. That's good or bad depending on your opinion of the Park Service, but it does present some unique opportunities for protecting the wilderness. For starters, it is one of the few parks that already regulates the number of visitors who pass through its "gates." Though logistics have done a sufficient job of keeping numbers down thus far, the National Park Service only has to cut back on ferry service or campsites to slow the flow.

Limited access also allows the Park Service to enforce rules more effectively. Dogs, for example, are not allowed on the island for fear they might bring rabies and other diseases to the island's wolf pack. Arrive with a poodle on your powerboat—even if it never sets paw on the dock—and you will be quickly waved off the island. Thumbsdown also to wheeled vehicles like mountain bikes or canoe carts. (Exceptions are made for wheelchairs.) The Park Service also takes great pains to preserve its backcountry solitude, with a park brochure reminding hikers to "refrain from loud conversation," "avoid songfests," and "select equipment of subtle natural tones rather than conspicuous colorful gear."

(BOAT TOURS

The Park Service shuttles visitors to various island attractions on its 25-passenger MV *Sandy.* (906/482-0984, www.nps.gov/isro, June–early Sept., fare rates vary). The *Sandy* makes several different trips in season. One four-mile boat ride takes passengers to the Hidden Lake Trailhead, where they are asked to debark and guided on a two-mile round-trip hike past Hidden Lake, up 320 feet, to **Lookout Louise.** From here, visitors can view the southern shore of Canada and the northern shore of Isle Royale.

Another trip heads across the mouth of Moskey Basin to the historic fishery of Peter and Laura Edisen, restored to show what life was like for the commercial fisheries that once thrived on the island. From **Edisen Fishery,** it's a short quarter-mile walk to the stout and simple **Rock Harbor Lighthouse,** a white edifice built in 1855 to guide ships to Isle Royale's then-busy copper ports.

Other tours feature out-of-the-way destinations such as Middle Island Passage and Starvation Point. History buffs, too, will enjoy these tours. Besides viewing the Rock Harbor Lighthouse, you can also select a tour to see the Passage Island Lighthouse, the historic Minong Mine, and the site of the *Monarch* shipwreck.

RECREATION
Hiking

Several day hikes are doable if you choose to "motel camp" in Rock Harbor. Don't miss **Scoville Point,** a 4.2-mile loop with interpretive signs that traces a rocky finger of land east of Rock Harbor. Another popular short hike is the 3.8-mile loop to **Suzy's Cave,** formed by the wave action of a once much-deeper Lake Superior. **Lookout Louise,** north of Tobin Harbor, offers one of the island's most spectacular views, looking out over its ragged northeastern shoreline. If you've got a canoe, it's a short paddle and short two-mile hike. Without a canoe, it's a fine hike along lovely Tobin Harbor and the eastern end of the Greenstone Ridge, but you'll have to retrace your steps to return to Rock Harbor, about a 20-mile trek in all.

For another all-day hike, follow the Lake Superior shoreline to the Daisy Farm campground and the Ojibway Trail, which heads north and brings you to the **Ojibway Tower,** an air-monitoring station. The tower marks the highest spot on the eastern end of the island, and you can climb its steps (but not enter the tower room) for an unmatched view of the island's interior lakes and bays on both the north and south sides of the island. Travel back via the Greenstone Ridge and along Tobin Harbor for a varied 18-mile hike that

will take you through blueberry patches, wildflower meadows, and serene shorelines. For a similar but shorter hike of about 10 miles, turn north at the Three Mile campground to ascend Mount Franklin, another high point on the Greenstone Ridge.

Canoeing

For paddlers, Isle Royale is a dream destination, a nook-and-cranny wilderness of rocky islands, secluded coves, and quiet bays interrupted only by the low call of a loon. For first-time visitors, you can't do better than the **Five Fingers,** the collection of fjord-like harbors and rocky promontories on the east end of the island. Not only is, it well protected (except from northeasterlies), it offers some of the finest and most characteristic Isle Royale scenery and solitude. Though Isle Royale is generally better suited to kayaks, open canoes can handle these waters in calm weather.

For kayaks, the entire island offers paddling opportunities, though some areas require long stretches of paddling without good shoreline access. Note that open-water passages on Lake Superior should be attempted by experienced paddlers only, and are not at all recommended in an open boat like a canoe. Capsizing in Lake Superior is not an unfortunate experience, it is a life-threatening one. With waters rarely exceeding temperatures in the 40s, hypothermia can occur in a matter of minutes. There are many places where you can rent canoes, 14-foot fishing boats, and outboard motors at Windigo and Rock Harbor.

ACCOMMODATIONS AND FOOD

Those just looking for a quiet island stay and some swell day hikes can set up a base in comfort at the **Rock Harbor Lodge** (906/337-4993 May–Sept. or 866/644-2003 Oct.–Apr., http://rockharborlodge.com, $150–300 d). Lodge rooms are pretty much your basic motel-style accommodations, but they sit right at the water's edge with a glorious view of nearby islands and the open waters of Lake Superior. You'll pay for this little slice of civilization in the wilderness, but the rate does include three meals at the lodge dining room. (Dinner often features fresh lake trout from the restored Edisen Fishery.) Guests also have use of an adjacent day lodge with a comfy wood-burning fireplace. Nearby housekeeping cottages include small kitchens, one double bed, and two bunk beds. While you can call about reservations year-round, the lodge is only open Memorial Day–Labor Day. Reservations are a must.

The **Rock Harbor Lodge dining room** (servings at 7 A.M., noon, and 5:30 P.M., $10–33) is open to the public, and its meals taste like a gourmet feast after a week of freeze-dried fare. The **Marina Store** (9 A.M.–5 P.M. daily) in Rock Harbor carries a good supply of food, camping supplies, film, fuel, and pretty much any other important item you forgot to pack.

Camping

If you want to see more of the island, camping is the way to do it. Rustic campsites are located throughout Isle Royale, with three types of sites available: tent sites for 1–3 tents, group sites for parties of 7–10 campers, and three-sided shelters that hold up to six people. You must obtain a free camping permit from the Windigo Rangers Station when you arrive, outlining your itinerary, but you can't obtain a reservation. All sites are available on a first-come, first-served basis. Should you reach a site at the end of the day and find it full (this can happen at sites a day's hike from Rock Harbor, especially in August), the unwritten rules say double up. No one expects you to hike off into the dwindling light to the next campsite.

INFORMATION AND SERVICES

For general information about the park, including camping and transportation options, contact **Isle Royale National Park** (906/482-0984, www.nps.gov/isro). You'll find few services (and probably no cell phone reception) on the islands, so be sure to stock up on supplies in Houghton or Copper Harbor before heading to Isle Royale.

Isle Royale was one of the first national parks to charge a "park user fee." Daily fees are $4 per person per day. If you're traveling to the island by ferry or seaplane, the concessionaire will collect your fee. If you're traveling by private boat, you can pay at the ranger station at Windigo or Rock Harbor, or at the Houghton Visitor Center (800 E. Lakeshore Dr., 8 A.M.–6 P.M. Mon.–Fri., 11 A.M.–6 P.M. Sat. June–July, shorter hours Aug.–May) prior to your departure. Also, remember that Isle Royale is one of the few national parks to close during the winter, from November through mid-April. This is due, of course, to extreme weather conditions, wildlife protection, and visitor safety.

GETTING THERE AND AROUND

Your options to Isle Royale are seaplane, ferry, or personal boat. The National Park Service operates the largest ferry, the 165-foot *Ranger III*. It departs from Houghton twice a week from the start of June through mid-September for the six-hour passage to Rock Harbor (same-day round-trip $75 adults, $40 children 7–12, children under 7 free). Canoes and kayaks are an additional $40. Make reservations through the national park (906/482-0984, www.nps.gov/isro).

A faster but more expensive boat, the 63-foot *Voyageur II* travels to Windigo in two hours, then continues on to Rock Harbor. On its way to Rock Harbor, it circumnavigates the island, offering drop-off and pick-up service along the way. (This makes for a slow but interesting trip.) The round-trip cost to Windigo is $118 adults, $78 children under 12; call for prices to other locations. It also can carry canoes and kayaks for additional fees. Make arrangements through **Grand Portage-Isle Royale Transportation Line** (218/475-0024 May–Oct. or 651/653-5872 Nov.–Apr., www.isleroyaleboats.com).

Seaplane service from Houghton is the most expensive but quickest way to the island—usually. The 45-minute flight is often delayed by wind and fog. From mid-May to mid-September, the plane flies on scheduled trips between Houghton County Memorial Airport and the protected bays at Windigo and Rock Harbor. The plane can carry up to five passengers for $269 round-trip per person ($185 one-way). While you won't be able to bring stove fuel on board, you can purchase it at one of the park stores on the island.

Reservations are required. For more information, contact **Royale Air Service** (877/359-4753, www.royaleairservice.com, children under two free).

Once you've arrived, you'll have little choice regarding transportation. For most, hiking or kayaking are the optimal modes for getting around the islands.

The Keweenaw Peninsula

South of Isle Royale, the enormous Keweenaw Peninsula juts out from the northern coast of the Upper Peninsula. Here, you'll find several former mining towns, a few inland lakes, and numerous historic attractions that comprise the Keweenaw National Historical Park.

The Keweenaw is home to some of the Midwest's most distinctive geology and oldest exposed rock. Part of the Precambrian Canadian Shield, the peninsula was created more than two billion years ago by spewing volcanoes and colliding continents. Much later, about 1.2 billion years ago, the hardened crust broke apart. More lava began seeping out through fissures, forming bedrock called basalt. For hundreds of years, the basalt piled up thicker and thicker; groundwater percolated in, too, filling the bubbles and cracks with minerals, creating the Keweenaw's vast deposits of pure copper.

Eventually, the basalt layers sank, forming a basin surrounded by tilted, uplifted rock. These high spots today are visible as the Keweenaw Mountain Range, the spine that runs the length of the peninsula and across Isle Royale. Consequently, the basalt found throughout the Keweenaw is believed to be among the oldest—perhaps *the* oldest—exposed volcanic rock on earth.

Though the Keweenaw's variety of minerals is not particularly vast, it contains some unusual gemstones in substantial quantity. Rock hounds seek out three in particular: porcelaneous datolite, mohawkite, and chlorastrolite. Chlorastrolite is more commonly known

as the Isle Royale greenstone, a tortoiseshell-patterned rock rarely found elsewhere in the world. The peninsula's beaches are also a good place to hunt for agates, thomsonite, epidote, zeolites, red feldspar, and others. Area mineral shops are excellent sources for guidebooks and hunting tips.

COPPER HARBOR AND VICINITY

Wedged between Lake Superior to the north and long and lovely Lake Fanny Hooe to the south, Copper Harbor marks the end of the road in the Keweenaw Peninsula. Literally. Even U.S. 41 peters out here, circling in a loop some 1,990 miles from its other terminus in Miami. The tip of the peninsula probably draws people precisely because it is the end of the road. And when they get there, they discover one of the Upper Peninsula's most scenic natural areas and one of its most appealing little towns.

Downtown

Tiny Copper Harbor, population 80, offers more than you might expect from its size. If shopping is your thing, check out the Finnish pottery at **Sataman Ruukku** (906/289-4636, hours vary), a shed-like storefront on U.S. 41. (No one has—or needs—a street address in a town just a few blocks long.) Rock hounds will appreciate the **Keweenaw Agate Shop** (906/353-7285, hours vary) and **Swede's Gift Shop** (906/289-4596, hours vary), both with a good selection of local minerals and,

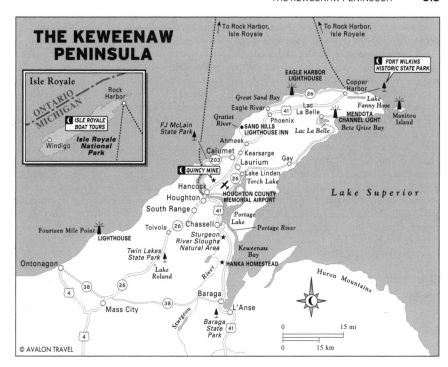

THE KEWEENAW PENINSULA

To Rock Harbor, Isle Royale

To Rock Harbor, Isle Royale

Isle Royale

ONTARIO
MICHIGAN

Rock Harbor

ISLE ROYALE BOAT TOURS

Windigo

Isle Royale National Park

FORT WILKINS HISTORIC STATE PARK

EAGLE HARBOR LIGHTHOUSE

Copper Harbor

Lake Fanny Hooe

Great Sand Bay

Eagle River

Lac La Belle

MENDOTA CHANNEL LIGHT

Manitou Island

Gratiot River

Phoenix

FJ McLain State Park

SAND HILLS LIGHTHOUSE INN

Lac La Belle

Bete Grise Bay

Ahmeek

Calumet

Kearsarge

Gay

QUINCY MINE

Laurium

Lake Linden

Torch Lake

Lake Superior

Hancock

Houghton

South Range

HOUGHTON COUNTY MEMORIAL AIRPORT

Portage Lake

Fourteen Mile Point

LIGHTHOUSE

Toivola

Chassell

Portage River

Twin Lakes State Park

Sturgeon River Sloughs Natural Area

Keweenaw Bay

Ontonagon

Lake Roland

HANKA HOMESTEAD

Mass City

Baraga

L'Anse

Baraga State Park

Huron Mountains

0   15 mi

0   15 km

© AVALON TRAVEL

---

as the Keweenaw Agate Shop advertises, "advice and stories." You won't find a full-service grocery store in Copper Harbor, so load up in Houghton or Calumet if you're planning a campout or cabin stay.

Boat Tours

You can't reach the **Copper Harbor Lighthouse** (906/289-4966, www.copperharborlighthouse. com, hours vary May–Oct., $15 adults, $10 children under 12) by land since adjacent property owners refuse to grant right-of-way, so the Park Service has arranged for boat tours of the light and keeper's house, which contains a small worthwhile museum. Originally built in 1849 and replaced in 1866, the stone lighthouse is the oldest operating light on Lake Superior. (Nowadays, however, an adjacent 62-foot-tall steel tower actually performs the site's navigational duties.)

Just wandering around the lovely rocky point

is worth the trip. It was on this point, by the way, where Douglass Houghton first spotted a thick green stripe in the rock indicating the presence of copper, a discovery that unleashed the Keweenaw's copper boom. The 90-minute tour leaves from the municipal marina several times. Also ask about sunset cruises.

C Fort Wilkins Historic State Park

The history of Fort Wilkins (15223 U.S. 41, 906/289-4215, campsites $16–25) reads like one of those overblown military spending stories of the 20th century. With miners pouring north during the Copper Rush, the federal government feared fighting would surely erupt between miners and the local Indian tribes, and ordered the construction of a garrisoned fort. In 1844, they sent troops of more than 100 men, who built barracks, a mess hall, a hospital, and other buildings behind a tall stockade fence, then hunkered down to fend off the fighting. Only no fighting ever erupted, and winters proved long, cold, and desolate. By the following year, half the troops were pulled out and sent south, where the country faced the threat of war with Mexico. By 1846, the rest were gone.

Today, Fort Wilkins stands as one of the only wooden forts remaining east of the Mississippi, with 16 whitewashed buildings wonderfully restored and filled with exhibits of life on the northern frontier. From mid-June to late August, costumed "inhabitants" even re-create military life. Along with the fort, the state park includes rocky and scenic Lake Superior frontage, a few short hiking trails, the 1866 Copper Harbor Lighthouse, and an excellent campground on Lake Fanny Hooe.

Brockway Mountain Drive

Dubbed "the most beautiful road in Michigan," this 10-mile route traces the spine of a high ridge between Copper Harbor and Eagle Harbor. Rising 735 feet above Lake Superior, it is the highest paved road between the Rockies and Allegheny Mountains. A parking area midway allows you to stop and soak in the panorama of Lake Superior and the rolling forests of the Keweenaw, an incredible vista no matter how many times you've seen it. Watch for ravens, bald eagles, and peregrine falcons—which sometimes soar below you. Traveling west to east, the end of the drive is marked by a picture-postcard shot of Copper Harbor, tucked between Lake Superior and Lake Fanny Hooe. From this drive, you might catch a glimpse of the 1871 **Eagle Harbor Light,** now site of a maritime museum (10 A.M.–5 P.M. daily mid-June–early Oct., $4 adults, children free), operated by the Keweenaw County Historical Society.

CALUMET

At the height of the Keweenaw's copper-mining glory, the Calumet and Hecla Consolidated Copper Company, operating largely in Calumet, proved the grandest operation of all. At the turn of the 20th century, C&H employed some 11,000 workers, who extracted more than 1.5 billion tons of copper from a web of mines tunneled out under Calumet. Striking red sandstone buildings with false fronts and cornices lined the 12-square-block downtown, filled with elegant shops, soaring churches, some 70 saloons, even a lavish theater that attracted the nation's leading vaudeville stars. The city buzzed day and night both above—and belowground.

After mining died, no one ever bothered to "modernize" Calumet. As a result, downtown Calumet is a marvel of architecture from the early 1900s, and was a deciding factor in the area earning national historical park status.

Downtown Calumet

Thanks to the national historical park and renewed civic pride, downtown Calumet looks more like a movie set everyday. Ugly 1960s facades are coming down off the elegant sandstone and brick buildings, and new money is coming in to further restore and preserve them.

© L. DIGGS, PICTURE THIS...

the Eagle Harbor Light

THE GIPPER OF LAURIUM

Born in Laurium on the Keweenaw Peninsula, George Gipp (1895-1920) attended Notre Dame University on a baseball scholarship. There, famed football coach Knute Rockne, recognizing an innate athletic talent, lured him onto the gridiron, where Gipp excelled as a runner, passer, punter, kicker, defensive back, and kick returner. During his collegiate career, he amassed over 8,200 yards in rushing, passing, kickoffs, and punts, and scored more than 150 points, including numerous touchdowns. Despite his incredible football skills, his first love remained baseball; in fact, he continued to play centerfield for Notre Dame's team and planned to join the Chicago Cubs following graduation.

In 1920, Gipp was named Notre Dame University's first all-American football player, but he didn't have long to celebrate the honor. Fol-lowing a winning game against Northwestern on November 20, he contracted pneumonia and died on December 14. Though he was celebrated for his talent, grace, humor, generosity, and leadership skills, it is undoubtedly his final words that have sustained his legend. From his deathbed, he supposedly told his coach: "I've got to go, Rock. It's all right. I'm not afraid. Some time, Rock, when the team is up against it, when things are wrong and the breaks are beating the boys, tell them to go in there with all they've got and win just one for the Gipper. I don't know where I'll be then, Rock. But I'll know about it, and I'll be happy." The Gipper's inspiring story was made famous by Ronald Reagan in the film *Knute Rockne-All American* (1940), which solidified his legacy in the minds and hearts of many a football fan.

To appreciate this architectural bonanza, stop by the **Keweenaw Convention & Visitors Bureau** (56638 Calumet Ave., 906/337-4579, www.keweenaw.info, 9 A.M.–5 P.M. Mon.–Fri.) to pick up a walking tour guide. A few stops of particular note: The **Union Building,** at 5th and Red Jacket, was home to one of the area's first banks in 1888 and remains in excellent shape, with a decorative metal cornice. **Shute's Bar** (322 6th St.) doesn't look that special on the outside, but the interior preserves ornate plaster ceilings and a magnificent back bar with a stained-glass canopy. The **Red Jacket Town Hall and Opera House,** now called the **Historic Calumet Theater** (340 6th St., 906/337-2610, $4 adults, $1.50 children 6–12), was the pride of the community. The theater portion, added in 1898 as the first municipally owned theater in the country, was a showy extravagance of plaster rococo in cream, crimson, green, and gilt. It even had electric lights!

Coppertown USA

The mine's pattern shop, where wooden patterns were made as molds for machine parts, now serves as the home of Coppertown USA (Red Jacket Rd., 906/337-4354, 10 A.M.–5 P.M. Mon.–Sat., 12:30 P.M.–4 P.M. Sun. June–mid-Oct., $3 adults, $1 children 12–18), a privately run museum (and national park cooperating site) that traces the region's copper industry. It includes loads of artifacts, a display of area minerals, a replica of a mining captain's office, a diorama of Native American mining, and more, with all the exhibits close enough to really examine.

HOUGHTON AND HANCOCK

When the hip outdoor sporting magazine *Outside* listed Houghton (Hoe-ton) among America's "next wave of dream towns," you knew times were a-changin'. Ho-where? Well, turns out *Outside* may have something here. Houghton—and the adjacent city of Hancock—not only offers great sporting diversions, it boasts a quirky ethnic flair, streets lined with beautifully preserved early-1900 buildings, and a university to add a dollop of culture and liveliness. If you find old mining ruins intriguing instead of ugly, then the Houghton and Hancock area is downright pretty, too.

Houghton (population 7,000) and Hancock (population 4,300) face each other across the Portage Waterway, with homes and churches tumbling down steep 500-foot bluffs. (Especially on the Hancock side, streets can be downright unnerving, rivaling those in San Francisco for pitch.) The Portage Waterway effectively slices the Keweenaw in two, a 21-mile passage that saves boaters the 100-mile-trip around the peninsula.

A unique lift bridge spans the waterway to link Houghton and Hancock, its huge center section rising like an elevator to let water traffic pass. Today, the Portage Waterway largely serves pleasure boaters and the 125-foot *Ranger III,* the ferry that transports hikers to Isle Royale National Park, 70 miles northwest. Houghton and Hancock are considered the gateways to the Keweenaw and to Isle Royale—but visitors just whizzing through will miss an appealing slice of the region.

Downtown

You can conduct your own historic walking tour of Houghton by strolling down **Shelden Avenue,** the city's main street. Tall facades of red brick and red sandstone line the street, like the **Douglass House Hotel** (517 Shelden Ave.), built in 1860 as a luxury hotel and dining establishment for travelers through the Portage Waterway. An addition in 1899 provided the lavish building you see today. The **Finnish-American Heritage Center** (601 Quincy St., 906/487-7367, 9 A.M.–5 P.M. daily, free) maintains a gallery open to the public that features Finnish artists, as well as archives of the area's Finnish settlement.

◖ Quincy Mine

Just north of Hancock, the mammoth shaft house of the Quincy Mine (906/482-3101, www.quincymine.com, 9:30 A.M.–5 P.M. daily in summer, hours vary in fall/winter, $15 adults, $8 children 6–12) dominates the skyline. The Quincy ranked as one of the world's richest copper mines in the late 1800s, producing over a billion pounds of copper. Today, a few of its buildings still stand, and the land

the Quincy Mine hoist house, part of the Keweenaw National Historical Park beneath it remains stitched with the shafts which stretched more than a mile-and-a-half deep—92 levels!—and two miles wide.

From the hoist house, the tour starts with a rather dramatic ride in a glass-enclosed tram down the side of a steep hill. Views of Houghton and Hancock are terrific as the tram descends to an entrance to the mine, an adit at Level 7. A tractor carries you a couple thousand feet into the mine, where guides demonstrate mining techniques and give you a feel for what it was like to work deep inside the earth, in a drippy, damp environment with only hand tools and candles.

BARAGA AND L'ANSE

While Baraga and L'Anse suffer from stuttering economies, the Keweenaw Bay Indian Community economy is on the upswing. Ojibwa tribal leaders here were among the first to profit from treaty rights that allow them to establish gaming on tribal lands along Keweenaw Bay. Today, the popular **Ojibwa Casino and Resort** (16449 Michigan Ave., 906/353-6333, www.ojibwacasino.com) generates millions of dollars in revenues and feeds much-needed tax dollars into the local economy. Other tribes have followed suit and opened successful casinos throughout the U.P. and the northern Lower Peninsula. Consequently, tribal governments now wield considerable influence in the region.

On a more traditional note, the tribe also hosts a colorful **powwow** each July, a traditional celebration of dancing and drumming. On the eastern shore of Keweenaw Bay, north of L'Anse, you can visit an Ojibwa burial ground from the mid-1800s, with spirit houses marking graves. These small shelters held offerings of food, provisions to help sustain the soul on its journey to the afterlife.

KEWEENAW NATIONAL HISTORICAL PARK

The Keweenaw National Historical Park (headquarters: 25970 Red Jacket Rd., Calumet, 906/337-3168, www.nps.gov/kewe, 9 A.M.–5 P.M. Mon.–Fri.) is not so much a place on a map but a place in time. The state's newest national park, it was established in 1992 "to commemorate the heritage of copper mining on the Keweenaw Peninsula—its mines, its machinery, and its people."

Rather than a park with simply defined boundaries, the Keweenaw National Historical Park consists of historic attractions throughout the Keweenaw. Two units anchor the park—the Quincy Unit at the Quincy Mine in Hancock and the Calumet Unit in historic downtown Calumet—but some of this land remains in private ownership. The National Park Service owns just a limited amount of land to preserve key sites and conduct interpretive activities. In addition, the park has designated "cooperating sites" throughout the peninsula, including mine tours and museums that will also remain in private ownership, but will continue to benefit from increased visibility and federal monies.

GHOST TOWNS

Ghost towns litter the Keweenaw, faded testament to the boom-and-bust days of copper. The ruins of old mines and stamping plants (facilities that separated copper from rock) line M-26 between Hancock and Calumet. The gray piles of residue are mine tailings or stamping plant leftovers called "stamp sand." Several bona fide ghost towns hide in the woods, too, especially between Calumet and Copper Harbor. At **Central** (watch for the small brown sign on U.S. 41 about 11 miles north of Mohawk), an exceptionally rich mine produced nearly $10 million by 1898; the surrounding town grew to 1,200. Today, nature has all but reclaimed Central, with just a few clapboard houses creaking in the breeze. Turn right near the top of the hill for a look at the mine ruins and rows of house foundations. Watch where you're walking.

Just south of Copper Harbor on U.S. 41, another sign announces your "arrival" in **Mandan,** directing you down a dirt road disappearing into birches. Follow it south for about 50 yards and homes suddenly erupt out of the woods, lined up in a tidy row. Welcome to Mandan, the last stop on a trolley line from Hancock.

FESTIVALS AND EVENTS

Despite its relative isolation from the rest of Michigan, the Keweenaw Peninsula plays host to numerous events and celebrations throughout the year. In winter, residents honor the frigid temperatures with ice-fishing derbies, cross-country skiing races, a winter carnival on the campus of Michigan Technological University, and **Heikinpäivä** (www.pasty.com/heikki), a Finnish American festival that takes place around January 19 every year, mainly in Houghton. Presenting traditional Finnish crafts, music, cuisine, and more, this annual event honors the Finnish culture that helped build this area and remains a significant part of it today. In Hancock alone, 40 percent of the population still claims Finnish ancestry.

Of course, the milder months are even busier on the Keweenaw Peninsula. Between May's **International Migratory Bird Day Festival** (www.keweenawimbd.org) in Copper Harbor and the **Houghton County Fair** (www.houghtoncountyfair.com) every August, you'll surely find something to do on the Keweenaw all through the summer. Of course, besides bicycle races, art fairs, and heritage events, one of the most popular annual events is Houghton's **Bridgefest** (906/370-2399, www.bridgefestfun.com), a mid-June celebration of the Portage Lake Lift Bridge—or perhaps just an excuse for the community to enjoy live concerts, sporting events, boat tours, arts-and-crafts exhibits, fireworks displays, and a seafood festival, where even live lobster is part of the fun.

RECREATION

Anglers and hunters increasingly find themselves sharing the backwoods and waters with hikers, mountain bikers, and paddlers.

Hiking and Biking

Mountain bikers new to the area can hardly believe the wealth of terrific trails in the Keweenaw, literally hundreds of miles of old mining and logging roads, overgrown double-track routes, and technical single-track. They loop through towering pines to backwoods waterfalls, to otherwise inaccessible Lake Superior shorelines, even past ghost towns now buried deep in the woods. (Consider it fair warning that many trails also peter out and stop in the middle of nowhere.)

Vast tracts of land in the Keweenaw are privately owned by large corporations—some mining firms, but mostly paper companies. In exchange for a break in state taxes, the companies allow public use of the land for recreation, including hiking, fishing, and mountain biking. Still, for liability reasons, some outfitters and bike shops are loath to hand out maps or "endorse" these lands for riding. If you ask, though, most bike shops tend to be quite helpful about suggesting trails, especially the **Keweenaw Adventure Company** (145 Gratiot St., Copper Harbor, 906/289-4303, www.keweenawadventure.com), a company that began in 1994 and now helps to organize the annual **Copper Harbor Fat Tire Festival,** a mountain-biking race in late summer.

Canoeing and Kayaking

This growing sport is at its finest in the Keweenaw, where you have plenty of islands, rock formations, and wilderness coastlines to explore. The **Keweenaw Adventure Company** (145 Gratiot St., Copper Harbor, 906/289-4303, www.keweenawadventure.com) rents kayaks, guides trips, and offers lessons. Beginners should try the 2.5-hour introductory paddle, which includes novice dry-land instruction and a fine little trip around the harbor and along the Lake Superior shoreline. The Keweenaw Adventure Company also offers some daylong trips around the peninsula—to Horseshoe Harbor, Agate Harbor, and the mouth of the Montreal River—as scheduling permits.

Rivers in the Keweenaw tend to be pretty bony, so white-water kayaking is limited (though this varies with the year's precipitation). Sea kayaking, on the other hand, is outstanding, the perfect way to access bluffs, caves, sea stacks and rocky islands all along the Lake Superior shoreline. The Keweenaw Water Trail, still under development, guides small craft around the peninsula and through the Portage Waterway. Isle Royale makes for an excellent paddling destination, too, and the ferries will transport kayaks and canoes for an additional fee. Canoeing is popular on inland lakes, but open boats are not recommended on Lake Superior.

Diving

The cold, clear freshwater of Lake Superior offers outstanding visibility for divers. Though there isn't much to look at in the way of plant and animal life—the cold waters make for a pretty sterile-looking environment—the waters provide plenty of entertainment in the form of interesting underwater geologic formations and shipwrecks.

Ships have been running aground for well over a hundred years around the Keweenaw Peninsula, a navigational hazard if there ever was one. Within the 103-square-mile **Keweenaw Underwater Preserve,** divers can explore the *Tioga,* a freighter that ran aground near Eagle River in 1919, and the *City of St. Joseph,* which met its fate north of Eagle Harbor in 1942. Both ships lie in less than 40 feet of water, with large sections of the hull, deck machinery, and other artifacts clearly visible.

One of the Upper Peninsula's oldest shipwrecks, the *John Jacob Astor,* lies just offshore from Copper Harbor, near the Fort Wilkins State Park Lighthouse Overlook. An Underwater Trail marks the location of the rudder, anchor, and other remnants of the *Astor,* which sank in 1844. For more information, contact the **Michigan Underwater Preserve Council** (800/970-8717, www.michiganpreserves.org).

Winter Activities

A giant snow gauge on U.S. 41 south of Phoenix proudly marks the Keweenaw's record snowfall, a staggering 390.4 inches in the winter of 1977–78. It wasn't an aberration; the surrounding waters of Lake Superior routinely generate colossal lake effect snows, often averaging over 300 inches. That reliable snowfall, combined

© KEWEENAW PENINSULA CHAMBER OF COMMERCE

snowmobiling on the Keweenaw Peninsula

with the remarkable local terrain, makes the Keweenaw a haven for snowmobilers, skiers, and snowshoers. Downhill skiers can check out Michigan's most challenging terrain at **Mount Bohemia** (100 Lac La Belle Rd., 231/420-5405, www.mtbohemia.com, 10:30 A.M.–4:30 P.M. Mon.–Fri., 9:30 A.M.–6 P.M. Sat.–Sun., $47 lift tickets) near Lac La Belle.

ACCOMMODATIONS

Located high on a ridge above Copper Harbor, the log lodge and cabins of the **(C Keweenaw Mountain Lodge** (U.S. 41, 906/289-4403, www.atthelodge.com, $95–169 d) were built as a public works project in the 1930s. Reservations here can be tough, but shoot for a cabin rather than an uninspired motel room (added much later than the other buildings). Meanwhile, the no-frills rooms at the **King Copper Motel** (Copper Harbor, 906/289-4214, www.kingcoppermotel.com, $50–100 d) come with great views of the harbor. Just a few steps from the ferry dock, this is a perfect spot for a warm shower and a real bed after a hard-core week on Isle Royale.

For a truly unforgettable experience, consider spending the night at the **(C Sand Hills**

Lighthouse Inn (5 Mile Point Rd., Ahmeek, 906/337-1744, www.sandhillslighthouseinn. com, $135–200 d), a beautifully preserved lighthouse constructed in 1919 and now serving as a year-round Victorian-style bed-and-breakfast. Listed on the National Register of Historic Places, this romantic spot offers eight lovely rooms, each with a roomy bed and private bathroom. Two of the chambers even have whirlpool bathtubs and a balcony overlooking Lake Superior.

The **Wonderland Motel and Cabins** (787 Lake Linden Ave., Laurium, 906/337-4511, $50–75 d) offers decent budget-friendly accommodations, complete with kitchens in the cabins. For such a small metropolitan area, Houghton's lodgings run a bit on the pricey side. A good mom-and-pop operation is the **Downtowner Motel** (110 Shelden Ave., 906/482-4421, $69–99 d). The **Carla's Lake Shore Motel** (14258 U.S. 41, Baraga, 906/353-6256, www.carlasinn.com, $52–58 d) has clean, inexpensive rooms with a view of Keweenaw Bay, and it gets bonus points for allowing your pooch.

Camping

Fort Wilkins Historic State Park (15223 U.S. 41, Copper Harbor, 906/289-4215, state park vehicle permit required, $16–25) has 159 modern sites in two campgrounds, both on Lake Fanny Hooe. Many sites sit along the water and offer decent privacy. For reservations, call 800/447-2757.

West of Ahmeek, the **Sunset Bay RV Resort & Campground** (2701 Sunset Bay Beach Rd., Eagle River, 906/337-2494 June–Oct. or 941/232-4832 Nov.–May, www.sun-set-bay.com, $22–27) indeed offers a fine view of the sunset from your tent flap. Many of its 12 tent sites and 18 RV spaces sit on Lake Superior. Three cabins, modern restrooms, a laundry and dump station, a nice swimming beach, a small boat launch, several hiking trails, and wireless Internet access are also available. Keep in mind that many locals simply head out into the woods on weekends and set up camp near a favorite stretch of beach or

river. If you choose to do the same, respect "No Trespassing" signs and observe all backcountry camping practices (such as burying waste, hanging packs, etc.).

Sunsets get top billing at **McLain State Park** (18350 M-203, Hancock, 906/482-0278, state park vehicle permit required, $16–26 sites, $60 cabins), where the sky often glows in peaches and pinks before the sun melts into Lake Superior. Like most Michigan state parks, the campsites are fine, too, and many come with those waterfront views. Follow M-203 seven miles north of Hancock. For reservations, call 800/447-2757.

FOOD

The **Pines** (906/289-4222, 8 A.M.–9 P.M. daily, $4–15), a small café in downtown Copper Harbor, is great for rainy-day breakfasts, with its homemade cinnamon rolls and crackling fireplace. Delicious soups, sandwiches, and local fish specialties keep folks coming all day. The adjacent **Zik's Bar** (906/289-4222, 10:30 A.M.–close) is the hangout for Copper Harbor locals.

In Eagle Harbor, the **Shoreline Restaurant** (906/289-4441) draws 'em in for homemade pies, but there's plenty of other home-style cooking—like soups, sandwiches and well-prepared fresh lake trout—to make it worth the stop. **Fitzgerald's Restaurant** (5033 Front St., 906/337-0666, 11 A.M.–9 P.M. daily, $9–27), located in the Eagle River Inn, offers upscale dining overlooking Lake Superior. The menu features Black Angus steaks, fresh fish and seafood, inventive vegetarian dishes, and a comprehensive wine list.

Combine a college town with a large ethnic population, and you'll conjure up a good range of eating options in the Houghton/Hancock area. **Marie's Deli & Restaurant** (518 Shelden Ave., Houghton, 906/482-8650, 9 A.M.–9 P.M. daily, $4–16) is a terrific find—the place for homemade breads, soups, sandwiches, salads, vegetarian options, and lots of Middle Eastern dishes like kibbie and spinach pies, reflecting the Lebanese heritage of its cheery owner. It's a good value at breakfast, lunch, and dinner.

INFORMATION AND SERVICES

For more information about the Keweenaw Peninsula, including attractions and lodging, contact the **Keweenaw Convention & Visitors Bureau** (56638 Calumet Ave., Calumet, 906/337-4579, www.keweenaw.info, 9 A.M.–5 P.M. Mon.–Fri.) or the **Keweenaw Peninsula Chamber of Commerce** (902 College Ave., Houghton, 906/482-5240, www.keweenaw.org, 9 A.M.–6 P.M. Mon.–Fri.). If you're hankering for a dose of local news, consult the daily *Mining Gazette* (www.mininggazette.com).

The twin towns of Houghton and Hancock represent the area's largest population center, where you'll find the lion's share of area services, like medical care, public transportation, and post offices. They also serve as the unofficial gateway to the Keweenaw, even though they sit halfway up the peninsula. In case of an emergency while visiting the Keweenaw, dial **911** from any cell or public phone. For medical assistance, consult **Portage Health** (906/483-1000, www.portagehealth.org), which offers facilities in Houghton and Hancock.

GETTING THERE AND AROUND

Bus service is spotty in the U.P. in general, and in the Keweenaw in particular. While you can certainly fly into the **Houghton County Memorial Airport (CMX)** (Houghton, 906/482-3970, www.houghtoncounty.org), it can be an expensive way to go. For those traveling by car, U.S. 41 and M-26 are the main routes to the peninsula. Many secondary roads in the Keweenaw are dirt or gravel. For old logging roads and other questionable routes, a four-wheel-drive vehicle is highly recommended.

Ontonagon to Ironwood

From Ontonagon to Ironwood, once thriving mining communities, stretches some of the most untamed wilderness in all of Michigan. This western edge of the Upper Peninsula is definitely a recreationist's dream, favored for fishing, canoeing, hunting, hiking, and snowmobiling.

Come November, Lake Superior snows inundate the region, marketed to downhill skiers throughout the Midwest as "Big Snow Country." Many visitors never get past the area's well-known downhill resorts and the homely stretch of U.S. 2 that links them. Their loss, because when the snow melts, a beautiful landscape emerges of inland lakes and rivers for fishing and paddling, and hundreds of miles of national forest trails for hiking and biking. After all, even in Big Snow Country, it stops snowing eventually—at least for a few months, anyway.

ONTONAGON

The Ontonagon Boulder was pried from its namesake riverbank a few miles upstream from the Lake Superior shoreline community of Ontonagon. Today, the two-ton mass of native copper resides at the Smithsonian, and Ontonagon's mining heritage thrives now only in museums—especially since the nearby copper mine and smelter in White Pine closed in 1995. (Nowadays, White Pine is little more than a creepy ghost town of 1950s tract housing.)

Check out Ontonagon's happier heyday at the worthwhile **Ontonagon County Historical Museum** (422 River St., 906/884-6165, www.ontonagonmuseum.com, 10 A.M.–5 P.M. Mon.–Fri., 10 A.M.–4 P.M. Sun.), a lavender building on M-38, downtown's main street. The Historical Society's biggest project these days has been restoring the 1866 **Ontonagon Light,** which replaced one of Lake Superior's first lighthouses, built in 1853.

◖ PORCUPINE MOUNTAINS WILDERNESS STATE PARK

Anchored along the Lake Superior shore in the northwest corner of the U.P., Porcupine Mountains Wilderness State Park (33303

Headquarters Rd., Ontonagon, 906/885-5275, state park vehicle permit required) covers 59,020 acres, the largest in Michigan's excellent state park system. The Porcupine Mountains were considered as a national park site in the 1940s, but were quickly preserved as a state park in 1945 when loggers threatened to get to work on their virgin timber before the federal government took action.

Someone once decided that this rumpled landscape of low mountains and tall pines looked like the silhouette of a porcupine. Hmm. But the name stuck, endearingly dubbed "the Porkies." It is a mecca for casual hikers and hard-core backpackers alike, home to 90-plus miles of well-marked, well-maintained trails—more than you'll find in many national parks, and certainly more than you'll find in most of the Great Lakes region.

And in this case, bigger also means better. The park preserves vast stands of virgin hemlock, pine, and hardwoods—the largest tract of virgin hardwoods between the Rockies and Adirondacks, in fact—secluded lakes, wild rivers, and some of the Midwest's highest peaks. (Summit Peak tops out at 1,958 feet.) Unlike most state parks, the Porkies are large enough to provide a sense of wilderness and serenity, an escape from the civilized world.

Hiking

Many park visitors head immediately for the justly famous **Lake of the Clouds Overlook.** From the parking lot at the end of M-107, it's just a few steps to the overlook, where the placid lake slices a long sliver of blue through a thick mat of jade forest hundreds of feet below. The view is the stuff postcards are made of and is probably the most photographed scene in the U.P.

The overlook also serves as the trailhead for some of the park's most rugged and scenic routes. To properly soak in the Lake of the Clouds view, hike the aptly named **Escarpment Trail,** which winds east and skims over Cloud Peak and Cuyahoga Peak. Bordered by a sheer cliff, the four-mile trail is considered by many to be the most beautiful in the park. Allow ample

Lake of the Clouds

time to stop and enjoy the shimmering lake and valley floor spreading out around you.

Long before the Porcupine Mountains were preserved for their virgin timber and natural beauty, miners harvested the rich minerals buried in their bedrock. At the east end of the park, the **Union Mine Trail** provides a glimpse into the 1840s, when the Porkies pulsed with the excitement of the area's copper rush. Marked with white mine shovels to indicate points of interest, this self-guided interpretive trail forms a mile loop along the spring-fed Union River and the site of an old copper mine, now largely swallowed by nature. In the shadow of lofty hemlocks, you'll see how miners tunneled shafts into the riverbank and learn about their life in the wilderness—a wilderness still untamed today.

In winter, the park's many hiking trails double as cross-country skiing trails. Just be careful of the higher ones. On days when the strong north wind is blowing, you'll feel the windchill all the way from Canada.

Camping

Campers have their choice of two campgrounds ($14–25), both with a number of sites overlooking Lake Superior: Union Bay (with full hookups and modern restrooms) at the east end of the park or rustic Presque Isle (no hookups) near the mouth of the Presque Isle River on the park's western edge. In addition, three rustic campgrounds (called "outposts") with 3–8 sites each are located off the South Boundary Road, accessible by car, but with no facilities. They tend to offer more privacy than the actual campgrounds.

As another option, the park offers 19 hike-in rustic cabins ($60). These are great retreats after a day on the trail. They come with 2–8 bunks, mattresses, a woodstove, basic utensils, and protection from the elements, but no electricity or running water. Bring your own stove for cooking. Cabins situated on inland lakes even come with a rowboat, so you can finish the day with a lazy drift across the water. Three yurts ($60) and a lodge are also available. Reserve any of these as much as a year in advance (800/447-2757).

Information

Start your visit at the park's **visitors center** at the junction of M-107 and South Boundary Road. Rangers on duty can provide you with maps and suggest trails. A gift shop has topo maps and a good selection of nature guidebooks.

Getting There and Around

Two roads lead to Porcupine Mountains Wilderness State Park, located 65 miles northeast of Ironwood. From Wakefield, County Road 519 leads to the park's western edge and the Presque Isle campground. From Bergland, M-64 heads north to Lake Superior, where it meets up with M-107 near the park's eastern boundary. The South Boundary Road connects both roads along, yes, the southern end of the park.

OTTAWA NATIONAL FOREST

Although backpackers could get lost amid the deep woods of Ottawa, and anglers favor Lake Gogebic east of Ironwood, visitors should be sure to visit the **Sturgeon River Gorge Wilderness Area.** The Sturgeon River, a federally designated wild and scenic river, travels a circuitous route through much of Baraga County before bleeding into Portage Lake near Chassell. One of the three wilderness areas within the national forest, the Sturgeon River Gorge Wilderness protects 14,000 acres that surround this river and its tributaries. The highlight is west of U.S. 41 and south of M-38, where the river cuts and tumbles through a magnificent 300-foot-high gorge. To reach it, follow Forest Road 2200 north from Sidnaw. Follow signs onto Forest Road 2270 to reach a parking area and foot trail that winds down about a half-mile or so to a cascade and the river. Continue west from the parking area on Forest Road 2270 to reach Silver Mountain, with stone steps that lead to a remarkable valley view. Come in fall for a fiery display by the abundant maple forest.

The U.S. Forest Service has marked few trails within the wilderness area, which, of course, is its appeal for those who love the backcountry. Several grown-over logging

A DYNASTY OF PINE

In the mid-1800s, a young and growing United States suddenly had an insatiable appetite for lumber. Settlers, moving west into the treeless plains, needed lumber to build their new towns; burgeoning cities needed lumber to build more homes and businesses; and railroads needed lumber as they laid mile after mile of track to connect it all.

Michigan's natural resources proved the perfect mix to fuel a hungry nation. Immense white pines and other conifers grew thick and tall across the Upper Peninsula and more than half of the Lower Peninsula. Rivers honeycombed through these vast forests, providing a route to the Great Lakes, which in turn connected the northern wilderness to Chicago, Detroit, and other railroad centers in the south. Mother Nature had created the perfect delivery system for the logging industry.

Around 1850, logging camps began springing up deep in the woods, from the western U.P. to the shores of Lake Huron. Young men streamed north, some of them farm laborers looking for winter wages, others newly arrived immigrants looking to gain a foothold in their new homeland. It was not easy work. The lumberjacks worked by hand, with ax and saw, tree after tree, acre after acre. With a shout of "timber!" the old pines came down with an earth-shaking thud, some of them as much as 20 feet in circumference and 100 feet tall.

The logging camps operated primarily in the winter months, when it was easier to transport the huge logs. With horses and sleighs, workers hauled the logs from the woods to the river's edge, branded the ends with the lumber company's mark, and stacked them there until spring, when they were floated downriver to waiting sawmills on the Great Lakes.

In spring, when the ice melted, the colorful and chaotic log drives began. Thousands of logs were shoved into northern rivers, guided downstream by daredevil workers known as "river pigs," who danced across the dangerous mass of moving wood, using hooks, poles and sometimes dynamite to dislodge log jams. It was the most dangerous job in the trade; with one misstep, river pigs ended up crushed between tons of logs or trapped underwater.

Once at the mills, the jumble of logs was sorted according to the mill owner's mark, and floated into mill storage ponds. From there, buzzing sawmills sliced it into lumber and loaded it onto lumber schooners — and later, barges and steamers — headed primarily to Chicago, the nation's largest lumber market and railroad hub.

In its heyday, the logging industry gener-

---

roads wind through the area for hikers who want to explore on their own. (A topo map is an absolute necessity.) Camping is permitted throughout the wilderness, and you can find some pretty choice spots out there.

Information

To make sense of what the Ottawa has to offer, start with a map. You can pick up a small brochure or large topo map at **Ottawa National Forest Headquarters** (E6248 U.S. 2, Ironwood, 906/932-1330, 9 A.M.–6 P.M. Mon.–Fri.). Other district offices, in Ontonagon and Watersmeet, may have maps and brochures, but budget cuts have forced them to curtail other visitor services.

IRONWOOD AREA

With mammoth Lake Superior providing the requisite moisture, the northwestern corner of the U.P. isn't exaggerating when it markets itself as Big Snow Country. Cool air moving across the warmer waters of Lake Superior create lake effect snows when they hit land, generating an average of 200 inches per season. This combines nicely with the area's rugged hills and Midwestern mountains, home to many of the Midwest's largest downhill ski resorts. As a result, the western U.P., especially around Ironwood, is one of the Upper Peninsula's more heavily marketed tourism areas, luring sizable crowds of skiers up I-39/U.S. 51 every weekend from Wisconsin and the Chicago area.

ated billions of feet of lumber and billions of dollars, the actual numbers almost incalculable. Lumber companies made all sorts of proclamations: Michigan mills asserted they produced enough lumber to lay an inch-thick plank across the state.

Success stories were everywhere. A sawmill in Hermansville, Michigan, came up with the idea of tongue-and-groove flooring, and quickly became the largest flooring plant in the country, crafting the floors for the Mormon Temple in Salt Lake City and the main lodge across Yellowstone National Park. Timber barons' homes were marvels of hand-carved mahogany, gold-leaf inlay, and cut-crystal chandeliers.

But the era that everyone thought would last forever lasted less than 50 years. By 1900, nearly all the big trees were gone – a scorched, denuded landscape of stump prairies left in their place. When farmers were able to convert some of the southernmost pineries into useful crop land, ambitious entrepreneurs sought to do the same in the north. A newspaper publisher in Menominee, Michigan, extolled the virtues of the Upper Peninsula's cutover land for farming or ranching. "No matter where the first Garden of Eden was located," he proclaimed, "the present one is in the Upper Peninsula."

Thousands of hard-working folks were lured north by the promise of cheap land in exchange for the back-breaking labor of removing pine stumps and tilling soil. But by the late 1920s, their work proved futile. Nearly half the U.P. was tax-delinquent cutover land. Ranches had failed. Most farms had failed. The stock market had crashed, and the nation's economy was in shambles.

The federal government took a different approach. In 1911, it established the first national forests in Michigan and Wisconsin, setting aside land and creating tree nurseries as a first step in reestablishing the Midwest's great forests. The Civilian Conservation Corps, established in 1933, continued the reforestation efforts, planting trees, fighting fires, and nursing the remaining great forests back to health.

Although we can never re-create the magnificent old-growth forests of yesteryear, pines once again stretch skyward across Michigan. Logging continues, too, though with sophisticated forest management and reforestation practices that help ensure the livelihood of the state's important lumber and paper industries. And a few stands of virgin old-growth timber remain, giving us an awe-inspiring glimpse of a lost Michigan landscape.

Cross-country skiers and, increasingly, snowshoers also take advantage of the abundant snows. Gogebic County has more dedicated Nordic skiing resorts than you'll find elsewhere in the Upper Peninsula. And the Ottawa National Forest offers a dizzying array of terrain for those seeking solitude. The U.P. never overlooks snowmobiling, though, and you'll see plenty of trucks pulling snowmobiles; snowmobile routes radiating out from Lake Gogebic seem especially popular. To avoid them, ask state park/national forest officials about the proximity of snowmobiling trails where you plan to set out.

Follow M-505 north from Ironwood to reach **Little Girl's Point,** an area favorite. Perched high on a bluff over Lake Superior, this county park features a sand beach, a boat launch, picnic tables, grills, and fantastic views—the Porcupine Mountains to the east, the Apostle Islands to the west.

From Little Girl's Point, continue west on M-505 to reach **Superior Falls.** The rushing Montreal River puts on its final spectacular show here, plummeting more than 40 feet, then squeezing through a narrow gorge before spilling into Lake Superior a short distance away. You can also reach it by taking U.S. 2 about 11 miles west from Ironwood and turning north on W-122. (You'll travel through Wisconsin and back into Michigan in the process.) In about 4.8 miles, watch for a small brown sign

WESTERN UPPER PENINSULA

that directs you west into a small parking area near a Northern States Power substation. From here, it's a short walk to the falls. You also can continue down the path past the falls to Lake Superior, a fine sunset spot.

SYLVANIA WILDERNESS AND RECREATION AREA

Sylvania protects its assets well—36 crystalline glacial lakes hidden among thick stands of massive, old-growth trees. For anglers who dream of landing that once-in-a-lifetime smallmouth bass, for paddlers who yearn to glide across deep, quiet waters and along untrammeled shoreline, for hikers who wish to travel under a towering canopy of trees and hear nothing more than the haunting whistle of a loon, Sylvania can be a truly magical place.

One of three wilderness areas within the national forest, Sylvania stretches across 18,300 acres near Watersmeet, an area roughly bordered by U.S. 2 to the north, U.S. 45 to the east, and the Wisconsin border to the south. The adjacent Sylvania Recreation Area acts as a buffer, an additional 3,000 acres of lakes and woodlands with a few developed services like a drive-in campground, nice beach, flush toilets, and running water.

Once viewed as just another tract of good timber, Sylvania's fate turned in the late 1890s, when a lumberman who purchased 80 acres near the south end of Clark Lake decided it was too lovely to cut, and instead kept it as his personal fishing retreat. He invited his wealthy buddies—some of them executives of U.S. Steel—who also were captivated by the land. Together, they purchased several thousand additional acres and formed the private Sylvania Club.

Begin a trip to Sylvania with a call or visit to the **Ottawa Visitors Center** (906/358-4724, 10 A.M.–4 P.M. Wed.–Sat.), at the intersection of U.S. 2 and U.S. 45 in Watersmeet. The staff can help you with maps, regulations, campsite reservations, and other information. Sylvania's rules can be quite unique—especially fishing regulations—so take time to ask questions and read through the materials rangers provide. To reach Sylvania itself, follow U.S. 2 west about four miles from the visitors center and turn south on Thousand Island Lake Road. Travel about four miles, following signs to reach the entrance building. All visitors are required to register upon arrival.

The entrance sits in the recreation area, near the drive-in campground on Clark Lake. If you intend to travel into the wilderness area, plan on treating your own water; you'll find water pumps only in the recreation area. Cookstoves are highly encouraged, too, to lessen the number of feet tramping through the forest in search of dead wood. During summer months, make sure you also have ample bug dope or, better yet, a head net to combat mosquitoes and black flies.

RECREATION
Biking

There are many tantalizing mountain biking opportunities in the western Upper Peninsula. Two hundred miles of trails in three networks with routes ranging from tame gravel roads to single-track trails deep in the woods. As a bonus, many link up with waterfalls, remote lakes, and historical features.

Near Marenisco in Gogebic County, the **Pomeroy/Henry Lake network** offers 100 miles of gentle rides on wide gravel roads around a national forest area peppered with small lakes. It's a good choice for families. The **Ehlco network,** just south of the Porcupine Mountains Wilderness State Park, includes more single-track deep in the forest, on grass or dirt paths. Arguably the best of the three is the one located outside the national forest: the **Iron County system.** Trails radiating out of Hurley lead you past waterfalls, large flowages, and old mining relics like the Plummer headframe near Pence. Good interpretive signs help make sense of historic sites. Routes in this system range from gravel roads to terrific single-track, though it's not clear from the map which is which.

Canoeing and Kayaking

Seven major river systems flow within the

forest, a staggering 1,000 miles of navigable waters for paddlers. Congress has designated more than 300 of those miles as wild and scenic or recreational rivers, leaving them largely in a pristine state. In general, rivers like the Ontonagon and Presque Isle offer quiet water in their southern reaches, winding through relatively flat woodlands. North of M-28, they begin a more rugged descent through hills and bluffs, requiring higher skills and boats appropriate for white water. For strong paddlers with good white-water skills, these rivers offer some of the finest paddling in the Midwest.

Of course, all of this can change depending on rainfall and the time of the year. Rivers that normally flow gently can be torrents in the spring. Always check with national forest officials before setting out. Also, the Forest Service publishes an extensive *River Digest* (free) that outlines navigable rivers, launch areas, liveries, and high flow/low flow times. Pick one up at a district ranger office.

◖ Downhill Skiing

The area's three major downhill ski resorts—Big Powderhorn, Blackjack, and Indianhead—line up conveniently along a short stretch of U.S. 2 just east of Ironwood. All welcome downhill skiers and snowboarders.

Heading east from Ironwood, the first resort you'll reach is **Big Powderhorn Mountain** (N11375 Powderhorn Rd., Bessemer, 906/932-4838, www.bigpowderhorn.net, lift tickets $31–45). Powderhorn's 33 downhill runs wrap across two faces, with 700 feet of vertical drop and nine double chairlifts. Perhaps more than the others, Big Powderhorn Mountain caters to families with affordable lift tickets, mostly tame runs, and plenty of ski-in/ski-out lodging bordering its slopes.

Also in Bessemer, the smaller, family-run **Blackjack Ski Resort** (N11251 Blackjack Rd., 888/906-9835, www.skiblackjack.com, lift tickets $28–40), with its 20 trails, carves out a niche in the market by making the most of its terrain. Cameron Run and Spillway often are left ungroomed and offer up good bump skiing, and it's arguably the best resort around for snowboarders, with the area's best half-pipe and a great terrain park on Broad Ax.

A few more miles down the road bring you to the **Indianhead Mountain Resort** (500 Indianhead Rd., Wakefield, 800/346-3426, www.indianheadmtn.com, $34–46), the area's largest resort with 638 feet of vertical, 9 chairlifts, 2 T-bars, and 29 runs. Indianhead offers some of the region's most challenging (although overly groomed) skiing, and pleasant runs that wind for more than a mile through the woods.

Cross-Country Skiing

Active Backwoods Retreats (E5299 W. Pioneer Rd., 906/932-3502, $10 adults, $8 children 11–17, $5 children under 11) grooms 25 miles of trails for skating and striding, on hundreds of acres of private land three miles south of Ironwood. A warming hut, lessons, and rentals are available.

Between Ironwood and Bessemer, take Section 12 Road north from U.S. 2 to reach **Wolverine Nordic Trails.** Situated on private land and maintained by volunteers, its 9.3 miles of groomed trails wind through the hilly country south of the Big Powderhorn ski area. You can, in fact, ride one of Powderhorn's chairlifts ($2 per ride) to access the network. Otherwise, begin at the lot with the warming hut on Sunset Road off Section 12 Road. Donations are requested.

ACCOMMODATIONS

You'll find a string of motels along M-64 between Silver City to Ontonagon. Many are plain, somewhat tired mom-and-pop-type places, but they work just fine after a long day outdoors. **Tomlinson's Rainbow Lodging** (2900 M-64, Silver City, 906/885-5348, $79–189 d) offers motel rooms and cottages on the shores of Lake Superior, with a private sand beach. Some units have whirlpools and kitchen facilities. Pets are welcome.

You'll also find a large selection of mom-and-pop motels along U.S. 2, many of which have great deals and clean, comfortable, if simple, rooms. A good choice is the **Sandpiper Motel** (1200 E. Cloverland Dr., Ironwood, 906/932-2000, $39–79 d). Reserve well ahead of time during ski season. Meanwhile, the larger area ski resorts offer slopeside (or near-slopeside) accommodations, ranging from dormitories to simple motel rooms to deluxe condominiums. The **Indianhead Mountain Resort** (500 Indianhead Rd., Wakefield, 800/346-3426, www.indianheadmtn.com, $105–483 d) offers some of the nicest rooms and condos (and the closest to what you might find in Aspen).

If you get hungry while exploring the area, head to Ontonagon, where you'll find **Syl's** (713 River, 906/884-2522, 7 A.M.–7 P.M. daily, $4–9), a classic small-town café, with some of the best pasties around. Their breakfasts are so big, you may not need to eat for the rest of the day. In Ironwood, you may spot what looks like a classic corner tavern, but **Don & GG's** (1300 E. Cloverland Dr., Ironwood, 906/932-2312, hours vary, $5–14) might surprise you with its vegetarian dishes and smoked trout salad. Don't worry—you can still get burgers and chicken dinners, too.

Camping
The **Ottawa National Forest** (E6248 U.S. 2, Ironwood, 906/932-1330, free–$17) maintains 27 auto-accessible campgrounds, all with tent pads, fire grates, and toilet facilities. Many are located along rivers and lakes. Most tend to be quite rustic and secluded, with the exception of Black River Harbor, Sylvania, and Bobcat Lake. A few, like Black River Harbor, require a fee and allow reservations.

INFORMATION AND SERVICES
While many of the area's small communities have chambers of commerce that can help with lodgings and other services, the area's most comprehensive source of tourism information is the **Western U.P. Convention and Visitor Bureau** (Ironwood, 906/932-4850, www.westernup.info). Of course, if you need more specific details, you can also consult the **Ontonagon County Chamber of Commerce** (Ontonagon, 906/884-4735, www.ontonagonmi.org), the **Lake Gogebic Area Chamber of Commerce** (Bergland, 888/464-3242, www.lakegogebicarea.com), and the **Ironwood Area Chamber of Commerce** (150 N. Lowell, Ironwood, 906/932-1122, www.ironwoodmi.org).

While the towns in this part of the U.P. offer limited services, such as local banks and small groceries, you'd be better off stopping first in larger towns like Marquette and Sault Ste. Marie. There, you'll find a better selection of supplies and services before venturing into the western wilderness. In case of an emergency, however, don't hesitate to dial **911** from any phone.

GETTING THERE AND AROUND
Although the western U.P. has a couple of small airports, in places like Houghton and Escanaba (both of which offer commuter service via Northwest Airlines), and **Greyhound** (800/231-2222, www.greyhound.com) offers limited bus service to Ironwood, you'll find it easier to traverse this area via car. From the eastern half of the U.P., take U.S. 2 or M-28 to Ironwood. To reach Ontonagon, head north on U.S. 45 from M-28.

Iron River to Iron Mountain

The Menominee Range is an anomaly in the Upper Peninsula, the only area not within rock-tossing distance of one of the Great Lakes. Roughly encompassing Iron, Dickinson, and Menominee Counties (all in the central time zone), as well as the southern reaches of Baraga County, it is a land of deep forests and literally thousands of inland lakes.

Tourists tend to pass right though the region, which admittedly doesn't look like much from U.S. 2, the main thoroughfare. But that thin strip of development masks an astounding amount of untrammeled wilderness. As proof, wolves thrive here (without any human assistance), because the region provides exactly the habitat wolves need: large tracts of land not sliced up by roads where they can avoid civilization, and plenty of large prey in the form of the region's abundant white-tailed deer.

Iron County's population centers around Iron River and Crystal Falls, the picturesque county seat 15 miles to the east. Both retain their small-town charm. The heart of Dickinson County, meanwhile, is Iron Mountain. Iron River and Iron Mountain, both former iron-mining centers, now offer visitors several historic museums, a couple of downhill ski slopes, and areas ideal for anglers, canoeists, and kayakers.

SIGHTS
◖ Iron County Historical Museum
You won't find a lot of dramatic lighting and fancy display cases at the Iron County Historical Museum (M-189, Caspian, 906/265-2617, www.ironcountymuseum.com, 10 A.M.–4 P.M. Mon.–Sat., 10 A.M.–1 P.M. Sun. mid-May–Oct., $8), two miles south of U.S. 2. What you will find is an interesting, appealing, and eclectic blend of local history and culture at this rambling, funky, and homegrown museum. Located on the site of the productive Caspian iron mine—whose rusting headframe still looms over the complex—it runs largely on

donated money and donated time. In the main museum building, displays cover everything from Native American history to logging, mining, and sporting equipment and kitchenware from the early 1900s. The perennial favorite display is the mechanized iron mine and railroad model. For five cents, a miniature ore skip hauls rocks to the surface and loads them on the railroad. Outside, several relocated buildings occupy the grounds, including a streetcar barn and the streetcar that once traveled between the mines in Caspian and Iron River.

Bewabic State Park
A small but pleasant chain of lakes is the highlight of Bewabic State Park (720 Idlewild Rd., Crystal Falls, 906/875-3324, state park vehicle permit required), located five miles west of Crystal Falls. Boaters can put in at the first of the Fortune Lakes and make their way to Fourth Lake, an easy day's paddling adventure. Though First Lake can be somewhat frenetic on summer weekends, the waters get quieter and downright pristine as you proceed down the chain. Most of the shoreline is dotted with cottages, though you can camp on state-owned land bordering Third Lake. Fishing for perch and bass is best on First Lake, the largest (192 acres) and deepest (72 feet). Paddlers can escape fishing boats by darting under the low U.S. 2 bridge to Mud Lake. The park itself has a modern 137-site campground ($10–20) with good privacy, a small stretch of sandy beach, tennis courts, and other amenities. For reservations, call 800/447-2757.

Iron Mountain
Iron Mountain was first settled in about 1880 and reached its heyday soon after, when vast deposits of iron were discovered underfoot. The Chapin Mine—located near present-day U.S. 2 and Kent Avenue on the north end of downtown—helped boost the town's population to almost 8,000 by 1890. Italian immigrants led the melting-pot mix working at the Chapin

Mine, and Italian neighborhoods still thrive around the old mine on Iron Mountain's north side—as evidenced by a mouthwatering supply of Italian restaurants and corner markets.

The long-abandoned Chapin Mine still serves an important role, this time as a magnet for brown bats. An estimated two million bats winter in the shaft, protected from predators yet able to enter and exit freely, thanks to bat-friendly grates installed at the mine entrance. As the weather turns cool (usually sometime in September), the bats congregate all around Iron Mountain before retreating to the mine, an amazing sight.

While iron mining seems to dominate the city's psyche, Henry Ford added to the economic mix in the 1920s, when he bought up huge tracts of nearby forest and built his first company sawmill on land southwest of town, which he dubbed Kingsford (named for Iron Mountain's Ford dealer, Edward Kingsford). Soon Ford's Kingsford empire included the main plant for making floorboards for the Model T, residential developments for workers, an airport, a refinery, even a plant to make newfangled charcoal briquettes. All of it eventually closed or was sold off, including the briquette plant, which relocated to Oakland, California, and still manufactures the ever-popular Kingsford charcoal briquettes.

Iron Mountain's Chapin Mine once led Menominee Range mining production, but was also one of the wettest mines ever worked. In 1893, an immense steam-operated pump was put to work, a 54-foot-high, 725-ton behemoth—the largest in the world at the time. Though electric pumps replaced it just 20 years later, the pump survives intact at the **Cornish Pump and Mining Museum** (300 Kent St., Iron Mountain, 906/774-1086, www.menomineemuseum.com, 9 A.M.–5 P.M. Mon.–Sat., noon–4 P.M. Sun. Memorial Day–Labor Day, $2). Along with the impressive pump, this comprehensive museum includes a good-sized collection of mining equipment, photos, and clothing; a small theater; and, arguably the most compelling display of all, the story of the World War II gliders built by Henry Ford's nearby Kingsford plant, used to quietly deploy troops behind enemy lines.

ACCOMMODATIONS AND FOOD

The **Lakeshore Motel** (1257 Lalley Rd., 906/265-3611, www.lakeshoremotelicelake.com, $42–68 d) sits on the edge of spring-fed Ice Lake (just east of downtown Iron River on U.S. 2), with tidy motel rooms, some with kitchenette units. This is a great find, complete with a sand beach and boat launch. The namesake of **Alice's** (402 W. Adams St., Iron River, 906/265-4764, 11 A.M.–8 P.M. daily, $8–14) produces Italian specialties just as her immigrant mother did before her, with homemade ravioli and other pasta dishes, gnocchi (Italian dumplings), and soups.

In Iron Mountain, the **Pine Mountain Resort** (N3332 Pine Mountain Rd., 906/774-2747, www.pinemountainresort.com, $60–90 d) anchors a full-service ski and golf resort on the northwest side of town, complete with a dining room, an indoor pool, an outdoor pool, a sauna, tennis courts, and trails ideal for hiking and mountain biking. Choose from standard lodge rooms or condominiums.

Italian is the way to go if you've decided to eat out in Iron Mountain. Homemade ravioli, slow-roasted pork, Italian sausage, Roma red sauce . . . you'll find it all in the town's unassuming Italian eateries. **Bimbo's Wine Press** (314 E. Main, 906/774-8420, 11 A.M.–10 P.M. daily, $5–14) dishes out mouthwatering Italian sandwiches like porketta for incredibly reasonable prices.

INFORMATION AND SERVICES

For more information about the Iron River and Iron Mountain areas, contact the **Iron County Chamber of Commerce** (50 E. Genesee St., Iron River, 906/265-3822, www.iron.org or www.ironcountylodging.com, 9 A.M.–5 P.M. Mon.–Fri.) or the **Tourism Association of the Dickinson County Area** (600 S. Stephenson Ave., Iron Mountain, 800/236-2447, www.ironmountain.org). Remember that, unlike most of Michigan, both Iron and Dickinson Counties are situated in the central standard time (CST) zone.

While the towns in this part of the U.P. offer limited services, such as local banks and small groceries, you'd be better off stopping first in larger towns like Marquette and Sault Ste. Marie. There, you'll find a better selection of supplies and services before venturing into the western wilderness. In case of an emergency, however, don't hesitate to dial **911** from any phone.

GETTING THERE AND AROUND

Although the western U.P. has a couple of small airports, in places like Houghton and Escanaba (both of which offer commuter service via Northwest Airlines), and **Greyhound** (800/231-2222, www.greyhound.com) offers limited bus service to Iron River and Iron Mountain, you'll find it easier to traverse this area via car. Both Iron River and Iron Mountain are situated along U.S. 2, so either can be easily reached, whether you're driving from St. Ignace or Ironwood.

Menominee to Escanaba

Spiking south like a canine tooth between Wisconsin and the waters of Green Bay, the triangle of land comprising Menominee County and southern Delta County has been dubbed the peninsula's "banana belt." Well, it does have the U.P.'s most temperate climate, thanks to the warm (okay, relatively warm) waters of protected Green Bay, and the lightest snowfall in the entire Upper Peninsula—just 50 inches a year on average, a quarter of what typically falls on the rest of the U.P. M-35 traces the shore of Green Bay, from Menominee, a handsome community near the Wisconsin border, to Escanaba, a sizable town by the U.P.'s standards, with a downtown district of shops, restaurants, and historic structures.

SIGHTS
Menominee
The Menominee River spills into Green Bay between the twin cities of Marinette, Wisconsin, and Menominee, Michigan, once the region's richest lumber port. The bustling business district centered on 1st Street along the waterfront. Happily, most of the late-19th-century brick and sandstone buildings have survived intact, and renovation and restoration is underway on many of them. You can explore the **historic district,** guided by a walking tour

brochure available at the Spies Public Library (940 1st St.). Its 1905 Beaux-Arts facade happens to be one of the tour's most handsome buildings. A growing number of shops and restaurants along 1st Street are adding new life to this pleasant area.

The waterfront district is also home to bayside parks, easily accessible on foot. **Victory Park** stretches along the water between 6th and 10th Avenues, flanked by a new marina and a band shell that hosts summer concerts on Tuesday and Thursday evenings. For a longer walk or bike ride, head south along the water to **Tourist Park** swimming beach. Farther south, the **Menominee North Pier Light** marks the entrance to Menominee Harbor with a beacon at the end of a rocky breakwater.

Escanaba and Gladstone
A metropolis for these parts, Escanaba and neighboring Gladstone (just a few miles north) are home to some 17,400 people, serving as the industrial and commercial center for the south-central Upper Peninsula. The natural deepwater port gave Escanaba its start back in the Civil War days, when a hastily built rail line linked the iron mines in Negaunee with the port, to bring coveted raw materials to the weapons-makers and railroad builders of the

Union Army. Today, Escanaba's modern ore port still ships iron, now in the form of iron/clay taconite pellets, to steelmakers in Indiana and Ohio.

Downtown Escanaba focuses on Ludington Street, an east-west route that runs from M-35 to the waterfront. The town's landmark is the **House of Ludington,** a grand old Queen Anne resort hotel built in 1865. The building's imposing facade continues to anchor the downtown.

At the foot of Ludington Street, lovely **Ludington Park** offers paved pathways along the water and to a small island (in-line skates permitted), interpretive signs explaining local history, a band shell that hosts concerts on Wednesday evenings in summer, a playground, a beach, tennis courts, and a boat launch. One of the park's most popular attractions is the **Sand Point Lighthouse** (16 Water Plant Rd., 906/786-3763, 9 A.M.–5 P.M. daily June–Sept., $2), an 1867 brick light that was restored and reopened as a museum in 1990 by the Delta County Historical Society. It was a big job. In the 1940s, the Coast Guard remodeled the obsolete light for staff housing, removing the lantern room and lopping off the top 10 feet of the tower.

ACCOMMODATIONS AND FOOD

The typical sprawl of chain motels runs along M-35 between Escanaba and Gladstone, but some nice family-owned operations are still holding their own along the waterfront. The **Terrace Bay Resort** (7146 P Rd., Gladstone, 906/786-7554, www.terracebay.com, $79–149 d) on Little Bay de Noc between Escanaba and Gladstone, has nice, clean motel rooms with great bay views. The 200-acre resort complex includes an 18-hole golf course, indoor and outdoor pools, tennis courts, a game room, and more. To find Terrace Bay, watch for the signs on U.S. 41 south of Gladstone. For vittles, try the (C **House of Ludington** (223 Ludington St., Escanaba, 906/786-6300,

www.houseofludington.com, lunch and dinner hours vary, $6–12), a historic structure that offers an upscale menu with a variety of Michigan favorites.

INFORMATION AND SERVICES

For general information, your best source is the large and comprehensive **Michigan Welcome Center.** The picturesque log building, which is located on U.S. 41 near the state line (just north of the bridge), provides ample local and statewide visitor information. For more specific details about the region, consult the **Bays de Noc Convention & Visitors Bureau** (230 Ludington St., Escanaba, 906/789-7862, www.travelbaysdenoc.com) or the **Delta Chamber of Commerce** (230 Ludington St., Escanaba, 906/786-2192, www.deltami. org, 9 A.M.–5 P.M. Mon.–Fri). Remember that Menominee County is in the central standard time (CST) zone, like neighboring Wisconsin. When you cross the line into Delta County, however, you're back on eastern standard time (EST), as with the rest of Michigan.

Escanaba offers plenty of services for travelers, though you might find more in the way of supplies in northerly Marquette. In case of an emergency, however, you can always dial **911** from any phone or visit the **OSF St. Francis Hospital** (3401 Ludington St., Escanaba, 906/786-5707, www.osfstfrancis.org).

GETTING THERE AND AROUND

The closest airport to this region is **Delta County Airport (ESC)** (3300 Airport Rd., Escanaba, 906/786-4902, www.deltacountymi.org/airport.php), which offers limited service via Northwest Airlines. In addition, **Greyhound** (800/231-2222, www.greyhound. com) provides bus service to Escanaba. Still, the most common way to visit Menominee and Delta Counties is via car. From St. Ignace, U.S. 2 heads west to Gladstone and Escanaba, from which M-35 leads you down to Menominee.

Marquette and Vicinity

With 20,800 hardy year-round souls, Marquette is distinguished as the largest city in Michigan's Upper Peninsula. Tucked in a well-protected natural harbor nearly midway across the U.P.'s northern shore, it grew and still thrives largely because of its location—an important Lake Superior port for the iron industry, and a rather central location that has helped it evolve into the U.P.'s center of commerce and government. In short, Marquette is definitely worth a visit—whether you plan to explore the historic architecture of its waterfront district or rest up before heading into the rugged hills, forests, and rivers that lie just beyond the city limits.

SIGHTS

Third Street, running north-south, and Washington, running east-west, represent Marquette's main cross streets and where they meet is a good area to begin an exploration of the downtown. This puts you in the heart of the shopping and historic district. Buildings like the 1902 **Marquette County Courthouse** (3rd and Baraga) and the 1927 **MFC First National Bank** (101 W. Washington) showcase the city's affinity for **Beaux-Arts architecture.** Step inside the courthouse for a better look, and also to check out a display about Michigan Supreme Court Justice and author John Voelker. Better known by his pen name, Robert Traver, the Ishpeming native wrote *Anatomy of a Murder,* among other works. Scenes from the popular 1959 movie starring Jimmy Stewart were filmed here, as well as in nearby Big Bay, where the actual murder occurred. Not far away, the **Marquette County History Museum** (213 N. Front St., 906/226-3571, www.marquettecohistory.org, 10 A.M.–5 P.M. Mon.–Fri., $3 adults, $1 children 12–18,

a barge passing downtown Marquette

children under 12 free) features artifacts from prehistoric to contemporary times, and is overseen by the oldest historical society in the U.P.

Another highlight here is the **Marquette Maritime Museum** (300 Lakeshore Blvd., 906/226-2006, http://mqtmaritimemuseum.com, 10 A.M.–5 P.M. daily late May–mid-Oct., $7 adults, $5 children under 13), which preserves the city's maritime history and honors its submarine veterans, with exhibits such as a lighthouse lens collection and a "silent service memorial." The museum also offers tours of the 1866 **Marquette Harbor Lighthouse.**

SHOPPING

Downtown Marquette is home to several distinctive shops worth a bit of browsing time. One pleasant stop is **Bookworld** (136 W. Washington St., 906/228-9490, www.bookworldstores.com, 9 A.M.–9 P.M. Mon.–Sat., 9 A.M.–5 P.M. Sun.), which offers a decent selection of local and regional titles. The U.P.'s Scandinavian heritage also looms large in Marquette's shopping district. **Scandinavian Gifts** (1025 N. 3rd, 906/225-1993, 9 A.M.–7 P.M. daily) showcases the sleek and simple lines of classic Scandinavian design in its selection of glassware and silver (lots of Norwegian sweaters, too).

RECREATION
Hiking and Biking

A thumb of land thrust out into the big lake, **Presque Isle Park,** about four miles north of downtown off Lakeshore Boulevard, is a

the northern lights above the Marquette Harbor Lighthouse

NORTH COUNTRY NATIONAL SCENIC TRAIL

When completed, the 4,600-mile North Country National Scenic Trail will be the longest continuous off-road hiking trail in the United States. Eventually, it will link communities, forests, and prairies across seven northern states, including New York, Pennsylvania, Ohio, Michigan, Wisconsin, Minnesota, and North Dakota. Much of the trail is already open to hikers and other recreationists. In general, it can be accessed at all times and during all seasons, although regional and seasonal closures can occur at the discretion of local landowners and managers.

Not surprisingly, the Great Lakes State contains the largest percentage of the North Country Trail, though only 50 percent of it has been certified for public use. The rest is still under development. Eventually, the trail will link Michigan's southern border to the Wisconsin state line, traversing the Heartland, the Grand Traverse Bay region, the Mackinac Bridge, Pictured Rocks National Lakeshore, Marquette, and three national forests. Maps are available from the **North Country Trail Association** (www.northcountrytrail.org).

For more information about the trail, consult the **National Park Service** (608/441-5610, www.nps.gov/noco), the **Michigan Department of Natural Resources/Forest Management Division** (517/373-1275, www.michigan.gov/dnr), or the three participating units of the **U.S. Forest Service** (www.fs.fed.us): Manistee National Forest (800/821-6263), Hiawatha National Forest (906/786-4062), and Ottawa National Forest (906/932-1330).

---

microcosm of the area's beauty: rocky red bluffs, tall pines, and lovely Lake Superior vistas. You can drive through the 323-acre park, but you'd do better to get out and stroll or ski along its many trails. Watch for albino deer (white-tailed deer lacking pigment), which survive in this protected setting. Near the park's entrance, there's a playground, a picnic area, tennis courts, a marina, and a good spot from which to watch the huge 800-foot freighters arrive at the towering railroad ore dock. Also at the entrance of the park, you can pick up the **Marquette Bicycle Path,** a paved route that hugs the shoreline all the way to Harvey, offering access to downtown and the Northern Michigan University campus.

Skiing

Among skiers and snowboarders, **Marquette Mountain** (4501 M-553, 906/225-1155, www.marquettemountain.com, $30–35) gets the thumbs-up for its 600-foot vertical drop, one of the highest in the state. The 23 trails may not be exceptionally long, but they offer good variety—including bumps and tree runs—and the half-pipe and terrain park grow and improve every year. Located just three miles south of town on M-553, it's popular all week long among local residents and college students. Night skiing is offered Tuesday–Sunday in season, which usually runs from about mid-November to early April.

ACCOMMODATIONS AND FOOD

The best spot in Marquette is easily the **Landmark Inn** (230 N. Front St., 906/228-2580, www.thelandmarkinn.com, $124–269 d). Built in the 1930s as the Northland Hotel, it hosted such luminaries as Amelia Earhart and Abbott and Costello. After falling into disrepair and eventually closing in the 1980s, it now has been beautifully remodeled and reopened as the Landmark. For not much more than you'd pay for a basic franchise motel room, you get a taste of history, a touch of elegance and a primo location: Lake Superior on one side, downtown Marquette on the other.

There's also a surprisingly good and varied choice of lodgings in tiny Big Bay. Probably the best known is the **Big Bay Point Lighthouse**

JACQUES MARQUETTE

A Jesuit missionary and explorer from France, Jacques Marquette (1637-1675) established a mission among the Ottawa at St. Ignace. He and his fellow traveler Louis Joliet were probably the first white men to explore much of the Great Lakes region and the Upper Mississippi.

Born in Laon, France, Marquette joined the Jesuit order in 1656 and spent the next decade studying and teaching in France. In 1666, Jesuit priests sent him to New France (present-day Quebec) as a missionary. Like many Jesuits, he lived among the Native Americans and studied their languages. In 1671, he was appointed missionary to the Ottawa tribe, and established the St. Ignace mission on the northern shore of the Straits of Mackinac.

In 1672, French explorer Louis Joliet arrived at the mission, sent by the governor of New France, Comte de Frontenac, to search for a trade route to the Far East. From the Native Americans, they had heard about a great waterway, Missi Sipi ("big river"), which they thought might flow into the Pacific Ocean. Marquette, with his knowledge of Native American languages, was to accompany Joliet.

Marquette, Joliet, and five other Frenchmen set out in canoes across the northern shore of Lake Michigan in May 1673. They traveled down Green Bay and up the Fox River in pres-ent-day Wisconsin, where local Native Americans led them to a portage to the Wisconsin River. The team followed the Wisconsin to its confluence with the Mississippi and explored the Mississippi all the way to the Arkansas River. They grew alarmed by both the swiftness of the water and word from the Indians about white men downstream. Fearing they would be attacked by Spaniards and deducing that the southerly flow of the river would not lead to the Pacific, the explorers turned back. They paddled the Illinois River to the Chicago River, then followed the western shore of Lake Michigan to Green Bay – a staggering journey of more than 2,900 miles. Along the way, they peaceably communicated with dozens of Native American tribes.

An ailing Marquette spent the winter at a mission in Wisconsin, returning to Illinois the following spring to work with Native Americans he had met along his voyage. In 1675, he died on Lake Michigan near present-day Ludington, Michigan, en route back to St. Ignace. Marquette and Joliet's exploration added greatly to the white man's knowledge of North American geography. The Native Americans who treated him so well would later suffer when that new knowledge spurred increasing European settlement.

Bed and Breakfast (3 Lighthouse Rd., 906/345-9957, http://bigbaylighthouse.com, $125–190 d). As a lighthouse, it naturally occupies a dramatic position on a rocky point just a few miles from the town of Big Bay. The red-brick lighthouse keeper's home, attached to the 1896 light, has been restored and retrofitted with seven very comfortable guest rooms, all with private baths. Five have Lake Superior views. The inn has extensive grounds, more than 43 acres and a half-mile of shoreline, set far back from busy roads and hustle and bustle. Guests are welcome to use the sauna, climb the light tower, or relax in the living room, where owners Linda and Jeff Gamble have collected loads of lighthouse lore and history. Reserve well in advance.

For a city its size, Marquette has a very good selection of quality, locally owned restaurants. The **Vierling Saloon** (119 S. Front St., 906/228-3533, www.thevierling.com, 11:30 A.M.–close daily, $6–21) stands out for its consistently good food, century-old decor, and interesting views of Marquette Harbor ore docks. (Ask for a table near the large windows in back.) The menu offers a lot of variety, including vegetarian dishes, whitefish served five ways, and excellent breakfasts, soups, and sandwiches. The microbrewery downstairs features British-style ales and stouts. In Big Bay, you should stop by the **Lumberjack Tavern** (202 Bensinger St., 906/345-9912, 11:30 A.M.–close daily, $5–14), which has a large local following.

Camping

Van Riper State Park (851 County Road AKE, Champion, 906/339-4461, state park vehicle permit required, $14–23) offers 187 easily accessible modern and rustic campsites, although within earshot of U.S. 41. The 1,044-acre park also has several hiking and cross-country skiing trails as well as a fine sand beach along Lake Michigamme, which is considerably warmer than Lake Superior. Reserve well in advance by phoning 800/447-2757 or visiting www.michigan.gov/dnr.

INFORMATION AND SERVICES

For more information about Marquette and its surrounding areas, contact the **Marquette Country Convention & Visitors Bureau** (337 W. Washington St., 906/228-7749, www.marquettecountry.org, 9 A.M.–5 P.M. daily). For local news, refer to *The Mining Journal* (www.miningjournal.net).

As the largest city in the U.P., Marquette has a wide array of banks, groceries, pharmacies, gas stations, and other necessary services. In case of a medical emergency, dial 911 from any phone or contact the **Marquette General Health System** (580 W. College Ave., 906/228-9440, www.mgh.org). Remember that Marquette is situated in the eastern standard time (EST) zone.

GETTING THERE AND AROUND

Marquette is one of the easiest places to reach in the western Upper Peninsula. You can fly directly into **Sawyer International Airport (SAW)** (125 G Ave., Gwinn, 906/346-3308, www.sawyerairport.com), rent a vehicle from several major car rental agencies, and head north on M-553 to Marquette. In addition, **Greyhound** (800/231-2222, www.greyhound.com) offers bus service to Marquette (1325 Commerce Dr.). Of course, most travelers simply drive to this area; from the Mackinac Bridge, head north on I-75 and take M-28 west to Marquette. Once here, you can park the car and rely on the **Marquette County Transit Authority** (906/225-1112, www.marq-tran.com).

NEGAUNEE AND ISHPEMING

In many ways, these twin towns 15 miles west of Marquette represent the heart of the iron range. One of the Upper Peninsula's earliest iron mines, the Jackson Mine, opened here in 1847; the nearby Empire and Tilden Mines mark the end of the era, the last operating iron mines in the range.

Ishpeming and Negaunee pretty much faded right along with the glory days of mining. The economy never quite recovered from the closing of the area mines in the 1960s, and the once-vital downtowns were further displaced by the commercial strips along U.S. 41, which passes just north of town. But anyone who enjoys tidbits of history will find these towns intriguing, with their leftover ornate storefronts, ramshackle antique shops, and fenced-off cave-in areas—where the land once and for all has succumbed to its mining heritage.

Sights and Attractions

One of the finest museums in the Upper Peninsula, the state-run **Iron Industry Museum** (73 Forge Rd., Negaunee, 906/475-7857, 9:30 A.M.–4:30 P.M. daily, free) is well worth the short detour off U.S. 41 to its picturesque location along the Carp River. The spot wasn't chosen for its scenery; it marks the site of one of the area's earliest iron forges, built in 1848. This small facility packs a lot of information and well-done displays into a single exhibit hall. It tells the story of Michigan's $48 billion iron mining and smelting industry, which dwarfed the California gold rush ($955 million), Michigan's lucrative logging industry ($4.4 billion), and even Michigan's venerable copper mining empire ($9.6 billion). You'll learn how iron prompted the development of dozens of port towns and the giant 1,000-foot ore freighters that now ply the Great Lakes. The "Technology Timeline" traces the advancements of exploration, working conditions, and mining methods.

Few people think of Ishpeming as the center

of the U.S. ski industry, but a lot of those big resorts in the Rockies can trace America's interest in the sport to Michigan. Michigan residents—many of them Scandinavian immigrants—established the Ishpeming Ski Club in 1887, one of the oldest continuously operating clubs in the nation, and organized the country's first ski jumping competition in 1888. Everett Kircher, visionary founder of Michigan's Boyne Mountain resort, invented the first successful snowmaking machine. Hence, Ishpeming was chosen as the site of the **U.S. National Ski Hall of Fame and Ski Museum** (610 Palms Ave., Ishpeming, 906/485-6323, www.skihall. com, 10 A.M.–5 P.M. Mon.–Sat., free) the "official" hall of fame, just like the Football Hall of Fame in Canton, Ohio, and the Baseball Hall of Fame in Cooperstown, New York.

The museum, on U.S. 41 between 2nd and 3rd Streets, covers the sport from *way* back, beginning with a replica of a 4,000-year-old ski and pole found in Sweden. Most interesting are the displays of early ski equipment (including early poles which "often doubled as weapons"), the evolution of chairlifts, and an account of the skiing soldiers of the 10th Mountain Division, who played an important role in the mountains of Italy during World War II. The Hall of Fame plaques offer insightful short biographies of those who shaped the sport, from racers to resort owners to, ahem, orthopedic surgeons.

Recreation

In summer, the entire area is part of the comprehensive **Range Mountain Bike Trail System,** with more than 25 miles of trails stretching from Teal Lake to Lake Sally, south of Suicide Bowl. Routes are covered in the *Marquette Region Hike and Bike Trail Guide,* available from local shops or the Marquette Country Convention & Visitors Bureau.

Down Wind Sports (514 N. 3rd St., Marquette, 906/226-7112, www.downwind-sports.com, 9 A.M.–7 P.M. Mon.–Thurs., 9 A.M.–8 P.M. Fri., 9 A.M.–5 P.M. Sat., 11 A.M.–3 P.M. Sun.) is a great local source for information on mountain biking, white-water kayaking, sea kayaking, rock climbing, and more. The shop also hosts weekly climbing outings, mountain bike rides, and river trips in summer months. Down Wind sells a full line of sporting equipment, including kayaks, skis, and snowshoes, and has rentals available.

THE HURON MOUNTAINS

Ask 10 people where the Huron Mountains begin and end, and you're likely to get 10 different answers. But everyone will agree that they fall within the fuzzy boundaries of Lake Superior to the north and east, and U.S. 41 to the south and west. That's a swath of land some 50 miles wide by 25 miles long, where the terrain rises into rugged hills and, yes, even mountains. Mount Arvon, about 15 miles due east of L'Anse, tops out at 1,979 feet, the highest point in the state.

Look at a map, and you'll see it's an intriguing parcel of land, virtually devoid of towns and roads. What the Huron Mountains do have, however, includes washboard peaks and valleys, virgin white pine forests, hundreds of lakes, the headwaters of a half-dozen classic wilderness rivers, dazzling waterfalls, far more wildlife than people, and utter silence. Even by U.P. standards, it's a rugged, remarkable place.

The preservation wasn't the result of happy accident; beginning around the 1880s, the Huron Mountains became the wilderness retreat of choice for several millionaire industrialists. Cyrus McCormick, head of the lucrative farm implement company that would become International Harvester, amassed a huge wilderness estate around White Deer Lake, now part of the Ottawa National Forest's McCormick Tract Wilderness Area. Frederick Miller of Miller Brewing owned his piece of wilderness at Craig Lake, now a wilderness state park. Dozens of others owned "camps" at the Huron Mountain Club, an organization so exclusive, even Henry Ford was turned downed for membership when he first applied. The members easily had enough clout to stop construction of a road that was to link L'Anse with Big Bay—County Road 550 abruptly ends west of Big Bay at a gate and security guard house.

Today, the 25,000-acre enclave is shared mostly by the descendants of those original members, who quietly protect and preserve this spectacular landholding. Though locals grumble about the lack of access onto the property (remember, trespassing is considered a right here), no one can argue that the Huron Mountain Club has proved to be an exceptional steward of the land. It kept away the loggers, the miners, and the developers, leaving what some consider the most magnificent wilderness remaining in the state, maybe even all of the Midwest. Within its boundaries lie towering virgin pines, blue-ribbon trout streams, pristine lakes, and waterfalls that don't even appear on maps. If the club should ever come up for sale, government officials admit (albeit off the record) that they would clamor to turn it into a state or national park.

In the meantime, the rest of us have to be content simply knowing that such wonderful natural beauty is there, and lovingly protected. Besides, there's plenty of Huron Mountain wilderness open to the public—more than enough to go around for those who are fortunate and smart enough to explore this special place.

Big Bay Area

Many people approach the Huron Mountains from the east, where County Road 550 climbs 30 miles out of Marquette to the tiny town of Big Bay, population 270. Sited above Lake Independence and within minutes of Lake Superior, Big Bay is a scrappy little place, where residents take pride in their simple life on the fringes of wilderness. The town has swung from prosperity to near-ghost-town status more than once, first as a bustling logging outpost, then one of Henry Ford's company towns, home to busy sawmills. More recently, residents joke about how the local bank, well aware of the town's volatile economy, was loath to loan money to Big Bay businesses; while the town's 20 businesses are thriving, the bank closed down. Folks now frequent Big Bay for its Huron Mountains access, Lake Superior harbor, Lake Independence fishing, and unique lodgings.

McCormick Wilderness

Once the private wilderness retreat of Cyrus McCormick, whose father invented the reaping machine, this 27-square-mile tract of wilderness was willed to the U.S. Forest Service by the McCormick family in 1967. Today, it remains in pristine wilderness condition—remote, undeveloped, and largely unused. In other words, perfect for backcountry hiking and camping. No-trace camping is permitted throughout the wilderness area. For more information, contact the **Ottawa National Forest Ranger District** (4810 E. M-28, Kenton, 906/852-3500, 9 A.M.–5 P.M. daily).

To access the McCormick Tract, follow U.S. 41/M-28 west from Marquette about 50 miles to Champion. Just after you cross the Peshekee River, follow the first paved road north. This is County Road 607, also called the Peshekee Grade or the Huron Bay Grade. In about 10 miles, you'll see a sign for Arfelin Lake; take the next road to your right and watch for a sign and small parking area.

Once you've arrived, you'll be pretty much on your own to explore this rugged terrain of high hills, rivers, muskeg, and bedrock outcroppings. Don't expect marked and maintained hiking trails. This tract is wild, so with the exception of a well-worn path to White Deer Lake (where the McCormicks's lodge once stood), you'll mostly be traveling cross-country. A compass and topo map are absolute necessities. Wildlife sightings can be excellent—the state's largest moose herd roams here, which in turn has attracted predators like the elusive gray wolf. You're not likely to see a wolf, but may be treated to its hollow wail at your camp some evening.

WESTERN UPPER PENINSULA

BACKGROUND

The Land

GEOLOGY AND GEOGRAPHY

Many eons ago, a combination of cataclysmic volcanic eruptions and soupy tropical seas initially formed what we know now as Michigan. In the northern part of the state, around Lake Superior and northern Lake Huron, erupting volcanoes laid down thick layers of basalt, which later tilted and faulted, forming the area's rugged, rocky topography of mountain ranges and steep shorelines.

Farther south, a shallow sea covered the vast Michigan Basin, an area that now encompasses the lower four Great Lakes. Over millions of years, sand, shells, and other detritus compacted into thick layers of sedimentary rock, the limestone, dolomite, sandstone, and shale now found from the shores of northern Lake Michigan to the state's southern border.

Much later, powerful glaciers added their indelible touch to the Michigan landscape, the last one as recently as 12,000 years ago. Four separate ice sheets scraped across the region, scouring out depressions that became lakes, lowlands, and ragged shorelines. When the ice melted and glaciers retreated, the water filled vast basins and created the modern-day Great Lakes.

Michigan comprises three distinct land regions: the Superior Uplands, Northern Highlands, and Great Lakes Plains. The

TWO STATES IN ONE

Is it a case of sibling rivalry or a marriage of irreconcilable differences? The Upper and Lower Peninsulas of Michigan are a five-mile bridge and a world apart. Many L.P. residents dismiss the U.P. as a bug-infested backwoods filled with yokels. U.P. residents (who proudly call themselves "Yoopers") find the generalizations insulting, especially when those same L.P. folks seem to enjoy the U.P.'s woods, wildlife, and beaches while on vacation.

That the two are even joined as a single state is a bit of a lark. The Michigan Territory actually wound up with the U.P. as a consolation prize, part of a deal struck with Ohio in 1837. Both Michigan and Ohio had fought for control of the "Toledo Strip," a valuable port on Lake Erie. To earn admission to the Union, the Michigan Territory was forced by Congress to relinquish all rights to the Toledo Strip in exchange for the "barren wasteland" of the Upper Peninsula. Michigan got the last laugh,

though, when priceless quantities of iron ore and copper were discovered in its bedrock just a few years later.

Much of the rivalry is good-natured; Yoopers joke about blowing up the Mackinac Bridge, and display bumper stickers portraying a giant U.P. with a tiny L.P. dangling from its eastern end. Yet there is some truth to the squabble. Yoopers feel they pay taxes to a distant state capital and receive very little in return – save for perhaps another protected land or wildlife program, of which they already have plenty. Occasionally, U.P. residents launch pseudo-serious drives to declare sovereignty from the rest of Michigan. As a musical group from Ishpeming, Da Yoopers, sings, "Dear Mr. Governor, you better turn us loose/We asked you for some rest stops, instead you sent us moose/ The honeymoon is over, the declaration's written/We'll take what's above the bridge, and you can keep the mitten."

Superior Uplands spans the western two-thirds of the Upper Peninsula, the region formed by ancient volcanic activity. It is a landscape of dramatic beauty, characterized by rugged basalt cliffs and thick boreal forests of fir, spruce, and birch—all part of the vast Canadian Shield that dips down from the Arctic, across portions of the northern Great Lakes region, and up the west side of Hudson Bay in a giant horseshoe. Much of the region rises more than 1,000 feet above sea level, including the state's highest point, Mt. Arvon, which tops out at 1,979 feet. The Superior Uplands harbors some of the nation's richest sources of minerals, especially copper and iron ore deposits.

South of the Superior Uplands lies the Northern Highlands, covering the eastern Upper Peninsula and the northern Lower Peninsula. Here, basalt bedrock gives way to sandstone and limestone, and boreal forests segue into pine and hardwoods. Once heavily logged for its vast, valuable stands of white and red pine, the Northern Highlands area is now prized by recreationists for its woods, water, and wildlife.

The Great Lakes Plains stretches across southern Michigan (as well as southern Wisconsin and northern Ohio). This region received the full brunt of the Ice Age and its powerful glaciers, which left behind a flattened landscape of sandy lakebeds, wetlands, prairies, and fertile topsoil, making it Michigan's primary farming region for a variety of fruit and vegetable crops.

Geographically, no other state is so distinctly divided. Michigan consists of two separate landmasses, the Lower Peninsula and the Upper Peninsula, circled by Lakes Michigan, Superior, Huron, and Erie, and connected by the Mackinac Bridge, which spans five miles across the Straits of Mackinac.

Ask Michiganders to give you directions in the Lower Peninsula, and odds are they'll hold up a right hand and use their palm to pinpoint within the state. Shaped like a mitten, the Lower Peninsula is 286 miles long and 195 miles wide, with the landmass jutting out into Lake Huron universally dubbed "the Thumb."

The Upper Peninsula shares a border with northeastern Wisconsin, then stretches east for 334 miles between Lakes Superior and Michigan, and reaches a third Great Lake, Huron, where it terminates at Drummond Island. Also considered part of the U.P. is 45-mile-long Isle Royale, the largest island in Lake Superior. The entire Isle Royale archipelago is a national park, one of the most remote and least-visited in the national park system.

Altogether, Michigan's landmass covers 58,110 square miles, making it the largest state east of the Mississippi. But it is water that defines Michigan, and helps to make it the 10th largest state in America. Along with its 3,288-mile shoreline—second only to Alaska—it encompasses more than 11,000 lakes, over 36,000 miles of rivers, and nearly 200 waterfalls, and boasts 16 federally designated Wild and Scenic Rivers. Both the Upper and Lower Peninsulas are home to a national lakeshore—Pictured Rocks and Sleeping Bear Dunes, respectively.

The Great Lakes State, Water Wonderland, Land of Hiawatha . . . many of Michigan's nicknames accurately describe this most beautiful of Midwestern states.

CLIMATE

It's difficult to make any generalizations about Michigan's climate, given that its two peninsulas cover a lot of latitude, and the Great Lakes tend to complicate weather patterns. Still, the state's weather is probably more moderate than you think, since the ever-looming Great Lakes cool the hot summer air and warm the cold winter winds.

Michigan has four distinct seasons. Summers require shorts and T-shirts almost everywhere (except near Lake Superior, where you'll want a sweatshirt handy). July and August temperatures average in the 80s in the Lower Peninsula and the 70s in the Upper Peninsula. Come December through February, they drop to the 30s in the L.P. and the 20s in the U.P. (Temperatures listed here are in degrees Fahrenheit.)

But don't take any of this too seriously. You can enjoy springlike skiing conditions in the U.P. in February, or freeze to death at Thanksgiving. You may swelter on a summer hike through the woods, then grab for your fleece on a Great Lakes beach. Michigan is anything but predictable.

The Lake Effect

The Great Lakes act like insulators—slow to warm up, slow to cool down. That's what allows for Michigan's valuable fruit harvest: Lake Michigan moderates springtime temperatures, so fruit trees and vines aren't usually tempted to bud until the threat of frost has passed.

The Great Lakes also have a dramatic effect on snowfall. Dry winter air travels over the Great Lakes on the prevailing western winds, absorbing moisture. When this air hits land, it dumps its load of precipitation in the form of snow. Weather people refer to this phenomenon as lake effect snows, which can be surprisingly localized—hence, the reason you'll find many of Michigan's ski resorts clustered along the western edge of the state.

The prevailing western breezes also affect water temperatures, most noticeably on Lake Michigan. In summer, the warm surface waters tend to blow right into those nice, sandy beaches along the lake's eastern edge. While Lake Michigan is rarely warm enough for swimming on the Wisconsin side, it can be downright pleasant in Michigan—as evidenced by the numerous popular beaches lining the state.

Lake Superior is another story. Temperatures on this deep, huge, northern lake never climb out of the 40s, save for the occasional shallow bay. "No one's ever drowned in Lake Superior," the saying goes. "They all die of hypothermia first."

Freshwater freezes faster than saltwater, and the Great Lakes will often freeze over from land to several miles out. The ice gets thick enough for brave souls to snowmobile to the islands, especially nearby ones like Mackinac. The commercial shipping season shuts down from mid-January to late March, but bad weather

AVERAGE TEMPERATURES
(High/Low °F)

Month	Detroit	Marquette
January	31/16	25/11
February	34/18	29/14
March	44/27	37/22
April	58/37	48/33
May	69/47	61/42
June	79/56	70/51
July	83/61	76/57
August	82/59	74/57
September	74/52	66/49
October	63/41	55/40
November	48/31	40/28
December	35/22	30/17

temperatures in northern Michigan from Thanksgiving to Easter. If you want reliable snow, head to the Upper Peninsula. While the Detroit area averages about 41 inches of snow a year, the U.P. gets blanketed with more than 160 inches annually.

U.P. snows are legendary, especially in the Keweenaw Peninsula, where 300-inch winters aren't that unusual. (Sticking far out into Lake Superior, it *really* gets nailed with lake effect snows.) In summer, you'll often notice curious elevated, pierlike contraptions leading from some houses to the sidewalk—no need to shovel those front walks in winter until there's at least 24 inches on the ground. Ladders nailed to roofs are there for a reason, too. When accumulated snows threaten to collapse the roof, the ladders give a foothold from which to clear off the stuff.

You should be aware of a dangerous little thing called the windchill factor, when cold temperatures are coupled with biting winds. If it's 5°F outside, a 15-mph wind will make it feel like -25°. Besides being exceedingly uncomfortable, it means you're at an even greater risk for frostbite or hypothermia. Weather forecasts tend to warn you about the windchill factor, but not always; remember to consider both the temperature and the wind speed when dressing for the outdoors.

That said, many people welcome Michigan's winter, which constitutes a huge piece of the state's tourism pie. Few other areas in the Midwest can offer as reliable a season for skiing, snowboarding, snowmobiling, ice fishing, and snowshoeing. Of course, sitting around a fire or soaking in a hot tub is acceptable behavior, too.

often hampers it for much longer. Commercial ships regularly pound through ice up to a foot thick; more than that, and they rely on the Coast Guard's new *Mackinaw*, a 240-foot reinforced ship designed for ramming a passage through ice.

Michigan Winters
You can usually count on snow and cold

Flora and Fauna

TREES AND PLANTS

There's a reason the white pine is the state tree—vast stands of it once covered the northern portions of the state, making Michigan the nation's leading lumber center. Michigan pine largely rebuilt Chicago after the Great Fire and supplied a hungry nation as it expanded westward across the treeless plains.

Today, a few tracts of virgin white pine, red pine, and cedar remain in Michigan, magnificent species scraping the sky several stories above. Much of Michigan's original prime logging land is now second-growth pines, many growing tall again. Today's logging operations still clear-cut, but in much smaller sections, and are increasingly turning to selective-cutting methods.

Along with pines in the north, much of the state is covered in hardwoods, especially oak, maple, aspen, and birch. Since Michigan has few native prairies, except in the southwestern corner of the state, many of its plant species are woodland varieties, including columbine, iris, aster, blazing star, various berries, and several species of orchids. Along the coastal dunes, milkweed and wormwood thrive.

MAMMALS AND BIRDS

Though it's called the Wolverine State, there's no evidence wolverines ever lived in Michigan—just a lot of tall tales about how it acquired the nickname. Most likely, early fur traders brought wolverine pelts to the numerous trading posts here.

With more than half the state forested, Michigan harbors lots of red foxes, skunks, squirrels, badgers, minks, muskrats, bats, and other small mammals. The state has a huge—and problematic—population of white-tailed deer throughout, and a very healthy number of black bears in its northern reaches. Elk can be found in the northeastern

© ST. IGNACE VISITORS BUREAU

white-tailed deer in winter

THREATENED PLANTS OF THE GREAT LAKES

In summer, Michigan's forests, riverbanks, and beaches are rife with native ferns, weeds, and wildflowers. While some of these vibrant landscapes remain relatively intact, others have long suffered from human encroachment. As a result, the following endemic plants are at risk for extinction, due to habitat loss or destruction:

- **American hart's-tongue fern** – once prevalent throughout the U.P.'s Hiawatha National Forest, now threatened by former logging and quarrying practices

- **Dwarf lake iris** – once prevalent throughout the U.P.'s Hiawatha National Forest and along the northern shores of Lakes Michigan and Huron, now threatened by various industries, including tourism

- **Eastern prairie fringed orchid** – once prevalent throughout Michigan's prairies and wetlands, now threatened by agricultural practices

- **Houghton's goldenrod** – once prevalent along the sandy shores of Lakes Michigan and Huron, now threatened by human coastal activities

- **Lakeside daisy** – once prevalent in the U.P.'s Hiawatha National Forest, now threatened by former limestone quarrying

- **Michigan monkey-flower** – once prevalent along Michigan's streams and lakeshores, now endangered by recreational and residential development

- **Pitcher's thistle** – once prevalent amid Michigan's coastal dunes, now threatened by human shoreline activities

While enjoying Michigan's great outdoors, take care not to disturb these and other precious natural resources. For further information, consult the **U.S. Fish & Wildlife Service** (www.fws.gov) or **The Nature Conservancy** (www.nature.org).

Houghton's goldenrod on Bois Blanc Island

© MICHAEL JAMES WHITE, SR.

portion of the L.P., part of a successful reintroduction program. Wolves, moose, bobcats, and cougars live in secluded areas of the U.P.

Some 300 kinds of birds live in the state, including such notable species as bald eagles, peregrine falcons, loons, swans, herons, and dozens of songbirds. Hunting is popular for game birds such as ducks, geese, grouse, and pheasant. Michigan lies on a major migratory pathway, so it offers excellent bird-watching in spring and fall. Of special note is the hawk migration, as thousands fly between the southern Lower Peninsula and Canada.

REPTILES, AMPHIBIANS, AND FISH

The backwoods and lakeshores of Michigan are rife with reptiles and amphibians, including numerous varieties of toads, frogs, salamanders, and snakes. With so much water, fish thrive here, too, in both the Great Lakes and inland waters. Though commercial fishing has decreased dramatically in the last few decades (the result of overfishing, and the accidental introduction of the lamprey eel and zebra mussel), sportfishing remains popular on the Great Lakes, for chinook salmon, coho, steelhead, lake trout, and brown trout. On inland waters, the walleye and yellow perch are prized for flavor, while the muskie and northern pike are considered top sport fish. Bass and trout can also be found on inland waters. Michigan has several blue-ribbon streams, especially near Traverse City and Grayling in the Lower Peninsula, and in the eastern U.P.

INSECTS AND ARACHNIDS

While parts of Michigan lie along the migratory route of the stunning monarch butterfly, the state also has its share of pesky insects. There's a reason you spot those corny T-shirts proclaiming the mosquito as the Michigan state bird. The first hatch of mosquitoes usually occurs in early June (depending on local weather conditions), and the little buggers immediately discover their love for humans. They won't seriously injure you, but their sting will cause a small, itchy lump. Most populous in woods and low-lying wet areas, and most active at dusk, mosquitoes can persist all summer, but tend to be less of a problem as the season wears on, especially if conditions are dry. Your best way to avoid them is to stay in a breeze, and wear long pants and long sleeves. Many people swear by repellent; the stuff with deet is most effective, but studies have linked it with various health risks. If you choose to use repellent, be sure to wash your hands carefully before eating, and read the label warnings, especially before applying it on small children. Some people also swear that eating a lot of garlic makes one less attractive to mosquitoes. (Probably to your hiking partners, too, but hey, this is about survival.)

Black flies can be an equally obnoxious travel companion. Like mosquitoes, black flies don't pose any health risk but have a nasty bite— somewhere between a mosquito bite and a bee sting on the pain scale. Black flies look like houseflies on steroids. They tend to be worst in the deep woods and in early summer. U.P. black flies can be the stuff of legend; anyone planning time in the backcountry there would be wise to carry the nastiest repellent they can find, and pack a head net, too.

The wilds of Michigan are also favored by a variety of beetles, including the multicolored Asian lady beetle, which was imported in the early 20th century to control other insect pests. You might also encounter spiders on your hikes through the Great Lakes State. Be especially careful of the black widow and the extremely rare brown recluse; the bites of both are poisonous and painful.

REINTRODUCTION PROGRAMS

Michigan has had great success reintroducing two large mammals to the state. The eastern elk, once common in Michigan, had disappeared from the state by 1875. In 1918, state officials relocated seven Rocky Mountain elk to Cheboygan County in the northeastern Lower Peninsula. Today, nearly 900 Rocky Mountain elk roam the woods and meadows of a four-county area. The largest concentration lies within the Pigeon River Country State Forest near Vanderbilt.

In the 1980s, moose were reintroduced to a remote area south of the U.P.'s Huron Mountains, where officials released a total of 59 moose from Ontario in two separate operations. Most interesting was the method of reintroduction: Wildlife biologists airlifted the moose one by one in a sling dangling beneath a helicopter to a base camp where they were trucked 600 miles to the Huron Mountains. Van Riper State Park near Michigamme has an interesting display with photos of the infamous "moose lifts." It worked—today, about 500 roam the central U.P.

ENDANGERED SPECIES

At last count, Michigan was home to over 80 threatened or endangered animals and insects, and more than 260 plant species. One of the ones that didn't make it was the passenger pigeon. Michigan was one of the premier places in the world to watch the passenger pigeon migration, which would literally blacken the skies as hundreds of thousands of birds took flight. Unfortunately, their meat became a delicacy and they were easy to hunt, a combination that wiped out the species nationwide by 1914.

One hopes a happier ending will result for the gray wolf. With plenty of deer to eat and few roads and people to disturb them, wolves have begun to repopulate the Upper Peninsula without help from humans, strolling over from Minnesota, or across the ice from Ontario. (The wolves that originally populated Isle Royale came across on the ice in the late 1940s.) The wolf is doing so well, in fact, that it has been moved from endangered to threatened status. With all the controversy surrounding the wolf reintroduction to Yellowstone, Michigan's wolves are indeed a success story.

History

MICHIGAN'S NATIVE PEOPLES

Buried under layers of glacial ice until about 10,000 years ago, the land that is now Michigan was inhospitable to many of the native cultures that thrived in much of the Midwest, like the Paleo and Archaic Indians. Some of the first signs of civilization can be found in the Upper Peninsula's Keweenaw Peninsula, where the Copper Culture Indians of about 5000–500 B.C. left evidence of their skill as prehistoric miners, devising ways to extract copper from bedrock and fashioning it into tools. Archaeologists believe they may be the world's earliest toolmakers.

Later, the Algonquin Indians migrated to the Great Lakes region from the banks of the St. Lawrence Seaway, probably after A.D. 1000. The Algonquins were divided into three tribes: the Ottawa (or Odawa), the Ojibwa (or Chippewa), and the Potawatomi. Together, they called themselves the Anishinabe (first people) and named their new land *Michi Gami* (large lake). In and around that lake, they found the state's abundant wildlife—including fish, white-tailed deer, moose, elk, and black bear—and rich natural resources that nourished the tribes for centuries.

The three tribes coexisted peacefully, each moving to a different area. The Ottawa settled around Sault Ste. Marie, the Straits of Mackinac, and the Leelanau Peninsula; the Ojibwa moved west, along the shores of Lake Superior; and the Potawatomi headed south, to the southern half of the Lower Peninsula. They communicated regularly, and their peaceable relationship proved valuable when others came to their lands. Together, they successfully fought off the warring Iroquois who came from the east in the 1600s, and presented themselves as a strong, unified people when the Europeans arrived.

FRENCH SETTLERS

Étienne Brulé, the first European to arrive on the state's soil (in 1615), was more interested in exploiting the land than worshipping it. Brulé was sent by Samuel de Champlain, lieutenant governor of New France, who hoped to find copper and a shortcut to the Far East. Brulé sent back reports recounting the land's untamed beauty and strange new flora and fauna.

Other opportunists soon followed. Some were after Michigan's rich supply of furs, others after the souls of what they saw as a godless land. Among the most famous of these early explorers was Father Jacques Marquette, who established the state's first permanent settlement at Sault Ste. Marie in 1668, and a second outpost at the straits of Michilimackinac in 1671. The French *coureurs de bois,* a loose term for unlicensed traders, provided a sharp contrast to the priests and nobility. Rugged individualists, they lived among the Native Americans, respected their customs, and hunted the region's rich stores of game.

Marquette's 17th-century writings brought even more settlers, mostly fur traders such as John Jacob Astor. In the early 1800s, Astor's American Fur Company, headquartered on Mackinac Island, made him the richest man in the United States. Few efforts were made to establish a permanent settlement until 1696, when Antoine de la Mothe Cadillac convinced France's King Louis XIV that the area was under threat from the British, who were forming alliances with the Native Americans, and that it would be a strategic stronghold for the French crown.

The king sent Cadillac and a 100-men-strong passel of priests, soldiers, and settlers to found Fort Pontchartrain in 1701. Cadillac, in turn, persuaded several Native American tribes to form a sort of coalition and settle near the fort. Within a short time, thousands of Native Americans and several hundred French families lived nearby, many establishing narrow "ribbon farms" along the Detroit River. Known as *la ville détroit* (the village at the strait), it soon became an important trading post and a strategic base for the area's continued settlement. Detroit remains the oldest city in the state and, surprisingly, among the oldest in the Midwest.

BRITISH SETTLERS
The area wasn't peaceful for long. As the fur trade became more lucrative, the intensity of the British and French animosity reached its peak, resulting in the French and Indian War in the mid-1700s. The war effectively ended the 145-year French era and, in 1759, ushered in British rule. Skirmishes continued, though, especially around the Straits of Mackinac. Today, museums and historic state parks in the area chronicle the events.

The British ruled the colony with an iron fist. While the French had treated the Native Americans with a certain amount of respect, the British allied themselves with tribes that were traditional enemies of those native to the area. The British actively discouraged settlement of the state's interior to protect their rich fur empire. In 1783, the Treaty of Paris gave the lands to the newly independent United States.

STATEHOOD
In 1825, New York's Erie Canal, which connected Albany on the Hudson River to Buffalo on Lake Erie, opened. This new water route enabled more and more whites to move westward and settle in the Michigan Territory. From 1820 to 1830, the population more than tripled, to just over 31,000. In 1837, the burgeoning territory was awarded statehood, making Michigan the 26th state in the Union.

By 1840, more than 200,000 people had moved to Michigan. Early industry revolved around farming and agriculture, with lumber becoming a hugely successful enterprise in the later part of the century. Altogether, more than 160 billion feet of pine were cut and hauled from Michigan's northwoods by the 1890s—enough to build 10 million six-room houses. While the southern part of the state grew increasingly civilized, the northwoods were filled with wild and rollicking logging camps.

INDIAN REMOVAL ACT
In one of the saddest chapters in our nation's history, President Andrew Jackson signed the Indian Removal Act in 1830, giving the U.S. government permission to "trade" Native American lands east of the Mississippi for unspecified lands out west. The federal government claimed it was for the tribes' own protection, reporting—and correctly so—that whites would continue to surge into their homelands in the name of frontier expansion.

The Indians, of course, had no interest in leaving what had been their homeland for centuries. Tribes in northern Michigan were largely ignored by the federal Indian Bureau at first, most likely because the government found their lands undesirable at the time. After all, the Potawatomi, who lived on valuable farmland in southern Michigan, were forcibly removed from their lands.

Unfortunately, the federal government didn't leave the tribes alone for long. By the mid-1800s, treaties "legally" took away more and more Native American land in both the Upper and Lower Peninsulas and established many of the reservations that exist today.

The new state government, however, did treat the tribes with a modicum of decency. In 1850, Native Americans were given the right to vote and even run for office in counties where the population was predominantly Indian—a concession unheard of elsewhere for many years.

THE COPPER RUSH

In 1840, State Geologist Douglass Houghton confirmed the presence of copper in the Upper Peninsula's Keweenaw Peninsula—vast deposits of pure, native copper, much of it right near the surface. The U.S. acquired the western half of the U.P.—and its mineral rights—from the Ojibwa in 1842, as prospectors began flooding toward the wild and remote Keweenaw. The young country had an insatiable appetite for the metal, first for new industrial machinery, and later, for Civil War hardware, electrical wiring, and other innovations. Houghton's find was nearly as good as gold.

The Copper Rush began almost overnight, first with prospectors, then large mining enterprises swarming the Keweenaw. Lucky prospectors secured deck space on Great Lakes vessels, sailing up Lakes Huron and Michigan, then along the southern shore of Superior. But hundreds of others straggled through the roadless wilderness, trudging overland through northern Wisconsin by snowshoe, or following rivers through thick forests to reach the fabled riches. It was the nation's first mineral rush. Copper employed thousands of immigrant laborers, built cities, made millionaires, and prompted extravagant luxuries like opera houses and "copper baron" mansions. Before it was over, King Copper generated more than $9.6 billion—10 times more money than the California gold rush.

The entire nation turned to the Keweenaw for its copper. From 1845 to 1895, the Keweenaw Peninsula produced 75 percent of U.S. copper; during the Civil War, it produced 90 percent. More than 400 mining companies operated in the Keweenaw over the course of the 19th century, and the resulting demand for labor drew immigrants from more than 30 countries—most notably, the British Isles and Scandinavia. With multiple cultures sharing the same mine shafts and communities, the

underground mining

Copper Country served as one of the nation's first true melting pots.

In the mid-1900s, however, virtually all the big mines disappeared, sealed up by economic conditions, leaving behind tattered houses and empty streets. They had extracted the easiest-to-reach copper; soon, newer mines in the southwestern U.S. and South America proved more cost-effective.

THE 20TH CENTURY AND THE RISE OF THE AUTOMOBILE

In the early 1900s, industrial giants such as Kellogg and Dow were getting their start, giving rise to industries that flourish even today. Yet few innovations had as much influence on the state—or on the nation—as the "horseless carriage." Shortly after the turn of the century, it gave birth to the state's largest corporate citizens: Ford, Chrysler, and General Motors. As the entire nation grew dependent on their products, the powerful "Big Three" automakers would soon change the face of the state forever.

With the auto industry came thousands of well-paying jobs and, for most, an improved standard of living. Henry Ford's revolutionary $5-a-day wage attracted workers from across the country and around the world, making Detroit among the country's richest melting pots. Agricultural workers from the Deep South, looking for a better wage, came north to work in the gleaming new factories. Many were African American, an influx that created the Detroit area's largest ethnic group.

As time passed, changing working conditions and a lack of employee representation in the auto factories spurred another American invention: the creation of the labor movement and the rise of unions.

THE 1930s-1950s

While labor unions have existed in Michigan since statehood, few were organized until the 1930s. A number of factors contributed to their growth, including auto industry automation, the uncertainties of the Great Depression, and the pro-labor New Deal environment. The most famous confrontation between labor and management was the 1936 sit-down strike in Flint, which led to General Motors accepting the United Auto Workers as the sole bargaining agent for its employees.

In contrast to the Depression, the 1950s were an era of great growth and prosperity. Only Florida and California attracted more people during the decade. The rise of the number of school-age children led, in part, to the greatest expansion of the state's educational system and the founding of new community colleges and other facilities of higher education. While plans to build a bridge connecting the state's two peninsulas had existed as early as 1884, it wasn't until the 1950s that the Mackinac Bridge Authority was founded and funds were raised. Work on the bridge began in 1954, one of the largest and most innovative engineering projects in the country. "Big Mac" opened to the public on November 1, 1957, at last linking the two disparate halves of the state.

THE CIVIL RIGHTS ERA

Racial tensions have occasionally erupted into violence throughout Michigan's history, but few eras were as turbulent as the 1960s. The national struggle for social justice and equality came to a head in Michigan, in some of the state's worst race riots. Before state and federal troops restored a semblance of order in Detroit on July 23, 1967, 43 people had been killed, more than 1,000 injured, and over 7,000 arrested. Damage to property topped $50 million. This tragic event was just one of several violent episodes that marred the era.

In some ways, the city of Detroit and the state of Michigan are still digging out from those indelible events. While the makeshift yellow fences that bordered riot sites have long been replaced by new development throughout the city, the psychological scars have proven harder to heal. Race relations are an ongoing, front-burner issue in Detroit, one of the most racially divided cities in the country. Always described as the metro area's largest "minority" group, African Americans are, in fact, no longer the minority at all, at least in a demographic sense: Detroit is now over 80 percent African-American.

CONTEMPORARY TIMES

Along with healing racial wounds, Michigan faces a number of other challenges in the coming years. The state must wrestle with an increasingly poor urban population, growing concern with quality of life, and an overdependence on the ever-fluctuating fortunes of the automobile industry.

On the positive side, one of Michigan's enduring strengths is its abundant natural resources, including one of the nation's largest forest areas and a staggering supply of freshwater—a commodity that, in the long run, will probably prove more valuable than oil. With a 19th-century history of land scarred from clear-cutting virgin forests and lackadaisical mining practices, one hopes Michigan has learned some lessons. Only history will tell if the state chooses to protect or exploit its vast cache of natural riches.

Government and Economy

GOVERNMENT

Politically, the state has traditionally been a stronghold of the Republican party. One of the major developments of the post–World War II years in Michigan, however, was the emergence of a competitive two-party political arena. Starting during the Depression, the Democratic Party made major inroads in the state.

Labor union leadership, including the powerful United Auto Workers, became much more active in postwar politics, reflecting the union's interest in larger social issues and quality of life outside the workplace. The electoral support of African-Americans, whose population had more than doubled between 1940 and 1950, also helped strengthen the Democratic Party. In 1948, Democrat G. Mennen Williams won the first of what would be six terms as Michigan's governor.

Beginning in the 1950s and continuing through today, Michigan politics reflect a highly competitive two-party state. Among the current Michigan politicians in the spotlight is Governor Jennifer M. Granholm, who became the state's first female governor in 2002, following John Engler's 12-year term. As governor, Granholm has worked to diversify Michigan's economy, expand educational opportunities for residents, and create universal access to affordable health care.

Also worth watching is former Detroit mayor

Dennis Archer, who took over from controversial mayor Coleman Young in 1992. While Young was best known for antagonizing the suburbs and championing the rights of urban African Americans, Archer proved much more of a peacemaker, striving to mend the seemingly insurmountable rift between the predominantly black city and its predominantly white

STATE SYMBOLS

- State bird – American robin
- State fish – brook trout
- State flower – apple blossom
- State fossil – mastodon
- State game mammal – white-tailed deer
- State gem – Isle Royale greenstone
- State reptile – painted turtle
- State soil – Kalkaska sand
- State stone – Petoskey stone
- State tree – white pine
- State wildflower – dwarf lake iris

suburbs. While he refused to run for reelection in 2001, he recently announced his possible intention of running for governor in 2010.

ECONOMY

Despite its patchwork of farm and field, Michigan remains a highly industrialized state. Heavy manufacturing leads its list of income-producing industries, followed by tourism and agriculture.

For almost two centuries, Michigan has been a mirror of the country's great industrial transition. As the state's economy has evolved from agriculture and fur trading to metals, logging, and, finally, automobile manufacturing, the state has ridden a roller coaster that shows no signs of stopping.

Ironically, the ups and downs that sometimes curse the state's economic fortunes are nothing new. Just as today's auto industry has experienced both wild success and dismal failure, so it was with the mining era in the Upper Peninsula, which left a legacy of fantastic wealth juxtaposed with depressed towns huddled around played-out mines. In the 1880s, just before the birth of the automobile, many Detroit residents thought that the city had already seen its greatest growth. Little did they know that in the city's workshops and laboratories, inventors were talking about a revolution.

Industry

Most Americans today need only look in their garages or on their kitchen tables to find evidence of Michigan's diversified economy. While a variety of businesses call Michigan home, the state will always be associated with the automobile industry. Nicknamed "Motor City," the state's largest town and most of its economy are driven by the most enduring of American inventions.

With $5-a-day wages and innovative automated assembly lines, Henry Ford revolutionized the industrial world with his "horseless carriage." To this day, the "Big Three"—Ford, Chrysler, and General Motors—maintain world headquarters in metropolitan Detroit. Those

corporations in turn spawned hundreds of auto-related businesses and legions of millionaires.

Outside of Detroit, industries are a bit more varied. To the west, Battle Creek is the cereal capital of the country, a place where the Kellogg brothers pioneered their new breakfast food at the Battle Creek Sanitarium. Grand Rapids has long been associated with the furniture industry. Midland is the home of Dow Chemical Company. Tiny Fremont claims Gerber, one of the world's best-known baby-food companies. Other Michigan exports include nonelectric machinery, appliances, pharmaceuticals, and lumber.

Agriculture

Beyond the larger cities, however, agriculture dominates. Farming remains an important presence in the state, with approximately 52,800 farms occupying a total of 10,000,000 acres. Crops vary from corn to cherries. The state ranks first in the nation in the production of red tart cherries, dry beans, blueberries, picking cucumbers, and potted geraniums.

Other principal field crops include hay, oats, corn, rye, potatoes, soybeans, wheat, and sugar

a typical Michigan farm

© L. DIGGS, PICTURE THIS...

MADE IN MICHIGAN

Yep, Henry Ford created the automobile assembly line in Michigan, which in turn prompted the nation's first mile of concrete highway in 1909, and its first freeway in 1942. Here are a few other notable Michiganders and their inventions:

- Melville Bissell - carpet sweeper

- Herbert Dow - bleach

- Daniel Gerber - prepared baby food

- Dr. John Kellogg - ready-made breakfast cereal

- Dr. William Upjohn - dissolvable pill

- James Vernor - ginger ale

staggering $48 billion in iron, compared with $955 million from the gold rush. The riches and the miners disappeared as the most accessible deposits were exhausted and global economics began to play a role. Nearly all the U.P.'s mines shut down by the mid-1900s.

Tourism

Since the U.P.'s former industries folded, it's relied largely on tourism to maintain its sputtering economy, luring many visitors with its unsurpassed rugged beauty. Today, tourism is one of Michigan's largest income producers, accounting for over $18 billion in annual revenues and nearly 200,000 jobs statewide. At one time, tourism was focused on the summer months, when beaches, festivals, and resort towns in the Lower Peninsula were most popular. Nowadays, however, the state is a four-season destination, attracting anglers in spring, hunters in fall, and all manner of skiers, snowmobilers, and skaters in winter.

Shipping and Fishing

Just as semis rumble down the interstate, commercial ships transport commodities across the Great Lakes. Officially designated as the nation's "Fourth Seacoast" by Congress in 1970, the Great Lakes serve as a vital, economical transportation artery for the nation's commerce. Via the U.S.-Flag fleet, about 125 million tons of cargo travel across the lakes each year. Without them, many of the country's largest industries, including Michigan's auto manufacturing, couldn't survive.

With its hundreds of miles of Great Lakes shoreline and dozens of deepwater ports, Michigan is a key player in the Great Lakes transportation network. What's more, the Soo Locks that link Lakes Superior and Huron at Sault Ste. Marie rank as the largest and busiest lock system in the world.

Iron ore forms the foundation of the Great Lakes trade. In Upper Peninsula ports like Escanaba and Marquette, huge lake carriers as long as 1,000 feet load iron ore from nearby mines, then transport it to steelmaking centers in the southern Great Lakes, where the steel

beets. The western side of the state, which enjoys warmer temperatures modified by Lake Michigan, is known as the "Fruit Belt" and has made the state a leading producer of apples, plums, peaches, and sweet cherries. It also has proved surprisingly tolerant for growing wine grapes, and Michigan's winemaking industry continues to surprise people with its award-winning and ever-improving vintages. Rounding out the state's wide-ranging agricultural products are fresh market and processing vegetables, mushrooms, potted Eastern lilies, spearmint, milk, eggs, and poultry.

Logging and Mining

Farther north, the Upper Peninsula's economy was long based on logging and mining. Great fortunes were made in logging in the late 1800s, as Michigan's vast stands of virgin timber produced enough wood to lay an inch-thick plank across the state—with enough left over to cover Rhode Island, too. Few can even grasp the riches of Michigan's copper and iron mining industries, which each dwarfed the gold rush taking place in California. Michigan produced more than $9.6 billion in copper and a

HENRY FORD AND THE HORSELESS CARRIAGE

Industrialist, billionaire, folk hero, preservationist, social engineer – these and many other labels exemplify Henry Ford's status as one of the most influential and complex Americans of the 20th century. While many schoolchildren learn the story of Ford's pioneering assembly line and the affordably priced Model T it spawned, most know little else of the automaker who rose from rural southeastern Michigan to become one of the world's richest and most powerful men.

Ford was born in 1863 on a prosperous farm in what is now Dearborn, a Detroit suburb. His was a typical rural 19th-century childhood, including endless chores and long lessons in a one-room school. From an early age, he was fascinated by machinery. He loved tinkering with watches, and saw his first steam engine at 12. Four years later, he moved to Detroit to serve as a machinist's apprentice. At 18, he accepted an engineer position at the Edison Illuminating Company. In 1893, he was promoted to chief engineer and began tinkering with a crude iron contraption in his spare time – the first gasoline engine.

In 1894, Ford began his first automobile, the Quadricycle, in a small workshop behind his home. Two years later, he took it for its first test run and sold it for $200, later buying it back as a souvenir. By 1898, he'd quit his job at Edison to devote himself full-time to his dream of producing automobiles.

His first business venture, the Detroit Automobile Company, lasted just a year and was dissolved in 1901. His next effort only fared a little better, with Ford resigning in 1902 as president of the Henry Ford Company, which, under Henry Leland's leadership, developed into the Cadillac Motor Company.

Ford finally hit pay dirt with the Ford Motor Company, which he established in 1903 at age 40. The inexpensive, two-cylinder Model A and Model C sold so fast that by 1905 the company was forced to move out of its original factory into larger quarters. Ford succeeded, in part, because he viewed the automobile not as a luxury, but as a tool that could ease the burden of everyday men. He strove to make his products as inexpensive as possible, believing that a low price tag and prompt service would please his customers more than flashy trim.

The car that put America on wheels was Ford's legendary Model T, which became the nation's workhorse. By 1925, the price had dropped to just $260, and sales climbed. More than 15 million were bought and sold. A major reason for the car's low cost was the rise of the assembly line – also pioneered by Ford. Waist-level workstations minimized the effort expended, and the line moved at the exact speed needed to mount a carburetor or lubricate a chassis. The assembly line cut production costs tremendously.

In 1914, Ford made yet another contribution: a profit-sharing plan that more than doubled the salaries of his workers to $5 per day. This reduced Ford's turnover and training costs and made him a national hero. People flocked to Detroit from around the world to work in his plants.

By 1918, Ford had become bored with the company and turned to other interests, including a failed attempt to end World War I and an unsuccessful bid for the U.S. Senate. Though his engineering skills were untouchable, some of his other habits were less sound. His company's "Sociological Department," established to monitor the conduct of workers, invaded the privacy of their homes. Too, Ford was condemned for his anti-Semitic beliefs and practices.

Ford's views grew increasingly rigid as he aged. Despite the fact that his $5-a-day plan made him a working-class hero, he voiced violent opposition to the formation of labor unions during the 1920s. This caused widespread unrest in his factories. Ford Motor

© DETROIT METRO CVB

F-150 truck assembly line at Dearborn's Ford Rouge Factory

Company, in fact, was the last of the major auto companies to sign with the United Auto Workers in 1941.

Since Ford, who died in 1947, amassed such enormous fame and wealth, it has been incorrectly assumed that he was the first to build a gas-powered car. That title belongs to George B. Selden of Rochester, New York, who applied for the first patent in 1879, the same year that Ford left the family farm. Problems with patents caused some of his greatest frustrations, long after his original competitors were out of business.

While Ford is perhaps the best known of Michigan's motoring men, others also played key roles. Charles B. King, an engineer, drove the first gas-powered horseless carriage through the streets of Detroit in 1896, six months before Ford. That same year, Ransom

Olds of Oldsmobile fame drove a gas-powered vehicle through downtown Lansing. A successful industrialist, Olds developed a steam-powered experimental vehicle as early as 1887. He made his greatest mark, however, in 1900 when he invented a tiny, motorized buggy known as a "Runabout." Other key figures include Dodge, Durant, Mott, and Sloan, all of whom played crucial, if often forgotten, parts in the history of the car.

Of today's "Big Three" – Ford Motor Company, General Motors, and the Chrysler Corporation – Ford is the only one still partially owned by the original family. Henry Ford was always at the center of his company, and his descendants remain involved today. William Clay Ford, Jr., one of his great-grandsons, was named board chairman in 1998, the first Ford to hold the title in over 15 years.

is, in turn, used by heavy manufacturers like Detroit's auto industry.

Heavy manufacturing also drives much of the demand for the second-largest cargo, limestone, which is used as a purifying agent in steelmaking. The construction, chemical, and paper industries rely on limestone, too. Michigan has a good corner on the market: The limestone quarry in Rogers City, northwest of Alpena, ranks as the largest in the world.

Great Lakes shipping does face its share of competition, especially from overseas, in the form of imported finished products ranging from refrigerators to automobiles. That translates to a decrease in steel production here, which in turn reduces the need for iron ore shipments. Secondly, other transportation networks like trains and trucks compete with shipping for certain commodities. But overall, shipping has proved to be a steady industry, and total cargo shipments have remained fairly even over the last decade.

People and Culture

While the Algonquins were the land's first inhabitants, today's Michiganders reflect a much more diverse population. The French "empire builders" were the first Europeans to come, and in due time, the British replaced the French. Early American settlers included a large group of Yankees from western New York and New England. From Europe came immigrants seeking a better life, including Finns, Cornish, Swedes, and Italians who worked in the Upper Peninsula mines and lumber camps. Germans, Irish, and Dutch settled in the cities and the rich agricultural lands to the south. Later, the automobile industry attracted large numbers of immigrants from southern and eastern Europe and, later, a large influx of southerners. Between 1850 and 1900, the state's population increased by more than 600 percent.

Today, Michigan's residents number 10.1 million, making it the eighth most populous state in the United States. The vast majority of the state's residents live in the southern third of the Lower Peninsula, mostly near major cities. Just three counties—Wayne, Oakland, and Macomb, near Detroit—contain 40 percent of Michigan's entire population.

NATIVE AMERICANS

In most books of Michigan history, the land's first inhabitants are given little more than a cursory nod, a line or two that identifies the approximately 100,000 early Native Americans as belonging to the tribes of the "Three Fires"— the Ojibwa, Ottawa, and Potawatomi— collectively known as the Anishinabe. During the 1700s, other tribes included the Huron, also known as the Wyandotte, who came to southeastern Michigan from Ontario; the Sauk, who lived in the Saginaw River Valley; the Miami, who lived along the St. Joseph River; and the Menominee, who lived in parts of the U.P.

The fact that Native Americans get little more than a footnote in many history books reflects a cultural ignorance throughout the nation. One of the few state museums to devote any space to the subject is the excellent Grand Rapids Public Museum, where the fine permanent exhibit, "Anishinabek: The People of This Place," traces the story of the Native Americans of western Michigan. While many tribes were being removed from their lands to reservations in Kansas and Oklahoma during the 1880s, Michigan's Anishinabe used skillful negotiation and hard work to remain in their homeland. Through video interviews, photographs borrowed from local families, and hundreds of artifacts, including clothing, tools, and decorative arts, the exhibition tells of the high price the tribe paid to remain citizens of the state, and of its ongoing struggle to preserve and protect this heritage in a swiftly changing modern society.

Today, Michigan is home to one of the largest Native American populations in the

PONTIAC: HERO OF THE OTTAWA

The son of an Ojibwa mother and Ottawa father, Pontiac (1720-1769) eventually became the chief of the Ottawa, Ojibwa, and Potawatomi people in the Great Lakes region. He is best known for organizing the most powerful coalition in Native American history.

During the French and Indian War (1754-1763), Native Americans joined the French in their battles against the British over land claims in North America. Nonetheless, the British were able to drive the French out of their most lucrative fur-trading areas. In early 1763, Pontiac organized a Detroit-area conference of the many tribes of the Great Lakes and Ohio Valley and convinced them to join together to fend off the British. The far-reaching alliance was a remarkable achievement, considering how widespread and disparate the tribes were at the time.

Pontiac's diplomacy skills were matched by his military ones. In 1763, Pontiac's forces seized every British post between the Straits of Mackinac and western New York, save for two. The fort at Detroit proved their downfall. While some accounts claim Pontiac's plan to capture Detroit was exposed by a "half-breed" girl, his men did besiege the fort for five months, withdrawing only when the French cut off their supplies. Pontiac and his people retreated to their hunting grounds and eventually signed a peace treaty with the British at Detroit in 1765.

Despite pressure from the French to renew warfare, Pontiac lived among the British in peace until 1769, when he was mysteriously killed in Illinois by a Native American reportedly bribed by a British trader.

country, estimated at 60,000, though it's hard to name an exact figure, since the label "Native American" can be defined in more than one way—by political, ethnic, or cultural criteria. Depending on how you count, Michigan may have the largest Indian population east of the Mississippi, and only a small percentage live on reservations. As with the state's general population, the majority of Michigan's Native American population resides near Detroit and Grand Rapids.

There are a number of reservations in the state, including federally recognized tribes in Brimley, Suttons Bay, Wilson, Fulton, Baraga, Watersmeet, Manistee, Petoskey, Dowagiac, Mount Pleasant, and Sault Ste. Marie. Some are authorized to operate their own tribal courts, which exercise exclusive jurisdiction over certain laws and civil matters involving Indians and events that occur on their reservations. In addition, Native American tribal councils throughout the state provide a variety of outreach services, economic development initiatives, and cultural activities.

Many reservations have cultural centers, and many tribes host powwows and festivals. For details, check with local tourism bureaus or inquire at tribal headquarters, which are prominent buildings on most reservations.

THE IMMIGRANTS

Traveling Michigan's numerous rivers as early as the 1600s, the French fur traders, missionaries, and voyageurs were the area's first white settlers, establishing posts in far-flung areas across the state. The majority of white immigrants, however, didn't arrive until the early 1800s. Expatriate New Englanders were the first in the 1830s, grabbing up vast tracts of land in the state's southern counties. More and more settlers followed in the next two decades, in response to a European food shortage.

During the remaining 19th and early 20th centuries, refugees from at least 40 countries arrived in record numbers. Among them were the Germans, still the largest ethnic group in Michigan. In the early 1830s, the first families settled the Ann Arbor area and the Saginaw River valley town of Frankenmuth—today a major tourist destination, famous for its Bavarian festivals and all-you-can-eat chicken dinners.

Other early immigrants included Dutch, Irish, and Poles, who continue to make up large chunks of the state's ethnic population. Concentrations of Dutch can still be found in Holland, a western city along Lake Michigan, where the tulip festival is one of the state's largest tourist attractions. Poles can be found throughout the state, most notably in Detroit's Hamtramck neighborhood. Not far away, the Irish settled Detroit's charming Corktown, the city's oldest neighborhood and the former home of the Detroit Tigers.

By the beginning of the 20th century, a new wave of immigrants poured into the state from southern and eastern Europe, including Austria, Hungary, Italy, and the Balkan States. Their arrival coincided with Detroit's newest industry, and thousands of them went to work in the auto factories. More recent migrations included Africans, Asians, Latinos, and Middle Eastern immigrants.

Today, African Americans make up one of the most influential ethnic groups in Michigan, especially in Detroit. While the majority of blacks came from the south to work in the auto industry, there has been an African-American presence in the state since Jean de Sable traded furs in the 1600s.

From the 1830s to 1860s, Michigan played an important role in the Underground Railroad, helping slaves escape north to Canada. Many escapees stayed in Michigan, mostly in the L.P.'s southwest corner, where they started their own farms in towns like Benton Harbor. Still, the largest number of African Americans came to Michigan after 1910, leaving families in the Deep South to find better jobs in Detroit's factories.

One of the state's newest waves of immigrants has been from the Arab world, including Iraq, Jordan, Lebanon, and Syria. Michigan today has one of the largest groups of Arabic people living in cities such as Dearborn and Southfield, where it's not unusual to see storefront signs in Arabic and women in full headdress.

The immigrants of the Upper Peninsula vary greatly from those of the Lower Peninsula. The iron and copper mines lured many from Sweden, Finland, Italy, and England with promises of steady work and decent wages, though despite difficult job conditions. Swedes and Finns in particular took to the U.P., at home with the area's woods and rushing rivers. Finnish names, foods, and the ubiquitous sauna can be found throughout the Keweenaw Peninsula, and Hancock remains largely Finnish, down to its street signs. Farther south, in Detroit, the Finnish Saarinen family helped develop Cranbrook Academy, a well-known private school and arts community near Detroit.

Arts and Entertainment

FINE ARTS

While state tourism boosters have long sung the praises of Michigan's legendary sand and surf, they've only, in recent years, begun heavily promoting its considerable cultural riches. The majority of the arts scene is concentrated in its larger cities, including Detroit, Grand Rapids, and Traverse City. Yet the arts thrive from Kalamazoo to Kalkaska—both mainstream and underground cultures that plug along without much state government support. The neighboring towns of Saugatuck and Douglas, for example, rely heavily on arts-related tourism; their downtown streets virtually teem with galleries.

Surprising as it might sound, the Detroit Institute of Arts is considered one of the country's top five art museums, and the Cranbrook Academy of Art, in nearby Bloomfield Hills, is a huge educational community that pioneered the Finnish Modern school. Outside Detroit, notable art museums include the University of Michigan Museum of Art in Ann Arbor, a city known for its galleries and excellent summer art

THE HEIDELBERG PROJECT

Buses full of Japanese tourists are a strange sight in this run-down neighborhood on Detroit's east side, a part of the city better known for its crack houses than its tourist attractions – that is, until artist Tyree Guyton, who grew up on Heidelberg Street, began The Heidelberg Project (313/267-1622, www.heidelberg.org), a remarkable piece of inner-city environmental art.

As a child, Guyton lived here in poverty, neglected, abused, and harassed for a growing interest in art. Only his grandfather encouraged him. Despite the odds, Guyton went on to study at Detroit's respected Center for Creative Studies (CCS), but he never forgot his roots. His first work was *Fun House*, created in 1986 from an abandoned house next door to his grandfather's duplex. He transformed the dilapidated frame structure with bright patches of color and covered it with old toys, dollhouses, picture frames, shoes, signs, and other urban cast-offs.

The Heidelberg Project grew to encompass most of Heidelberg Street between Mt. El-

liott and Ellery (to get there from downtown, take Gratiot northeast to Mt. Elliot and turn right). It drew acclaim from newspapers and art journals as well as curators at the nearby Detroit Institute of Arts, but failed to win over neighbors and then-mayor Coleman Young, who regularly demolished Guyton's work along with vacant houses. It takes pride in its reputation as Detroit's most controversial art project.

Former mayor Dennis Archer was more enlightened, and though he didn't openly encourage Guyton's work, he didn't discourage it either. Guyton's grandfather, who served as an unofficial tour guide, died back in 1992. His neat duplex is now part of the project, known as the *Dotty Wotty House* and dedicated to the memory of his grandfather and of Martin Luther King, Jr. Despite arson and vandalism, The Heidelberg Project has endured, and improvements are on the horizon, including a plan to transform the *OJ House* into the penny-covered *House That Makes Sense*. Admission is free if you visit on your own.

festival; the Flint Institute of Arts, which ranks second in size and scope only to the Detroit Institute of Arts; and the Kresge Art Museum at Michigan State University in East Lansing, noted for collections that span more than 5,000 years of art and local history. The Marshall M. Fredericks Sculpture Museum, part of Saginaw Valley State University, contains one of the state's finest sculpture collections.

MUSEUMS

The Henry Ford, in Dearborn, ranks among the state's top tourism draws, with a funky collection that ranges from vintage washing machines to presidential limousines. Adjacent Greenfield Village is a patchwork quilt of 83 historic buildings, including Thomas Edison's Menlo Park laboratory and Noah Webster's home, where he wrote the first American dictionary. Detroit's Charles H. Wright Museum of African American History is the largest of its

kind in the world, filled with dramatic visual arts and historic artifacts.

Not surprisingly, many of the state's museums cover the lore and legends of the Great Lakes and the state's maritime industry. Belle Isle, Detroit's 1,000-acre urban park, is home to the Dossin Great Lakes Museum, which includes a full-size freighter pilothouse and an anchor from the *Edmund Fitzgerald*, the Great Lakes ship that sank mysteriously in 1975.

In South Haven, the Michigan Maritime Museum traces the state's history from Native Americans to the 19th century, when huge freighters crossed Lake Michigan, the start of the state's tourism era. In the Upper Peninsula, more stories can be found at Whitefish Point's Great Lakes Shipwreck Museum, which tells the haunting tale of the hundreds of ships who met their match in the area's frigid, turbulent waters. Also in the U.P., the U.S. National Ski and Snowboard Hall of Fame Museum in

Ishpeming chronicles both sports, while neighboring Negaunee is home to the Michigan Iron Industry Museum, an excellent state-run facility on the site of one of the state's first iron forges.

LITERATURE

While most out-of-towners know about the famous musicians that hail from Detroit, few are perhaps aware of the many notable writers who, at times, have called the Great Lakes State home, including novelists Ernest Hemingway, Joyce Carol Oates, Elmore Leonard, and L. Frank Baum, author of *The Wizard of Oz*. Some authors were even born here, including Petoskey's Bruce Catton, Kalamazoo's Edna Ferber, and Port Huron's Terry McMillan. Pulitzer Prize–winning poet Theodore Rothke was born in Saginaw, and the former judge John D. Voelker, who wrote *Anatomy of a Murder* under his pen name, Robert Traver, spent his formative years in Ishpeming.

PERFORMING ARTS

In Motown, the restored Theater District is second only to Broadway in its number of available seats, with performances ranging from cutting-edge productions to the classics. Queen of the venues is the 5,000-seat Fox Theatre, a gloriously gaudy 1920s-era theater that defied the odds to survive until its 1988 restoration by Little Caesars magnate Mike Ilitch. Other Theater District highlights include the Music Hall Center for the Performing Arts; the intimate 450-seat Gem Theatre; and the restored Detroit Opera House. The towns north of Detroit offer their own impressive performance venues, most notably The Whiting in Flint. Even farther north, the historic Cheboygan Opera House was once a stop for luminaries such as Mary Pickford and Annie Oakley.

Detroit is one of the few large cities without a resident dance company. Ballets from around the world stop at the city's restored opera house, which sells out regularly, but you'll have a better chance of finding modern dance performances at university venues in Ann Arbor and East Lansing. Elsewhere in the state, dance events are held throughout the summer season.

MUSIC

While Michigan has spawned numerous musicians—including Aretha Franklin, the queen of soul, and Madonna, the queen of pop—American music has never been the same since Berry Gordy started a small recording studio in the 1950s, giving birth to the Motown Sound. Soon this fresh, exciting creation was known worldwide, made famous by local talents like Smokey Robinson, Mary Wells, Diana Ross, Marvin Gaye, Gladys Knight, The Temptations, Stevie Wonder, and countless more. Their stories are told in the Motown Historical Museum, also known as Hitsville USA, where displays include everything from the legendary Studio A to flashy Supremes and Temptations costumes.

Classical fans flock to Saginaw's Temple Theatre, where the Saginaw Bay Symphony Orchestra regularly performs, or the acoustically perfect 90-year-old Detroit Orchestra Hall, home to the Detroit Symphony Orchestra. Almost as old is the Grand Rapids Symphony, founded in 1929. Today this award-winning orchestra stages classical concerts as well as jam sessions by the Grand Rapids Youth Symphony. Farther north, the Traverse Symphony Orchestra is one of the region's premier ensembles.

The lands around Traverse City and the Lake Michigan shore also provide plenty of inspiration for the 1,200-acre Interlochen Center for the Arts, a music academy and arts camp. Students from around the world come to practice and perform in a variety of open-air concerts, most of which are open to the public. Each June, the camp hosts a festival featuring renowned conductors and soloists.

If you're an alternative music fan, plenty of options exist in lower Michigan. In Detroit, bands favor St. Andrews Hall and the Royal Oak Music Theater, both known for their warm receptions to cutting-edge artists. Meanwhile, well-known folk artists usually add the Hill Auditorium in Ann Arbor to their

IGGY POP: THE GODFATHER OF PUNK

Born in Muskegon in 1947, James Newell Osterberg, Jr., spent his early years in Ann Arbor, where he became a drummer for various high school bands. After dropping out of the University of Michigan, he moved to Chicago to study the blues. In the mid-1960s, he formed a band called the Psychedelic Stooges (for which he was the lead vocalist) and adopted the moniker Iggy Pop. In 1968, his band, now called the Stooges, signed with Elektra Records (also The Doors' label). Despite the explosive phenomenon of their unique sound – which eventually heralded the styles of punk rock and American heavy metal – their first two albums sold poorly, and Iggy's heroin addiction caused the group to disband.

His career rebounded when David Bowie decided to produce an album with him in England. Reuniting some of the original Stooges, the album, *Raw Power,* became a punk-rock landmark. Despite the album's success, Iggy's drug problem persisted, initiating a second break-up of the Stooges and stalling his career for several years.

Together, he and Bowie, his consistent friend and collaborator, tried to overcome their drug addictions. Iggy signed with RCA and, with Bowie's help, produced two acclaimed albums, *The Idiot* and *Lust for Life,* in 1977. After producing a third album with RCA, Iggy moved to Arista Records, with whom he produced *New Values,* a partial Stooges reunion and not much of a commercial success. While promoting the album in Australia and New Zealand, Iggy displayed his characteristically irreverent, erratic behavior. After two subsequent album failures, however, he was dropped from the Arista label.

During the 1980s, Iggy's life continued to resemble a roller coaster. After another failed album, his fortunes improved with Bowie's cover of his song "China Girl." Subsequent royalties allowed Iggy to resolve his tax problems and take a three-year break, during which he tried to beat his heroin addiction. In 1986, his popular cover of "Real Wild Child" constituted one of his only brushes with major commercial success. His follow-up album, *Instinct,* resem-

© ALEVAJKOVIK/DREAMSTIME.COM

Iggy Pop

bled the guitar-based sound of the Stooges, and while punk-rock fans embraced it, his record label did not.

Iggy continued to perform during the 1990s, playing with musicians like Deborah Harry, contributing old songs to films like *Trainspotting,* and even acting in a few movies. More recently, he's collaborated with the surviving members of the Stooges, appeared in Motorola and Cadillac commercials, and participated in music festivals around the world.

Over the years, Iggy has been noted for his extreme performance style. Inspired by Jim Morrison's antagonistic stage antics of the 1960s, he has been known to expose himself to the crowd, dive off the stage, and participate in other raucous activities. While Iggy's often been labeled a controversial performer, there's no doubt that he's an iconic figure in the world of modern music. His songs have been covered by the likes of Joan Jett and the Sex Pistols, and countless soundtracks, documentaries, commercials, and compilation albums have kept the mystique of Iggy and the Stooges alive. Hard to believe that the "godfather of punk" got his start on the laid-back coast of southwestern Michigan. For more information, visit www.iggypop.com.

list of dates, and fans of blues and jazz can find several hangouts in downtown Detroit.

CINEMA

Film entertainers have also made their mark in Michigan. Jeff Daniels may be a Hollywood type, but the Georgia native prefers to live in tiny Chelsea, a village west of Ann Arbor, where the actor-director founded the acclaimed Purple Rose Theatre (named after the Woody Allen film in which he starred). Other successful filmmakers and performers, who were actually born in the Great Lakes State, include directors Sam Raimi and Francis Ford Coppola and actors Ellen Burstyn, Gilda Radner, Timothy Busfield, Tom Selleck, Ernie Hudson, Lee Majors, Piper Laurie, and Charlton Heston, among others.

NIGHTLIFE

Michigan's larger cities have a full plate of nightlife options. On most nights and every weekend, you can choose from blues, jazz, alternative, rock, country, and everything in between. In Detroit, check out the free *Metro Times,* an alternative weekly that provides a comprehensive entertainment listing (and is also known for its colorful personal ads). Another good bet is the entertainment section of the *Detroit Free Press,* which lists city events as well as dates throughout the state. Beyond Detroit, nightlife varies, but almost universally gears up in the summer season. From gay bars in Saugatuck to Nugent-lovers in Jackson, there's something for everyone.

INDIAN GAMING AND DETROIT CASINOS

As sovereign lands, Indian reservations often are able to offer high-stakes gambling that isn't legal elsewhere in the state. Michigan's first Indian-run casino opened in 1984. The Bay Mills Blackjack Casino had just 15 blackjack tables and one dice table in a 2,400-square-foot room in the tribal center. While it wasn't Atlantic City, visitors quickly displayed their love of gambling, pouring millions of dollars into casino coffers. It started a gambling tradition that has escalated ever since.

There are currently 17 Indian casinos in Michigan. They range from small, simple gambling halls to glitzy showplaces like Leelanau Sands in Peshawbestown. Many are open 24 hours a day and have become enormous tourism draws.

By the early 1990s, the state wanted in on the deal. In September 1993, Governor John Engler passed the Tribal-State Gaming Compact, giving the state 8 percent of net win income derived from games of chance. While providing the state government with easy cash, the success of Indian gaming has also given new power and influence to tribal governments.

Non-Indian groups were soon eager to seize a piece of this cash cow. In 1997, Detroit voters approved a controversial referendum permitting non-Indian casino gambling within the city limits. After years of controversy, several casinos have opened in the Motor City, including the MGM Grand Detroit, the first-ever, Las Vegas–style destination to open in a major metropolitan core.

Given the competition from Detroit, many of the Indian-owned facilities have expanded. Soaring Eagle, in Mount Pleasant, added a 514-room luxury hotel. The Kewadin complex in Sault Ste. Marie houses an incredible, 1,500-seat performance venue. Not surprisingly, even more tribes, many of whom live at or near the poverty level, are seeking to open casinos.

While the pros and cons of gambling remain an ethical debate, there's no arguing the positive effect gaming has had on the reservations' economies. Within the Indian community, gambling provides jobs and funds schools, health-care facilities, and cultural centers. Many overlook that it provides loads of economic benefits to those outside the Native American community, too, providing jobs for the building trades and tourism industry. Michigan residents and visitors, it seems, just can't spend enough on Lady Luck.

© TRAVERSE CITY CVB/WMTA

the State Theatre marquee during the Traverse City Film Festival

FAIRS AND FESTIVALS

Given the down-to-earth Midwestern vibe that permeates the state of Michigan, it's no wonder that fairs and festivals, especially family-friendly ones, abound here. All major towns and most small villages celebrate their unique culture with annual events, from music festivals to county fairs. While the summer months, in particular, are rife with such celebrations—from Traverse City's National Cherry Festival in July to the Detroit area's Woodward Dream Cruise in August—winter is not without its share of fun. Frankenmuth, for one, offers Zehnder's Snowfest in January, while Sault Ste. Marie hosts the I-500, the world's oldest snowmobile race, every February.

ESSENTIALS

Getting There

While international tourists will most likely arrive in Michigan via plane or by crossing the U.S.-Canada border, domestic travelers can reach the Great Lakes State by air, water, rail, or road. Consider your budget and intended destinations before choosing the method that's right for your trip.

BY PLANE

The **Detroit Metropolitan-Wayne County Airport (DTW)** (734/247-7678 or 800/642-1978, www.metroairport.com) is the state's biggest and busiest. It's also a hub for **Northwest Airlines** (800/225-2525, www.nwa.com) and its sister airline **KLM** (800/225-2525, www.klm.com), so you can fly from Detroit to almost anywhere in the United States and Canada, and to a surprising number of cities around the globe, from Amsterdam to Tokyo. Northwest also offers the most comprehensive service elsewhere in the state. It flies into most of Michigan's commercial airports, including Alpena County Regional, Bishop International, Capital Region International, Cherry Capital, Chippewa County International, Delta County, Gerald R. Ford International, Houghton County Memorial, Kalamazoo/Battle Creek International, MBS International, Muskegon County, Pellston Regional, and Sawyer International. For information about each airport, refer to the destination chapters in this guide.

Of course, Northwest's muscle means other airlines don't offer as many flights in and out of the state. Check with **American Airlines** (800/433-7300, www.aa.com), **Continental Airlines** (800/525-0280, www.continental. com), **Delta Air Lines** (800/221-1212, www. delta.com), **Southwest Airlines** (800/435-9792, www.southwest.com), **United Airlines** (800/241-6522, www.united.com), and **US Airways** (800/428-4322, www.usairways. com). Northwest, American, Continental, and Delta are your only options to the Upper Peninsula; United can take you to Sault Ste. Marie and Windsor in Canada.

In early 2008, Northwest and Delta began a lengthy merger, which could affect schedules for both airlines. Since routes and carriers seem to change with the weather, your best bet is to call a travel agent or book your trip online (through such websites as www.orbitz.com, www.cheaptickets.com, www.expedia.com, www.travelocity.com, or www.kayak.com).

BY BOAT

Given that Michigan is surrounded by miles and miles of shoreline, it's no surprise that many visitors arrive via boat, and they'll find plenty of docks when they get here. The state's Parks and Recreation Division has established a network of over 90 protected public mooring facilities (fees vary) along the Great Lakes, a "marine highway" that ensures boaters are never far from a safe harbor. For a free *Handbook of Michigan Boating Laws and Responsibilities,* contact the **Michigan Department of Natural Resources** (Parks and Recreation Division, Mason Building, 3rd floor, P.O. Box 30031, Lansing, MI 48909, 517/373-9900, www. michigan.gov/dnr).

Nonboaters, too, can arrive by water via the **S.S. *Badger*** (Lake Michigan Carferry, 701 Maritime Dr., Ludington, 231/845-5555 or 800/841-4243, www.ssbadger.com), the only authentic passenger steamship on the Great Lakes. The 410-foot-long ship ferries up to 620 passengers and 180 vehicles across Lake

Michigan, from Manitowoc, Wisconsin, to Ludington, Michigan. The four-hour passage spares travelers from a congested auto trip through Chicago, or a lengthy jaunt across the Upper Peninsula. Plus, it saves on gas and is great fun.

Built in 1952, the S.S. *Badger* was one of seven railroad and passenger ferries crossing Lake Michigan; you can still see the railroad tracks that lead into the car deck. The *Badger* marked the end of an era; ferries were to the Great Lakes what steamboats were to the Mississippi. Today, it's the only ferry of its kind, and it's been quite inventive about making a go at it. Although it also transports loaded trucks and occasional business travelers, tourism is its bread and butter. The ship is comfortably outfitted with tables, chairs, a theater showing free movies, a cafeteria and snack bar, a gift shop, a video arcade, and small staterooms ($44 one-way, $78 round-trip). Equipped with twin berths, these are well worth it if you hope to catch some sleep. There's ample deck space and chaise lounges, if it's warm enough, and the crew even hosts children's activities, bingo, and interactive games.

The *Badger* sails daily from mid-May through mid-October. It departs Ludington at 9 A.M. (EST) and Manitowoc at 2 P.M. (CST) from the beginning of the season to early June and from early September to the end of the season. From June to September, it offers two round-trip passages daily, leaving Ludington at 8 A.M. and 7:55 P.M. Rates are $67 one-way or $110 round-trip for adults; $27 or $44 for children 5–15; $61 or $99 for seniors 65 and over; $70 one-way for cars, vans, and pickups; $34 one-way for motorcycles; and $5 one-way for bicycles. There is a $5-per-foot charge for motorhomes. Pets must remain in your vehicle or in a ventilated kennel (which you must provide) on the car deck; this isn't suggested during the hot summer months. For security reasons, you cannot access your vehicle during the crossing. Reservations are strongly recommended.

© S.S. BADGER LAKE MICHIGAN CARFERRY

the S.S. *Badger* crossing Lake Michigan

BY TRAIN

Amtrak (800/872-7245, www.amtrak.com), which has a hub in Chicago, runs three regular routes through the southern half of Michigan's Lower Peninsula. One Michigan route, the Pere Marquette, travels from Chicago through St. Joseph and Holland to Grand Rapids. A second route, the Blue Water, travels from Chicago to Kalamazoo, Battle Creek, East Lansing, Flint, and Port Huron. A third Chicago train, the Wolverine, splits at Battle Creek and heads for Jackson, Ann Arbor, Dearborn, Detroit, and Pontiac. From Windsor and Sarnia, the Canadian cities adjacent to Detroit and Port Huron, respectively, you can hop aboard **VIA Rail Canada** (888/842-7245, www.viarail.ca), which offers service to Toronto, Vancouver, and numerous other cities throughout Canada.

BY BUS

Greyhound (800/231-2222, www.greyhound.com) operates in most major Michigan cities, and plenty of smaller ones, too. It can be a very inexpensive way to travel if you've got the time.

Traveling from Chicago to Marquette, for example, takes almost 12 hours—but only costs about $100.

BY CAR

About a dozen major interstates and highways make it mighty efficient to zip into and around Michigan. I-75 stretches from the state's southern border at Toledo through Detroit, and all the way north across the Mackinac Bridge to Sault Ste. Marie. I-69 cruises up the middle of the Lower Peninsula, from Indianapolis through Lansing, then east to Flint and Port Huron. I-94, which comes over from Chicago, traverses the southern tier of the state to Detroit. From I-94 just east of Benton Harbor, I-196 extends north along Lake Michigan and over to Grand Rapids, where I-96 heads east to Lansing and Detroit.

Major highways include U.S. 31, which heads north from Indiana, follows the Lake Michigan shore as a major four-lane to Ludington, becomes a smaller two-lane to Traverse City and Petoskey, and merges

MILEAGE BETWEEN CITIES

Comprising two large peninsulas, Michigan is a bigger place than it appears on many maps. It can be deceptively far from Point A to Point B, especially if Point A is, say, Kalamazoo and Point B is Copper Harbor, which lies 600 miles to the north. To put it into perspective, traveling the same distance from Kalamazoo would take you to the outskirts of Kansas City or Washington, D.C.

DISTANCE FROM DETROIT TO:

- Alpena: 249 miles

- Bay City: 116 miles

- Benton Harbor: 187 miles

- Copper Harbor: 602 miles

- Escanaba: 436 miles

- Grand Rapids: 161 miles

- Mackinaw City: 290 miles

- Marquette: 455 miles

- Sault Ste. Marie: 346 miles

- Traverse City: 256 miles

DISTANCE FROM MARQUETTE TO:

- Grayling: 251 miles

- Ironwood: 146 miles

- Lansing: 396 miles

- Menominee: 120 miles

- Munising: 43 miles

- Muskegon: 441 miles

- Petoskey: 202 miles

- Port Huron: 457 miles

- Saginaw: 356 miles

- St. Ignace: 162 miles

with I-75 just south of the Mackinac Bridge. U.S. 131, at first a small road near the southern border, becomes a major highway south of Kalamazoo, linking it to Grand Rapids, Cadillac, and Petoskey. U.S. 127, which also begins as a small road near the border, heads north from Jackson to Lansing, connecting with I-75 near Grayling. U.S. 23, which extends north from Toledo, passes through Ann Arbor, merges with I-75 in Flint, and splits off near Standish, becoming the Sunrise Side Coastal Highway, a scenic route that traces the Lake Huron shore all the way to Mackinaw City.

Meanwhile, two main east-west routes traverse the Upper Peninsula. M-28 is the northern route, starting at I-75 and passing through Munising and Marquette. U.S. 2 is the southern route, starting in St. Ignace, passing through Escanaba, and heading west to Ironwood. Several north-south highways link the two. If you're traveling all the way from the U.P.'s eastern end to Ironwood, M-28 is usually faster.

Getting Around

BY PLANE

Regional airports pepper the entire state; even the Upper Peninsula has a number of options, including Delta County Airport (ESC) near Escanaba, a stop for Northwest Airlines. Hence, it's easy, though often expensive, to fly from one end of Michigan to the other.

In addition, it's possible to charter small planes to some of the surrounding islands. **Great Lakes Air** (906/643-7165, www.greatlakesair.net, $27 adults, $13.50 children under 13) offers service from St. Ignace to Mackinac Island, while **Royale Air Service** (877/359-4753, www.royaleairservice.com, mid-May–mid-Sept., $185 one-way, $269 round-trip, children under 2 free) provides the only air transportation to Isle Royale National Park, with scheduled trips between the Houghton County Memorial Airport and the protected bays at Windigo and Rock Harbor. Reservations are required for both services.

BY BOAT

Surrounded by four Great Lakes and filled with thousands of inland lakes and rivers, Michigan is a popular place for water-based travel during the summer. Visitors will find many pleasure cruises throughout the state, including **Saugatuck Boat Cruises** (269/857-4261, www.saugatuckboatcruises.com, $16 adults, $8 children 6–12, $5 children 3–5), offering trips down the Kalamazoo River, and the *Bavarian Belle* (866/808-2628, www.bavarianbelle.com, $9 adults, $4 children 5–12), which tours the Cass River in Frankenmuth.

To reach the islands that surround Michigan, boating is usually one's best option. The **Beaver Island Boat Company** (231/547-2311 or 888/446-4095, www.bibco.com, Apr.–Dec., one-way $21–23 adults, $11–13 children 5–12, rates vary for pets and vehicles) links Charlevoix to Beaver Island. **Shepler's Mackinac Island Ferry** (231/436-5023 or 800/828-6157, www.sheplersferry.com, late Apr.–Oct., $23 adults, $11 children

5–12, $7.50 bicycle) connects St. Ignace and Mackinaw City to Mackinac Island. **Plaunt Transportation** (231/627-2354 or 888/752-8687, www.bbiferry.com, May–Nov., $14.25 adults, $9.50 children 5–11, rates vary for vehicles) provides service from Cheboygan to Bois Blanc Island, and the *Isle Royale Queen IV* (906/289-4437, www.isleroyale.com, mid-May–Sept., $54–62 adults, $27–31 children under 12, rates vary for paddling/diving equipment) operates between Copper Harbor and Isle Royale.

BY TRAIN

Besides Amtrak, which links several cities in Michigan's Lower Peninsula, the state boasts several authentic train tours. In the Upper Peninsula, the **Tahquamenon Falls Wilderness Excursion** (888/778-7246, www.superiorsights.com/toonerville/index.html, mid-June–mid-Oct., $42 adults, $26 children 9–15, $17 children 4–8) leads visitors on a scenic round-trip tour via riverboat and the Toonerville Trolley, a narrow-gauge railroad in operation since the late 1920s. In the Lower Peninsula, the **Southern Michigan Railroad** (517/456-7677, www.southernmichiganrailroad.org, round-trip $10 adults, $8 seniors 65 and over, $6 children 2–12) offers seasonal and holiday train tours between Clinton and Tecumseh.

BY BUS

Most of Michigan's major towns and regions offer a public bus system. Some include **Thumb Area Transit** (989/269-2121 or 800/322-1125, www.tatbus.com), Lansing's **Capital Area Transportation Authority** (517/394-1000, www.cata.org), **Muskegon Area Transit System** (231/724-6420, www.matsbus.com), Traverse City's **Bay Area Transportation Authority** (231/941-2355, www.bata.net), and **Marquette County Transit Authority** (906/225-1112, www.marq-tran.com). Refer to each destination chapter for more public transit options.

BY CAR

In Michigan, the birthplace of the automobile, the car is the preferred method of travel, never more apparent than on Friday afternoons May–October, when it seems about half the state's southern residents load up the car (or motorcycle) and head out on the highway—to hotels, resorts, cabins, and campgrounds "up north." Though it's best to avoid northbound highways on Friday and southbound ones on Sunday, Michigan—a state of remarkable diversity—is highly worthy of a road trip.

Roads here are plentiful and good. Along with interstates and federal highways, the state is crisscrossed with numerous state highways, marked on road maps by a circled number. In conversation, they are often preceded by an "M," as in, "Follow M-28 west to Marquette." County roads are marked with rectangles on most road maps. The state also has several toll bridges, including "Big Mac" between Mackinaw City and St. Ignace, and the four international bridges that link Canada to the cities of Detroit, Port Huron, and Sault Ste. Marie.

When planning a route in the Upper Peninsula, consult your map legend regarding road surfaces. All state and federal highways are paved and well maintained, as are most county roads and many secondary roads. But just be aware. Gravel and dirt roads can make for very slow going. For road construction updates, consult the **Michigan Department of Transportation** (800/641-6368, www.michigan.gov/mdot).

In Michigan, all drivers, front-seat passengers, and children 4–15 must wear safety belts. Motorcyclists are required to wear helmets at all times, and all motorists must yield to emergency vehicles. In addition, you must always stop at railroad crossings when the lights are flashing and/or the crossing gates have been activated. Remember, too, that littering is against the law on state and federal highways. Unless otherwise posted, the maximum speed limit on Michigan's interstates and federal highways is usually 70 mph; on county roads and state highways, it's typically 55 mph.

Finally, there's a myth that driving a foreign car is a potentially dangerous practice in Michigan. While that may have been true in the 1970s when the Japanese were doing serious damage to the U.S. auto industry, it's not the case today. These days, many "foreign" cars are made in the United States, and U.S. plants supply parts to foreign automakers, so it's often a moot point. But don't push it too far. You might not feel comfortable parking your Toyota in front of a tavern near the Flint GM plant, especially given Michigan's economic recession in recent years.

Taxi and Shuttle

Most of Michigan's major cities have taxi and shuttle services. Unless you're at an airport, however, you'll have to call ahead to arrange a ride. From the Detroit Metropolitan–Wayne County Airport, contact **Metro Airport Taxi** (800/745-5191, www.metroairporttaxi.org). Other services include **Spartan Cab/Yellow Cab** (Lansing, 517/482-1444, www.capitoltransport.com), **By the Bay Transportation** (Traverse City, 231/929-9283, www.bythebaytransportation.com), and **Marquette Cab Company** (906/226-7777, www.marquettecab.com).

Rental Car

Rental cars are available at most commercial airports around the state. In smaller cities, you'll be limited to the big players like **Alamo** (800/462-5266, www.alamo.com), **Avis** (800/831-2847, www.avis.com), **Budget** (800/527-0700, www.budget.com), **Enterprise** (800/261-7331, www.enterprise.com), **Hertz** (800/654-3131, www.hertz.com), and **National** (800/227-7368, www.nationalcar.com). Reservations are highly recommended; big cities do a huge volume, and small locales don't keep many cars on the lot. If you plan to explore the Upper Peninsula, ask about the company's policies regarding off-road driving. Many forbid you to leave the pavement, which can curtail your access to a lot of U.P. sights.

RV

Traversing Michigan via RV can be a wonderful

way to see the state's diverse attractions and spend quality time with family and friends. If you don't have a motorhome or trailer of your own, you can easily rent one from various locations. For more information about RV rentals, contact **General RV Center** (888/483-7744, www.generalrv.com), **GetRV.com** (888/438-7844, http://michigan.getrv.com), and **Cruise America** (800/671-8042, www.cruiseamerica.com). For a list of Michigan's campgrounds and RV parks, consult the **Michigan Association of Recreational Vehicles and Campgrounds** (517/349-8881, www.marvac.org) or the **Association of RV Parks and Campgrounds Michigan** (989/826-5255, www.michcampgrounds.com).

WINTER DRIVING

Michigan roads are generally well maintained in winter, plowed free of snow, then salted or sanded. (Salt does a better job of melting while sand is less destructive to the environment.) During or immediately after a storm, though, don't expect smooth sailing; it's often hard for road crews to keep up with conditions. County and city crews have a well-established hierarchy, first taking care of interstates, state highways, major thoroughfares, roads to schools and hospitals, then addressing less-vital routes. In the Upper Peninsula, many small roads are considered seasonal, which means they're not plowed or patrolled in winter. To check winter driving conditions before you travel, consult the **Michigan State Police Travel Advisory** (800/381-8477, www.ohsp.state.mi.us/rw/home.htm).

If you're not used to driving in snow, don't learn on the road in a Michigan snowstorm. Drive slowly, allow lots of room between you and the car in front of you, and remember it may take a lot longer to stop than you're accustomed. Tap your brakes lightly in succession to come to a stop; never stomp on them, or you'll send your car reeling into a "doughnut." If you have antilock brakes, apply steady pressure, and let the system's computer do the work.

Chains or studded snow tires are not permitted on Michigan roads. Many residents do switch to snow tires, which have a heavier tread. If you have a rear-wheel-drive car, adding weight to the back end can greatly improve traction. Bags of sand or salt work well, and sand can be used if you get stuck.

Ice is considerably more dangerous than snow, since it provides even less traction and stopping ability. Especially be aware of black ice, seemingly wet pavement that is actually glare ice. Watch for icy roads as rain turns to snow (called freezing rain), especially on bridges, where the cold air circulating above and below the road will cause it to freeze first. Ice also forms when lots of cars travel over a snowy surface (like a heavily traveled interstate), packing it down to a super-slick hardpack. On four-lane roads, the left lane usually looks snowier but may be less icy and, therefore, less slippery.

Equip your vehicle with a shovel, sand (or kitty litter), and boots, in case you get stuck. Throw the sand/kitty litter under the front tires for a front-wheel-drive car, the rear tires on a rear-wheel-drive car. Keep the tires straight and slowly apply the gas. Flooring it will only spin you deeper. Gently rocking the car forward and back, especially if you have someone who can push, works best.

Pack an emergency kit and make sure your car is in good mechanical condition before embarking upon your journey; check your batteries, fluids, and tire pressure. Keep a flashlight (with fresh batteries), flares, blankets, extra clothing, and a first-aid kit in your vehicle in case you have to spend the night in your car. It could save your life. Help may not always be on the way, especially in rural areas. If you spy a car hung up on a snowbank or in a ditch, try to offer a push or a ride to town (as long as your personal safety isn't in doubt).

DEER CROSSINGS

Several million deer inhabit Michigan, posing a significant threat to drivers. Thousands contribute to automobile accidents each year, some of them fatal. Deer behave erratically and will dart in front of your car with no warning. Be particularly alert at dawn and dusk, when deer are most active, and during the fall hunting season, when they're really unpredictable. Yellow-and-black "leaping deer" signs warn motorists of roadways where crossings are common, but they can occur virtually anywhere.

Deer may come from the woods or from an open field, almost out of nowhere. If you see deer by the side of the road, slow down and get ready to stop. If you see a deer cross ahead of you, also slow down—where there's one deer, there are usually several. If you do hit a deer, notify the nearest law enforcement office immediately.

Visas and Officialdom

For U.S. citizens, a trip to Michigan is a snap. International travelers, however, should understand current American policies before heading here. With Canada so close to Detroit, Port Huron, and Sault Ste. Marie, it's helpful for all tourists to know the ins and outs of traveling between the two nations.

PASSPORTS AND VISAS

While international travelers are required to show a valid passport upon entering the United States, most citizens from Canada and the 27 countries that are part of the Visa Waiver Program (VWP)—including France, Italy, Australia, Japan, and the United Kingdom—are allowed to travel to Michigan without a visa. As of January 2009, however, they will still need to apply to the Electronic System for Travel Authorization (ESTA). All other temporary international travelers are required to secure a nonimmigrant visa before entering Michigan. For more information, consult the **U.S. Department of State's Bureau of Consular Affairs** (202/663-1225, http://travel.state.gov).

CUSTOMS

Upon entering Michigan, international travelers must declare any dollar amount over $10,000 as well as the value of any articles that will remain in the country, including gifts. A duty will be assessed for all imported goods; visitors are usually granted a $100 exemption. Illegal drugs, Cuban cigars, obscene items, toxic substances, and prescription drugs (without a prescription) are generally prohibited. In order to protect American agriculture, customs officials will confiscate certain produce, plants, seeds, nuts, meat, and other potentially dangerous biological products. For more information, consult the **U.S. Customs and Border Protection** (703/526-4200, www.cbp.gov).

EMBASSIES AND CONSULATES

While the embassies for most countries are located in Washington, D.C., some nations have consular offices in Detroit's Renaissance Center, including Canada (313/567-2340, www.canadianembassy.org) and Japan (313/567-0120, www.detroit.us.emb-japan.go.jp). Other consulates are situated in nearby Chicago, including those of the United Kingdom (312/970-3800, www.britainusa.com), France (312/327-5200, www.consul-france-chicago.org), Germany (312/202-0480, www.germany.info), Austria (312/222-1515, www.austria.org), and Mexico (312/855-1380, www.consulmexchicago.com). For a more comprehensive list of the foreign embassies and consulates in America, consult the **University of Michigan's International Center** (www.internationalcenter.umich.edu).

UNITED STATES-CANADA BORDER

Years ago, U.S. citizens were barely given a perfunctory glance upon crossing the Canadian border. Given today's more vigilant climate, however, they must now show either a valid U.S. passport or a certified birth certificate with photo identification (like a driver's

©RONALD M. GROGAN

the Blue Water Bridge between Port Huron and Sarnia

license). Unless you have a criminal record or decide to transport something suspicious, you'll probably just be asked about the purpose of your visit, then waved through. Pets require proof of proper vaccinations; plants and animal products will be confiscated. In addition, you must declare any alcohol or tobacco products, which could be taxed depending on the amount. Obscene materials, illegal drugs, and most weapons are prohibited from entering Canada.

With child abductions on the rise, border officials are especially concerned about protecting minors. If you're traveling with children, you must bring proper identification for them as well, such as a birth certificate or passport. If the children are not your own, you must provide written permission from a parent or legal guardian. If you are divorced or separated and traveling with your children, you must provide a copy of the legal custody agreement. For more information, consult **American Consular Services** (www.amcits.com).

Non-U.S. citizens must have a valid passport, too. If you're a citizen of a non-European country, you may also need a visa (obtained in advance from the Canadian Consulate). U.S. resident aliens will be asked to show a green card. For more information, consult the **Canada Border Services Agency** (www.cbsa-asfc.gc.ca).

Unless you travel between Michigan and Canada by plane or boat, you'll do so by bridge or tunnel. There are four toll bridges connecting Michigan and Ontario: the Ambassador Bridge from Detroit to Windsor (www.ambassadorbridge.com, $4), the Detroit-Windsor Tunnel (www.dwtunnel.com, $3.75), the Blue Water Bridge from Port Huron to Sarnia (www.michigan.gov/mdot, $1.50), and the International Bridge from Sault Ste. Marie to Sault Ste. Marie (www.michigan.gov/mdot, $2). (All toll rates listed are for passenger vehicles; higher rates may apply for trucks and buses.) If you do arrive by plane or boat, you're required to check in at the nearest customs station immediately upon arrival.

Sports and Recreation

SPECTATOR SPORTS

While Michigan boasts a variety of spectatorial teams—including minor-league baseball players like the Traverse City Beach Bums—most sports lovers flock to Detroit to watch the state's megaprofessional teams in action. From September to December, football fans head to Ford Field to cheer on the **Detroit Lions** (800/616-7627, www.detroitlions.com). From April to October, baseball fans can see the **Detroit Tigers** (313/962-4000, http://detroit.tigers.mlb.com) at Comerica Park. From October to April, hockey fans can catch the **Detroit Red Wings** (313/396-7575, http://redwings.nhl.com) at Joe Louis Arena. Basketball fans, meanwhile, can support two teams during the November–April season: the NBA's **Detroit Pistons** (248/377-0100, www.nba.com/pistons) and the WNBA's **Detroit Shock** (248/377-0100, www.wnba.com/shock), both of which play at The Palace in Auburn Hills.

Of course, Michigan has some fantastic college teams, too. In Ann Arbor, fans of football, baseball, basketball, soccer, and other varsity sports can watch the **University of Michigan's Wolverines** (734/764-0247, www.mgoblue.com) throughout the year. Meanwhile, **Michigan State University's Spartans** (517/355-1610, http://msuspartans.cstv.com) regularly lure sports lovers to East Lansing.

GOLF

As it turns out, northern Michigan has both the perfect climate for turf-growing and a diverse terrain of hills and water views that make for great golf courses. Over the last few decades, golf course architects have noticed. Michigan is home to all kinds of nationally ranked courses, including several with designer names like Arnold Palmer, Robert Trent Jones, and Jack Nicklaus attached.

Traverse Bay, Mackinac Island, and the city of Oscoda on Lake Huron form a golden triangle of golf courses. Here, you'll find award-winners like The Bear at Grand Traverse Resort near Traverse City, Cedar River at Shanty Creek Resorts in Bellaire, Signature at Treetops Resort near Gaylord, Fountains at Garland Resort in Lewiston, and The Gailes at Lakewood Shores Resort near Oscoda. Outside this "triangle," you'll find plenty of well-kept and challenging courses, too; just consult the destination chapters in this guide. (Note: All rates in this book refer to 18-hole play.) For more information, consult the **Golf Association of Michigan** (248/478-9242, www.gam.org), peruse *Michigan Golf* (www.michigangolfmagazine.com), or visit www.michigangolf.com.

NATIONAL PARKS AND FORESTS

Michigan is home to four national forests, two national lakeshores, a national park, a national historic park, and seven national wildlife refuges. This federal land is rather evenly divided between the two peninsulas, which can each claim two national forests and a national lakeshore. In the Upper Peninsula, **Pictured Rocks National Lakeshore** traces the Lake Superior coastline east of Marquette, while in the Lower Peninsula, **Sleeping Bear Dunes National Lakeshore** sits alongside Lake Michigan west of Traverse City. The L.P. also contains four wildlife refuges, just as the U.P. boasts three wildlife refuges, the **Keweenaw National Historical Park,** and **Isle Royale National Park,** a 45-mile long wilderness surrounded by the frigid waters of Lake Superior.

Save for key attractions like waterfalls or beaches, national forests are often overlooked as visitor destinations, yet they offer a remarkable range of activities for outdoor enthusiasts. Hiking trails tend to be little used. Campsites are more secluded, more rustic, and usually less crowded than in other places. Mountain biking, which is often forbidden on national park trails, is permitted on miles and miles of federal forest land, and inland lakes, which can be difficult to reach with a boat trailer, are often ideal for those looking for a quiet paddling experience.

The national forests also cover an astounding amount of real estate. The **Ottawa National Forest,** situated in the western U.P., contains nearly 1 million acres, while the **Hiawatha National Forest,** which comprises two units in the eastern U.P., adds another 879,000 acres. In the Lower Peninsula, the **Manistee National Forest** stretches from Cadillac to just north of Muskegon, an area of roughly 539,000 acres, while the **Huron National Forest** covers more than 437,000 acres in the northeastern section, encompassing lightly developed rivers like the Au Sable. To receive information about hiking, camping, paddling, and other activities, contact the **U.S. Forest Service** (www.fs.fed.us) or each forest headquarters: Ottawa National Forest (E6248 U.S. 2, Ironwood, 906/932-1330), Hiawatha National Forest (2727 N. Lincoln Rd., Escanaba, 906/786-4062), and Huron-Manistee National Forests (1755 S. Mitchell St., Cadillac, 231/775-2421). For more information about Michigan's national lakeshores or wildlife refuges, contact the **National Park Service** (www.nps.gov/state/mi) or the **U.S. Fish and Wildlife Service** (www.fws.gov/refuges), respectively.

STATE PARKS AND FORESTS
State Parks

Michigan has an outstanding state park system. Well planned and well maintained, the parks showcase some of the state's most diverse and most beautiful land. Some state parks, like those along Lake Michigan, were clearly set aside for public access, while others preserve historic sites and state jewels like Mackinac Island and the Porcupine Mountains.

Currently, Michigan has 98 state parks and recreation areas. The **Michigan Department of Natural Resources** (Parks and Recreation Division, 517/373-9900, www.michigan.gov/dnr) publishes a handy brochure that includes regional maps and charts listing each park's amenities.

All state parks and recreation areas require that every entering vehicle, despite the number of passengers, have a motor vehicle permit affixed to the windshield ($6 daily or $24 yearly for Michigan residents, $8 daily or $29 yearly for nonresidents). The annual sticker is good for all Michigan state parks. Senior citizens who have a vehicle registered in-state may obtain an annual pass for $6.

There is an additional fee for camping ($10–20 per night for rustic campsites, $16–33 per night for modern campsites that include utility hookups, showers, and restrooms). For $45 a night, some parks also rent mini-cabins, tiny shelters that offer little more than a roof and four walls to protect against the elements. These book up fast, so reserve yours well ahead of time. A few parks, including Bald Mountain Recreation Area, rent rustic cabins ($60–80 per night), which are equipped with heaters and basic furniture, ideal for groups, and terrific when bugs are particularly fierce. These are *extremely* popular in summer; if you hope to get one, call in January.

For an $8 fee, you can make a camping reservation at any park by calling 800/447-2757 or visiting www.michigan.gov/dnr. Though you can request a specific site, it isn't guaranteed. In summer, reservations are recommended at many state parks; this book indicates if a park is particularly popular.

State Forests

Like national forests, state forests are a hidden gem for anyone looking for a quiet corner in the wild. Much of the state's forest land was actually acquired by default, picked up after the Depression when its owners couldn't pay the property taxes. Their loss was the public's gain—much of the property is exceptional, comprising rivers, waterfalls, lakes, beaches, and, naturally, forests. Altogether, it encompasses 3.9 million acres of land, the largest state forest system in the nation.

In the Lower Peninsula, you'll find **Pere Marquette State Forest** south of Traverse City, **Mackinaw State Forest** between Gaylord and Mackinaw City, and **Au Sable**

STATE PARK EXPLORER PROGRAM

Every summer, campers and day-use visitors can participate in the State Park Explorer Program at 51 of Michigan's state parks, recreation areas, and fish hatcheries. Equipped with field guides and hands-on materials, expert rangers and volunteers lead informal programs, nature hikes, and nighttime activities that feature each region's unique natural, cultural, and historic resources. These free programs, which are designed for children and adults alike, focus on a wide assortment of topics, including insects, frogs, birds, mammals, carnivorous plants, and constellations.

Participating locales range from Van Riper State Park in the Upper Peninsula – where visitors can learn about native dragonflies, owls, black bears, wolves, and moose – to Warren Dunes State Park along Lake Michigan's southern shore – where guides explore coastal tides and the area's fossils, birds, and wildflowers. At Hartwick Pines State Park, in the northeastern part of the Lower Peninsula, visitors can listen to presentations about old-growth trees and watch 19th-century activities like cooking, logging, and vintage baseball. For program details and schedules, visit www.michigan.gov/dnr.

State Forest between Grayling and Midland. In the Upper Peninsula, you can explore **Lake Superior State Forest** on the eastern half, **Escanaba River State Forest** in the central part, and **Copper Country State Forest** on the western side. For more information, contact the **Michigan Department of Natural Resources** (www.michigan.gov/dnr).

HIKING

Given its bounty of national parks and lakeshores, federal and state forests, state parks, and whatever county land is set aside for public use, Michigan has almost unlimited offerings for hikers, especially in the Upper Peninsula. Where you go depends on your taste.

For backpackers, **Isle Royale National Park** in Lake Superior is an outstanding choice, free of roads and other development. Rustic campsites along the way allow you to hoof across the 45-mile-long island; water-taxi services can get you back to your starting point. A little less remote, **Porcupine Mountains Wilderness State Park** in the western U.P. also offers great backpacking in a rugged backcountry environment that one doesn't normally associate with state parks.

Michigan also has lots of linear hiking trails, like the **Bay de Noc-to-Grand Island Trail,** which bisects the U.P., and the **Shore-to-Shore hiking/riding trail,** which stretches from Empire on Lake Michigan to Oscoda on Lake Huron. And for those really looking for an adventure, the **North Country National Scenic Trail** (www.northcountrytrail.org) traverses both the Upper and Lower Peninsulas as part of a 4,600-mile-long national trail that, when complete, will stretch from New York to North Dakota. In Michigan, many long segments of the trail, which cross national forest land, are already open to hikers. Check with national forest officials for more information.

BIKING

With its rolling topography, stunning shorelines, and ample country roads, Michigan makes for a great biking destination. Some favorite areas for road riding include the wine country region near South Haven, the farmland around historic Marshall, and the lovely Leelanau Peninsula. For more information about suggested routes and bicycle tours, check with local tourism bureaus or consult the **League of Michigan Bicyclists** (www.lmb.org), **Michigan Mountain Biking Association** (www.mmba.org), or **Michigan Trails & Greenways Alliance** (www.michigantrails.org).

Michigan leads the nation in the number of rails-to-trails, with over 50 old railroad beds converted into multiuse trails. Some, like the 55-mile **Bill Nichols Trail** on the U.P.'s

© PETOSKEY AREA VISITORS BUREAU

biking along Michigan's western coast

Keweenaw Peninsula, are very rough, often still marked by old railroad ties and sharp mining rock. While spectacular, some of these more primitive trails are appropriate only for snowmobiles and all-terrain vehicles, but many are ideal for adventuresome mountain bikers hoping to experience wonderful wilderness terrain. At the other end of the spectrum, the 28-mile **Hart-Montague Bicycle Trail** is paved, making it especially popular with families and in-line skaters. For more information, consult the **Rails-to-Trails Conservancy** (www.railtrails.org).

Unlike much of the Midwest, Michigan is kind to mountain bikers. Good technical mountain biking can be found in many state and national forests, and ski resorts in the Lower Peninsula have wisely courted mountain bikers by maintaining their cross-country trail networks for biking in the off-season.

As for the Upper Peninsula, you can pretty much consider it a giant mountain bike park. Between the national and state forests, you probably have more miles than you could ever ride, not to mention the hundreds of miles of old logging roads. Off-road riding in places like the Keweenaw and the Huron Mountains is the best you'll find between the Rockies and the Appalachians, and Michigan adds a little extra perk: some stunning Great Lakes views.

BIRD-WATCHING

Given Michigan's myriad forests, prairies, lakes, rivers, marshes, and beaches, it's no wonder that the state is rife with hundreds of avian species, including songbirds, raptors, shorebirds, and waterfowl. It's no wonder, too, that bird-watchers flock here, especially in spring and fall, to observe them in action. Equipped with little more than binoculars and cameras, bird-watchers are welcome at many nature centers, state parks, wildlife refuges, bird sanctuaries, and other protected areas.

In Saginaw, the **Shiawassee National Wildlife Refuge** (www.fws.gov), which hosts over 270 bird species annually, provides trails, observation platforms, and bird species lists, while the **Whitefish Point Bird Observatory** (www.wpbo.org) near Paradise offers field trips for bird-watchers of all skill levels. For more information about Michigan's birds as well as birding tours and festivals, visit www.michiganbirding.com or consult the **Michigan Audubon Society** (www.michiganaudubon.org).

HUNTING

With its plentiful populations of deer, duck, pheasant, turkey, and other game, Michigan is definitely a hunter's paradise. Even black bear and elk can be legally hunted here. Hunting seasons, license requirements, and regulations vary depending upon the animal and region, so it's important to do your research ahead of time. For example, white-tailed deer (the state game mammal) can be hunted with bows from October 1st to mid-November and during December; firearms can only be used from mid-to-late November and in late December.

For up-to-date regulations and to apply for specific licenses, consult the **Michigan Department of Natural Resources** (www.michigan.gov/dnr). For hunting-related articles (including some by Ted Nugent, perhaps the state's most famous hunter), visit www.michigan-sportsman.com.

BOATING AND FISHING
Boating

In summer, boating is an exceedingly popular pastime in Michigan. Boaters cruise from port to port on the Great Lakes, sail around large bays like Grand Traverse and isolated areas like Beaver Island, water-ski on thousands of inland lakes, paddle the state's white-water rivers and quiet waters, cruise the inland waterway through Cheboygan County, and fish just about everywhere.

Small watercraft like canoes and fishing boats are readily available in many Michigan communities. For more information, contact the local chamber of commerce or tourism bureau in the area that you plan to visit. For larger watercraft, such as sailboats, contact the **Michigan Charter Boat Association** (800/622-2971, www.micharterboats.com).

If you plan to bring your own boat,

consult the **Michigan Department of Natural Resources** (800/447-2757, www.michigan.gov/dnr), which provides maps, a listing of public marinas and harbors, a handbook of boating laws, and a harbor reservation system. State law requires that all boaters must carry a Coast Guard–approved life jacket—known as a personal flotation device (PFD)—for each person on board, regardless of the type of boat.

Canoeing and Kayaking

Michigan is a paddler's dream. You can canoe down several national wild and scenic rivers, surf waves along Lake Michigan's shoreline, sea kayak along Pictured Rocks or Isle Royale, or run white water. For mellow paddling, the Au Sable River is a perennial favorite, stretching from Grayling to Lake Huron. In July, it's the site of the annual 120-mile **AuSable River Canoe Marathon** (www.ausablecanoemarathon.org).

Also in the northeastern Lower Peninsula is the less-crowded Rifle River, east of West Branch. Other popular paddling rivers include the Platte and Betsie Rivers south of Traverse City, and the Sturgeon River in the Upper Peninsula. The U.P. also has several notable white-water rivers, including the beautiful Presque Isle River and the Ontonagon, both of which are designated wild and scenic rivers. For more information on paddling destinations and liveries, consult the **Michigan Association of Paddlesport Providers** (www.michigancanoe.com).

Fishing

Fishing is deeply embedded in the state's psyche. It comes in all styles and seasons, too, from fly-fishing along a pristine stream in summer to hanging out in an ice-fishing shanty, watching a Lions-Packers game on a portable TV. The quantity of blue-ribbon trout streams is unrivaled this side of Montana—enough clear, swift, and rocky waters to keep you busy for weeks on end. The Fox, the Jordan, the Boardman. . . you'll find most of the best ones in the eastern U.P. and northern parts of the Lower Peninsula.

"Deep-sea" charters on the Great Lakes go after the big chinook salmon, coho salmon, and lake trout. Lake Michigan's Little Bay de

Noc arguably offers the finest walleye fishing in the state, if not in all the Great Lakes. Inland, literally thousands of lakes harbor walleye, northern pike, muskie, bass, and perch. Some of the most popular spots are the lakes around Cadillac and Indian River in the Lower Peninsula, and the Manistique Lakes chain and huge Lake Gogebic in the U.P.

But to avoid the people and the whine of outboards, you really should head for the dozens of small lakes in the U.P.'s Ottawa and Hiawatha National Forests, which are peaceful, harder to access, and teeming with fish. Some, like the 34 lakes that comprise the Sylvania Wilderness near Watersmeet, have special fishing regulations, so check with authorities. All Michigan waters require a valid Michigan fishing license. For fishing information, contact the **Michigan Department of Natural Resources Fisheries Division** (517/373-0908, www.michigan.gov/dnr). For additional information about fish species, fishing reports, river guides, and charters in your area, contact the **Michigan Charter Boat Association** (800/622-2971, www.micharterboats.com).

DIVING

Over a century ago, the Great Lakes were like today's interstates—the fastest and most efficient way to get around. Commodities like lumber and iron ore were hauled from the forests and mines to Great Lakes ports; passengers traveled on steamships from urban areas around the southern Great Lakes to imbibe the fresh, cool air of northern resorts.

Of course, the Great Lakes were also known for shallow reefs and violent storms, which led to hundreds of shipwrecks. Moreover, the fresh, cold, barnacle-free waters kept those shipwrecks from badly decaying. Many of them sit on the lake floor, undisturbed and almost unchanged.

Decades later, all of this comes as a delight to divers. Michigan has set aside 11 areas (where shipwrecks were particularly prevalent) as underwater preserves, protecting their historic significance and mapping them for divers. Together, they cover 2,300 square miles

of Great Lakes bottomland—an area nearly twice the size of Delaware. Underwater preserves are located off the Keweenaw Peninsula, Marquette, Munising, and Whitefish Point on Lake Superior; in the DeTour Passage, around the Straits of Mackinac, off Thunder Bay, and near Port Austin and Port Sanilac on Lake Huron; and along the Manitou Passage and the southwestern shore on Lake Michigan.

Most of the popular dive sites are marked with buoys in summer by volunteers of the **Michigan Underwater Preserve Council** (800/970-8717, www.michiganpreserves.org), which also produces a biannual booklet. All the preserves are served by diving charters, which can be found through the **Michigan Charter Boat Association** (800/622-2971, www.micharterboats.com). For more information, you can also contact the chamber of commerce or tourism bureau near the preserve you wish to visit, or consult the appropriate chapters in this book.

BEACHES AND SWIMMING

For a state nearly surrounded by water, Michigan does not disappoint with its beaches. Public access is excellent. State parks and forests alone provide over 140 miles of Great Lakes frontage; county and local parks provide countless more.

The western shore of the Lower Peninsula gets most of the attention; along this "Gold Coast," a wide, soft ribbon of sand stretches along Lake Michigan from the Indiana state line over 200 miles north to the tip of the Leelanau Peninsula, the longest freshwater beach in the world. With the prevailing western winds carrying warm surface water to these shores, Gold Coast beaches are comfortable for summertime bathing, too. Favorite spots include the immensely popular **Warren Dunes State Park,** near Michigan's southern border, and **Ludington State Park,** a six-mile-long sandy point wedged between Lake Michigan and inland Hamlin Lake. High dunes rise along stretches of the Gold Coast, including **Sleeping Bear Dunes National Lakeshore** west of Traverse City.

The eastern side of the Lower Peninsula,

bordered by Lake Huron, also has fine sand beaches curving along the "Sunrise Shore." **Tawas Point State Park,** near Tawas City, is noted for its pure white sand, while **Port Crescent State Park,** at the tip of the Thumb, offers three miles of sandy beach and dunes. The Huron shore is also famous for its many lighthouses, which were needed to signal mariners traveling near this low-lying shore.

The beaches of the Upper Peninsula have a completely different mood—often wild and windswept, rocky and remote. Striped cliffs rise directly from Lake Superior at **Pictured Rocks National Lakeshore;** nearby, the **Grand Sable Dunes** provide enough sand to thrill even the most devoted beachcomber. You probably won't see many people here, but you may glimpse a deer, or even a black bear, headed to the water's edge for a drink. While perfect for long, sandy walks, only a hardy few actually swim in Lake Superior—the water temperatures rarely climb out of the 40s.

The U.P. shares its southern shore with Lake Michigan, a winding border filled with bays and inlets. A favorite of anglers, it also has some good beaches—if you know where to look. Public access is a little more difficult here. The best spots are along U.S. 2 from Naubinway to the Straits of Mackinac, where rest stops and county parks point you toward nice sandy beaches hidden behind the pines. You'll find another good stretch along Green Bay between Menominee and Escanaba, where **J. W. Wells State Park** and several county parks offer good swimming beaches.

WINTER ACTIVITIES

The Great Lakes churn out plentiful lake effect snows, which drop onto some of the Midwest's hilliest terrain, making Michigan the top ski destination in the region. While you can't really call anything here mountainous, resorts do an admirable job of working with the terrain they've got, carving out 600-foot vertical drops and runs that wind through the pines or offer jaw-dropping views of the Great Lakes.

Though downhill ski areas can be found throughout the state, they're concentrated in two primary areas: in the western U.P. from Ironwood

downhill skiing in northwestern Michigan

© PETOSKEY AREA VISITORS BUREAU

to the Porcupine Mountains, and in the northwest corner of the Lower Peninsula, from south of Traverse City to just north of Petoskey.

Cross-country skiers have even more options. Garland Resort, near Lewiston, pampers guests with a beautiful log lodge hidden away in the northeastern Lower Peninsula, surrounded by miles and miles of groomed Nordic trails. In fact, Michigan has several privately run Nordic trail systems. Many of the downhill resorts, such as Crystal Mountain in Thompsonville and Shanty Creek in Bellaire, also have notable Nordic trails. The national lakeshores and many state parks groom trails for skiing, and the state and national forests offer virtually limitless opportunities for backcountry skiing.

Other popular wintertime activities include snowboarding, snowshoeing, snowmobiling, ice skating, ice fishing, and, of course, dogsledding. For more information about Michigan's winter sports, consult the **Michigan Snowsports Industries Association** (248/620-4448, www.goskimichigan.com) and **Travel Michigan** (800/644-2489, www.michigan.org).

Accommodations

Michigan has a wide range of accommodations, from luxurious resorts to primitive campgrounds. Where you plan to stay depends on your interests, destination, and budget. Though spontaneity can be fun on a vacation, be aware that you might have to make reservations far in advance of your trip. Inns and campgrounds can fill up quickly, especially in summer or during certain annual events.

While Michigan has plenty of unique lodges and inns, you'll find all the big hotel and motel chains, from Holiday Inn to Super 8, here, too. If you prefer staying in such a tried-and-true establishment, pick up a copy of the chain's national directory to find current locations, rates, and services. Just remember that all Michigan lodgings charge a 6 percent "use tax." For more information about Michigan's accommodations, consult **The Michigan Travel Companion** (www.yesmichigan.com) or the **Michigan Lodging and Tourism Association** (www.michiganhotels.org).

INDEPENDENT HOTELS AND MOTELS

In the last few decades, the combination of interstate highways, corporate motel chains, and America's love of efficiency dealt a fatal blow to hundreds of independently owned motels. The pendulum seems to be swinging the other way these days—interesting inns and distinctive lodges seem to be cropping up in the most unlikely places. Nothing fancy—just those good old mom-and-pop motels, the kind of places now romanticized along Route 66.

The happy news is that they never went away in northern Michigan, including the Upper Peninsula. Perhaps too out-of-the-way to attract the big chains, many U.P. towns have several independent motels. Although some are kind of run-down, many mom-and-pop motels are clean, tidy, and inexpensive, and offer perks most chains don't—allowing pets, for example. Additionally, they're often pedestrian friendly, situated in town or along a waterfront, rather than stranded out along a highway. (One caveat: Some don't take credit cards, but many will almost always accept a personal check.) Many independent establishments are listed in this book, and you may discover many more. Don't be afraid to try something a little different.

BED-AND-BREAKFASTS

Michigan has hundreds of bed-and-breakfasts. Some are the traditional, old-fashioned variety—a spare room or two in someone's quaint old farmhouse—but those have become the exception rather than the rule. Today's B&Bs run the gamut from large inns with pools to renovated lighthouses. For a directory of Michigan's bed-and-breakfasts, contact the **Michigan Lake to Lake Bed and Breakfast Association** (888/575-1610, www.laketolake. com).

RESORTS AND LODGES

Many of Michigan's ski resorts double as golf resorts in summer, ringed with lodging that ranges from motel-style rooms to condo units and townhouses with kitchens (which allow you to save considerable money on meals). Many also offer a number of other amenities like pools, game rooms, and fitness centers, so they can be a particularly good choice for families with active kids. While golf resorts tend to be pricey, ski resorts that *don't* have the summer golf draw can be great bargains.

For those interested in other activities, like fishing and hunting, Michigan also has a number of seasonal lodges, such as Fish Point Lodge near Saginaw Bay. For information on ski/golf resorts and seasonal lodges, contact **Travel Michigan** (800/644-2489, www.michigan.org).

CABINS AND COTTAGES

A delightful way to experience the rustic beauty and down-home charm of Michigan's varied regions is by staying in a quaint cabin or cottage during your trip here. Several state parks offer inexpensive lodging in the great outdoors, from furnished cabins at Albert E. Sleeper State Park to tepee rentals at Baraga State Park. Besides cabins, Porcupine Mountains Wilderness State Park also provides basic yurts as well as a historic lodge overlooking Lake Superior. For more information, contact the **Michigan Department of Natural Resources** (800/447-2757, www.michigan.gov/dnr).

Private cottages, often equipped with amenities like cable television and laundry facilities, are available in resort communities and small towns like Saugatuck, Cadillac, and Petoskey. Whether situated along the beach, beside a golf course, or in the woods, such dwellings can vary in price, size, and amenities, so do your research far in advance of your trip. Reservations are often necessary. For more information, consult **The Michigan Travel Companion** (www.yesmichigan.com).

CAMPING

It's not easy to sum up camping in Michigan in a few paragraphs. You can park an RV next to a pool with a waterslide, or you can pitch a tent in backcountry so remote you might never see another soul. Most of us, of course, seek something in between. With tens of thousands of campsites in the state, you can probably find it, too.

This book lists many campgrounds, from primitive lots to highly developed RV properties. Many of the state park campgrounds are included, because they are almost universally good—usually the nicest campgrounds in a particular area. Some can get busy in summer months, though. You can reserve a site ahead of time (though specific spots aren't guaranteed) by contacting the **Michigan Department of Natural Resources** (800/447-2757, www.michigan.gov/dnr).

State and national forests also tend to have nice camping facilities, often more rustic but in appealing, out-of-the-way locations. Backcountry camping is permitted in many forests.

For a complete list of private campgrounds, request a *Michigan Campground Directory* ($3) from the **Association of RV Parks and Campgrounds Michigan** (325 N. Mt. Tom Rd., Ste. B, Mio, MI 48647, 989/826-5255, www.michcampgrounds.com) or a free *RV & Campsite* magazine from the **Michigan Association of Recreational Vehicles and Campgrounds** (2222 Association Dr., Okemos, MI 48864, 517/349-8881, www.marvac.org).

Food and Drink

REGIONAL CUISINE

Most of the "Indian" food featured in Michigan these days is the kind flavored with curry, not the wild fish and game enjoyed by the state's Native Americans. Short of the few annual powwows held around the state, there's no place to sample the staples of the region's original inhabitants. Michigan's immigrant ethnic heritage is well represented, however. From Hamtramck to Frankenmuth, Dearborn to Detroit, the state's diversity has found its way to the dinner plate.

In Detroit, you can feast on *saganaki* in **Greektown** and soul food in **Bricktown.** In the waterfront area known as **Mexicantown** (www.mexicantown.org), busy restaurants stay open until 4 A.M. to serve the hungry mole and margarita fans who wait for up to two hours for a table. Not far away is **Hamtramck** (www.hamtramck.com), a Polish enclave within the Detroit city limits known for traditional Polish kielbasa and pierogi; on Fat Tuesday, Detroiters of all nationalities jam the glass-fronted bakeries to buy up *paczki,* fresh jelly doughnuts. A little farther west, **Dearborn** is home to one of the largest groups of Arab peoples in the United States, where eateries sport signs in English and Arabic and serve up lentil soup, tabbouleh, and *fattoush.*

PASTIES

Pasties have long been a Michigan delicacy, especially in the Upper Peninsula. While folks fill these tasty pies with a variety of ingredients, from blackberries to broccoli to mackerel, the traditional recipe is a Cornish concoction of meat and vegetables. To begin, prepare your favorite pastry dough, enough for four nine-inch pies. Then set aside:

- 2 lbs. cooked pork and/or beef, cut into half-inch cubes
- 2 cups onions, diced
- 1 cup turnips, diced
- 1 cup potatoes, diced
- 4 tablespoons butter
- Salt, pepper, and parsley to taste

Divide the dough into four equal pieces and roll each one out to the size of a nine-inch plate. For each pie, layer one-fourth of the potatoes, turnips, onions, and meat on one half of the dough. Season each layer as desired, and top the pile with a tablespoon of butter. Fold the dough over the filling, then roll and crimp the edges so that the pasty is a sealed half-moon. Using a fork, poke several holes in the top of the dough, then bake on a greased cookie sheet for one hour at 400°F. Yields four large pasties.

In **Frankenmuth** (www.frankenmuth.org), a village near Saginaw settled by Germans in the mid-1800s, buses and cars come from miles around for all-you-can-eat chicken and strudel in two cavernous restaurants owned by the Zehnder clan. Made popular by traveling salesmen and Detroit families "out for a drive" in the 1950s, the Bavarian-inspired town has become one of the state's top tourist attractions. In Holland, Dutch food reigns of course, with flaky pastries the specialty at the popular Queen's Inn Restaurant at **Dutch Village** (www.dutch-village.com).

Throughout the Upper Peninsula, many main street cafés and bakeries serve up the **pasty** (PASS-tee), a pot-pie creation of beef, potatoes, onions, turnips, and other vegetables. Brought to the U.P. by Cornish miners, the pasty made for a hearty and filling meal, one that was easy to transport deep into the mine and warm up later with their candles. The same concept works well today if you're headed from town to your campfire.

Another Michigan food well worth tasting is the state's abundant fresh fish, from brook trout to walleye. In Great Lakes ports, you'll often be able to find a commercial fishery operating a small retail store, usually down by the docks. They often sell both fresh catch and smoked fish. The latter is absolutely superb with a bottle of wine and a Great Lakes sunset.

WINERIES

With temperature extremes moderated by prevailing western winds across Lake Michigan, two areas of the Lower Peninsula have developed into bona fide wine-producing regions. Both in the southwestern corner and around Grand Traverse Bay, local wineries have won international acclaim by producing wines from Michigan grapes. White wines like rieslings and chardonnays tend to be their best offerings, but some vintners have had success with reds, too.

Many Michigan wineries offer free tours and tastings. A few to try include **Warner Vineyards** (Paw Paw, 800/756-5357, www.warnerwines.com), **Tabor Hill Winery** (Buchanan, 800/283-3363, www.taborhill.com), **L. Mawby Vineyards** (Suttons Bay, 231/271-3522, www.lmawby.com), and **Chateau Grand Traverse Winery** (Traverse City, 231/223-7355 or 800/283-0247, www.cgtwines.com). For more information, contact the **Michigan Grape and Wine Industry Council** (517/241-4468, www.michiganwines.com).

BREWERIES

Wine isn't all that Michigan has to offer the connoisseur; the state ranks sixth in the nation for the total number of breweries. Each of its eight regions has at least two—if not several—breweries, microbreweries, and brewpubs. From the Quay Street Brewing Company, a brewpub in Port Huron, to the Keweenaw Brewing Company, a microbrewery in Houghton, Michigan hosts over 50 independent establishments for beer lovers. Be sure to sample a few varieties on your tour of the Great Lakes State (just remember not to drink and drive). For more information, consult the **Michigan Brewers Guild** (www.michiganbrewersguild.org).

GROCERIES AND MARKETS

Whether you're traveling via RV or staying in a place with a kitchen, you'll be pleased to know that, despite its acres of rugged countryside and numerous out-of-the-way villages, Michigan has plenty of supermarkets, independent groceries, specialty stores, and farmers markets.

So, no matter how long you plan to stay, you'll surely be able to purchase the produce and products to which you're accustomed.

You'll find major supermarket chains throughout the Lower Peninsula, including **Meijer** (www.meijer.com) in the southern half and **Glen's Markets** (www.glensmarkets.com) up north. Glen's even has a few stores in the eastern U.P. Meanwhile, mom-and-pop stores are pretty much everywhere, even on remote country roads.

But, if you're hoping to experience Michigan's regional treats and ethnic cuisine, you should visit some of the state's many farmers markets, U-pick farms, and specialty stores—from cheese and sausage shops in Frankenmuth to Glen Arbor's **Cherry Republic** (www.cherryrepublic.com). For a statewide list of farmers markets, consult the **Michigan Farmers Market Association** (www.farmersmarkets.msu.edu). For a wide selection of Michigan-made goods, visit **Michigan Peddler** (Mackinac Island, 906/847-6506, www.michiganpeddler.com).

© L. DIGGS, PICTURE THIS...

a seasonal produce stand

FUDGE AND CHERRIES

Since the 19th century, the regional cuisine of Michigan has been largely influenced by two factors: immigrant cultures and seasonal crops. Visitors interested in ethnic dishes can sample Polish pierogies in Hamtramck, Bavarian bratwursts in Frankenmuth, and Cornish pasties throughout the Upper Peninsula. Depending on the season, gourmands can enjoy a wide assortment of homegrown products, from maple syrup to blueberry jam; many such Michigan-made goods are sold through **Michigan Peddler** (www.michiganpeddler.com). In addition, U-pick farms and orchards are abundant in the northeastern and southwestern portions of the Lower Peninsula; oftentimes, motorists need only watch for the hand-painted signs alongside country roads.

Fudge and cherries are two of the state's most popular treats, especially in summer. "Fudgies," as tourists are often called by Michiganders, flock to the fudge emporiums that dot the northern half of the Lower Penin-sula, from Petoskey to Mackinac Island. In July and August, visitors can even watch the fudge-making process in shops like **Doug Murdick's Fudge** (www.murdicksfudge.com), which specializes in 16 different flavors, including black cherry and maple walnut.

As for cherries, Traverse City's **National Cherry Festival** (www.cherryfestival.org) is one of the state's most well-attended summertime events, where connoisseurs can, among other activities, compete in pie-eating and pit-spitting contests. Of course, no visit to the world's largest tart cherry-growing region would be complete without stopping by the headquarters of **Cherry Republic** (www.cherryrepublic.com) in nearby Glen Arbor, west of Traverse City. Not far from Sleeping Bear Dunes, Cherry Republic boasts everything from cherry wines to cherry-flavored condiments to chocolate-covered cherries.

Needless to say, you won't go hungry while touring the Great Lakes State.

ripening cherries on the Old Mission Peninsula

© TRAVERSE CITY CVB

Tips for Travelers

CONDUCT AND CUSTOMS

Michigan is similar to other Midwestern states in temperament and traditions. While major cities like Detroit and Flint might not follow the general rule, most areas of Michigan, especially smaller towns in the U.P. and the northern half of the Lower Peninsula, have a down-to-earth, wholesome vibe. Most residents seem to embrace the values of good education, hard work, and close family ties. As in other U.S. states, more and more women are working outside the home (whether in the auto plants of southeastern Michigan or the corporations of the Heartland), and yet traditional gender roles still do exist in many families, where men typically work while women tend to the children.

Given the state's multiethnic history, reliance on tourism, and proximity to Canada, foreigners and tourists are generally welcome here. Overall, the residents are helpful, hospitable, and forthright. They might use strange terms like "pop" and have unique accents, especially in ethnic enclaves and throughout the U.P., but politeness and good manners are prevalent. You'll often hear "please," "thank you," "yes, ma'am," and "no, sir." So, while in Michigan, do as the natives do. Be kind and considerate, ask for help when you need it, thank others for their time, and, as a courtesy, ask permission before taking a photo.

OPPORTUNITIES FOR STUDY AND EMPLOYMENT

With several notable universities and thriving industries in the Heartland, Michigan offers plenty of educational and work-related opportunities for residents and travelers. If you're interested in such a long-term stay, your best bet would be to research the schools and companies that interest you, consider details like transportation and accommodations, and, for foreign travelers, look into U.S. visa policies *before* making travel or relocation plans.

VOLUNTEER VACATIONS

Sometimes, being a tourist isn't enough. If you want to get to know Michigan *and* lend a helping hand, then perhaps a volunteer vacation is right up your alley. National and state parks can especially use some extra assistance, and working in such diverse environments can be a truly rewarding experience. Isle Royale National Park, for instance, is almost always on the lookout for campground hosts, museum assistants, wilderness rangers, and the like. Meanwhile, many of Michigan's state parks and recreation areas need volunteer guides for their summertime State Park Explorer Program.

For more information about volunteering in Michigan's national parks and lakeshores, contact the **National Park Service** (www.nps.gov/volunteer). For more information about Michigan's State Park Explorer Program, contact the **Michigan Department of Natural Resources** (www.michigan.gov/dnr).

TRAVELERS WITH DISABILITIES

Michigan is a very accessible state for those with disabilities. Most welcome centers and rest areas are equipped with features that can accommodate wheelchairs, such as convenient parking spaces, entrance ramps, wide passages, automatic doors, and spacious restrooms. The same can be said for major store chains, such as Wal-Mart and Meijer; major hotel chains like Days Inn; and key attractions, including the football stadium at the University of Michigan, the Michigan's Adventure amusement park in Muskegon, and the visitors centers at Pictured Rocks National Lakeshore. When in doubt about the possibility of access, simply call the establishment in question.

TRAVELING WITH CHILDREN

With its multitude of beaches, state parks, museums, train rides, boat tours, ice-skating facilities, and other amusements, Michigan is clearly a kid-friendly place. If you're traveling here with children, you'll surely find something for them to do. Even better, many restaurants and hotels go out of their way to accommodate young travelers. In Frankenmuth, for instance, Zehnder's Splash Village Hotel and Waterpark offers a video arcade, several waterslides, and shuttle service to the restaurant.

When traveling with children, just remember to supervise them at all times, both to keep them safe from harm and to minimize the possibility of disturbing others. If you decide to venture into Canada, be sure to have proper identification for them as well as for yourself.

TRAVELING WITH PETS

Although pets aren't allowed in much of Michigan's national parkland and in many of the state's hotels, restaurants, and stores, plenty of places do welcome them, including highway rest areas. In locations where dogs, cats, and other pets are allowed, it's crucial that you understand and follow any relevant rules. Typically, you are asked to keep your pets on a leash at all times, walk them in designated areas, control their behavior so as not to disturb or endanger others, and always pick up after them. Barking or aggressive dogs are usually forbidden everywhere. When in doubt, call ahead to verify the pet policies of a particular park, attraction, or establishment.

WOMEN TRAVELING ALONE

While it's admirable for an independent woman to explore the world on her own, it's important to take precautions, especially in urban centers like Detroit and Flint. Although Michigan is a relatively safe place, there are still too many things that can go wrong—on the road, in a campground, even in a crowd.

If you must venture out alone, tell someone back home about your intended travel plans, stick to daytime driving, and stay close to busy attractions, streets, and campgrounds. Try to stow your money, credit cards, and identification close to your person; big purses make easy targets. If you feel that someone

is stalking you, find a public place (such as a store, tourism bureau, police station, etc.) and don't hesitate to alert the police. Keep the doors to your lodging and vehicle locked at all times.

Before heading out on your trip, you should invest in a cell phone, which can be useful in an emergency. Just remember that cellular reception is limited in the state's more remote areas.

SENIOR TRAVELERS

Michigan is an exceptionally helpful place, so senior travelers should have little trouble getting assistance here. For help with directions, there are several welcome centers and tourism bureaus throughout the state, not to mention plenty of locals able to point you in the right direction. In addition, many establishments, especially restaurants, offer discounts to senior travelers. The National Park Service (www.nps.gov/fees_passes.htm) even offers a special lifetime pass ($10) for U.S. citizens and permanent residents aged 62 or over, allowing them free access to any national park or federal recreational land that charges an entrance fee, including the parks and lakeshores in Michigan.

GAY AND LESBIAN TRAVELERS

Although Michigan, like many Midwestern states, isn't openly friendly to gay and lesbian travelers, some towns and establishments can make you feel more welcome than others, especially along the Southwest Coast. Towns like Benton Harbor have a large number of gay-owned vacation homes, and the neighboring villages of Saugatuck and Douglas (www.gaysaugatuckdouglas.com) offer over 120 gay-friendly shops, art galleries, restaurants, and lodging options. For more information about gay-related issues, events, and establishments in Michigan, contact **Pride Source Media Group** (www.pridesource. com), which produces an annual business directory for the state's lesbian/gay/bisexual/ transgender (LGBT) community.

Health and Safety

Despite the best-laid plans, trouble can occur at any time. Before hitting the road, it's critical that you pack a well-stocked first-aid kit and prepare yourself for the common pitfalls of travel in Michigan.

HEALTH RISKS
Contaminated Water

Although the state's crystal-clear streams may look inviting for a drink, don't take a chance. Many of Michigan's most pristine lakes and streams may be tainted with *Giardia lamblia,* a nasty little organism that is most commonly transmitted in the feces of beavers, moose, and other mammals. Giardiasis can result in severe stomach cramps, vomiting, and diarrhea. As one Isle Royale ranger once said, "It won't kill you, but it may make you wish you were dead." Neither chemical treatment with Halizone nor a water filter will make water safe from giardia. You need a water purifier filtering down to 0.4 microns or less. Boiling is also effective, but make sure to get your water to a full, rolling boil for five minutes. In addition, Isle Royale waters may be infected with the hydatid tapeworm, which can also be eradicated by purifying or boiling.

Insects

Wood ticks and deer ticks are found in Michigan woods and grasslands. The larger wood tick, about a quarter-inch long, attaches itself to your skin and gorges on your blood. Gross, yes, but relatively harmless. If you find a wood tick on yourself, your companion, or your pet, grasp it as close to the head as possible and yank. Don't leave a piece of the animal imbedded, or it might cause an infection. Though not super particular, ticks prefer warm areas—scalp, neck, armpits, genitals. Ditto for your dog; check under the collar and all around the ears, too.

Deer ticks are the more dangerous beast. They may be transmitters of Lyme disease, a potentially debilitating condition. Lyme disease shows up as a temporary red rash that often resembles a ring, slowly expanding outward. As the disease progresses, other symptoms include sore joints, fatigue, and nausea; if left untreated, it can lead to arthritis and severe neurological and cardiac problems. Caught early, antibiotics treat it effectively.

To complicate matters, deer ticks are tiny—hardly larger than the head of a pin. Like wood ticks, they burrow into the skin, especially in warm places. After hiking, check yourself and your hiking partners carefully. If it's large enough, grasp the tick and pull it off, or use tweezers. If you've been in a tick-infested area, watch for a developing rash within the next week and have anything suspicious looked at by a doctor promptly. Your best defense against ticks is to wear long pants and long sleeves, and spray yourself liberally with a hard-core repellent like those containing deet.

Dogs are also highly susceptible to Lyme disease. Check your dog carefully and thoroughly for deer ticks by slowly running your fingers or a comb through his coat to get a look at the skin—a task that requires a lot of patience on the part of you and your dog. Again, ears, necks, bellies, and genitals are favorite hiding places. Signs that your dog may have acquired Lyme disease include nausea, fatigue, and lameness that may come and go from different joints. If you see potential symptoms, get to a vet right away. Like humans, dogs respond well to antibiotics if the disease is caught early enough.

There is a canine vaccine for Lyme disease, but veterinarians are divided on how effective it is. There are some very good tick repellent sprays on the market. Use them.

Plants

While hiking amid Michigan's forests, marshes, and beaches, be careful where you step. It's easier than you think to trip on a root or other obstruction. In addition, unless you're certain that you've found a patch of wild blueberries or other recognizable fruit, you should refrain from digesting any tempting berries, flowers, plants, and the like without first consulting local residents or expert field guides.

Wild Animals

As for large animals, deer are by far your biggest danger—they cause thousands of accidents a year on Michigan roads. But black bears certainly seem more frightening, especially when you're deep in the woods. Black bears are found throughout northern Michigan; the Upper Peninsula has an especially large population. They usually live in areas of heavy forest, but will routinely wander into open areas, in search of food. They're beautiful animals, and you should consider yourself lucky to observe one.

Black bears are generally shy creatures that would prefer to have nothing to do with you. If they hear you coming down the trail, they'll likely run the other way. If you happen to see one before it sees you, leave it an "escape route," then clap, yell, or bang pans. Give especially wide berth to a mother and cubs. There are very few documented cases of black bear aggression against humans, and theories vary on what to do if you should ever find yourself in such a situation. Most behaviorists believe that, unlike grizzlies, black bears will be intimidated by dominance behavior like shouting and waving your arms.

The biggest problems come when bears are lured into populated areas by human carelessness. It's always sad to see a bear relocated from its home territory, but it happens frequently in campgrounds, where humans don't properly store food or dispose of garbage. If you're car camping, keep all food in your car—with doors and windows closed! If you're tent camping, keep everything in airtight storage containers, and suspend the containers on a line between two trees, high enough off the ground and far enough apart to be out of a bear's reach. Latched coolers shoved under a picnic table are not sufficient to keep out bears.

Clean pans and utensils right away, dumping the water well away from camp, and store them with the food. Never keep any food (even gum) in your tent. Bears have an extremely good sense of smell and may be tempted to join you. Some say cosmetics also can attract them, so play it safe and store your soap and toothpaste with the food. You might want to leave your tent unzipped during the day while you're gone. Bears are curious; if they want to check out your tent, they'll make their own entrance if they can't find one.

If you're at a campground, deposit garbage in the animal-proof refuse containers provided. If you're backcountry camping, pack it out. Needless to say, never attempt to feed a bear, no matter how "tame" it may seem.

Heatstroke

Despite Michigan's mild summers (especially in the northern regions), hot, sunny days are common, and it's crucial that you prepare for them. Although sunscreen will help to prevent sunburn (which, if experienced often, can cause long-term problems for your skin), you must apply it often (and liberally). Prolonged sun exposure, high temperatures, and little water consumption can also cause dehydration, which can lead to heat exhaustion—a harmful condition whereby your internal cooling system begins to shut down. Symptoms may include clammy skin, weakness, vomiting, and abnormal body temperature. In such instances, you must lie down in the shade, remove restrictive clothing, and drink some water.

If you do not treat heat exhaustion promptly, your condition can worsen quickly, leading to heatstroke (or sunstroke)—a dangerous condition whereby your internal body temperature starts to rise to a potentially fatal level. Symptoms can include dizziness, vomiting, diarrhea, abnormal breathing and blood pressure, headache, cessation of sweating, and confusion. If any of these occur, you must be taken to a hospital as soon as possible; in the meantime, your companions should move you into the shade; remove your clothing; lower your body temperature with cool water, damp sheets, or fans; and try to give you some water to drink, if you're able.

Extreme Cold

While winter can be a beautiful time to visit the Great Lakes State, there's no doubt that Michigan winters can be long, hard, and cruel, especially for those unaccustomed to such cold, snowy conditions. If you plan to travel here November–March, be sure to pack plenty of warm clothes, including sweaters, mittens, hats, and waterproof boots. Be prepared to dress in layers (including your feet), as it's always better to remove clothing than to not have enough, especially if you plan to be outside for a while.

One condition to avoid is hypothermia, whereby the body temperature begins to lower to a dangerous level. Being cold and wet for an extended period of time, such as during a snowstorm, can be fatal. Try to keep warm and dry at all times. If you start to shiver, slur your speech, stumble, or feel drowsy, do not fall asleep. Instead, find some shelter, change into dry clothes, try to move around, and eat a quick-energy snack.

You should also watch out for frostbite, which can occur when blood vessels near the skin constrict, sending more blood to your vital organs and allowing outer tissues to freeze. The body parts most susceptible are your nose, cheeks, ears, and extremities. Initially, affected areas might tingle, itch, burn, whiten, go numb, or turn cold. Prolonged frostbite could cause swelling, blisters, and, ultimately, blackened skin. Diabetes, alcohol consumption, tobacco use, fatigue, dehydration, high altitude, and improper clothing can make the situation worse. To avoid long-term damage (and possible amputation), you should find shelter immediately and warm the affected areas. If your condition is severe, a doctor will need to oversee the rewarming process, in order to determine the extent of the damage.

Getting Lost

Part of Michigan's charm is its plethora of untamed backcountry and the possibility of exploring it in any season. Losing oneself in such wilderness might sound romantic, but it can be downright deadly, especially amid extreme weather. To protect yourself from harmful, long-term exposure to the elements, it's crucial that you plan your route ahead of time, consult local residents before heading into an isolated area, and inform someone else of your intentions—in case you don't return when scheduled. When venturing into the wilderness, traveling in a group of at least four is also advisable; in an emergency situation, one of you can stay with the afflicted person while the other two seek help.

If you stick to the main highways, you might need little more than a reliable map to navigate Michigan. But, if you have any intention of exploring the state's more remote areas, it's imperative that you bring a compass and GPS (global positioning system) with you. Be advised that, despite improved coverage over the past decade, cell phones still have a tendency to lose signal in the L.P.'s northern forests and throughout the U.P.

MEDICAL SERVICES

Emergency Care

All of Michigan is tied into the **911** emergency system. Dial 911 free from any telephone (including pay phones) to reach an operator who can quickly dispatch local police, fire, or ambulance services. This service also works from cellular phones. Be aware, however, that cell towers can be few and far between in rural areas. Much of the Upper Peninsula, including Pictured Rocks National Lakeshore, remains without reliable cellular and digital wireless service.

Hospitals and Pharmacies

If you experience an illness or injury while traveling in the Great Lakes State, rest assured that, as with other U.S. states, hospitals and pharmacies abound here, especially in major cities like Detroit, Flint, Grand Rapids, and Marquette. Consult each regional chapter in this guide for specific information about area hospitals and pharmacies. Just be advised that most medical facilities will require you to have insurance or make a partial payment before admitting you for treatment or dispensing medication.

Insurance

Although you might be the sort of traveler who likes to live dangerously, insurance is highly recommended while traveling in Michigan. Whether you're a U.S. citizen driving your own car or an international traveler in a rented RV, you should invest in medical, travel, and automotive insurance before embarking upon your trip—in order to protect yourself as well as your assets. Research your insurance options and choose the policies that best suit your needs and budget. For travel insurance (which should include medical coverage), consider **SafeMex Travel Insurance & Assistance** (www.safe-mex.com).

CRIME

Despite the crime-ridden reputations of places like Detroit and Flint, Michigan is a relatively safe place. It might be hard to believe in modern-day America, but residents of the northern rural parts rarely lock their doors at night. People here are, for the most part, friendly and helpful. Still, whether you're visiting the Motor City or a small town on the Leelanau Peninsula, it's important to take precautions.

Never leave valuables in plain view on a car seat; secure them in the trunk, where they're less tempting to thieves. Similarly, in case of an accident on the highway, do not abandon your vehicle, as this might also invite thieves. When sightseeing, keep your money, credit cards, identification, and other important items hidden on your person; purses and backpacks are much easier to steal. Do not walk alone at night, even in a small town, and try not to travel on the highways after dark. Even if you have AAA roadside assistance, help can be slow to come if you break down on a country road in the wee hours of morning. Just to be on the safe side, lock your hotel and car doors at night.

If you're traveling via RV, do not boondock alone in an isolated place. Try to stay in an RV park, a campground, or, at the very least, a well-lit parking lot. When venturing into the wilderness, try to camp with others. If you do find yourself in trouble, don't hesitate to find a phone and dial **911**. Of course, the time it takes police and emergency vehicles to reach you will depend upon your location, especially in the U.P.'s more remote areas.

Information and Services

MAPS AND TOURIST INFORMATION

For general information on traveling in Michigan, your best source is the state-run **Travel Michigan** (800/644-2489, www.mich-igan.org, 9 A.M.–5 P.M. Mon.–Fri.). Your call will be answered by a live person who can send you brochures and field your questions about festivals, activities, lodgings, and more. You may find it even more convenient to surf the website, which offers a comprehensive database of communities, accommodations, activities, golf courses, parks, attractions, shops, events, restaurants, and other aspects of the state. Just be aware that some of the information can be out of date, so always call ahead when making travel plans.

Suggested Maps

Michigan's official state road map is one of the few maps that doesn't relegate the U.P. to the opposite side. Pick one up at a **Welcome Center** or request one from **Travel Michigan** (www.michigan.org). **AAA Michigan** (800/222-6424, www.aaa.com) also offers a helpful Michigan map (members free, nonmembers $5).

For more detail, **DeLorme** (800/642-0970, www.delorme.com) produces the *Michigan Atlas and Gazetteer,* with the state portrayed in 102 large-scale maps. Though the 15-inch-long format is unwieldy for hikers, it's a great resource for planning your trip; it even identifies wineries, historic sites, bicycle routes, industrial tours, and other points of interest. You can find it at many Midwestern bookstores for $20.

If you'll be exploring the backcountry, you're best off with an official topographical (topo) map produced by the **U.S. Geological Survey** (888/275-8747, www.usgs.gov). Michigan's national parks and forests have topo maps for sale at their visitors centers or ranger stations. Outside federal lands, you may find them (or other detailed maps) in local outfitter shops, but don't count on it. If the shop you visit doesn't have the map you need, you may be a hundred miles from a store that does. If you can, buy or order one ahead of time at an outfitter or travel store.

Welcome Centers

The **Michigan Department of Transportation** (www.michigan.gov/mdot) operates 14 year-round welcome centers throughout the state. Stocked with maps and brochures, these facilities are staffed with "travel counselors" who are knowledgeable about the state in general and their region in particular. The centers are marked on the state map and by signs on the nearest highway. Hours vary.

WELCOME CENTERS IN THE LOWER PENINSULA

- Clare: U.S. 10/127, north of town
- Coldwater: I-69, six miles north of the Indiana-Michigan state line
- Detroit: Off I-75 at 2835 Bagley Street
- Dundee: U.S. 23, six miles north of the Ohio-Michigan state line
- Mackinaw City: I-75 at Nicolet Street
- Monroe: I-75, 10 miles north of the Ohio-Michigan state line
- New Buffalo: I-94 at the Indiana-Michigan state line
- Port Huron: I-69/94, west of Blue Water Bridge

WELCOME CENTERS IN THE UPPER PENINSULA

- Iron Mountain: U.S. 2/141 in downtown district

- Ironwood: U.S. 2 at the Wisconsin-Michigan state line
- Marquette: U.S. 41/M-28, two miles south of town
- Menominee: U.S. 41 at the Wisconsin-Michigan state line
- Sault Ste. Marie: I-75, south of the International Bridge
- St. Ignace: I-75, north of the Mackinac Bridge

Regional Tourism Bureaus

All of Michigan's major cities and many of its small towns offer tourism services through area convention and visitors bureaus (CVBs) or chambers of commerce. The state also has several regional tourism offices, which cover larger areas.

In the Lower Peninsula, you can contact the Thumb Area Tourism Council (989/672-0323, www.thumbtourism.org), the Southwestern Michigan Tourist Council (269/925-6301, www.swmichigan.org), the Michigan Beachtowns Association (www.beachtowns.org), the West Michigan Tourist Association (800/442-2084, www.wmta.org), and Michigan's Sunrise Side Travel Association (989/469-4544 or 800/424-3022, www.visitmichigansunriseside.com). In the Upper Peninsula, contact the Northern Michigan Tourist Association (www.travel-north.org), the Western U.P. Convention and Visitor Bureau (906/932-4850 or 800/522-5657, www.westernup.info), and the Upper Peninsula Travel and Recreation Association (906/774-5480 or 800/562-7134, www.uptravel.com).

To reach local tourism offices, consult the Michigan Association of Convention and Visitor Bureaus (www.visitmichigan.org) or refer to the destination chapters in this guide.

COMMUNICATIONS AND MEDIA
Postal and Shipping Services

In Michigan, a post office is never very far away via car, so it's fairly easy to purchase stamps, receive mail (via "General Delivery" for temporary visitors), and send letters and packages all around the world. While major cities and towns, such as Detroit and Lansing, have numerous post offices, even small U.P. towns like Skandia have at least one. To locate a post office in your area, consult the **United States Postal Service** (www.usps.com) or refer to the destination chapters in this guide.

If you need to send a package quickly (and cost isn't an issue), you'll find plenty of shipping stores throughout Michigan, especially in major towns. For more information about shipping locations and services, contact **FedEx** (www.fedex.com) or **UPS** (www.ups.com).

Phones and Internet

Public pay phones can be found throughout Michigan—at airports, gas stations, stores, bars, restaurants, hotels, etc. To place a call, listen for a dial tone, deposit the necessary coins, and dial the desired number (including "1" and the area code, if you're making a long-distance call). In the case of an emergency, you can dial **911** at no charge. For international calls, it's probably best to use a prepaid phone card, which you can often purchase in gas stations or convenience stores. To figure out the correct international calling code, visit www.countrycodes.com.

Nowadays, a cell phone is a necessary tool for travelers. It can make it easier to get roadside assistance, call an establishment for directions, and seek help in an emergency situation. Just be advised that cellular reception is still unreliable in many rural areas, especially in northern Michigan.

As for the Internet, it's hard to imagine the days when travel was possible without it. With the help of a computer and a modem, you can research Michigan's native flora, book a fishing charter, monitor the day's weather, view the menu of a Traverse City restaurant, and perform a host of other duties. Access to your own laptop can make such tasks even more convenient, especially since several of Michigan's hotels and other establishments offer wireless Internet access. Internet cafés also make it difficult to stay out of touch for long—even in remote areas of the U.P. Just remember that not all websites are updated regularly. Consult local residents or contact businesses directly before making any firm travel plans.

Publications and TV/Radio

Most of Michigan's major towns have at least one daily newspaper, from *The Detroit News* (www.detnews.com) to Escanaba's *Daily Press* (www.dailypress.net). Some places, such as Traverse City, even have their own magazine. Such periodicals are terrific sources of information for festivals, restaurants, sporting events, outdoor activities, and other diversions. Refer to the destination chapters for specific publications.

Local television and radio stations, such as Detroit's ABC affiliate WXYZ (www.wxyz.com), are also excellent sources for regional information. Pick up a newspaper in your area for a list of channels.

MONEY
Currency and Credit Cards

Bank debit cards and major credit cards (like Visa and MasterCard) are accepted statewide, even in the smallest towns. In addition, automated teller machines (ATMs) have become more prevalent, allowing travelers to withdraw cash whenever they need it. If you're uncomfortable using ATMs, you're sure to find a bank open during business hours (and sometimes on the weekend). That said, you'll need cash at self-registration campgrounds, and many independent motels, eateries, and stores will accept only cash, traveler's checks, or personal checks (often even out-of-state ones). As any wise traveler knows, never count on getting by with only plastic.

If you're traveling to or from Canada, you'll find currency exchanges at the border and at nearby banks in both countries. Since the exchange rate between Canadian and U.S. dollars can change at any time, you should plan to exchange currencies whenever coming or going. For up-to-date exchange rates, consult www.xe.com.

If you're a U.S. resident with Canadian money "left over" at the end of a trip, try to end up with bills, not coins. Many banks (especially away from border towns) will exchange only paper money, so you can easily find yourself with $10 or $20 worth of heavy souvenirs.

Sales Tax

In Michigan, you'll find that most goods and services, save for perhaps movie tickets, often cost more than their listed price. That's due, of course, to state taxes—specifically, the 6 percent sales tax on taxable retail items such as clothing and the 6 percent use tax imposed on accommodations. Fortunately, unlike many other U.S. states, Michigan does not allow local units to impose sales or use taxes of their own.

Tipping

Although the amount of a gratuity depends on the level of service received, general tipping guidelines exist in Michigan (and throughout the United States). Typically, restaurant servers should receive 15–20 percent of the entire bill; taxi and limousine drivers should receive at least 15 percent of the entire fare; and valets, porters, and skycaps should receive $2 per vehicle or piece of luggage.

WEIGHTS AND MEASURES
Electricity

In Michigan, most standard electrical outlets operate at 120 volts. So, if you're coming from Europe, Asia, or a country that operates at 220–240 volts, you'll need to bring an adapter in order to use your hair dryer, laptop, or other small appliance. Outlets here vary between the two-pronged and three-pronged variety, for which you might also need an adapter (easily purchased in any Home Depot or decent hardware store).

Time Zone

Most of Michigan is located in the eastern standard time (EST) zone, with the exception of the four Upper Peninsula counties that border Wisconsin. Gogebic, Iron, Dickinson, and Menominee Counties are in the central standard time (CST) zone.

RESOURCES

Glossary

The following regional terms and abbreviations will help you navigate your way across the state of Michigan, and better understand its unique people and culture:

Big Mac a nickname for the Mackinac Bridge, the link between Michigan's Upper and Lower Peninsulas; also called simply "The Bridge"

downriver a reference to the Wayne County suburbs south of Detroit, along the Detroit River

downstate a reference to Michigan's Lower Peninsula

D-Town a nickname for the city of Detroit

eh a spoken interjection commonly used by Upper Peninsula natives to solicit a response or add emphasis to a statement (e.g., "There's no place like Michigan, eh?")

Eight Mile the boundary between Detroit and its wealthier northern suburbs

euchre a trick-taking card game popular throughout the Midwest

fudgie a nickname for tourists, especially in the northern part of Michigan's Lower Peninsula, which is known for its ubiquitous fudge shops

Hockeytown since the mid-1990s, a nickname for the city of Detroit, in celebration of its NHL team, the Detroit Red Wings

L.P. a seldom used abbreviation for Michigan's Lower Peninsula

Michigan bankroll a large roll of money in small denominations, often covered by one larger bill to give the appearance of a lot of money

Michigander a nickname for Michigan residents, occasionally used to specify a male resident

Michiganian a nickname for Michigan residents

Michigoose a nickname for Michigan residents, occasionally used to specify a female resident

Mighty Mac a reference to the Mackinac Bridge, the link between Michigan's two peninsulas; also called "Da Crossing" or "Troll Turnpike" by U.P. residents

Mitten a nickname for Michigan's Lower Peninsula; also called "Troll Land" by U.P. residents

Motor City a nickname for Detroit, honoring its rich automotive history

Motown a record label and musical style that originated in Detroit, also used as a nickname for the city itself

pasty a hand-held pastry filled with meat and vegetables, popular in Michigan's Upper Peninsula

pop how Michigan residents refer to soda or soft drinks

Spartan the mascot of Michigan State University in East Lansing

tip of the Mitten a reference to the Straits of Mackinac

tip of the Thumb a reference to Port Austin, Michigan

Thumb the region of Michigan's Lower Peninsula that resembles the thumb of a mitten

Troll a nickname for residents of Michigan's Lower Peninsula, who live "below" the Mackinac Bridge

U.P. a frequently used abbreviation for Michigan's Upper Peninsula

up north north of wherever one is in Michigan

Wolverine the mascot of the University of Michigan in Ann Arbor

Yooper a nickname for residents of Michigan's Upper Peninsula

Yooperland a nickname for Michigan's Upper Peninsula; also called "Da Yoop" or "Yoopsconsin" by U.P. residents

Suggested Reading

While by no means an exhaustive list of Michigan-related titles, the following books will shed some light on the state's singular geography, history, culture, and offerings. Peruse them before your trip, and bring them along for the ride.

CUISINE

Whether you plan to dine out for every meal or rent a place with a kitchen, you'll find a handful of cookbooks dedicated to Michigan's assorted cuisine.

Breckenridge, Suzanne, and Marjorie Snyder. *Michigan Herb Cookbook.* Ann Arbor: The University of Michigan Press, 2001. Written by two Midwest natives, this cookbook offers growing tips, a detailed history about herbs, and of course, regional recipes made from homegrown Michigan herbs and produce, such as dill, pumpkins, and cherries.

Eustice, Sally. *History from the Hearth: A Colonial Michilimackinac Cookbook.* Mackinaw City: Mackinac State Historic Parks, 1997. This collection of traditional 18th-century recipes is complemented by snippets of letters and journals from inhabitants of the original fur-trading village.

Johnson, Chuck, Blanche Johnson, and Matt Sutherland. *Savor Michigan Cookbook: Michigan's Finest Restaurants, Their Recipes & Their Histories.* Belgrade, MT: Wilderness Adventures Press, Inc., 2007. Part cookbook, part travel guide, this selection allows epicureans to plan their route across Michigan and bring their favorite dishes home with them.

Michigan Lake to Lake Bed & Breakfast Association. *Celebrate Breakfast!: A Cookbook & Travel Guide.* 4th ed. Woodruff, WI: The Guest Cottage, Inc., 2005. The innkeepers of several bed-and-breakfasts throughout Michigan provide their favorite recipes, from prune muffins to asparagus pepper quiche.

Williams, Angela, ed. *With a Cherry on Top: Stories, Poems, Recipes & Fun Facts from Michigan Cherry Country.* Bay City, MI: Mayapple Press, 2006. Besides offering recipes that celebrate northern Michigan's cherry industry, this collection also features memoirs and stories by Michigan writers.

FICTION AND PROSE

Though no substitute for practical guidebooks, fictional tales, personal essays, and travel memoirs about Michigan can definitely give travelers a tantalizing sense of the cultural and natural diversity of this unique place.

Catton, Bruce. *Waiting for the Morning Train: An American Boyhood.* Detroit: Wayne State University Press, 1987. Reflecting on his boyhood in Benzonia, southwest of Traverse City, Pulitzer Prize–winning Catton offers a beguiling look at boyhood memories that segues into more serious discussions about the impact of technology on our society.

Emerick, Lon L. *The Superior Peninsula: Seasons in the Upper Peninsula of Michigan.* Skandia, MI: North Country Publishing, 1996. A collection of essays and "love letters" about the big lake, categorized by seasons.

Hamper, Ben. *Rivethead: Tales from the Assembly Line.* Revised ed. New York: Warner Books, Inc., 1992. A compelling collection of first-hand experiences from a former General Motors factory worker.

Hemingway, Ernest. *The Complete Short Stories.* New York: Simon & Schuster, Inc., 1987. Hemingway's works have been packaged and repackaged, of course, but this volume includes his finest Michigan-based short stories: "Up in Michigan," set in Horton's Bay, and numerous Nick Adams tales, including "Big Two-Hearted River," about fishing in the Upper Peninsula.

Leonard, Elmore. *Out of Sight.* New York: Bantam Dell Publishing Group, 1996. Famous for his crime novels, several of which have been turned into films, Leonard tells the story of a career thief and his unlikely relationship with a U.S. marshal, which takes them both to the gritty streets and posh suburbs of Detroit.

Shiel, Walt. *Devil in the North Woods.* Lake Linden, MI: Slipdown Mountain Publications, 2004. Based on contemporary reports and recorded oral histories about the 1908 wildfire that ravaged northeastern Michigan, obliterated the town of Metz, and killed several people, this novel traces the real-life story of an adolescent boy who survived the ordeal.

Steinberg, Michael, ed. *Peninsula: Essays and Memoirs from Michigan.* East Lansing: Michigan State University Press, 2001. An eclectic regional anthology of nearly 40 contemporary, evocative essays and memoirs, written by current and former Michiganders and focused on the state's great outdoors and metropolitan areas.

Stocking, Kathleen. *Lake Country: A Series of Journeys.* Ann Arbor: The University of Michigan Press, 1994. A series of essays from a talented local writer, who expands her observations beyond her native Leelanau Peninsula to other areas of Michigan.

Stocking, Kathleen. *Letters from the Leelanau: Essays of People and Place.* Ann Arbor: The University of Michigan Press, 1990. Poignant personal essays about the inhabitants and features of Stocking's native Leelanau Peninsula.

Traver, Robert. *Anatomy of a Murder.* New York: St. Martin's Press, 1983. Originally published in 1958, this popular novel-turned-movie was penned by former State Supreme Court Justice and U.P. resident John Voelker (a.k.a. Robert Traver), about a lover's-triangle murder that took place in nearby Big Bay.

Traver, Robert. *Trout Magic.* Reprinted ed. New York: Simon & Schuster, Inc., 1989. Filled with tall tales and amusing opinions, this collection of essays, originally published in 1974, offers a joyous look at trout fishing by the prolific Michigan author and judge.

Voelker, John D. *Trout Madness.* West Bloomfield, MI: Northmont Publishing Co., 1992. Originally published under the author's pseudonym, Robert Traver, in the 1960s, this collection of fishing tales serves as "a dissertation on the symptoms and pathology of this incurable disease by one of its victims."

GEOGRAPHY AND ECOLOGY

Several books aim to familiarize visitors with Michigan's unique flora, fauna, and topography.

Barnes, Burton V., and Warren H. Wagner. *Michigan Trees: A Guide to the Trees of the Great Lakes Region.* Revised ed. Ann Arbor: The University of Michigan Press, 2004. Originally published in 1913 by different authors, this updated field guide was written by two University of Michigan professors of forestry and botany, respectively.

Blacklock, Craig. *The Lake Superior Images.* 2nd ed. Moose Lake, MN: Blacklock Nature Photography, 1998. Blacklock, son of famous nature photographer Les Blacklock, circumnavigated Lake Superior by kayak to capture images for this award-winning book that belongs on every northern coffee table.

Dickmann, Donald I., and Larry A. Leefers. *The Forests of Michigan.* Ann Arbor: The University of Michigan Press, 2003. Two forestry professors from Michigan State University examine the natural history, ecology, management, and economic importance of the varied forests that cover roughly half of the state.

Huber, N. King. *The Geologic Story of Isle Royale National Park.* Washington, D.C.: U.S. Department of the Interior Geological Survey,

1983. For a government publication, this is a rather colorfully written study of Isle Royale's distinctive topography. Understanding even a little makes an Isle Royale backpacking trip all the more memorable.

Mueller, Bruce, and Kevin Gauthier. *Lake Michigan Rock Picker's Guide.* Ann Arbor: The University of Michigan Press, 2006. Filled with several helpful photographs, this rock identification guide appeals to beachcombers of all skill levels.

Peterson, Rolf O. *The Wolves of Isle Royale: A Broken Balance.* Ann Arbor: The University of Michigan Press, 2007. In this first-hand study, a wildlife biologist scrutinizes the ancient predator-prey relationship between the mysterious Isle Royale wolf and the native moose.

Tekiela, Stan. *Birds of Michigan Field Guide.* 2nd ed. Cambridge, MN: Adventure Publications, Inc., 2004. With color photographs and an easy-to-use format, this field guide can help even amateur bird-watchers observe Michigan's native species.

Tekiela, Stan. *Wildflowers of Michigan Field Guide.* Cambridge, MN: Adventure Publications, Inc., 2000. As with all of Tekiela's colorful field guides, this one is ideal for both beginners and those familiar with Michigan's varied flora.

HISTORY AND CULTURE

History buffs, amateur sociologists, and curiosity seekers will find a varied selection of books about Michigan's intriguing (and, at times, surprising) past—and the people that have made the state what it is today.

Alexander, Jeff. *The Muskegon: The Majesty and Tragedy of Michigan's Rarest River.* East Lansing: Michigan State University Press, 2006. An examination of the creation, history, uses, devastation, and restoration of Michigan's second longest river.

Ashlee, Laura Rose, ed. *Traveling Through Time: A Guide to Michigan's Historical Markers.* Revised ed. Ann Arbor: The University of Michigan Press, 2005. The definitive, illustrated guide to nearly 1,500 of Michigan's historic sites, along various highways and within assorted neighborhoods and city centers.

Bjorn, Lars, and Jim Gallert. *Before Motown: A History of Jazz in Detroit, 1920–1960.* Ann Arbor: The University of Michigan Press, 2001. Written by a sociology professor and a veteran jazz broadcaster, this book explores the history of Detroit jazz, within its social, often racially charged context.

Bohnak, Karl. *So Cold a Sky: Upper Michigan Weather Stories.* 2nd ed. Negaunee, MI: Cold Sky Publishing, 2006. Using eyewitness accounts, this book chronicles weather-related events in the Upper Peninsula from the 1600s to the present.

Carson, David A. *Grit, Noise, and Revolution: The Birth of Detroit Rock 'n' Roll.* Ann Arbor: The University of Michigan Press, 2005. A narrative history of the long-haired, hard-rocking musicians who helped to change the face of rock 'n' roll.

Clifton, James, James McClurken, and George Cornell. *People of the Three Fires.* Grand Rapids: Grand Rapids Inner-Tribal Council, 1986. An excellent introduction to the Ottawa, Potawatomi, and Ojibway cultures, with an emphasis on history and traditions, but also a good discussion of modern Native American issues.

Darden, Joe T., Curtis Stokes, and Richard W. Thomas. *The State of Black Michigan, 1967–2007.* East Lansing: Michigan State University Press, 2007. An investigation of how Michigan's black population and its interactions with the white community have changed since the terrible race riots that swept through Detroit during the summer of 1967.

Dodge, Roy L. *Michigan Ghost Towns of the Lower Peninsula*. Berkeley, CA: Thunder Bay Press, 2002. A compilation of the settlements and communities that have since faded into Michigan's history.

Dorson, Richard. *Bloodstoppers and Bearwalkers: Folk Traditions of Michigan's Upper Peninsula*. 3rd ed. Madison: The University of Wisconsin Press, 2008. Recently revised by James Leary, this collection of folk tales sheds light on the loggers, miners, sailors, trappers, and villagers that founded and sustained the U.P.'s communities.

Dunbar, Willis F., and George S. May. *Michigan: A History of the Wolverine State*. 3rd revised ed. Grand Rapids, MI: William B. Eerdmans Publishing Co., 1995. First published in 1965, this widely praised, comprehensive work covers the rich history of Michigan, from the early days of the first Native American settlers to the political developments of the mid-1990s.

Gile, Marie A., and Marion T. Marzolf. *Fascination with Fiber: Michigan's Handweaving Heritage*. Ann Arbor: The University of Michigan Press, 2006. Based on oral histories, interviews, and artifact research, this is surely the first comprehensive history of Michigan's rich tradition of handweaving, from pioneer days to the contemporary era of computer-aided looms.

Gustin, Lawrence R. *Billy Durant: Creator of General Motors*. 2nd ed. Ann Arbor: The University of Michigan Press, 2008. A well-researched look at the man who initiated General Motors and made Flint one of America's greatest industrial centers.

Lyons, Sandy Arno. *Michigan's Most Haunted: A Ghostly Guide to the Great Lakes State*. SkateRight Publishing, 2007. Written by a Michigan resident, this book features more than 25 true ghost tales from several of the state's hotels, restaurants, and other properties.

Michigan Department of Natural Resources. *A Most Superior Land: Life in the Upper Peninsula of Michigan*. Lansing, MI: Two Peninsula Press, 1983. A wonderful series of short essays and anecdotal tales about the history of the Upper Peninsula. Loaded with great historical photos, too.

Rydholm, C. Fred. *Superior Heartland: A Backwoods History*. Marquette, MI: Superior Heartland, Inc., 1989. These two enormous volumes comprise hundreds of short chapters of U.P. history, the kind of thing you don't have to read chronologically. Exhaustively researched, it's filled with all manner of quirky stories, character studies, and historical photos you won't find elsewhere.

Stonehouse, Frederick. *The Wreck of the Edmund Fitzgerald*. Revised ed. Gwinn, MI: Avery Color Studios, 2006. Though one of several related books about this famous shipwreck, this is considered by many historians to be the definitive work on the subject, scrutinizing the events leading up to the tragedy and offering various theories about the cause of its demise.

Taylor, Sprague. *Tahquamenon Country*. East Lansing: Michigan State University Press, 2008. The history of the people who depended on Michigan's mighty Tahquamenon River, as told by a lifelong resident of the eastern Upper Peninsula.

Thurner, Arthur W. *Strangers and Sojourners: A History of Michigan's Keweenaw Peninsula*. Detroit: Wayne State University Press, 1994. The socioeconomic history of the diverse immigrants who established and sustained the communities that comprise the U.P.'s Keweenaw, Houghton, Baraga, and Ontonagon counties.

PARKS AND RECREATION

Outdoor enthusiasts will find several books geared toward exploring and camping amid the beaches, forests, and lakes of Michigan.

DuFresne, Jim. *Backpacking in Michigan*. Ann Arbor: The University of Michigan Press, 2007. Written by a Michigan native and author of more than a dozen wilderness and travel guides, this book features 50 backpacking trails across both peninsulas. Loaded with photographs and detailed maps.

DuFresne, Jim. *The Complete Guide to Michigan Sand Dunes*. Ann Arbor: The University of Michigan Press, 2005. In addition to a comprehensive explanation of dune formation, this guide offers all the necessary information for swimmers, picnickers, hikers, and skiers to explore nearly 50 duneland areas, from the remote to the well known.

DuFresne, Jim. *Isle Royale National Park: Foot Trails and Water Routes*. 3rd ed. Seattle: The Mountaineers, 2002. The definitive guide to Isle Royale, filled with practical information about campsites, portages, fishing spots, and more. Small enough to carry along, and you should.

DuFresne, Jim. *Michigan's Best Campgrounds: A Guide to the Best 150 Public Campgrounds in the Great Lakes State*. 3rd ed. Berkeley, CA: Thunder Bay Press, 2005. This expert outdoorsman and writer suggests the best campsites for anglers, canoeists, hikers, bikers, and bird-watchers during the state's most popular season, May–October.

DuFresne, Jim. *Michigan State Parks: A Complete Recreation Guide*. 2nd ed. Seattle: The Mountaineers, 1998. Michigan outdoor writer DuFresne worked with the Michigan Department of Natural Resources to compile this handy guide, which devotes a couple of pages to each of Michigan's state parks, suggesting the ideal spots for boaters, anglers, hikers, and skiers.

Funke, Tom. *50 Hikes in Michigan's Upper Peninsula: Walks, Hikes, and Backpacks from Ironwood to St. Ignace*. Woodstock, VT: The Countryman Press, 2008. A new addition to the 50 Hikes series, this guide features day-long and overnight trips for hikers, backpackers, and other recreationists throughout the U.P. Each hike description is accompanied by a detailed topographical map, a difficulty rating, directions to the trailhead, and commentary about any related natural and cultural history.

Hillstrom, Kevin, and Laurie Hillstrom. *Paddling Michigan*. Guilford, CT: The Globe Pequot Press, Inc., 2001. An invaluable survey of 70 of Michigan's finest lakes, streams, and coastal waterways, whether known for amazing scenery, historical significance, or marine wildlife and activities. Ideal for canoeists and kayakers of all skill levels, this guide contains detailed maps, preparation advice, seasonal tips, and lists of local paddling organizations.

Sharp, Eric. *Fishing Michigan*. Detroit: Detroit Free Press, 2002. Written by a veteran reporter and outdoors writer for the *Detroit Free Press,* this guide describes the state's major game fish, their frequent hangouts, and the best ways to snag them.

REGIONAL TRAVEL

Mainstream travel guides offer details about Michigan's regions, cities, attractions, restaurants, and shops, with useful maps and contact information.

Burcar, Colleen, and Gene Taylor. *Michigan Curiosities: Quirky Characters, Roadside Oddities, & Other Offbeat Stuff*. 2nd ed. Guilford, CT: The Globe Pequot Press, Inc., 2007. Popular among residents and tourists alike, this recently updated guide offers a panoply of Michigan's wildest quirks, wackiest characters, and bizarre destinations, including Trenary's Outhouse Classic.

Cantor, George. *Explore Michigan: Detroit*. Ann Arbor: The University of Michigan Press, 2005. A former media personality and writer for *The Detroit News,* Cantor has prepared a series of travel and activity guides for key Michigan destinations, including the Motor City itself.

Cantor, George. *Explore Michigan: Leelanau.* Ann Arbor: The University of Michigan Press, 2005. Though brief, this guide can definitely assist visitors on their tour of the Leelanau Peninsula, north of Traverse City.

Cantor, George. *Explore Michigan: Mackinac.* Ann Arbor: The University of Michigan Press, 2005. As with all of Cantor's compact travel guides, this one offers enough history, photographs, and practical information for any first-time visitor to fully experience Mackinac Island.

Cantor, George. *Explore Michigan: Traverse City.* Ann Arbor: The University of Michigan Press, 2005. Cantor's comprehensive take on the Traverse City area.

DuFresne, Jim. *Lonely Planet Road Trip: Lake Michigan.* Footscray, Victoria, Australia: Lonely Planet Publications, 2005. Longtime Michigan travel writer DuFresne guides readers along the "Michigan Riviera."

DuFresne, Jim. *Michigan Off the Beaten Path: A Guide to Unique Places.* 9th ed. Guilford, CT: The Globe Pequot Press, Inc., 2007. A quirky take on the Great Lakes State, with the less-traversed routes and little-known attractions of both peninsulas.

Franklin, Dixie. *Compass American Guides: Michigan.* 2nd ed. New York: Fodor's Travel Publications, Inc., 2005. Filled with photos and full-color illustrations, this guide focuses more on the cultural, historical, and geographical aspects of each region, and less on practical travel details.

Godfrey, Linda S. *Weird Michigan: Your Travel Guide to Michigan's Local Legends and Best Kept Secrets.* New York: Sterling Publishing Co., 2006. Part of a series of state-by-state guides focused on odd places, this is an ideal guide for those who prefer visiting sights off the beaten path.

Hutchins, Brian. *Michigan's West Coast: Explore the Shore Guide.* Roscommon, MI: Abri-Press, 2005. This book invites visitors to explore 500 public parks and points of access along the Lake Michigan shoreline of the Lower Peninsula.

Roberts, Bruce, and Ray Jones. *Lighthouses of Michigan.* Guilford, CT: The Globe Pequot Press, Inc., 2005. A handy guide for exploring nearly 50 of Michigan's lighthouses, presented in geographical order, with detailed descriptions, historical background notes, color photographs, and complete travel information.

Royce, Julie Albrecht. *Traveling Michigan's Sunset Coast: Exploring Michigan's West Coast Beach Towns.* Berkeley, CA: Thunder Bay Press, 2007. This comprehensive guide gives visitors all the practical information needed to explore the Lake Michigan coast, from New Buffalo near the Indiana border to Mackinac City at the tip of the Lower Peninsula.

Royce, Julie Albrecht. *Traveling Michigan's Thumb: Exploring a Shoreline of Small Pleasures and Unexpected Treasures.* Berkeley, CA: Thunder Bay Press, 2008. This helpful book invites visitors to leave behind day-to-day stresses and explore Michigan's undiscovered jewel, a region of quiet harbors, quaint villages, less-crowded beaches and inns, and small-town festivals.

Westervelt, Amy. *Michigan's Upper Peninsula.* Woodstock, VT: The Countryman Press, 2008. A comprehensive guide to the U.P., with regional maps, historical tidbits, and practical details about area hotels, restaurants, and the like.

Suggested Viewing

Michigan has long been a favorite spot for filmmakers. While gritty Detroit has received most of the screen time, the wilds of the Upper Peninsula have served as a unique cinematic backdrop, too. Before traveling through Michigan, take some time to view the following films and experience the way others have interpreted the Great Lakes State.

Anatomy of a Murder (1959)

Written by Wendell Mayes. Directed by Otto Preminger. Starring James Stewart, Ben Gazzara, Lee Remick, and George C. Scott. In this engaging courtroom drama set in the Upper Peninsula, a small-town lawyer struggles to defend his client, a hotheaded army lieutenant arrested for the murder of a bartender who supposedly assaulted his wife. Based on the famous novel by a former Michigan judge.

8 Mile (2002)

Written by Scott Silver. Directed by Curtis Hanson. Starring Eminem, Kim Basinger, Mekhi Phifer, and Brittany Murphy. During the course of one critical week, a young, angry rapper from the wrong side of Detroit's 8 Mile tries to achieve his musical goals while struggling with various problems in his life.

Escanaba in da Moonlight (2001)

Written and directed by Jeff Daniels. Starring Jeff Daniels. In this whimsical comedy about deer-hunting season amid the wilds of the Upper Peninsula, a man must deal with his eldest son's curse of never having killed a buck of his own.

Grosse Pointe Blank (1997)

Written by Tom Jankiewicz, D.V. DeVincentis, Steve Pink, and John Cusack. Directed by George Armitage. Starring John Cusack, Minnie Driver, Joan Cusack, Dan Aykroyd, and Alan Arkin. In this dark comedy, a professional assassin is forced to reevaluate his life when he returns home to Grosse Pointe, Michigan, for a contract hit and, coincidentally, his 10-year high school reunion.

Hoffa (1992)

Written by David Mamet. Directed by Danny DeVito. Starring Jack Nicholson and Danny DeVito. Based on the story of legendary labor union leader Jimmy Hoffa, this controversial film follows his tumultuous career to his 1975 disappearance.

Out of Sight (1998)

Written by Scott Frank. Directed by Steven Soderbergh. Starring George Clooney, Jennifer Lopez, Ving Rhames, Steve Zahn, and Don Cheadle. Based on the eponymous Elmore Leonard novel, this gritty crime thriller follows the unlikely relationship between a career thief and a female U.S. marshal, from the sweltering heat of Miami to the bitter cold of Detroit.

The Road to Wellville (1994)

Written and directed by Alan Parker. Starring Anthony Hopkins, Matthew Broderick, Bridget Fonda, and John Cusack. Based on the eponymous novel, this madcap comedy explores the inner workings of the Battle Creek Sanitarium, an unusual health facility run by cereal king Dr. John Harvey Kellogg during the late 19th century.

RoboCop (1987)

Written by Edward Neumeier and Michael Miner. Directed by Paul Verhoeven. Starring Peter Weller, Nancy Allen, Ronny Cox, and Kurtwood Smith. In a futuristic, crime-ridden Detroit, a fatally wounded cop returns to the city's overrun police force as a powerful cyborg, determined to clean up the streets.

Roger & Me (1989)

Written and directed by Michael Moore. In the first of several films that have defined Moore's "docuganda" style, the filmmaker tries to confront GM head Roger Smith about the massive downsizing that contributed to Flint's decline.

Somewhere in Time (1980)

Written by Richard Matheson, based on his novel. Directed by Jeannot Szwarc. Starring Christopher Reeve, Jane Seymour, and Christopher Plummer. After meeting an elderly actress who seems to know him from the past, a young Chicago playwright uses self-hypnosis to travel back to the early 1900s, where he embarks upon an ill-fated love affair inside Mackinac Island's Grand Hotel.

The Upside of Anger (2005)

Written and directed by Mike Binder. Starring Joan Allen, Kevin Costner, Erika Christensen, Keri Russell, Alicia Witt, Evan Rachel Wood, and Mike Binder. When her husband unexpectedly vanishes from their wealthy Detroit suburb, a sharp-tongued wife and mother of four daughters turns to alcohol, anger, and an unlikely romance with her boozy neighbor to help her cope with her husband's abandonment.

Internet Resources

The following websites will provide valuable information before, during, and after your trip:

CUISINE AND TRAVEL

Frog Leg Productions
www.micuisine.com

Ostensibly, the company that runs this website is a graphics design firm for Michigan-based restaurants, but you'll also find recipes, cultural facts, plus information about some of the state's best eateries and festivals.

Michigan Association of Fairs and Exhibitions
www.michiganfairs.org

You can use this website's fair/festival locator feature to learn more about Michigan's numerous county fairs.

Michigan Festivals & Events Association
www.michiganfun.us

Search this website for most of Michigan's cultural and community events.

Michigan Peddler
www.michiganpeddler.com

If you hope to take a taste of Michigan home with you, look no further than this website, where you can a purchase a wide assortment of Michigan-made foods and condiments, from Cherry Republic's hot cherry salsa to Postma Brothers' maple syrup.

The Michigan Travel Companion
www.yesmichigan.com

Use this comprehensive website to research Michigan's accommodations, from motels to resorts. You can browse options by region, city, or type of lodging.

Michigan's Upper Peninsula
www.uptravel.com

This portal offers complete travel and lodging information for the U.P., including details about events, activities, campgrounds, waterfalls, lighthouses, and other attractions. Here, you'll also find weather reports and tips for anglers, skiers, and snowmobilers.

Northern Michigan Travel
www.northernmichigantravel.com

This one-stop online travel guide serves as a useful repository for those eager to explore the northern part of the Lower Peninsula and the eastern half of the Upper Peninsula. Listed here are emergency numbers, weather conditions, and details about camping, lodging, boating, fishing, golfing, skiing, shopping, dining, entertainment, and sightseeing options.

Thumb Area Tourism Council
www.thumbtourism.org

The TATC website is a helpful resource for those planning a trip to the Thumb. Here, you'll find information about area attractions, parks, beaches, marinas, events, accommodations, historic sites, and more.

Travel Michigan
www.michigan.org

Michigan's official travel and tourism website offers just about everything you need to know about the state's cities, accommodations, restaurants, casinos, attractions, shops, parks, events, recreational activities, and entertainment venues. Just be aware that some of the information can be out of date, so always call ahead when making travel plans.

Travel North
www.travelnorth.org

The official portal for the Northern Michigan Tourism Association offers visitors helpful information about the northern part of Michigan's Lower Peninsula and the eastern half of the Upper Peninsula. Besides special deals, you'll find details about shops, restaurants, accommodations, seasonal sports, festivals, outdoor diversions, and cultural attractions.

West Michigan Tourist Association
www.wmta.org

Based in Grand Rapids, the WMTA has been promoting West Michigan—the western half of the Lower Peninsula, from the Indiana border to the Straits of Mackinac—since 1917. The group's website provides a wealth of travel information, from events to attractions to accommodations. Here, you can also make reservations, find travel deals and coupons, and peruse maps and suggested itineraries.

GENERAL INFORMATION

Absolute Michigan
www.absolutemichigan.com

As its slogan states, this comprehensive website offers both visitors and residents "all Michigan, all the time"—a collection of links, features, news, and information about everything from wineries and art galleries to newspapers and vacation cottages.

Country Codes
www.countrycodes.com

If you decide to make any international phone calls while visiting Michigan, you'll need this handy website, an easy-to-use directory of country calling codes.

MD Travel Health
www.mdtravelhealth.com

Updated daily, this medical website is an excellent resource for travelers. You'll find information about specific destinations, available clinics, infectious diseases, and illness prevention.

Online Conversion
www.onlineconversion.com

This website will help you make any U.S.-metric conversion, from temperatures to distances to clothing sizes.

State of Michigan
www.michigan.gov

Michigan's official website has all the typical links to state departments, such as Agriculture and Natural Resources, plus some truly useful and fun information. Here, you can check road closures, purchase fishing and hunting licenses, and even learn more about the state's symbols, landmarks, and little-known historical facts.

U.S. Department of State
www.travel.state.gov

Whether or not you're a U.S. citizen, this website will help you travel safely across the U.S.-Canada border near Detroit, Port Huron, and Sault Ste. Marie. International travelers will also find guidelines for flying into and out of Michigan.

HISTORY AND CULTURE

Michigan History
www.michiganhistorymagazine.com
The online version of this engaging magazine promises history buffs a variety of articles and images chronicling the state's rich history, including stories about lighthouses, college campuses, famous Michiganders, professional sports teams, and more. You'll also find lists of recommended history books.

Michigan State University Press
http://msupress.msu.edu
You'll find a number of titles by Michigan-based writers, from personal essays about the Great Lakes to historic accounts about Michigan's rivers and colleges.

The University of Michigan Press
www.press.umich.edu
Peruse this website for a wealth of Michigan-related books that shed light on the state's history and culture. Included here are historic accounts, personal memoirs, biographies, even field guides.

PARKS AND RECREATION

GORP
www.gorp.com
An in-depth portal for adventure travel and outdoor recreation, this website is an invaluable resource for information about campgrounds, national parks, recreational activities, and outdoor gear. There's even a whole section devoted to Michigan, from fly-fishing in the northern parts to exploring Sleeping Bear Dunes.

League of Michigan Bicyclists
www.lmb.org
Mountain bikers can explore this website for routes, clubs, and shops throughout the state.

Mackinac State Historic Parks
www.mackinacparks.com
Visitors to Mackinac Island should stop here first for information about the island's various historic sites, including details about admission rates, hours of operation, and special events.

Michigan Birding
www.michiganbirding.com
Peruse this website for information about bird-watching hot spots, tours, and festivals throughout Michigan.

Michigan Charter Boat Association
www.micharterboats.com
This website offers access to hundreds of charter fishing boats, river fishing guides, sailing excursions, and diving trips that service the coastal areas and open waters of Lake St. Clair and the five Great Lakes.

Michigan Department of Natural Resources
www.michigan.gov/dnr
From this recreation portal, you'll learn everything you need to know about fishing, hunting, camping, boating, hiking, biking, and snowmobiling in the Great Lakes States. Also included here are maps, publications, and information about law enforcement, forest management, state parks, visitors centers, historic sites, and trails.

Michigan Interactive
www.fishweb.com
Besides offering numerous maps and lodging options, this website provides tons of advice for anglers, boaters, paddlers, hikers, golfers, snowmobilers, off-road enthusiasts, even mushroom hunters.

Michigan Snowsports Industries Association
www.goskimichigan.com
Skiers and snowboarders should peruse this website for details about Michigan's downhill ski slopes, outfitters, and snow conditions.

Michigan Underwater Preserves
www.michiganpreserves.org
For divers, this website offers advice and information about all of Michigan's underwater preserves, from Isle Royale to Sanilac Shores.

National Park Service
www.nps.gov

The National Park Service provides detailed maps, brochures, and contact information for each of its nearly 400 parks, monuments, recreation areas, trails, and other natural and cultural sites throughout the U.S. Use the state-by-state search function to learn more about Michigan's protected places, including Isle Royale National Park, Keweenaw National Historical Park, Pictured Rocks National Lakeshore, Sleeping Bear Dunes National Lakeshore, and Motor Cities National Heritage Area.

National Wild and Scenic Rivers System
www.rivers.gov

Learn more about Michigan's federally designated wild and scenic rivers, from the Au Sable to the Sturgeon.

U.S. Coast Guard's Boating Safety Division
www.uscgboating.org

Use this comprehensive website to prevent accidents and fatalities while boating in Michigan.

Index

WXYZ

List of Maps

Acknowledgments

Although it seems impossible to thank all of the people who have contributed to this guide, I promise to give it a try.

Since the summer of 2000, my husband and I have often traveled to the Great Lakes State—ostensibly to visit his parents, who live here during the summer months. While on such trips, we've always taken the time to explore the nooks and crannies of this fascinating state, from the quiet shores of Pictured Rocks National Lakeshore to the quaint shops of Frankenmuth. In recent years, we, too have joined the ranks of Michigan's seasonal residents. Although we spend much of the year in New Orleans and Los Angeles, from May to September, home becomes Big Bear Lake, in the northeastern part of the Lower Peninsula. Now, we have even more time to explore one of our favorite places.

During every stay, we've encountered plenty of friendly, helpful residents, usually willing to point us in the right direction—for the best blueberry patch, the least crowded beach, the most innovative museum, or whatever else we sought at the time. So, thanks to everyone who's made each of our trips to Michigan a rejuvenating experience.

Of course, there are a few folks to whom I'm particularly grateful. First, I offer a special thanks to the many innkeepers, restaurant owners, park rangers, adventure outfitters, and tourism officials who made the job of compiling this guide a little easier. Thanks, too, to those who provided photographs for this book, and to the patient editors of Avalon Travel who offered valuable assistance during the preparation of this guide. Thanks also to Tina Lassen who wrote the previous editions of this book—and helped me in ways she'll never know.

In addition, I'd like to thank my friends and family, all of whom have supported me during each of my frenzied writing projects. Most of all, I'm grateful to my husband, Daniel, who encouraged me to accept this particular gig and who supported me at each and every turn. He's the best traveling companion a girl could ask for.

Lastly, I thank you, the reader. May your next trip to Michigan be as memorable as ours have been.

Photo Credits

Front cover photo: © Claudia Adams/DigitalRailroad.net

Page 1: Autumn on Lake Charlevoix © Petoskey Area Visitors Bureau

Page 4: Fort on Mackinac Island © Mackinac State Historic Parks

Page 5: (L-R) Bushels of apples and peaches © L. Diggs, Picture This..., White River Light Station © Muskegon County CVB, entrance to Comerica Park © L. Diggs, Picture This...

Page 6: (top) Gilmore Car Museum © Gilmore Car Museum, (bottom) Carp River © L. Diggs, Picture This...

Page 7: (clockwise) Birch forest near Calumet © L. Diggs, Picture This..., Detriot skyline © L. Diggs, Picture This..., kayaking on Lake Huron © Port Austin Kayak & Bike Rental, fresh produce © Ann Arbor Area CVB

Page 8: River Place shops © Frankenmuth Chamber of Commerce/CVB

Page 9: cannon demonstration © Mackinac State Historic Parks

Page 10: Lake of the Clouds in the Porcupine Mountains © Ross Reinhold, SuperiorTrails.com

Page 11: (L-R) Air Zoo © Air Zoo, Sleeping Bear Dunes © Kerry Kelly, Grand Traverse Lighthouse © Traverse City CVB/WMTA

Page 12: Greenfield Village © Detroit Metro CVB

Page 13: (top) Old Mackinac Point Lighthouse © Mackinac State Historic Parks (bottom) Tahquamenon Falls © L. Diggs, Picture This...

Page 14: Soo Locks boat tours © Jeffrey Foltice/MEDC (michigan.org)

Page 15: Eagle Harbor Light © Gary Platte/MEDC (michigan.org)

Page 16: (top) *Huron* Lightship © Blue Water Area CVB, (bottom) Fort Gratiot Light © Cindy Lindow

Page 17: Ole Mission Point Lighthouse © Traverse City CVB/WMTA

Page 18: (top) Little Sable Point Light © L. Diggs, Picture This..., (bottom) Manistee North Pierhead Light © Monte Spanier

Page 19: Saugatuck's Oval Beach © L. Diggs, Picture This...

Page 20: (top) Tabor Hill Winery, (bottom) grapevine in winter © Jeff Greenberg

Page 21: (top) Round Barn Winery © Southwestern Michigan Tourist Council, (bottom) Black Star Farms © Fenn Valley Vineyards

Page 22: Shanty Creek Resorts © Shanty Creek Resorts

Page 23: Chateau Chantal winery © Chateau Chantal

Page 24: The Detroit People Mover passing below GM's Renaissance Center © Detroit Metro CVB